POLICE AND GOVERNMENT RELATIONS: WHO'S CALLING THE SHOTS?

Edited by Margaret E. Beare and Tonita Murray

The issue of police governance, accountability, and independence has been the subject of ongoing academic research and public discourse. *Police and Government Relations: Who's Calling the Shots?* examines the broad question of control of the police and our understanding of both the independence and accountability of the police for their actions. The product of an academic symposium held at Osgoode Hall Law School and supported by the Ipperwash Inquiry, the volume offers a thorough and timely study of police-executive relationships. The Ipperwash Inquiry, which examined the circumstances surrounding the death of Native protestor Dudley George, has provided an important opportunity to revisit the question of what constitutes an ideal or, at least, a reasonably acceptable balance between government direction of the police and police independence. This volume contributes new insights derived from the evolution of policing in the last thirty years and from recent events that have again brought into question the degree of autonomy a democratic society should grant to its police.

In this collection of essays Margaret E. Beare and Tonita Murray have brought together scholars from law, political science, and criminology to illustrate the diversity of opinion that exists on the topic. While providing theoretical models and concrete e   the chapter lize multidisciplinary, comparative, and cas explore how the operating tension between democratic governance and accountability and abroad. Together the essays offer a fram cussion and suggest criteria, options, and too police for future discussion and implementation.

MARGARET E. BEARE is an associate professor in the Department of Sociology and the Osgoode Hall Law School at York University.

TONITA MURRAY is a consultant and gender adviser to the Afghan Ministry of Interior Affairs and former director of the Canadian Police College.

Police and Government Relations

Who's Calling the Shots?

*Edited by Margaret E. Beare
and Tonita Murray*

UNIVERSITY OF TORONTO PRESS
Toronto Buffalo London

© University of Toronto Press Incorporated 2007
Toronto Buffalo London
Printed in Canada

ISBN 978-0-8020-9152-9 (cloth)
ISBN 978-0-8020-9423-0 (paper)

Printed on acid-free paper

Library and Archives Canada Cataloguing in Publication

Police and government relations : who's calling the shots? /
edited by Margaret E. Beare and Tonita Murray.

Includes bibliographical references and index.
ISBN 978-0-8020-9152-9 (bound)
ISBN 978-0-8020-9423-0 (pbk.)

1. Police power – Canada.   I. Beare, Margaret E.
II. Murray, Tonita, 1939–

HV8157.P65 2006   363.20971   C2006-904975-0

University of Toronto Press acknowledges the financial assistance to its
publishing program of the Canada Council for the Arts and the Ontario
Arts Council.

University of Toronto Press acknowledges the financial support for its
publishing activities of the Government of Canada through the Book
Publishing Industry Development Program (BPIDP).

One of the main organizers of the Symposium on Police/Government Relations and a contributor of one of the chapters to this book was our dear friend Dianne Martin, Osgoode Hall Law School professor and co-founder of the Innocence Project. Dianne died in December 2004. Book proceeds will be contributed to the Dianne Martin Bursary Fund to assist students in financial need.

Contents

Foreword

Dudley George was shot and killed by a member of the Ontario Provincial Police at Ipperwash Provincial Park on 6 September 1995. The Ipperwash Inquiry was established by the Government of Ontario on 12 November 2003, under the *Public Inquiries Act*. The order-in-council establishing the inquiry gave me a two-part mandate. The first part gave me the authority to independently investigate and report upon the circumstances surrounding Mr George's death. The second part authorized me to make recommendations directed to the avoidance of violence in similar circumstances. An important issue in both parts of my mandate has been police and government relations.

The papers and commentaries included in this volume were delivered on 28 June 2004 at the Ipperwash Inquiry/Osgoode Hall Law School Symposium on Police/Government Relations. This symposium brought together academics, police and government officials, Aboriginal leaders, and virtually every party with standing at the inquiry to learn about and discuss this important topic.

I am grateful to the authors and commentators for their perceptive and comprehensive analysis of the complex policy, legal, political, and practical issues in the police/government relationship. I am also grateful to the editors, Osgoode Hall Law School, and the University of Toronto Press for their assistance in preparing and publishing this volume. I believe that this collection of papers and commentaries is a significant contribution to the analysis of police and government relations that will assist academics, policy-makers, courts, and others for years to come. Finally, I would like to personally acknowledge the contribution of Professor Dianne Martin. Professor Martin wrote one of the papers in this collection and was a key organizer of the symposium.

This was one of her many efforts to improve the justice system in Ontario and it is fitting that this book be dedicated to her memory.

The Honourable Sidney B. Linden
Commissioner
Ipperwash Inquiry
7 December 2006

Acknowledgments

No book is produced by its authors or editors alone. We wish to thank all of those people who have participated in making this particular book a reality. In their separate ways all of them have contributed to the pursuit of new knowledge on the continuing question of relations between government and police.

First of all, we thank Commissioner Sidney B. Linden, Nye Thomas, director of policy and research, and the staff of the Ipperwash Inquiry for their imagination in funding the academic symposium that produced the substance of this book, and for their practicality in providing financial assistance for its publication. Further, we thank John McCamus for suggesting that Osgoode could serve as host for the symposium. Osgoode Hall Law School also provided strong support for the symposium and the subsequent publication of its papers in book form. We hope that the academic, policing, and policy-making communities are adequately recompensed by the insights that the book provides.

It goes without saying that we are particularly grateful to the contributors. Their reward will be in seeing their scholarship influencing the course of police–government relations in the years to come. Already their work is being used in the Ipperwash Inquiry discussion paper on police–government relations for Part II of the commission mandate. It is also likely to provide guidance to Commissioner Linden in making his final recommendations to the Government of Ontario.

We cannot fail to mention the three groups who were the major parties under scrutiny in the Ipperwash Inquiry: the First Nations communities of Kettle and Stony Point, the police, and political officials. The pressure on all three during the inquiry was great. While they were frequently seen as antagonists, we hope that those in each camp who have goodwill and a desire to see justice done will use the papers in this book to press for a system of police-government relations that will prevent similar confrontation in the future, and help foster good relations between police and First Nations peoples.

Finally, we must acknowledge Sam George, who has shown determination and quiet courage in pursuing justice for his people and for Dudley George, yet without bitterness or vengefulness. He also gave permission for the picture on the cover of the book, which shows First Nations people about to take part in a ceremony to find truth. As he and his family were, all of us who collaborated on this book are searching for truth. It is an elusive quality, but perhaps the joint quest is more important than what we find at the end.

Contributors

Margaret E. Beare
Sociology and Law, York University; Nathanson Center for the Study of Organized Crime and Corruption, Osgoode Hall Law School

A. Alan Borovoy
General Counsel, Canadian Civil Liberties Association

Gordon Christie
Faculty of Law, University of British Columbia

Susan Eng
Former Chair, Metropolitan Toronto Police Services Board

Dianne Martin
Osgoode Hall Law School (deceased)

Kim Murray
Aboriginal Legal Services of Toronto

Tonita Murray
Former Director General, Canadian Police College

W. Wesley Pue
Nemetz Chair in Legal History and Professor of Law, University of British Columbia

Kent Roach
Prichard-Wilson Chair in Law and Public Policy and Professor of Law, University of Toronto

Robert Simmonds
Royal Canadian Mounted Police Commissioner (retired)

Lorne Sossin
Faculty of Law and Political Science, University of Toronto

Philip Stenning
Professor in Criminology, Keele University, UK

Toni Williams
Osgoode Hall Law School

POLICE AND GOVERNMENT RELATIONS:
WHO'S CALLING THE SHOTS?

Introduction

MARGARET E. BEARE AND TONITA MURRAY

Police and Government Relations: Who's Calling the Shots is concerned with the broad question of control of the police and our understanding of both the independence of the police and their accountability for their actions. The book is the product of an academic symposium held at Osgoode Hall Law School and funded by the Ipperwash Inquiry.

The inquiry was established to inquire into and report on events surrounding the death of Dudley George in 1995.[1] Mr George was shot by a police officer during a First Nations protest at Ipperwash Provincial Park, Ontario, and later died. His death was generally regarded as the outcome of actions by the Ontario Provincial Police, which had initially taken a patient and low-key approach to managing the protest, abruptly changing tactics to become less compromising and more forceful. The accusation was that the premier of Ontario at that time had in some way instructed police to remove the Natives from the park. Apart from the question of Aboriginal rights, if the premier had indeed issued instructions to the police and they had obeyed, the circumstance flew in the face of the widely accepted, if constitutionally shaky, theory that governments give policy direction to the police but cannot interfere in operational matters.

While the tragic incident of Dudley George's death raised a number of complex and human issues, this book addresses only the one concerning the relationship between government and the police. Usually, questions about the relationship between elected governments and the police attract only academic attention until a crisis occurs. Then, for a brief period, the issues are minutely examined and furiously debated by governments, media, and the public until the furor subsides and complacency descends once more, leaving seemingly sensible recommendations unimplemented and universally recognized problems unresolved.

The Ipperwash Inquiry has provided us with an important opportunity to revisit the question of what constitutes an ideal or, at least, a reasonably acceptable balance between government direction of the police and police independence. Its support of the symposium allowed eminent scholars to re-examine the body of knowledge that supports the present relationship. These scholars have contributed new insights derived from the evolution of policing in the last thirty years and new events that have again brought into question the degree of autonomy a democratic society should grant to its police.

As the policing literature indicates, this issue, which is currently capturing so much attention in Canada, is simultaneously being debated in other parts of the world in much the same terms. For example, as Ian Loader and Aogán Mulcahy point out in reference to the police in England: 'A particular social imagery is, of course, mobilized here – one that projects the police as a bedrock, national institution ... an institution belonging to "the people" rather than government, and accountable to them (mysteriously one is bound to say) through the majestic splendour of Law rather than the dirty, meddling, dangerous business of politics.' Seen in this light – as a *cultural* as much as a legal doctrine ... it is unsurprising that constabulary independence came to figure so dominantly ... in subsequent struggles over the democratic governance of police.'[2] These authors further argue that while the 'ritualized defences of the unimpeachable importance and cultural significance of police autonomy' continue to fall from the lips of police chiefs as well as politicians, autonomy is no longer the 'trump card' to which any proposal for reform must defer. The 'sacred' service of police work, as policing scholars such as Peter Manning[3] have described it, is arguably giving way to a perception of policing as a 'profane' service. The factors that have stripped away the mystique and led to calls for external monitoring – if not actual dictation of direction – include financial restrictions, a trend towards performance measurement, and more frequent liability considerations. Also strengthening the pull towards greater central oversight are conflicting but powerful lobbying constituencies, new and closer collaborations between police and prosecutors, and empowered victims' groups. Moreover, much-publicized corruption in some jurisdictions and the post- 9/11 environment, both of which have increased the blurring between what Jean-Paul Brodeur[4] terms 'high' and 'low' policing, justify greater intervention in police matters. National security considerations now extend from the national security agencies through the Royal Canadian Mounted Police (RCMP) into the operational duties of the provincial and municipal police across Canada, and security rhetoric authorizes or dictates specific police operations.

We may need to go back to first principles to remember why we are concerned about governance, accountability, independence, and political influence over the police, and why we are more concerned about the conduct of the police than we are about other public sector workers. We are concerned because the state has given the police a non-specific mandate to maintain the peace. This is a somewhat general direction that might mean anything, depending on the time, place, prevailing social and political attitudes of the day, and the individual judgments of those holding such a mandate. In addition, we have granted the police the coercive and intrusive powers we believe are necessary for them to maintain the peace. So we have set up the police with the mandate and powers to make them effective generalist public sector workers able to intervene in a wide range of situations to maintain or restore social stability when necessary. But, in a democratic society, where we are all theoretically equal, we are fearful that in giving powers to the police that we do not ourselves possess, we are disabling ourselves and providing them a means by which to work against rather than for us, if they were so minded. Governance and accountability mechanisms are an expression of our ambivalence and inherent distrust of the police function.

Police can detain, enter premises, search, seize, arrest, and use force – even deadly force. The rule of law, the *Charter*, the *Criminal Code*, and other statutes all prescribe the circumstances under which such powers can be used. Such powers are usually used in the maintenance of public order and in criminal investigation. But police face many tasks, and public order maintenance and criminal investigation tend to constitute a smaller percentage of police activity than responding to service calls. Governance and oversight mechanisms thus influence only part of the police role, but that part has the greatest potential to harm individuals, society, and democratic processes, and hence we consider the degree of oversight well justified.

There is also another power that is not so well defined or understood but that is perhaps the most potent and the most likely to allow partisan behaviour or to tempt political influence. It is the power of police to exercise discretion or, in other words, the ability of police officers to act on individual judgment according to circumstances. Discretion allows for equity and flexibility, but it can also be abused by police officers and it can render them vulnerable to pressure from others to decide in a particular way. This is perhaps the chink in the armour that can allow political influence of the police to creep in.

Some readers will recall the 'classic' 1980 paper titled 'The Police: A Policy Paper' prepared by Alan Grant for the Law Commission of Canada. Professor Grant notes both, but distinguishes between, 'police discretion' in situations where police can make actual discretionary decisions and 'political discretion' that determines where as a matter of political decisions the police are given the structural capacity to engage in specific enforcement efforts. He states: 'society not only has substantive laws but must also consider the arrangements for enforcing them. A lack of such arrangements in particular areas can result in the shape and content of the substantive law being quite different in practice from that which a study of the law-in-the-books might lead an observer to expect.' He argues therefore that 'the manner in which we organize our various law enforcement agencies is an essentially political decision.'[5]

Ultimately in Canada, police observation of democratic principles is maintained by balancing political accountability and police independence. As in any dynamic system, the balance is not a steady constant but a swing too much in one direction tends to stimulate a response to bring it back to something approaching equilibrium. Moreover, we ensure some limits on police authority by keeping police numbers low. As of 2005 there were almost 60,000 police officers in Canada, one for every 533 Canadians, or about 188 per 100,000 population. There are fewer than 350 police services in Canada and most have less than 100 police officers. In Ontario in 2003 there were 23,328 police officers,[6] or 191 for every 100,000 Ontario residents. These ratios are among the lowest in the world and on a par with New Zealand and Japan. As far as numbers are concerned, therefore, Canada is not in danger of becoming a police state. Nevertheless, the numbers are likely to be of little comfort to those people or groups who feel they have been abused by police actions or are the victims of political decisions targeting them.

Several of the authors of the following chapters agree that while revitalization or remaking of systems of governance is important, it is only part of the remedy. Unless there is an understanding of the policing environment and its prevailing culture, values, arrangements, practices and, in particular, pressures and demands, reform of police governance is likely to fall short of its objectives. We must engage in a discussion of the art of the possible: how to identify and bring all the active ingredients for governing the relationship between the executive arm of government and the police into the same formula.

Police need more civic education, or the equivalent of a Political Science 101 course in basic training. They need to be more sophisticated about politics and government, so that they can distinguish between legitimate direction and undue political influence. And there could be better selection and training of members and executive staff of governing bodies to improve knowledge and competencies. Governing bodies in their turn could be required to demonstrate accountability, to be transparent, and to submit to public scrutiny and reporting. Above all, they should be truly at arm's length to elected officials, appointed on merit, and a clear distinction should be made between legitimate direction of the police and illegitimate political influence.

Ultimately, however, it may prove impossible to take the political colour entirely out of policing. A policing system is defined by the ruling ideology of its state. Ours is a parliamentary democracy founded on common law. It works because we are essentially pragmatic. Our police are a reflection of this approach to government. Other countries, such as the United States, Germany, or France, have more rational approaches to democracy, and this is evident in the organization and authority of their police. The police of the former USSR and South Africa of apartheid days also reflected the prevailing ideologies of their states. In Canada, where no political party diverges too far from the centre, police approaches tend not to diverge greatly either, whatever the party in power.

This book does not attempt to provide final answers. The goal is to provide a framework for a continuing discussion that may lead to the development of helpful and workable recommendations for the future. In the process, it will also serve as an academic and intellectual contribution to an important matter of public policy.

Structure and Organizational Logic

This book comprises six chapters, five of which include commentaries; an epilogue; and an appendix of selected materials used to guide the Ipperwash Inquiry. The chapters utilize multi-disciplinary, comparative, and case-study methodologies to provide concrete examples as well as ideas, theoretical models, and frameworks. While each chapter was selected to 'fit' into a complete picture of police-executive relations, the exercise has not been ideologically driven. It was deemed important for the papers to reflect the diversity of opinion on the topic. From various perspectives, the chapters help to flesh out the ways that the operating tension between police independence and democratic governance and accountability has played out in Canada, as well as in other countries and settings. Thus each chapter illustrates its central ideas with specific examples, suggests criteria, options, and tools for both legislators and police, and explains why they are needed.

The opening chapter by Kent Roach provides a broad overview of the issues explored in greater depth by the chapters that follow. He discusses incidents that have gained a degree of notoriety, including the APEC incident, which led to the inquiry by Justice Ted Hughes, and more recent criticism over the timing of charges laid in 2004 by the RCMP immediately prior to an election in what has come to be called the 'sponsorship scandal.' As all lawyers examining police independence must, Roach also discusses Lord Denning's landmark 1968 opinion, considered to be the definitive articulation of the argument on the subject.

Professor Roach reminds us of the lost opportunities to clarify the basic principles of police independence and the failure to introduce transparent processes and protocols, most recently in the Supreme Court's statement in *R. v. Campbell and Shirose* (1999) that police independence could be derived from the rule of law, and in Justice Hughes's call in the 2001 APEC inquiry for a codification of the principles of police accountability. Roach then sets out four models of police-government relations, which represent a continuum from full police independence to close government direction, all four derived from judicial decision, the conclusions of commissions of inquiry, or current legislation. In essence, he suggests that a choice should be made among them and then codified to end the lack of clarity. Of note is his argument that the case for police independence is based largely on arguments of civil liability cases without adequate theorizing from a constitutional or administrative law perspective. Canadian cases, often ignored in the international debate, are introduced in this chapter and used as a prism through which the Canadian situation is analysed.

Included in Roach's chapter is a historically significant document recording a discussion that took place in 1985 between the Honourable Robert Kaplan and Robert Simmonds, then commissioner of the RCMP. Robert Simmonds provided us with this document. The situation under discussion was the appropriateness of the solicitor general of the day potentially influencing the RCMP in what was referred to as the *Hatfield* case. Kaplan asserted that if the commissioner could disregard a minister's order regarding a decision to carry out an investigation 'then we live in a police state. We live in a state where the police can defy a lawful order from the civilian authority.' The commissioner responded, 'The more common definition [is] that a police state emerges when a government uses its police agencies as instruments of repression against the citizens of the state. It is against that very concern that the police are given a high degree of independence.' In addition to its historical significance, this exchange contains the essence of the debate over police–government relations, each side perceiving different types of dangers.

An insider's point of view is emphasized in the Commentary to Roach's chapter provided by Commissioner Robert Simmonds (retired). Both in his commentary and in the open discussion portion of the symposium, Simmonds provided valuable insight into what the police see their role to be in situations that are clearly politically explosive. In the discussion portion of the symposium, he recounted an incident that occurred early in his career when he was sent by the government or, in his terms, 'as the Queen's representative,' to resolve a situation involving a First Nations roadblock in British Columbia that had involved the drowning death of a protestor. What was from his perspective a successfully negotiated, peaceful example of good police work was viewed differently by some of the conference participants. Others however saw it as an example that illustrated the complexity of the very topic under discussion. Easy or clear policing situations would not warrant the attention of either academics or policy makers.

Roach's chapter is followed by five more that analyse police accountability in other ways: accountability to the law and, by more subtle negotiation, to the community. In chapter 2, Lorne Sossin looks at the question of the relationship between police and the executive arm of government from the perspective of the executive, and offers an alternative model to the typology presented by Kent Roach. Perhaps among all of the chapters, his best describes how the oversight mechanisms are *supposed* to work in a formal way. Professor Sossin outlines the formal mechanisms but then proceeds to analyse the inherent contradictions that tend to erode the model, such as the requirement that the relationship between police and executive be 'political but not partisan' and 'autonomous but not independent.'

Sossin makes an argument that is reiterated in a number of the chapters. Accountability processes and the various checks and balances require a high degree of transparency to earn trust and win and maintain the confidence of the public. He sets out what he calls 'an ideal apolitical autonomous police model,' in which neither the police nor the executive arm of government unilaterally imposes its will on the other. He advocates a role for each branch of government in the comprehensive governance of the police. In addition to governing and oversight bodies and the courts, he argues that parliamentary and legislative committees with, perhaps, even an officer responsible to the legislative arm of government, would add greater transparency to the relationship between the executive and the police.

The need for transparency is picked up by Alan Borovoy in his commentary on Sossin's paper. Borovoy's solution, in contrast to that offered by Sossin, reveals a slightly less trusting police critic! The commentary of Wesley Pue likewise challenges Sossin's faith in the rule of law: 'Professor Sossin's emphasis on the rule of law is discomfiting. The idea of law sits ill at ease with a criminal justice system so shot-through with discretionary powers as to seemingly vanish into a mere "rule of persons."'

The comments of Borovoy and Pue introduce us to a notable 'tension' between the papers and commentary provided by the legal scholars and the more criminological chapters in this volume. The existence of this tension is perhaps one of the most significant findings from the symposium. Legal interpretations (although there is no absolute consensus here) of the appropriate relationship between the police and the executive may be quite different from what happens 'in the field' where policing individuals meet political individuals and political issues. Lord Denning and other legal writers may decree what is proper, and these views may be used to guide policies relating to the interactions between police and politics. However, the day-to-day nuanced and negotiated relationships, as emphasized by the criminologists, tell a different story. The ongoing shared interests, organizational requirements, friendships, and power dynamics of the police and politicians converge and serve to blur the priorities and dictate the actions of both.

Legitimacy considerations – possibly expressed as demands from the public – may require that 'actions must be taken or be seen to be taken.' Social unrest must be converted to social order, and responsibility for this transition will rest largely with both the police *and* the politicians. Hence in crisis situations the agendas of both may well overlap. This consensus is only disrupted by a second source of tension: the equally demanding voices of groups with as great a need, and in our society a protected right, to express their ideological, economic, or social perspectives. The commitment on one side may be matched with zeal on the other. The situation being 'policed' may in fact be a 'political' situation with a long history that ought to have been resolved outside of law enforcement and yet falls upon law enforcement.

Chapter 3, by Gordon Christie, is a key chapter of the book. A strong theme underpinning the Ipperwash Inquiry was the political relationship among the police, the state, and Aboriginal peoples, and this is the subject of Professor Christie's paper. His thesis is that Aboriginal peoples are not merely protected against arbitrary government or police action as a minority group under the *Charter of Rights and Freedoms*, but that they have a status altogether different, and legally problematic, which should influence police-government relations with respect to Aboriginal peoples. He points out that Aboriginal peoples 'enjoy the recognition and affirmation of existing Aboriginal and Treaty rights under section 35 of the *Constitution Act* of 1982,' which gives them explicit constitutional protection. He explains that government is engaged in reconciliation with Aboriginal peoples, based on their existence prior to the existence of the Crown in Canada, and that the government is in a fiduciary relationship to Aboriginal peoples, which means the government has a duty to work on their behalf. In its fiduciary role, the government therefore has a duty to direct police *away* from actions that potentially interfere with Aboriginal and treaty rights and *towards* actions that promote reconciliation. This duty, he implies, could extend into the operational realm of the police.

While, from what may be a practical point of view, Christie favours a democratic policing model overseen by the law and in harmony with the fiduciary role of the government, ultimately he has no blueprint for police-government relations with respect to Aboriginal peoples. He argues that this is because the fiduciary relationship itself is flawed. In the face of what may be essentially Aboriginal sovereignty, the fiduciary role, the Canadian legal framework, and the Canadian courts have no force in the context of Crown-Aboriginal relations. If this is the case, the question of the government-police relationship is left in the air until the question of the status of Aboriginal rights is resolved. Christie thus introduces a new and troubling strand to the already difficult question of police-government relations. It is an aspect of the relationship that cannot be ignored, yet there will clearly be no early or easy resolution, despite the fact that it has the potential to arise in every police-Aboriginal interaction.

The commentary on Christie's chapter, prepared jointly by Toni

Williams and Kim Murray, touches on the colonization of Aboriginal peoples and the need to build a new relationship between them and the Canadian state before police governance in relation to Aboriginal peoples can be considered. The lack of what they call a framework for decolonization may help explain why well-meant experiments in First Nations self-policing have not been totally successful.

Since the 1980s, First Nations communities have been able to decide whether to administer their own police services or to contract the services of other police organizations such as the RCMP. Many First Nations communities in Ontario and Quebec in particular have opted to administer their own police services. Three hundred, or 60 per cent of First Nations communities, now have self-administered police services. Such organizations are wholly funded by the federal government and the province in which the community is located. The funding, however, has been contingent on the First Nations communities accepting terms and conditions for policing incorporated into tripartite agreements. None of the three parties has been completely happy with the results. The Canadian and provincial governments have been concerned with failed police leadership and financial accountability, the police services with penurious conditions that have limited their ability to provide a full range of effective services, and First Nations communities with either poor service or policing exhibiting the same colonialist characteristics that they resented in previous non-Aboriginal policing arrangements. On occasion, self-policing has led to tension, divisiveness, and outright confrontations between police and community.

More recently there has been a movement to introduce police governance mechanisms. Ontario, for example, has a number of First Nations police commissions. These are still in their infancy, however, and have yet to prove themselves. Given that they are built on non-Aboriginal models, apart from the question of appropriateness, there is a danger that they may incorporate the same flaws as exist in longer-standing governing bodies. Without new ideas, First Nations policing and police governance may be doomed to follow the same path that makes police governance in Canada so problematic. And, despite good will, if the Canadian state is unable to 'think out of the box' to provide Aboriginal peoples with a 'decolonized' framework for police governance, present efforts will achieve little.

Chapter 4, by Philip Stenning, provides the reader with two separate contributions. Professor Stenning begins by clarifying why, from his perspective, there is no contradiction between police independence and police accountability. By his definition, these concepts are totally compatible. Part of the clarity that his chapter offers lies in the differentiation he brings to the term 'independence.' While the literature on police autonomy often refers to the sloganlike reiteration that police must be 'operationally independent while operating under the policy direction' of ministers, Stenning identifies six separate aspects of independent decision making. From thereon, the chapter offers us a series of comparisons with the situation in England and Wales, Australia, and New Zealand.

In chapter 5 Dianne Martin supports some of the Commentary views expressed in Lorne Sossin's chapter. She is also concerned with the 'legal sites' that may have been intended to structure the relationship between the executive and the police. However, rather than focusing on the tensions or contradictions that she would agree exist, Martin analyses the more informal negotiations, and the significant role of the wide array of players and processes that shape the relationships. Martin sees control of the police residing in a multilayered system of examination and oversight. The more 'sites,' agencies, or mechanisms for questioning police actions and the relationship between government and police, the greater the likelihood that transparency and the rule of law will be respected and democratic policing produced. While the accountability of the police to the rule of law may be a viable mechanism, it is individualized and fraught with institutional needs and organizational interests. Gender, class, and wider power issues are all part of what is seldom a neutral discretionary operation. Her chapter serves to bring the discussion closer to the ground, to what really happens in the relationship between the police and their political masters.

Susan Eng's commentary supports Martin's arguments, but with a slight twist. Not only are diverse interests being negotiated during the accountability processes, but these interests may be, in some cases, as petty as personal agendas or as arbitrary as a strict consideration of costs. Eng served as the former chair of the Metropolitan Toronto Police Services Board and saw firsthand the negotiations inherent in attempting to achieve police accountability. She cites the example of the costs that municipalities must pay for civilian complaint hearings being used as the basis for opposition to a viable complaint process. The limits on municipal funds are in contrast to the plentiful resources that police unions apparently have to hire the best lawyers for the defence of their members. Both large and small 'p' political pressures serve to determine the degree of commitment to various well-intentioned directives, policies or, in some cases, laws. This theme runs through Martin's paper, as it has in her writings over the years.

Chapter 6, by Margaret Beare, continues the examination into the operational specifics of the police-executive relationship and looks again at the actual working relationship between the police and the various levels of political bodies. This chapter is based in part on a fifty-year analysis of policing in Metropolitan Toronto and illustrates with particular examples the ongoing, intensive political involvement in police decision making. As stated in the chapter, searching for the smoking gun, namely the memo or moment when an explicit operational directive was given, misses the point, for in many cases a partnership has been formed between the police and their political masters in which they share interests and priorities. A number of the authors in this volume suggest that a two-way relationship between the executive arm of government and the police is not a sufficient guarantee of right action. Beare's chapter goes further in showing that the governing body and the police are not always in tension but can collude in negative ways and, when this happens, the rights of minority groups can be violated. As Dianne Martin emphasizes, only multiple responsibilities for police governance can ensure that the common and public interest rises above the particular interest. Such a multilayered arrangement can also support the autonomy of the police, since it protects them from the real or suspected danger of partisan political influence.

The commentary by Tonita Murray questions the multiple definitions given the word 'politics' in discussions of the police-government relationship. Having held a number of senior positions in policing and as a civilian member of the RCMP, Murray is well placed to point out, with excellent examples, that political influence can look very different inside policing.

Following these six chapters, the book concludes with an epilogue and an appendix that presents a discussion paper and questions used to guide the Ipperwash Inquiry Report that pertain specifically to police-executive relations.

NOTES

1 Established by the Government of Ontario on 12 November 2003. The Honourable Sidney B. Linden served as the commissioner to the inquiry.
2 Ian Loader and Aogán Mulcahy, *Policing and the Condition of England: Memory, Politics, and Culture* (Oxford: Oxford University Press, 2003), 265 and 298.

3 Peter Manning, *Police Work: The Social Organization of Policing* (Prospect Heights, IL: Waveland Press, 1997).

4 J.P. Brodeur, 'High Policing and Low Policing: Remarks about the Policing of Political Activities,' in *Understanding Policing*, ed. K. McCormick and L. Visano, 277–99 (Toronto: Canadian Scholars' Press, 1992).

5 Alan Grant, 'The Police: A Policy Paper,' prepared for the Law Commission of Canada, Criminal Law Series (Ottawa: Minister of Supply and Services Canada, 1980), 6–7.

6 Ramona Morris, *Ontario Police College Recruit Profile: September 1998–September 2003* (Toronto: Queen's Printer for Ontario, 2004).

1 The Overview: Four Models of Police-Government Relations

KENT ROACH

Abstract

This chapter provides an introduction to police-government relations in Canada and serves as an overview of some of the issues covered in later chapters. It outlines the law and history of police-government relations in Canada, describes four different models of those relations, and identifies critical issues distinguishing different approaches to police independence.

The first part of the chapter examines the contested legal basis for claims of police independence from government, focusing on the Supreme Court of Canada's pronouncements on this issue in R. v. Campbell *and* Shirose. *The second part examines highlights of the history of police-government relationships. Controversies such as the Nicholson affair and the Airbus, Doug Small, and sponsorship scandal cases are examined, as well as the contributions of the McDonald, Marshall, and APEC inquiries to thinking about the proper relations between the police and the government. Included in this chapter is a historic document written by the then RCMP commissioner R.H. Simmonds regarding the relationship between the RCMP and the government pertaining to the Hatfield affair.*

The third part of the chapter constructs four ideal models of police-government relations in order to reveal the range of value choice and policy options. The first model is full police independence, in which the police are immune from government intervention on a wide variety of matters, including the policing of demonstrations. The second model is core or quasi-judicial police independence, in which police independence is restricted to the process of criminal investigation. The third model, democratic policing, similarly restricts police independence but places greater emphasis on the responsible minister's accountability and control over policy matters in policing. The

*fourth model, governmental policing, both minimizes the ambit of police
independence and accepts the greater role of central agencies in coordinating
government services including policing.*

*The final part of the chapter outlines some critical issues differentiating the
four models of police-government relations. They include the precise ambit of
police independence from government, the respective roles of responsible
ministers and central agencies in interacting with the police, the distinction
between government requests for information from the police and attempts
to influence the police, and whether government interventions in policing
should be formally reduced to writing or remain informal.*

*The chapter concludes with a commentary by Commissioner R.H. Sim-
monds (Retired).*

Introduction

The contested issue of whether and to what extent the police are independent from the government can pop up at any time. When it does, it
will often raise the temperature of the debate, but the result can often be
more heat than light. One need not look far back in time to find examples of controversies in Canada concerning the relationship between
the police and the government. They include the conclusion of Justice
Hughes in the 2001 APEC report that there had been 'improper federal
government involvement' in the Royal Canadian Mounted Police
(RCMP) security operation and that the police had 'succumbed to government influence and intrusion in an area where such influence and
intrusion were inappropriate.'[1] More recently, we have seen statements
by the then leader of the Opposition that the laying of criminal charges
in relation to the sponsorship scandal just before the 2004 election
seemed suspicious. The minister responsible for the RCMP responded
that such allegations were 'appalling and profoundly unacceptable.'[2]
Likewise, Liberal supporters questioned the announcement, just prior
to the 2006 election, that the RCMP were investigating possible wrongdoing in a budget leak situation – again with a denial from the RCMP.
Controversy can at times serve the purpose of prompting and clarifying thought, but these recent events appear to have done relatively
little to generate a consensus about the appropriate relationship between the police and the government. The relationship remains 'murky,'[3]
even though it is a matter of considerable civic and constitutional
significance.

It is, however, difficult to be too critical of the state of public understanding about the relationship between the police and the government. As Professor Philip Stenning has concluded, there is 'very little
clarity or consensus among politicians, senior RCMP officers, jurists ...,
commissions of inquiry, academics, or other commentators either about
exactly what "police independence" comprises or about its practical
implications ...'[4] In chapter 4 of this volume Stenning makes the further
point that, based on his international research, the lack of consensus is
not unique to Canada. Indeed, one can find support in some statutes,
cases, and commentary for opposite conclusions on whether the police
are independent from government direction and on the ambit of any
independence. For example, there is some support for a broad understanding of police independence that would extend beyond the freedom of the constable to decide who to investigate and who to charge to
cover a broad range of other policing decisions. At the other extreme,
there is some support in statutes and cases for a thin to non-existent
doctrine of police independence that sees the police in Canada as civil
servants subject to ministerial control and direction. There are also, of
course, a variety of views that fall somewhere between these two extremes. There is confusion about whether police-government relations
should be funnelled through the responsible minister or include discussions with central agencies and political staff. Finally, there is the critical
question of whether a distinction between the government informing
itself about police matters and influencing the police is sustainable in
the minds of politicians, police, and the public.

The relationship between the police and the government is a matter
of fundamental constitutional significance in any state. It is particularly
challenging in a country such as Canada, which is free and democratic
and committed to the rule of law. The idea that the police are a law unto
themselves is unacceptable in a democracy that prides itself on restraint
in the use of coercive state-sponsored force and on accountability for
the use of such powers. The idea that the police are directed by the
government of the day, however, raises concerns about improper partisanship influencing or appearing to influence the machinery of justice.
There is a need to respect and balance the principles of independence
and accountability, and to do so in a manner that advances our aspirations to be a democratic nation that is governed by law. The competing
values were well summarized by an RCMP spokesperson who, in response to allegations of political interference in policing in the sponsorship scandal, commented that 'police have a unique role to play in our

democratic system. On the one hand, their criminal investigations must be absolutely free of political influences. Yet on the other, they must not become the law unto themselves.'[5]

The first part of this chapter will examine the contested legal basis for police independence. The starting point is Lord Denning's controversial conclusion in *Ex parte Blackburn*[6] that a police constable is independent and answerable only to the law. Several chapters in this volume refer to Lord Denning and *Blackburn*, as the case is seen as an authoritative starting point for the debates around police independence. Although it purported to establish a broad and absolute relationship of independence between the police and the government, both *Blackburn* and the cases it relied upon actually dealt with very different issues, such as whether the government was civilly liable for police actions and whether the courts could review decisions by the police not to enforce laws. The Quebec Court of Appeal concluded in 1980 that the British common law concept of police independence was thoroughly inappropriate in the Canadian context of national and provincial police forces responsible to Cabinet ministers.[7] Although the Quebec Court of Appeal's decision has largely been ignored, it finds some support in legislation governing Canada's two largest police forces, the RCMP and the Ontario Provincial Police (OPP). As will be seen, in both cases the relevant laws contemplate that the police are subject to the direction of an elected minister who sits in Cabinet.[8] Such statutory powers, however, may be limited by the Supreme Court of Canada's decision in *R. v. Campbell and Shirose*.[9] In that case, the Court not only cited the *Blackburn* doctrine with favour but also related police independence from the executive with respect to criminal investigations to the constitutional principle of the rule of law. The *Campbell* case has arguably elevated police independence in criminal investigations from a constitutional convention that in practice restrains the exercises of ministerial powers to a component of one of Canada's organizing constitutional principles, namely the rule of law.[10] Nevertheless, the precise nature and ambit of police independence remains unclear. The modern concept of police independence was born in controversy in the United Kingdom and its applicability to Canada has been contested from the start.

The second part of this chapter will examine contested political understandings of police independence in Canada. The focus will be on a series of controversies over the last forty-five years with respect to police-government relations. These range from the resignation of a commissioner of the RCMP because his minister refused his request to send re-enforcements to a volatile labour strike to allegations that the timing of charges arising from the sponsorship scandal and the announcement of a RCMP investigation into a budget leak, just before the 2004 and 2006 elections, were suspicious. Various law reform proposals, including those made by the McDonald Commission into the RCMP, the Royal Commission on the Prosecution of Donald Marshall Jr, and the APEC report will be examined, as will the findings of those inquiries about government involvement in policing.

The third part of this chapter will attempt to identify the fundamental principles and interests at stake, as well as the range of reasonable disagreement, by constructing four models of police-government relationships. Given the lack of consensus about the proper ambit of police independence, the complexity of the subject, and the tacit assumptions that lie behind different understandings of police independence, it is my hope that the models described will facilitate debate and clarity. In the first model (full police independence) the police are immune from government intervention on a wide variety of matters, including the policing of demonstrations. This model is best associated with Lord Denning's views in *Ex parte Blackburn* about the independence of the police constable. The second model (quasi-judicial or core police independence) restricts police independence to core functions such as decisions to initiate criminal investigations and lay charges. This model finds some support in *Campbell* as well as in the reports the McDonald, Marshall, and APEC inquiries. The third model (democratic policing) protects police from direction by the government on core law enforcement functions, but maintains the ability of the responsible minister to be informed about policy-laden elements of criminal investigations and to shape all other policy or public interest matters in policing. This model is best associated with the recommendations of the McDonald Commission, which stressed the importance of democratic control and accountability for policing. The fourth model (governmental policing) is one in which the police are conceived by and large as civil servants subject to ministerial control and protected only by their ability to refuse to obey unlawful orders and whatever other protections that civil servants may enjoy. This model finds some support in the wording of police acts which suggest that the police are 'under the direction of the Minister'[11] and the Quebec Court of Appeal's rejection of the common law understanding of police independence as inconsistent with such statutes.[12] The governmental policing model could also embrace developments in government that stress the importance of Cabinet and central agencies in coordinating and even dominating the multifaceted work of government and the increasing erosion of traditional notions of ministerial accountability.

The fourth and final part of this chapter outlines some of the key questions that will inform the choice of models. The first critical issue is how the ambit of police independence should be defined. Should it be confined to core or quasi-judicial functions related to criminal investigations, or does it also cover other matters such as the methods of police deployment at demonstrations? As will be seen, the answer to this critical question may depend on the respective trust accorded to the police and politicians, and whether there is transparency and accountability for political interventions in policing. Another fundamental issue is whether distinctions drawn by some scholars and royal commissions between government requests for information and explanations from the police and government attempts to control, direct, and influence the police are sustainable. At issue is not only the ability to make intellectual distinctions, but whether these distinctions are sustainable in the real world of politics, and public cynicism, where police independence is not widely understood. Related issues concern the appropriate timing of political interventions either before or after the police have made preliminary decisions, and whether such interventions should be reduced to writing. Another crucial issue that will affect the choice of any particular model of police independence is who precisely constitutes the government. Is it limited to the minister responsible for the police, or does it extend to the senior civil service, political staff, the Cabinet, and central agencies? One challenge in developing a twenty-first-century approach to police-government relations is to account for increased centralization within government that can allow even the responsible minister to be bypassed in favour of central agencies and their political apparatus.[13] Important questions remain about the quality of political direction that the police might receive from government. Is the distinction between permissible political intervention in the public interest as opposed to impermissible partisan concerns sustainable? Is it realistic to expect that ministers will impose standards on the police that are more respectful of the right to dissent in a democracy than the minimum standards imposed by the constitution and presumably respected by the police? Is it possible to design systems to promote greater accountability for political directions to the police, or will requirements that political directions to the police be reduced to writing and be made public be circumvented and/or dismissed as too unwieldy? The ultimate and difficult goal should be to design under-standings and processes that will promote fidelity to both democracy and the law.

I. Contested Legal Understandings of Police Independence

The Blackburn Doctrine

The most famous articulation of the idea of police independence was made in 1968 by Lord Denning, in a rather odd case challenging a confidential instruction by the commissioner of the London police to his officers not to enforce certain gambling laws.[14] The police had decided to revoke their blanket policy not to enforce the law, which might have rendered the case moot. This did not deter Lord Denning, who stated:

> I have no hesitation in holding that, like every constable in the land, [the Commissioner of the London Police] should be, and is, independent of the executive. He is not subject to the orders of the Secretary of State, save that under the Police Act, 1964, the Secretary of State can call upon him to give a report, or to retire in the interests of efficiency. I hold it to be the duty of the Commissioner of Police of the Metropolis, as it is of every chief constable, to enforce the law of the land. He must take steps so to post his men that crimes may be detected; and that honest citizens may go about their affairs in peace. He must decide whether or not suspected persons are to be prosecuted; and, if need be, bring the prosecution or see that it is brought. But in all these things he is not the servant of anyone, save of the law itself. No Minister of the Crown can tell him that he must, or must not, keep observation on this place or that; or that he must, or must not, prosecute this man or that one. Nor can any police authority tell him so. The responsibility for law enforcement lies on him. He is answerable to the law and to the law alone.[15]

In support of the above categorical propositions, Lord Denning cited two cases that held that there was no master and servant relationship between the Crown and the police for the purpose of determining civil liability.[16] Writing in 1965, Geoffrey Marshall, a distinguished constitu-tional scholar, argued that the cases relied upon by Lord Denning rest 'almost entirely upon fairly recent inferences from the law of civil liability.' They were not concerned with general constitutional prin-ciples, but only that 'there is no master and servant relationship between constables and their employers in the rather special sense which has been given that phrase in the law of torts.'[17] In Professor Marshall's opinion, at their highest, the civil liability cases relied upon by Lord Denning stood for the proposition that the police, like the military, could reject illegal orders. This limited form of independence, however, 'does not entail independence in the sense of an immunity from subjection to lawful orders.'[18] Professor Marshall, however, worried that 'the exaggerated and inconsistent' idea of police independence 'has almost taken on the character of a new principle of the constitution while nobody was looking.'[19]

Lord Denning did not cite a Canadian master and servant case, but he could have. The Supreme Court of Canada, in the 1999 *Campbell* case, relied upon the same master and servant cases as Lord Denning relied upon, but added one decided by the Supreme Court in 1902, well before the cases cited by Lord Denning. In that case, Strong CJ stated: 'Police officers can in no respect be regarded as agents or officers of the city. Their duties are of a public nature. Their appointment is devolved on cities and towns by the legislature as a convenient mode of exercising a function of government, but this does not render them liable for their unlawful or negligent acts. The detection and arrest of offenders, the preservation of the public peace, the enforcement of the laws, and other similar powers and duties with which police officers and constables are entrusted are derived from the law, and not from the city or town under which they hold their appointment.'[20] I am not arguing that police independence is illegitimate because it rests on civil liability cases decided for very different purposes; I only wish to suggest that it was born under somewhat dubious circumstances. The reliance on civil liability cases means that the concept of police independence has been under-theorized from the start from a constitutional or administrative law perspective. Courts, and sometimes commentators, have been too quick to cite extraneous statements from cases as opposed to thinking through the rationale and implications of police independence from government.

The Canadian Context

In 1980, a three-judge panel of the Quebec Court of Appeal in *Bisaillon v. Keable* rejected the common law principle of police independence and made statements that may seem heretical to many proponents of police independence. The case was reversed on appeal by the Supreme Court of Canada, on other grounds[21] and the Supreme Court did not confirm or deny the Court of Appeal's categorical dismissal of the common law concept of police independence. Even if the Court of Appeal's decision has been overtaken by *Campbell*, it should be examined here because it reminds Canadians of the need to adapt the English common law to Canadian circumstances, and in particular to the statutory framework of Canadian police acts.

The lead judgment in *Bisaillon v. Keable* was written by Turgeon JA of the Quebec Court of Appeal. He stressed that in contrast to the English history, 'notre système d'administration de la justice est tout à fait différent, et le rôle et le statut de la police à l'intérieur de ce système est clair et bien défini par des textes législatifs.'[22] The minister of justice in Quebec had at the time statutory powers over the police in Quebec and the solicitor general had statutory powers over the RCMP. There was a strong streak of legal positivism and legislative supremacy in Turgeon JA's judgment, but he also suggested that the national policing model used in Canada could be contrasted with a more local policing model that prevailed in the United Kingdom. In his 1965 book, Geoffrey Marshall had made a similar point, observing in the English context that 'feelings about the political undesirability of directing constabulary forces from a single administrative centre have perhaps overlapped with the notion that the members of such forces ought to be under no form of external direction at all. If the nineteenth-century statutory regulation of police forces had taken the form of setting up a single national force it seems doubtful whether so much would have been heard about the autonomous common law powers of constables. Such a doctrine would cut across the necessities of public accountability to Ministers and Parliament.'[23] The suggestion here is that the statutes trump and overtake the common law, but also that questions of accountability need to be formalized when policing is done at the national or provincial as opposed to the local level.

L'Heureux-Dubé JA concluded, 'comme mon collègue Turgeon et pour les raisons qu'il invoque, j'estime que l'appelant exerce une fonction de l'état en matière d'administration de la justice. En ce sens, l'appelant doit être considéré comme un fonctionnaire de l'état, même si son statut au sein de la fonction publique peut différer de celui d'autres fonctionnaires.'[24] Her idea that police officers are civil servants, even with the qualification that they exercise different functions than other civil servants, would, rightly or wrongly, be viewed as heresy by believers in Lord Denning's views of the constable as independent from the executive and answerable only to the law. A year later, albeit without reference to the case, the McDonald Commission similarly commented that Lord Denning's comments had unfortunately been 'constantly transposed to the Canadian scene with no regard to those essential features that distinguish Canadian police forces from their British counterparts' and that statutory reference to the RCMP being subject to ministerial direction 'has to that extent made the English doctrine expounded in *Ex parte Blackburn* inapplicable to the R.C.M.P.'[25]

The Quebec Court of Appeal's decision is of more than historical significance because it finds some support in current legislation governing Canada's two largest police forces, the RCMP and the OPP. Section 5(1) of the *Royal Canadian Mounted Police Act* provides: 'The Governor in Council may appoint an officer, to be known as the Commissioner of the Royal Canadian Mounted Police, who, under the direction of the Minister, has the control and management of the Force and all matters connected therewith.'[26] From 1959[27] to 1966, the relevant minister was the minister of justice of Canada; from 1966 to 2003, it was the solicitor general of Canada, and since the end of 2003 it has been the minister of public safety and emergency preparedness. Section 17(2) of Ontario's 1990 *Police Services Act*[28] also contemplates ministerial direction of the provincial police force by providing that 'subject to the Solicitor General's direction, the Commissioner has the general control and administration of the Ontario Provincial Police and the employees connected with it.' As in the federal sphere, the responsible minister has recently been renamed and is now called the minister of community safety and correctional services.[29] In contrast to the *RCMP Act* and even though there was little discussion of police-government relations at the time of its enactment, the Ontario legislation does define the duties and powers of the responsible minister. In addition to a variety of educational, informational,[30] and inspection matters, they include monitoring police forces to ensure that adequate and effective police services are provided; monitoring police boards and polices forces to ensure that they comply with prescribed standards of service; assisting in the coordination of police services and issuing directives and guidelines respecting 'policy matters.' Conspicuous by their absence is any reference to providing direction on matters of criminal investigation or indeed direction in individual cases as opposed to 'directives and guidelines respecting policy matters.'[31] The Ontario act may implicitly recognize some degree of police independence from government more by what it omits than what it includes. This may be an improvement from the

RCMP Act which on its face contemplates unrestricted ministerial direction of the police. Nevertheless, the Ontario act is not as explicit or as precise as it could be in spelling out the exact ambit of police independence or the proper relationship between the minister and the police. One of the reasons for controversy and confusion about police independence in Canada is the general absence of clear statutory definitions of the concept.

Campbell and Shirose

The Supreme Court's 1999 decision in Campbell and Shirose has revived the Blackburn doctrine of police independence despite the statutory language examined above which suggests that the RCMP and the OPP operate subject to the direction of their responsible ministers. The case involved two people, Campbell and Shirose, who were charged with drug offences as a result of a reverse sting operation in which RCMP officers sold them drugs. The Crown sought to defend the police conduct on the basis that the police were part of the Crown or agents of the Crown and protected by the Crown's public interest immunity. Binnie J for the unanimous Supreme Court emphatically rejected such an argument: 'The Crown's attempt to identify the RCMP with the Crown for immunity purposes misconceives the relationship between the police and the executive government when the police are engaged in law enforcement. A police officer investigating a crime is not acting as a government functionary or as an agent of anybody. He or she occupies a public office initially defined by the common law and subsequently set out in various statutes.'[32] The Court noted that the police 'perform a myriad of functions apart from the investigation of crimes' and that '[s]ome of these functions bring the RCMP into a closer relationship to the Crown than others.' Nevertheless the Court stressed that 'in this appeal, however, we are concerned only with the status of an RCMP officer in the course of a criminal investigation, and in that regard the police are independent of the control of the executive government.'[33] The Court declared that this principle 'underpins the rule of law,' which it noted 'is one of the "fundamental and organizing principles of the Constitution."'[34]

The principle of police independence derived in Campbell from the constitutional principle of the rule of law seemed to qualify even the terms of section 5 of the RCMP Act which, as discussed above, assigned control and management of the force to the commissioner 'under the direction of the Minister.' Binnie J explained:

While for certain purposes the Commissioner of the RCMP reports to the Solicitor General, the Commissioner is not to be considered a servant or agent of the government while engaged in a criminal investigation. The Commissioner is not subject to political direction. Like every other police officer similarly engaged, he is answerable to the law and, no doubt, to his conscience. As Lord Denning put it in relation to the Commissioner of Police in R. v. Metropolitan Police Comr., Ex parte Blackburn, [1968] 1 All E.R. 763 (C.A.), at p. 769:

> I have no hesitation, however, in holding that, *like every constable in the land, he [the Commissioner of Police] should be, and is, independent of the executive*. He is not subject to the orders of the Secretary of State, save that under the Police Act 1964 the Secretary of State can call on him to give a report, or to retire in the interests of efficiency. I hold it to be the duty of the Commissioner of Police, as it is of every chief constable, to enforce the law of the land. He must take steps so to post his men that crimes may be detected; and that honest citizens may go about their affairs in peace. He must decide whether or not suspected persons are to be prosecuted; and, if need be, bring the prosecution or see that it is brought; *but in all these things he is not the servant of anyone, save of the law itself*. No Minister of the Crown can tell him that he must, or must not, keep observation on this place or that; or that he must, or must not, prosecute this man or that one. Nor can any police authority tell him so. The responsibility for law enforcement lies on him. He is answerable to the law and to the law alone. [Emphasis added.][35]

The *Campbell* case constitutes the Supreme Court's most extended discussion of the principle of police independence.

The Supreme Court indicated that the principle of police independence will not be engaged in all of the functions performed by the police, but that it will apply when the police are engaged in the process of 'criminal investigation.' The case-by-case common law method is such that *Campbell* cannot be taken as a definitive pronouncement about the outer limits of police independence because the Court had only to resolve whether the police were agents of the Crown on facts that involved a criminal investigation. As Justice Hughes commented about the *Campbell* case in his APEC report: 'In respect of criminal investigations and law enforcement generally, the *Campbell* decision makes it clear that, despite section 5 of the RCMP Act, the RCMP are fully independent of the executive. The extent to which police independence extends to other situations remains uncertain.'[36]

The Court derived the principle of the independence of the police from the constitutional principle of the rule of law, which stresses the importance of impartially applying the law to all and especially to those who hold state and governmental power. Indeed, the case raises the possibility that courts might enforce the principle of police independence as part of the unwritten constitutional principle of the rule of law. The *Campbell* case was decided in the wake of previous decisions by the Court to require that governments not negotiate salaries with the judiciary in order to respect the unwritten principle of judicial independence and the Court's statement that the unwritten constitutional principles of democracy, federalism, minority rights, and democracy should guide any decision involving the secession of Quebec from Canada. The Supreme Court has indicated that 'underlying constitutional principles may in certain circumstances give rise to substantive legal obligations which constitute substantial limitations upon government action. These principles may give rise to very abstract and general obligations, or they may be specific and precise in nature. The principles are not merely descriptive, but also involve a more powerful normative force.'[37] In this sense, an unwritten principle of the Canadian constitution may be more powerful than a constitutional convention which, while it may restrain the exercise of statutory powers, does not override them.

In the *Campbell* case, the Supreme Court seemed to indicate that the principle of police independence would qualify the general statement in section 5 of the *RCMP Act* that the commissioner controlled the police 'under the direction of the Solicitor General.' In general, only constitutional law can displace such clear statutory authority. In this respect, the Supreme Court decision in *Campbell* may displace the Quebec Court of Appeal's decision in *Bisaillon v. Keable*, which stressed that the Canadian statutory framework had displaced the common law concept of police independence derived from English law. In other words, *Campbell* suggests that the principle of police independence taken from the common law of *Ex parte Blackburn* may have been elevated from a matter of common law or even constitutional convention to become part of the constitutional principle of the rule of law, which is capable of restraining the statutory authority granted to the minister over the police.

Although the Supreme Court relied on *Ex parte Blackburn* and the civil liability cases upon which it is based, it defined the ambit of police independence in *Campbell* in a more limited fashion than in *Ex parte Blackburn*. The Supreme Court defined police independence in relation to the process of criminal investigation, as opposed to the deployment of the police. As discussed above, the Court did not purport to decide the outer limits of the principle of police independence, and even with respect to criminal investigations, it is unlikely that police independence as discussed in *Campbell* is absolute. Although the police would be free to commence investigations, a growing number of criminal offences, including those involving hate propaganda and terrorism, require the attorney general's consent before the commencement of a prosecution.[38] Some extraordinary police powers, such as the use of investigative hearings or preventive arrests in relation to terrorism investigations, require the attorney general's consent.[39] These qualifications of police independence are designed to protect important values such as restraint in the use of the criminal law and are clearly authorized in statute.

In summary, with respect to most criminal investigations, *Campbell* stands for the proposition that police officers enjoy independence from the executive and should not be directed by their minister either to commence or terminate a criminal investigation.[40] It demonstrates a willingness to read down general statutory references to ministerial direction of the police to accommodate police independence from the executive with respect to criminal investigations. Finally, it suggests that police independence may have been elevated from a constitutional convention to a constitutional principle.

II. Contested Political Understandings of Police Independence

The issue of police independence has most often surfaced in public discourse in Canada at times of scandal, and the reception of police independence has been contested and controversial. In this part I will provide a brief history of the concept of police independence in Canada. Fortunately, much of this history was described in a valuable essay published by Professor Philip Stenning in 2000.[41] As will be seen, however, in the few years that have passed since that publication, controversy in Canada about the appropriate relationship between the government and the police has not abated

The Nicholson Affair

The origins of debate about police independence in Canada predate Lord Denning's famous declarations in *Ex parte Blackburn*. In 1959, the head of the RCMP, Commissioner L.H. Nicholson, resigned in protest after the minister of justice refused to follow his recommendation that fifty officers be sent to Newfoundland to deal with a heated labour dispute after the Smallwood government had passed a law decertifying an American union. It bears noting that Commissioner Nicholson is a hero to the RCMP and its main building in Ottawa, which houses the commissioner's office, is named after him.

Commissioner Nicholson justified his resignation on the following terms: 'I feel most strongly that the matter of law enforcement should be isolated and dealt with on its own merits. This is the attitude the force has taken throughout. It has not concerned itself with the issues back of the strike but has merely tried to maintain law and order in the area.'[42] These comments demonstrate a tendency to define even possibly policy-laden decisions about whether a larger police presence was in the public interest in terms of a technical exercise of law enforcement expertise. Although Commissioner Nicholson's refusal to consider issues in 'back of the strike' manifests an impartiality that is admirable in terms of laying charges, it also demonstrates a certain lack of concern with the larger public interest or policy issues that are engaged in an escalation of the police presence during volatile times of political protest. Whether issues relating to the deployment of forces during demonstrations and strikes should be left to the police or be decided by the responsible minister, or perhaps the Cabinet, is an important and difficult question.

The minister responsible for the RCMP at the time of the Nicholson affair was the minister of justice, Davie Fulton. He justified his refusal to approve the re-enforcements on a number of grounds. One was that 'after consulting with [his] colleagues,' he had concluded that 'it was not possible to send the additional men requested without prejudicing the other responsibilities and duties of the force.' This explanation smacks of second-guessing the commissioner, who has the responsibility and the expertise to manage the police force. Such second-guessing might justify a commissioner's resignation, albeit on the grounds of having lost the confidence of the minister rather than as a matter of constitutional principle.

Minister Fulton gave a second explanation of his refusal to agree with the commissioner's request for re-enforcements. Sending the extra officers, he said, 'might only act as provocation to further incidents of violence and provocation.'[43] Commissioner Nicholson believed that such policy and public interest considerations were part of the issues behind the strike and, as such, not of concern from a law enforcement perspective. Nevertheless, they are issues that can be of concern to the responsible minister and the government. The manner in which a government responds to protests – whether it treats protesters as concerned citizens entitled to respect or as common criminals – is a matter of intense political controversy and engagement. It raises important issues about the nature and quality of the direction that the police may receive from a minister. It cannot be assumed that governments will always be tougher on protests than the police would be without political intervention.

Prime Minister Diefenbaker later explained the decision on the basis that he 'was not prepared to sacrifice the reputation of the RCMP to save either Mr. Smallwood or the reactionary corporations which owned the Newfoundland forest industry.'[44] This raises the question of whether the government was genuinely concerned about provoking more violence or whether there were also partisan concerns behind the decision. These issues will undoubtedly be explored at length by historians, but they raise immediate and pressing concerns about whether ministerial involvement is to be desired and whether the distinction between public interest and partisan concerns is sustainable.

The minister of justice was ambiguous about whether the ultimate decision was made by him alone or by the government of Canada. The decision not to send RCMP re-enforcements was part of a larger political decision by the federal Cabinet that included discussion about whether it would disallow Newfoundland's decertification legislation.[45] Professor Stenning reports that the decision not to send in RCMP re-enforcements was actually made by the Cabinet and the prime minister after being discussed at no less than five Cabinet meetings.[46] This raises the important issue of whether political intervention in policing can be channelled through the responsible minister. The minister of justice as attorney general and the solicitor general are both law officers of the Crown who may be able to assert independence from the Cabinet in making decisions about particular cases. At the same time, this convention, especially with respect to policing, is far from clear or universally supported.[47] Policing decisions made at the Cabinet level will be made subject to Cabinet solidarity and confidence, raising questions about the transparency of political involvement in policing. If political intervention can be justified in policing matters, then there is a strong argument that it should be done in a transparent manner that ensures that the politicians who intervene are held accountable for such decisions, whether in the court of public opinion or in a court of law.

The Nicholson affair is a particularly rich source for thinking about relationships between the government and the police. It reveals how the police may claim independence not only with respect to quasi-judicial or core functions such as the laying of charges, but over deployment issues that may involve larger policy issues about the proper approach to political demonstrations. If the minister had acceded to the commissioner's request to send the extra officers, who would have been accountable had the additional deployment resulted in violence between the police and the strikers? The Nicholson affair also reveals how political explanations for decisions involving policing may not always be clear or consistent. The minister of justice initially attempted to explain the decision in somewhat technical terms relating to the staffing obligations of the RCMP, and only later hinted that a policy decision had been made to take a less confrontational approach to the strike by refusing to send in more police. As discussed above, the public interest and partisan dimensions of such policy decisions can sometimes be blurred. Finally, the minister of justice respected the confidentiality of Cabinet deliberations, but did so in a manner that obscured the role that the Cabinet and the Prime Minister played in the decision. In sum, the Nicholson affair raises difficult issues about whether police independence extends to deployment issues; whether the public interest can be separated from partisan interests in policy decisions related to the policing of protest; whether government decisions with respect to deployment will be made by the Prime Minister, the Cabinet, or the responsible minister; and whether political decisions will be made in a manner that promotes transparency and accountability.

Trudeau and McDonald

Another major controversy over government involvement in policing arose over the activities of the RCMP security services in the wake of the 1970 October Crisis. This episode resulted in sustained public debate about the appropriate relationship between the police and the government as well as important recommendations by the McDonald Royal Commission. For our purposes, the end result was the production of differing yet articulate and enduring understandings of police independence.

At one end of the spectrum were comments made by Prime Minister Pierre Trudeau during a press conference held in 1977. These comments by a former minister of justice and constitutional law professor deserve to be quoted at some length because they represent the fullest and most considered statement by an active Canadian politician on the issue of police independence. Mr Trudeau stated:

> I have attempted to make it quite clear that the policy of this Government, and I believe the previous governments in this country, has been that they ... should be kept in ignorance of *the day-to-day operations of the police force* and even of the security force. I repeat that is not a view that is held by all democracies but it is our view and it is one we stand by. Therefore, in this particular case it is not simply a matter of pleading ignorance as an excuse. It is a matter of stating as a principle that the particular Minister of the day *should not have a right to know* what the police are doing constantly in their investigative practices, what they are looking at, and what they are looking for, and the way in which they are doing it ...

> I would be much concerned ... if the Ministers were to know and therefore be held responsible for a lot of things taking place under the name of security or criminal investigation. That is our position. It is not one of pleading ignorance to defend the government. It is one of keeping the government's nose out of the operations of the police force at whatever level of government.

> On the criminal law side, the protections we have against abuse are not with the government. They are with the courts. The police *can go out and investigate crimes* ... without authorization from the Minister and indeed without his knowledge.

> What protection do we have then that there won't be abuse by the police in that respect? We have the protection of the courts. If you want to break into somebody's house you get a warrant, a court decides if you have reasonable and probable cause to do it. If you break in without a warrant a citizen lays a charge and the police are found guilty. So this is the control on the criminal side, and indeed the ignorance, to which you make some ironic reference, is a matter of law. The police don't tell their political superiors *about routine criminal investigations*.

> On the security side, ... the principle has been that the police don't tell their political superiors about the day to day operations. But they do have to act under the *general directions and guidelines laid down by the government of the day*. In other words, the framework of the criminal law guides the policy of the police and on the criminal side the courts check their actions.[48]

Although Trudeau's statement is obviously influenced by Lord Denning's comments about police independence in *Ex parte Blackburn*,[49] it goes beyond them by asserting not only police independence from control or direction by the government, but also police independence from requests for information by the government. At the same time, the Trudeau statement does seem to limit the ambit of police independence to matters of 'criminal investigation.' Although Trudeau makes some reference to independence from ministerial direction and knowledge in 'day to day operations,' he generally limited police independence to the process of criminal investigation. In contrast, Lord Denning in *Ex parte Blackburn* seemed to include some issues of police deployment within the ambit of police independence.

The McDonald Commission took issue with Prime Minister Trudeau's views about police independence. Much of the groundwork for the commission's eventual views is found in a research study prepared for it by the late John Edwards. Professor Edwards's approach was based on his firm belief that it was possible to separate public interest from partisan considerations when the responsible minister intervened in policing or prosecutorial matters.[50] Some might argue that in matters relating to Quebec separatism, it would be difficult if not impossible for the Trudeau government to separate the public interest from partisan considerations.

Professor Edwards also maintained that Prime Minister Trudeau was wrong to treat 'knowledge and information as to police methods, police practices, even police targets, as necessarily synonymous with improper interference with the day to day operations of the police.' Indeed, he argued that 'undue restraint on the part of the responsible Minister in seeking information as to police methods and procedures can be as much a fault as undue interference in the work of police governing bodies and individual chiefs of police.'[51] Professor Edwards raised in stark relief the dilemmas of, on the one hand, avoiding political interference in policing, while on the other hand avoiding political shirking of responsibility for police activities. The McDonald Commission itself adopted a similar view when it stated that 'a police force with an arm's length relationship to government may produce problems as serious as the partisan misuse of the security intelligence agency.'[52]

The idea that the responsible minister should be informed about police practices that raised general issues of policy was reflected in the final report of the McDonald Commission. It noted that the common law principle of police independence was qualified in Canada both by the reference to ministerial direction in the *RCMP Act* as well as the role of the commissioner of the RCMP in supervising the actions of individual constables. The McDonald Commission defended ministerial involvement on the basis of democratic principles. Here much of the groundwork was laid by its director of research, Peter Russell. In a preliminary paper for the commission, Professor Russell stressed that a 'security service accountable only to itself is incompatible with democracy' which, in our constitutional system, involved 'a government whose activities are directed by Ministers and officials responsible to elected representatives and whose policies are open to informed public discussion.'[53] Building on these themes, the McDonald Commission stated: 'We take it to be axiomatic that in a democratic state the police must never be allowed to become a law unto themselves. Just as our form of Constitution dictates that the armed forces must be subject to civilian control, so too must police forces operate in obedience to governments' responsible to legislative bodies composed of elected representatives.'[54] As will be discussed in the third part of this chapter, the McDonald Commission represents a democratic vision of policing based on ministerial responsibility and accountability.

Although its singular contribution was in articulating a vision of democratic policing, it would be wrong to conclude that the McDonald Commission rejected the concept of police independence from government in its entirety. It clearly stated that 'the Minister should have no right of direction with respect to the exercise by the R.C.M.P. of the powers of investigation, arrest and prosecution. To that extent, and to that extent only, should the English doctrine expounded in *Ex parte Blackburn* be made applicable to the R.C.M.P.'[55] Even with respect to such core, or what the commission called 'quasi-judicial,' functions, however, the minister should have a right to be 'informed of any operational matter, even one involving an individual case, if it raises an important question of public policy. In such cases, he may give guidance to the Commissioner and express to the Commissioner the government's view of the matter, but he should have no power to give *direction* to the Commissioner.'[56]

The McDonald Commission process represents Canada's most sustained and considered examination of the proper relationship between the government and the police. Both Prime Minister Trudeau and the McDonald Commission seemed to restrict the concept of police independence to the process of criminal investigation, although the Prime Minister did refer to the potentially broader concept of the day-to-day operations of the police. Where they differed was as to whether police independence included independence from requests for information. Trudeau defended government ignorance as a matter of principle and McDonald argued that democracy required ministerial knowledge of even operational and investigative matters if they affected matters of policy. The McDonald Commission report stands as an eloquent statement of the need for democratic responsibility and direction of policing, with the exception of criminal investigations. Nevertheless, the democratic principles that were at the core of the McDonald Commission proposal have come under assault in the subsequent decades by increased centralization within government, the erosion of principles of ministerial responsibility, and increasing cynicism about politics and politicians.[57] Its recommendations were also based on a number of crucial but debatable assumptions. One was that governments could receive and impart information and views to the police without assuming control or direction of the activities. Another assumption was that partisan considerations could be excluded from a broader category of public interest considerations when ministers intervened in policing matters. As will be seen, subsequent cases have put these distinctions between information and influence and between partisan and public interest considerations sorely to the test.

The Richard Hatfield Case

This case involved meetings between Richard Hatfield, then the Progressive Conservative premier of New Brunswick, and Elmer MacKay, the Progressive Conservative solicitor general of Canada, when the former was under investigation by the RCMP in relation to a small quantity of marijuana found in the premier's luggage. The Liberal opposition repeatedly raised concerns in Parliament about political interference with the police investigation, but Solicitor General MacKay relied upon assertions that he did not 'have prosecutory jurisdiction or jurisdiction to instruct the RCMP to lay charges, whom to charge, or indeed whether charges should be laid. My responsibility is the practice, and procedures and policies.'[58] This was an interesting statement of the solicitor general's role, but it did not really respond to the propriety of a meeting with the subject of an ongoing criminal investigation or any policy matters that might have been at play in such a meeting. The extensive parliamentary debates on this case are replete with colourful language, but contain more heat than light and reveal little about the proper relationship between the government and the police.

Commissioner R.H. Simmonds of the RCMP stated that the solicitor general only conveyed information about his meetings with Premier Hatfield and had 'not in any way influenced our work or our decision-making.' Commissioner Simmonds took the position that any attempt by the solicitor general to interfere with the investigation and the decision whether to lay charges 'would have been an unacceptable interference with the principle of police independence and discretion.'[59] Premier Hatfield was subsequently charged with possession of marijuana and was acquitted on the basis that the Crown had not proven actual possession of the substance.[60]

The Hatfield affair reveals some of the difficulties in maintaining distinctions between exchanges of information and perceptions of improper influence. Although both the solicitor general and the commissioner of the RCMP maintained that there was nothing improper, the prospect of a private meeting between the solicitor general and the subject of a criminal investigation raised suspicions of interference, not only among the Opposition but in the media. It also suggests how a solicitor general could invoke the principle of police independence as a shield against allegations of improper influence while at the same time taking actions that must have made it clear to the police that the case was very much on the political radar screen. It raises the importance of personal integrity of all involved in police-government relationships, as ultimately both Parliament and the public had to trust both the minister and the police when they stated that no improper influence had been brought to bear on the case.

The following document was prepared and submitted in 1985 by RCMP Commissioner Simmonds in relation to the RCMP investigation of the *Hatfield* case. It has been included here as a historic document that outlines the difference in opinion between a minister and the commissioner regarding the issue of police independence.

ADDENDUM **to report on** RCMP **investigation of the** HATFIELD **Case.**

1. In para.54 (vii) I outlined that no minister, nor any other person, in either the Federal or Provincial Administration, attempted to give any improper direction or in any way influence the police decisions that had to be made as this case progressed. I had been on leave for two weeks during the latter part of January and early February, 1985. When I returned to duty on February 11th I found that the media was a-buzz with respect to a meeting that had taken place between the Hon. Elmer MacKay and Premier Hatfield at Ottawa on the 7th October, 1984. It was being

suggested that the Solicitor General may have given improper direction to the Force as the result of that meeting.

2. As the Solicitor General had maintained a perfectly proper position vis-à-vis the Force throughout this investigation I felt compelled to speak out, entirely of my own volition, to set the record straight. This I did through several telephonic discussions with print, T.V. and radio personalities on the 11th February. I made two principal points. Firstly, that the Solicitor General had not in any way influenced our work or our decision making, and secondly, that had he attempted to do so it would not have been accepted as it would have been an unacceptable interference with the principle of police independence and discretion. Such being the case and, as at the time the Minister met with the Premier, no charge had been laid, I did not find that the meeting was offensive or dangerous insofar as our work was concerned. It had absolutely no effect on what we were doing.

3. At a meeting of the Justice and Legal Affairs Committee on the 14th March, 1985, the Honourable Bob KAPLAN made the following comment and posed the following question;

> Thank you, Mr. Chairman. I have a lot of subjects I would like to cover, but I have no doubt that the most important to me is a difference that has been expressed between you, Mr. Minister, and me about the powers and responsibilities of the Solicitor General. I would like to take a few minutes to clarify that. I find myself also on this occasion, which is a very rare one, in almost complete disagreement with some statements attributed to the Commissioner of the RCMP, and so what I would like to do is refer to those statements and set out for you the theory on which I believe the Solicitor General is accountable to Parliament for the operations of the RCMP and have your views about it.
>   You have been critical of a position I have stated on a number of occasions that I think what is described in section 5 of the RCMP Act is the position – and it is to be taken literally – which is that the Commissioner operate under the direction and subject to the direction of the Solicitor General. Now, I interpret that to mean that if the Solicitor General gives a direction to the Commissioner and that direction is lawful, it is to be obeyed. Of course, if it is unlawful, it is not to be obeyed. No official can obey an unlawful order. So if you tell the Commissioner to send some people to beat up some of your enemies, that order should be disobeyed, but if you tell the Commissioner to

discontinue an investigation or to begin an investigation, I consider that to be a lawful order.

Now, I want quickly to add that I consider that to be an improper order in normal circumstances. I consider that to be an order which flies in the face of the tradition of the RCMP, which is a tradition of independence and a tradition which the Solicitor General must respect, at his peril. But when in an appropriate case he intervenes, if the Commissioner ... I believe I can quote him. He says: 'In the end, we have our independent right to conduct investigations based on reasonable grounds, and no Minister can order us not to.' If that is an accurate statement of the position, then we live in a police state. We live in a state where the police can defy a lawful order from the civilian authority.

Now, I think a responsible and sensible Commissioner who received an improper order – close this file or layoff so and so – a Commissioner who received an order such as that would perhaps think twice before replying. I would think, for example, it would be entirely proper for him to call on the Prime Minister and say: Your Solicitor General has given me this order; what are your views about it? In circumstances such as that, the Prime Minister could say he would speak to him about it or that he has to go if that is the kind of order he is giving, or the Prime Minister could say: Do it; he is the Minister.

In a case such as that, I think a Commissioner of the character of the present Commissioner would probably resign, in the way Mr. Nicholson resigned when he received a lawful order from John Diefenbaker with which he did not agree. I do not want to get into the history of that, but there is no question, in my view, that when a lawful order is given by the Solicitor General under section 5 of the RCMP Act, it is to be obeyed.

Now, I am not surprised that this type of issue is viewed as almost theoretical, because it happens very rarely, and it should happen very rarely. But there are circumstances in which it would be right for the Solicitor General to give an order on these matters. That is the reason – and I will come to that after you have had an opportunity to comment on that – why I do not think you should sit down in normal circumstances with people who are under investigation, especially not in the kind of circumstances in which you did, where you are refusing to say what you did as a result of the meeting, where no officials were present other than a partisan appointee whose job is to make you look good. You know, the chef du cabinet who is not there representing the independent tradition of the RCMP, quite the contrary. So what I want to put to you as my first question is whether you do not agree with the version I have just outlined of your powers and responsibilities in relation to the Commissioner of the RCMP.

4. The Solicitor General provided his answer to the question and I was then invited to respond. Before having the opportunity to do so the ringing of the Division Bells brought the meeting to a close. The question was not further discussed at the next sitting of the Committee. The issue is important because, if the Honourable Mr. KAPLAN is correct, I too, would be greatly concerned if the Solicitor General were to meet with suspected or charged persons and then have it within his power to direct the police as to what they could or could not do. With the greatest of respect, however, I do not accept that his position is correct. My reasoning is as follows

(i) Section 5 of the Royal Canadian Mounted Police Act reads as follows

The Governor in Council may appoint an officer to be known as the Commissioner of the Royal Canadian Mounted Police who, under the direction of the Minister, has the control and management of the Force and all matters connected therewith.

(ii) Section 17 of the Royal Canadian Mounted Police Act reads as follows

(1) The Commissioner, and every Deputy Commissioner, Assistant Commissioner and Chief Superintendent, is 'ex officio' a justice of the peace having all the powers of two justices of the peace.
(2) Every Superintendent and every other officer designated by the Governor in Council is 'ex officio' a justice of the peace.
(3) Every officer, and every person appointed by the Commissioner under this Act to be a peace officer, is a peace officer in every part of Canada and has all the powers, authority, protection and privileges that a peace officer has by law.
(4) Every officer, and every member appointed by the Commissioner to be a peace officer, has, with respect to the revenue laws of Canada, all the rights, privileges and immunities of a customs and excise officer, including authority to make seizures of goods for infraction of revenue laws and to lay informations in proceedings brought for the recovery of penalties therefore.

(iii) Section 18 of the Royal Canadian Mounted Police Act reads as follows

It is the duty of members of the Force who are peace officers, subject to the orders of the Commissioner,

(a) to perform all duties that are assigned to peace officers in relation to the preservation of the peace, the prevention of crime, and of offences against the laws of Canada and the laws in force in any province in which they may be employed, and the apprehension of criminals and offenders and others who may be lawfully taken into custody;

(b) to execute all warrants, and perform all duties and services in relation thereto, that may, under this Act or the laws of Canada or the laws in force in any province, be lawfully executed and performed by peace officers;

(c) to perform all duties that may be lawfully performed by peace officers in relation to the escort and conveyance of convicts and other persons in custody to or from any courts, places of punishment or confinement, asylums or other places; and

(d) to perform such other duties and functions as are prescribed by the Governor in Council or the Commissioner.

(iv) I accept that the Minister has broad powers of direction over the Commissioner with respect to the Commissioner's *control* and *management* of the Force, and all matters connected with that *control* and *management*. However, I do not accept that the Minister's powers of direction over-ride the inherent responsibilities, authorities and powers that are given to every member upon appointment to the office of 'Peace Officer.' By virtue of Section 17(3) the Commissioner, and every other regular member of the Force, is a Peace Officer.

(v) The Office of 'Peace Officer' or 'Constable' has its roots in the Common Law. It is not to be taken lightly and it is my belief that much of the Common Law of England applies to that position as it is understood in Canada. I have never been able to find much Canadian jurisprudence with respect to the question, I however, have for some time believed that the principle to be guided by is that which can be found in the case of R. v. Metropolitan Police Commissioner, Ex parte BLACKBURN in which Lord DENNING, M.R. states

The office of Commissioner of Police within the metropolis dates back to 1829 when Sir Robert Peel introduced his disciplined Force. The Commissioner was a justice of the peace specially appointed to administer the police force in the metropolis. His constitutional status has never been defined either by statute or by the courts. It was considered by the Royal Commission on the Police in their report in 1962 (Cmnd. 1728). I have no hesitation, however, in holding that, like every constable in the land, he should be, and is, independent of the executive. He is not subject to the orders of the Secretary of State, save that under the Police Act 1964 the Secretary of State can call on him to give a report, or to retire in the interests of efficiency. I hold it to be the duty of the Commissioner of Police, as it is of every chief constable, to enforce the law of the land. He must take steps so to post his men that crimes may be detected; and that honest citizens may go about their affairs in peace. He must decide whether or not suspected persons are to be prosecuted; and, if need be, bring the prosecution or see that it is brought; but in all these things he is not the servant of anyone, save of the law itself. No Minister of the Crown can tell him that he must, or must not, keep observation on this place or that; or that he must, or must not, prosecute this man or that one. Nor can any police authority tell him so. The responsibility for law enforcement lies on him. He is answerable to the law and to the law alone. That appears sufficiently from Fisher v. Oldham Corpn. (14), the Privy Council case of A.-G. for New South Wales v. Perpetual Trustee Co. (Ltd.)(15).

This citation is a portion of a lengthy judgment that can be found in All England Law Reports [1968] All E.R.

5. The Honourable Mr. KAPLAN characterizes the position that I believe to be correct as being tantamount to that of a 'police state.' Again, I respectfully defer. The Office of Constable, with its' [sic] original powers, seems to have been most deliberately structured as outlined to ensure that the more common definition of a 'police state' not be allowed to develop. The more common definition being that a police state emerges when a Government uses its' [sic] police agencies as instruments of repression against the citizens of the state. It is against that very concern that the police are given a high degree of independence. Nor is it a dangerous degree because, after all, there are many ways that a capricious Commissioner can be called to account, or an errant Constable disciplined. The Commissioner is appointed 'at pleasure.' His estimates can be constrained, and the actions of every Peace Officer come under the eyes of the Courts.

6. The Honourable Mr. KAPLAN further takes the position that the Commissioner has no choice but to accept direction on all matters, including who he may or may not investigate or charge, and if he disagrees with the

direction his option is to resign. I do not necessarily agree. The Commissioner is not appointed by the Minister, but rather by the Governor-in-Council under the Great Seal of Canada. If a Minister tried to limit the Commissioner's discretion under his inherent powers as a Peace Officer, as opposed to his responsibilities for the management and control of the Force, I believe he could just ignore such direction and let the Minister take his case to the Governor-in-Council to seek the Commissioner's dismissal. The result would be interesting to see. The case of Commissioner NICHOLSON, which was referred to by the Honourable member, is not parallel. As I understand that situation the Minister of the day refused to support the Commissioner on an administrative matter that required the Minister's consent, that being to transfer personnel between Provinces to deal with an emergent situation. When the Minister refused to give his consent, thus severely challenging the Commissioner's professional judgment and his leadership of the Force in the face of a crisis, the Commissioner did what most honourable men would do. He tendered his resignation. The distinction being, of course, that the Minister did not challenge the Commissioner's authority as a Peace Officer, but rather his judgment and leadership.

7. I have outlined my views in some detail as it puts the meeting between the Minister and the Premier in a different perspective. The Minister is not the Attorney General responsible for prosecutions, and as, if I am correct, his powers to direct are as described, it is of little importance to me, as Commissioner, with whom he meets. Had a charge been preferred, and had the meeting been with the judge on the case the matter would be quite different, but that is not what occurred. In any event the Minister described to me the tone of his conversation with the Premier and he, the Minister, gave me no direction.

8. In bringing this to a close I should make it clear that I am not a lawyer. My views have been arrived at over years as a practicing policeman and my layman's interpretation of the law as I find it. In any event I believe the question to be much more theoretical than real as there have been five honourable gentlemen who have occupied the position of Solicitor General during my tenure as Commissioner, and not once have I felt that my right to investigate, when there was a reasonable apprehension of criminal conduct, or not to investigate if I could find no grounds, has in any way been threatened at any time.

R. H. Simmonds
Commissioner

The above document demonstrates that Commissioner Simmonds limited police independence to decisions involving a peace officer's conduct of a criminal investigation and the decision whether to lay charges, whereas Commissioner Nicholson had previously defined police independence more broadly to include what Commissioner Simmonds characterized as administrative matters related to the deployment of the police and its 'control and management.'

The Douglas Small Case

Another controversy in the relationship between the police and the government was the RCMP's decision to lay theft charges against a television reporter and others who had obtained budget documents before the budget was announced in Parliament. Prime Minister Mulroney responded to the leak by saying that 'Canadians are concerned with the criminal and not with the honourable minister,' the finance minister responsible for budget secrecy. The RCMP was called in to investigate, with the minister of justice explaining 'We said "Something's happened, we don't like it, get on it,"' adding, 'what they find in the course of their investigation [is not determined by the government]. It is up to them to decide to lay charges.' The solicitor general also stated that he 'had absolutely nothing to do whatsoever' in the decision to lay charges.[61]

The accused moved to stay the charges, alleging political interference in the charging decision. This allegation was supported by the testimony of Staff Sergeant Jordan, the original investigating officer, who had refused to lay charges. He testified that charges eventually laid by other police officers 'were intended to please elected officials.'[62] Stenning reports that there was also testimony that the political chief of staff of the solicitor general had contacted the deputy commissioner of the RCMP twelve to fifteen times during a thirty-four-day investigation, stating that he wanted a 'status report' but did not want to interfere with the investigation.[63] In the court judgment, the trial judge reported two calls between the chief of staff of the president of the Treasury Board and the assistant commissioner of the RCMP 'for the purpose of obtaining information to advise the minister.' The trial judge characterized these contacts as 'entirely normal, routine and proper to the day-to-day functioning of government.'[64] The trial judge accepted testimony that information only 'flowed upward' to the Prime Minister's Office (PMO), but that it did not 'flow downward' or amount to 'pressure' or direction to lay charges.[65] The trial judge dismissed the allegations of political interference or even 'justifiable perception of political interference,' stressing that there was no evidence of such interference 'from the top down.'[66]

At the same time, the judge did stay the charges, concluding that 'the zeal of superior law enforcement police officers' in pushing ahead with the laying of charges despite evidential concerns and legal concerns about whether the appropriation of confidential information could be the basis for a theft charge 'suggests an objective unfairness and vexatiousness, particularly with regard to the accused Douglas Small, which is indeed inappropriate to criminal proceedings.'[67] The charges were thus stayed on the basis not of political interference, but overzealousness by police officers who reversed the investigating officer's decisions that charges of theft were not warranted. The question, however, remains whether this overzealousness and intervention by senior officers would have occurred in a case that had not embarrassed the government and attracted repeated requests for information and status reports from political staff.

The *Small* case, like that of Richard Hatfield, reveals some of the practical difficulties of maintaining the distinction between requests for information about a criminal investigation as opposed to attempts to influence such investigations. The trial judge ruled that it was permissible for information to flow 'upward' from the police to the Prime Minister's Office, but it would not be permissible for such information to flow 'downward' in the form of influence or direction. To this extent, the *Small* case confirms the distinction between information and influence. Nevertheless, the trial judge's decision to stay proceedings suggests that not all was right in the way the police handled this politically sensitive case. The distinction between exchanges of information and of influence or between upward flows of information from the police and downward flows of information from the government can be questioned. Communication, unlike water, flows both ways. Moreover, explicit or implicit signals of approval or disapproval from important people who receive information can have a significant effect on those who are imparting the information.

The *Small* case reveals the increasing complexities of modern government. Unlike in the earlier *Hatfield* case, it was members of the political staff, as opposed to the solicitor general, who interacted with the police. Although the judge reviewing the matter ultimately rejected this perception, the *Small* case also reveals how police officers down the line may react to perceptions that the minister or his or her staff are on the case.

Finally, the *Small* case also raises the intriguing possibility that political interference may be subject to judicial review on an abuse of process application and that as a consequence, trial judges may hear considerable evidence about political involvement in policing.[68] Although subsequent legal developments make it much less likely that a stay of proceedings would be entered should a trial judge accept evidence of political interference,[69] the *Small* case suggests that the transparency of political intervention in policing may in some cases be a matter of interest for the courts as well for the public.

The Marshall Commission and Nova Scotia Cabinet Ministers

Although it is best known for its examination of the wrongful conviction of Donald Marshall Jr, the Marshall Commission also examined two cases where Nova Scotia Cabinet members had been the subject of RCMP criminal investigations but were not criminally charged. The Marshall Commission, like the McDonald Commission, limited police independence from government to the process of criminal investigation. It concluded that 'inherent in the principle of police independence is the right of the police to determine whether to commence an investigation.' The police should in an appropriate case be prepared to lay a charge, even if it was clear that the attorney general would refuse to prosecute the case. Such an approach, in the royal commission's views, 'ensures protection of the common law position of police independence and acts as an essential check on the power of the Crown.'[70] On the facts, the commission concluded that 'what the RCMP failed to do was to follow through on their stated "principle that police officers have the right to lay charges independent of any legal advice received if they are convinced that there are reasonable grounds to do so" ... the RCMP failed in its obligation to be independent and impartial. It was improperly influenced by factors unrelated to the investigation itself, but it attempted to explain the decision not to proceed in evidentiary and discretionary terms. The RCMP put its working relationship with the Department of Attorney General ahead of its duty to uphold the law.'[71] In the second case, the commission concluded that the RCMP's refusal to proceed with an investigation without authorization from the Department of the Attorney General was 'a dereliction of duty' and 'a failure to adhere to the principle of police independence. It reflects a double standard for the administration of criminal law, contributes to the perception of a two track justice system and undermines public confidence in the integrity of the system.'[72] These are some of the strongest findings ever in Canada about an improper relationship between police and government.

The Marshall Commission's finding of double standards underlines that relation between police independence and a rule of law that applies equally to all without regard to status. Its finding of interventions by the attorney general's department in favour of two Cabinet ministers at the same time as a young, Aboriginal man was wrongfully accused and convicted of murder highlights how the rule of law and police independence from government can advance the important values of equality before the law. Although it could be argued that principles of police independence are perhaps overly dominated by the dangers of favouritism, or the appearance of favouritism, when members or friends of the government are subject to criminal investigation, the unequivocal and highly critical findings of the Marshall Commission suggest that such cases do arise. Moreover, they suggest that failures of police independence from government can threaten the equal and impartial application of the rule of law.

The Airbus Affair

Another controversy about the appropriate relationship between the police and the government was the Airbus affair, in which former prime minister Brian Mulroney was named in a letter of request to Swiss authorities with respect to an RCMP criminal investigation. He brought a defamation suit against the RCMP commissioner, the RCMP investigator, Minister of Justice Allan Rock, and the Justice official who signed the letter of request, a suit that was eventually settled with money being paid to the former prime minister. For our purposes what is most significant is the hands-off attitude displayed by both Solicitor General Herb Gray and Minister of Justice Allan Rock towards the police investigation. When asked about his role, Herb Gray admitted that he was informed of the request by the RCMP for the assistance from the Swiss authorities but he 'played no role whatsoever in the decision to seek their support. I played no role in the formulation of the request or its content ... the minister or the solicitor general does not get involved in operational matters. The investigations carried out by the RCMP are at arm's length from ministers ...'[73]

Allan Rock also indicated that he was not personally aware of the letter of request before it was sent, and he was supported by some experts who argued that a minister of justice should not interfere in an ongoing police investigation.[74]

The Airbus affair is significant because the ministers responsible for both the police investigation and the letter of request took less of an interest in the case compared to the *Hatfield*, *Small*, and Nova Scotia cabinet ministers cases discussed above. Indeed, the case may represent a growing consensus about police independence from ministerial direction and perhaps even ministerial requests for information about a particular criminal investigation. At the same time, some have raised concerns that the hands-off approach of the ministers[75] came at the high price of a lack of ministerial accountability for the investigative actions of the police.[76] Whether such concerns would have been raised had the letter of request not have been leaked, however, is an important consideration. The balance between police independence with respect to criminal investigations and claims that ministers should be accountable for any abuses of those investigative powers should factor in the confidential nature of criminal investigations.

APEC

Second perhaps only to the McDonald Commission process, the APEC affair resulted in sustained discussion and reflection on the relationship between government and the police. A series of inquiries were held under the public complaints provisions of the *RCMP Act* regarding the treatment of protestors during the Asia Pacific Economic Cooperation (APEC) summit held at the University of British Columbia in November 1997. There were many allegations of improper police conduct, but for our purpose the most important were allegations that the PMO had intervened and interfered with the RCMP security operations. After one aborted inquiry, Justice Ted Hughes held hearings and issued a report on the matter.[77]

After reviewing the McDonald Commission report and the *Campbell* case discussed above, Justice Hughes articulated the following propositions concerning police independence:

- When the RCMP are performing law enforcement functions (investigation, arrest and prosecution) they are entirely independent of the federal government and answerable only to the law.

- When the RCMP are performing their other functions, they are not entirely independent but are accountable to the federal government through the Solicitor General of Canada or such other branch of government as Parliament may authorize.
- In all situations, the RCMP are accountable to the law and the courts. Even when performing functions that are subject to government direction, officers are required by the RCMP Act to respect and uphold the law at all times.
- The RCMP are solely responsible for weighing security requirements against the Charter rights of citizens. Their conduct will violate the Charter if they give inadequate weight to Charter rights. The fact that they may have been following the directions of political masters will be no defence if they fail to do that.
- An RCMP member acts inappropriately if he or she submits to government direction that is contrary to law. Not even the Solicitor General may direct the RCMP to unjustifiably infringe Charter rights, as such directions would be unlawful.[78]

This discussion of police independence builds on the McDonald Commission to the extent that police independence is restricted to the core functions of criminal investigations. Given that the issue of protest was central to the mandate of the APEC inquiry, it is unfortunate that there was not more discussion about whether police deployment and tactics in dealing with demonstrations were included in the scope of police independence. On the one hand, such arrangements seem to lie outside of the core law enforcement functions of investigation, arrest, and prosecution, and thus fall within 'other functions' of the police. These are matters in which, according to Justice Hughes, the police are not entirely independent from government but are accountable to the government through the solicitor general. At the same time, however, Justice Hughes recommended that the 'RCMP should request statutory codification of the nature and extent of police independence from government' with respect not only to 'existing common law principles regarding law enforcement' as articulated in *Campbell*, but also 'the provision of and responsibility for delivery of security services at public order events.'[79] It is difficult to know exactly what to make of this last and crucial recommendation. It could suggest that police independence extends to security at public order events so that the government could not instruct the police to increase their security deployments at these events or to decrease them. If so, Justice Hughes would have embraced a broader definition of police independence than articulated by the McDonald Commission or in the *Campbell* case. On the other hand, Justice Hughes does distinguish security at public order events from the common law core of police independence and his recommendation may be more that the government and the police should codify in advance the respective responsibilities of the police and the responsible minister for public order policing. This interpretation would be more consistent with the McDonald Commission's recommendations that the responsible minister must be able to direct police operations with policy consequences if the police are not to become a law unto themselves.

One change since the 1981 McDonald Commission was, of course, the advent of the *Charter of Rights and Freedoms*. Justice Hughes seems to suggest that the need to consider the *Charter* may expand the ambit of police independence. He stated that 'weighing security requirements against the Charter rights of citizens' is exclusively a matter for the police and that they should refuse to follow 'the directions of political masters' if the result is to violate the *Charter*. One interpretation of this statement may be that, because *Charter* considerations are central restraints on security operations at public order events, police independence now extends to police deployment and tactics at such events. This would be a significant expansion of police independence beyond its law enforcement core. On the other hand, Justice Hughes's comments may be consistent with political direction concerning protests so long as the direction does not violate the *Charter*. Even those who are sceptical about police independence accept that the police can always refuse to obey an illegal order. The *Charter* is now the supreme law and it would be proper for the police to stop obeying an order if they believed that the order would require them to violate the *Charter*. This caveat has implications for the content of the direction that responsible ministers could give the police about policing demonstrations. The minister could not direct the police to act in a manner that would result in an unreasonable limit on constitutional rights, but could direct them to show more restraint and respect for dissent than required by the minimum standards of the *Charter*. To return to the Nicholson affair, the minister could direct the police to back off and not provoke protestors, but could not direct them to do something that would violate the protestors' constitutional rights.

Although it is impossible to disagree with the simple proposition that the police should not violate the *Charter* or the idea that the principle of legality should guide police-government relations, matters are considerably more complex than this seemingly simple admonition. Issues of constitutional compliance will often be difficult to determine, especially in real time as an event unfolds. Will the police be able to receive independent legal advice on whether a political direction violates the law? Will this advice also consider whether the order invades the imprecise boundaries of police independence? A further danger is that the police may not unreasonably see the courts as the ultimate arbitrator of whether their conduct is consistent with the law. The police might then follow orders that come close to overstepping the legal line. And in many cases, the ultimate legal call by the courts may never come. Although the *Charter* has undoubtedly increased judicial scrutiny of police conduct, the McDonald Commission's caution that most police conduct is not reviewed through the expensive and time-consuming process of litigation still holds true.

In terms of the *RCMP Act*, ministerial responsibility is clearly assigned to the solicitor general. Unfortunately, the APEC report does not address the propriety of ministerial powers being delegated or taken over by a central agency, the Prime Minister's Office. This omission is regrettable because the principle of responsible democratic government and ministerial accountability figured prominently in the McDonald Commission's discussion of democratic policing. The McDonald Commission was certainly not blind to the important role that central agencies, including the PMO, might play in matters of national security, but their dominant philosophy stressed respect for the tradition of ministerial responsibility. The McDonald Commission would have agreed with Joe Clark, who argued in 1977 that 'if we destroy the principle of Ministerial accountability, we destroy the system of government which we have in this country.'[80] Much water has passed under the bridge since that time and many would view such sentiments as quaint, given the increasingly centralization of government and the erosion of ministerial accountability.

On the merits of the allegations of political interference, Commissioner Hughes found that 'the Canadian government did not signal to the RCMP, either overtly or subtly, that they ought to perform as they did to curtail demonstrations and stamp out visible dissent.'[81] He did, however, make the following findings under the heading 'improper federal government involvement':

The federal government's role in the removal of the tenters from the grounds of the Museum of Anthropology on November 22 was one of two instances of its improper involvement in the RCMP security operation. I am satisfied that it was because of the government's intervention that the tenters were removed that evening. Were it not for that involvement, the contrary view of Site Commander Thompsett would have prevailed. As it happened, his view did not carry the day because of the acquiescence of other RCMP personnel, principally Supt. May, who had succumbed to government influence and intrusion in an area where such influence and intrusion were inappropriate.[82]

The other instance of improper and inappropriate federal government involvement in the RCMP's provision of security services was with respect to the size of the demonstration area adjacent to the law school. In that case, the government's efforts did not prevail due to the intervention of others, including Site Commander Thompsett, on behalf of the protesters. Had those intervenors not prevailed, the security challenges the RCMP faced on November 25 may well have been increased.[83]

The above findings were made in a context that focused on the complaints against the RCMP as opposed to the conduct of the Prime Minister or his staff. Indeed, Justice Hughes concluded that he did not have jurisdiction to call Prime Minister Chrétien as a witness and the prime minister refused the commissioner's invitation to testify.[84] Professor Pue has argued that Jean Carle, then director of operations at the PMO, was at the centre of both of these findings and that like all individuals he 'had no inherent authority and no right to act outside of the law.' Pue suggests that the principle of ministerial responsibility should require the Prime Minister either to have accepted responsibility for Jean Carle's actions or to have 'rebuked him for misuse of his position in the Prime Minister's Officer.' As of the summer of 2001, however, the prime minister had done neither, something that Professor Pue argues was 'an unacceptable constitutional outcome.'[85] The APEC affair certainly underlines the need to address the position of central agencies and political staff in determining both the appropriate ambit of police independence and of political responsibility for directions to the police. It also indicates that the topic cannot be separated from larger questions concerning the health of ministerial accountability in our democracy.

The Sponsorship Scandal

On 11 May 2004, the RCMP laid twelve fraud charges against Chuck Guité, a retired bureaucrat, and Jean Brault, president of Groupaction

Marketing Inc. The charges arose from a scandal over government spending that threatened the re-election prospects of the Liberal government and led to both parliamentary committee hearings and the appointment of a royal commission. For our purposes, the focus is on what the episode reveals about the relation between the police and government.

A number of people around the government had commented on the ongoing RCMP investigation. Jean Lapierre, often described as Prime Minister Martin's 'Quebec Lieutenant,' stated in an interview in April 2004 that charges in the sponsorship scandal 'would provide relief, because I think people want to see people found guilty. They want to see people accused and eventually found guilty, that's clear ... I think people say "Wait a minute, if something improper happened here, why hasn't someone paid for it?"' These comments led the justice critic of the official Opposition to allege that 'by the Prime Minister's silence he is allowing his political friends to direct and influence the RCMP criminal investigation.' Anne McLellan, the minister of public safety with responsibility for the RCMP, stated that Lapierre's comments were 'totally irrelevant' to the police investigation and that 'the honourable member is very aware that no one pushes the RCMP.' The commissioner of the RCMP also denied that there was any political pressure on the police force.[86] In light of the APEC findings, however, others were not convinced. Professor Pue, for example, stated 'the question is still hanging out there. Can Canadians be assured that the RCMP is absolutely free of political interference from its political masters. The answer, broadly, is no.'[87]

After the charges were laid the leader of the Opposition, Stephen Harper, stated: 'I think the timing of the charges after Mr. Lapierre demanded pre-election charges is more than a little suspicious ... I would not want to speculate. It just seems to me that the timing is suspicious.' A RCMP spokesperson again denied any political interference, stating, 'our investigation is totally independent from whatever is going on in politics. We're just going step by step and turning over almost every stone we can to make the best investigation possible.'[88] Anne McLellan responded that allegations of political interference in the charging decision were 'appalling and profoundly unacceptable'[89] and also denied that the laying of charges in the political scandal would affect the calling of the election. The Quebec attorney general also participated in the laying of the charges because of a decision to proceed by way of direct indictment. Somewhat surprisingly, the issue of police independence was not subsequently discussed in Parliament.

The focus was not on constitutional principle but political matters relating to the sponsorship scandal. In the absence of litigation, that, as in the *Small* case, alleged political interference or careful probing in Parliament, almost nothing is known about whether or how the police and the government interacted on this matter.

The controversy over the timing of the police charges in the sponsorship scandal reveals the persistence of the problem of police-government relationships in Canada. Allegations of political interference can do damage both to the government and the police, but little has been done to clarify the basic principles of police independence or ensure transparent processes and protocols to prevent such allegations. The calls made by Justice Hughes in 2001 for codification of the principles of police independence have not been heeded despite the Supreme Court's 1999 *Campbell* decision suggesting that police independence, at least with respect to criminal investigations, can be derived from the constitutional principle of the rule of law.

III. Four Models of Police-Government Relationships

Models provide a convenient means of highlighting different policy options and the value choices and assumptions implicit in the choice of those policies. Starting with Herbert Packer's famous contrasting crime control and due process models, models of the criminal process have spawned a generation of normative and positive debate about the criminal process.[90] Models need not be stark alternatives, as multiple models may operate at the same time on different levels. Thus Packer's due process model may describe the few criminal cases that are the subject of adversarial challenge and appeal, but his crime control model describes the routine cases that result in a guilty plea. Models can also be mapped on a continuum so as to reveal both their similarities and differences. All of Packer's models presume an adversarial system, but they posit different roles for judges and other actors. Although models may potentially limit the range of debate, this shortcoming can be overcome by developing new models, as has occurred in the plethora of third models of the criminal process that have attempted to add to Packer's models. The development of new models may be particularly appropriate in order to accommodate the unique position of Aboriginal peoples.[91] Although the models identified here may not exhaust all the possibilities, it is hoped that they will provide a foundation for subsequent debates about the precise meaning of police independence and the range of policy choices in determining and structuring the relationship between the police and government.

Full Police Independence

This model of full police independence is based on Lord Denning's famous comments in *Ex parte Blackburn*. In that case, Lord Denning seemed to suggest that the police were independent from government not only with respect to law enforcement decisions such as initiating a criminal investigation and laying charges, but also with respect to issues of police deployment. Thus, Lord Denning stated that the constable 'must take steps so to post his men that crimes may be detected; and that honest citizens may go about their affairs in peace'[92] without government interference. Supporters of full police independence would also argue that the policing of public order events would fall under the exemption in section 31(4) of Ontario's *Police Services Act* that municipal boards 'shall not direct the chief of police with respect to specific operational decisions' and that there is no reason in principle why the same understanding of independence should not apply to the OPP's relationship with the responsible minister or others in government.

Supporters of full police independence would also read Justice Hughes's recommendation in the APEC report that there should be 'statutory codification of the nature and extent of police independence from government with respect to ... the provision of and responsibility for delivery of security services at public order events'[93] as support for the proposition that police independence extends to deployment at public order events. Following Justice Hughes, they might argue that the police, assisted by their own lawyers, should be entitled to decide whether security arrangements at such events respect the Charter and other constitutional standards. Finally, supporters of full police independence would argue that the *Campbell* case has constitutionalized police independence as a constitutional principle that prevails over even clear statutory recognition of Ministerial authority over the police.

Proponents of police independence would also cite Prime Minister Trudeau's 1977 statements as the definitive political statement about the proper relationship between the government and the police and would be sceptical about arguments that it is possible to distinguish improper attempts by the government to control the police from legitimate attempts to obtain information necessary to hold the police accountable. They would argue that Trudeau's defence of governmental ignorance of the day-to-day operations of the police as a matter of principle has been born out by subsequent developments such as the *Hatfield* and *Small* cases, in which attempts by government to be informed about ongoing police investigation resulted in serious allegations of impropriety. Even if these allegations are eventually found to be unwarranted, much of the damage was done by perceptions that information cannot be disassociated from influence. The hands-off approach articulated in the Airbus case would also be cited as an example of an appropriate manifestation of full police independence.

The model of full police independence is based on a faith in the expertise and professionalism of the police. Proponents would argue that the confidence displayed by Lord Denning, when he declared in 1968 that the police should only be answerable to the law, should only be increased by the development of new legal instruments since that time. These instruments include the *Charter*, abuse of process doctrine, civil litigation against the police claiming malicious prosecution or abuse of public office, and increased review of complaints against the police. If the police misuse their independence, there are more legal remedies available today for that abuse than ever before. Enhanced legal accountability supports the idea that in a wide variety of matters, the police should be answerable only to the law.

The more candid proponents of full police independence might also point to increasing public cynicism about whether elected politicians will act in a publicly spirited manner. The distinction drawn by some between public interest and partisan politics will be dismissed as untenable in an age which assumes that politicians always act in their partisan self-interest. Cynicism about politicians, perhaps even more than confidence in the police, can push people in the direction of the full police independence model. Writing in 1977, only twelve years after he published a book that was extremely critical and almost dismissive of the concept of police independence, Geoffrey Marshall candidly conceded that the case for full police independence had become stronger in the subsequent years because 'nobody's faith in councilors or Congressman or Members of Parliament can now be as firmly held as it was fifteen years ago.' He argued that 'many liberal democrats' would trust the police more than the responsible minister to protect civil liberties. Professor Marshall even went so far as to suggest that a constitutional convention was emerging that 'would suggest that direct orders, whether of a positive or negative kind, whether related to prosecution or other law-enforcement measures, and whether related to individual cases or to general policies, ought to be avoided by police authorities even when they involve what the Royal Commission [on Policing in 1960] called "police practices in matters which vitally concern the public interest."'[94] Full police independence is supported not only by cynicism about politicians, but by despair at the erosion of principles of ministerial accountability. As seen above, some commentators expressed concerns that Prime Minister Chrétien was not held accountable for the role of his office in APEC. If ministers and others in government can escape responsibility for their interventions in policing, or interventions by their staff or civil servants, then the case for full police independence is strengthened.

Proponents of full police independence might also argue that in a post-APEC environment, most politicians would be happy to let the police take full responsibility for policing public order events that might result in controversy. They would cite in support the following comments made by Sir Robert Mark, a former commissioner of the London Police, who argued: 'I do not mean to give offence when I assert that in matters of public order, demonstrations, political, industrial or racial, the public trust the police a great deal more than politicians in government or opposition and I think it significant that all of the Home Secretaries that I have known have been only too glad disclaim any responsibility for police operations in that sphere.'[95] The doctrine of full police independence is supported by faith in the expertise and professionalism of the police and scepticism about the motives and optics of political intervention in policing and about whether politicians can or will be held accountable for such interventions.

Quasi-Judicial or Core Police Independence

The model of quasi-judicial or core police independence is based on the recognition in the *Campbell* case that while the police may be under the direction of the responsible minister on many aspects of policing, they should be immune from ministerial or other forms of government direction with respect to core law enforcement functions such as initiating or ending a criminal investigation and deciding whether to lay charges. The Marshall Commission's strong conclusion that the RCMP was improperly influenced in its criminal investigation of two ministers in the Nova Scotia Cabinet is particularly dramatic evidence of the need for police independence in this area. It also supports the equation of police independence with the rule of law in the *Campbell* case by underlining the dangers of political interference to the impartial application of the law to all. Core police independence is a consensus position that would be supported by *Ex parte Blackburn* and *Campbell*, as well as by the reports of the McDonald, Marshall, and APEC Commissions. It has also arguably been constitutionalized as a part of the rule of law in *Campbell*. As suggested by the APEC Commission, the 'existing common law principles regarding law enforcement'[96] should be codified as a qualification to the general requirements of ministerial direction and responsibility found in Canadian police acts.

Proponents of core police independence may have differing views about whether the principle should be extended beyond activities involving criminal investigation. Some may follow the McDonald Commission in believing that police independence should not be extended beyond its core because of our commitment to responsible government and democratic control and accountability of the police. Supporters of the McDonald Commission might well argue that Ontario's *Police Services Act*[97] already goes too far in recognizing police independence from directions by municipal boards with respect to all 'operational decisions' and 'day-to-day operations,' as opposed to directions with respect to criminal investigations. Other supporters of core police independence, however, may be less optimistic about political involvement in the policy-laden aspects of policing but nevertheless conclude that the law and the consensus of informed opinion does not at this time support extending the principle of police independence beyond the law enforcement core. Codification of core or quasi-judicial police independence might be a first step towards a broader understanding of police independence. If confidence grows in the police and legal accountability structures and/or confidence diminishes about the prospects for transparent and helpful political interventions in policing, then it may be advisable to extend core police independence into full police independence.

Proponents of core police independence may also extend the principle to government requests for information about law enforcement decisions. The controversies surrounding attempts to obtain or impart information in the *Hatfield* and *Small* cases suggest that exchanges of information may be perceived as exchanges of influence. This perception may be especially strong if information is exchanged before the police make their decision. A more hand-offs approach is supported by the conduct of both the solicitor general and the minister of justice in the Airbus affair, and the controversy that would have been created had it been discovered that responsible ministers or their staff had been requesting status reports on the RCMP's investigation of the sponsorship scandal.

The model of core police independence is based on a conclusion that ministers and their staff have no business attempting to influence criminal investigations. On such matters, there is a confidence in the professionalism and expertise of the police. There is also a recognition that both prosecutors and the courts should act as a check on police powers, at least in cases that result in the laying of charges. These review mechanisms will have less application when the police decide that a charge is not warranted. It is still possible in some cases, however, for private citizens to lay a charge and police complaints and civil suits could serve as some checks on abusive investigations that do not result in charges.

Democratic Policing

The democratic model of policing is supported by the recommendations of the McDonald Commission. As described above, the commission accepted the need for core or quasi-judicial police independence, but was firm that police independence should not be expanded beyond this limited domain. In this respect the McDonald Commission's model of democratic policing is consistent with the model of core police independence described above.

The model of democratic policing differs from the model of core police independence, however, in maintaining the importance of allowing the responsible minister to be informed and to discuss even ongoing criminal investigations with the police if the investigations raise more general policy matters. This position is based on an assumption that the relevant actors – the ministers, their staff, their civil service, the police and the public – will understand the distinction between seeking information about a criminal investigation and seeking to influence the police conduct of the investigation. The *Hatfield* and *Small* cases constitute precedents where information was sought. Although allegations of influence were made in both cases, they were dismissed by the solicitor general and the commissioner in the case of Hatfield and by the trial judge in *Small*. The democratic policing model would oppose the attitudes of both Prime Minister Trudeau and the responsible ministers in the Airbus affair that ministers should remain ignorant of the day-to-day operations of the police. The democratic policing model affirms the importance of the minister being informed about important cases lest they reveal policy issues or structural defects that should be reformed.

The democratic policing model sees ministerial responsibility for policing matters as a fundamental feature of responsible government and as a necessary means of ensuring that the police do not become a law unto themselves. A variation on this theme would place a police board between the minister and the police, as is done with the local police in Ontario and many other jurisdictions. A police board could represent a larger cross-section of the community than the minister and constitute its own democratic forum on issues of police policy. Gordon Chong has recently called for enhanced capacities and powers for local police boards in Ontario as a means to ensure 'civilian "control" of the police.' He also has argued that 'a far greater concern today' than the traditional concern about politicians abusing 'their power by attempting to influence specific police activities' is 'the intensified political activity on the part of police – especially through their militant union – to unduly influence police policy.'[98] The democratic policing model accepts that there is much policy in policing and argues that those responsible to the people and not the police should be able to determine police policy.

The democratic policing model defines the ambit of police independence narrowly and would resist suggestions by Commissioner Nicholson that the deployment of additional officers was a matter of police independence or any suggestions in the APEC report that security operations at public order events fall within the ambit of police independence. This does not, however, mean that the democratic policing model would accept what happened at APEC as a proper example of government-police relations. The McDonald Commission, for example, stressed the importance of ministerial responsibility for policing. From this perspective, it is disturbing that the solicitor general and his civil service appeared to be non-players in the APEC affair. The model of democratic policing would support attempts to channel political direction of the police through the responsible minister, albeit after that minister had consulted other relevant Cabinet ministers.[99] There might also be acceptance of attempts to formalize political direction of the police in the form of written and public guidelines and directives. Such channelling would help promote greater accountability of the responsible minister for a broad range of policing decisions and could provoke more public debate about policing policy. It could also ensure that directives from the government to the police in individual cases were exposed to public and judicial scrutiny.

An important issue that will be discussed in the last part of this chapter is whether the traditions of responsible government and democracy celebrated by the McDonald Commission in its 1981 report are vibrant enough a quarter of century later to inspire a model of democratic policing. The democratic policing model is premised on optimistic assumptions that political intervention in policing will, more often than not, result in a restrained and just police response and a faith that the people will learn about and hold the government accountable if they abuse their powers over the police. Geoffrey Marshall is an example of a person who, by the late 1970s, had lost faith in politicians and democracy and was prepared to abandon democratic policing for full police independence. Many would argue that responsible government and democracy have only declined since Professor Marshall's change of heart.

If the democratic policing model is based on what some might see as a nostalgic faith in the integrity of politicians and their willingness to accept responsibility for making difficult policy decisions for the police, it is also based on a more limited faith in police expertise and professionalism than the model of full police independence. The McDonald Commission was quite critical of the institutional culture of the RCMP and recommended the creation of a civilian security intelligence agency in part to ensure more respect for dissent and better ministerial and parliamentary oversight. The democratic policing model limits police expertise to the process of criminal investigation and is based on the belief that the police should be subject to democratic direction in all other matters. Indeed, the McDonald Commission seemed to believe that the politicians might be less likely to countenance the policing of legitimate dissent than the police themselves. More than two decades later, this assumption needs to be re-examined in light of changes in policing and developments such as the *Charter*.

The democratic policing model is also based on scepticism that courts and complaints bodies provide an adequate check on police decisions outside of the core activities that result in charges. This scepticism is both procedural and substantive. Procedurally, most police activity is not subject to the expensive and lengthy process of either complaint or litigation. Substantively, proponents of democratic policing would argue that the *Charter* only provides minimum standards for police conduct and that governments are entitled to demand that police go beyond these standards in their dealings with protestors and vulnerable groups. They would argue that the minister of justice was entitled in the Nicholson affair to refuse to allow the RCMP to send more officers to police a strike even though the additional deployment might not in itself violate the law.

Governmental Policing

The governmental policing model is supported by a literal reading of Canadian police acts, which generally provide that the police is managed by a commissioner subject to direction from the responsible minister. It follows the Quebec Court of Appeal's decision in *Bisaillon v. Keable* in holding that police independence is at most a common law concept that can be and has been displaced by clear statutory language. It is also consistent with the views of former solicitor general Robert Kaplan quoted above, who argued that the commissioner of the RCMP should follow any lawful order of the solicitor general, perhaps with an ability to appeal to the prime minister. This model is also based on considerable scepticism about the whole notion of police independence. Stress is placed on the dubious origins of the concept of police independence in civil liability cases holding that there is not a master and servant relationship between the Crown and the police. Police independence is not as recognized a concept as judicial independence. Judges have to attempt to apply pre-existing standards and give reasons for their decisions, whereas the police exercise considerable discretion and do not have to give reasons for their decisions.[100] Even the Supreme Court's recent decision in *Campbell* would in this model be restricted to its narrow holding. The facts that the police are not protected by Crown immunities and are subject to the rule of law should not justify police independence from governmental direction. At most, police independence in this model refers to the ability of the police to refuse to follow blatantly illegal orders from their political masters and the protections that any civil servant may enjoy with respect to direction from the relevant minister and his or her political staff.

Although Canadian police acts vest authority in responsible ministers, the model of governmental policing would be sensitive to developments within government that affect the relationship between civil servants and the government of the day. Thus the involvement of central agencies such as the Cabinet in the Nicholson affair or the Prime

Minister's Office in the APEC affair would not be seen as unusual, given the important role of such central agencies in government. Political scientist Donald Savoie has observed in his important study *Governing from the Centre* that the relationship between the RCMP commissioner 'and the prime minister through the PCO ... has become so close over the past twenty years or so that the minister responsible – the Solicitor General – ... is now effectively cut out of some of the most important discussions and decisions.'[101] Thus the model of governmental policing would also accept that post-September 11 changes in governance through the creation of a new Ministry of Public Safety and Emergency Preparedness, a national security adviser within the PCO, and a Cabinet committee on security matters may require a fundamental re-orientation of older models of the RCMP being accountable to government through the solicitor general. The fact that the formal title of solicitor general, with its claim to be a law officer of the Crown with some independence from Cabinet on some matters,[102] has been re-named both federally and in Ontario would also be accepted by proponents of governmental policing as a sign that government and the police alike must respond to changes in society. Government coordination is also justified because of the intergovernmental nature of much policing, including the need to coordinate the efforts of municipal, provincial, and federal forces in Canada and with various police forces outside of Canada. Policing in this model is not fundamentally different from any other governmental service and as such is subject to the reorganization and direction that may be provided to any group of civil servants. One difference between the models of democratic and governmental policing is that the latter does not insist that all governmental direction to the police be channelled through the responsible minister.

The governmental policing model is based on a more limited faith in the expertise and professionalism of the police than the models of full or core police independence. If forced to accept some idea of police independence, proponents of government policing, like proponents of democratic policing, would opt for the more limited law enforcement core. The governmental policing model shares a faith in government with the democratic policing model, but it places less importance on traditions of ministerial responsibility. It is recognized that policing issues frequently cross ministerial boundaries and that the police are entitled to the best information from all departments in government. Once the interministerial, intergovernmental, and international nature of policing is recognized, the desire for centralized coordination is more understandable. Policing can be subject to the same trends as other parts of government, including those of privatization and business plans.[103] The world changes, and the McDonald Commission's vision of ministerial responsibility may not fit the demands of modern governance.

Working with the Models

The four models outlined above need not be seen as static or dichotomous. The optimal model of police-government relations may combine features from more than one model, and some models may be appropriate for some police functions while others are appropriate for others. For example, police independence may be required with respect to criminal investigations, while democratic policing may be appropriate for other matters. The choice of models may also change over time. For example, a democratic model for policing protests could be established, but it could evolve towards de facto full police independence should the responsible minister not wish to take responsibility for devising written and public guidelines or directives for the policing of protests. Alternatively, a democratic policing model that places clear and transparent responsibilities on the responsible minister could be developed, but the minister might subject his or her discretion to the demands of the governmental policing model with its emphasis on central agency control and coordination.

Finally, the models can be viewed through a critical perspective. Just as some have argued that the due process model of the criminal process facilitates and legitimates the reality of the crime control model, it can be argued that the model of either full or core police independence could facilitate governmental policing if they believe that the police will anticipate and follow the desires of the government with respect to policing. In this sense, police independence could be a legitimating veneer for governmental policing. Similarly, the democratic model of policing based on ministerial accountability could be said to facilitate governmental policing if the minister takes direction from the Cabinet and other central agencies. Police independence may be justified on the basis of rule of law values, but in practice it could facilitate repressive practices without the government having to take responsibility. The idea that the police are only answerable to the law could often mean that they are answerable to no one.

Finally, it is possible that none of the four models outlined above may be optimal for Aboriginal people and that alternative models should be developed.[104] For example, police independence may be resisted in part because of the well-documented history of systemic discrimination against Aboriginal people in the criminal justice system and the often tense relations that have existed between Aboriginal people and the police. In addition, the democratic model of policing may have to be adjusted to accommodate Aboriginal people who are under-represented in Canada's democratic institutions. Such adjustments may include the encouragement of Aboriginal policing where possible and the introduction of police boards that may include Aboriginal representation. Finally, the case for a governmental model of policing may be stronger in relation to Aboriginal people, who can argue that policing implicates the duty of the Canadian state to respect Aboriginal rights, including treaty rights and fiduciary duties. When these rights are not respected by the state, including the police, the relationship between Aboriginal peoples and the Canadian state may suffer by resting on force as opposed to consent and reconciliation.[105]

IV. Crucial Questions for Choosing between the Models

In this concluding section I will outline some of the key issues that separate the models. The emphasis will be more on the questions that policy makers and commentators should ask rather than the answers to those questions. The point is not to declare a winner between the competing models, but to get a better handle on the value choices implicit in evolving relationships between the government and the police.

The Ambit of Police Independence: Criminal Investigation or Beyond?

Perhaps the most important question that will determine the proper relationship between the government and the police is the ambit of the principle of police independence. One approach that should be rejected is to draw a bright line between policy and operational matters. As the McDonald Commission concluded, operations, especially those in new or high-profile circumstances, can often raise important policy issues. This is particularly true of the policing of political protests.

The main options in defining the ambit of police independence are to restrict police independence to the process of criminal investigation as contemplated by the McDonald Commission and affirmed in the *Campbell* case or to extend police independence to include issues of police deployment. As discussed above, there is some suggestion in the APEC report that police independence extends to deployment decisions and it will be recalled that Commissioner Nicholson resigned because the government would not approve of his decision that extra officers should be sent to Newfoundland to deal with labour unrest. The choice between full and core police independence will depend in large part on one's views of the comparative dangers of allowing the police or the politicians decide policing matters beyond the core of criminal investigations. There is a danger, seen in the Nicholson affair, that the police will define policing of protests solely in terms of their professional judgment about what is tactically necessary and legally permissible to maintain order. The police may be inclined to ignore the 'issues in back' of the demonstration or the effects of a large paramilitary presence on political protest, as Commissioner Nicholson did. This could have a particularly harmful effect on the policing of Aboriginal protests, which are often rooted in treaty and land claims. At the same time, it can be argued that the police have evolved since Commissioner Nicholson's time and they may be more inclined to take a softer approach that involves consultation and perhaps even negotiation with the protesters. While this softer police approach may avoid violence, it may not resolve the underlying grievances between Aboriginal people and the police.[106]

There are also grounds to be sceptical about whether an independent police will truly be answerable to the law. Although the police will be subject to possible criminal prosecution, civil and Charter litigation, and police complaints for any abuse of power, these forms of accountability all operate after the fact. They all demand considerable time, expense, and trust in the justice system. The policy issues that will be shielded from political direction under full police independence may be particularly difficult to review through legal methods that focus on issues of liability.

Even if police independence is defined in a limited way that does not preclude political direction with respect to protests, it is not clear that elected politicians will be eager to take responsibility for high-risk and high-visibility decisions regarding the policing of protest. As discussed above, Sir Robert Mark argued that in his extensive experience as head of the London police, his responsible minister was only too willing to leave difficult policy decisions to the police.[107] In other words, there may not be enough democracy to support a model of democratic policing.

The danger of excluding public order policing from police independence is that political power in directing the police will be abused and/or exercised in a sub rosa manner that inhibits accountability for whatever political direction the police receive. There is much instinctive distaste for political involvement in policing. In the wake of APEC, for example, Professor Pue has argued that 'countries where the police respond to political command are not democracies. They tend to be brutal, inhumane places.'[108] The danger here is that politicians may be tougher on protest than the police. There is also a danger that it may be impossible for the government to divorce partisan from public interest concerns. For example, governments to the right of centre may conclude that it is in the public interest to be tough on labour, anti-globalization, and Aboriginal protest, while governments to the left of centre may conclude that it is in the public interest to be tough on anti-abortion, anti-gun control, and anti-gay rights protest. In a pluralistic and conflicted democracy, there may be no middle and detached ground to determine the public interest.

Another danger of political intervention in protests is that governments will not be held accountable by the people and the media for whatever direction is provided to the police. In this vein, Professor Pue takes issue with the optimistic view of democratic policing articulated by the McDonald Commission by observing that 'the theory of responsible government may well be at odds with the practice of modern executive,'[109] in which ministers rarely resign for misconduct in their ministries and power is centralized in central agencies, most notably the Prime Minister's Office. On this view, the problem at APEC was perhaps not so much the fact of political involvement, but the failure of responsible ministers to be held accountable for the intervention. A related issue is the lack of transparency about what guidance is provided to the police. At various junctures, responsible ministers and their staff have relied on the controversial idea that they were seeking and conveying information to the police as opposed to directing or even influencing their actions.[110] There is a danger that this distinction may be lost on the public and perhaps the police.

Who Is the Government: Responsible Ministers, Police Boards,
or Central Agencies?

A related question is who represents the government in any model of democratic policing. Both the relevant federal and Ontario police acts, as well as traditional theory of responsible parliamentary government, are clear. The responsible minister should represent the government to the police and be accountable for police actions as well as any direction that the police receive from civil servants in the ministry or the minister's own staff including their political staff. Even if one proceeds on the assumption that traditional understandings of ministerial responsibility can be maintained, some difficult questions remain. One is whether the responsible minister takes direction from the Cabinet and the Prime Minister on how his or her powers should be exercised. As discussed above, there was a lack of clarity about whether the minister of justice or the Cabinet made the decision in the Nicholson Affair. Both the attorney general and the solicitor general are law officers of the Crown who, by constitutional convention, enjoy some degree of independence from the Cabinet with respect to some decisions. The exact nature of this convention is, however, unclear, especially with respect to non-prosecutorial decisions.

There is also the issue that the responsible minister for policing both in Ontario and federally is no longer called the solicitor general. Although some might argue that this is a cosmetic change, proponents of governmental policing might counter that it represents a more profound change in governance and policing. The new emphasis since 9/11 on public security and the need for a multi-pronged and multi-ministerial response to a wide variety of threats places pressures on the idea that relations between the police and the government can and should be filtered through one responsible minister. This change also builds on developments prior to 9/11 that saw increasing centralization of power in central agencies and evidence that the traditional relationship between the solicitor general and the commissioner of the RCMP had at times been bypassed by intervention from central agencies.[111] Donald Savoie has argued that the multiplicity of departments and agencies involved in major files 'may well have reached the point where accountability – in the sense of retrospectively blaming individuals or even departments for problems – is no longer possible or fair.'[112] The patterns of traditional ministerial accountability and responsible government appear to have eroded to a significant extent since the McDonald Commission defended its vision of democratic policing based on ministerial responsibility for all but the quasi-judicial functions of the police. The appropriate reaction to this change in government is, however, an open question. One possibility is to fight the tide and attempt to channel accountability back along ministerial lines.[113] Others might give up on ministerial responsibility and accept governmental policing as a reality. For others, the complexity and difficulties of governance may make the model of full police independence much more attractive.

A final complication is that the RCMP and the OPP are somewhat anomalous in Canada because, unlike many municipal forces, they are not subject to direction from a police board. For example, the Ontario *Police Services Act*[114] provides for police boards appointed in part by the province and the municipality for all municipal police forces. Under section 31 of the act, the boards are responsible for policies for effective management of the police and can direct and monitor the performance of the police chief. At the same time, the board can only give orders and directions to the chief and shall not direct him or her 'with respect to specific operational decisions or with respect to the day-to-day operation of the police force.' The introduction of a police board may be a means to ensure more direct political oversight of the police than can occur in a large ministry. A properly staffed police board might be able to spend much more time on policing than could a minister with multiple responsibilities in an expanding security portfolio. Such a board might also be more inclined to develop protocols and guidelines to deal in advance with issues such as the policing of protests. Police boards could also facilitate the inclusion of Aboriginal people and other vulnerable groups in the democratic model of policing. At the same time, it could be argued that adding another body as a buffer in the complex relationships between the minister and the OPP might only cause confusion and diffuse accountability.

Information or Influence; Accountability or Control?

Another crucial question that will inform the choice of models is whether it is possible to maintain the distinction between exchanges of information between police and government in order to promote accountability as opposed to attempts by the government to exert control or influence over policing decisions. There is considerable support for such a distinction in the literature and the case law. Geoffrey Marshall has drawn a distinction between accountability based on a 'subordinate and obedient' mode and that based on an 'explanatory and co-operative mode.' He suggests that in England, the 'Home Secretary's responsibility for policing throughout the country is one that rests not on an ability to issue orders but on the capacity to require information, answers and reasons that can then be analysed and debated in Parliament and the press.'[115] Philip Stenning and Lorne Sossin have also argued that accountability need not be tied to control.[116] The McDonald Commission accepted the viability of such a distinction by concluding that the responsible minister might in some instances have a responsibility to be kept informed about even quasi-judicial policing functions that could not be the subject of ministerial control or direction. The judge in the *Small* case concluded that information had flowed upward from the police but influence did not flow downward from the government. Those who support a distinction between accountability and control envisage a process whereby the responsible minister can demand information from the police in order to ensure accountability without purporting to control the decisions made by the police.

The analytical distinction between the exchange of information for accountability purposes and the actual exercise of influence and control certainly can be made. The more relevant question for policy makers is whether it is sustainable in the real world. The sustainability of the distinction is premised on a wide acceptance by the relevant actors, as well as by the public, of the principle of police independence. Professor Edwards has argued that in extreme cases at least, a minister who has access to information about a case that he or she believes is badly mishandled will likely be pressured into acting.[117] Information in the absence of the ability to act can be a severe political and perhaps even legal liability. Even if ministers restrain themselves and do not attempt to influence a police decision, the police may either try to please the minister or perceive that there has been influence. As we have seen, the investigating officer in the *Small* case perceived political influence in the charging decision even though he was an experienced and legally trained officer. The lack of consensus and clarity about the ambit of police independence make it more likely that the public and the police will interpret requests for information as an implicit attempt to influence the police.

Political Involvement: Before, During, or After the Police Have Made Their Decisions?

One distinction that may perhaps help to inform the above debate is the distinction between requests for information after the police have made the relevant decision and requests made after the decision has been taken. This mirrors a distinction sometimes found in the accountability

literature between review which is retrospective in nature and oversight which is ongoing.[118] It also builds on a distinction drawn by the
Patten Inquiry into Policing in Northern Ireland between police independence from direction and their accountability to 'inquiry or review
after the event.'[119]

Requests and exchanges of information after a decision has been
made by the police can minimize the likelihood that political intervention will influence the police decision. Even if a minister intervenes and
changes a preliminary decision made by the police, the contrast between the police's preliminary decision and the minister's final decision may help to promote transparency and accountability for the final
decision. As will be discussed below, one of the more important issues
in police-government relationships is providing optimal conditions for
ensuring transparency and accountability for any political intervention
in policing. What should be avoided is the too common murky middle
ground in which the public and the media are not sure whether political
influence has been brought to bear on the police. Accountability and
transparency may be enhanced by allowing the police the opportunity
to make a preliminary decision free from influence and then requiring
that any political influence be conveyed in a deliberate and formal
manner.

Political Intervention: Partisan or Public Interest?

Another crucial question that will inform the choice between the models is rooted in assumptions and predictions about the quality and
nature of political intervention in policing matters. Both John Edwards
and the McDonald Commission argued that it was possible and vital to
distinguish between partisan and public interest considerations. Partisan matters such as support for the government and its supporters
should never influence political intervention on policing matters, but a
broad range of public interest considerations should. These would include the effects of policing on group relations in Canada and matters of
international relations. Lorne Sossin's argument that police, like all civil
servants, have a right to be 'apolitical' is based on a similar confidence
that partisan and public interest considerations can be separated.[120]

Others argue that the distinction between partisan and public interest
matters breaks down in the real world. The fortunes of the government
are often linked with the manner in which police handle high-profile
matters. Even if politicians were genuinely prepared to make the dis-

tinction, a cynical public might assume that they were nevertheless still motivated by partisan considerations. In addition, the assumption of a single public interest is increasingly questioned in our pluralistic and contested democracy. Reg Whitaker has criticized the McDonald Commission for adopting an overly optimistic view of ministerial interventions and for downplaying the danger and reality that ministerial interventions on issues involving Quebec separatism can and did serve the interests of the Liberal Party of Canada.[121] The point here is only to illustrate some of the difficulties of separating public interest considerations from the partisan fortunes of the government of the day. This debate also raises the question of whether the idea of a non-partisan public interest is based on a consensus view of politics that glosses over deep cleavages that have always existed in Canadian society, but are perhaps more evident today.

What Is Worse: Political Interference or Political Shirking?

Much of the literature and case law on police independence has been driven by the fear that politicians will interfere in police decisions in a manner that adversely affects the impartial application of the rule of law to all. Such fears cannot be dismissed. The findings of the Marshall Commission of interference in police investigations of Cabinet ministers stand as an important reminder of the dangers of improper influence on criminal investigations. Once one moves away from criminal investigations, however, the danger of political interference should be balanced against the danger of political shirking.

Political shirking occurs when the responsible minister refuses to assume responsibility and be held accountable for policing decisions that he or she could have influenced. Professor John Edwards made this point particularly well when he argued that 'undue restraint on the part of the responsible Minister in seeking information as to police methods and procedures can be as much as a fault as undue interference in the work ...'[122] As discussed above, Sir Robert Mark has stated that successive home secretaries were only too happy to leave controversial and difficult policing decisions to the chief constable. The prospect that responsible officials may avoid political responsibility suggests that the exact contours of police independence will be shaped by the willingness or unwillingness of responsible officials to intervene in policing matters. Thus a democratic model of policing could in practice evolve into one of full police independence should the politicians not enter the field. The prospect of political avoidance of difficult policing decisions also raises the question of whether problems of democratic deficit that are said to affect other aspects of government also affect the relationship between the police and the government.

Political Involvement in Policing: Informal or Formal?

A final important issue in selecting between the models is whether political involvement in policing will remain informal, or whether it can be reduced to writing so as to ensure transparency. The *Hatfield*, *Small*, and APEC cases suggest that politicians and those acting for politicians may often maintain that they were only making suggestions to the police and that the police retained the ultimate power to make an operational decision. The *Small* case reveals how those within the police may differ on whether the political intervention has actually influenced the police decision. The question then becomes whether it is possible or desirable to formalize the relationships between the government and the police so as to ensure that political interventions in policing are reduced to writing and perhaps also made public.

René Marin has writtenly approvingly of South Australian legislation that requires directives from the responsible minister to the police commissioner to be both reduced to writing and to be laid before Parliament and published. In his view such an approach can bring 'the transparency necessary to avoid potential conflict' and unfounded allegations of interference in 'the very sensitive relationship between the Minister responsible for the police and police authorities.'[123] Acting on the Australian example and the advice of Professor Edwards,[124] the Marshall Commission championed a similar approach to govern the relations between a director of public prosecutions (DPP) and the attorney general. In its view 'the right blend of independence and accountability'[125] was a system that would allow day-to-day prosecutorial independence while enabling the responsible minister to intervene through general guidelines and specific directives that would be reduced to writing and published in the Gazette.

The implementation of the Marshall Commission's recommendations, as well as subsequent amendments to Nova Scotia's *Public Prosecutions Act*,[126] is a complex subject beyond the scope of this chapter. It is relevant to note, however, that there are some signs that the attorney general has become reluctant to intervene formally under the requirements of the legislation.[127] The Nova Scotia act also contemplates consultation and discussions between the attorney general and the DPP about individual cases that do not have to be reduced to writing and published. This has raised fears in some quarters that informal political interventions in prosecutions will occur.[128] This experience, transferred to the policing context, raises the issue of whether formalized requirements might either inspire political avoidance of intervention and/or adaptive behaviour that results in informal consultations between politicians and the police without written and public directives being issued. These dilemmas suggest that reliance on the integrity of the relevant actors and their understandings of the proper principles that should govern police–government relations is inescapable.

The South Australian policing model and the Nova Scotian DPP model might be an effective way to combine police independence with accountability. Expectations could develop that the responsible minister would never intervene with respect to criminal investigations and would only intervene in the policing of specific public order events through general guidelines and in exceptional cases with written and public directives. A statutory requirement that both general guidelines and specific directives be reduced to writing and made public might help to ensure that the responsible minister is held accountable for any political intervention in policing. It could also be valuable as a means of channelling governmental intervention through the responsible minister and not allowing central agencies or political staff to perform an end run around the traditional and statutory framework of ministerial accountability for policing. At the same time, the possibility of adaptive behaviour cannot be precluded and there could be consultation between the minister and the police that is not reduced to writing or made public.

One possible way to deal with the danger of informal influence on the police would be that even less formal information requests not be made until the police have made preliminary decisions. As suggested above, waiting until preliminary decisions and plans have been made by the police responds to the dangers that earlier exchanges of information and views between the police and the government may unduly influence the police or create public perceptions of such influence. Once informed of the preliminary decision and the preliminary plan, the responsible minister, perhaps after consultation with the Cabinet and/

or a central agency, could then decide either not to intervene or to issue a public directive to guide the police. Such a process would allow the police space and time to apply their professional judgment to difficult policing matters, but it would also allow the responsible minister to assume responsibility for either the police's plan, or for a different plan or directive.

Conclusion

One first step in clarifying relationships between the police and the government would be to codify basic and widely agreed upon principles of police independence. Although there is some dispute about its outer periphery, there is a growing consensus that the police should be protected from political direction in the process of criminal investigation. The only legal sources that run counter to this principle are the statements in various Canadian police acts that the police are subject to the direction of the minister, as well as some statutory requirements that the attorney general consent to the commencement of proceedings and some police investigative techniques. As recommended by the APEC inquiry, the time has come to amend those acts to codify the *Campbell* principle and to recognize police independence to that extent.

There is much more dispute about police independence beyond the criminal investigation sphere. In support of a broader understanding of police independence is considerable scepticism about all forms of political intervention in policing and of the distinction between exchanging information and exerting influence. The role of central agencies in events such as APEC also raises questions about whether traditions of ministerial responsibility are viable given the complexity of modern governance. Geoffrey Marshall's striking change of position and his embrace in 1978 of a convention of full police independence is testimony to a growing lack of confidence in politicians and traditions of ministerial accountability. Some might also argue that legal developments such as the Charter and police complaints bodies provide more of an accountability check on police decisions than existed when Lord Denning originally articulated the doctrine of full police independence.

Nevertheless, there are still some reasons to be cautious about embracing a doctrine of full police independence. In support of limiting police independence to the criminal investigation core are the dangers of the police making questionable policy decisions in the name of police expertise and independence. There is also the democratic importance of promoting informed and meaningful debate about how the police inter-act with their fellow citizens. The case for transparent and accountable democratic control and responsibility over policing may be particularly strong with regard to police relations with Aboriginal people, because they involve broader question of whether the government respects Aboriginal rights. Indeed, even the democratic and governmental mod-els of policing outlined here may have to be modified to accommodate the unique circumstances of Aboriginal people. The case for democratic policing is also strengthened where legal methods of holding the police accountable for the way they police demonstrations prove to be in-adequate. Police complaints, Charter and civil litigation, and criminal prosecutions are blunt and after the fact methods to control police conduct. We should be cautious about giving up on democratic control of the police and the traditions of responsible government.

If the democratic policing model is to be viable, however, steps should be taken to ensure that political intervention in policing is more trans-parent, so that the responsible minister can be held accountable for any guidance given to the police. Legislative reform to recognize police independence with respect to criminal investigations and providing for written and public guidelines and directives for other policy matters might strike an appropriate balance between the goals of police inde-pendence and the ultimate accountability of both the police and the responsible minister to both the people and the law. Such a process could make clear to the public, the police, and the courts the exact influence elected politicians have had on policing decisions. Should such a process be dismissed as too onerous and too visible by the responsible officials, or as inconsistent with the complexities of modern governance and policing, much of the democratic justification for po-litical involvement in policing would be taken away. If our elected representatives are to influence policing, they should be prepared to do so in an open and accountable manner. If transparently democratic policing (outside the core of independent police investigation) fails, the alternatives are full police independence or governmental policing. In other words, we will have to decide whether to place our trust in the police or in governments that may not be held accountable for their influence on the police. Such a choice would not be a happy one to have to make in a democracy.

COMMENTARY BY COMMISSIONER
R.H. SIMMONDS (RETIRED)

In 1985 I felt the need to publicly outline my views with respect to the issue of police independence on a single narrow issue. My views on that issue have not changed in any way (a copy of that document has been included in this chapter). I refer to that incident as a 'single narrow issue' as that is exactly what it was. There are, however, quite a number of other circumstances in which the political level and the police interact, and about which I shall comment briefly, based upon my experience gained in over forty years of police service, all as a member of the RCMP, with the last ten years as commissioner of the force.

In the Canadian context I have always thought that the concept of police independence should receive a rather narrow interpretation, at least as far as the RCMP is concerned. Some of my comments may be viewed a bit differently by local police chiefs, depending upon the statutory provisions contained in the various provincial municipal acts, provincial police acts, city charters, and city ordinances by which they are bound. It is also important to keep in mind that the RCMP is not a unionized organization, nor are there any bodies or structures between the force and the ministry, such as a police board or a police commission. The relationship of the force vis-à-vis the political level is thus on quite a different footing than most other Canadian police forces, whether they be provincial or municipal organizations.

The constitution is silent on the matter of policing; however, it is the responsibility of the Canadian Parliament to ensure 'Peace, Order and good Government' through the enactment of legislation within their area of jurisdiction. One such piece of legislation is the *Royal Canadian Mounted Police Act*, which provides for the establishment of a police force and the appointment of a commissioner who acts under the direction of the minister with respect to the 'control and management of the Force and all matters connected therewith.' The act goes on to outline the duties of members of the force, who are 'Peace Officers,' and who, upon taking their oath at the time of enlistment, are bound to act accordingly. While acting in their peace officer capacity their activities are subject only to the orders of the commissioner and are not to be influenced by the whim of any minister (my interpretation, not necessarily agreed upon and accepted by everyone, as indicated in the

Simmonds-Kaplan exchange.) It is my view that it is only on this narrow issue concerning the *sworn duties of a peace officer* that independence from the political level can be claimed.

When examined from a historical prospect it will be seen that from 1873, when the North West Mounted Police was established, the force has often been used as an instrument to assist in meeting government policy objectives. A few examples follow.

• The very purpose in establishing a constabulary force was to settle issues in western Canada so that the territory could be opened up for colonization. In carrying out that responsibility members undertook duties that were far removed from that of a traditional police officer.
• The force played a role during times of war, starting with the so-called rebellion in Western Canada (1885) and continuing through the war in South Africa at the turn of the previous century and the First World War. Imagine an RNWMP Cavalry Troop at Vladivostok ready to take on the revolutionaries until cooler heads prevailed. In the Second World War. No. 1 Provost Company was recruited from the RCMP, and all the force's aviation and sea-going assets were seconded for military duty.
• The force was called in to deal with the Winnipeg General Strike and riots of 1919.
• The force was called in during the On to Ottawa Trek and Regina Riot of 1935.
• The force was used to enforce special back-to-work legislation enacted by Parliament to end labour strife when deemed necessary to protect the national interest.

These are but a few examples to illustrate that the force has often been called upon to act under the direction of government, without the issue of police independence being raised. In my view all of the above activities were quite legitimate, and they serve to illustrate why I believe the question of police independence should be given a narrow interpretation and invoked only to prevent unacceptable political meddling with respect to who can, and who cannot, be subject to police investigation and prosecution within the context of current law – which in itself is perhaps the ultimate reflection of government policy. The only other area that I would argue is sacrosanct to police judgment is that of determining the methods and timing of operations needed to carry out a legitimate objective, subject always to having to operate within the law and policy guidelines.

While researchers and professors may speculate endlessly with respect to the concept of police independence, the police themselves do not have that prerogative. They must comply with the law as they find it in terms of their duties and to a large extent their deployment (i.e., as expressed in policing contracts, memoranda of understanding between agencies, both domestic and foreign, and other instruments in place), and it is therefore not an issue that is debated at length within the police service. Having said that, I am pleased to see the issue studied in a forum such as this, as it is a matter that deserves to be better understood at the political level, at the operational police level, and by the public at large when it becomes a matter of public interest as a result of some incident that has occurred and when finger pointing is taking place. It is difficult to find a great deal of literature on the subject, and the papers prepared for this exercise go a long way towards filling that void. Whether or not any change or codification of these issues results, fostering a greater knowledge and awareness of the subject and the pitfalls attendant thereto is a worthwhile endeavour.

The questions to be asked, then, are in what form should government policy wishes best be communicated to the police, and to what extent should government officials be allowed to influence field activity? Once again I shall restrict my comments to the activity of the RCMP in its role as federal police, and in provincial and municipal policing under contracts between governments. I would just point out that, when performing regular police duties under the terms of a contract, when a member refers to 'the minister,' he or she generally has in mind the provincial attorney general or solicitor general, as the case may be.

My view of the correct relationship has always been quite simple. While keeping firmly in mind the two principles mentioned above, which must not be breached, I have always believed that mature and experienced persons, possessed of good judgment and common sense, can resolve and successfully deal with almost any problem that might be encountered in the field of law enforcement. That is not to say that there will always be agreement, but a good deal of accommodation can be reached without any of the parties feeling that their responsibilities and their professional judgment have been compromised.

I see no problem with a good deal of discussion between ministers of the Crown and the commissioner of police when a large event, or series of events, are at the planning stage or actively being dealt with. In fact, I believe it essential that ministers with political responsibility and the commissioner of police with operational responsibility have a clear understanding of the problems and concerns as seen by all sides. However, once the police have been tasked with the wide array of responsibilities that come with any major event, particularly if it involves difficult security issues, and national or international ramifications of concern, the political level must defer to the professional judgment of the police in the planning and the execution of the tasks for which they are responsible. The professional judgment of the police must take into account the rights of citizens to lawful assembly and protest; however, their first concern must be directed to assuring the security of the venue and the participants, and accomplishing that task with the least degree of force and disruption possible. From a police perspective this of course is where the difficulty arises, and most assuredly there will be those who feel that the police have been overly protective or aggressive in their conduct, even in the face of severe provocation, and on occasion, with benefit of hindsight, such sometimes appears to be the case.

In a large and highly decentralized country much of the planning, and virtually all of the on-site activity, is in the hands of local or regional personnel, and here difficulties occasionally arise. At large events at which the government is the host, ministry officials will always be present during the planning phase and during the execution of the plan. On occasion these officials will attempt to go beyond their proper consultative and information-sharing role and will invoke the name of the minister, or even the Prime Minister, to try and get their way. If such an attempt occurs the officer-in-charge should politely but firmly advise the official that if the minister has a problem he or she should take it up directly with the commissioner, and the officer-in-charge will take his or her direction from that office through the chain of command. Such advice will generally end the problem. The minister is unlikely even to be aware of the official's concerns, and if made aware, it is unlikely that he or she would approach the commissioner unless convinced that there was a major problem requiring higher level intervention.

Ministry officials should not be permitted access to command centres while operations are underway, and if they choose to be out where the action is taking place they should be treated as any other citizens. It must be borne in mind that if problems develop the ministry official is not the person who will be held to account. Again, there is room for a good deal of discussion and dialogue among all the parties in the work up and planning stages, and seldom does the situation lead to the scenario suggested above. Should it do so, however, there must be no doubt about how it should be handled, and there must be no doubt in the minds of all personnel committed to the operation precisely who is in charge. In this respect I am in complete accord with the comments found in paragraphs 31.3.1 to 31.4 of the Hughes report with respect to the APEC conference, cautioning only that should these principles be subject to written codification they be carefully worded so as not to prevent the free flow of information and discussion up to the point where the bar is set.

In a similar vein, I see no threat to police independence if there are quite detailed discussions with the ministry regarding national priorities and concerns in the area of criminal activity and crime suppression programs, bearing in mind that there will never be sufficient resources to deal with all the problems. This type of discussion is particularly vital if amendments to the law are being recommended.

There are occasions in which it can be quite galling to have to dedicate resources to investigating what, in the overall scheme of criminal activity, are rather minor offences, but because they involve parliamentarians or government officials are given high priority. To that I can only say that given the role of Parliament and the need for good governance any sensible commissioner would move quickly to have these matters investigated in order that the affairs of the nation could be dealt with in an orderly fashion and public confidence be maintained in the institutions of governance. This type of incident will often generate a good deal of comment, some high drama, and plenty of rhetoric, which will occasionally include suggestions that the police are being used for partisan political purposes. In these cases the police must proceed expeditiously and professionally, and be scrupulously careful to ensure that no minister be kept apprised with respect to their findings until the appropriate moment, which will generally be at the time that charges are preferred, or the matter is concluded for want of evidence or determined to be unfounded. During my tenure as commissioner I never experienced any interference or improper comment from any minister or any official in cases of this nature, although on one occasion a highly partisan parliamentary committee attempted to compel me to divulge the contents of an ongoing investigation, which, despite threats to my liberty, I refused to do.

In reading the papers prepared for this consultation, I note some comment with respect to the issue of information sharing vis-à-vis attempts to influence the investigative process. Again I do not see any problem in this area provided that the exchange of information is between persons of good judgment who have a proper understanding of their role. In matters of significant interest the minister should not have to rely upon the daily media as his or her source of knowledge, particularly so because in the Canadian parliamentary system he or she will surely be bombarded with questions by Opposition members during the Question Period, and should be in a position at least to state that the commissioner has indicated that an investigation is or is not under-way, and that the results will be discussed with Crown counsel at the appropriate time.

Furthermore, ministerial support is a prerequisite in submitting budget requirements in the estimates process, in memoranda to Cabinet, in Treasury Board submissions, in negotiating certain contracts, and so on. All of these procedures require a good deal of discussion and supporting data to make the case, and thus there must be ongoing dialogue between the minister and the commissioner, and between relevant departmental officials and relevant officers of the force. None of this discussion will include details of matters under investigation, but it does illustrate the need for open dialogue with respect to current needs and perceived future needs as identified through the planning process. In these activities the police cannot proceed independently.

One other comment is relevant to the matter of information exchange. During the ten years that I was the commissioner of the RCMP there were seven solicitors general and four prime ministers (one of them serving twice). Each of these gentlemen had a different background of experience and brought different priorities to the table. On occasion the new incumbent had little experience or knowledge of the subtleties of the justice system and the role of the police within that system. This resulted in an inordinate amount of time being spent in briefing sessions with respect to the work of the force historically, currently, and futuristically, and likewise in determining the interests and concerns of the new incumbent. I see no alternative to this procedure, given the responsibility of the government for peace, order, and good government, and for the minister's role as outlined in the *RCMP Act*. I only point this out because some observers tend to characterize this activity as an indication that the police leadership is somehow becoming too close to the political level. The exact opposite is actually the case, as all this activity is undertaken to ensure that there is a proper understanding of roles, hopefully leading to a productive relationship with respect to the work and the needs of the police community.

On a more general theme one can state that factual police independence has been eroded over a period of years by what is generally considered to be progressive reform (especially by lawyers), and often with the full acquiescence of the police. Perhaps the most obvious example is in the area of the prosecution of common crime. When I first entered the police service there were many jurisdictions in which magistrates courts were commonly referred to as police courts. In these courts all charges were preferred by the police and all prosecutions were conducted by police prosecutors, up to and including preliminary hearings. Now, in many of these same jurisdictions, no charge can be preferred unless approved by a city prosecutor or Crown counsel (although I maintain that this is a matter of practice and not a matter of law). Informations are seldom laid by the investigating officer, and such officer will probably not even know the result of the case unless he or she deliberately seeks it out. Frequently, the work of the police officer handling the case at street level is completed with the submission of his or her report on the incident. Others decide what, if any, follow up there should be. All this change has taken place in the name of efficiency and so-called professionalization; however, an unintended result has been the lowering of knowledge and understanding of court procedures and the presentation of evidence on the part of constables. While one would not argue that the old systems should be reintroduced, it must be stated that these changes, along with a number of others, have had the effect of diminishing the so-called independence of the police.

My comments are not particularly weighty when compared to the work that has gone into the preparation of the papers included in this volume but rather are the personal views and comments of a former senior police official. I certainly make no attempt to speak for the force today. Attempting to do so would be quite inappropriate and well beyond my mandate. In fact, in this entire exercise my greater interest is centred on the issues for which the Ipperwash Inquiry was created, as during my police career I was, at times, quite involved in dealing with problems arising firm the concerns of Native Canadians and the difficulties which flow therefrom. Consequently I have firm views with respect to the way in which those issues should be handled. I find that to be a much more interesting topic than the somewhat theoretical question of police independence. I thank you for including me in your deliberations.

NOTES

Kent Roach would like to thank Lynne Weagle for her diligent research assistance and Jonathan Rudin, Lorne Sossin, and Philip Stenning for helpful comments on an earlier draft.

1 Commission Interim Report Following a Public Inquiry into Complaints that took place in connection with the demonstrations during the Asia Pacific Economic Cooperation Conference in Vancouver (Ottawa: Commission of Public Complaints, RCMP, 23 July 2001), www.cpc-cpp.gc.ca/defaultsite/ at 30.4.
2 Susan Delacourt, 'Flurry of civil suits expected within days,' *Toronto Star*, 11 May 2004.
3 Susan Delacourt, 'To serve and protect its political bosses,' *Toronto Star*, 17 April 2004.
4 Philip Stenning, 'Someone to Watch over Me: Government Supervision of the RCMP,' in *Pepper in Our Eyes: The APEC Affair*, ed. Wes Pue (Vancouver: UBC Press, 2000), at 113.
5 Tim Cogan, as quoted in Delacourt, 'To serve and protect.'
6 [1968] 1 All E.R. 763.
7 *Bisaillon v. Keable and Attorney General of Quebec* (1980), 17 C.R.(3d) 193; Que.C.A. rev'd on other grounds, [1983] 2 S.C.R. 60.
8 *Royal Canadian Mounted Police Act*, R.S.C. 1985, c. R-10 s. 5(1), and *Police Services Act*, R.S.O. 1990, c. P-15, s. 17(2).
9 [1999] 1 S.C.R. 565.
10 *Reference re Secession of Quebec*, [1998] 2 S.C.R. 217.
11 *Royal Canadian Mounted Police Act*, R.S.C. 1985, c. R-10, s. 5(1).
12 *Bisaillon v. Keable*.
13 Donald Savoie, *Governing from the Centre: The Concentration of Power in Canadian Politics* (Toronto: University of Toronto Press, 1999), at 125.
14 Mr Blackburn brought a subsequent case charging that the police were not enforcing laws against pornography. *R. v. Metropolitan Police ex parte Blackburn*, [1973] Q.B. 241. This challenge was rejected but as in the 1968 case, the courts left the door open to judicial intervention in an extreme case of police refusal to enforce the law.
15 *R. v. Metropolitan Police ex parte Blackburn*, [1968] Q.B. 116 at 135–6.
16 *Fisher v. Oldham Corporation*, [1930] 2 K.B. 364; *Attorney General for New South Wales v. Perpetual Trustee Company* [1955] A.C. 457.
17 Geoffrey Marshall, *Police and Government* (London: Methuen, 1965), at 34;

Geoffrey Marshall, *Constitutional Conventions* (Oxford: Oxford University Press, 1984), ch. 8.

18 Marshall, *Police and Government,* at 45.

19 Ibid. at 120.

20 *McCleave v. City of Moncton* (1902), 32 S.C.R. 106 at 108–9. For an examination of other early Canadian civil liability jurisprudence see Stenning, *Legal Status of the Police* (Ottawa: Law Reform Commission of Canada, 1981), at 102–12. Professor Stenning concludes that 'none of these cases ... determines the implications of the constitutional status of the police in terms of their liability to receive direction of any kind with respect to the performance of their duties.' Ibid. at 110.

21 See note 7 above. It could be argued that the Canadian fixation on federalism and now the Charter in relation to policing may have distracted attention from general constitutional principles concerning the relation between the police and the government. Compare Peter Hogg, *Constitutional Law of Canada,* 3rd ed. (Toronto: Carswell, 1992), ch. 19 with William Wade and Christopher Forsyth, *Administrative Law,* 8th ed. (Oxford: Oxford University Press, 2000), ch. 5.

22 *Bisaillon v. Keable,* at para. 28 (Que. C.A.).

23 Marshall, *Police and Government,* at 25.

24 *Basillon v. Keable,* para. 130.

25 Commission of Inquiry Concerning Certain Activities of the RCMP, *Freedom and Security under the Law* (Ottawa: Supply and Services, 1981), at 1011 (henceforth McDonald Report).

26 *Royal Canadian Mounted Police Act.*

27 *Royal Canadian Mounted Police Act,* S.C. 1959, s. 5 . Before that time, the *North-West Mounted Police Act* of 1873, 36 Vict. c. 33, s. 33, also contemplated that the Department of Justice would be responsible for the 'control and management' of the force.

28 R.S.O. 1990, c. P.15.Other provincial policing acts follow this model of recognizing the power of the responsible minister, usually the solicitor general, to direct the police. See *Police Act,* R.S.B.C. 1996, c. 367, s. 7; *Police Act,* R.S.A. 2000, c. P-17, s. 2(2); and *Police Act,* S.Q. 2000, c. 12 s. 50.

29 O.C. 497/2004.

30 For example, s. 3(I) contemplates that the minister may 'provide to boards, community policing advisory committees, and municipal chiefs of police information and advice respecting the management and operation of police forces, techniques in handling special problems and other information calculated to assist.'

31 S. 31(4) of the *Police Services Act* is more explicit with respect to the powers
of municipal police services boards and states that 'the board shall not
direct the chief of police with respect to specific operational decisions or
with respect to the day-to-day operation of the police.' Nevertheless, it
must be noted that controversy rages over the extent of 'operational'
autonomy. The choice of the 'operational' definition may not be ideal. The
McDonald Commission concluded that operational decisions can often
raise policy issues. See McDonald Report at 868–9, discussed below.

32 *R. v. Campbell*, [1999] 1 S.C.R. 565 at para. 27.

33 Ibid. at para. 29.

34 Ibid. at para. 18.

35 Ibid. at para. 33.

36 APEC Interim Report at 10.2.

37 *Quebec Secession Reference*, [1998] 2 S.C.R. 217 at 249. See also *Judges Remuneration Reference*, [1997] 3 S.C.R. 3. See generally Robin Eliot, 'References,
Structural Argumentation and the Origin of Principles of the Constitution'
(2001) 80 Can. Bar Rev. 67. The Ontario Court of Appeal has also used
similar unwritten constitutional principles to govern its interpretation of
statutes: *Lalonde v. Ontario* (2001), 56 O.R. (3d) 505 at para. 174 (C.A.); see
also *Polewsky v. Home Hardware* (2003), 66 O.R. (3d) 600 (Div. Ct.). Some
other courts, however, have been more reluctant to recognize constitutional principles or to contemplate that they may limit statutory powers.
Baie d'Urfe c. Quebec, [2001] J.Q. no. 4821 (Que. C.A.). Constitutional
conventions are commonly thought to constrain the exercise of legal
powers but not to override clear statutory powers. *Reference re Amendment
of the Constitution*, [1981] 1 S.C.R. 753.

38 Criminal Code, ss. 83.24, 319(6).

39 Ibid., ss. 83.28–83.3.

40 The latest word from the courts on the matter does not particularly clarify
the legal status of police independence. In the *Odhavji Estate* case, the
Ontario Court of Appeal held that a tort against the solicitor general of
Ontario in relation to the refusal of police to cooperate with the SIU was
properly struck because it was the chief of police 'who has the sole authority to deal with the day-to-day operational conduct of police officers. The
duties of the Solicitor General with respect to policing matters are contained in s. 3(2) of the Act and do not impose any duty concerning the
day-to-day supervision of municipal police officers.' *Odhavji Estate v.
Metropolitan Toronto Police*, (2001), 194 D.L.R. (4th) 577 at para. 43. This
part of the decision was upheld by the Supreme Court of Canada, which
observed that 'whereas the Police Chief is in a direct supervisory relation-

ship with members of the force, the Solicitor General's involvement in the conduct of police officers is limited to a general obligation to monitor boards and police forces to ensure that adequate and effective police services are provided and to develop and promote programs to enhance professional police practices, standards and training. Like the Board, the Province is very much in the background, perhaps even more so.' *Odhavji Estate v. Metropolitan Toronto Police*, [2003] 3 S.C.R. 263 at para. 70. This decision strikes a somewhat different note than *Campbell* because the Supreme Court focused on the statutory language of the *Police Services Act* and did not make resort, as it did in *Campbell*, to the principle of police independence to limit references to ministerial direction in the relevant act.

41 Stenning, 'Someone to Watch over Me.'

42 As quoted in ibid. at 89.

43 Ibid. at 90.

44 John Diefenbaker, *One Canada: The Years of Achievement 1957 to 1962* (Toronto: Macmillan, 1976), at 317.

45 Robert Bothwell, Ian Drummond, and John English, *Canada since 1945: Power, Politics and Provincialism* (Toronto: University of Toronto Press, 1981), at 240–1.

46 Stenning, 'Someone to Watch Over Me,' at 95.

47 See generally John Edwards, *Ministerial Responsibility for National Security* (Ottawa: Supply and Services, 1980), and John Edwards, *Walking the Tightrope of Justice: An Examination of the Office of Attorney General* (Halifax: Queen's Printer, 1989).

48 As quoted (emphasis added) in Edwards, *Ministerial Responsibility for National Security*, at 94–5.

49 Stenning, 'Someone to Watch Over Me,' at 100.

50 Professor Edwards defined improper partisan political considerations as those 'designed to protect or advance the retention of constitutional power by the incumbent government and its political supporters.' He added, 'This does not mean the Attorney General in the realm of prosecutions, or the Solicitor General in the area of policing, should not have regard to political considerations in the non-partisan interpretation of the term 'politics.' Thus, it might be thought that there are legitimate political grounds for taking into account such matters as the harmonious international relations between states, the reduction of strife between ethnic groups, the maintenance of industrial peace and generally the interests of the public at large ...' Edwards, *Ministerial Responsibility for National Security*, at 70.

51 Ibid. at 96–7.
52 McDonald Report at 762.
53 Peter Russell, *Freedom and Security: An Analysis of the Police Issues before the Commission of Inquiry* (Ottawa: Commission of Inquiry Concerning Certain Activities of the Royal Canadian Mounted Police, 1978), at 17. Professor Russell elaborated that 'a system of responsible government requires not only that the major agencies of government be under the direction of responsible ministers, but also that there is adequate opportunity to make the responsible Minister accountable to the representative legislature.' Ibid. at 21–2.
54 McDonald at 1005–6.
55 Ibid. at 1013.
56 Ibid. at 1013 (emphasis in original). The commission rejected Pierre Trudeau's distinction between policy matters that the government could be involved in as opposed to 'the day to day operations of the Security Service' on the basis it would result 'in whole areas of ministerial responsibility being neglected under the misapprehension that they fall into the category of "operations" and are thus outside the Minister's purview. This neglect has become apparent in what might be called the policy of operations ...' These included 'important policies questions concerning the distinction between legitimate dissent and subversive threats to the security of Canada' that 'will arise in the context of deciding whether or not to initiate surveillance of a particular individual or group. Similarly, questions will arise about the legality and propriety of a particular method of collecting intelligence in the context of a particular case.' Ibid. at 868–9.
57 Savoie, *Governing from the Centre*; Savoie, *Breaking the Bargain: Public Servants, Ministers and Parliament* (Toronto: University of Toronto Press, 2003).
58 Hansard, 11 Feb. 1985 at 2201. MacKay subsequently seemed to agree that he should not descend in the arena of day-to-day operations but 'that it is another thing to elicit information that any person wants to give to a Solicitor General if the circumstances are proper.' Ibid. at 2207.
59 As quoted in Stenning, 'Someone to Watch Over Me,' at 105.
60 *R. v. Hatfield* (1985), 85 N.B.R. (2d) 208 (N.B. Prov.Ct.).
61 'Ottawa admits it intervened before budget charges laid,' *Toronto Star*, 1 June 1989; 'Charge of reporter may signal tougher stand on secrets,' *Globe and Mail*, 1 June 1989; 'Leak charges not political, Tories say,' *Globe and Mail*, 31 May 1989.
62 *R. v. Small* (1990), 78 C.R. (3d) 282 at para. 57 (Ont. Prov. Ct.).
63 Stenning, 'Someone to Watch Over Me,' at 107–8; Stenning, 'Accountabil-

ity in the Ministry of the Solicitor-General,' in *Accountability for Criminal Justice: Selected Essays*, ed. Philip C. Stenning (Toronto: University of Toronto Press, 1995), at 54.

64 *R. v. Small*, at para. 79.

65 Ibid. at para. 72.

66 Ibid. at para. 82

67 Ibid. at para. 112.

68 The judge commented that 'owing to the unique and somewhat startling grounds for the motion – that is the allegation, in the generic sense, of political interference in the criminal law process – the hearing necessarily assumed some of the flavour of a public inquiry, in order to ensure a full and probing examination of the allegation. Rules of criminal evidence were relaxed; hearsay and opinions were received (albeit from competent persons) and privileges were waived. It would not have served the public good to suppress evidence and testimony by the strict application of the rules of criminal evidence such as would be appropriate in the course of the trial.' Ibid. at para. 4.

69 See generally Kent Roach, 'The Evolving Test for Stays of Proceedings' (1998) 40 Crim. L.Q. 400, and *R. v. Regan*, [2002] 1 S.C.R. 297 for cases where improprieties by Crown counsel and judges were held not to be egregious enough to merit a stay of proceedings.

70 See, e.g., *Campbell v. Attorney General of Ontario* (1987), 31 C.C.C. (3d) 289 (Ont. H.C.); *Dowson v. The Queen* (1983), 7 C.C.C. (3d) 527 (S.C.C.).

71 *Royal Commission on the Donald Marshall Jr. Prosecution* (Halifax: Queen's Printer, 1989), at 212–14.

72 Ibid. at 216.

73 As quoted in William Kaplan, *Presumed Guilty: Brian Mulroney, the Airbus Affair and the Government of Canada* (Toronto: McClelland and Stewart, 1998), at 147.

74 Stenning, 'Someone to Watch over Me,' at 111.

75 Kaplan, *Presumed Guilty*, at 289. Even as the settlement of the suit was announced, Minister of Justice Rock defended the principle that 'police decide ... when to start and when to stop investigations.' He did, however, accept responsibility for inadequacies in the system of accepting requests for foreign assistance. Ibid. at 315.

76 An editorial in the *Toronto Star* argued 'Rock says he is accountable to Canadians, but in this instance justice officials simply followed normal procedures. Solicitor General Herb Gray acknowledges he's responsible for the RCMP, but, of course, he can't interfere in police probes. RCMP Commissioner Philip Murray says he is "deeply disturbed" that a member

of his force blabbed to the press, but he is convinced the leak did not jeopardize the investigation. Everyone is sorry. But the buck stops nowhere.' As quoted in ibid. at 321.

77 For an excellent collection of essays on the matter which were written without the benefit of Justice Hughes's 2001 report see Pue, ed., *Pepper in Our Eyes*.

78 APEC Interim Report at 10.4.

79 Ibid. at 31.3.1.

80 As quoted in Savoie, *Breaking the Bargain*, at 4.

81 APEC Interim Report at 9.7.

82 Elsewhere in the report, Justice Hughes concludes that he was 'of the view that the RCMP's conduct in removing the tenters was directly attributable to the actions of the federal government. It was Mr. Carle of the Prime Minister's Office, who through Mr. Vanderloo of ACCO, directed the RCMP to remove the protesters, apparently out of a concern about potential vandalism. However, Supt. Thompsett, the man in charge of security, was less concerned about potential vandalism than that removing the protesters might lead to more serious security problems. The federal government has no authority to make decisions, which may have compromised an RCMP security operation, particularly given that such decisions, although consistent with the License Agreement and the Criminal Code, were unjustifiably inconsistent with the Charter. I am satisfied that, in this instance, the federal government acting through the Prime Minister's Office, improperly interfered in an RCMP security operation.' Ibid. at 11.7.

83 Ibid. at 30.4

84 Wes Pue, 'Executive Accountability and the APEC Inquiry: Comment on *Ruling on Applications to Call Additional Governmental Witnesses*' (2000) 34 U.B.C. Law. Rev. 335.

85 Wes Pue, 'The Prime Minister's Police? Commissioner Hughes APEC Report' (2001) 39 Osgoode Hall L.J. 165 at 86.

86 Darren Yourk, 'Lapierre politicizing RCMP and probe: Opposition,' *Globe and Mail*, 22 April 2004.

87 Susan Delacourt, 'To serve and protect.'

88 Les Whittington and Miro Cernetig, 'Fraud charges rock Liberals,' *Toronto Star*, 11 May 2004 A1, A7.

89 Susan Delacourt, 'Flurry of civil suits expected.'

90 The most influential models have been Herbert Packer's contrasting crime control and due process models. See Herbert Packer, 'Two Models of the Criminal Process' (1964) 113 U. Penn. L. Rev. 1 For attempts to add to Professor Packer's models see John Griffith, 'Ideology in Criminal

Procedure or a Third Model of the Criminal Process' (1970) 79 Yale L. J.
359 ; Kent Roach, 'Four Models of the Criminal Process' (1999) 89 J. Crim.
L. and Criminology 691. For an assessment of the methodology of models
as a form of scholarship see Kent Roach, 'The Criminal Process,' in *The
Oxford Handbook of Legal Studies*, ed. P. Cane and M. Tushnet (Oxford:
Oxford University Press, 2003).

91 See Gordon Christie's chapter in this volume.

92 *Ex parte Blackburn*, at 135–6.

93 APEC Interim Report at 31.3.1.

94 Geoffrey Marshall, 'Police Accountability Revisited,' in *Policy and Politics:
Essays in Honour of Norman Chester*, ed. D. Butler and A.H. Halsey (London: Macmillan, 1978), at 60–1. In 1984, he elaborated on this thesis by
arguing that 'despite its uncertain legal foundations ... it is now necessary
to defend' what has been described here as full police independence 'as a
constitutional and administrative convention.' Geoffrey Marshall, *Constitutional Conventions* (Oxford: Oxford University Press, 1984), at 144.

95 Sir Robert Mark, *In the Office of the Constable* (London: Collins, 1978), at
157–8.

96 APEC Interim Report at 31.3.1.

97 R.S.O. 1990, c. P-15, s. 31.4.

98 Gordon Chong, 'Who controls police?' *Toronto Star*, 6 May 2004.

99 In the context of policing Aboriginal people, this might require consultation with the minister of native affairs and the attorney general and
perhaps the federal government in order to assess policing decisions in
the context of other developments and the Crown's fiduciary responsibilities to Aboriginal peoples. See Gordon Christie, 'Police–Government
Relations in the Context of State–Aboriginal Relations,' in this volume.

100 Geoffrey Marshall concluded that 'the analogy with judicial independence is defective,' in large part because of the greater range of discretion
available to police as opposed to judges. Marshall, *The Government and the
Police*, at 117–18. Perhaps a better distinction is that judges only act after
hearing from the parties and must give reasons for their decisions.

101 Savoie, *Governing from the Centre*, at 125.

102 Edwards, *Ministerial Responsibility for National Security*.

103 Robert Reiner has observed a 'calculative and contractual' trend in British
policing that 'is a new mode of accountability, side-stepping without
displacing the constabulary independence doctrine.' Robert Reiner,
'Police Accountability: Principles, Patterns and Practices,' in *Accountable
Policing*, ed. Robert Reiner and Sarah Spencer (London: Institute for
Public Policy Research, 1997), at 19.

104 For arguments that Packer's due process and crime control models do not fit the situation of Aboriginal people see Kent Roach, *Due Process and Victims' Rights: The New Law and Politics of Criminal Justice* (Toronto: University of Toronto Press, 1999), ch. 8.
105 See Gordon Christie's chapter in this volume.
106 I am indebted to Jonathan Rudin for these points.
107 Sir Robert Mark, *In the Office of the Constable* (London: Collins, 1978).
108 Pue, *Pepper in Our Eyes*, at x.
109 Wes Pue, 'Policing, the Rule of Law and Accountability in Canada: Lessons from the APEC Summit,' in ibid.
110 In the APEC affair, Jean Carle of the PMO testified he only made 'suggestions' to the police and did not make orders. Pue, *Pepper in Our Eyes*, at xxi. Similarly, the responsible minister and officials in the *Hatfield* and *Small* cases maintained that they sought information as opposed to influence.
111 Savoie, *Governing From the Centre*, at 125.
112 Savoie, *Breaking the Bargain*, at 268.
113 Professor Savoie appears attracted to this route as he argued 'there is no need to abandon the doctrine of ministerial responsibility. The doctrine is not what ails institutions and doing away with it would accomplish very little. It would not strengthen the hand of political actors in their relation with career officials, increase accountability, improve policy making or government operations, or make government more responsive to Canadians.' Ibid at 256. Interestingly, he proposes the greater use of 'written instructions' from ministers (ibid. at 259), an option that will be discussed below.
114 R.S.O. 1990, c. P-15.
115 Marshall, 'Police Accountability Re-Visited,' at 61–2.
116 Stenning, 'Accountability in the Ministry of the Solicitor General of Canada'; Stenning, 'The Idea of Political "Independence" of the Police' in this volume; Sossin, 'The Oversight of Executive-Police Relations in Canada,' in this volume.
117 Edwards, *Walking the Tightrope of Justice*, at 163.
118 'Oversight means "supervision" ... Review means a "survey of the past" ... Oversight results in a sharing of responsibility, and as such, it somewhat blurs accountability. Review, on the other hand, is an important element of accountability because it provides an independent assessment of the way in which an organization has performed.' *A National Security Committee for Parliamentarians* (Ottawa: Privy Council Office, 2004), at 8–9.
119 Independent Commission on Policing for Northern Ireland, *A New*

Beginning: Policing in Northern Ireland (September 1999). The Patten
Inquiry rejected Lord Denning's understanding of police independence
and the very term itself in favour of a new term 'police responsibility.'
It wanted to stress that while police may be able to make decisions free
from external direction, 'no public official, including a chief of police, can
be said to be "independent,"' at least in the sense of being 'exempted
from inquiry or review after the event by anyone.' Independent Commission on Policing for Northern Ireland *Report* at 6.20–6.21. It recommended
that a police board and ombudsman 'actively monitor police performance
in public order situations and if necessary seek reports from the Chief
Constable and follow up these reports as they wish.' Ibid. at 9.19. This
contemplates after-the-fact accountability but no powers of direction and
qualifies its categorical statement that 'we disagree with Lord Denning's
view that the police officer "is not a servant of anyone, save of the law
itself."' Ibid at 1.14.

120 Sossin, 'The Oversight of Executive-Police Relations in Canada,' in this
volume. Professor Sossin also stresses the importance of various accountability mechanisms as a check on an 'apolitical and autonomous' police.

121 Reg Whitaker, 'Designing a Balance between Freedom and Security,' in
Ideas in Actions: Essays on Politics and Law in Honour of Peter Russell, ed.
J. Fletcher (Toronto: University of Toronto Press, 1999), at 129.

122 Edwards, *Ministerial Responsibility for National Security*, at 97.

123 René Marin, *Policing in Canada* (Aurora, ON: Canada Law Book, 1997), at
111. S. 6 of South Australia's *Police Act, 1998* No 55 of 1988 provides that
the commissioner is responsible for the control and management of the
police 'subject to this Act and any written directions of the Minister.' S. 7
provides that there shall be no ministerial directions in relation to internal matters of pay, discipline, hiring, and firing. S. 8 provides that a copy
of any ministerial direction to the commissioner shall be published in the
Gazette within eight days of the direction and laid before Parliament
within six sitting days.

S. 4.6(2) of the Queensland *Police Services Administration Act* provides
that the minister may give direction to the commissioner about 'policy
and priorities to be pursued in performing the functions of the police
service' and 'the number and deployment of officers and staff members
and the number and location of police establishments and police stations,' but s.4.7 provides that a copy of these written directions should be
kept and provided annually to the Crime and Misconduct Commission
and then referred to a Parliamentary Committee on Crime and Misconduct. S. 37(2) of the Australian *Federal Police Act* provides that 'the Minis-

ter may, after obtaining and considering the advice of the Commissioner and of the Secretary, give written directions to the Commissioner with respect to the general policy to be pursued in relation to the functions of the Australian Federal Police.' For a full explanation of the genesis and reception of these and other international comparison see Stenning, 'The Idea of the Political "Independence" of the Police' in this volume.

124 Professor Edwards concluded that in general federal legislation in Australia establishing a DPP that was subject to written and published directives from the attorney general was an optimal means of 'conferring upon any officer holder the maximum degree of independence when making prosecutorial decisions' but also maintaining 'parallel regard for sustaining the principle of ministerial accountability.' Edwards, *Walking the Tightrope of Justice*, at 184–5.

125 Marshall Commission Final Report, at 229–30.

126 S.N.S. 1990, c.s 21 as amended by S.N.S. 1999, c. 16. Note that s. 6(2) of the *Canadian Security Intelligence Act*, R.S.C. 1985, c. C-23, also contemplates more transparency than s. 5 of the *RCMP Act* by providing that the minister 'may issue to the Director written directions with respect to the Service.' These directions are not published as statutory instruments, but a copy is provided to the Security Intelligence Review Committee.

127 Professor Stenning has concluded that 'the appropriate limits to an Attorney General's intervention in particular cases appear still to be neither agreed upon not well understood by the public and the media. This situation may perhaps have led Attorneys General to be overly reluctant to fulfill their responsibilities with respect to intervention in some individual cases and the public and the media to be overly suspicious of any such involvement by an Attorney General. On the other hand, it can readily be acknowledged that these shortcomings may be preferable to their opposites, as revealed by the Marshall Inquiry's report.' Stenning, 'Independence and the Director of Public Prosecutions: The Marshall Inquiry and Beyond' (2000) 23 Dal. LJ. 385 at note 46.

128 S. 6(c) of the *Public Prosecutions Act* provides for consultations that do not bind the DPP and s. 6a, added in 1999, provides that the attorney general and the director of public prosecutions shall 'discuss policy matters, including existing and contemplated major prosecutions,' at monthly meetings. Professor Edwards contemplated that the responsible minister could still seek information and offer advice without triggering the formal requirements of written and public directives. He wrote: 'There is no intention to limit the process of advice and consultation ... I am not advocating that the contents of such advice be always reduced to writing

and made the subject of public disclosures.' Edwards, *Walking the Tight-rope of Justice*, at 189. The Opposition in Nova Scotia, however, argued that the 1999 consultation amendments compromised the arm's- length relationship between the DPP and the attorney general and could defeat other provisions designed to ensure that political interventions were reduced to writing and made public so as to ensure transparency and accountability. Nova Scotia Legislative Debates, 4 Nov. 1999 at 1667, 1683.

2 The Oversight of Executive-Police Relations in Canada: The Constitution, the Courts, Administrative Processes, and Democratic Governance

LORNE SOSSIN

Abstract

This chapter critically examines two central questions. First, what are the mechanisms that constrain and define executive accountability and police oversight in Canada? Second, can the need for the police to remain above partisan politics and beyond manipulation by the government of the day be reconciled with these mechanisms of governance and accountability? Sossin argues that an apolitical and autonomous model is best suited to the dynamics of policing in a constitutional democracy such as Canada, and has the potential to balance the need for political input into policing against inappropriate political interference.

The executive-police relationship is shaped by multiple and overlapping forms of oversight, from internal review and disciplinary investigations to judicial and public inquiries. These multiple and overlapping forms of executive oversight are often criticized as unwieldy, incoherent, and ineffective. The problem with the present system of executive-police oversight is its lack of overarching vision and coherence. Police commentators tend too easily to fall into pro-police and anti-police camps, and these polarized groups tend to talk at each other rather than to each other. Governance and institutional structures reflect this bipolar situation.

The bipolar political backdrop is complicated by the policy/operational distinction on which the involvement of the executive in policing often turns. Sossin argues that the policy/operation dichotomy is maintained not because it accords with a readily identifiable boundary, but rather because we have yet to discover any other way of distinguishing legitimate government interests from illegitimate ones. The 'apolitical and autonomous' model of policing represents an alternative framework for discerning the boundary between legitimate and illegitimate executive involvement in policing. The goal of this ideal type is to create a legal, administrative, and political framework in which neither the police nor the executive can unilaterally impose its will on the other, and in which, as a result, avenues for deliberation and dialogue must be pursued.

This chapter ends with commentaries by Alan Borovoy and Wes Pue.

Introduction

This chapter will consider the issue of police-executive relations principally from the executive perspective, and will critically examine two central questions. First, what are the mechanisms which constrain and define executive accountability and police oversight in Canada? Second, can the need for the police to remain apolitical and autonomous be reconciled with mechanisms of governance and accountability? In seeking to address these competing demands I will sketch what I term an 'apolitical and autonomous' ideal type of executive-police relations. I suggest this model is best suited to the dynamics of policing in a constitutional democracy such as Canada, and has the potential to respond to the need for political input into policing while countering inappropriate political interference in policing. Further, as I elaborate below, the apolitical and autonomous model does not rely on the often unstable boundary between police policy and police operations upon which the present model depends. Finally, a significant impediment to an apolitical and autonomous police is the lack of transparency with respect to the political, legal, and administrative relationship between the executive and the police. The present analysis is directed towards redressing this transparency gap.

The executive-police relationship is shaped by multiple and overlapping forms of oversight. In the spring of 2004, a snapshot of this oversight would include three formal judicial inquiries investigating undue executive interference in police matters in Ontario (the Ipperwash Inquiry) and with respect to the RCMP (the Sponsorship Inquiry and the Arar Inquiry); inquests and inquiries into wrongful convictions and police conduct in Saskatchewan (the Commission on First Nations and Métis Peoples and Justice Reform) and Newfoundland (the Lamer Inquiry); internal reviews of police accountability in Toronto (the Ferguson Report); and provincewide task forces on civilian oversight in Ontario (chaired by former Chief Justice of the Ontario Superior Court, Patrick

LeSage), as well as the ordinary business of municipal, provincial, and federal governments deciding on police force budgets, the work of internal investigations departments (e.g., the Special Investigations Unit in Ontario), and the activities of specialized police-related tribunals (civilian and police complaints tribunals, police services boards, internal police disciplinary panels, etc). These multiple and overlapping forms of executive oversight are often criticized as unwieldy, incoherent, and ineffective, and such criticisms are often justified. On the other hand, there is a persuasive case to be made that the more perspectives (not just from within the executive but those of judicial, legislative, and community groups as well) brought to bear on police conduct, the more likely abuses of the rule of law will be addressed or deterred and public confidence in the police enhanced.

The problem with the present system of executive-police oversight is its lack of overarching vision and coherence. Police commentators tend too easily to fall into pro-police and anti-police camps and these polarized groups tend to talk at each other rather than to each other.[1] Governance and institutional structures reflect this bipolar situation. Some mechanisms appear designed to ensure the police implement the direction of the government of the day, while others appear designed to ensure that the police remain insulated from political interference. Some mechanisms view the police as a central instrument of enforcing the rule of law while others view them as a potential source of violations of the rule of law. In the debate surrounding executive-police relationships, it is crucial not to conflate concepts such as independence and autonomy or accountability and oversight. Oversight, for example, does not require independence. Independence, on the other hand, does require autonomy. Autonomy may or may not be inconsistent with accountability, depending on the forms of governance, funding, and transparency involved. Neither oversight nor accountability suggest control. Below, I attempt to disentangle these related but meaningfully distinct concepts in the context of executive-police dynamics.[2]

This paper is divided into three sections. In the first section, I outline the apolitical and autonomous ideal type of executive–police relations as the model best suited for a constitutional democracy such as Canada. In the second section, I explore how this ideal is furthered or hindered by the current executive-police terrain in Canada, with special emphasis on the respective role of courts, administrative bodies, and ministerial responsibility in the oversight of the executive–police relationship. The boundaries between the police and other aspects of the executive branch of government often turn on the distinction between police policy and police operations. I argue below that the policy/ operation dichotomy is maintained not because it accords with a readily identifiable boundary, but rather because we have yet to discover any other way of distinguishing legitimate government interests from illegitimate ones. In the third section, I expand on the apolitical and autonomous police model as an alternative framework for discerning the boundary between legitimate and illegitimate executive involvement in policing. The goal of the ideal type described is to create a legal, administrative, and political climate in which neither the police nor the executive can unilaterally impose its will on the other, and in which, as a result, avenues for deliberation and dialogue must be pursued.

I. In Search of an Ideal Type of Executive-Police Relations

Kent Roach, in his helpful typology of four models of police independence, contrasts the 'democratic policing' and 'governmental policing' models, which imply close government supervision, with models of 'police independence,' which imply little or no government supervision.[3] In this chapter, I argue that these do not have to be understood as opposing ends of a spectrum of government control. Indeed, I would suggest they should not be. The police are part of the political order, not above it or beneath it. Democratic concerns both motivate and confine the legitimate bounds of police independence. The fourth model of policing, presented as the most extreme example of governmental policing, in which 'the police are conceived by and large as civil servants subject to ministerial control,' implies a degree of direct control over the police by the political executive. There are good reasons to blanch at the suggestion that the police ought to be seen as civil servants. As Wes Pue has observed: 'The difference between "bureaucrats with guns" and law enforcement officers is simple: police are supposed to be prohibited equally from pursuit of their own desires and from acting on the whim of politicians. Unlike civil servants, they are not supposed to respond to "political masters." Their job, simply, is to enforce the law.'[4]

While this statement captures an important concern regarding political direction in police activities, it glosses over equally important constitutional norms of bureaucratic independence which establish the public service as 'apolitical' and constitutionally protect a public servant's right to decline direction or expose confidential communications where the rule of law has been violated or public safety is imperilled.[5] Although, as a general proposition, public servants may take direction from the government of the day, this should not be seen as an indication that they are the instruments of political whim, vulnerable to political interference, or without means to resist political pressure. That said, the police are certainly no ordinary public servants.

The constraints on the kind of direction government may appropriately give, and the amount of functional autonomy civil servants (or executive boards, tribunals, and agencies) enjoy are matters to be worked out through constitutional principle and political practice. Policy advisers are public servants who work hand in glove with the government of the day, for example, but frontline decision makers are civil servants who make judgments and exercise discretion according to a range of non-partisan considerations. Consider Crown prosecutors, who are both public servants (subject to the relevant public service acts, accountable to the relevant minister) and functionally autonomous in the exercise of prosecutorial discretion.[6] Crown prosecutors are not independent of government, but their freedom from political interference is well-accepted and jealously guarded (which is not to say that it is not challenged from time to time, or that those challenges are not sometimes successful). By contrast, judges, while paid from the public purse, subject to statutory direction, and vulnerable to government funding and management of the administration of the courts, are constitutionally independent and expressly not accountable to the government for adjudicative decision making.[7]

It is important to remember why we understand the courts to be a separate and independent branch of government and prosecutors and police to be a part of the executive branch. The police are not and should not be viewed as a separate branch of government, nor of course, are they simply part and parcel of the executive branch of government. We should not lose sight of the fact that attempts to use police forces as an arm of 'political administration' of the government of the day has a long and unsettling history in Canada,[8] nor should we gloss over the equally long and equally unsettling history of the police acting as a law unto themselves,[9] particularly in the context of Aboriginal communities.[10] This is the classic double bind of executive–police relationships: how to guard against one extreme without inviting the other.

With these caveats in mind, I suggest an alternative model to the typology presented by Kent Roach, one which takes as its ideal type an 'apolitical and autonomous police.'[11] I am certainly not the first to suggest that both terms capture an aspiration of executive-police relations. Maurice Martin, for example, has referred to the importance of the police remaining apolitical and autonomous. He suggests that 'apolitical' and 'autonomous' are 'near synonymous.' By contrast, I use the terms to suggest different orientations. 'Apolitical' is an orientation of detachment from partisan considerations in the political process. Autonomy relates not to an administrative orientation but to a set of administrative practices, arrangements, and structures that constitute a functional separation from the government. These two concepts are related but reflect different aspects of the executive–police relationship and are elaborated below.

Just as Max Weber proposed the ideal type of 'rational–legal administration' as the most effective model of bureaucracy and the most suitable form of bureaucracy for democratic society,[12] I advance the concept of an apolitical and autonomous police both as the most effective form of executive-police relations generally and the form most consistent with Canada's political, administrative, and legal values, which include accountability, governance and rule of law concerns. In my view two central characteristics typify this model. These characteristics address, from different perspectives, the double bind discussed above, although they are not intended to be exhaustive of the characteristics by which one might elaborate this model.

Political but not Partisan

An apolitical and autonomous police model reflects a culture and orientation of non-partisanship and a mindset of detachment from partisan concerns. Underscoring this sensitivity to partisanship is the recognition that the traditional bonds of ministerial responsibility in Canada no longer provide sufficient accountability (either of the police to the government or of the government to the citizenry).[13] An apolitical and autonomous model of police-executive relations recognizes that police forces are and should be interested in, affected by, and connected to political institutions. However, the model also recognizes the necessary limitations of police engagement in the political process and suggests an approach by which appropriate limits may be negotiated. The ideal type of an apolitical and autonomous police is meant to convey a posture of engagement with the political process that need not and should not result in capture of police decision making by that process, nor the converse use of political powers for illegitimate political ends.

Autonomous but Not Independent

This ideal type is also meant to convey a vital separation between the government and the police that does not presuppose formal independence or hindrances to accountability. An apolitical police, while by definition not independent of government, must be subject to effective internal, intra-executive, and external oversight mechanisms in order to ensure functional autonomy and the highest standards of professionalism. These mechanisms should also ensure predictable and principled ways/means to monitor police compliance with the rule of law on the one hand, and freedom from political interference on the other.

In my ideal type, these mechanisms do not act at cross-purposes but rather serve as complementary constraints on executive–police relations. An example of internal oversight mechanism would be police disciplinary investigations into the activities of individual officers. Intra-executive forms of oversight ideally include both arm's-length bodies, such as a civilian oversight board or police services board, as well as oversight by other arms of the government responsible for monitoring police activities, such as a special investigations unit with responsibility where individuals are harmed while in police custody. In addition to internal and intra-executive oversight, police authority must also be subject to external oversight from an independent judiciary through criminal and civil adjudication. Finally, safeguarding the apolitical and autonomous model of police may depend on review by a parliamentary officer as well (along the lines of an auditor general or information and privacy commissioner). This might require a separate entity or may simply dictate the means of appointment and funding for existing entities. The appropriate mix of oversight and governance relationships is discussed in more detail in the second section below.

There is no jurisdiction in Canada where executive–police relations and their oversight mechanisms attain the apolitical and autonomous ideal outlined above. The purpose of an ideal type is to provide an overarching vision for police-executive relationships, an aspiration by which to measure present structures and arrangements and propose a framework for future reform. In the next section, my goal is to analyse the current executive-police terrain in Canada with this normative approach in mind.

II. The Executive-Police Relationship in Canada

What is the government of the day's interest in policing activities and structures? Arguably, the executive branch's priorities with respect to policing fall into one of three broad categories.[14] First, the executive is interested in articulating those policing policies and practices which are in the 'public interest.' Decisions to lay hate crimes charges in individual cases, which by statute require the approval of the attorney general, represent an example of this public interest motivation.[15] Second, the executive is interested in developing and implementing the government's own policy preferences in the policing context, or more generally on 'law and order' and criminal justice issues. This second interest includes decisions about the share of scarce public resources that should be allocated towards the police sector. Third, because the executive is drawn from the political party which controls the legislature, it is invariably interested in creating positive publicity while avoiding negative publicity for its policies. These are not watertight compartments of interests. The decision to call for a task force review or public inquiry into a police controversy, for instance, may involve dimensions of all three interests. Similarly, one could say that establishing executive-police structures and arrangements that enhance public confidence in the government and the police (for example, civilian complaints bodies) also reflect the fruition of all three motivations.

Conventional wisdom suggests that the executive has an abiding interest in 'policy' matters and no interest in 'operational' matters. In some cases, this distinction is clear and compelling. A government might want to 'crack down' on gun violence, for example, and the police become the means by which this policy goal is achieved. How the police execute the policy, however, is properly the concern of the police (within the budgetary, legal, and other constraints that shape operational decisions). In other cases, the executive's interest will shade indirectly into operational issues. For example, the government may want to demonstrate its commitment to the gun violence policy by devoting more resources to a 'guns and gangs' police and prosecutor task force with an understanding that this should lead to more arrests, charges, prosecutions, and convictions. Alternatively, the government's interest might be directly operational, as in the case of a government that wishes to trumpet a 'zero-tolerance' initiative for gun-related infractions, which involves directing the police to take action on laying charges they might otherwise exercise their discretion not to lay. To suggest that the government's interests may be neatly packaged into a 'policy' compartment and not spill over into an 'operational' compartment is a dubious claim which appears to resonate with few people who have even a passing acquaintance with policing or government. In this section, in order to better understand the terrain across which the boundary between the police and other parts of the executive branch of government must be mapped, I discuss the various sites of executive involvement in policing and their implications for the apolitical and autonomous model.

The executive-police terrain in Canada is complex and multifaceted. Different executive and policing bodies interact in overlapping ways. Municipal, provincial, and federal governments have distinct relationships with city police, provincial police (in Quebec and Ontario), and the RCMP, respectively. The relationship between these governments and these police forces may be statutory or may involve contractual agreements. These executive and policing bodies may also interact across jurisdictional lines (for example, the RCMP was called in to investigate charges of corruption against the Toronto Police). Finally, all of these police forces may also interact with private security firms on the one hand, or military or security intelligence forces on the other, which may be subject to separate legal regimes, duties, and authority. Take hate crime as an example. Hate crime laws are the product of the federal government's justice policy; pursuant to the Criminal Code, however, prosecutions require the approval of a provincial attorney general, and the investigation of a hate crime may involve local, provincial, and RCMP investigations. This set of relationships has both policy and operational implications. For example, is the decision to create a special 'hate crimes' unit within a police force a policing decision, a policy decision, or a political decision? When the chief of police attends a town hall meeting organized by religious and ethnic groups to lobby government for greater hate crimes enforcement, is she or he there as part of government, or as a stakeholder of government? If the outcome of the meeting is a governmental decision to deploy public resources to provide additional private security at religious institutions, what should the response of the chief of police be? Should she or he be thinking of what is good for the police? What is good for the government of the day? What is good for the affected communities facing the possibility of violence? Or what is good for the public at large?

As the following cursory review of executive oversight bodies reveals, there is considerable variation in their mandate, authority, and resources. But how are we to assess their effectiveness? Should they be measured by outcomes (e.g., the more complaints made/investigated/resolved/reported, the better)? Should they be measured by their independence from police control? Or should they be measured globally by the extent to which public confidence in the police rises or falls, or the extent to which police morale and community relations improve or deteriorate? I have suggested an ideal type of an apolitical and autonomous police to provide a normative framework for such assessments and pose two questions in this regard. How have these bodies ensured the proper balance between political engagement on the one hand and detachment from partisan pressures and concerns on the other? And how have these bodies ensured that the police can discharge their distinctive duties to the Crown and the public in upholding the rule of law with appropriate political input but without undue political interference? I attempt to address these questions through a brief review of the administrative, legal, and political dynamics defining the police–executive relationship, each of which is discussed in turn.

Administrative Dynamics

In addition to this jurisdictional complexity, there is significant administrative complexity in the executive-police relationship. A plethora of administrative bodies have been established in Canada with the goal of providing venues for the regulation and redress of police conduct.[16] Most prominent among these have been civilian complaints bodies, police services boards, and internal investigating bodies such as Ontario's Special Investigations Unit. All of these bodies exercise powers pursuant to legislative mandates that also limit the scope and consequences of their oversight over police conduct. Governance and oversight of police conduct and services may reside in a number of executive bodies. In Ontario, for example, this web of executive supervision consists of police services boards made up of provincial and municipal officials, special investigations units that review police conduct in specified circumstances, civilian oversight boards, internal disciplinary bodies, ministry and minister's staff (both solicitor general and attorney general), central agencies, and in some cases coroner's inquests and ad hoc public inquiries, all of which are creatures of the executive branch in one form or another, but each of which often must remain, to some degree, autonomous from both the police leadership and other executive bodies.

Each of these bodies operates in the context of the legal and political complexity discussed below. The application of the apolitical and autonomous ideal type allows for the assessment of these bodies based on the degree to which they further or hinder the police's non-partisan orientation and the ability to distinguish legitimate from illegitimate political input.

Civilian Oversight

Some of the most innovative and controversial executive bodies charged with police oversight are civilian complaints commissions. As Tammy Landau has observed, 'while there are numerous mechanisms both inside and outside police organizations to achieve "accountability," the precise arrangements for handling public complaints against the police have emerged as a flashpoint for assessing both police accountability to the public and "progress" in the reform of policing.'[17]

The Ontario Civilian Commission on Police Services (OCCOPS) is an example of this type of executive vehicle for community oversight and has been the subject of fairly intense scrutiny.[18] As critics have made clear, the present incarnation of civilian oversight in Ontario fails to ensure the functional separation of executive oversight and police interests by providing too much discretion to the chief of police to dismiss complaints without further review both on procedural and substantive grounds, and to conduct investigations where they are deemed warranted. The primary role of the OCCOPS appears to be receiving reports from the chief of police. A recent audit disclosed that of the seven hundred complaints made about police conduct, only two were referred to a formal disciplinary hearing. Two hundred complaints were withdrawn, 200 were dismissed as unsubstantiated, and 150 were informally resolved. As the CCLA noted, 'such numbers are bound to create suspicion.' The CCLA, along with numerous other bodies, have submitted proposals for reform as part of the Ontario attorney general's overhaul of the civilian complaints policy (which, as indicated above, is now under review by a task force headed by former Chief Justice of the Ontario Superior Court, Patrick LeSage).

Police Boards

Police boards act as a buffer between political direction from government on the one hand and the operational control of police investigations by the chief of police on the other. Under the Ontario *Police Services Act*,[19] for example, the boards, which are appointed jointly by the provincial government and the municipality for all municipal police forces, are responsible for policies for effective management of the police and can direct and monitor the performance of the police chief, although not with respect to 'specific operational decisions' or the 'day-to-day operation of the police force.'[20]

While the provision of a buffer (even one based on the problematic policy/operational dichotomy) would appear to be consistent with an apolitical and autonomous police model, police boards in several jurisdictions have simply become the focal point for political disputes involving the police. This characterization is particularly apt in the case of the Toronto Police Board. In January 2004, the Toronto police launched an investigation when news of an investigation into the chair of the Police Services Board for allegedly inappropriate sexual comments about a child leaked to the press.[21]

By May 2004, the chair of the Toronto Police Services Board was on the verge of asking the province to take over the civilian oversight functions and launch a review of 'supervision and accountability' among police management, but was prevented from doing so when some members of the board literally left the table to deprive the body of the quorum necessary for decision making.[22] The tensions and dysfunctions characterizing the Toronto Police Services Board in 2004 were exacerbated further by the decision by a divided board not to renew the contract of Chief Julian Fantino.[23]

The example of the Toronto Police Services Board illustrates that an apolitical and autonomous police model requires not only structures and arrangements but personal commitment to this ideal on the part of those charged with implementing it. This example also places a spotlight on how members of intra-executive oversight or governance bodies are appointed and what constituencies, if any, those members are selected to represent. This point is discussed below in another context.

Public Inquests, Inquiries, Reviews, Task Forces, and Advisory Panels
Because many executive bodies lack or are seen to lack sufficient separation from the government of the day, credible oversight of the executive–police relationship will sometimes require an arm's-length interloper. The classic arm's-length interloper is the independent judiciary, but where the issue is systemic, where the questions do not break down into discrete legal thresholds, or where legal remedies are insufficient to address executive concerns or restore public confidence in the police system, the courts may prove ineffective. In such circumstances,

public inquests, inquiries, reviews, and task forces examining police structures, activities, and/or accountability are the most common recourse for the executive. They have arguably become the norm rather than the exception in Canada in the past generation at all levels of government and even within many policing organizations.

It is important to keep in mind that the decision to launch an inquiry, and the determination of its terms of reference, are political choices. Once an inquiry is launched and its terms of reference are set, however, it operates by and large independent of government involvement. The only control the government retains is to shut the inquiry down entirely (e.g., the Somalia Inquiry). Inquiries into policing questions of various dimensions are called for differing reasons. Some are forward-looking catalysts for policy reform. Others are backward looking, and aimed primarily at truth-finding. Some are launched in order to serve political ends by extricating the government from a thorny controversy; other inquiries themselves become thorny controversies for the government (e.g., the Somalia Inquiry).[24] Launching an inquiry entails risk for the executive, but declining to launch an inquiry can also prove problematic.

One of the central oversight functions performed by inquiries, inquests, and reviews is disentangling problems relating to individual police officers and leaders from problems relating to structures, arrangements, and systems. Was excessive force used by the RCMP on peaceful protestors during the APEC summit because of a failure of particular officers, a failure of police leadership, a failure of political or bureaucratic leadership, a failure of autonomous bodies (e.g., the University of British Columbia) to act autonomously, or a failure of all of the above? Questions that cross individual and systemic lines are particularly well suited to public inquiries.

Notwithstanding these limitations, which I return to below, it is clear that the ideal type of an apolitical and autonomous police is significantly enhanced by the recourse to public inquiries where the executive–police relationship is alleged or believed to have broken down. The McDonald Commission, the Marshall Inquiry, and the APEC Inquiry, while called under different auspices for different reasons in different places at different times, all led to significant exposure to and deliberation over executive-police relationships. Aside from independent or quasi-independent inquiries, both the police and the executive have also availed themselves of less independent but more confidential external reviews by impartial sources. For example, George Ferguson, a retired judge, undertook a two-year review of police governance and made numerous recommendations arising from allegations of police misconduct and corruption on the Toronto Police drug squad.[25]

In addition to the inquiries, inquests, and reviews, Canada also has a tradition of executive task forces advising on particular aspects of policing. To take a recent example, consider the Mayoral Task Force on Community Safety launched by Toronto's mayor David Miller.[26] Miller described the mandate of the panel, chaired by the Chief Justice of Ontario (and former attorney general/solicitor general for the province) Roy McMurtry, in the following terms: 'The police are responsible for enforcing, and I think they do a good job, and that they deserve our support. The City, though, can and must play different role from the police. The city must emphasize the prevention aspect. We can advocate with senior levels of government and the City can play a coordinating role.'[27] Curiously, however, the police themselves are not represented on this particular advisory panel.[28]

Drawing the boundary between the legitimate and illegitimate executive role in policing is not simply a matter of administrative or institutional design. It also dovetails with the constitutional and legal environment within which executive-police relations take place. It is to this set of dynamics that I now turn.

Legal Dynamics

The executive-police terrain is shaped by a complex legal topography. The legal constraints include written and unwritten constitutional principles, including the rule of law, federalism and the *Charter of Rights*, Aboriginal rights, statutory standards, common law administrative and private law duties, and internal codes, rules and guidelines. Together, these constraints constitute a roadmap for judicial intervention in the executive-police relationship. This judicial role includes the articulation of the boundaries of police autonomy and political accountability.

Courts constrain the executive-police relationship in several important respects. Most importantly, the independent judiciary, relatively free from political interference, provides a meaningful form of accountability on police conduct to ensure it comports with constitutional, statutory, and common law standards, and more generally, with the rule of law. Typically, the courts exercise this oversight through adjudication in the criminal justice system. Thus, as a practical matter, this oversight arises only when police irregularities are raised by defence counsel seeking to exclude evidence, create reasonable doubt, and avoid convictions. Crown counsel typically act as advocates for the police, although their relationship is more nuanced than this suggests and the police have no role in directing counsel in the prosecution of a criminal charge. My point here is merely that judges do not have a mandate for any independent investigation into police activities, and are constrained by the individual facts and circumstances of the case before them from developing or implementing systemwide solutions.

Many legal and constitutional principles may animate judicial intervention in the police context. Below I discuss what I take to be the most significant of these, including the constitutional principle of the rule of law, the doctrines of federalism, the *Charter of Rights,* and civil liability (I do not cover Aboriginal rights which, while significant, are the subject of Gordon Christie's contribution to this symposium).

Rule of Law

The rule of law is, it has been said, easy to invoke but virtually impossible to apply. It may mean considerably different things to considerably different observers.[29] In Canadian administrative law, it has taken on special resonance in settings where judicial review is used to call the government to account.[30] This focus on providing a check against unfettered executive authority arises in part from the circumstances of the leading case elaborating its content, *Roncarelli v. Duplessis.*[31] In *Roncarelli,* the Supreme Court quashed an attempt by the premier, acting through the liquor commissioner, to revoke a liquor licence of a tavern owner who was a supporter of Jehovah's Witnesses. Because the revocation had nothing to do with actual liquor offences, and was instead related to a political interest on the part of the government, the Court found that the decision had been taken on ulterior grounds. Using the apparatus of the state for political ends, in other words, was held to be an arbitrary and unlawful exercise of public authority.

The rule of law has occupied a central place in Canada's constitutional firmament ever since *Roncarelli.* It appears in the preamble to the *Charter* (alongside the 'supremacy of God') and has been held to form a part of the guarantees imported from the United Kingdom through the preamble to the *Constitution Act, 1867.* In the *Secession Reference,* the Court described the importance of the rule of law in the following terms:

> The principles of constitutionalism and the rule of law lie at the root of our system of government. The rule of law, as observed in *Roncarelli v. Duplessis,*

[1959] S.C.R. 121, at p. 142, is 'a fundamental postulate of our constitutional structure.' As we noted in the *Patriation Reference, supra*, at pp. 805-6, '[t]he "rule of law" is a highly textured expression, importing many things which are beyond the need of these reasons to explore but conveying, for example, a sense of orderliness, of subjection to known legal rules and of executive accountability to legal authority.' At its most basic level, the rule of law vouchsafes to the citizens and residents of the country a stable, predictable and ordered society in which to conduct their affairs. *It provides a shield for individuals from arbitrary state action.*[32] (Emphasis added.)

Following *Roncarelli*, the rule of law has also come to embrace the principle that no discretion is 'untrammelled.' No matter how wide a grant of statutory authority (or how broad a prerogative power), all government decision making must conform to certain basic tenets, such as being rendered in good faith, and not for ulterior or improper motives. Given that some of the widest discretion in our legal system is afforded to police officers, the significance of the idea that all discretion is structured and constrained by constitutional standards has enduring appeal in the policing context. As William Wade has stated: 'The powers of public authorities are ... essentially different from those of private persons. A man making his will may, subject to any rights of his dependants, dispose of his property just as he may wish. ... This is unfettered discretion. But a public authority may do none of those things unless it acts reasonably and in good faith and upon lawful and relevant grounds of public interest ... The whole conception of an unfettered discretion is inappropriate to a public authority, which possesses powers solely in order that it may use them for the public good.'[33]

While I emphasize that the police should be seen generally as autonomous rather than independent of the executive, there are clearly settings where the police must act independently, and be seen to act independently, in order to protect the rule of law. What amplifies this necessity is that the police are sometimes put in the position of enforcing the rule of law against the very political bodies to which they are accountable. Charges of political interference are the most complicated and contentious when they arise in the context of police investigations of executive officials. The recent drug-related investigation in British Columbia that involved searches and seizures at the offices of senior political staffers is a case in point.[34] Initially, the RCMP indicated that the seizures were related to money-laundering aspects of a drug investigation. Later, the Crown suggested that staffers may have been offered or had taken bribes to trade in secret government information.[35] The staffers, it turns out, were involved in the $1 billion privatization sale of BC Rail, which was also in due course tainted by the police investigation. With national media attention focused on the RCMP activities, and political fortunes and futures hanging in the balance, how can the public be confident that the police can resist political interference in their investigative decision making (and that the executive can resist the temptation to interfere in the first place)?

The allegation of political interference into the leak of the federal budget in 1990 is another case in point.[36] Journalists obtained copies of budget documents and released their content prior to the introduction of the budget in the House of Commons. The RCMP investigated and initially the responsible officer declined to bring charges, in part because the prosecution seemed selective as it involved only some of the people who had control of the leaked material and not others. Finally, the investigating officer was removed from the case and another officer ultimately swore the informations in the case. While inappropriate influence from the Prime Minister's Office (PMO) or Privy Council Office (PCO) was never established in the case, the charges were stayed and the undertone of political interference was clear.

The incidence of interference by the PMO in policing matters was more clearly established in the APEC affair. This incident arose out of police conduct in clearing protestors from the site of the 1997 Asia-Pacific Economic Cooperation meeting in Vancouver.[37] In his report as a member of the Commission for Public Complaints against the RCMP, Justice Ted Hughes concluded that the RCMP providing security for the 1997 APEC Summit in Vancouver had 'succumbed to government influence' in its efforts to coercively sequester protestors from the view of the summit delegates.[38] In particular, there were various links between Jean Carle, then the prime minister's director of operations, and policing decisions made before and during the summit in relation to protestors.[39]

Finally, the 'sponsorship' affair reflects the awkwardness for police agencies themselves caught up in investigations into wrongdoing. The auditor general turned over to the RCMP evidence of potential wrongdoing arising from improper sponsorship contracts. At the same time, a parliamentary committee and public inquiry have been investigating potential RCMP involvement in the very same scandal.[40] The fact that the RCMP laid charges against senior public servant Chuck Guité, just days prior to the Liberal election call, led to speculation that political interference might have played a part in the timing of the charges. The

RCMP spokesperson asserted 'our investigation is totally independent from whatever is going on in politics.'[41]

These cases[42] raise questions not just of the police's obligation to uphold the rule of law in the face of political interference, but also of the legal status of police officers themselves. Are they 'employees' in a 'master and servant' relationship with their 'employer' (whether a municipality, region, or the provincial/federal Crown), or an 'office-holder' with direct obligations to discharge legal duties irrespective of the direction that might be received from the supervising authority? There is case law supporting both positions and the answer appears to depend on the context. In labour relations settings, the police are more likely to be seen as employees;[43] in rule of law settings, they are more likely to be seen as office holders beholden to no 'master' save the law.[44]

Thus, for the police, the rule of law must serve as a two-way street (or perhaps more accurately a four-way intersection with no stop signs). The police must be called to account for their adherence to the rule of law through various forms of oversight (Special Investigations Unit, civilian complaints, the criminal justice process, internal discipline, etc.), but they must also be unfettered by political interference or direction so as to serve as a mechanism by which other political and legal entities are held to account. This is a tall order. Since no entity has the legitimacy and capacity to hold itself to account, the only real option is for multiple and overlapping oversight (both of the police and of executive conduct in relation to the police). The rule of law in this sense should be seen as reflexive and dynamic rather than linear and static.[45] While this general approach strikes me as inevitable, and perhaps even desirable, the coherence of how it has unfolded in Canada is open to debate.

Federalism

It is impossible to approach the executive-police relationship in Canada without acknowledging the constraints and complexities imposed through federalism. As David Smith has written, 'there is no subject more central to the study of Canadian politics than that of federalism.' He went on to observe, 'at one level of analysis, policing would seem to confound the pre-eminence of federalism. Along with courts and the legal system, the policy as instruments of the state appear to violate the division of power that is the hallmark of Canadian federalism.'[46] What Smith had in mind was the fact that the RCMP provides one-third of all public police officers in Canada (including the RCMP's federal police duties and eight of ten provinces in which the RCMP has contractual arrangements to provide police services).

Apart from this centralizing force in Canadian policing, federalism also generates a complex set of federal-provincial/municipal dynamics in the mandate, funding, and governance of the police. For example, the federal government, while it has no jurisdiction over local policing, may modify, expand, or contract local police mandates through amendments to the *Criminal Code*. Whether local police and provincial prosecutors have a constitutional duty to investigate and prosecute all offences designated by the federal government remains a heated and unsettled issue. This arose recently with respect to amendments to the *Criminal Code* dealing with firearms offences: attorneys general in Alberta, Manitoba, Saskatchewan, and Nova Scotia expressed reservations regarding whether they would instruct prosecutors to enforce the new provisions.[47] At least in Manitoba, the attorney general also speculated as to whether the federal government should be billed for any costs associated with prosecuting firearms cases if compelled to do so.[48]

Is it open to provincial governments to direct police and/or prosecutors to decline to enforce compliance with particular criminal provisions? Or do provincial attorneys general and/or police officers have an independent duty to the Crown to enforce validly enacted penal provisions? There is no clear answer to this question in Canada's constitutional system. In the absence of hard and fast constitutional rules, political practices and constitutional principles form the foundation for negotiation. Federalism offers few solutions for executive–police oversight, but it does provide a framework and venue for deliberations on important questions. As Smith noted, 'in the exercise of the discretionary power that the police have to lay charges in criminal matters lies the potential for the practices of law enforcement to sustain societal and, in turn, political federalism.'[49]

The form and content of political oversight over police activities varies sharply across provinces and territories and between those jurisdictions and the federal government. This is so even without addressing other special policing relationships, such as Aboriginal band police departments and military police, which entail special forms of federal accountability and control.[50] Federalism remains a meaningful constraint on executive-police oversight, but also ensures a potentially constructive balance between centralizing and decentralizing tendencies in the development and implementation of oversight mechanisms.

Charter Rights

It is now impossible to speak of the autonomy of the police without considering the constraints (and protections) imposed by the *Charter*.[51] The central mechanisms by which the courts regulate police conduct, in particular, sections 7–14 and 24(2),[52] collectively put the police in the vital but awkward position of discharging a public duty to seek the arrest, charge, and conviction of those they believe responsible for crimes while at the same time discharging a constitutional duty to protect the rights of the accused, including most importantly the right to be presumed innocent, with all the assumptions and guarantees that flow from this right.[53] It is significant to note that in these cases, both police conduct and the laws that authorize that conduct are 'defended' by Crown counsel – in other words, by the executive branch. There is no suggestion that the interests of the police are in any sense divorced from the interest of the executive in the criminal justice context.[54]

While the police establishment was leery of the *Charter*'s introduction,[55] studies to date suggest both that the *Charter* has had a meaningful impact on police operations and that the police have adapted to the *Charter* without significant operational disruptions or attempts at evading the consequences of court decisions.[56] Further, the mere fact that the police are now so enmeshed in the protection of *Charter* rights makes the spectre of political interference in policing even more troubling. The executive interest in *Charter* litigation involving the police is multidimensional. There is a clear 'public interest' role in the executive's defence of police conduct in particular prosecutions. There may also be a policy element where the *Charter* litigation arises from an initiative with a policy dimension (e.g., roadside screening for drunk drivers). Finally, there are often partisan concerns at stake for the government of the day if the *Charter* litigation attracts a public or media spotlight.

Civil Liability for Misuse of Police Power

Judicial involvement in executive-police oversight does not always come in the form of constitutional litigation. More often of late, it has manifested itself in adjudication of civil claims by and against the police.[57] Civil claims are particularly compelling as forms of public accountability as they permit aggrieved individuals to call police officers, police authorities, and boards and executive bodies directly to account for their police activities. For example, in *Jane Doe v. Metropolitan Toronto (Municipality) Commissioners of Police*,[58] a woman was able to establish that the police owed a duty of care towards potential victims of a rapist in circumstances where the police did not warn women in the community who fit the profile of the rapist's victims.[59]

In *Odhavji Estate v. Woodhouse*,[60] the Supreme Court considered whether the family of a person who was shot dead during a police investigation could bring an action for negligence and the tort of misfeasance in public office against the police, based on the failure of the officers involved to cooperate with the Special Investigations Unit (SIU). The Supreme Court held that the claim of misfeasance in public office could proceed. Iacobucci J., writing for the Court, clarified the relationship between the tort of misfeasance in public office and the obligations of public officials to uphold the rule of law:

> As is often the case, there are a number of phrases that might be used to describe the essence of the tort. In *Garrett, supra*, Blanchard J. stated, at p. 350, that '[t]he purpose behind the imposition of this form of tortious liability is to prevent the deliberate injuring of members of the public by deliberate disregard of official duty.' In *Three Rivers, supra*, Lord Steyn stated, at p. 1230, that '[t]he rationale of the tort is that in a legal system based on the rule of law executive or administrative power "may be exercised only for the public good" and not for ulterior and improper purposes.' ... The tort is not directed at a public officer who is *unable* to discharge his or her obligations because of factors beyond his or her control but, rather, at a public officer who *could* have discharged his or her public obligations, yet willfully chose to do otherwise.[61]

Iacobucci J also makes clear in his reasons the special accountability relationship between the chief of police and members of the community affected by potential police misconduct. He observes that 'members of the public reasonably expect a chief of police to be mindful of the injuries that might arise as a consequence of police misconduct.'[62] By contrast, Iacobucci J held that the nexus between members of the public and the Police Services Board or the provincial solicitor general was insufficient to ground a claim in negligence and these aspects of the claim were dismissed.

The executive interest in civil challenges against police activities is equally complex. The government may be liable for damages in such cases and may also be hurt by negative publicity (this was particularly apposite for municipal government in the decision whether to appeal or settle the *Jane Doe* case). Additionally, civil liability is, as with the other legal constraints discussed above, also a recourse for the police, at least for individual officers and police associations. In 2002, when the *Toronto Star* published an empirical analysis of police reports disclosed pursuant to a freedom of information request, and concluded the Toronto police engaged in racial profiling, the police association responded with a $2.7 billion civil defamation class action on behalf of all officers and civilian members of the Toronto Police Services against the *Toronto Star*.[63] The suit was dismissed by the Ontario Superior Court in July 2003 on the grounds that the articles in question did not relate to the entire police force but rather to a group of officers.[64]

The above review of the grounds on which courts may be called upon to intervene in police activities is intended as illustrative rather than exhaustive. The examples cited are also intended to demonstrate that the legal doctrines and remedial instruments available to courts to address accountability for police activities are limited. Judges can quash decisions, strike out evidence, and award damages. It is unlikely that any of these remedial options will modify police conduct. The limits of litigation to produce systemic solutions have also been highlighted. That said, the importance of judicial intervention, especially on consti-tutional grounds, should not be underestimated or undervalued. Judi-cial application of constitutional and other legal remedies in police contexts also reiterates that civil liberties and fundamental human rights are always at stake in police decision making (another dimension which the policy/operation dichotomy tends to gloss over).

The enduring significance of the judicial role is not in behaviour modification of police officers but in articulating the broad parameters of the executive–police relationship. The courts provide one of the few venues, in other words, for deliberation about the political roles and responsibility of governmental and policing bodies.

Political Dynamics

The executive-police terrain cannot be navigated without a political compass. Virtually every municipal, provincial, and federal govern-ment is elected with a specific 'law and order' policy agenda and scarce public resources with which to fulfil that agenda. As alluded to above, the distinction between the executive's view on the 'public interest' and its own partisan interests may often appear blurred. All three levels of government have differing tools to implement that agenda. Municipal leaders often play a lead role in selecting police chiefs, for example, while provincial ministers often have a lead role in selecting civilian oversight bodies. The federal Cabinet appoints the RCMP complaints commissioner chair, for example.

The executive is responsible for critical decisions regarding the funding, structure and, in some cases, the mandate of policing bodies. The police leadership must be deft negotiators with these various governments, while at the same time maintaining the support of their own political constituencies, whether police associations or community groups. Further complicating this political terrain is the important and often influential role of third parties, including police associations and unions, victims advocacy groups, political parties, interest group organizations of various stripes, and the media.

In a Westminster political system, all executive activity, including that of the police and Crown prosecutors, must be subject to ministerial responsibility, whether under the rubric of an attorney general, solicitor general, or some other member of Cabinet. As discussed above, this does not mean, of course, that the RCMP commissioner or any police chief is subject to ministerial direction, nor is the head of a police investigation a 'servant or agent of the government.' Police officers exercising criminal investigation functions are said to be 'answerable to the law' and their 'conscience' alone.[65] Therefore, while ministers are responsible for the police, police leadership is not necessarily accountable to ministers.[66] As discussed above with respect to the constitutional principle of the rule of law, the police are not the servant of anyone 'save the law itself.'[67] Without at least the aspiration of ministerial responsibility, however, the police would become a law unto itself.

Paradoxically, the law to which police owe their loyalty appears expressly to validate the supervision of the political executive over the police. As Kent Roach highlights, most of the statutory authority empowering police commissioners stipulates that the responsibility for 'direction' resides with the minister. For example, section 5(1) of the *Royal Canadian Mounted Police Act* provides: 'The Governor in Council may appoint an officer, to be known as the Commissioner of the Royal Canadian Mounted Police, who, *under the direction of the Minister*, has the control and management of the Force and all matters connected therewith[68] (emphasis added). Section 17(2) of Ontario's 1990 *Police Services Act*[69] also contemplates ministerial direction of the provincial police force by providing that: '*Subject to the Solicitor General's direction*, the Commissioner has the general control and administration of the Ontario Provincial Police and the employees connected with it' (emphasis added).

Unlike some aspects of the justice system (court or prison administration, for example) issues involving the police attract significant political constituencies. Campaign pledges on 'law and order' often have a direct impact on police, setting out policies for community policing or the hiring of new officers or the purchase of new equipment or anti-crime initiatives. Perhaps in part because of this, it has become more common to see police forces themselves express preferences for one party's political vision or another. This issue rose to the forefront of the 2003 Toronto mayoral campaign, when the chief of police appeared to endorse the 'pro-police' John Tory candidacy,[70] and may arise again in a provincial election now that he is leader of the Ontario Progressive Conservative party.[71] Equally controversial has been the support of police associations and unions for specific parties and candidates.[72]

The government's responsibility for the police extends to police budgets, which must be approved by the applicable municipal, provincial, or federal government. The fiscal levers available in budget setting provide the government of the day with another important (and often subtle) mechanism for influencing police conduct. Is it legitimate to use the budgetary process to affect police policy? Does the question of resources inevitably influence operational decisions by police as well?

The political nature of police issues, coupled with the centrality of the police in the justice system, has the potential to erode the already porous boundary between the dual hats worn by attorneys general (and solicitors general) as law officers on the one hand and politicians in Cabinet on the other.[73] The problem is not only that these ministers have the dual interests per se, and the potential for conflicts, but also the lack of transparency about which hat is on at any given time (this is even more apparent in the remaining jurisdictions that combine the functions of attorney general and solicitor general in one minister (e.g., Manitoba).

When Ontario's attorney general decided to establish a 'guns and gangs' task force, for example, was this a decision taken as chief law officer or as political cabinet minister. Even if a decision such as this was taken on 'public interest' as opposed to partisan grounds, does it become a partisan initiative when the government of the day highlights this initiative as it seeks support on the campaign trail?

Like the dispersal of executive accountability for policing through police boards, disciplinary panels, and civilian complaints mechanisms, the multiplicity of political accountability relationships for policing can be beneficial. The overlapping mandate of the attorney general, minister of justice (in those jurisdictions where the two are distinct), and solicitor general (often now referred to as the minister for 'public safety'), in this light, perhaps is salutary. While inter-agency squabbles and incoherent policies are possible, it is more likely that the result of overlapping jurisdiction over policing is greater political oversight and enhanced police accountability. To highlight but one example, in Ontario, the fact that the SIU are accountable to the attorney general rather than the same minister (public safety) as the police force reinforces the appearance and reality of its separation from the police hierarchy (which is not the same, of course, as ensuring its independence from political interference).

This dynamic also arises in the sphere of court backlogs. Politicians are called upon to deal with the situations of delay in criminal accused reaching trial. Court backlogs are an example of a criminal justice issue that requires integrated and systemic responses. Solving the problem is not merely a matter of appointing more judges and building more courthouses (although both undertakings have been announced recently in Ontario as strategies to address backlogs), but must also involve policies aimed at Crown prosecutors, legal aid lawyers, and court staff. One strategy adopted by provincial governments has been to direct that certain minor offences (i.e., vagrancy) not be prosecuted by local police. This policy also assumes a degree of political control and influence over the justice system that is rarely interrogated.

There is, as I alluded to above, an important distinction between accountability and oversight. In the apolitical and autonomous police model I have identified, the line of accountability formally is to the political executive (i.e., the responsible minister, who in turn is responsible to Parliament and by extension to the public). While other institutions may provide an important oversight role (courts, complaints bodies, and administrative tribunals, for example) the police must be accountable to a single Crown authority. If the police are accountable to everyone in theory, they are accountable to no one in practice. However, notwithstanding that they are accountable only to the Crown in theory (and in part because of this fact), their activities may and should be subject to public scrutiny by a range of other judicial, administrative, political, and community bodies in practice.

The need for multiple oversight arises from the reality that accountability through a ministry may lead to ineffective supervision and exacerbate the vulnerability of the police to political interference. The main principles underlying ministerial responsibility in its original formulation now appear outdated or naïve. For example, the principle that ministers should resign in response to errors or misdeeds of public servants, and that the civil servants involved in committing those errors or misdeeds should remain anonymous, seems to have lost currency in Canada (the sponsorship scandal is a case in point).[74] The notion that the minister may be personally responsible for all the decisions taken in the ministry presumes a level of knowledge and control over the actions of government that is no longer realistic given the volume and complexity of government action. In lieu of strong confidence in ministerial responsibility, those seeking to call government to account are now far more likely to call for a public or judicial inquiry, or at least parliamentary committee hearings, than in the past, and governments are far more likely to grant such requests (the Sponsorship Inquiry and Arar Inquiry are two recent examples). The fact that inquiries remain the prerogative of the government of the day to call, and that the government controls the budget and terms of reference of such inquiries, significantly limits their ability to hold policing forces accountable.[75] That said, inquiries can and do provide a pivotal form of oversight for allegations of police misdeeds and have served as the catalyst for significant shifts in police structures and policies.[76]

As these inquiries demonstrate, the executive-police relationship is mediated by the political currents of the day and events outside the control of both groups. The line between legitimate implementation of government policy and undue political interference is not and should not be viewed as fixed and immutable. As I elaborate in the final section below, the dynamic nature of this boundary, shaped both by constitutional principle and political practice, can be a constructive and animating feature of executive-police relations.

III. Reconciling Political Accountability with the Rule of Law: Towards an Apolitical and Autonomous Police Model

The tension between police autonomy and accountability in a constitutional democracy is both familiar and vexing. If the police must report to political authorities or bodies appointed by political authorities, the potential for political interference always is present. It may be blatant. It may be subtle. It may be intentional or inadvertent. If the police are insulated from review, on the other hand, then the police ultimately may become an authority unto themselves, which may in turn give rise to the appearance that the police can and may exempt themselves from the rule of law. Is there a way out of this enduring conundrum? Perhaps not. In the third and final section of this chapter, however, I explore several areas where progress towards an apolitical and autonomous model of policing would at least be desirable. The goal of this ideal type is to create a legal, administrative, and political climate in which neither the police nor the executive can unilaterally impose its will on the other. In other words, the executive and the police are expected, in this model, to engage in deliberative and transparent debate over policing matters.

The discussion below is divided into five brief subsections. Each seeks in different ways to counter the tendency to compartmentalize executive–police relations within artificial categories or boundaries. In the first section, I emphasize the importance of moving beyond the policy/operation dichotomy. In the second section, I explore the separation of powers and the importance of judicial and parliamentary oversight as a complement to intra-executive forms of oversight. In the third section, I highlight the need for objective structures to ensure that government's authority over budgets and appointments does not lead to inappropriate influence over police activities. In the fourth section, I argue that executive-police relations need to be situated more clearly within the broader criminal justice system. Finally, I attempt to consider, in each of the four areas discussed, what approaches and arrangements would be consistent with an apolitical and autonomous ideal type of executive-police oversight.

Moving Beyond the Policy/Operation Distinction

As I have argued above, I believe that it is desirable to move beyond the policy/operation distinction, which obscures more than it reveals about the executive-police relationship. In lieu of certainty with respect to the policy/operational boundary, the most we can demand, in my view, is transparency and authenticity. Rather than try to classify various police activities into artificial categories such as 'policy' or 'operational,' I believe we must better articulate what is at stake in these determinations, both for the executive and for the police.

I would advance an alternative, contextual framework to replace the policy/operational dichotomy as a means of determining when political input into police decision making is legitimate. This framework could comprise three issues:

1) First, does the executive have a legitimate public interest goal to advance?

2) Second, would pursuing that goal respect the functional autonomy and apolitical status of the police? and

3) Third, is there an overriding interest, either of individual rights or public safety, which is inconsistent with political involvement?

If the answer to any of the above questions is 'yes,' then political involvement would be inappropriate (this framework relates to settings of police direction; it could be applied equally where the issue is 'upstream' reporting to political authorities of police actions). That executive input may be appropriate, however, does not mean that it necessarily trumps the police's own view of what is desirable and in the interests of the public.

Context, of course, is the key to the legitimacy analysis. The decision whether to pursue criminal charges lies at the core of police autonomy and political involvement in such decisions should be rare and subject to a high threshold of justification. It should be rare, however, not because we classify the laying of charges as 'operational' but rather because there are few, if any, political considerations that may legitimately justify intervention in the laying of charges under an apolitical and autonomous police model. Are there any such considerations? Ponder once again the 'zero tolerance' directives in certain areas (gun violence, domestic assaults, etc.) that governments develop pursuant to their policy agendas. Rather than debate whether 'zero tolerance' initiatives are policy or operational interventions, we ought to debate whether they are legitimate political preferences to which policing should be subject. Applying the framework set out above, I accept that there may be cases where political input in the form of zero tolerance initiatives would be legitimate. But I do not believe that all cases would meet this threshold.

How are the inevitable disputes regarding the application of this kind of framework to be resolved? Whether one prefers judicial involvement, public inquiries and reviews, or other inter-institutional arrangements, it is vital that a record be kept of the competing approaches to policing issues, if any. In this vein, I share Kent Roach's belief that steps should be taken to ensure that political intervention in policing is less murky and more transparent so that the responsible minister can be held accountable for guidance given to the police. This, of course, is easier said than done.

Roach raises the issue of putting more political guidance and direction in writing. This could take many forms. For example, ministerial directives could be issued as confidential or public memoranda to police chiefs and/or police service boards, or they could be disseminated through soft law instruments such as police manuals and training materials. Such measures may well be desirable, but the uncertain status of these instruments might simply move the problem to a new venue. Are ministerial directives contained in memoranda 'law' and, if so, where they are designed to structure and constrain police discretion, can they be subject to judicial oversight such as challenge under the *Charter*?[77] If they are considered not law but 'policy,' must they be made public?

While distinctions such as policy/operational tend to imply right answers to the question of executive's role in police matters, the framework of contextual legitimacy suggests a more relational analysis. Executive action is not viewed in isolation but rather is situated within particular circumstances and principles. Below, I suggest how this might change the way we assess how executive-police tensions play out.

Coming to Terms with the Separation of Powers and Parliamentary Oversight

I have argued that an apolitical and autonomous police ideal type requires a distinct oversight relationship with each branch of government, one that builds on a maturing separation of powers doctrine in Canada. Canada's separation of powers doctrine does not have the rigorous checks and balances of the American constitutional order but consists instead of fluid and overlapping roles for the legislative, executive, and judicial branches of government. This doctrine remains a cornerstone. Executive tribunals adjudicate constitutional rights, courts provide advice to the executive through answering reference questions, and so forth.

In this context, there is a distinctive and vital role for each branch of government in attaining the ideal of an apolitical and accountable police. As indicated above, it is important that the police should be subject to robust judicial oversight for compliance with constitutional, administrative, and civil legal norms. The police should also be subject to oversight from a range of executive bodies of varying degrees of autonomy from control by the government of the day and from the police, whether civilian complaints bodies, special investigative units, or police boards. The judicial and executive role in police oversight is relatively well-accepted (although there is significant debate as to the effectiveness of such oversight). The role for the legislative branch is less clear.

In the discussion on federalism, I have already alluded to the key role of Parliament in establishing the mandate and authority for the police through its supervision over the *Criminal Code* and its amendments. Does the legislative branch also have a role in ongoing oversight of police activities? If so, how is this role distinct from the judicial and executive oversight of those same activities (especially where at least some of the executive oversight bodies appear to derive their legitimacy from their representative mandate for community interests).

In my view, there are two possible areas in which there is a potential role for parliamentary oversight. First, standing committees of Parliament or provincial legislatures are an underutilized mechanism for giving a public hearing to allegations of political influence over the police (recent examples include the hearings into the sponsorship affair, which included allegations of RCMP involvement). This kind of public forum for examining the propriety of executive-police relations represents a unique and potentially valuable form of political accountability (the conduct and outcome of the recent sponsorship hearings, however, may serve as a cautionary tale about the limitations of this kind of accountability).

There is a persuasive case to be made that the police should also be subject to the oversight of a complaints body appointed (and funded) by and reporting to the legislature. As demonstrated by auditors general, privacy commissioners, and ombudsmen in Canada, parliamentary bodies are better able to provide an autonomous and apolitical effective check on executive conduct than agencies that derive their budgets from and report to the executive. One option would be simply to transfer the existing civilian complaints bodies from executive to legislative control.

The exact modalities chosen are of course significant but not the point. An apolitical police is enhanced both by other non-partisan forms of oversight (judicial and through public inquiries) and by all-party forms of oversight, where public and political deliberation about police actions and arrangements, ideally, can occur.

New Approaches to Budgets, Appointments, and Other Political Levers of Influence

I have asserted that the goal of a system of effective, multiple, and overlapping oversight is to achieve an autonomous and apolitical police force (in which its apolitical posture reinforces its autonomy and its autonomy reinforces its apolitical nature). There are, of course, political challenges to achieving such an apolitical institutional posture. To take an obvious example, police budgets are set by municipal, provincial, and federal governments, and typically require a 'champion' at the Cabinet/council table to justify new initiatives or significant capital infusions. Another major challenge to an apolitical model is that the appointment power for the chiefs of police or heads of police boards remains with government, either directly or indirectly.

Here, too, the analogy to the judiciary or other 'apolitical' bodies such the auditor general or information and privacy commissioner might be helpful (they are also subject to public budgeting and appointments). In these settings, public confidence in the independence of parliamentary officers and judges requires objective guarantees of freedom from political interference. For this reason, judicial salaries must be set by an independent commission rather than by executive fiat, and appointment to parliamentary offices requires all-party support or must involve a credible nominating committee. Such mechanisms prevent the appointment power from being perceived as an expression merely of the policy preferences or ideological inclinations of the government. This leads us to the question of what objective guarantees could or should be put in place to ensure police budgets and appointments are not merely levers of political influence.

The question of budgets and appointments in the police context varies significantly across the country given different statutory environments, contractual arrangements, and whether there is a role for local police boards. Certainly, appointments to these boards and to the police leadership which are viewed as 'merit' driven rather than 'patronage' or 'political' appointments will be more consistent with an apolitical and autonomous ideal. With respect to budgets, the question of political choice in the face of competing needs and scarce resources is more central and more critical. Rather than seek to turn political questions into objective calculations, the priority here, in my view, should be on the transparency of the budgetary process and the substantive quality of the deliberations surrounding that process. A more robust system of independent audits of police budgets and government expenditures on policing more broadly would signal a positive step in this direction.

Towards an Integrated Approach to Executive-Police Oversight

The issue of police budgeting raises broader questions about where policing fits within the justice sector as a whole. As James Robb has pointed out, we should view questions of the executive–police relation-ship as integrated into the larger questions of the executive's role in criminal justice, including its influence over Crown prosecutors, the legal aid system, the structure and mandate of police boards and civil-ian oversight agencies, the launching of public inquiries and reviews, the administration of the courts, and decisions flowing from the attor-ney general and solicitor general's 'law officer' functions.[78]

All of these components of the criminal justice system enjoy varying degrees of autonomy on various issues and derive their legitimacy from various legal and political sources, but none can perform their mandate effectively without some support from other components of the system. The executive-police relationship, in other words, cannot and should not be seen in isolation, whether from other parts of the criminal justice system or from social and economic structures more generally.

That the police are embedded not just in the criminal justice system but in the social fabric of the community is not a controversial claim but has been illustrated dramatically in recent years by the issue of profil-ing – whether in the form of local police forces engaging in racial profiling when stopping vehicles for inspection, or decisions made at borders and airports to detain members of particular ethnic and reli-gious groups for secondary searches.[79]

Such polycentric police settings demonstrate the futility of the policy/operational dichotomy and highlight the importance of legitimacy and public confidence in the police and the executive. The legitimacy of the police and of the executive in settings that raise questions of systemic racism in policing depends on the role of mediating forms of executive and judicial oversight discussed in this chapter (including constitu-tional and civil court cases,[80] public inquiries,[81] and human rights code challenges).[82] Additionally, proposals to address racial profiling cannot ignore the views of police associations, victims groups, and multi-cultural groups, among other stakeholders. In the profiling context neither the police nor the executive can achieve their goals in isolation from one another or from the other stakeholder groups (this in turn raises the importance of the media in consultation initiatives as well as in communicating outcomes). Whether the solution lies with police training, court orders, civil damages, internal discipline, funding for cameras on police cruisers, more inquiries and reviews or a more arm's-length civilian complaint system, or some combination of all of the above, I have suggested that the ideal of an apolitical and autonomous police may chart a constructive course towards more transparent and deliberative relations with the executive.

Conclusion

In this chapter I have reviewed the nature of the executive–police relationship in Canada and the respective roles of the courts and administrative agencies and advanced the ideal type of an apolitical and autonomous police as a means of reconciling the tension between police accountability and the rule of law. This ideal type is predicated on a dynamic rather than static relationship between the executive and the police, where complex relationships of individuals, structures, and ideologies do not fit easily into policy/operational boxes and the boundary between legitimate and illegitimate political input is to be continuously worked out rather than predetermined by artificial 'bright lines.'

Transparent deliberations between executive and police leadership, augmented with internal and external forms of oversight, provide venues where these contextual boundaries may be contested and resolved. The success of this apolitical and autonomous ideal in policing lies not in submerging executive interests in police matters, nor in submerging police interests in political matters, but in providing frameworks where both interests are seen as valid and where neither is able entirely to subjugate the other. My claim in this analysis is that where the police and the executive are engaged in working out their relationship in public view, the safety of the public, needs of communities, and rights of individual are likely to be more effectively safeguarded. The Canadian legal and political system is characterized by a strong set of constitutional and democratic norms. Translating those norms into practical realities that take into consideration political realities, however, remains an elusive and vital goal.

COMMENTARY BY A. ALAN BOROVOY

In my view, the centrepiece of Professor Sossin's paper is his welcome repudiation of the long-time conventional wisdom in Canada that there is a significant distinction between police policies and their operations. According to this distinction, the government may direct the former but must avoid the latter. Not infrequently, however, there is no clear distinction between these concepts. And not infrequently, the distinction, even if clear, is not very helpful.

One of the most revealing examples of the difficulty emerged in the aftermath of the Ipperwash incident. In the Ontario legislature, the opposition parties were pummelling the government with questions regarding the government's role in the decision of the Ontario Provincial Police (OPP) to remove the Aboriginal protesters by force. The attorney general replied that there was no government interference. In his view, such interference would have been 'highly inappropriate.' The premier said that the government did not know of the OPP build-up; he insisted that such activity was 'not our business.' The opposition MPPs accused the government of misleading them.

Of course, it would be very bad if the government had not told the truth. But in this situation it would be even worse if it *had*. How can there be political responsibility for the police if the government cannot involve itself in, or even *know about*, an operation of such magnitude and importance? Suppose there were a question of our country deploying a contingent of troops (the same number as the OPP used) for possible conflict with a group (the same number as the Aboriginal protesters) from a foreign power? Who would ever suggest that anyone but the government should make such a decision? Why should it be so different if we are risking a battle with our own citizens?

In his quest for the right balance, Professor Sossin nicely states the dilemma. He says that this country has 'a long and unsettling history' of governments using the police as an arm of the political administration *and* of the police becoming a law unto themselves. Greater government involvement risks the former; less government involvement risks the latter. At one point, Professor Sossin says that the goal of the exercise is to create the kind of climate where neither government nor police can unilaterally impose their will on the other. Surely, however, that depends on what is involved. Suppose, for example, one of the parties was about to commit an unlawful act. I would regard it as incontestable that the other party must be able to stop it.

That's an easy case. Suppose instead that the activity involved is obviously lawful but arguably awful. Remember, for example, the Fort Erie search-and-strip drug raid of 1974 and the bathhouse raids of 1981. At Fort Erie, the police physically searched the more than one hundred patrons they found in the lounge; the women were herded into washrooms, stripped, and subjected to vaginal and rectal examinations. In Toronto's bathhouse raids, the police arrested some three hundred adult patrons whose offence involved nothing more than consensual sex – albeit of the homosexual variety – with other adults. At least as things stood before the *Charter* when these incidents occurred, the behaviour of the police was likely lawful. But wasn't it nevertheless awful?

The key question is whose view of 'awful' should prevail, that of the police or that of the government? Suppose the relevant ministers found out beforehand what the police were going to do. Would it be so 'highly inappropriate' for these civilian masters to contact the police chiefs and direct them to desist? After all the politicians, not the police, are elected.

As indicated, it is argued that a key reason to keep the government out of police operations is to reduce the risk of politicizing the police. A democratic society does not want the police to perform partisan duties at the behest of any politicians. But why should we assume that only the government has improper political motives? So do many police officials. And what about all the other police prejudices that could influence their behaviour? It was suggested, for example, that the bathhouse raids were motivated by homophobia. As between the appointed police and the elected government, why should the police have the right to make the last mistake?

Professor Sossin has rightly said that the main problem is the lack of transparency in the relationship. In response, he has made the helpful suggestion that the instructions of the civilian masters to the police should be put in writing. To this, I propose another safeguard: independent auditing. An independent agency should be given continuing access to police records, facilities, and personnel so that it can conduct ongoing, self-generated audits of this pivotal relationship as well as police policies and practices in general. The agency should have no decision-making power; its sole function should be to disclose and propose.

Anyone who has lived in the real world for more than an hour knows very well that civilian decision makers, such as Cabinet ministers, tend to shrink from confrontations with the police. The genius of audits is that those performing them don't face this problem. Since they have no decision-making role, there is much less reason for them to hide. But they have only one function, they have every incentive to be thorough. If they miss something that surfaces later, they will incur a considerable risk of winding up with egg on their faces.

At the same time, the publicity from an audit subjects the decision makers to a new and potent pressure that can produce changes in police policies and practices. Canada is already experiencing this concept in national security matters. The independent Security Intelligence Review Committee (SIRC) performs such audits of the Canadian Security Intelligence Service (CSIS). A SIRC audit a number of years ago pressured the government into disbanding CSIS's counter-subversion unit.

The mere existence of such an audit system would help to ensure that the politicians do not misuse any new power to supervise police operations. Audits can be instrumental in deterring, detecting, and correcting any propensity for undue politicization.

COMMENTARY BY W. WESLEY PUE

Two incidents help to frame the idea of police independence:

• During the premiership of Joh Bjelke Peterson, Queensland State Police assigned significant resources to raid Brisbane's three universities, removing condom vending machines from the campuses.[83]
• In a British proceeding observed by criminologist Doreen McBarnet, a young man was tried on the charge of jumping on and off a curb in a disorderly fashion.[84]

While the first illustrates the absurdity of misdirecting police resources, the second reveals the degree to which discretion gives life to criminal law. The rights of citizens turn significantly on the discretion of police officers, Crown attorneys, and judges to intervene, arrest, charge, prosecute, and convict – or not.

Dr Sossin's contribution to this volume usefully locates police issues within wider frameworks of thought about the legal regulation of discretion. This helpfully corrects a common tendency to divorce questions relating to the police-politics interface from larger issues of constitutional governance, reducing complexly nuanced matters to the misleadingly simple questions of 'who should be in charge' or 'who should have the final say.' Put so bluntly and in disregard of the larger constitutional background, it provokes responses that flow directly from the questioner's assumptions as to whether 'police' or 'politicians' are most likely to produce substantively agreeable outcomes.[85] In reinserting constitutional principle into this otherwise starkly pragmatic calculation Professor Sossin provides valuable service. 'Independence,' it turns out, is an ancient legal term of art that suffuses the entire field of common law constitutionalism.

Though it is also helpful, Professor Sossin's emphasis on the rule of law is discomfiting. The idea of law sits ill at ease with a criminal justice system so shot through with discretionary powers as to seemingly vanish into a mere 'rule of persons.' The awkwardness associated with personal exercises of discretion is accentuated in our era, when the background ideology of managerialism vies mightily with the rule of law for our loyalty. We inherit the notion, famously articulated by Albert Venn Dicey, that no person is to be punished in body or in goods except for a distinct breach of law, established before the ordinary courts in the ordinary way.[86] Though much criticized, this idea remains, as E.P. Thompson put it, 'an unqualified human good.'[87] Managerialism's predilection for efficiency[88] over the values of fairness, propriety, rights, duties, constitutionalism, or 'law's' proceduralist values reflects a culture that prizes 'getting things done' The two live in inevitable tension. They always have.

'Getting things done' is not, however, the whole story when it comes to the management of a domestic armed force denoted as 'police.' It bears emphasis that police-government relations ought always to be constrained within the parameters of legality. This is so not because efficiency in any managerial sense demands it but because the *grundnorm* of our civil society requires it. No unlawful executive direction of police is acceptable. It matters not how or by whom it is communicated, to whom it is addressed, or whether it is analytically 'operational' or 'policy' in nature. No argument derived from efficiency concerns can justify unlawful instructions, orders, deployment, or actions.

Discretion muddies even these analytically clear waters. Unlawfulness typically arises in one of several ways. Police actions such as the arrest of law-abiding individuals, harassment of political opponents of the government, the use of unnecessary force, or turning a blind eye to the crimes of well-connected individuals[89] would be clearly unlawful. Even in such cases, however, the reality that police need to make choices as to the allocation of their resources, cannot prosecute all wrong-doers, must exercise discretion, and sometimes make thoroughly honest mistakes renders assessment of particular circumstances a complex, multifaceted matter. What is essential is that fear or favour must never flow from political connection or influence. The 'playing field' of law enforcement discretion must remain level.

Beyond the realm of the blatantly unlawful, one can imagine situations in which the executive branch of government would wish to direct the use of otherwise lawful powers in situations where constitutional propriety would dictate otherwise. It can be extraordinarily difficult to mark precisely where one constitutional right – freedom of expression or Aboriginal entitlement, for example – must give way to another – the preservation of the peace, perhaps. Such boundaries fuzzily demarcate the frontier between lawful and unlawful police conduct. But, for all their 'fuzziness,' they define the character of our democracy. The 'playing field' tilts strongly in the direction of political command any time police forces lack access to independent legal advice.[90]

Finally, a police power used in pursuit of improper goals is unlawful even if the same power, used in pursuit of proper goals and in closely similar circumstances, would be appropriate. The pretense of proper motivation should not serve to uphold state action that is in substance directed to improper ends. The intent or effect of state action can render it 'colourable' and, hence, ultra vires, and unlawful.[91]

Though the principle of colourablity is clear enough, its application is less so. If mundane police wrong-doing is notoriously well concealed behind an all-but-impenetrable blue curtain, the problem is compounded where possibly inappropriate police-politician relations are concerned.[92] Institutional inertia weighs heavily against those who would challenge high level impropriety. Direct evidence of what was said or done in the course of government communications with police is often lacking, quite possibly by design. Witnesses can be hard to identify – and harder to compel. There are few incentives encouraging willing testimony that runs contrary to the interest of either police or government hierarchies – that way career suicide lies. The evidentiary bar to be overcome in proving the colourability of state actions in court is extraordinarily high and judicial habits of deference to officialdom have become well entrenched during the past half-century. Difficult questions are rarely put, the executive commands effectively infinite resources in protecting itself from effective inquiry. Government officials often have more or less unreviewable ability to restrict access to precisely the evidence most likely to prove their colourable intent[93] and presumptions of constitutional propriety conveniently prevent the drawing of logical inference in any circumstances falling short of admitted impropriety.

Human nature being what it is, it seems inevitable that influential persons will wish to improperly influence the police.[94] They will want to do so for reasons of 'corruption' (often no more ill-intended than 'don't put so-and-so through a prosecution; he's a good guy') or for reasons related to political grandstanding ranging from a sort of orchestrated 'photo-op-by-cop'[95] through to the tough-guy peacock displays of politicians seeking electoral advantage by demonstrating 'law and order' machismo.[96] If the police as individuals or organizations are to rise above partisanship they must be demonstrably impartial (committed to Joseph's 'Queen's Peace') *and* enjoy a degree of structural independence that is up to the task of sustaining impartiality over the long term. We should not confuse the two. Institutional integrity can survive human failing but the converse is not true. The conditions under which impartiality can exist is a central concern of administrative law and this too points to the need for a broad-based analysis of just the sort that Professor Sossins seeks to develop.

Finally, it bears noting that Kim Murray's remarks at this symposium emphasized the importance of recognizing that the 'law in the books' is often at variance with what *actually* happens. This is a centrally important insight. 'Rights' solemnly declared at the rarefied levels of the Supreme Court of Canada or trial courts in Snow Drift, Northwest Territories (*all* courts are at a rarefied level) mean little if not respected in daily practice. It is there that police–politician propriety is most likely to go off the rails. To Sossin's public law insight, then, must be added Murray's measure of legal realism. Combining the two leads, in turn, to two observations. First, if they are to be effective, schemes derived from sophisticated legal analysis need to be translated into language both readily intelligible to politicians and constables alike and capable of being rendered operational in real life. A finely expounded doctrine has little worth in real life if it is unintelligible to those called upon to put it into practice. Second, in developing rules to govern the police–politician relationship, attention needs to be directed to procedural law, the law of evidence, and to the institutional capacities of the courts. A legal structure incapable of identifying colourable intrusions upon rights that it purportedly protects has limited worth. A system organized around deference to occupants of high office can hardly qualify as 'legal.'

Little in the history of police-government relations over the past three decades justifies complacency in these respects. And that, as Professor Sossin emphasizes, gives cause for concern about the integrity of both police and the democratic apparatus itself.

NOTES

Lorne Sossin wishes to express his gratitude for the superb research assistance of Alexandra Dosman and his indebtedness to Alan Borovoy and Wes Pue for their insightful and constructive comments.

1 This dynamic is of course not new. See, e.g., Alan Grant, 'The Control of Police Behaviour,' in *Some Civil Liberties Issues in the Seventies*, ed. Walter Tarnopolsky (Toronto: Osgoode Hall Law School, 1975), 75.

2 Philip Stenning also includes a discussion of some of these terms in his contribution to this volume.
3 See Kent Roach's contribution to this volume. For a related attempt at a typology of political accountability over the police, see Philip Stenning, 'Someone to Watch Over Me: Government Supervision of the RCMP,' in *Pepper in Our Eyes: The APEC Affair*, ed. Wesley W. Pue (Vancouver: UBC Press, 2000), 97.
4 Wes Pue, 'The Prime Minister's Police? Commissioner Hughes APEC Report' (2001) 39 Osgoode Hall L.J. 165 at 167.
5 For an elaboration on these constitutional norms, see L. Sossin, 'Speaking Truth to Power? The Search for Bureaucratic Independence' (2005) University of Toronto L.J. 1.
6 There is of course significant variation across different jurisdictions of the prosecutorial branch's relationship to the executive. In Nova Scotia, for example, there is greater prosecutorial independence due to the Director of Public Prosecutions being constituted as a separate office. See also *Krieger v. Law Society of Alberta*, [2002] 3 S.C.R. 372, where Iacobucci and Major JJ, speaking for the court, at para. 43 held that '"prosecutorial discretion" is a term of art. It does not simply refer to any discretionary decision made by a Crown prosecutor. Prosecutorial discretion refers to the use of those powers that constitute the core of the Attorney General's office and which are protected from the influence of improper political and other vitiating factors by the principle of independence.' See also the discussion of the executive-judiciary division of powers in *R. v. Felderhof*, [2003] O.J. No. 4819 (C.A.) at paras. 46–55.
7 On the comparison between police and judicial independence, see Geoffrey Marshall, *The Government and the Police* (London: Methuen, 1965), at 117–18.
8 See Nelson Wiseman, 'Hand in Glove? Politicians, Policing and Canadian Political Culture,' in *Pepper in Our Eyes*, 125. Wiseman points to the long history of government calling on police to thwart union organizing in various parts of Canada in the 1930s and 1950s and the RCMP's activities against the Parti Québécois in Quebec in the 1970s.
9 See Kent Roach, 'Four Models of Police-Government Relationships,' in this volume. See also Martin Friedland, 'Controlling the Administrators of Criminal Justice' (1988–9), 31 Crim. L.Q. 280.
10 See Gordon Christie's contribution to this volume.
11 Maurice Martin, *Urban Policing in Canada: Anatomy of an Aging Craft* (Toronto: University of Toronto Press, 1995), 142.
12 The 'ideal type' is commonly associated with Max Weber, who created a typology of bureaucracy consisting of three ideal types: traditional author-

ity, charismatic authority, and legal-rational authority. He demonstrated
how legal-rational authority was the ideal type among the three capable of
attaining the highest degree of effectiveness. See Max Weber, *The Theory of
Social and Economic Organization*, trans. A.M. Henderson (New York: Free
Press, 1947). The ideal type is a 'theoretical construct, combining several
features of a phenomenon in their purest and most extreme form ... it is a
conceptual tool which simplifies and exaggerates reality for the sake of
conceptual clarity.' See Eva Etzioni-Halevy, *Bureaucracy and Democracy:
A Political Dilemma* (London: Routledge, 1985), 29. This is not to say, of
course, that Weber's claims regarding the ascendancy of hierarchal,
impersonal bureaucracy have not been challenged. I review this critical
literature in L. Sossin, 'The Politics of Discretion: Towards a Critical
Theory of Public Administration' (1993) 36 Canadian Public Administration 364.
13 For a discussion of the limitations of ministerial responsibility, see the
discussion below. See also Donald Savoie, *Breaking the Bargain: Public
Servants, Ministers and Parliament* (Toronto: University of Toronto Press,
2003); and S. Sutherland, 'Responsible Government and Ministerial Responsibility: Every Reform Is Its Own Problem' (1991) 24 Canadian Journal of Political Science, 91.
14 By 'executive' in this context, I refer to the political executive. The political
executive (i.e., Cabinet and political staff) must be distinguished from the
bureaucratic executive (i.e., the civil service). Further, the political executive itself is a product of complex relationships, which may involve tensions between responsible ministries and the political 'centre' (i.e., PMO,
POs, etc.) and tensions between Cabinet members and the PM/Premier on
the one hand and between Cabinet members and the party caucus and
leadership on the other. For a discussion of these tensions, see Donald
Savoie, *Governing from the Centre: The Concentration of Power in Canadian
Politics* (Toronto: University of Toronto Press, 1999).
15 This distinction is discussed in Kent Roach's contribution to this volume at
29. See also John Edwards, *Ministerial Responsibility for National Security*
(Ottawa: Supply and Services, 1980).
16 Beyond the scope of this review are a host of other administrative bodies
which, while not established specifically to perform police oversight,
nonetheless may be involved indirectly, such as human rights commissions and human rights tribunals.
17 Tammy Landau, 'Back to the Future: The Death of Civilian Review of
Public Complaints against the Police in Toronto,' in *Civilian Oversight of
Policing: Governance, Democracy and Human Rights*, ed. A. Goldsmith and
C. Lewis (Portland: Oxford, 2000), 64.

18 For a history of civilian complaints commissions in Ontario see Claire
   E. Lewis, Sidney B. Linden, Q.C., and Judith Keene, 'Public Complaints
   against Police in Metropolitan Toronto: The History and Operation
   of the Office of the Public Complaints Commissioner' (1986) 29 Crim.
   L.Q. 115. See also brief prepared by the CCLA for the attorney general
   for Ontario on 'Proposed Amendments to the Police Civil Complaint
   System' (28 January 2004) and Dianne Martin's contribution to this
   volume.
19 R.S.O. 1990, c. P-15.
20 Ibid., s. 31.
21 Katherine Harding, 'Child-porn controversy hits police board,' *Globe and
   Mail*, 15 January 2004); Catherine Porter, 'Lawyer to probe Heisey's comments,' *Toronto Star*, 16 January 2004; Rosie DiManno, 'Heisey should step
   aside,' *Toronto Star*, 17 January 2004, E01; John Barber, 'Alan Heisey? It's
   just plain scary,' *Globe and Mail*, 17 January 2004, M1; Katherine Harding,
   'Heisey cleared of breaching rules,' *Globe and Mail*, 26 March 2004, A13;
   Catherine Porter, 'Police probe fails to find who leaked Heisey memo,
   Toronto Star, 15 May 2004.
22 See Katherine Harding, 'City police board in disarray,' *Globe and Mail*,
   28 May 2004.
23 See Royson James, 'Police board paralyzed again,' *Toronto Star*, 31 July
   2004.
24 See P. Desbarats, *Somalia Cover-Up: A Commissioner's Journal* (Toronto:
   McClelland & Stewart, 1997).
25 The report was made public on 26 February 2004. The full text is available on the Toronto Police website: http://www.torontopolice.on.ca/
   modules.php?op=modload&name=News&file=article&sid=916 . For
   commentary, see Kirk Makin, 'Plan would require disclosure of past
   misconduct to civilians' *Globe and Mail*, 27 February 2004, A11, and Betsy
   Powell and Catherine Porter, 'Police board gets action Plan,' *Toronto Star*,
   26 February 2004, B02.
26 The mayor announced the creation of the Mayor's Advisory Panel on
   community safety in this speech: Mayor David Miller, Address to North
   York, Etobicoke, and Scarborough Chambers of Commerce (9 March 2004)
   [http://www.city.toronto.on.ca/mayor_miller/speeches/c_of_c_030904
   .htm]. See also http://www.toronto.ca/legdocs/2004/agendas/
   committees/pof/pof040224/it023a.pdf. Katherine Harding, 'Panel on
   youth crime praised,' *Globe and Mail*, 20 February 2004.
27 Ibid.
28 The excuse given for this omission was the discomfort of Chief Justice
   McMurtry at police involvement – this discomfort did not extend, reveal-

ingly, to the involvement of provincial ministers, whose representatives serve on the advisory panel.

29 In the policing context, see Margot E. Young, '"Relax a Bit in the Nation": Constitutional Law 101 and the APEC Affair,' and W. Wesley Pue, 'Policing, the Rule of Law and Accountability in Canada: Lessons from the APEC Summit,' in *Pepper in Our Eyes* at 45–7. For recent appraisals outside the policing context see A. Hutchinson, 'The Rule of Law Revisited: Democracy and Courts,' in *Recrafting the Rule of Law: The Limits of Legal Order*, ed. D. Dyzenhaus (Oxford: Hart Publishing, 1999) 196; J. Jowell, Q.C., 'Beyond the Rule of Law: Towards Constitutional Judicial Review' [2000] Pub. L. 671; and T.R.S. Allen, 'The Rule of Law as the Rule of Reason: Consent and Constitutionalism' (1999) 115 L.Q. Rev. 221.

30 See, for example, D. Dyzenhaus and M. Moran, eds., *Calling Power to Account* (Toronto: University of Toronto Press, 2004).

31 *Roncarelli v. Duplessis*, [1959] S.C.R. 121.

32 Ibid. at para. 70.

33 This passage was cited with approval by Laws J. in *R. v. Somerset County Council, ex parte Fewings*, [1995] 1 All E.R. 513 at 524. Wade emphasized that the police in the United Kingdom, while not a law unto themselves, do not take direction from any executive authority. He observed, 'The truth is that a police officer holds a public position, that of peace officer, in which he owes obedience to no executive power outside the police force.' William Wade, *Administrative Law* (Oxford: University of Oxford Press, 2000), 153.

34 See RCMP News Release dated 29 December 2003, 'Search Warrants Executed on BC Legislature: News Release'; at http://www.rcmp-bcmedia.ca/ printablepressrelease.jsp?vRelease=4218 (RCMP Media Relations Website); Robert Matas, 'Mounties target B.C. ministers' staffers,' *Globe and Mail*, 29 December 2003, A1; Jane Armstrong, 'B.C.'s Campbell left reeling from liberal dose of sleaze,' *Globe and Mail*, 1 January 2004, A1; Brent Jang, 'Police probe won't disrupt B.C. budget, minister says,' *Globe and Mail*, 1 January 2004, A4; Peter O'Neil, Jim Beatty, and Lori Culbert, 'B.C. legislature raid involved possible fraud, source says,' *National Post*, 14 January 2004, A7; and Mark Hume, 'Bribery suspicions prompted B.C. raid,' *Globe and Mail*, 3 March 2004, A5.

35 Mark Hume, 'Judge gives first insight into BC police raid,' *Globe and Mail*, 2 April 2004, A9.

36 See *R. v. Appleby, Belisle and Small* (1990), 78 C.R. (3d) 282.

37 See the chronology of events in *Pepper in Our Eyes* at xii–xxii.

38 Commission Interim Report Following a Public Inquiry into Complaints

that took place in connection with the demonstrations during the Asia
Pacific Economic Cooperation Conference in Vancouver (Ottawa: Commission of Public Complaints, RCMP, 23 July 2001), www.cpc-cpp.gc.ca/
defaultsite/ at 30.4. See also Pue, 'Prime Minister's Police?'

39 These links are detailed in Pue, 'Prime Minister's Police?'

40 Andrew McIntosh, 'Mounties conducted secret probe of spending, *National Post*, 13 February 2004; Daniel Leblanc, 'More charges likely to be
laid in ad sponsorship scandal,' *Globe and Mail*, 10 March 2004, A4; and
Andrew McIntosh, 'Senior Mountie queried sponsorship funds in '98,'
National Post, 2 June 2004.

41 Les Whittington, 'Opposition questions timing, *Toronto Star*, 11 May 2004,
A01. See also Susan Delacourt, 'To serve and protect its political bosses,'
Toronto Star, 17 April 2004, F03.

42 For a more comprehensive review of political interference cases involving
the police see Kent Roach's contribution to this volume and Stenning,
'Someone to Watch over Me.'

43 See, for example, *Re Prue*, [1984] A.J. No. 1006 (Q.B.) which discusses this
case law at paras. 10–20.

44 This principle was most explicitly articulated in *R. v. Metropolitan Police
Commissioner, ex parte Blackburn*, [1968] 1 All E.R. 763. For an analysis of
this judgment in the Canadian context, see Kent Roach's contribution to
this volume and especially his analysis of *R. v. Campbell* at 26–9.

45 B. Archibald, 'Coordinating Canada's Restorative and Inclusionary Models of Criminal Justice: The Legal Profession and the Exercise of Discretion
under a Reflexive Rule of Law,' presentation to the Canadian Association
of Law Teachers, 1 June 2004. For the classic exposition of 'reflexive'
systems, see G. Teubner, *Law as an Autopoietic System* (London: Blackwell,
1993).

46 D. Smith, 'The Police and Political Science in Canada,' in *Police Powers
in Canada: The Evolution and Practice of Authority*, ed. R.C. McLeod and
D. Schneiderman (Toronto: University of Toronto Press, 1994), at 187. See
also Marie-France Bich, 'Organisation des forces de police au Canada'
(1989) 23 R.J.T. 279.

47 Since most firearms violations would be prosecuted by federal prosecutors,
the provincial role would in most cases consist primarily of cooperation
between provincial and federal counterparts. For discussion, see Mark
Carter, 'Current Tensions in the Federation: Provincial Prosecution Policy,'
presentation to the Canadian Association of Law Teachers, 31 May 2004.

48 See 'Manitoba Refuses to Prosecute Firearms Registration Offences,' at
http://www.gov.mb.ca/chc/press/top/2003/04/2003-04-15-02.html.

49 See Smith, 'The Police and Political Science in Canada.'
50 See Martin Friedland, *Controlling Misconduct in the Military: A Study Prepared for the Commission of Inquiries into the Deployment of Canadian Forces to Somalia* (Ottawa: Minister of Public Works. Government Services Canada, 1997); Bryan David Cummins, *Aboriginal Policing: A Canadian Perspective* (Scarborough: Prentice Hall, 2003); and Gordon Christie's paper in this volume.
51 For a discussion of the remarkable change in policing following the enactment of the *Charter*, see M. Friedland, 'Reforming Police Powers: Who's in Charge?' in *Police Powers in Canada* at 100–18.
52 D. Stuart, 'Policing under the *Charter*,' in ibid.
53 For a more detailed review of *Charter* cases involving police conduct and a discussion of the extent to which these cases 'curb' police activities, see Dianne Martin's contribution to this volume.
54 Even in public inquiries investigating possible political interference in police activities where *Charter* rights are at stake, the interests of the police are represented by government lawyers. This is noted by Wes Pue in his discussion of the government's strategy during the APEC inquiry; see 'The Prime Minister's Police,' at note 10.
55 See Canadian Association of Chiefs of Police, 'A Brief Concerning the Proposed Resolution Respecting the Constitution of Canada,' presented by the Law Amendments Committee of the Senate/House of Commons Special Joint Committee on the Constitution of Canada, Ottawa, 27 November 1980 (in which the chiefs of police expressed concern over accountability for policing standards shifting from parliamentary to judicial control under the then proposed *Charter of Rights*).
56 See, for example, Reginald A. Devonshire, 'The Effects of Supreme Court Charter-based Decisions on Policing: More Beneficial than Detrimental?' (1994) 31 Crim. R. (4th) 82, and Kathryn Moore, 'Police Implementation of Supreme Court Charter Decisions: An Empirical Study' (1992) 30 Osgoode Hall L.J. 547.
57 This discussion builds on the survey of civil police liability presented in Dianne Martin's contribution to this volume.
58 (1990), 74 O.R. (2d) 225.
59 Interestingly, the police relied on the policy/operation distinction to immunize its decision not to warn the plaintiff from judicial scrutiny. The Court rejected the notion that the decision not to warn potential victims was a policy choice. However, the reasoning of the Court implied that even if the decision had been characterized as one of 'policy,' it might still give rise to civil liability if it could be shown to be arbitrary or unreason-

able in the circumstances. For an analysis of this aspect of the decision, see Mayo Moran, 'Case Comment on *Jane Doe*' (1993), 6 CJWL 491–501.

60 [2003] 3 S.C.R. 263.

61 Ibid. at para. 26.

62 Ibid. at para. 57. This obligation of the chief is reinforced by s. 4 (1)(b) of the *Police Services Act*, which creates a 'freestanding' obligation on the chief to ensure that members of the police force carry out their duties in accordance with the Act and the needs of the community.

63 P. Small, 'Police union sues Star over race-crime series,' *Toronto Star*, 18 January 2003, A06.

64 *Gauthier v. Toronto Star Daily Newspapers Ltd.*, [2003] O.J. 2622 (Sup. Ct.), affirmed [2004] O.J. 2686 (C.A.).

65 See *Campbell*, [1999] 1 S.C.R. 565. See also *R. v. Metropolitan Police Commissioner, ex parte Blackburn*, [1968] 1 All E.R. 763.

66 In *Odhavji Estate v. Metropolitan Toronto Police* the Supreme Court of Canada explained the relationship between the minister and police chief in the following terms: 'whereas the Police Chief is in a direct supervisory relationship with members of the force, the Solicitor General's involvement in the conduct of police officers is limited to a general obligation to monitor boards and police forces to ensure that adequate and effective police services are provided and to develop and promote programs to enhance professional police practices, standards and training. Like the Board, the Province is very much in the background, perhaps even more so.' *Odhavji Estate v. Metropolitan Toronto Police*, [2003] 3 S.C.R. 263 at para. 70.

67 *Blackburn*, at 769.

68 *Royal Canadian Mounted Police Act*, R.S.C. 1985, c. R-10.

69 R.S.O. 1990, c. P.15. Other provincial policing acts also follow this model of recognizing the power of the responsible minister, usually the solicitor general, to direct the police. See *Police Act*, R.S.B.C. 1996, c. 367 s. 7; *Police Act*, R.S.A. 2000, c. P-17, s. 2(2); and *Police Act*, S.Q. 2000, c. 12, s. 50.

70 Nick Pron, John Duncanson, and Kerry Gillespie, 'Tory gets police union's support,' *Toronto Star*, 29 October 2003; Jonathan Fowlie, 'Fantino lashes out as Liberals cancel helicopter funds,' *Globe and Mail*, 6 November 2003; Jack Lakey, 'Probe requested of chief's words,' *Toronto Star*, 12 December 2003; Katherine Harding, 'Mayor gets Fantino's apology,' *Globe and Mail*, 21 February 2004.

71 Robert Benzie, 'John Tory vows boost for cities,' *Toronto Star*, 7 May 2004.

72 See Robert Benzie, 'Police role in politics examined,' *Toronto Star*, 5 February 2004, A04; Bruce DeMara, 'Officers defend endorsements,' *Toronto Star*

30 April 2004; Catherine Porter, 'Union stays out of federal race,' *Toronto Star*, 3 June 2004, B03.

73 .As the Supreme Court observed in *R. v. Power*, [1994] 1 S.C.R. 601, 'the Attorney General is a member of the executive and as such reflects, through his or her prosecutorial function, the interest of the community to see that justice is properly done. The Attorney General's role in this regard is not only to protect the public, but also to honour and express the community's sense of justice.' See also the discussion in Ian Scott 'Law, Policy and the Role of the Attorney General: Constancy and Change in the 1980s' (1989) 39 U.T.L.J. 109; John Edwards, 'The Attorney General and the *Charter of Rights*,' in *Charter Litigation*, ed. Robert Sharpe (Toronto: Butterworths, 1987); John Edwards, 'The Office of the Attorney General: New Levels of Public Expectations and Accountability,' in *Accountability for Criminal Justice*, ed. P. Stenning (Toronto: University of Toronto Press, 1995); Mark Freiman, 'Convergence of Law and Policy and the Role of the Attorney General' (2002) 16 S.C.L.R. (2d) 335; and most recently, Kent Roach, 'The Role of the Attorney General in Charter Dialogues Between Courts and Legislatures,' paper prepared for conference in honour of Ian Scott (Queen's University, Fall 2003).

74 The relationship between the sponsorship affair and principles of ministerial responsibility is discussed in Sossin, 'Speaking Truth to Power.'

75 See A. Manson and D. Mullan, eds., *Commissions of Inquiry: Praise or Reappraise* (Toronto: Irwin, 2003). See also Robert Centa and Patrick Macklem, 'Securing Accountability through Commissions of Inquiry: A Role for the Law Commission of Canada' (2001) 39 Osgoode Hall L.J. 117.

76 See, for example, the McDonald Commission, the Marshall Inquiry, and the APEC Inquiry.

77 For discussion, see Sujit Choudhry and Kent Roach, 'Racial and Ethnic Profiling: Statutory Discretion, Democratic Accountability and Constitutional Remedies' (2002) 40 Osgoode Hall L.J. 1 and Lorne Sossin, 'Discretion Unbound: Reconciling Soft Law and the *Charter*' (2002) 45 Canadian Public Administration 465.

78 See J. Robb, 'The Police and Politics: The Politics of Independence,' in *Police Powers in Canada*, at 177.

79 For a general discussion, see Choudhry and Roach, 'Racial and Ethnic Profiling.'

80 See, for example, *R. v. Golden*, [2001] 159 C.C.C. (4th) 449 (S.C.C.); *R. v. Brown* (2003), 173 C.C.C. (3d) 23 (Ont. C.A.); and the other cases discussed in Dianne Martin's contribution to this volume.

81 See G. Smith, 'Saskatchewan police probe finds anti-Native prejudice,' *Globe and Mail*, 22 June 2004, A1.

82 In December 2003, adjudicator Philip Girard ruled that Johnson was the victim of racial discrimination at the hands of Halifax Regional Police Constable Michael Sanford during a traffic stop in April 1998. In its decision, the board of inquiry recommended that the Halifax Regional Police re-examine its internal complaints mechanism to ensure it is sensitive to the diversity of the local community. *Johnson v. Halifax (Regional Municipality) Police Service*, [2004] N.S.H.R.B.I.D. No. 4.

83 The remarkable political career of Premier Joh Bjelke Petersen is chronicled in a number of studies including John Harrison, 'Faith in the Sunshine State: Joh Bjelke-Petersen and the Religious Culture of Queensland' (PhD dissertation, University of Queensland, 1991); Rae Wear, *Johannes Bjelke-Peterson: The Lord's Premier* (St Lucia: University of Queensland Press, 2002); Allan Patience, ed., *The Bjelke-Petersen Premiership 1968–1983: Issues in Public Policy* (Melbourne: Longman Cheshire, 1985); Derek Townsend, *Don't You Worry About That! The Joh Bjelke-Peterson Memoirs* (North Ryde, NSW: Collins/Angus & Robertson, 1990); Derek Townsend, *Jigsaw: The Biography of Johannes Bjelke-Petersen, Statesman – Not Politician* (Brisbane: Sneyd & Morley, 1983); Hugh Lunn, *Joh: The Life and Political Adventures of Johannes Bjelke-Petersen* (St Lucia: University of Queensland Press, 1979); Hugh Lunn, *Johannes Bjelke-Petersen: A Political Biography*, 2nd ed. (St Lucia: University of Queensland Press, 1984); Rae Wear, *Johannes Bjelke-Petersen: A Study in Populist Leadership* (St Lucia: University of Queensland Press, 1998); Rae Wear, *Johannes Bjelke-Petersen: The Lord's Premier* (St Lucia: University of Queensland Press, 2002). Various reminiscences of the event are to be found at the blogsite http://troppoarmadillo.ubersportingpundit .com/, while the National Library of Australia has collected newspaper clippings of the events in MS 8915 – Papers of Greg Weir Volume Number 21: A.I.D.S. Issues & Queensland Parliamentary Leadership 1987 (http:// www.nla.gov.au/ms/findaids/8915_21.html): 'Qld Police Remove Condom Machines,' *Sydney Morning Herald*, 1 Sept. 1987; 'Police Tear Out Uni Condom Machines,' *Courier Mail*, 1 Sept. 1987; 'Police Seize Condom Sales Machines,' *Daily Sun*, 1 Sept. 1987; 'Students Plan Legal Action after Police Raid Machines,' *Australian*, 2 Sept. 1987; 'Police Raid Townsville University, but Condom Machines Have Gone,' *Courier Mail*, 3 Sept. 1987; and 'Police seize campus condom machines,' *Canberra Times*, 7 Sept. 1987.

84 Doreen J. McBarnet, *Conviction: Law, the State and the Construction of Justice* (London: Macmillan, 1981), 33: 'in some public order offences there need not even be evidence that the accused was doing or intending to do any-

thing, merely being part of an offensive crowd is enough. Hence Case 30, where the charge was a breach of the peace, involving "jumping on and off a pavement in a disorderly fashion," and the accused was the only one of a small group of youths who pleaded not guilty.'

85 For example, Kent Roach's contribution to this volume includes a delightful account of the changing views of Geoffrey Marshall on police 'independence.' See pages 56–7. Quoting from Roach: 'The more candid proponents of full police independence might also point to increasing public cynicism about whether elected politicians will act in a publicly spirited manner. The distinction drawn by some between public interest and partisan politics will be dismissed as untenable in an age which assumes that politicians always act in their partisan self-interest. Cynicism about politicians, perhaps even more than confidence in the police, can push people in the direction of the full police independence model. Writing in 1977, only twelve years after he published a book that was extremely critical and almost dismissive of the concept of police independence, Geoffrey Marshall candidly conceded that the case for full police independence had become stronger in the subsequent years because "nobody's faith in councillors or Congressman or members of Parliament can now be as firmly held as it was fifteen years ago." He argued that "many liberal democrats" would trust the police more than the responsible minister to protect civil liberties. Professor Marshall even went so far as to suggest that a constitutional convention was emerging that: "would suggest that direct orders, whether of a positive or negative kind, whether related to prosecution or other law-enforcement measures, and whether related to individual cases or to general policies, ought to be avoided by police authorities even when they involve what the Royal Commission [on Policing in 1960] called 'police practices in matters which vitally concern the public interest."

Full police independence is supported not only by cynicism about politicians, but despair at the erosion of principles of ministerial accountability. As seen above, some commentators expressed concerns that Prime Minister Chrétien was not held accountable for the role of his office in APEC. If ministers and others in government can escape responsibility for their interventions in policing, or the interventions by their staff or civil servants, then the case for full police independence is strengthened.' See Geoffrey Marshall, 'Police Accountability Revisited,' in Policy and Politics: Essays in Honour of Norman Chester, ed. D. Butler and A.H. Halsey (London: Macmillan, 1978), at 60–1. Roach also observes that in 1984, during the period of high Thatcherism, Marshall 'elaborated on this thesis by arguing that "despite its uncertain legal foundations ... it is now necessary to defend" what has been described here as full police independence "as a constitutional and administrative convention"': Geoffrey Marshall *Constitutional Conventions* (Oxford: Oxford University Press, 1984), at 144. See also Geoffrey Marshall, *Police and Government: The Status and Accountability of the English Constable* (London: Methuen & Co. Ltd., 1965); G. Marshall and B. Loveday, 'The Police: Independence and Accountability,' in *The Changing Constitution*, ed. J. Towell and D. Oliver (Oxford: Clarendon Press, 1984), 295–321.

86 Albert V. Dicey, *Introduction to the Study of the Law of the Constitution*, 8th ed. (Holmes Beach, FL: Gaunt, 1996), 183.

87 See, for example, the discussion in Daniel H. Cole, 'An Unqualified Human Good: E.P Thomson and The Rule of Law' (2001) 28(2) *Journal of Law and Society*, 177.

88 Janice Gross Stein's *The Cult of Efficiency* (Toronto: House of Anansi/ Canadian Broadcasting Corporation, 2001) usefully points to the frequently misleading invocations of 'efficiency' in policy making.

89 For suggestions that this has happened at the highest levels in Canada see Paul Palango: *Above the Law* (Toronto: McClelland & Stewart, 1994); Paul Palango, *The Last Guardians: The Crisis in the RCMP – and in Canada* (Toronto: McClelland & Stewart, 1998).

90 The RCMP, for example, can obtain no legal advice other than from government lawyers.

91 In *Ladore et al. v. Bennett al.*, [1939] 3 D.L.R. 1 the Judicial Committee of the Privy Council (Lords Atkin, Russell of Killowen, Macmillan, Wright, and Romer) articulated the relevant principle in a somewhat different context as follows: per Lord Atkin, 'the Courts will be careful to detect and invalidate any actual violation of constitutional restrictions under pretence of keeping within the statutory field. A colourable device will not avail.' The Supreme Court of Canada observed in *Reference re: Firearms Act (Can.)* that '[i]n some cases, the effects of the law may suggest a purpose other than that which is stated in the law ... a law may say that it intends to do one thing and actually do something else. Where the effects of the law diverge substantially from the stated aim, it is sometimes said to be "colourable"' (*Reference re: Firearms Act (Can.)*, [2000] 1 S.C.R. 783, para. 18).

92 *R. v. Appleby* (Between Her Majesty The Queen, and John Appleby, Normand Belisle, Douglas Small), [1990] O.J. No. 1329; 78 C.R. (3d) 282; *Re: Royal Canadian Mounted Police Public Complaints Commission* (Federal Court of Appeal), Hugessen, Decary, and Linden, JJ.A., 1994 N.R. LEXIS 1362; 173 N.R. 290.

93 Such factors conspired against a full review of the circumstances leading up to Canada's APEC inquiry – possibly the best documented case of public event policing in Canadian history. See W. Wesley Pue, 'The Prime Minister's Police? Commissioner Hughes' APEC Report' (2001) 39(1) Osgoode Hall L.J. 165; W. Wesley Pue, 'Executive Accountability and the APEC Inquiry: Comment on "Ruling on Applications to Call Additional Government Witnesses"' (2000) 34 University of British Columbia L.R. 335; Pue, ed., *Pepper in Our Eyes*; W. Wesley Pue, 'Why the APEC allegations are so serious,' *Globe and Mail*, 5 October 1998.

94 Internal 'police politics' are also of concern, of course. That, however, is properly the subject matter of another paper.

95 Seemingly a powerful factor motivating much political influence on the policing of so-called public order events.

96 See, for example, J. Simon, 'Governing through Crime,' in *The Crime Conundrum: Essays on Criminal Justice*, ed. L.M. Friedman and G. Fisher (New York: Westview Press, 1997), 171.

3 Police-Government Relations in the Context of State-Aboriginal Relations

GORDON CHRISTIE

Abstract

Common debates over government-police relations share a certain structure: the main realm of contention revolves around questions about how to resolve tension between the concern that the police should be free to act independent of political interference and the concern that the police should, in a liberal democracy, be held accountable for their actions. Chapter 3 examines this tension in the context of state-Aboriginal relations, casting a critical eye on the efficacy of the typical forms of analysis that arise from this debate.

The first stage of analysis provides a contrast for the process of critical contextualization, as the question of police-government relations in the context of Aboriginal policing issues is treated as if that context introduced no particular or unique problems. At this first stage Aboriginal peoples in Canada are conceptualized as 'minority populations' within a liberal democracy, possessed of the rights enjoyed by other disadvantaged minority groups. The next two stages progressively critique this position, introducing first factors related to Aboriginal people's unique legal and constitutional status in Canada, and then factors relating to Aboriginal people's distinctive historical (and thereby necessarily political) status in relation to the Canadian state.

This form of contextual analysis is critical to making sense of the appropriate relation between the police and the Canadian government when these two bodies intersect with the interests of both Aboriginal nations and Aboriginal individuals within Canada. It is also critically important when attention is turned to particular disputes, for no scenario played out in the arena of Canadian-Aboriginal relations can be adequately understood outside its place within the larger legal, constitutional, historical and political landscape.

The chapter concludes with a commentary by Toni Williams and Kim Murray.

Introduction

The debate about the appropriate relationship between the police and the government on a liberal democracy centres on the tension between the value placed on an independently operating police force (which would be seen as an original source of action, responsible only to the law and good conscience for its actions) and the value in having police forces accountable to a representative governing body (which could set policy, and monitor – potentially even control – the actions of the police).

The value of an independent police force is grounded in the freedom from unwarranted political interference such independence promises. This freedom, one could argue, is essential to the rule of law, as it both allows for police discretion in relation to police operations and opens the door to the possibility of the police applying the rule of law to those who might otherwise seem to be their political superiors.[1] The value in police accountability is grounded in recognition of the role police play in liberal democracies, recognition which demands that the police be both directed by the public good and overseen in its efforts to promote that good. Political direction is essential, for the police function as an arm of the state, necessarily accountable to the public (and the governing body charged with both ensuring that the interests of the public are being met, and that state institutions are constantly and consistently directed by the public's interests). Forms of oversight are essential in providing protection from 'rogue' police elements and in fostering democratic notions of accountability.

The notion of a fully independent police force is antithetical to that of a police controlled and directed by political forces, and so some synthesis is demanded – some arrangement within which a reasonable measure of police independence is preserved in the face of the need for the police to be publically accountable. One fundamental debate about police independence concerns how to arrive at such an arrangement. This chapter problematizes this debate by placing it in the context of disputes involving Aboriginal peoples in Canada. The discussion passes through three stages. The first sets out how one could attempt to conceptualize Aboriginal peoples and their situations in Canada in such a manner that the debate could proceed essentially unhindered by troublesome contextual matters. The second two stages progressively critique the parameters within which the debate commonly transpires, first by introducing the unique position of Aboriginal peoples currently unfolding within domestic jurisprudence, the second by questioning certain key assumptions that underlie this jurisprudence.

Viewed simplistically through a demographic lens, Aboriginal peoples in Canada can be said to constitute 'minority populations.' In liberal democracies such as Canada (in which multiculturalism is highly valued) mechanisms exist to protect minority rights.[2] Part of this protection requires that individual members of minority communities be protected from unwarranted actions from either the police or the state. Insofar as the rights of minorities are accorded legal protection, and the actions of the state and all its manifestations are governed by the rule of law, the law will rule over both police and the government, assuring that neither can undercut the legal protections afforded without due consequences.

Ensuring that the rights of minorities are protected could have an impact on the appropriate balance that must be struck between the need for the police to be free from political interference (when that political intrusion might run counter to the protections required for minorities in a liberal democracy), and the need for the state to monitor (and perhaps to some extent control) policing activity (where an unfettered police force might act counter to the protected rights of minorities). It cannot be a simple matter of the police and the government negotiating a mutually satisfactory arrangement between them, for whatever balance they strike it must function to protect (or at the very least not endanger) minority rights in Canada.

Minority rights in Canada can be said to fall into two broad categories: rights that members of minority populations enjoy on the basis of being Canadians, and rights they enjoy on the basis of their inclusion in a minority population. The latter are clearly rights held by minority groups, while the former can be classified as such because, though it can be said that all Canadians enjoy the protection of their individual rights, any mechanism for protecting individual rights will function primarily to protect the interests of non-dominant groups, those that would most likely suffer the effects of discriminatory action.

Let us consider first those rights individual members of minority populations enjoy on the basis of being citizens or residents of Canada. There are fundamental rights and interests held by all Canadians that must be equitably and fairly recognized and protected, no matter the personal characteristics of the person(s) claiming such rights. Many of these rights are articulated in the *Charter of Rights and Freedoms*.[3] *Within the framework of the Charter*, section 15 operates to ensure that governmental practices unjustifiably discriminating on the basis of race (or ethnicity) can be found unconstitutional, and the situation rectified. Under this broad category of 'minority rights,' then, individual members of minority populations can reasonably expect to be treated by and under the law in the same manner as all other Canadians.

In interacting with the police, the rights that individual members of minority groups enjoy by virtue of being Canadians fall prey to two basic threats. First, the police might enjoy, in their sphere of authority, the ability to ignore or overrun non-discriminatory requirements. Second, concern might also lie with political direction behind either particular policing operations or general policing policy (where the implementation of some policy might have the effect of discriminating on the basis of race or ethnicity). Herein lies the principal motivation (from within the context of minority group interests) for locating an appropriate structure that can operate to provide checks and balances capable of monitoring and controlling the power of both the police and the government. Members of minority populations are primarily concerned with what might appear to be an inappropriately unregulated or uncontrolled ability of either the police, or a political force behind the police, to single them out for unwarranted policing attention.

The second set of minority rights are less often invoked in policing disputes in Canada. These are rights held by minority groups to the exclusion (it would seem) of other collectives. While these are commonly classified as 'special' rights, arguably one might suggest that this is best seen as rhetorical flourish, for these rights are merely those recognized rights that minority populations must enjoy if they are to be treated equitably in a liberal democracy (in relation to the members of the dominant racial/cultural group).

So, for example, in Canada certain francophone rights are legally recognized, especially in relation to language[4] and education.[5] While these particular rights have their origins in the unique historical dynamic that developed over time between the British and French colonies in North America, their contemporary grounding arguably now rests in the liberal democratic understanding that linguistic and educational rights are essential to the preservation of groups and group identities.[6] English-speaking Canadians enjoy a world within which the use of their language and the existence of their educational structures are unquestioned, and this dominance operates as a key element contributing to the apprehension that a constant threat looms over francophone cultural institutions. The dominance of English-language institutions and the threat this poses to French-language counterparts necessitates the protection of language and education rights for francophones.[7]

While it is discriminatory policing that commonly generates disputes over the proper way in which the police and the government should interact in relation to minorities, it is possible to imagine a situation in which minority group rights would be in the background of the policing action itself. For example, a provincial government in Canada might consistently and continually act to minimize the provision of French-language-based educational programs, potentially inciting members of that province's francophone community to engage in some form of physical protest. This protest, in turn, might be met with inappropriate police action, which itself might be prompted by either unacceptable (potentially ethnocentric) attitudes on the part of some members of the police force involved or unacceptable political interference with the policy or operations of the police force.

The first sort of problem (unacceptable police attitudes) would bring to the fore concerns about discrimination, as the police involved would most likely be prone to reasonable charges of bias and intolerance. The second sort of problem is more interesting, as it may be traced back to either discriminatory attitudes held by the government (or government officials involved) or potentially unwarranted policy positions that deny or downplay the legal protections that should be accorded minority rights.

Aboriginal peoples in Canada can be said to enjoy both forms of minority rights. They enjoy rights on the basis of being Canadians, rights which are protected from unjustifiable discriminatory governmental action. They may also be said to enjoy certain rights by virtue of being racial/cultural minorities – rights, for example, to the preservation and protection of their languages.

For the purposes of this study, however, little of import comes from this, as Aboriginal peoples would share these sorts of rights with other minority groups in Canada (and indeed in the case of the first sort of rights, with every Canadian). Furthermore, as we noted just above, policing disputes that engage minority rights will most likely rest on claims about discriminatory practices – completely unacceptable practices to be certain, but certainly not unique to the situations of Canada's Aboriginal peoples.

It will be necessary in the next stage of discussion to reintroduce the second sort of problem, that which arises when particular disputes that draw the attention of the police and the state can be causally traced back to potentially unacceptable political (or policy) decision making (where the relevant executive members reach decisions that essentially deny or ignore the importance of rights that should enjoy legal protection). We must reconsider this sort of problem when we introduce particular sorts of rights – distinct from minority rights – that Aboriginal peoples possess.[8]

The Legal and Constitutional Status of Aboriginal Peoples: Not Just Minority Populations

What makes the question of how to mediate the tension between police independence and political oversight particularly powerful and intriguing in the context of disputes involving Aboriginal peoples is the fact that Aboriginal peoples *do not* simply constitute minority populations within Canada. While it is open to Aboriginal people to appeal to section 15 of the *Charter*, demanding that government treat them without bias, and while they may even enjoy minority rights by virtue of the liberal democratic push to protect group identities from the threat of immersion in the larger dominant cultural milieu, Aboriginal peoples also enjoy the recognition and affirmation of existing Aboriginal and treaty rights under section 35 of the *Constitution Act, 1982*.[9]

As we noted above, individuals in Canada enjoy constitutionally protected rights (with section 15 of the *Charter* operating to ensure that members of minority groups are considered equal before and under the law), while minority groups enjoy rights that serve to protect their cultural identities. Aboriginal (and treaty) rights are distinct from any of these sorts of rights. In fact, Aboriginal (and treaty) rights are distinct from any sort of right that any other party in Canada might enjoy. Apart from those rights persons in Canada might enjoy on the basis of being people (fundamental human rights) and citizens or residents (fundamental political rights, which some might argue are themselves grounded in human rights), persons in Canada also enjoy rights granted by the state. More specifically, they can enjoy what we can generally classify as property rights. Individuals (and corporations) can hold free simple title to land, corporations (and more rarely individuals) can have licences to cut and harvest trees on Crown land, individuals and corporations can enjoy patents protecting innovative products they have developed, and so forth. These rights, created by the state and grounded in recognition by the state, reach back in Canada at least as far as the grant of what amounts to a monopoly business licence to the Hudson's Bay Company in its Royal Charter of 1670.[10]

Aboriginal (and treaty) rights are distinct in origin and nature from *any* of these sorts of rights. The following list identifies some of the more visible ways in which Aboriginal (and treaty) rights differ from rights held by other Canadians, either individually or collectively. While some of these differences may be shared with some of the other recognized rights Canadians enjoy, together they paint a picture of distinct and unique Aboriginal and treaty rights.

1 Aboriginal (and treaty) rights are group rights, held exclusively by Aboriginal peoples of Canada. Not only are the rights not attached to Aboriginal peoples as individual citizens of Canada, they are also not restricted to contemporary Aboriginal communities. They are rights that reach out to future generations of Aboriginal peoples, protecting their interests alongside those of people now living in Aboriginal communities.[11]

2 Aboriginal (and treaty) rights have been accorded *explicit* constitutional protection: while section 15 protects minority groups from governmental discriminatory action, fundamental rights that might be threatened are not articulated in this provision – indeed, the test for determining whether section 15 has been respected speaks of the protection of 'interests' as much as it does rights.[12] Furthermore, only in relation to francophone rights do we find in the law explicit and detailed recognition of minority group rights (apart from that explicit recognition, the only other implicit mention of such rights in the *Constitution Act, 1982*, is found in section 27, which speaks vaguely of the promotion of 'multiculturalism,'[13] while jurisprudence only speaks of a constitutional convention or principle concerning the protection of minority rights).[14]

3 This constitutional protection precludes the extinguishment of Aboriginal (and treaty) rights by the government. At most the legislative branch can justifiably infringe these rights (through a test introduced in *R. v. Sparrow*,[15] modified in *R. v. Gladstone*,[16] and applied to treaty rights in *R. v. Badger*[17] and *R. v. Marshall*).[18]

4 By implication, the executive cannot infringe upon Aboriginal (and treaty) rights. Only legislative action meeting the test for justification can do so.

5 Aboriginal (and treaty) rights are not grounded in recognition of the

need to preserve Aboriginal culture or heritage (though Supreme
Court jurisprudence may be mistakenly taken at times to have
suggested that this is so).[19]

6 Aboriginal (and treaty) rights are grounded in the need to reconcile
the prior presence of organized Aboriginal societies to the assertion
of Crown sovereignty.[20]

7 The very content of Aboriginal (and treaty) rights, then, is grounded
in the *prior existence* of organized Aboriginal societies. As such they
cannot be thought of as based in any fashion on grants from the
state. Aboriginal title cannot be thought of as any sort of granted
interest in land,[21] and Aboriginal rights cannot be thought of as
forms of licence to do one thing or another.

8 Aboriginal (and treaty) rights are marked by and intertwined with a
complex fiduciary relationship that binds the Crown and Aboriginal
peoples.[22] This entails recognition of a relationship that precludes
the Crown from viewing its obligations to Aboriginal peoples as
merely 'political.' Its obligations, in many instances, will be entirely
legal in nature.

9 In light of this historically grounded relationship, with its trustlike
quality, the *honour* of the Crown is engaged when dealing with the
legal and practical interests of Aboriginal peoples.[23]

With this overview of the ways in which Aboriginal (and treaty)
rights differ essentially from any other rights held by minority populations in Canada in mind, we can now turn to the question of the form
the discussion of the tension between police independence and political
oversight should take in the context of disputes involving Aboriginal
communities.

Police-Government Relations in the Context of Aboriginal and Treaty Rights

To highlight the impact contextual matters have on this debate we can
work our way through several contrasting situations. On one hand,
consider policing problems that might arise when police interact with
protestors voicing political dissent, while on the other hand, consider a
policing problem that might arise when police interact with Aboriginal
protestors voicing dissatisfaction with the government's treatment of
their particular situation, involving potential Aboriginal and/or treaty
rights. The right to engage in political protest is protected in Canada

under the right to free expression,[24] as well as under the rights to peaceful assembly and to association.[25] This sort of activity receives constitutional protection (afforded on the basis of the importance of the rights to free expression and to gather with others of like mind, especially in protest against government policy and action, in a free and democratic society).[26] The Aboriginal protestors could also be said to be exercising their constitutionally protected right to free speech, but their protest revolves around claims about government inaction in regards to *other* constitutionally protected rights – Aboriginal (and perhaps treaty) rights. At first glance, however, would one be tempted to say that this contextual difference would have any impact on the debate about police-state relations?

Inappropriate police activity in relation to the non-Aboriginal political protest may lead to calls to re-evaluate the relationship between the police and the government in power (especially, of course, if it appears that the police action was driven by government directive, which would call into question the strength of what many see as a necessary 'firewall' between the police and the state).[27] Similarly, inappropriate police activity in relation to the Aboriginal protest may lead to questions about the relationship between the police and the government in power (especially, once again, if it appears the government inappropriately directed the police in this matter). In both types of situations a re-evaluation of the relationship would likely indicate the need for a stronger firewall between the police and the government (especially in relation to particular police operations, when such operations are following established policy that seems to further the public interest, but partisan political concerns apparently intrude in the situation). Constitutionally protected rights are at issue, and the movement of the state as it attempts essentially to rise above the rule of law (facilitated through what many might see as an unwarranted use of the police) would seem to call for a greater measure of police independence.

Is there, then, no discernible impact on the debate when Aboriginal or treaty rights are the issue at hand behind the policing action? To determine if this is so we need to consider a slightly different pair of scenarios. At the level of generality at which we were operating the non-Aboriginal political protestors were merely exercising their right to free speech, while in the case of the Aboriginal protestors we were witness to an exercise of a right to free speech in relation to protests over other constitutionally protected rights. We must particularize the non-Aboriginal protest, for example, by contrasting the protest of an Aboriginal community with a type of situation introduced earlier: that wherein a francophone population in a province protests over a systematic government policy of disregarding their language rights, where that protest is met by inappropriate police action, likely driven by political directives.

Very little would seem to change if we contrast these two sorts of situations. Re-evaluating the police-government relationship would once again seem to point to the same outcome: a greater degree of police independence is called for, especially in relation to particular police operations already guided by policy aimed at promoting public interests.

Some fundamental distinctions do exist, however, between the two sorts of non-Aboriginal situations imagined (in regards to basic rights to free speech and association and to constitutionally protected language rights) and the situation surrounding Aboriginal (and treaty) rights. The key differences lie not in the fact that Aboriginal and treaty rights are group rights, nor simply in their having a different set of requirements for the government to meet should it attempt to justify infringement, but rather in the source of these rights in non-Canadian *original* societies, and their being embedded in a fiduciary context, with the honour of the Crown engaged.

The right to free expression is grounded in a conception of a liberal democracy, and of the conditions necessary for the promotion of values and ideals highly esteemed by those living in and through a liberal democratic structure. Francophone rights, on the other hand, can be defended today as necessary for the protection of French culture in a nation dominated by English peoples and their institutions. These are rights arrived at, however, historically, and their nature has already been broadly set out in constitutional instruments that have their origins in the early nineteenth century. Aboriginal and treaty rights, in contrast to these two sorts of rights, have only very recently been recognized as rights protected within Canada, and their place within the legal and constitutional landscape is by and large unsettled.[28] Indeed, the next chapter in Canadian history will be one wherein the nature of these rights – which are grounded in an existence pre-dating the Crown – is worked out across Canada.

What impact do these fundamental differences have in regard to the debate over the proper relationship between the police and the government? To identify and appreciate the impact they generate we need to refocus on the reasons commonly brought in to bolster arguments for either greater police independence or more political control. On the one hand, there are what might be termed negative reasons for the promotion of each position: greater police independence is promoted as a way of protecting the public from undue political interference in what should be even-handed policing matters, while greater political control (especially in regards oversight) is promoted as a means of protecting the public from potentially unfettered inappropriate police activity. On the other hand, there are what might be termed positive reasons for the promotion of each position: a police force operating free of political interference is more effective in working under its mandate to further the safety and well-being of the citizenry (which includes acting as a pillar in the maintenance of the rule of law), while political control is essential to the task of ensuring that the police continue to operate in the direction of the public's interests (where one of the government's essential functions is that of representing the public and its interests).

While the two sets of negative reasons serve to create and underscore the tension between police independence and political control, the positive reasons converge and mutually reinforce each other around the notion of the public's interests. The positive reasons focus our attention on the fundamental interest that lies at the heart of the relationship between the public, the government, and the police: the need to create in a liberal democratic society an institutional framework within which the police are best able to function as protectors of the public, promoting safety and ensuring a free and peaceful civil atmosphere.

As we noted above, however, at this point in Canada's history Aboriginal (and treaty) rights are being introduced into the legal and political landscape, a task charged with tremendous responsibility that falls exclusively to the government. A process of reconciliation between the prior presence of Aboriginal societies and Crown sovereignty is only just beginning and will be ongoing for some time to come, and this process requires the Crown to determine how Aboriginal peoples and their interests will be worked into the fabric of society. This task will require in turn that direction be provided to police forces. The police must be directed away from actions that potentially interfere with Aboriginal (and treaty) rights, and towards actions that promote the reconciliation envisioned.

In such an environment police independence must, then, be tempered, as the government ought to be *constantly* and *actively* involved in the task of establishing and implementing policing policy that can adequately uphold the honour of the Crown and which satisfactorily meets its fiduciary requirements. While some measure of police inde-

pendence must be maintained in relation to particular policing operations, even in such cases government monitoring ought to be expected,
as the government's responsibilities extend to all contexts in which the
legal and practical interests of Aboriginal rights-holders might be unduly threatened.

The outcome of this analysis would thus seem to be an endorsement
of something like the third model of police-government interaction
explored by Kent Roach, that of democratic policing, or Lorne Sossin's
model of an autonomous and non-partisan political force.[29] A core of
policing functions should by and large be removed from government
interference, but the government should have a large monitoring role
(especially in relation to policy-laden operations), and should play an
active role in developing and implementing policing policies.

Calling into Question the Parameters of the Debate

The analysis thus far, however, has introduced elements that reach
unavoidably beyond the constraints of the standard debate over appropriate police-government relationships. This has the effect of
'problematizing' the debate, calling into question the adequacy of its
parameters given the context in which it is here being carried out. In
short, the very aspects of this context that pointed towards a particular
model of appropriate police-government relations – the source of Aboriginal (and treaty) rights, and their nature in Canadian law as involving notions about the honour of the Crown (as it functions to temper its
own power with legally mandated fiduciary duties) – also serve to
place the debate itself in a particular and unique context.

In the context of Aboriginal (and treaty) rights the government is not
free to develop and implement policy as it sees fit. This is essentially
what it means to say that 'federal power must be reconciled with
federal duty,'[30] the notion that lies at the heart of the imposition of
fiduciary obligations on the Crown. The government is not bound
merely to political obligations, as fiduciary doctrine has been introduced to reflect the fact that the Crown's hands are tied by the law (and
not by politics). This fact cannot be traced back to the content of Aboriginal (and treaty) rights, but rather to their source – in their being
grounded in organized societies pre-dating the arrival of the Crown to
present-day Canada. Until the process of reconciliation has run its
course in a fair and just fashion the Crown cannot treat Aboriginal
peoples as nothing more than groups of citizens within society, their

rights contained entirely within the ambit of the social contract forming the nation state. In a sense, a fully formed social contract (which will complete the process of welcoming Aboriginal peoples into Canadian society) would be the outcome of this process.

What this means in the context of police-government relations should be clear. While some discretionary leeway around the exercise of decision-making power will remain unavoidably present, in broad terms the decisions of the government about how to set appropriate police policy must be by and large settled.

Consider a 'traditional' fiduciary-beneficiary relationship, one wherein the fiduciary has discretionary control over the legal and/or practical interests of the beneficiary, such that the fiduciary is in a position to act unilaterally to influence those interests either positively or negatively.[31] While there may be some discretion available in how this fiduciary can work with (and further) the beneficiaries' interests, there are strong guiding principles laying out general restrictions on how the fiduciary can act, and guiding the fiduciary towards a narrow range of acceptable options. Ranging over the particular principles and guideposts is one over-arching fiduciary principle: the fiduciary must act in the best interests of the beneficiary (in relation to the interests at stake).

The very same sort of situation must confront the government as it establishes how to approach Aboriginal issues, even when the particular problem concerns how to direct the police either when they are engaged in policing a particular dispute about Aboriginal (and treaty) rights or when the question is about how to set general policing policy. Fiduciary responsibilities intrude, constraining the government as it goes about exercising its powers.

It is clear, then, that what must dominate the discussion over the proper relationship between the police and the state in the Aboriginal context is the rule of law. Both the police and the government must be firmly ensconced under the rule of law, and the nature and ambit of the law under which they must fall must be adequately understood and acknowledged. In this context the substance of the law is provided by fiduciary doctrine, and more particularly by the principles that guide fiduciaries as they exercise control over the legal and practical interests of beneficiaries. Aboriginal peoples have reposed trust in the government that it will deal fairly and honourably with their interests, and this trust is protected by the rule of law, functioning to ensure that the honour of the government manifests into appropriate policy and direction.

This implicates the courts in the debate over the appropriate relationship between the police and the government, for the judiciary must function to measure the degree to which the government has met its legal obligations, dispensing remedies as warranted. In some sense the courts must take on the role of overseers, monitoring and measuring the success of the relationship established by the government between the government and the police, where the measuring stick is provided by fiduciary doctrine and the jurisprudence around Aboriginal and treaty rights. The courts have (somewhat reluctantly) taken on this role in relation to the government's treatment of Aboriginal and treaty rights, and in the context of government-police relations they must come to see that the constitutionally mandated task they have fallen under carries with it the need constantly to assess both how the government has responded to the legal interests of Aboriginal peoples and (where the government has systematically ignored or denied the existence of rights which, prima facie, seem plausibly established) the response of the government to the policing of disputes that might arise. Not only must the government be seen not to be unjustifiably interfering with the particular operations of the police once the police are engaged in policing a dispute over Aboriginal and/or treaty rights, it must also be seen as establishing policies for the police to follow in such situations which themselves respect the fiduciary position of the government.

Some Problems with the Use of Fiduciary Doctrine in this Context

The most obvious difficulty with the suggestion that the government should be ever-mindful of its fiduciary obligations to Aboriginal peoples when it is working out its relationship with the police is that it is exceedingly difficult to say anything with a reasonable measure of precision about the nature and content of the fiduciary relationship between the Crown and Aboriginal peoples (and about the fiduciary obligations this relationship might generate). At the heart of this problem is the 'sui generis' status of the fiduciary relationship the Supreme Court has introduced and (minimally) mapped out.

In a traditional fiduciary relationship if the fiduciary was in a conflict of interest that fact would be sufficient for finding that the fiduciary was in a situation at direct odds with the fundamental principle informing fiduciary doctrine (that the fiduciary is charged with acting in the best interests of the beneficiary). In the sui generis Crown-Aboriginal context, however, the Supreme Court has suggested that the government may weigh its fiduciary obligations to Aboriginal peoples against other obligations it may fall under in making political decisions.[32] If this were translated into the realm of traditional fiduciary relationships, it would appear as the notion that a fiduciary could be permitted to weigh her fiduciary responsibilities against other personal interests she might have in assisting other third parties. This notion does *not* translate, however, into standard fiduciary relationships, for it is unique to those situations in which the government is found to be in a fiduciary position.

In the Crown-Aboriginal context allowance for what might otherwise appear to be conflicts of interest can be teased out of the jurisprudence as the notion that the government may 'reasonably' balance its political (or governmental) obligations with its legal obligations. In many instances in the Crown-Aboriginal context this seems to lead to little more than the requirement that the Crown not ignore Aboriginal peoples (that it 'respect' their interests)[33] when making decisions that might affect their interests. This would seem to be a far cry from the sorts of impositions on fiduciaries that would ensue under standard fiduciary doctrine.[34]

As troublesome as this might be, it only goes to illustrate the problems that arise in trying to make sense of fiduciary doctrine in the Crown-Aboriginal context. With the absence of any clear guidance from the Supreme Court, it is next to impossible to say in any given context what the existence of the fiduciary relationship entails for the government (and so what Aboriginal groups that might be affected by government decision making might be able reasonably to expect).[35] Of particular difficulty in the context of government-police relations is the problem in saying, with any acceptable and workable level of detail, whether fiduciary *obligations* actually befall the government, and if so what these might be.

The Court has recognized that a general fiduciary relationship exists between the Crown and Aboriginal peoples of Canada. This relationship, however, must be translated into particular fiduciary obligations in particular situations. In some situations, interactions between the Crown and Aboriginal peoples will not result in any legal obligations on the Crown (in such situations the Crown would not be acting in its role as fiduciary, but simply as the government of Canada). In other situations, however, the Crown would be exercising its control over the legal and/or practical interests of an Aboriginal people in such a way as to raise the reasonable expectation of the affected Aboriginal people that the Crown would act to diligently protect and promote these interests.

Fiduciary obligations will typically not arise outside the context of disputes over either section 35 rights or particular Aboriginal land interests. Outside such contexts fiduciary obligations could only arise if it were determined that their existence facilitated 'supervision of the high degree of discretionary control gradually assumed by the Crown over the lives of [A]boriginal peoples.'[36] Such obligations, however, must still be tied down to 'specific Indian interests.'[37] As a matter of positive law, '[f]iduciary protection accorded to Crown dealings with [A]boriginal interests in land (including reserve creation) has not to date been recognized by this Court in relation to Indian interests other than land outside the framework of s. 35(1) of the Constitution Act, 1982.'[38]

Can one follow this vague and incomplete set of directions to arrive at any definite conclusions about government action in working out a relationship with the police (and a body of policy setting out mandates and operations for police interaction with Aboriginal peoples)? One might argue that the action in question (that of the government deciding how to structure its relationship to the police, and the nature of the policies under which it would have police operate) *could* intersect with section 35 concerns. This would seem to have to involve some form of derivative argument, however, for the claim would not be that in making such decisions the Crown is exercising power in direct relationship to rights Aboriginal peoples could claim under section 35, but rather that in making such decisions it is deciding only how it (and one of its institutions, the police) would react to disputes over these sorts of claimed rights. In a similar fashion one would have to be concerned about arguments that tried to ground particular fiduciary obligations in this context in land interests of affected Aboriginal parties.

This is not to say that such arguments would not suffice, or are not persuasive, especially when the honour of the Crown is brought into the mix.[39] It may not be necessary, however, to tie the actions of the government so closely to specific Aboriginal interests (articulated under section 35 or found in particular land interests). General principles on their own would seem to point the way in this context to the finding of fiduciary obligations on the Crown.

Imagine an Aboriginal community protesting what they consider to be government denial of their constitutionally protected rights. While one might think police operations in such situations would only raise concerns parallel to those that might accompany non-Aboriginal political protests, we earlier noted the differences between situations wherein Aboriginal or non-Aboriginal parties engage in such action. The imagined protest would be in relation to legal interests grounded in an existence pre-dating the Crown, legal interests not grounded in any fashion in non-Aboriginal society. Police action in meeting such a protest must be seen, then, as playing a role in a process of reconciliation that will, in due course, integrate these pre-existing rights into the legal and political landscape of Canada. The discretionary control the government exercises over any such police action (either in individual situations or as a matter of setting policy) directly intersects with this process, and so arguably injects into the picture fiduciary obligations on the Crown.

Even should this argument hold water, however, work must then go into answering questions about the nature of obligations that might befall the Crown. In a previous section the suggestion was made that the government, in meeting its fiduciary obligations, would have to develop policing policies in particular ways. What these ways might be has so far not been explored.

The exploration could begin with a look into the issue of whether obligations on the government might be of a general nature (to develop policies with certain general features), or rather of more specific natures, tied to specific aspects of policing, or to specific sorts of fact situations or eventualities. If the latter were the case, one could not simply say that the government had fiduciary obligations that arose whenever it set about framing policing policies. Instead, fiduciary obligations would only arise in the context of framing policing policy when this activity happened to touch upon particular and specific Aboriginal interests. How do we begin to address this sort of issue?

The first steps towards resolving this – and related – concerns begin with reflection on the arguments that go to establishing the existence of fiduciary obligations. Recall that the most direct route to establishing the existence of obligations is through a consideration of principles that the Supreme Court has itself laid out in relation to this sui generis area of the law. In setting out its relationship to the police in the context of Aboriginal and treaty rights, the government is engaged in a central aspect of the project of reconciliation, the process that lies behind the constitutionalization of Aboriginal and treaty rights in section 35. When one is operating on this level of principle, it should not matter to the argument what the particular underlying interests at issue might be, so long as they are legal interests of Aboriginal peoples. Fiduciary obligations arise in the context of state control over policing operations of Aboriginal disputes because the state, in this situation, enjoys immense discretionary power over the ability of Aboriginal peoples to enjoy their legal and practical interests, whatever these might be.

We now, however, need to advance to the next logical question. If the obligations on the Crown in this context are of a general nature, what do they require of the Crown? Could the Crown satisfy its fiduciary obligations by developing and instituting policing policies vis-à-vis Aboriginal peoples that were non-discriminatory, so that Aboriginal protestors should expect nothing more than they should be treated by the police no differently than might be reasonably expected by other political protestors?

Policies that were merely non-discriminatory would likely not suffice in this context, however, to satisfy the obligations on the Crown. To imagine so would be to ignore the nature and content of the rights at issue – their constitutional status, their grounding in pre-Crown existence, and most particularly their presently unsettled nature. Aboriginal and treaty rights are unsettled in nature, recall, as they are currently being worked into the legal and constitutional framework of Canada. Interests over which the Crown has come to have control are now being translated, through a process of reconciliation, into full-fledged rights in Canada. Being unsettled, disputes over these rights – the sorts of events that might lead to policing activities – have a dual nature (unlike disputes over other rights, including those of minorities in Canada). Disputes over Aboriginal and treaty rights are similar to other 'political' protests in that the disputants are protesting what they take to be inappropriate state action in relation to their rights and interests. Disputes over Aboriginal and treaty rights are, however, dissimilar to any other challenges to state action in that Aboriginal and treaty rights are in flux, as they are currently being integrated *by the state* into the legal and political landscape of Canada.

In meeting its fiduciary obligations in this situation, then, the Crown must establish policing policies cognizant of the special status of Aboriginal and treaty rights, cognizant of the ongoing project of reconciliation, and especially cognizant of the responsibilities it has given the role that it has taken on, and of the honour it must exhibit in fulfilling these responsibilities.

Saying something definitive, however, about the particular content of the obligations that befall the Crown as it goes about establishing relations with the police in the context of state-Aboriginal relations remains elusive. If more than merely non-discriminatory policies are called for, what is this 'more'?

For some insight into this issue we need to focus on the *reasons* for the need for a project of reconciliation, that is, on the grounding of Aboriginal and treaty rights in the pre-existence of Aboriginal nations in Canada. Aboriginal and treaty rights are currently amorphous in nature – they are yet to be fully crystallized in their full form in contemporary Canada – because Aboriginal peoples and their interests were treated inappropriately in the long colonial period that marked much of the history of the relationship between Canada and Aboriginal nations. How should Aboriginal peoples have been treated during the colonial period? Their existence in Canada *pre-dates* the Crown and European settlement. Non-Aboriginal peoples and their institutions are the newcomers, those who owe a certain measure of respect to the peoples and institutions that existed prior to their arrival.

This suggests that in meeting its fiduciary obligations to Aboriginal peoples in the context of establishing relations with the police, and in setting out policing policies vis-à-vis Aboriginal protests, the Crown should be constrained by a principle of maximal restraint. Quite simply, the government should be concerned to ensure that police are a force of last resort in matters relating to Aboriginal and treaty rights, and that when, as a last resort, the police are deployed, their actions should be marked by further operational policies of maximal restraint. The rights at issue have origins in societies predating the arrival of the Crown, and so in approaching the exercise of these rights the Crown should be as deferential as reasonably possible – especially in the period of history we are currently passing through, as these rights are now being worked into the landscape (a landscape they *should* have occupied through the colonial period and up to the present time).

This deference – manifest in policies falling under a principle of maximal restraint – is mandated not only by the facts of pre-existence and colonial impropriety, but also by the role the Crown has taken on. In assuming the role of that body which will work out how Aboriginal and treaty rights will come to a full-fledged existence in contemporary

Canada, the Crown has taken on responsibilities that it must honourably discharge. Honour, in this context, clearly calls for strong deference, fleshed out under a principle of maximal restraint.

Further Problematizing the Debate: Aboriginal Peoples' Positions on the Margins of Canadian Society

An examination of the debate over the proper relationship between the police and the government in the context of state-Aboriginal relations would not be complete without consideration of questions about the very nature of those relations. Much of the discussion in the previous section hinged on an uncritical acceptance of a particular judicial conceptualization of the relationship between the state and Aboriginal peoples, and yet that conceptualization is extremely contentious, especially as viewed from within many Aboriginal communities. The last section of this chapter introduces the nature of the conceptualization used, focusing on key assumptions upon which it rests. The nature of the conceptualization is itself problematic, but equally so is the notion that the judiciary is the appropriate body to be charged with the task of constructing it. As we will see, problematizing in this manner the debate around the appropriate relationship between the police and the state in the context of state-Aboriginal relations leads to radically different suggestions about how the debate should be approached (and potentially resolved).

The central assumption structuring the judicial conceptualization of the Aboriginal-state relationship is that the relationship is one essentially internal to the state. While earlier we noted that the purpose of section 35 has been held to be to reconcile the prior presence of Aboriginal societies to the sovereignty of the Crown, this has been understood (in the minds of both the state and its courts) as not implying that Aboriginal peoples do not fall under the sovereignty of the Crown. The reconciliation envisioned by the state and its courts is seen as working out how Aboriginal peoples, *who already fall under the sovereignty of the Crown*, are to have one fact of their existence (that the lineage of their communities pre-dates the arrival of the Crown to Canada) acknowledged and respected within Canadian society.

In the minds of many Aboriginal peoples, however, this central assumption is the most contentious. While it is difficult to dispute the fact that some form of reconciliation between Aboriginal and non-Aboriginal peoples is necessary, many Aboriginal people do not view the process as a matter of determining such an arrangement under the *precondition* that the issue is seen as inherently internal to Canadian society. Rather, many Aboriginal people see the inevitable process as a matter of determining how an arrangement can be arrived at between these two broad sets of communities. While the outcome of this process may very well be that Aboriginal nations come to be fully encompassed within Canadian society, many are opposed to the notion that debate over how they will fit within Canadian society must *begin* with the assumption that they are already under and subject to Canadian sovereignty.

This central assumption colours the rest of the debate over how the police and the state are to appropriately interact, even when that debate is problematized as it was in the previous section. Since the judicial vision of reconciliation begins with the 'unquestioned' fact of Crown sovereignty,[40] the demands of reconciliation are one-sided, with Aboriginal communities having to submit to the power of the government (and its third arm, the judiciary) to determine their place in Canadian society. The rest of the jurisprudence around Aboriginal (and treaty) rights illustrates the danger inherent in this move, as non-Aboriginal courts have worked gradually to settle Aboriginal (and treaty) rights into the status of being linked to 'traditional practices and customs,' with the vitality of powers of self-determination entirely removed from their core, and their nature and strength determined under unique principles of fiduciary doctrine.

Some might suggest that the introduction of fiduciary doctrine was meant to counteract the vestiges of colonialism in domestic law, for it elevated the government's interaction with Aboriginal peoples from the political plane to the legal arena. The fiduciary relationship defined by the Court, however, actually plays a key role in the perpetuation of what amounts to a modern-day form of colonialism, now firmly entrenched in domestic law in Canada. As noted in the previous section, the sui generis nature of the relationship (and the duties it can create) sits uneasily within traditional fiduciary doctrine. More problematic than the murky fashion by which the government is held to the legal requirements attendant on its being a fiduciary, however, is the reasoning that lies behind the use of fiduciary doctrine in this context. The reason the government is said to be in a fiduciary position is keyed to the contentious view Aboriginal peoples have of the law: the Crown is held to be in a fiduciary position as a result of its *having control over* the legal and practical interests of Aboriginal peoples in Canada. Under this conceptualization, while Aboriginal (and treaty) rights are rights attached to Aboriginal communities, they are controlled by the state and its courts, both of which purportedly act 'in the best interests' of Aboriginal communities.

It is not just that fiduciary doctrine is employed to subvert Aboriginal interests, removing them from the control of Aboriginal communities, and thereby maintaining – indeed reinforcing – the subordinate role these communities have found themselves in vis-à-vis the state over the last 150 years. If it were only a problem with the legal doctrine pro- pounded by the Supreme Court, one could argue that the road out of colonialism lay in simply replacing this doctrine with another legal conceptualization of the state-Aboriginal relationship, one which would grant Aboriginal peoples better control of their own interests. The prob- lem, however, lies in the larger framework within which exists the mechanism churning out a process to determine how Aboriginal issues can be dealt with.

Once again, the central problem (which sets the larger framework) lies in the initial presumption that state-Aboriginal relations are a mat- ter internal to Canadian society. This initial presumption lies behind the role the courts then play in determining the legal characterization they construct of state-Aboriginal relations. Only if we begin with the notion that Aboriginal peoples are already subject to Crown sovereignty can we move on to the notion that the courts of Canada can legitimately take upon themselves the task of conceptually constructing the con- tours of the legal relationship between the state and Aboriginal peoples.

In this sense, then, a problem exists not only with the judicial conceptualization of the relationship between the state and Aboriginal peoples, but also with the fact that the courts of the state have been charged with the task of developing such a conceptualization. If the conceptualization they now work under had been 'given' there would be no problem, for it would legitimate their work in developing or fleshing out such a conceptualization. But since they developed out of thin air the notion that Aboriginal peoples are already subject to Crown sovereignty (and that working out a relationship between the Crown and Aboriginal peoples is a problem internal to Canadian society), the legitimacy of their work has to be called into immediate question.

The language of the rule of the law does not mitigate this problem. We noted in the previous section that the rule of law plays a prominent role in the unfolding of the judicial determination of the relationship between the state and Aboriginal peoples, as the government is held to legal requirements set out under the unique fiduciary relationship said to exist between the Crown and Aboriginal peoples. One cannot say, however, that since this vision of police-state relations places the rule of law in a dominant position the vision is thereby unassailable on these grounds.

This entire structure begins with the determination of the place Aboriginal interests will have within domestic law, a determination made by courts constituting an arm of the Canadian state. Any appeal enjoyed by the position thereby rests upon prior unreflective acceptance of the notion that it is appropriate for the institutions of domestic law to arrive at conceptualizations of the state-Aboriginal relationship which can inform the legal apparatus that will rule over all.[41] This ignores the problem with legitimating the role Canadian courts play in setting out what the rule of law entails, monitoring governments as they function in relation to the legal obligations they are found to fall under, and working to hold governments to the requirements established under these obligations.

While it is commendable that Canada, as a liberal democracy, is committed to the rule of law, one has to be clear on the fact that the appropriate application of the rule of law rests on certain preconditions. An appropriate application of the rule of law presupposes the existence of a substantive positive body of rules and principles (the body of law which is to rule evenly over all in society). An appropriate application of the rule of law also presupposes the existence of an established society, one that enjoys boundaries recognized and (at least tacitly) accepted by those who make up its citizenry. And finally, an appropriate application of the rule of law presupposes the existence of institutions rightly charged with the task of generating legal rules, principles, and tests recognized and (at least tacitly) accepted by those who make up the society in question.

Questions swirl around these preconditions in the context of state-Aboriginal relations, even in the form in which the governments and courts of Canada have conceptually constructed this relationship. With respect to police-government relations in the context of Aboriginal issues, for example, we have seen that the part of the substantive positive body of law that would govern over the actions of the government in this context would be a uniquely constructed body of fiduciary doctrine. The courts have introduced onto the scene fiduciary doctrine, and taken upon themselves the task of laying out how the contours of this doctrine would develop in this unique situation. While this picture could be commended were the liberal and democratic society over which the rule of law governs safely 'given,' in the context of Aboriginal issues it is the very nature of the presence of Aboriginal peoples in society that is unsettled.

In a liberal democracy there must be an assurance that the body of law which rules over all parties is appropriately arrived at, and when the question concerns how societies which predate the liberal democracy will be reconciled to the existence of this new arrival, the answer cannot be to begin with the notion that institutions of the liberal democracy have the authority to decide how the relationship will be understood.

Implications for the Discussion of the Appropriate Relationship between the State and Police in the Context of Aboriginal Issues

Challenging the parameters of the debate around police-government relations in this manner radically alters what can be meaningfully said about how the two bodies should interact in the context of Aboriginal protests and disputes. While in the previous section we noted that domestic jurisprudence points us towards a democratic policing model supplemented with the notion that the state must operate under restrictions imposed by their falling under fiduciary obligations in relation to Aboriginal peoples, this model cannot be simply amended upon reflection on the factors we have considered. What the discussion points to, rather, is a much larger and more fundamental challenge, that of working out a fair and just relationship between the state and Aboriginal peoples (one which does not begin with the presumption that Aboriginal peoples are subject to Crown sovereignty and the authority of the state's courts).

Faced with this challenge little can be said about how the state and police should interact when the police are interacting with Aboriginal people. Something can be suggested along lines which run roughly parallel to those which drove the previous discussion, but this suggestion could only be tentative.

As we noted in the previous section, the rule of law is an empty vessel, presupposing for its appropriate application a given collective over which it can legitimately govern; institutions which can be properly charged with the task of developing legal rules, tests, and principles; and appropriate mechanisms for monitoring and enforcing adherence to the rules, tests, and principles constructed. In a situation in which two distinct collectives meet and mingle one can imagine a larger collection built out of the two, but within which the two maintain their integrity and distinctive powers and entitlements; an institutional body which could set out rules and principles guiding the interactions of these two collectives (a body acceptable to both collectives); and mechanisms for monitoring and enforcing adherence to the rules and principles constructed (again, acceptable to both collectives). If these imagined structures could be constructed around the worlds of Aboriginal and non-Aboriginal societies, the question of how the police should interact with the state might begin to come into focus, and some resolution attained.

Conclusion: The Three Stages of Analysis

In the first section of this work the notion that Aboriginal peoples can be characterized as 'minority populations' was examined in relation to the task of finding an appropriate balance between police independence and government oversight in the context of Aboriginal issues. Jurisprudence around Aboriginal (and treaty) rights, however, clearly demonstrates that Aboriginal peoples, while numerically minority populations, possess constitutionally protected rights that cast the debate in a particular light. The means by which Aboriginal (and treaty) rights are legally protected from unjustifiable government interference (and the means by which the Crown must act in order to justify certain infringements) dictates that a democratic policing model be adopted in the Aboriginal context, though one which is itself overseen by the law (with the judiciary ensuring, for example, that in setting policing policy the government act in concert with its fiduciary obligations to Aboriginal peoples). In the last section of this work certain key assumptions that lie at the heart of this jurisprudence were explored, the result being the charge that neither the legal framework developed, nor the institutional body tasked with developing this framework (the courts of Canada), are appropriate in the context of Crown-Aboriginal relations.

One might wonder, however, at the necessity of entering into the third stage of analysis. Since the discussion in the last section is unlikely to play a role in settling the debate 'on the ground' around the proper relationship between the government and the police in the Aboriginal context, what purpose could it possibly serve?

The response to this sort of challenge is twofold. On the one hand, the sort of discussion found in the third stage of analysis must be presented simply because it lays out axiomatic problems that will forever plague relations between the state and Aboriginal peoples, no matter how 'generous' and 'liberal' judicial and governmental action might become. With the failure to take the first few necessary steps down a fair and just path to reconciliation, the rest of the journey is doomed. On the other hand, and more immediately pressing for the sort of project undertaken in this work, presenting this form of analysis lays out the topography against which the debate over the proper relationship between the state and the police in the Aboriginal context must take place.

Without identifying this landscape some might imagine that the conceptualization of the relationship developed by the Supreme Court is a 'radical' or extreme position from which concessions must be (and most likely would) follow. This, as we noted, is far from the case. Indeed, the position taken by the Court carries with it a demand that Aboriginal peoples across Canada make an initial fundamental concession, a concession that runs so deep as to potentially undermine the ability of Aboriginal communities to work out any sort of acceptable arrangement within Canadian society. Juxtaposed against the true relationship between the Crown and Aboriginal peoples, it can be seen as essentially an attempt to cut off Aboriginal aspirations at their roots. At the very least, this reveals that those who would argue that no unique contextual matters requiring special legal protections arise in conjunction with the debate in the Aboriginal context around police-government relations are either ignorant of Canadian history, or attempting to deploy a tactic only possible within a colonial state.

COMMENTARY BY TONI WILLIAMS AND KIM MURRAY

Shifting the deckchairs on the Titanic once more:
A plea for redundancy in the governance of relationships between the police and Aboriginal peoples.

Gordon Christie's multilayered chapter provokes those working on matters of police governance to confront some fundamental questions about that project – questions arising from Canada's history of imperial colonialisation and contemporary practices of internal colonialization. Christie's analysis disputes the legitimacy of the Canadian state determining the relationships of its institutions – police, courts, governments – to Aboriginal peoples by reference to the logics, law, and politics of its own liberal democratic order, when that state's relationship with

Aboriginal peoples remains unresolved and the proposed liberal democratic terms of that relationship remain contested.

Building on this critique, the chapter exposes the limitations of designing police-governance structures on the basis of contested constructions of relationships between the Canadian state and Aboriginal peoples, such as those that situate Aboriginal peoples as one of many minority groups in Canada, or that frame the relationship in terms of its uniquely fiduciary character. While either of these ways of thinking might be compatible with what Kent Roach describes in this volume as the 'democratic policing' model, this model creates the risk of subordinating and obscuring the need for reconstruction of the fundamental relationship in terms of nation-to-nation reconciliation between the Canadian state and Aboriginal peoples.

Absent such reconstruction, it likely is true that 'little can be said about how the state and the police should interact when the police are interacting with Aboriginal people.'[42] Perhaps something can be said, however, about how the state and the police should *not* interact when interacting with Aboriginal peoples.

Liberal democratic discourses and institutions have not protected Aboriginal peoples in Canada from ongoing practices of displacement and dispossession. These processes will not be held in abeyance, awaiting the arrival of a just and fair relationship between the Canadian state and Aboriginal peoples, since their purpose is to preclude the need to arrive at such a relationship. Ipperwash is not the first – nor the last – occasion on which organized resistance by Aboriginal peoples has been met with force, with threatened or actual violence. Canada has a long history of treating Aboriginal peoples as 'uncivilized' and in need of assimilation or control, a policy first enacted in the 1857 *Gradual Civilization Act*. Policing has played a variety of roles in the processes of dispossession, displacement, and resistance that stem from this policy. Through activities such as raiding longhouses, suppressing potlatch ceremonies, enforcing residential schools policies, and attempting to contain organized resistance, the Canadian state has consistently deployed policing in attempts to repress Aboriginal peoples' aspirations, cultures and rights.[43]

The questions that need to be considered are: what can be said about how the state and the police should not interact in relation to Aboriginal peoples? Can we say these things in ways that are consistent with the decolonizing framework required to ground a nation-to-nation relationship? This comment does not presume to answer these questions;

our goal, rather, is to support their finding a place on the agenda for change. But we have some observations about how that agenda might unfold.

First, one challenge for inquiries, lawyers, and policy makers engaged in institutional design is that the goal is often conceived in terms of replacing a set of institutional arrangements that have failed with one that will work because it will not make the same mistakes. The idea is to build institutional change on the notion of learning from failure. In relation to conventional models of policing, this approach may mean lurching between more police independence or more governance and control, depending on which aspect of the delicate balance is thought to be most in need of fixing.

It may be useful to alter this perspective to one that acknowledges failure as a substantial risk of institutions that purport to restrain the exercise of state power against persons and collectivities exercising rights and asserting claims: we perhaps need to approach the design of institutions such as police governance with a presumption of failure, not a naive assumption of success. This starting point is especially important in relation to Aboriginal peoples because the long history of failure on the part of the state, particularly in relation to the state's exercise of coercive and intrusive powers, has earned their mistrust. From the days of explicit nation building to the present, the institutions and practices that should constrain, control, and hold to account policing, such as human resources policies, command and reporting systems, negotiations, agreement, contract, incentives/deterrents, and sanctions have little record of success in restraining the use of force and the abuse of state power. Contemporary practices of over-policing, under-protection, and repression of Aboriginal peoples show that systemic failure in both policing and its governance continue to be real, live, and ever-present risks in complex unequal societies. The conditions of internal colonialism, documented by the Royal Commission on Aboriginal Peoples and numerous other studies, increase the risk.

Second, Aboriginal peoples in Canada, like indigenous peoples around the world, have collective experiences of five centuries of confronting and surviving the failure of colonial and imperial states to act with honour, integrity, and respect. This unique expertise is an important resource for understanding how to respond to the perpetual risk of failure in governance institutions. To secure the benefit of this expertise at all stages of institutional reform, it may be necessary to develop new dialogic processes to inform and shape institutional change.

Third, given the political and empirical reality of systemic failure in policing, police governance, and government in relation to Aboriginal peoples, it hardly seems plausible to trust one institution over another – as might be suggested by the police autonomy versus control debate – or to believe that police independence is inherently more robust than government oversight. This simple point perhaps does not take the discussion very far, but it indicates the value of 'redundancy' in the design of police governance institutions and practices. A redundancy model of governance relies on multiple, overlapping, and cross-cutting systems of oversight and control, 'in which overlapping (and ostensibly superfluous) accountability mechanisms reduce the centrality of any one of them.'[44] It constructs governance more in terms of a circle, a web, or a network rather than a linear hierarchy. By deploying multiple regulatory devices, each of which has the capacity to work alone, redundancy may offer a proactive and precautionary response to the risk of systemic failure in oversight and governance mechanisms.[45]

One objection to this suggestion is to point out that redundancy already features in the plethora of oversight, control, accountability, normative, and incentive regimes that constitute police governance, where it has offered little protection against the risk of systemic failure when the police interact with Aboriginal peoples and with disadvantaged minority populations.[46] While this observation has some validity, the problem may result from redundancy being an unintended effect of different eras and theories of reform, rather than a deliberate element of institutional design. An embrace of the creative complexity of redundancy may offer instead the possibility of exploiting the conflicts and tensions among different components of police governance in ways that strengthen oversight, control, and participation.[47]

The presumption of systemic institutional failure carries other risks, such as generating cynicism and irresponsibility. It may be demoralizing to give up on the myth of progress – the notion that each institution of governance that a society creates is better than the last. Moreover, we do not suggest that structuring police governance in terms of a presumption of failure and the adoption of redundancy fully responds to Christie's insistence that, absent a new relationship between the state and Aboriginal peoples, 'little can be said about how the state and the police should interact when the police are interacting with Aboriginal people.'[48] Our more limited point is simply that institutional design premised on governance failure, contingency, and redundancy may comport better with what Christie characterizes as the questionable legitimacy of government in the absence of such a new relationship. Ultimately, the development of a structure to govern how the police interact with Aboriginal peoples will not turn on details of institutional design but on an honest and sincere commitment to a decolonizing framework of action, a framework that embodies the core values identified by Aboriginal peoples: truth, reconciliation, reparation, and the reconstruction of the relationship between Aboriginal peoples and the Canadian state.

NOTES

1 On a practical or functional level one could also suggest that an independently operating police – being a self-contained institutional structure – can be much more efficient in promoting public safety and stability.
2 See, for example, *Reference re Secession of Quebec*, [1998] 2 S.C.R. 217 [hereinafter *Quebec Secession Reference*] where protection of minority rights is said to constitute a fundamental constitutional principle, one of four principles said to 'dictate major elements of the architecture of the Constitution itself and [which] are as such its lifeblood' (at 248).
3 Other fundamental rights may be articulated and recognized in statutes (such as human rights statutes and the Canadian *Bill of Rights*), in the common law, and under constitutional conventions and principles.
4 For example, s. 16 of the *Charter of Rights and Freedoms* [being Part I of the *Constitution Act, 1982*, Schedule B to the *Canada Act, 1982* (U.K.), 1982, c. 11] states:

> (1) English and French are the official languages of Canada and have equality of status and equal rights and privileges as to their use in all institutions of the Parliament and government of Canada.
> (2) English and French are the official languages of New Brunswick and have equality of status and equal rights and privileges as to their use in all institutions of the legislature and government of New Brunswick.
> (3) Nothing in this Charter limits the authority of Parliament or a legislature to advance the equality of status or use of English and French.

5 The *Charter of Rights and Freedoms* states under s. 23:

> (1) Citizens of Canada
>   a) whose first language learned and still understood is that of the

English or French linguistic minority population of the province in which they reside, or

b)·who have received their primary school instruction in Canada in English or French and reside in a province where the language in which they received that instruction is the language of the English or French linguistic minority population of the province,

have the right to have their children receive primary and secondary school instruction in that language in that province.

(2) Citizens of Canada of whom any child has received or is receiving primary or secondary school instruction in English or French in Canada, have the right to have all their children receive primary and secondary school instruction in the same language.

(3) The right of citizens of Canada under subsections (1) and (2) to have their children receive primary and secondary school instruction in the language of the English or French linguistic minority population of a province

a) applies wherever in the province the number of children of citizens who have such a right is sufficient to warrant the provision to them out of public funds of minority language instruction; and

b) includes, where the number of those children so warrants, the right to have them receive that instruction in minority language educational facilities provided out of public funds.

6 See, for example, Denise Reaume, 'The Demise of the Political Compromise Doctrine: Have Official Language Use Rights Been Revived?' (2002) 47 McGill L.J. 593; 'Official Language Rights: Intrinsic Value and the Protection of Difference,' in *Citizenship in Diverse Societies: Theory and Practice*, ed. Will Kymlicka (New York: Oxford University Press, 2000); and 'The Constitutional Protection of Language: Security versus Survival,' in *Language and the State: The Law and Politics of Identity*, ed. David Schneiderman (Montreal: Yvon Blais Lté., 1991).

7 The Supreme Court also endorsed this line of reasoning in the *Quebec Secession Reference* at 259: '[A] constitution is entrenched beyond the reach of simple majority rule [because] ... a constitution may seek to ensure that vulnerable minority groups are endowed with the institutions and rights necessary to maintain and promote their identities against the assimilative pressures of the majority.'

8 Thinking of Aboriginal peoples as minority groups (with particular rights legally·protected) draws them into a particular conceptual circle. Understandably, then, under this conceptualization recommendations about

what to do if policing problems arise would be the same whether the policing targets were urban blacks in Toronto or Aboriginals on reserve anywhere in Canada. Numerous commissions of inquiry have looked into policing problems within the context of minority concerns, and many recommendations have been tabled.

9   S. 35(1) of the *Constitution Act, 1982* states that: 'The existing [A]boriginal and treaty rights of the Aboriginal peoples of Canada are hereby recognized and affirmed.'

10   I am distinguishing between the right to hold property, which may be argued to be a human or political right, and the particular rights to property that may be held by parties in Canada.

11   This is the only way to make sense, for example, of the 'inherent limit' placed on Aboriginal title in *Delgamuukw v. British Columbia*, [1997] 3 S.C.R. 1010 [hereinafter *Delgamuukw*]. Lamer CJ, in describing the nature of Aboriginal title, held that while it encompasses the power to use the land in ways which are not tied to traditional practices, traditions, and customs, this power is limited in that the title-holders cannot use the land in a way that might break the traditional connection to the land which established the title in the first place. The reason for this limit, Lamer CJ stated, was to preserve the ability of future generations of Aboriginal peoples to continue to enjoy their title rights in ways which reflect the interests the community traditionally has in the land. Furthermore, the language of treaties makes perfectly clear their prospective nature, reaching out endlessly into the future, protecting the future interests of Aboriginal treaty nations.

12   See, for example, *Law v. Canada (Minister of Employment and Immigration)*, [1999] 1 S.C.R. 497. In this decision the Supreme Court gathered together threads of analysis that had developed around issues of discrimination and advanced a 'guide' to future jurisprudence around s. 15. The heart of this approach is the focus on human dignity – if action by the government is found to treat a group differentially in such a manner as to negatively impact on the dignity of individual members of that group, a court may find that this group has been treated unequally in such a manner as to constitute an affront to constitutional values and principles. This sort of analysis can protect members of minority groups from discrimination, but the analysis does not rest on the notion that members of minority groups have particular rights that warrant protection. In any particular dispute only a right to 'equal treatment' would be at issue.

13   The *Constitution Act, 1982*, at s. 27: 'This Charter shall be interpreted in a manner consistent with the preservation and enhancement of the multicultural heritage of Canadians.'

14 See again, for example, *Quebec Secession Reference.*
15 *R. v. Sparrow*, [1990] 1 S.C.R. 1075 [hereinafter *Sparrow*].
16 *R. v. Gladstone*, [1996] 2 S.C.R. 723.
17 *R. v. Badger*, [1996] 1 S.C.R. 771.
18 *R. v. Marshall*, [1999] 3 S.C.R. 456 [hereinafter *Marshall*].
19 In R. v. Van der Peet, [1996] 2 S.C.R. 507 [hereinafter *Van der Peet*], Lamer
    CJ developed a test for the establishment of Aboriginal rights which
    demands of the claimant that they demonstrate that the present activity
    said to fall under the right be continuous with a practice, tradition, or
    custom integral to the culture of the people claiming the right at the time
    of contact with Europeans. While this suggests a cultural grounding for
    these rights, this test is meant not to suggest *why* these rights are accorded
    protection in s. 35, but rather *how to identify* rights which are so protected.
    Elsewhere Lamer CJ states that the reason for the protection accorded
    these rights lies in the need to reconcile the prior presence of organized
    Aboriginal societies to the sovereignty of the Crown (see the discussion
    beginning at para. 39). Clearly any sort of 'cultural' grounding would
    make no sense for treaty rights, which come out of sacred agreements
    establishing fundamental ways in which two sets of peoples would co-
    exist over one territory.
20 *Van der Peet.*
21 *Delgamuukw.*
22 The existence of a fiduciary relationship (as opposed to a political relation-
    ship, or a pure trust relationship) was introduced in the context of land
    surrenders in *R. v. Guerin*, [1984] 2 S.C.R. 335. In *Sparrow*, the general
    relationship between the Crown and Aboriginal peoples was characterized
    as fiduciary in nature (which structured the sort of process of justification
    in which the Crown would have to engage when it acted to infringe
    Aboriginal rights).
23 This was especially highlighted in *Marshall*. More recently this notion of
    the honour of the Crown has taken on added significance, as the Supreme
    Court has relied on this concept to underpin a structural framework of
    interim measures (duties to consult and accommodate) designed to protect
    from undue Crown interference Aboriginal and treaty rights that have been
    asserted but not yet proven or established in litigation or negotiations. See
    Haida Nation v. British Columbia (Minister of Forests), [2004] 3 S.C.R. 511;
    Taku River Tlingit First Nation v. British Columbia (Project Assessment Direc-
    tor), [2004] 3 S.C.R. 550; and *Mikisew Cree First Nation v. Canada (Minister of*
    Canadian Heritage), [2005] 3 S.C.R. 388.
24 See, for example, remarks in *R. v. Keegstra*, [1990] 3 S.C.R. 697. At page 728

the Court also noted that prior to the arrival of the *Charter* and the rights protected in s. 2, political expression formed the core of expressive content protected under the right to free speech (as valued in democratic societies). The *Charter* continues to protect political expression, but broadens the scope of application of the right to free speech protected under s. 2(b).

25 The *Charter of Rights and Freedoms*, s. 2 (c) and (d).

26 See, e.g., *Committee for the Commonwealth of Canada v. Canada*, [1990] 1 S.C.R. 139.

27 See, e.g., in Kent Roach's discussion in this volume of certain authorities (for example, Pierre Elliot Trudeau) who have taken this side of the issue.

28 This is, in essence, the context for the cases cited in footnote 23 as the Haida Nation, the Taku River Tlingit First Nation, and the Mikisew Cree First Nation were asserting rights that were yet 'unsettled' (at least in the eyes of the Canadian state – the Haida, Taku River Tlingit, and Mikisew Cree likely have well-formed visions of their rightful claims).

29 Roach and Sossin's chapters in this volume.

30 *Sparrow*.

31 See, e.g., *Frame v. Smith*, [1987] 2 S.C.R. 99; *Lac Minerals Ltd. v. International Corona Resources Ltd.*, [1989] 2 S.C.R. 574; and *Hodgkinson v. Simms et al.*, [1994] 3 S.C.R. 377.

32 *Osoyoos Indian Band v. Oliver (Town)*, [2001] 3 S.C.R. 746.

33 *Gladstone* and *Delgamuukw*. While the notion of respecting Aboriginal interests is raised in these cases in the discussion of how the Crown might justify legislative infringement of Aboriginal rights and/or title, this discussion is informed by the fiduciary considerations attached to the relationship between the Crown and Aboriginal rights-holders.

34 D.W.M. Waters, *The Law of Trusts in Canada*, 2nd ed. (Toronto: Carswell, 1984).

35 One issue definitively resolved in the *Haida Nation*, *Taku River Tlingit* and *Mikisew Cree First Nation* decisions was that of the purported requirement that an Aboriginal or treaty right be established (either in a court of law or through a negotiated agreement) before any obligations befall the Crown. At the Court of Appeal level in British Columbia this requirement was invalidated, with the Court holding that it is sufficient for the generation of obligations on the Crown that a prima facie case for the existence of the claimed right(s) be made out. See *Haida Nation v. British Columbia (Minister of Forests)*, [2002], B.C.C.A. 462, and *Taku River Tlingit First Nation v. Ringstad*, [2002] B.C.C.A. 59. The Supreme Court upheld this position, finding that the honour of the Crown acted to generate legal obligations in

relation to Aboriginal and treaty rights, even before they were definitively
defined and established either in court or by way of negotiations.

36 *Wewaykum Indian Band v. Canada*, [2002] 4 S.C.R. 245 [hereinafter
Wewaykum], at para. 79 (citing the acceptance of such a proposition by
the full court in *Ross River Dena Council Band v. Canada*, [2002] 2 S.C.R.
816).

37 *Wewaykum*, at para. 83.

38 Ibid. at para 81.

39 'Somewhat associated with the ethical standards required of a fiduciary in
the context of the Crown and Aboriginal peoples is the need to uphold the
"honour of the Crown."' *Wewaykum,* at para. 80 (noting with approval the
use of the notion of the honour of the Crown in *Van der Peet* and *Marshall*).

40 *Sparrow*.

41 This is not to say that the application of the rule of law is not entirely
welcome in the context of state-Aboriginal relations, for the prominence of
the rule of law may act to assuage a valid and central concern of Aboriginal communities. These communities are distrustful (and rightfully so) of
the motives and plans of both federal and provincial Crowns. If the governments of Canada are constricted in their activities in relation to Aboriginal communities and their interests, this can act to displace some of
the accumulated distrust. Given that the position we are discussing in this
last section is unlikely to have a practical effect upon the state and its
courts, at least one can hope that the prominent role accorded the law acts
to channel government action into paths more respectful of Aboriginal
peoples.

We also noted in the previous section, however, that under this model of
police-state interaction the courts take on an important role, for they must
(a) monitor the degree to which the governments of Canada act to respect
their fiduciary obligations, and (b) work as best they can to hold the
governments to the task of meeting their duties. The courts themselves,
though, cannot fall under a similar body of substantive law, one that could
constrict their activities in relation to Aboriginal communities and their
interests, unless they decide to put themselves into such a box. Presumably, then, they would also come to have to undertake to monitor their
own activities, and to hold themselves accountable to the law they introduced to govern the relationship between the judiciary and Aboriginal
peoples.

42 Gordon Christie's chapter in this volume at 147.

43 Andrew Ortin, 'When the Law Breaks Down: Aboriginal Peoples in

Canada and Government Defiance of the Rule of Law' (2003) 41 Osgoode Hall L.J. 455.
44 Colin Scott, 'Accountability in the Regulatory State' (2000) 27 Journal of Law and Society 38 at 52.
45 John Braithwaite, 'Accountability and Governance under the New Regulatory State' (1999) 58 Australian Journal of Public Administration 90.
46 Canada, Royal Commission on Aboriginal Peoples, *Report* (Ottawa: Queen's Printer, 1997). Ontario, Report of the Commission on Systematic Racism in the Ontario Criminal Justice System (Toronto: Queen's Printer for Ontario, 1995).
47 Scott, 'Accountability.'
48 Christie in this volume at 170.

4 The Idea of the Political 'Independence' of the Police: International Interpretations and Experiences

PHILIP STENNING

Science must begin with myths, and with the criticism of myths.

Karl Popper, 'The Philosophy of Science' (1957)

Abstract

This chapter serves to clarify some of the key concepts with respect to the political independence of the police. By graphically illustrating the relationship between degrees of 'control' and degrees of accountability it is argued that the two concepts are not incompatible. The term 'independence' is used in the chapter to refer only to decision making that falls in what is pictured as the fourth quadrant: 'full accountability' with 'no control.' The chapter then outlines the scope or range of the potentially independent decision-making tasks.

    Relationships between the police and governments have proven to be a source of persistent difficulty and controversy in many countries of the world. In this chapter the experiences of and debates over this relationship in Britain, Australia, and New Zealand during the last three decades are reviewed and discussed. The analysis discloses that, despite similar legal and constitutional traditions, the relationships between the police and governments have played out quite differently in the three jurisdictions. There is, however, a common trend towards greater and more detailed political accountability of the police in all three countries. Somewhat ironically, in Britain, the birthplace of the now common notion of 'police independence,' recent developments have most threatened this doctrine of police autonomy from political influence and direction. In all three countries, however, the impact of more generalized public service reforms (the so-called new public management) has made more inroads into the practical political independence of the police than any explicit retreat from established legal doctrine on this subject.

  A growing disparity between the practices of governments and the conservatism of judicial pronouncements on police independence is apparent in all three jurisdictions. This is most clearly manifest in movements towards legislative specification of the parameters of the police-government relationship, in preference to reliance on judicial rulings on the subject. In all three countries, however, governments have been reluctant to concede to police any right to complete immunity from political influence or direction with respect to the handling of major public order challenges, such as political demonstrations.

Introduction: The Concept of 'Independence'

The concept of 'independence' in governance has a number of dimensions, and it is important to identify these before considering how it has evolved in the context of policing in different jurisdictions. Essentially, 'independence' refers to autonomy in decision making, that is, freedom from control, direction, or undue influence by others. It may be considered as a feature of the *internal management* of an organization – as reflected, for instance, in the idea, which is sometimes floated, that a police constable is not subject to direction from superiors in deciding whether to arrest and charge someone[1] – or as a feature of the *external relations* of an organization – as reflected, for instance, in the idea that, with respect to certain policing decisions, the police should not be subject to direction by a police governing authority such as a police services board or a minister. Independence thus always implies some kind of constraint on a particular relationship.

Independence and Accountability

While independence is usually alluded to in terms of freedom from control or direction, some (especially in the policing context) use the term more broadly to refer to freedom from requirements of *accountability* as well. It is important, therefore, to be clear as to the relationship between the two concepts of independence and accountability. In this chapter, I adopt a formulation of this relationship that I have elaborated elsewhere, and which is derived from an observation by Goldring and Wettenhall in an article published in 1980: 'When we speak of the responsibility of statutory authorities, we are referring to two parallel

Figure 4.1

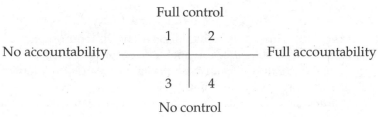

Full control

No accountability   1 | 2   Full accountability
—————————+—————————
3 | 4

No control

and interlocking mechanisms. The first is the mechanism of control, which extends from the controlling person or institution to the controlled statutory authority. The second is the mechanism of answerability or accountability. The control mechanism provides a means for ensuring that the statutory authority acts, or refrains from acting, in certain ways. The answerability mechanism provides information to the controller, and may indicate the occasions in which the control mechanism is to be brought into play.'[2] Graphically, the relationship between these two 'parallel and interlocking mechanisms' is displayed in figure 4.1. It can be seen that when people speak of 'independence' as freedom from both control and accountability, they are speaking of decision making as lying in quadrant 3 of the diagram, whereas when they use the term to refer only to freedom from control or direction, they are speaking of decision making as lying in quadrant 4. The distinction is critical, as I shall discuss further below, so it is important to keep it in mind in any discussion of 'independence.' It indicates that independence and accountability need not necessarily be considered to be incompatible or inconsistent characteristics of an office or organization.[3] Throughout this chapter, I use the term 'independence' in its more limited sense to refer only to decision making that falls within quadrant 4 of figure 4.1, and so regard independence as entirely compatible with substantial accountability requirements.

The Scope of Independence

Of course, independence may be claimed (or conceded) with respect to *all or most* of an organization's or official's decision making (as is the case generally, for instance, with judicial independence), or with respect only to certain (more or less clearly specified) areas of decision making. In this regard, it may be helpful, in discussing the *scope* of independence, to differentiate between the following subjects of decision making:

1 *Resourcing*. How much, and what kinds of, funds, equipment, staffing, and so forth will be made available to an organization
2 *Organizational structure and management*. How the organization will be structured, organized, and managed.
3 *Organizational policies*. General policies that the organization will be expected to adhere to in its operations.
4 *Priority setting*. The determination of priorities with respect to how the resources of the organization will be deployed.
5 *Deployment*. How the organization will deploy the resources available to it, either generally or in particular circumstances.
6 *Specific operational decision making*. How a particular operation will be handled and managed.

The dividing line between the last two of these subjects is certainly the most difficult to delineate with any precision, and doing so has been one of the most common stumbling blocks in achieving any consensus on the scope and limits of any concept of police independence. In democracies at least, it is rare that any official or organization is recognized as enjoying independence with respect to all these areas of decision making. Determining to which of these areas the independence of an official or organization relates, therefore, is very important to understanding what that official's or organization's independence implies for its external relationships.

The Concept of 'Police Independence'

As in other areas of governance, the concept of police independence embraces a number of different ideas. First, as noted above, it may be applied to relations *within* a police organization (e.g., between a constable and his or her superior officers) or to an organization's *external* relations with others (e.g., with a governing authority, or with 'government' more generally). In this chapter, I consider police independence only as it may apply to the external relations of police.

Second, even limiting one's attention to police independence as a feature of the police's external relations, a variety of external relationships may be considered. Thus, for instance, one might consider relations between the police and their governing authority, relations between the police and ministers or other elected officials or their 'political' staff or assistants, relations between the police and other public servants, relations between the police and the courts, relations between the police and prosecutors, relations between the police and the media, relations between the police and members of the general public or representatives of special interest groups, and so on and so on. In this chapter, because of the particular concerns of the Ipperwash Inquiry in commissioning it, my attention is focused almost exclusively on the *political* independence of the police, that is, on the external relations between the police and elected officials and their 'political' staff or assistants, and other public servants such as departmental staff. Other aspects of external police independence – in particular, the relations between police and the courts – will also occasionally be referred to.

The doctrine of police independence, to the extent that there is any agreement at all about its content, intent, and implications, amounts essentially to a proscription against certain kinds of external (especially political) intervention in, or influence over, decision making by police with respect to a limited range of matters. It is identifiable not so much as a clear-cut set of rules with self-explanatory application but as a broad legal principle typically expressed in rather general terms, the precise content, meaning, scope, and application of which have been the subject of little or no consensus in the various jurisdictions in which it has been recognized.

Contrary to the claims of some commentators, it is not a long-established legal doctrine with an accepted or undisputed pedigree. Rather, the historical-legal pedigree claimed for political independence by its most committed proponents has been effectively discredited by almost every legal scholar who has carefully examined it.

The kinds of decisions to which the doctrine has been said to be applicable have variously been described as 'quasi-judicial' or 'law enforcement' decisions in 'particular cases' (what, under the categories I itemized earlier, would be considered specific operational law enforcement decisions). The precise meaning, scope, and application of such terms, however, have remained matters of debate, particularly when invoked in reference to the kinds of tactical decisions that police may find themselves having to make in undertaking public order policing in circumstances such as those that prevailed at Ipperwash in September 1995. Furthermore, as I shall illustrate, some formulations of the doctrine claim a much broader scope for it, including, for instance, 'law enforcement' policy, priority setting, and general deployment decisions.

An Idea with a Quite Restricted Passport

It is important to note at the outset that the doctrine of police independence is unique to certain common law jurisdictions and, at least until
very recently, has been entirely the creation of judicial pronouncement
(either from the bench or through the reports of commissions of inquiry), having no clear constitutional or statutory basis. In fact, in
Canada and in many other common law jurisdictions, as I shall illustrate, it has not been easily reconcilable with apparently clear statutory
language concerning the governance of police.

Equally important to note is that the doctrine is by no means equally
recognized in all common law jurisdictions. One can search case law
and relevant literature in the United States largely in vain, for instance,
for any significant recognition of, let alone commitment to, the doctrine
of police independence as it has been articulated in countries such as
England and Canada. The same is to a lesser extent true for Scotland.[4]
Interestingly, one of the features of police governance that distinguishes
these two jurisdictions from those common law jurisdictions in which
the doctrine has been recognized is the relationship between the police
and prosecutorial authorities. Specifically, in both the United States and
in Scotland, the tradition has been that with respect to the conduct of
criminal investigations (i.e., with respect to those 'quasi-judicial' decisions to which the English Royal Commission on the Police referred as
the foundation for the doctrine of police independence), the police are
subject to direction by, and are accountable to, prosecutors (the district
attorney in the United States, the procurator fiscal in Scotland).

Outside common law jurisdictions, the doctrine of police independence, as formulated in common law jurisprudence, is virtually unheard of. Institutional arrangements for the governance of the police in
the Netherlands provide a good illustration of the approach to such
issues in continental European countries. In that country, the governance of municipal police services is accomplished through what have
been described as 'three-cornered' or 'triangular' discussions, or 'trilat-
eral consultations,' between three appointed officials: the police chief,
the burgomeister (mayor), and the local prosecutor. In theory at least,
the police chief is subordinate to the other two officials with respect to
all major police decisions. With respect to criminal investigations and
charges, the police chief is subject to the direction of the prosecutor (as
in Scotland). Responsibility for decisions concerning public order policing, however, rests firmly and indisputably with the burgomeister, from

whom the police chief is bound to accept and follow instructions with respect to such matters. In practice, as might be expected, prosecutors and burgomeisters commonly defer to the professional expertise of police chiefs with respect to routine and non-controversial police decisions, but no one in the Netherlands would suggest that such practical deference confers any legal 'independence' on police chiefs with respect to such decisions.[5]

Of course, there is no less concern to avoid undesirable partisan or special interest influence over police decision making in the United States or Scotland or continental European countries than in countries like England, Canada, Australia, and New Zealand, which I will be focusing on in the remainder of this chapter. Rather, what the governance arrangements in these countries demonstrate is that the common law doctrine of 'police independence' is not the only mechanism through which such concerns may be addressed and such undesirable influences averted. In fact, this mechanism is recognized and accepted in a small minority of countries in the world, and not even in all of those having a common law tradition. I think that this is an important point for the Commission of Inquiry to keep in mind when considering the issue of relations between police and the government.

Doctrinal Origins

The doctrine of police independence has historically been associated with the development of modern public police forces in the United Kingdom, subsequently being to a greater or lesser extent adopted and applied to police services in other countries that were modelled on those in Britain. As I have elaborated elsewhere, police institutions in common law countries are traceable to two quite distinct models that were developed in the United Kingdom: the Royal Irish Constabulary (RIC) model and the 'London Met' model.[6] The former, on which the provincial police services as well as the Royal Canadian Mounted Police (RCMP) and its predecessor, the North West Mounted Police, in Canada were modelled, was characterized by military or quasi-military organization, tradition, and rank structures, and was typically under the direct governance of a designated government minister. The London Met model, by contrast, was designed as a more civilian institution. While the original example of this model was headed by two commissioners who were justices of the peace and answerable to the English home secretary, subsequent municipal and county adaptations featured chief constables or chiefs of police as the heads of police organizations and various kinds of local 'police authorities' or 'police commissions' (later 'police services boards' in Ontario) as the principal governing authorities to whom such chief constables and chiefs of police were primarily accountable. Most of the police forces that Britain established in its overseas colonies during the nineteenth and early twentieth centuries were originally based on the RIC model rather than the London Met model, and in many of those countries (such as New Zealand) there is still only one, national police service accountable directly to the national government.

This is an important distinction to keep in mind because the earliest (nineteenth-century) judicial decisions identified as having provided the juridical foundation from which the modern doctrine of police independence later emerged were almost all concerned with the civil and administrative relationships between local municipal police forces and their local governments or local police authorities or police commissions. Only later, in the twentieth century, notably in Australia, did legal principles developed in these early decisions come to be invoked and applied in cases involving police forces based on the RIC model (i.e., those, such as the Ontario Provincial Police [OPP], headed by commissioners who were directly answerable to designated government ministers). Principles that were originally developed to govern legal relations between local police forces and their local employers, in the context of claims of civil liability and employment relations,[7] were thus questionably applied to relations of governance and accountability between members of state, provincial or national police forces, and the government ministers responsible for them. And, as I noted earlier, and will illustrate further below, such principles were commonly, on their face, incompatible with apparently clear statutory language delineating such relations.

Experience with the Doctrine in Three Common Law Jurisdictions

Despite all the questionable aspects of it to which I have referred, the doctrine of the political independence of the police has flourished and received almost totemic and enduring recognition and respect in several common law jurisdictions, including Canada. In what follows, I consider the history of, and recent developments in the doctrine in Britain (at least, in England and Wales), Australia, and New Zealand. In each case I focus on developments during the last thirty to forty years.

1. England and Wales

As I noted earlier, the modern doctrine of police independence was a creation of the English judiciary, and originated in judicial decisions in cases in which the extent to which the police were subject to political direction or control was not the principal concern. Rather, the legal issue involved in these cases was whether the relationship between a police officer and the government that hired and paid him was the legal relationship of 'master and servant' for the purposes, respectively, of the liability of the corporation for the wrongful actions of the police officer,[8] and a suit for compensation for the loss of his services when he was injured. In these cases it was held that a police officer is not to be considered a 'servant' for these purposes.[9] Geoffrey Marshall, in his 1965 book *Police and Government*, has exhaustively examined and critiqued this earlier case law, and there is no need for me to repeat his analysis here. Suffice it to say that he concluded that certain judicial *obiter dicta*[10] in these cases that were subsequently cited as the basis for a doctrine of the political independence of the police were neither doctrinally sound nor necessary for the decisions in these earlier cases.

In its 1962 report, the Royal Commission on the Police, having reviewed some of these earlier cases, concluded that 'these judgments establish the legal status of the constable today beyond doubt,' and noted that in submissions to it, police witnesses had 'relied upon them in asserting the immunity of all ranks of the police service from interference or control by a police authority or anyone else in the discharge of their police duties.' The commission commented that 'this claim leads to some odd and awkward consequences which it is our duty now to examine.'[11]

Remarking that 'it appears odd that the constable enjoys a traditional status which implies a degree of independence belied by his subordinate rank in the force,' the commission argued that this 'anomalous situation' is justified by the fact that

> the constable, in carrying out many of the purposes we described at the beginning of this chapter, ought to be manifestly impartial and uninfluenced by external pressures. For much of the time he is not acting under orders and must rely on his own discretion and knowledge of the law. This consideration applies with particular force to police activities that are sometimes described as 'quasi-judicial,' such as inquiries in regard to suspected offences, the arrest of persons and the decision to prosecute.[12]

In matters of this kind it is clearly in the public interest that a police officer should be answerable only to his superiors in the force and, to the extent that a matter may come before them, to the courts. His impartiality would be jeopardised, and public confidence in it shaken, if in this field he were to be made the servant of too local a body.' (25)

This passage from the commission's report provides a good illustration of how easily essential concepts become confused in the debate about police independence. For while the passage seems to start out with a concern about 'external pressures' (such as direction, control, or influence – the indicia of *control*), the commission concludes that the public interest in avoiding such pressures justifies that a police officer should be 'answerable' only to his superiors in the force and to the courts in 'matters of this kind' (thus referring to a constable's *accountability*). As I have pointed out earlier, however, there is no logical inevitability in such a conclusion (that protecting a person from unwanted control necessarily requires limiting his or her accountability). In fact, an opposite conclusion (that the greater a person's independence, the greater and more transparent should be his or her accountability for its exercise in a liberal democracy – a position that the commission actually eventually took) may well be preferable. Yet such conceptual confusion has unfortunately permeated much of the debate over police independence, both in England and elsewhere, as I shall illustrate further in this chapter.

The commission went on to consider the position of chief constables and whether (and if so in what respects) it was or ought to be different from that of constables generally. After noting that the position of chief constables vis-à-vis their police authorities was 'unsatisfactory and confused,' the commission also noted that 'the duties which it was generally agreed in the evidence should be performed by chief constables unhampered by any kind of external control are not capable of precise definition, but they cover broadly what we referred to earlier as 'quasi-judicial' matters, that is, the enforcement of the criminal law in particular cases involving, for example, the pursuit of inquiries and decisions to arrest and to prosecute' (30).[13] On this, the commission concluded: 'We entirely accept that it is in the public interest that a chief constable, in dealing with these quasi-judicial matters, should be free from the conventional processes of democratic control and influence. We therefore recognise a field, wider in England than in Scotland,[14] in which the present legal status of the chief constable is clearly justified by the purposes of his appointment, namely the field of law enforcement in relation to particular cases' (30).

The commission then went on to consider the position of chief constables with respect to 'activities other than the enforcement of the law in particular cases' (31), which it described in the following terms:

The range of these activities is wide, and the present legal status of the chief constable is widely regarded as providing him with unfettered discretion in their exercise – although, as we said earlier, the Association of Municipal Corporations question this. Thus he is accountable to no-one[15] and subject to no-one's orders, for the way in which, for example, he settles his general policies in regard to law enforcement over the area covered by his force, the disposition of his force, the concentration of his resources on any particular type of crime or area, the manner in which he handles political demonstrations or processions and allocates and instructs his men when preventing breaches of the peace arising from industrial disputes, the methods he employs in dealing with an outbreak of violence or of passive resistance to authority, his policy in enforcing the traffic laws and in dealing with parked vehicles, and so on. (31)

It will be noted that this list includes many of the categories of decisions that I listed earlier in this chapter.

The commission concluded: 'It cannot in our view be said that duties of the kind which we have described require the complete immunity from external influence that is generally acknowledged to be necessary in regard to the enforcement of the law in particular cases' (31). Accordingly, the commission canvassed three options with respect to decision making by chief constables on such matters. Under the first option, 'while the chief constable would continue to enjoy immunity to orders, he would nevertheless be exposed to advice and guidance of which he would be expected to take heed. If he persistently disregarded and flouted such advice his fitness for office would be in question. In this manner an element of supervision would be exercised over the chief constable's actions, but there would be no interference with law enforcement in particular cases' (32). The second option that the commission considered as 'another way of improving the control over chief constables without altering their present legal status' was 'to increase the cohesion of separate forces by strengthening the links between them, and by superimposing over the whole police service a more effective system of Government inspection' (32). The third option was 'to place chief constables under the direct control of either the local or the central government, and so to convert their present legal status to the status of local authority or Crown servants' (32–3).

The commission rejected outright the option of subordinating chief constables to the direct control of local authorities, as this would not, in the commission's view, 'make for the preservation of the impartiality of the police in enforcing the law' (33). What it recommended instead was a combination of the first and second options.

Specifically, the commission recommended that local police authorities should be recognized as having legitimate authority to call for confidential reports from their chief constables on 'activities other than the enforcement of the law in particular cases' (31), and to offer 'advice and guidance' (54) to the chief constable on such matters. By way of a check on possible abuse of this authority, the commission recommended that a chief constable should have the right to refuse to submit a report to the police authority 'on police activities concerned with law enforcement' (54),[16] subject to a determination of the matter by the home secretary. The commission described the relationship it thus envisaged between a police authority and its chief constable in the following terms:

> the authority's role cannot, under the arrangements which we propose, extend beyond the giving of advice; and it will not be entitled to give orders or instructions to a chief constable on matters connected with policing. Thus the relationship between a police authority and its chief constable will in this field differ from that between other council committees and their chief officers. In the latter case the role of the official is to advise the committee and to implement its decisions on matters of policy; but the decisions themselves are the responsibility of the elected body. In the case of the police these positions will be reversed. The role of the police authority will be to advise the chief constable on general matters connected with the policing of the area; but decisions will be the responsibility of the chief constable alone. However, the lack of local control which this relationship implies will be offset by increasing a chief constable's accountability for his actions, and also by improvements in the cohesion of separate police forces, in ways we discuss in the next chapter, designed to make the police function more effectively as a national body. (55)

In addition to this advisory role, a police authority would also have a role, in conjunction with the central home secretary, in removing a chief constable from office on grounds either of personal misconduct or 'because he has ceased to be effective and no longer enjoys its confidence in his ability to command the force properly' (57).

While the commission thus recommended that chief constables should enjoy a very substantial and broad measure of political independence vis-à-vis their local police authorities, it also recommended that they be subject to a much greater degree of control, other than with respect to matters of law enforcement in particular cases, by the home secretary with the assistance of inspectors of constabulary. The commission summarized these recommended powers of the home secretary in the following terms:

> Ministers will not merely be entitled to intervene in the local administration of the police where they have reason to suspect inefficiency: they will have a duty to do so. The administrative attitude of the central Departments towards police affairs will thus become positive. Their responsibility will be not merely to correct inefficiency, but to promote efficiency. With the advice of a strong professional element, incorporating a central research unit, they will for the first time be in a position to raise standards of equipment and of policing uniformly throughout the country. The development of a comprehensive manpower policy will promote the most economical and effective deployment of men. Forces too small to be thoroughly efficient will be amalgamated with others to make larger units. All forces will be commanded by chief constables appointed with the full approval of the Secretary of State, and their continued tenure office will also be subject to his approval. There will be effective arrangements to secure the collaboration of groups of forces and to provide ancillary services. All this activity will have the backing of statutory powers; and with these, and the power to call for reports, the Secretaries of State will be accountable to Parliament for the efficient policing of the whole country. (98)

Although the details are not always self-evident from the commission's report, let me now try to summarize the idea of 'police independence' that seems to emerge from the Commission's report, in terms of the six categories of decision making that I listed earlier:

1 *Resourcing*: Together, the police authority and the home secretary would have ultimate control over these decisions (i.e., no 'police independence' here).

2 *Organizational structure and management*: Within the resources available to him or her, a chief constable would enjoy a large measure of independence from control over such matters by the police authority, but would be subject to considerable direct and indirect control on such matters by the home secretary.
3 *Organizational policies*: The police authority would have no power of control over these, but the home secretary could set general policies to be adhered to by all police forces.
4 *Priority setting*: Same as for organizational policies, but the chief constable's independence with respect to such decisions would likely be somewhat greater.
5 *Deployment*: The police authority would have no control over these decisions, but the home secretary could, I think, exercise considerable influence, if not direct control, over *general* deployment decisions. The chief constable would enjoy complete independence with respect to deployment decisions in particular circumstances.
6 *Specific operational decision making*: The chief constable would enjoy complete political independence with respect to 'quasi-judicial' law enforcement decisions (i.e., decisions re investigation, arrest, and prosecution in individual cases). With respect to other operational decision making, the commission's report is not specific.

The commission drew a clear distinction between direction and control ('orders' or 'instructions') on the one hand, and 'guidance and advice' on the other. Specifically, chief constables could be called upon to provide reports (accountability) to their police authorities, and would not be immune to 'guidance and advice' from them, on any matter in categories 2 to 5 with respect to which police authorities were precluded from giving orders or instructions. The commission's report is not clear, however, as to whether police authorities would be permitted to call for such reports or offer such advice and guidance with respect to matters other than 'quasi-judicial law enforcement decisions in particular cases' in category 6.

I have described the recommendations of the Royal Commission on the Police on these matters in considerable detail because it can fairly be said that they more or less set the broad contours (although not always the more precise details) of the idea of 'police independence' in Britain since its report was presented in 1962, and have had enormous influence over the development of the concept in other common law jurisdictions.

Within six years of the publication of the commission's report, in fact, the idea of 'police independence' that it had explored so carefully had become deeply and seemingly irrevocably entrenched in the thinking of police leaders, politicians, judges, academic commentators, and others interested in matters of police governance in Britain. The main 'tripartite' structure of police governance (chief constables, police authorities, and the home secretary) that the commission had recommended was legislated, with some modification, in the *Police Act, 1964*. Other than by implication, however, the act did not spell out the scope and limits of 'police independence.'

The following year, Geoffrey Marshall published his seminal and influential book, *Police and Government*, in which he disputed the doctrinal authenticity of the idea of police independence that the commission had embraced, argued against it as a sound basis for police governance, and referred to it as a thesis that 'exaggerated and inconsistent as it is, remains a hardy one and it has almost taken on the character of a new principle of the constitution whilst nobody was looking.'[17] He also argued that the 1964 act had not even successfully implemented the commission's recommendation that police policies should be subject to effective local challenge, guidance, and advice. On the issue of 'the proper limits of intervention by police authorities in policing and law enforcement,' however, Marshall offered the following conclusions and suggestions:

First: an obvious limitation is that they cannot without exceeding their powers issue instructions which would involve a chief officer in a breach of statutorily imposed duty or which would amount to a conspiracy on their own part to pervert the course of justice.

Secondly: in matters affecting the institution and withdrawal of prosecutions their powers as police authority should not be regarded as essentially different from those of the Home Secretary as police authority for the metropolitan area. As a matter of sound administrative practice, intervention in routine prosecution matters should be excluded. There may, however, be exceptions which cannot be set out in any simple formula. They may relate to particular policies adopted in the prosecutions of offences or exceptional particular cases. In all except the most extreme cases intervention would be expected to take the form of advice rather than a specific instruction. In extreme cases, however, instructions ought not to be ruled out, and no general legal principle does rule them out.

Thirdly: in matters, other than the institution of prosecutions, which affect the disposition of police forces, the methods used in policing and the enforcement of the law, administrative morality ought to restrict the intervention in a chief constable's sphere of decision. But it is in this sphere, particularly, that executive decisions may be made and policies followed which ought on at least some occasions to be open to an effective challenge by the public and their elected representatives issuing where necessary in police authority directions.[18]

Marshall's heretical views[19] found no favour with police leaders, the judiciary, or the government of the day, although they attracted support from left-wing local and national politicians, academics, and social activists. Within three years of the publication of his book, the English Court of Appeal was to expound a doctrine of police independence that was far broader even than that which had been advocated by the Royal Commission. In the case of *R. v. Metropolitan Police Commissioner ex parte Blackburn*, the Master of the Rolls, Lord Denning, expressed the doctrine in the following terms:

> I have no hesitation ... in holding that, like every constable in the land, [the Commissioner of the London Metropolitan Police] should be, and is, independent of the executive. He is not subject to the orders of the Secretary of State, save that under the Police Act 1964 the Secretary of State can call on him to give a report, or to retire in the interests of efficiency. I hold it to be the duty of the Commissioner of Police, as it is of every chief constable, to enforce the law of the land. He must take steps so to post his men that crimes may be detected; and that honest citizens may go about their affairs in peace. He must decide whether or not suspected persons are to be prosecuted; and, if need be, bring the prosecution or see that it is brought; but in all these things he is not the servant of anyone, save of the law itself. No Minister of the Crown can tell him that he must, or must not, keep observation on this place or that; or that he must, or must not, prosecute this man or that one. Nor can any police authority tell him so. The responsibility for law enforcement lies on him. He is answerable to the law and to the law alone.[20]

Despite the fact that one of the many critics of this statement has commented that it deserves quotation in full 'because seldom have so many errors of law and logic been compressed into one paragraph,'[21] Lord Denning's exposition of the doctrine of police independence in the *Blackburn* case remains today the most oft-quoted statement of the doctrine by its proponents in Britain, Canada, Australia, and New Zealand, to the point that the doctrine is now not infrequently referred to as 'the *Blackburn* doctrine,' and the *Blackburn* decision itself as the 'police chief's bible.'[22] If he had had copyright over his statement, Lord Denning would have been able to retire a lot sooner than he did.

Although he provided an illustrative list of decisions with respect to which every chief constable enjoys complete political independence, Lord Denning's statement of the doctrine seems to suggest that chief constables enjoy such independence with respect to every aspect of 'law enforcement,' and that 'law enforcement' embraces almost every aspect of policing policy, priority setting, and deployment. Furthermore, his statement, like the formulation of the doctrine by the Royal Commission before him, completely confounds the concepts of control and accountability. According to Lord Denning, a chief constable's independence with respect to 'law enforcement' renders him immune not only to political direction on such matters, but also to any requirement for political accountability ('he is answerable to the law and to the law alone') for such matters.

Despite its obvious shortcomings, Lord Denning's statement of the doctrine of police independence in *Blackburn* has effectively become the locus classicus on the subject in common law countries around the world, as well as in England itself, thus seemingly ensuring continued disagreement and confusion about its scope, application, and implications. In England, the statement has been cited and endorsed in several subsequent judicial decisions. In 1981, Lord Denning himself cited his own earlier statement in declining to issue mandamus against the chief constable of the Devon and Cornwall Constabulary, in *R. v. Chief Constable of the Devon and Cornwall Constabulary, ex parte Central Electricity Generating Board*.[23] Seven years later, a differently constituted Court of Appeal cited the statement with approval in *R. v. Secretary of State for the Home Department, ex parte Northumbria Police Authority*.[24] And in 1999 the statement received approval from the House of Lords in *R. v. Chief Constable of Sussex, ex parte International Trader's Ferry Ltd*.[25] It can thus be stated with confidence that, in judicial minds at least, the Denning statement currently represents the law on this topic in England and Wales.

During the thirty-six years since the *Blackburn* case was decided, discussion of the doctrine has largely been focused on political contestation (particularly over the respective roles of the three participants in the 'tripartite' arrangements for local police governance in England and

Wales) over the practical application and implications of the doctrine. The main context in which such discussion occurred was the conflict in the 1980s between the Thatcher Conservative government, Labour-controlled local authorities, and the unions. The 'Denning Doctrine' was strongly criticized by Labour Party spokesman Jack Straw and other left-wing union, civil liberties, and academic supporters as giving chief constables too much power, for which they were not democratically accountable, especially with respect to the policing of industrial disputes, of which the miners' strike in 1984 provided the emblematic example. Straw himself introduced private member's bills in Parliament designed to increase the powers of local councils and police authorities to exercise control over, and demand accountability from, their chief constables, and to exert more influence over policing policies. The idea of enhancing local *consultation* over, and input into, policing priorities had received significant support from the report of the Scarman Inquiry into the Brixton riots of 1981[26] as well as from the Chief Constable of Devon and Cornwall, John Alderson, who had been promoting the then relatively novel concept of 'community-based policing.'[27] It was resisted, however, by other chief constables, notably the Chief Constable of Greater Manchester, James Anderton, who argued that 'genuine efforts by reasonable people at local levels currently to devise a more meaningful involvement in police affairs are unwittingly preparing the foundations for political mastery of the police' which, he wrote, 'is now a positive threat.'[28]

The Conservative government, however, was in the process of introducing its Financial Management Initiative and Citizens' Charters, as part of its more general commitment to supply-side economics, neo-liberalism, and the 'new public management.' These initiatives subjected all public services, including the police service, to increasing central controls, fiscal constraints (requiring them to do 'more with less'), and regular audits. While the legal/constitutional status of chief constables remained unchanged, their effective autonomy over policing policy and management was undoubtedly gradually eroded through these central government initiatives and demands.[29] With the eventual ascendancy to government of the Labour Party in the 1990s (with its slogan of 'attacking crime and the causes of crime'), these central government policies intensified rather than abated. Straw, as the new home secretary, however, also introduced reforms to the *Police Act* in 1996 that were designed to give local authorities a greater say in policing policy and priorities. Section 10 of the *Police Act, 1996*, replacing the provisions of the 1964 act, provided:

10. – (1) A police force maintained under section 2 shall be under the direction and control of the chief constable appointed under section 11.

(2) In discharging his functions, every chief constable shall have regard to the local policing plan issued by the police authority for his area under section 8.

In 1999, section 314 of the *Greater London Authority Act, 1999* established, for the first time, a local Metropolitan Police Authority for the Metropolitan Police, severing the historical governance relationship between the Metropolitan Police commissioner and the home secretary, which had been in place since the force was established in 1829. A new section (section 9A) was inserted into the *Police Act* which defined the role of the police commissioner in identical terms to that of provincial chief constables, and similarly required him to 'have regard' to the local policing plan issued by the new Metropolitan Police Authority 'in discharging his functions.'

Local policing plans were required to include 'a statement of the authority's priorities for the year, of the financial resources expected to be available and of the proposed allocation of those resources, and shall give particulars of (a) any objectives determined by the Secretary of State under section 37, (b) any objectives determined by the [local police] authority under section 7, and (c) any performance targets established by the authority.' Within the constraints of national objectives determined by the home secretary, local police authorities were thus empowered and required to play a significant role in setting objectives, priorities, and performance targets[30] to which their chief constables were required to 'have regard' in discharging their duties.

Meanwhile, the Labour government's *Crime and Disorder Act, 1998*, imposed further duties on local councils, in collaboration with chief constables, police authorities, probation committees, health authorities, and other local persons or bodies designated by the home secretary, to undertake studies of crime and disorder in their areas and develop and provide for the implementation of 'crime and disorder strategies,' thus giving a mandate to a much wider range of local authorities and interests to exert influence over policing policies, objectives, and priorities. As I noted, however, despite these legislative and administrative reforms, the House of Lords still felt able in 1999 to endorse (albeit in *obiter dicta*)[31] Lord Denning's now famous expansive formulation of the doctrine of police independence in the 1968 *Blackburn* case.

Another document that has had an important influence over recent discussions of police governance in the United Kingdom has been the

1999 report of the Independent Commission on Policing for Northern Ireland (which has come to be known, after its chairman, as the Patten Inquiry). The commission recommended radical changes to the governance arrangements for the Royal Ulster Constabulary (the name of which it recommended should be changed to the Police Service of Northern Ireland). It recommended the establishment of a Northern Ireland Policing Board which would have broad powers to determine policing objectives, priorities, and policies for not only for the police service, but also taking into account all other possible state or non-state resources for accomplishing policing objectives in the province. In addition, it recommended the establishment of local District Policing Partnership Boards that should be empowered to determine more local policing objectives, priorities and policies, and which should be allocated funding that they would be free to spend as they see fit to accomplish local policing objectives.[32] These recommendations were implemented, with some important modifications and qualifications, by the *Police (Northern Ireland) Acts* of 2000 and 2003.

In its report, however, the Patten Inquiry recommended that the idea of the 'operational independence' of the police should be abandoned in favour of a concept of 'operational responsibility' that would more clearly differentiate the concepts of control and accountability. Given the novelty and significance of this recommendation, the inquiry's argument on it deserves to be quoted in full here:

6.19 One of the most difficult issues we have considered is the question of 'operational independence.' Some respondents urged us to define operational independence, or at least to define the powers and responsibilities of the police. The Police Authority and the Committee on the Administration of Justice both advocated this. The Authority told us that under the present arrangements if a chief constable decided that a matter was operational, and therefore within the scope of police independence, there was nothing that they could do to pursue it. We have consulted extensively in several countries, talking both to police and to those who are responsible for holding them accountable. The overwhelming advice is that it is important to allow a chief constable sufficient flexibility to perform his or her functions and exercise his or her responsibilities, but difficult if not impossible to define the full scope of a police officer's duties. The term 'operational independence' is neither to be found in nor is it defined in any legislation. It is an extrapolation from the phrase 'direction and control' included in statutory descriptions of the functions of chief constables.

But, however it may be defined, it is not acceptable that scrutiny of the police should be impeded by the assertion, valid or otherwise, that the current legislation empowering such scrutiny is limited to matters outside the scope of operational independence.

6.20 Long consideration has led us to the view that the term 'operational independence' is itself a large part of the problem. In a democratic society, all public officials must be fully accountable to the institutions of that society for the due performance of their functions, and a chief of police cannot be an exception. No public official, including a chief of police, can be said to be 'independent.' Indeed, given the extraordinary powers conferred on the police, it is essential that their exercise is subject to the closest and most effective scrutiny possible. The arguments involved in support of 'operational independence' – that it minimises the risk of political influence and that it properly imposes on the Chief Constable the burden of taking decisions on matters about which only he or she has all the facts and expertise needed – are powerful arguments, but they support a case not for 'independence' but for 'responsibility.' We strongly prefer the term 'operational responsibility' to the term 'operational independence.'

6.21 Operational responsibility means that it is the Chief Constable's right and duty to take operational decisions, and that neither the government nor the Policing Board should have the right to direct the Chief Constable as to how to conduct an operation. It does not mean, however, that the Chief Constable's conduct of an operational matter should be exempted from inquiry or review after the event by anyone. That should never be the case. But the term 'operational independence' suggests that it might be, and invocation of the concept by a recalcitrant chief constable could have the effect that it was. It is important to be clear that a chief constable, like any other public official, must be both free to exercise his or her responsibilities but also capable of being held to account afterwards for the manner in which he/she exercises them. *We recommend that the Chief Constable should be deemed to have operational responsibility for the exercise of his or her functions and the activities of the police officers and civilian staff under his or her direction and control.* Neither the Policing Board nor the Secretary of State (or Northern Ireland Executive) should have the power to direct the Chief Constable as to how to exercise those functions.'[33]

There is evidence now that the thinking of the Patten Inquiry has begun to influence approaches to police governance of senior public servants in the English Home Office, if not home secretaries themselves. A consultation document published by the Home Office in

November 2003, entitled *Policing: Building Safer Communities Together*, includes a foreword by the current Home Secretary, David Blunkett, in which he wrote: 'We understand that public services, including the police, can no longer be seen as services 'done unto' people; they can only be successful if they are conducted *with* people. This means integrating policing activity into the daily life of every community. In short, we must transcend our traditional notions of policing by consent, and establish a new principle of policing through co-operation.'[34] In the body of the document appears the following discussion of police independence:

> **5.15** In terms of officers ultimately in charge of their police forces, the Government is clear that in wanting to clarify and strengthen accountability arrangements, it is not seeking to interfere in operational decisions which are the right and duty of chief officers to take – a position which is enshrined in law. Police forces are under the 'direction and control' of their chief officer – not politicians. The political impartiality of the police is absolutely vital for public confidence.
>
> **5.16** But the Government is similarly clear that chief officers and their forces are accountable to the communities they serve. Like the authors of the 1999 Report on the future of policing in Northern Ireland, we believe that the often-used term 'operational independence' is in fact a stumbling block in talking about accountability of the police service. We believe that instead we should begin focusing on the *operational responsibility* of chief officers – because to say 'independence' suggests a lack of accountability. Chief officers are in charge of, and have responsibility for, day to day operational decisions. The police exercise important powers and must be capable of being held to account for the way in which they are used. But more than this, chief officers should be accountable, and be seen to be accountable, for reform of the police service, the positive development of policing in general and working with police authorities in terms of the performance of their particular force. This is what we mean by *operational responsibility*.'[35]

The most recent chapter in this development of police governance in England and Wales came with the passage of the *Police Reform Act* in 2002. This act further enhances the authority of the home secretary in exercising control over policing in England and Wales. Specifically, it authorizes the home secretary to promulgate a 'National Policing Plan' to order inspections of provincial police services to ensure that their policing complies with the objectives of the national plan and, in the event of a finding of non-compliance, to give directions to local police authorities and require them to prepare 'action plans' (which must be approved by the home secretary) to bring their local policing into compliance.[36] The act also empowers the home secretary to make regulations 'requiring all police forces in England and Wales (a) to adopt particular procedures or practices; or (b) to adopt procedures or practices of a particular description.' Finally, and most significant for the topic of this chapter, the act empowers the home secretary to issue 'codes of practice relating to the discharge of their functions by the chief officers of police' of police forces in England and Wales. So far, only one code of practice – on the subject of police use of firearms[37] – has been issued under this authority.

Section 42 of the 1996 act was amended by the 2002 act to include a power in the home secretary to require a police authority to suspend a chief constable when 'he considers it necessary for the maintenance of public confidence in the force in question' (section 42(1A)). Most recently, the home secretary has exercised this power, in the face of resistance from the local police authority, with respect to the chief constable of the Humberside Police, in the wake of a highly critical report into the handling of the investigation of the murder of two small children in Soham, Cambridgeshire.[38] The local authority challenged the home secretary's exercise of this power in this case on the ground that the 'public confidence' referred to in section 42(1A) should be interpreted as the confidence of the public in the police force's specific area, rather than of the public more generally. It maintained that it and the Humberside public continued to have confidence in the chief constable. In ruling against the police authority and upholding the home secretary's exercise of the power, Burnton J, commented: 'The power of a Home Secretary, in a sense, is a default power. It is exercised on a national basis having regard to the need for the maintenance of public confidence at large in all the police forces in the country. The wording of the statute confers a large element of discretion on the part of the Secretary of State. The question is whether he considers it is necessary for the maintenance of public confidence in the force in question that the Chief Constable be suspended.'[39] In support of this conclusion, Burnton J commented: 'It would be somewhat surprising if the real question for the Home Secretary were whether there were local public confidence in the force in question given that Parliament has conferred a power on Central Government, or a Minister of Central Government, rather than only the Police Authority in question which, of course, is local.'[40] This incident represents just the most recent example of the struggle over local versus central control and influence over the police in Britain.

Summary: England and Wales

In terms of its legal definition, the idea of police independence in England and Wales is currently defined by the much-contested statement of it by Lord Denning in the 1968 case of *R. v. Metropolitan Commissioner of Police, ex parte Blackburn*, quoted above. This statement recognizes a wide sphere of political independence (i.e., independence from both political direction *and* political accountability) for chief constables with respect to the more or less undefined area of 'law enforcement.' This formulation of the doctrine of police independence, however, is based on a series of *obiter dicta* in previous English and other Commonwealth cases, as well as the discussion of the topic by the English Royal Commission on the Police in its 1962 report, and is itself *obiter dicta*.[41]

Since Lord Denning's statement in the *Blackburn* case, major practical, administrative, and legislative developments with respect to police governance have occurred, in which the practical (and likely legal) autonomy of chief constables with respect to matters of policing and law enforcement has undoubtedly been substantially reduced. Given these developments, and the questionable legal pedigree, correctness, and authority of Lord Denning's statement in the first place, there is good reason, despite its endorsement by the House of Lords as recently as 1999, to question whether the statement remains (or for that matter ever was) what lawyers refer to as 'good law.'

In sum, the content, scope, and practical implications for police governance of the idea of 'police independence' in England and Wales remain today, as they have always been, unclear, and open to contestation and debate. Most recently, following recommendations of the Patten Inquiry in Northern Ireland, there has been some evidence that, in the English Home Office at least, there may be a preference for the term 'operational responsibility' over the term 'operational independence' with respect to the status and political autonomy of chief constables vis-à-vis the local police authorities and the central home secretary. As defined by the Patten Inquiry, and more recently in a Home Office consultation document, the term 'operational responsibility' has the advantage of more clearly differentiating the concepts of control and accountability discussed at the beginning of this chapter, ensuring that increased 'independence' does not necessarily imply increased immunity from accountability as well as from direction and control (i.e., quadrant 4 rather than quadrant 3 in figure 4.1).

2. *Australia*

Further examples of such *ad hoc* intervention [by governments] ... demonstrate the absence of any clear consistent or principled stance in relation to police/government relations on the part of either major political party, with the possible exception of the Dunstan Labor Governments in South Australia and the Bjelke-Petersen Governments in Queensland. Rather, the vagueness in legal and administrative arrangements, and their lack of visibility, are exploited opportunistically as the need arises, but this rarely if ever entails an explicit political renunciation of the principle of independence. More often it occasions an ideological affirmation of it, in the face of its blatant distortion or evasion on the occasion in question.'[42]

As I noted previously, two of the cases that have been commonly cited as providing the judicial foundation for the modern doctrine of police independence were Australian.[43] The *Enever* case involved the question of whether the Crown in Tasmania could be held civilly liable for a wrongful arrest by a police officer, while in the *Perpetual Trustee* case the issue was whether the Crown could claim compensation for the loss of services of a police officer who was injured in a road accident. In both cases, therefore, the courts had to determine whether, in law, the police officers concerned could be regarded as in a master and servant relationship with those who employed them (and in both cases the courts held that they were not). In neither case was the question of the political independence of the police directly in issue, and judicial comments on that issue in each case were certainly obiter dicta.[44] The fact that the two cases were subsequently invoked in support of the idea of the political independence of the police, however, undoubtedly created a judicial climate in Australia that was more receptive to the police independence doctrine.[45]

Somewhat surprisingly, there appear to have been few judicial decisions in Australia in which the idea of police independence has been addressed. In two cases in the early 1990s[46] applicants sought the issue of writs of mandamus to compel police to enforce the law, as had been done in the English *Blackburn* cases, and in each case passing reference was made to the idea of police independence. As in the *Blackburn* cases, however, in neither of these cases was the question of the alleged immunity of police from political direction with respect to law enforcement directly in issue, nor was mandamus granted in either case.

Modern support for the doctrine of police independence in Australia has come, interestingly, primarily from state police commissioners, the reports of commissions of inquiry, and some academic commentators, rather than from the courts, as in England. A significant explanation for this may well be that police services in Australia are not locally based and subject to the governance of a local police authority, as in England, but are accountable directly through state and federal ministers. In this respect, of course, they are much more similar to the RCMP, OPP, the Quebec Police Force (QPF), and the Royal Newfoundland Constabulary (RNC) in Canada. Indeed, as with those Canadian police services, the doctrine of the political independence of the police has been less easily reconcilable with statutory provisions concerning the governance and accountability of the state and federal police services of Australia, most of which, until relatively recently, stipulated that police commissioners had the control and management of their police forces subject to the directions of the relevant government minister.[47]

South Australia

Interestingly, South Australia – which is where the modern debate over police independence in Australia really began, as I shall detail in a moment – was the exception in this regard. Section 21 of its *Police Regulation Act* provided that the commissioner of police had 'control and management' of the police force 'subject to this Act.' While his or her authority in this respect had to be exercised in conformity with regulations made by the state governor under the act, nowhere in the act was a power of any minister to give directions to the commissioner explicitly conferred or recognized.

In September 1970, opponents of the Vietnam War, and of Australia's participation in it, in South Australia decided to organize a mass protest demonstration in downtown Adelaide, the state capital. The Labour state government was sympathetic to the anti-war cause,[48] but the premier had stated in Parliament that 'there is no question of the Government's not backing the police in maintaining peace and order' during the demonstration. In a private meeting with the police commissioner before the demonstration took place, he had expressed his desire that, should the demonstrators take over a particular intersection and impede the flow of traffic, the police should not intervene. After considering this request for a few hours, the commissioner wrote to the state's chief secretary indicating that he was unable to agree to the premier's request since 'if there is any serious disruption of traffic or interference with citizens going about their lawful business, by the demonstrators taking over a busy intersection, the police will have no alternative than to take the necessary action to uphold the law.' Although the letter was not made public at the time, the commissioner gave a statement to the press that included this view.

The next day, the premier made the following statement in Parliament:

> The Government has no power to direct the Commissioner of Police in this matter. The Commissioner has made a decision which, in my view, does not entirely accord with what has happened in relation to other demonstrations which have held up public traffic, including the farmers' demonstration, in which I took part. However, that is the expression of view of the Commissioner of Police, and over him we have no control ... [T]he matter is now out of the hands of the Government; we have no power legally or administratively to take further action than we have taken. We have expressed the view that the utmost tolerance and understanding must be shown and prudence and care taken to see to it that the peace is kept, and I hope that that will occur. Unfortunately, the Commissioner of Police has communicated with me in these terms, and he will carry out his duties, as will members of the Police Force, in the terms that he and they believe to be right. In these circumstances, the responsibility will rest there. (57)

In testimony before the inquiry into the handling of the demonstration that the government established, however, the premier told the inquiry commissioner that 'although the Government had no power legally to direct the Commissioner in terms of the Police Regulation Act it had always previously been the practice in his experience in government that directions had from time to time been given to the Commissioner and that he had always followed them and deferred to ministerial advisement' (58).

After reviewing the entire circumstances of the demonstration, its handling by the police, and the various communications between the police and the government, the inquiry commissioner, Mr Justice Bright, reached the following conclusions in his report:

> The police force has some independence of operation under the Police Regulation Act ... but it is still a part of executive operation. In a system of

responsible government there must ultimately be a Minister of State answerable in parliament and to the parliament for any executive operation. This does not mean that no senior public servant or officer of State has independent discretion. Nor does it mean that the responsible minister can at his pleasure substitute his own will for that of the officer responsible to him. The main way in which a minister and an officer of State become identified with an important decision is by a process of discussion and communication. The minister enquires of his officer, the officer provides information and advice to his minister, the minister, perhaps also drawing on a different field of information, provides information and advice to the officer. From there on, the officer will be the 'field commander.' He will carry out the decision, acting reasonably and using his own discretion in circumstances as they arise. But ultimately, he will be responsible, through the minister, to the parliament – not in the sense that he will be subject to censure for exercising his discretion in a manner contrary to that preferred by the majority in parliament, but in the sense that all executive action should be subject to examination and discussion in parliament. (79–80)

Commenting that if the kind of decision that had to be made in this case is made solely by the commissioner 'the process of polarization is almost inevitable,' Bright J wrote:

I do not think that the Commissioner of Police and his force ought to be placed in a situation where they have to take sole responsibility for making what many reputable citizens regard as a political type of decision. The Commissioner of Police ought to have the right, in any such case, of obtaining general advice from the Chief Secretary but the Commissioner of Police ought not to be bound to initiate such discussions. The Chief Secretary ought to be willing to advise and direct the Commissioner of Police an any such case, to make public that he has done so, and to take the burden of justifying the decision off the shoulders of the Commissioner of Police and on to his own shoulders in Parliament. (80)

Referring to statutory provisions in other police legislation in Australasia, Bright J added the following important comments:

I am not impressed by the need for uniformity, but the fact that in so many places there can be executive intervention is significant. It is not only politically correct, but it is also in the long term best interests of the police force in this State, that there should be a power of executive intervention.

The relationship between senior officers and the executive is not spelled out in detail in statutes. To a great extent it is a matter of convention, of arrangements well understood, of limits not transgressed. One such convention is, I believe, firmly established in this State now. It provides that in matters of ordinary law enforcement the minister will seldom, if ever, advise the Commissioner, although he may consult with him. It is in the area of law enforcement in which there is a political element that advice and occasionally direction are to be expected from the minister. It should therefore be in writing and should, at the appropriate time, be tabled in Parliament. I say 'at the appropriate time' because I can envisage circumstances in which it would not be appropriate to publicize a proposed course of action before the event had occurred.' (81)

Bright J consequently recommended that section 21 of the South Australian *Police Regulation Act* should be amended to read, 'Subject to this Act and to any directions in writing from the Chief Secretary the Commissioner shall have control and management of the police force,' and that there should be a requirement for publication of any such ministerial direction 'at the appropriate time.' He also recommended that 'a convention should be established ... with regard to the limits within which any such written direction may properly be given' and commented that 'the Chief Secretary and the Commissioner of Police ought to be able to reach an understanding which would form the basis of this convention' (81).

Bright J's recommendations in this respect were implemented through an amendment to the South Australian *Police Regulation Act* in 1972, whereby section 21 was changed to read: 'Subject to this Act and the directions of the Governor, the Commissioner shall have the control and management of the Police Force.' The Police Commissioner, J.G. McKinna, who had been in office at the time of the demonstration and the inquiry into it, retired in the same year. He was replaced by Harold Salisbury who, immediately prior to arriving in South Australia to take up the post of commissioner, had been chief constable of the York and North East Yorkshire Police in England. There is little doubt, therefore, that he brought with him the attitudes and beliefs about police independence that were common among English chief constables at that time, four years after the decision in the *Blackburn* case had been handed down. Unfortunately, he was in the job as commissioner of police in South Australia for only five years before he, like his predecessor, came into conflict with the Labour state government, still presided over by the same premier.

The conflict this time revolved around the issue of accountability rather than that of control or direction as such. Questions had arisen about certain activities of the force's Special Branch, and the files that they maintained on 'political dissenters' who had not been convicted of any offence in South Australia. The chief secretary (the minister responsible for police in South Australia) requested answers to a set of questions about these activities and files, to which the commissioner provided a written reply in which he stated at the outset that the police force considered that 'some of these questions from the press are improper, even impertinent, and that they should not be answered.'[49] In response, the government established an independent inquiry to examine the activities of the Special Branch, the report of which, in the government's view, indicated that Commissioner Salisbury had misled the government in his written answers to the chief secretary's request for information. The government called upon the Commissioner to resign, and when he refused to do so, dismissed him. A further inquiry was then set up to look into the circumstances of the commissioner's dismissal and advise whether it had been 'justifiable in the circumstances.'[50]

In testimony before the inquiry, echoing the sentiments of Lord Denning in the *Blackburn* case ten years earlier, Salisbury maintained that his duty as police commissioner was 'to the law ... to the Crown and not to any politically elected government.'[51] With respect to this argument Madam Justice Roma Mitchell, the inquiry commissioner, responded in her report that 'that statement, in so far as it seems to divorce a duty to the Crown from a duty to the politically elected Government, suggests an absence of understanding of the constitutional system of South Australia or, for that matter, of the United Kingdom.' Salisbury also maintained that the amended section 21 of the *Police Regulation Act* did not entitle the government to give him, as commissioner of police, a direction with regard to the Special Branch – an argument to which Mitchell J responded: 'No argument to this effect was put forward by [Salisbury's] counsel and, in my opinion, any such argument would have been untenable.'[52]

In her report, Mitchell J concluded that Salisbury had indeed misled the government and that his dismissal was justifiable. Commenting on the commissioner's 'duty to the law,' Mitchell J wrote:

Of course the paramount duty of the Commissioner of Police is, as is that of every citizen, to the law. The fact that a Commissioner of Police 'is answerable to the law and to the law alone' was adverted to by Lord

Denning, M.R., in *R. v. Commissioner of Police of the Metropolis; ex parte Blackburn*. That was in the context of the discretion to prosecute or not to prosecute. No Government can properly direct any policeman to prosecute or not to prosecute any particular person or class of persons although it is not unknown for discussions between the executive and the police to lead to an increase in or abatement of prosecutions for certain types of offences. That is not to say that the Commissioner of Police is in any way bound to follow governmental direction in relation to prosecutions. Nor should it be so. There are many other police functions in respect of which it would be unthinkable for the Government to interfere. It is easier to cite examples[53] than to formulate a definition of the circumstances in which the Commissioner of Police alone should have responsibility for the operations of the police Force.'[54]

On the issue of accountability, Mitchell J wrote:

It is one matter to entrust the Commissioner of Police the right to make decisions as to the conduct of the Police Force. It is quite another to deny the elected Government the right to know what is happening within the Police Force. Of course there are some matters of detail into which the Government should not inquire.[55] In the context of Special Branch work the South Australian Government has recognised that situation in that it has never sought to identify the persons who are the subject of records. But it believes itself entitled to know the general nature of the work done by Special Branch and of its relationship with outside agencies including ASIO.[56] That view, in so far as it relates to the association with ASIO, is shared by Hope J.[57] I believe it to be correct.

   Clearly under the Police regulation Act 1952 as amended the South Australian Government must have the right to be informed generally as to the operations of any particular section of the Police Force.'[58]

Noting that the *Police Regulation Act* authorized the governor to make regulations concerning the 'division of the Police Force into groups, branches divisions or sections,' Mitchell J concluded that 'if the Governor in Council may make such regulations it follows that executive Council is empowered to know the nature of the work that is being undertaken by any section of the Police Force. By that I mean that the Government has a right to know the general duties and the general operations of the various sections of the Police Force.'[59]

   The Mitchell Report, I think, nicely illustrates the importance of differentiating between control and accountability when thinking about police independence. Clearly, Mitchell J recognized that a substantial measure of independence need not in any way be incompatible with an equally substantial requirement of accountability.

In 1992, prompted by the experience in New South Wales of the interposition of a police board into the governance of the police in that state (discussed further below), and in response to a recommendation in a National Crime Authority report that a similar board should be established in South Australia, the government had a discussion paper on the subject prepared for consideration by its Heads of Agencies Committee.[60] This paper constitutes the most extensive exploration of arguments for and against a police board as an element in the governance of state police services in Australia since the idea was first proposed in the report of the New South Wales Lusher Inquiry in 1981, and adopted in that state (discussed below). Arguing that 'in the final analysis the main objective is to establish arrangements which maintain the statutory independence of the Police Commissioner, but also provides [sic] the necessary checks and balances required of all public sector organisations' (9), the paper canvassed various possible models and roles for such a board, citing extensively from the literature on police commissions and boards in Canada.[61] It would reward close reading by anyone contemplating such a board for the governance of the OPP. The South Australian government, however, has never established such a board for the governance of the South Australian Police.

Before leaving South Australia,[62] I should note that in 1998 a new *Police Act*[63] was enacted in the state, section 6 of which now provides: 'Subject to this Act and any written directions of the Minister, the Commissioner is responsible for the control and management of S.A. Police.' Section 7 stipulates, 'No Ministerial direction may be given to the Commissioner in relation to the appointment, transfer, remuneration, discipline or termination of a particular person,' and section 8 provides that any ministerial direction must be published in the *Gazette* within eight days of being given, and laid before each House of Parliament within six sitting days of its date if Parliament is sitting, otherwise within six sitting days of the beginning of the next session.

Queensland
While these disputes between the police commissioners and the government were going on in South Australia in the 1970s, other disputes between a police commissioner and the government were brewing in

the state of Queensland. In this instance, the situation was in many respects the very opposite of that which had transpired in South Australia in 1970, as it involved a state premier who believed that the police, with the support of the minister of police, were not being 'tough' enough in enforcing certain laws against certain people in the state while being too tough on police officers who were suspected of corruption and other misconduct. Joh Bjelke-Petersen had been premier of Queensland for many years and had governed the state with what can only be described as a very sure hand. There had been persistent allegations of corruption within the Queensland Police Force, and in 1969 the minister of police had commissioned McKinna, the South Australian police commissioner, to undertake a study of the force and to make recommendations with respect to training and administration. The following year, the position of commissioner of police became vacant and, at McKinna's suggestion, the minister of police persuaded the Cabinet to appoint Ray Whitrod, a career policeman, as the new commissioner.

Whitrod, who was described in a subsequent inquiry report as 'a dignified, intelligent and honest man,'[64] had previously served in the South Australian, Papua New Guinea and Commonwealth of Australia police forces, in the latter two as commissioner, and was a former assistant director of ASIO. He had obtained a Bachelor of Economics and a postgraduate diploma in Criminology from Cambridge University in England, where he had doubtless heard and read about English views of 'police independence.'[65]

With the support of his minister, Commissioner Whitrod set about the difficult task of 'cleaning up' the Queensland Police Force that he now headed, and improving its educational and ethical standards. Not surprisingly, he encountered considerable resistance from within the force, some of whose members seemed to be particularly politically well connected. Shortly after his arrival, Whitrod announced his view that henceforth promotion should be based on merit rather than seniority. Within a year of his appointment the Queensland Police Union had passed a vote of no confidence in him, as an 'academic' unable to communicate with non-academics. At the same meeting, the union passed a vote of confidence in the premier's leadership.

By September 1971 Whitrod had formed a new Crime Intelligence Unit (CIU), staffed by trusted officers, to collect, record, and disseminate intelligence about organized crime and corruption. Underfunded and facing constant resistance from the police union, this unit had great difficulty in performing its tasks effectively. Furthermore, Whitrod's policies and the minister's efforts to get them approved in Cabinet were being opposed by the premier, and by the mid-1970s Whitrod was becoming increasingly concerned by what he perceived to be the premier's interference in police operational matters, which he felt was contrary to his understanding of the proper relationship between a police commissioner and the government.

At about the same time, an inspector in the force, Terry Lewis, who apparently thought that he had been denied promotions by Whitrod to which he was entitled, began meeting with the premier and passing him documents he had prepared which, in addition to promoting himself, cast aspersions on the commissioner (including allegations that he was linked with the Australian Labor Party).

In July 1976, allegations were made that police had used excessive force in policing a student march that had been undertaken without a permit. Whitrod ordered an internal police inquiry into the incident; the Premier promptly intervened and stopped the inquiry. The Police Union wrote to the premier expressing its gratitude and pledging its support for his government. Shortly afterwards, the premier replaced the police minister and Whitrod lost his only powerful supporter in government. The union continued to send letters of support to the premier, in which potential successors to Whitrod were mentioned, including Lewis. The head of the CIU was called before the new police minister for what a later inquiry report referred to as a 'dressing down,' during the course of which he was advised that the premier had ordered that no more charges be laid against police officers.

In August 1976, further allegations of police brutality surfaced in connection with a police raid of a 'hippie colony' at Cedar Bay. The premier publicly supported the police. Despite the premier's instructions, Whitrod directed an internal inquiry as a result of which charges were laid against some of the police officers involved.

Appointments to the rank of inspector and above were made by Cabinet in Queensland, but normally from a list of candidates provided by the commissioner. In October 1976 Whitrod submitted a list of suitable candidates for appointment to the position of assistant commissioner. Terry Lewis was not on the list, but in November Whitrod was advised by the police minister that the Cabinet had decided to appoint Lewis (over a hundred more-senior officers in the force). Whitrod had made it perfectly clear that he did not regard Lewis as a suitably qualified candidate for the position. He sought an opportunity to speak to the Cabinet, but was refused. He resigned the same day. In his resignation speech he made the following comments: 'The Government's view seems to be that the police are just another Public Service Department, accountable to the Premier and Cabinet through the Police Minister, and therefore rightly subject to directions, not only on matters of general policy, but also in specific cases. I believe as a Police Commissioner I am answerable not to a person, not to the Executive Council, but to the law.'[66] The influence of Lord Denning's formulation of the idea of police independence in the *Blackburn* case, with its characteristic confusion between the concepts of control and accountability, could hardly be more clear.

At the next Cabinet meeting a week later, Lewis was appointed commissioner in his place. As an inquiry subsequently noted: 'The only missing Cabinet notes over a period of many years relate to the Cabinet meeting dealing with Lewis' appointment as Commissioner.'[67]

I have described the circumstances of Whitrod's resignation in some detail in order to provide some sense of the political climate in Queensland in which it occurred. A full public airing of it, however, had to await the election of a Labour government in Queensland more than a decade later, which immediately set up a commission of inquiry (the Fitzgerald Inquiry) to investigate corruption, including police corruption, in Queensland.[68] In its report, the Fitzgerald Inquiry had some comments to make about relations between the police and governments:

> It is anticipated that the Commissioner remain answerable to a Minister of Police for the overall running of the Police Force, including its efficiency, effectiveness and economy. Under no circumstances should the Department be included in the responsibilities of the Attorney-General.
>
> The Minister can and should give directions to the Commissioner on any matter concerning the superintendence, management and administration of the Force.
>
> The Minister may even implement policy directives relating to resourcing of the Force and the priorities that should be given to various aspects of police work and will have responsibility for the development and determination of overall policy.
>
> Priorities determined would have to include the degree of attention which is to be given to policing various offences. The advice sought by the Minister in deciding these matters and the process by which such decisions are made will depend on the circumstances at the time, and cannot be defined or rigidly laid down in legislation. Nor should they be left to

the discretion of the Police Commissioner or Police Union. They should be properly reviewed and determined in the immediate future by the Criminal Justice Commission and approved by the Parliamentary Committee.

The proposed Criminal Justice Commission has a much wider role than that proposed for a Police Board which was suggested by many submissions to the Inquiry. It will not remove the need for a Commissioner of Police, nor diminish the responsibility of that Commissioner for the superintendence of the Force, however, it would take particular responsibility for oversight of the reform process, and report to Parliament upon it.

In the interests of open and accountable Government, and the proper independence of the Police department, a register should be kept of policy directions given by the Minister to the Commissioner; and recommendations provided by the Commissioner to the Minister. In the case of staff appointments, the register would also record the instances where the Minister or Cabinet chooses not to follow recommendations put forward. The register would be tabled in Parliament annually by referral through the Chairman of the Criminal Justice Commission to the Criminal Justice Committee.

The Commissioner of Police should continue to have the independent discretion to act or refrain from acting against an offender.[69] The Minister should have no power to direct him to act, or not to act in any matter coming within his discretion under laws relating to police powers.'[70]

Following the presentation of the Fitzgerald Inquiry report, the legislation governing the Queensland Police Force was radically overhauled. Section 4.8 of the new *Police Service Administration Act, 1990* included detailed provisions setting out the responsibilities of the police commissioner, which are to be discharged, among other things, with due regard to ministerial directions given pursuant to section 4.6. Section 4.6 requires the commissioner to provide reports and recommendations in relation to the administration and functioning of the police service when required by the minister to do so and otherwise when the commissioner thinks fit. It also authorizes the minister, 'having regard to advice of the commissioner first obtained,' to give directions in writing to the commissioner concerning '(a) the overall administration, management, and superintendence of, or in the police service; and (b) policy and priorities to be pursued in performing the functions of the police service; and (c) the number and deployment of officers and staff members and the number and location of police establishments and police stations.' The section also requires the commissioner to comply with all such ministerial directions duly given. Section 4.7 requires the commissioner to keep a register of all reports and recommendations made to the minister and all directions given by the minister under section 4.6, and to furnish a copy of the register to the chairperson of the Crime and Misconduct Commission (CMC), 'with or without comment of the commissioner' [of police], which the chairperson of the CMC is to pass on to the chairperson of the Parliamentary Crime and Misconduct Committee of the Legislative Assembly. Within fourteen sitting days of receiving it, the committee chairperson is required to table it in the Legislative Assembly.

The Federal Jurisdiction
As far as I have been able to determine, no comparably detailed legislative provisions governing the relationship between a police commissioner and a police minister have been enacted anywhere else in the Commonwealth. They were not entirely without precedent in Australia, however. A year after Madam Justice Roma Mitchell handed down her report in South Australia (discussed above), the commonwealth Parliament passed legislation to establish the Australian Federal Police. Section 13 of the *Australian Federal Police Act, 1979* provided that:

> (1) Subject to this Act, the Commissioner has the general administration of, and the control of the operations of, the Australian Federal Police.
> (2) The Minister may, after obtaining and considering the advice of the Commissioner and of the Secretary,[71] give written directions to the Commissioner with respect to the general policy to be pursued in relation to the performance of the functions of the Australian Federal Police.
> (4) The Commissioner shall comply with all directions given under this section.'[72]

New South Wales
Problems of corruption and in relations between police commissioners and their governments have also been experienced in New South Wales over the last thirty years, and have been the subject of a number of official inquiries. In 1981, the report of a commission of inquiry into the administration of the New South Wales Police Force gave lengthy consideration to the issue of the governance arrangements for the force.[73] The inquiry commissioner, Mr Justice Lusher, examined at length the case law and literature on the concept of police independence and, on the basis of the evidence he had heard, concluded that the relationship

between the commissioner of police and the state government required both an improved oversight capacity for the minister and a greater degree of distance in order to reduce the likelihood of improper political interference in the administration of the force. His recommendation for achievement of these objectives was to interpose a three-member police board between the police force and the minister:

> The proposed Board would be subject to the Minister's direction and be responsible to the Minister for certain functions and responsibilities hereinafter set out.[74] The Inquiry considers that the membership of the Board would comprise three persons, one of whom would be the Commissioner of Police; the other two members would be government appointees from outside the New South Wales Police Force, one of whom would be the Chairman. The Inquiry considers that the Commissioner of Police should, subject to the direction of the Minister, be responsible for the superintendence of the Police Force in the sense of its operational command and have the further function of implementing within the Force and complying with the policies of the Board of which he is a member. In this latter function, the Commissioner in substance, would be in no greatly different position in principle than he is now in implementing government or ministerial policies: indeed he would have the additional advantage of having taken part in their formulation as a Board member.'[75]

The inquiry's recommendations were adopted and the recommended police board was established by the *Police Board Act, 1983*.[76] It was specified to be 'subject to the control and direction of the Minister' in the exercise of its functions, which were specifically listed in section 7 of the act. None of these countenanced supervision of any operational matters as such. Section 7 specified that 'the Commissioner shall implement, by the exercise of the Commissioner's functions in accordance with law, decisions of the Board,' but also that, subject to this requirement, 'nothing in this Act affects the responsibility of the Commissioner for the superintendence of the police force and its operational command and day-to-day management.'

The new police board, with a new commissioner as one of its members, worked to improve the professionalism of the police force and root out corruption, but soon found itself confronting opposition from the Police Association and some political quarters. It is not necessary here to detail the growing concerns about corruption that emerged during the next ten years; it is sufficient to say that they were so pervasive and serious that by 1988 an Independent Commission Against Corruption had been set up,[77] and in 1994 another royal commission (under the chairmanship of Mr Justice James Wood) was established to investigate corruption in the police service. The royal commission sat for three years, handing down its final report report in May 1997.

While the commission was in the midst of its hearings, a new police commissioner, Mr Peter Ryan, was recruited from England and appointed in 1996 with a mandate, like Commissioner Whitrod before him in Queensland, to 'clean up' the New South Wales police service and raise its professional and ethical standards. Steeped in the English tradition of police independence, Ryan was evidently unenthusiastic about sharing what he saw as his responsibilities with a politically appointed police board which was subject to ministerial direction and control, and shortly after his arrival in Australia he persuaded the government to abolish it.[78]

Ryan lasted six years as commissioner, and the story of his tenure has an eerie resemblance to that of Whitrod twenty-five years earlier.[79] In his 1997 report, Wood J expressed concern about the statutory provision concerning the relationship between the commissioner and the minister:

3.26 This Commission remains concerned at the terms of s. 8(1) [of the Police Service Act,1990]. In the course of round table discussions it was said that there is a recognised convention that the Minister is concerned with matters of 'policy' and not with 'operational' matters. If this is so, then it seems to the Commission that the statute should reflect that situation, defining what is policy and what is operational, and providing for resolution of any overlap. The problem can be illustrated by asking whether the following matters are operational or policy:

- the particular location of a number of police officers;
- the opening or closing or relocation of a police station;
- the creation of a Task Force;
- the targeting of a particular category of conduct and the means by which it should be achieved.

3.27 In the view of the Commission it is difficult to see why any of these matters is other than an operational matter, in respect of which the Police Commissioner should retain independence. Otherwise a risk remains that:

- by reason of political or electoral considerations, decisions might be forced on a Commissioner by a Minister, which intrude into the responsibility of the former to deploy the Service to meet its operational needs;
- decisions will be made spontaneously and in circumstances where those advising the Minister are not well informed as to the facts; and
- conflicts of the kind seen in the past between the Commissioner and a Minister will continue.

3.28 The Commission acknowledges that ministerial accountability to Parliament is an important principle. It is not suggesting for a moment that the Commissioner of Police should be unaccountable or that the Minister should not be kept informed by the Commissioner. However, it is desirable in principle that the Police Service not be subject to undue political direction, and that the ministerial role be confined to one of policy.[80]

Wood J accordingly recommended that section 8 of the New South Wales *Police Service Act, 1990* should be amended along the lines of the comparable provision (section 13) in the *Australian Federal Police Act, 1990* (quoted above). This recommendation, however, has not been implemented in New South Wales,[81] and another of the conflicts between police commissioners and police ministers to which Wood J alluded in his report with concern that they not continue in the future eventually led to Peter Ryan's termination as commissioner in 2002. The newly appointed police minister was perceived to be increasingly involving himself, sometimes without even consulting the commissioner beforehand, in the kinds of decisions that Wood J had argued were clearly 'operational' matters.[82]

Victoria
Compared with South Australia, Queensland, and News South Wales, the issue of police independence seems to have been much less discussed than in the other Australian jurisdictions.[83] Although allegations of corruption have surfaced in both Victoria and Western Australia,[84] and have been the subject of inquiries in both states,[85] the reports of neither of those inquiries have addressed the issue of police governance generally, or police independence in particular.[86] In 1970, a former chief inspector of constabulary for England and Wales, Col. Sir Eric St Johnston, was commissioned to undertake a review of the 'administration and organization' of the Victoria Police Force. His review and

report,[87] however, was concerned only with the force's internal administration and organization, and did not touch at all on the relationships between the force and the state government, or between its chief commissioner and the responsible minister.

A wideranging review of the Victoria Police Force was undertaken in 1985 by a committee of inquiry under the chairmanship of T. Neesham, QC.[88] The relationship between the police and the government was considered only briefly in the committee's substantial (three-volume) report, however. Having cited the famous Denning *Blackburn* statement in a brief history of the London Metropolitan Police,[89] the report mentions that the original legislation establishing the Victoria Police Force 'imposed no requirement upon the Chief Commissioner to comply with the direction of the Executive Government,' but that this requirement was added to the legislation in 1873.[90] Commenting on the chief commissioner's current status, the committee wrote:

> The position of a Chief Commissioner in Victoria may be ambiguous as the resignations and dismissals of police commissioners in Queensland and South Australia seem to indicate. While possessing the original authority of a constable (Section 11), the Chief Commissioner is administratively accountable for the overall efficiency of the force and the use of resources entrusted to him. As for more operational (as distinct from administrative) decisions, we regard it as not only desirable but essential that the police should not be or be seen to be tools of the Executive. We received a number of submissions emphasising this. The need for police independence was one of the strongest statements of the Scarman report which followed the 1981 riots in Brixton. The need for independence was one of the principal reasons why we ultimately rejected the creation of a Police Board.[91]

Despite this recommendation, a police board was in fact established by the Liberal state government seven years later, in 1992.[92] The main function of the board, which was composed of three persons appointed by the governor in council and the chief commissioner, was to 'advise the Minister and the Chief Commissioner on ways in which the administration of the force might be improved,' and it was given substantial powers of investigation for this purpose.[93] The Labour government that was elected in 1999, however, immediately abolished the board, replacing it, and a police review commission that had also been established, with a 'Police Appeals Board.'[94] When the Labour leader announced his party's intentions in this respect before the 1999 election, the Liberal state premier issued a press release entitled 'Labor Launches Assault against Police Independence,' in which he argued that the Labour leader's proposals would 'effectively see him take over the operational running of the Victoria Police Force' by 'announcing that he would restructure the operational squads of Victoria Police, dictate the type of equipment issued to members and determine the placement of police stations.' 'All of these matters,' the premier wrote, 'have traditionally been the domain of Police Command who are the only ones in a position to best make such decisions.'[95] By way of response, the Labour leader apparently wrote to a member of Parliament committing himself to 'a Government that recognises the independence of the Office of the Chief Commissioner of Police and does not interfere with the operational functions of the Victorian Police Force.'[96]

Once in office, the new Labour state government established, in 2000, a Ministerial Administrative Review into Victoria Police Resourcing, Operational Independence, Human Resource Planning and Associated Issues. Its terms of reference included the following rather revealing term of reference: 'To consider and recommend appropriate protocols between Government and Victoria Police which better establish the operational independence of Victoria Police whilst preserving the role of Executive Government to determine State policy objectives for Victoria Police, including overall policing objectives, organisational governance requirements and associated resource allocation, as well as financial management, budgetary and employee relations policies.'[97]

Chapter 2 of the Review's report, entitled 'Towards Greater Certainty and Transparency in the Relationship Between Government and Victoria Police,' explores this term of reference in great detail and, because it is the most recent and comprehensive official discussion of these issues in Australia, deserves to be read in full. It includes a set of fifteen recommendations, including recommendations for a complete overhaul of the state's legislation governing its police force. The most important of these from the point of view of this chapter is Recommendation 7:

Recommendation 7 – Ministerial Direction Power
[a] Ministerial Direction Power: In view of the governance principles, which emphasise transparency and accountability, police legislation include a Ministerial direction power with the following key features:
- a broad definition of the scope of matters on which the Minister may direct, e.g., along the lines of the general formula of 'general policy in relation to the performance of the functions of Victoria Police' contained

in s.13(2) of the *Australian Federal Police Act 1979* [Cwlth]. As an alternative, a more prescriptive formula could be prepared, for example, based on that contained in the *Police Service Administration Act 1990* [Qld] but qualified to safeguard the operational independence and accountability of the Chief Commissioner;[98]
- the Minister be required to obtain and consider the advice of the Chief Commissioner before issuing any direction;
- such directions be in writing;
- the Chief Commissioner be required to give effect to any such direction;
- such directions as a minimum be tabled in Parliament. In addition, or as an alternative, such directions should be notified to the public, for example in the *Victoria Government Gazette*, including information of how to obtain a copy of the direction; and
- the *Victoria Police Annual Report* could contain a Schedule setting out any directions issued during the relevant year and afford the opportunity for the Chief Commissioner, should he/she wish, to comment upon them.

[b] inclusion of Non-exhaustive List: Consideration be given to also incorporating with the proposed Ministerial direction power a non-exhaustive list of matters on which the Minister cannot direct the Chief Commissioner including, for example, decisions to investigate, arrest or charge in a particular case; or to appoint, deploy, promote or transfer individual sworn staff members.'[99]

The review's recommendations on this term of reference have not so far been implemented in Victoria.[100]

Finally, in terms of experience with the idea of police independence in Australia, I should note that many of the same kinds of public service reforms identified in the discussion of England and Wales above have also been occurring in the Australian jurisdictions, with similar potential implications for the realities of police independence. In particular, most Australian jurisdictions have now moved to fixed-term contracts for police commissioners and other senior command positions, as well as 'purchase agreements' for policing services and performance reviews.[101] Since these latter innovations have also been introduced in New Zealand in recent years, I will leave further discussion of them to the following section of the chapter on New Zealand.

Summary: Australia

There is no doubt that the idea of police independence has had currency in Australian law and conventions for some time. Its relatively recent

reception and recognition in Australia has largely reflected the influence of English case law and governmental practice there, and has in
particular been fostered by a few senior English police officers who
have been recruited to senior police executive positions in Australia
over the last thirty to forty years. The context in which it has been
recognized, however, differs in important ways from that found in its
country of origin, the United Kingdom. Importantly, Australian police
services are organized on a state and federal level, rather than on a
more local level. The governance arrangements for these police services, therefore, involve direct relationships between the police services
and state and Commonwealth governments, without the kind of 'tripartite' arrangements out of which the idea of police independence
originally developed in the United Kingdom.

It would be fair to say, I think, that there has been considerably more
reluctance on the part of governments in Australia to embrace any very
expansive conception of police independence than has been the case in
England and Wales. Specifically, many state governments in Australia
have successfully insisted on maintaining quite broad powers of direction and control over their state police services, acknowledging only a
limited area of police decision making (specific law enforcement and
prosecutorial decisions in particular cases – those 'quasi-judicial'
decisions of which the 1962 English royal commission wrote) that is
recognized as immune from executive direction. Some influential commentators in Australia (e.g., Mr Justice Bright in his 1971 report in
South Australia) have not even been prepared to concede that all of
these kinds of decisions ought necessarily always to be immune from
governmental direction or influence.

Unlike the situation in England and Wales, the scope and limits of
police independence in Australia have been defined and clarified more
in the reports of commissions of inquiry than by judicial decisions, and
there has been a trend since the late 1980s towards attempts to define
and clarify the governance relationship between police commissioners
and government ministers through legislative provision, rather than
simply through recognition of constitutional convention.[102] Sections
4.6–4.8 of the Queensland *Police Service Administration Act, 1990* currently constitute the most detailed of such legislative provisions. A
critical aspect of these provisions has been the requirement that any
ministerial directions given must be in writing and must be published
and/or laid before the legislature for scrutiny and debate.

Public service and other more general governmental reforms similar to those which have been taking place in England during the last twenty years have been occurring in Australia, and probably have similar implications for the realities of the relationships between police commissioners and their governments, and hence for the day-to-day realities of the reach and scope of police independence.

3. New Zealand

Since 1886, New Zealand has had a single, national police service headed by a commissioner of police and governed directly by the central government. Consequently, reflections on the relative roles of local and central authorities in the governance of the police that have provided the backdrop for inquiry into police independence in the United Kingdom have not had any role in discussions of this idea in modern New Zealand. This likely also explains why, in New Zealand as in Australia, judicial discussion of, and pronouncements about, the idea of police independence have been quite rare. The starting point for consideration of this idea in New Zealand are the legislative provisions for the governance of the New Zealand police in the *Police Act, 1958* and the *Police Regulations, 1992* promulgated pursuant to it.

Current Statutory Delineation of the Relationship between the Commissioner and the Minister in New Zealand

Somewhat unusually, the current legislative provision concerning the relationship between the minister of police and the commissioner of police in New Zealand is to be found not in the principal statute governing the police, the *Police Act, 1958*,[103] but in section 3 of the Police Regulations, 1992 made pursuant to section 64 of the act:

> 3. *Responsibility and duty of Commissioner* – (1) The Commissioner shall be responsible to the Minister for –
> (a) The general administration and control of the Police; and
> (b) The financial management and performance of the Police.
> (2) The Commissioner shall take all reasonable steps to ensure that all members of the Police discharge their duties to the Government and the public satisfactorily, efficiently, and effectively.

This provision has been criticized not only because it is in the Regulations rather than in the act, but also because it does not specify clearly enough either what the relationship between the commissioner and the minister is supposed to be or the boundaries of their respective roles in governing the New Zealand police. One critic has also argued that the language of subsection (2) of this provision is inappropriate, taking what some might consider to be a rather extreme position that 'police do not owe any duties to the government' since, under the act, they are required to 'swear to serve the Queen and to uphold the Queen's Peace.'[104] Joseph has consequently argued that 'reference to 'the government' ought to be replaced by reference to 'Her Majesty the Queen' which imports symbolic reference to the Queen's Peace.'[105]

Until quite recently, there has been relatively little discussion in the academic literature of the police-government relationship in New Zealand.[106] What these studies suggest is that, as in other common law countries, the police enjoy practical autonomy with respect to 'routine' policing decisions, but that at critical moments government involvement in (or at least influence over) police decision making sometimes becomes quite intense. While some of these critical moments are more or less routine (e.g., annual budget approval, selection of a new police commissioner, etc.), most of those which spark public debate about police–government relations arise in relation to the policing of particular events or circumstances (such as political unrest, labour disputes, or visits of controversial foreign dignitaries).

Dunstall's fourth volume of the history of the New Zealand police[107] provides ample evidence of very close relations between the police and government during the first half of the twentieth century, in the early years of which there appears to have been an attitude that the police, like all other elements of the public service, were subject to government control and direction. He quotes the minister of justice, speaking on the introduction in Parliament of a bill in 1913 to reform the 'obsolete' *Police Force Act* of 1886, as having said that 'it is absolutely necessary in the interests of the public, in the interests of the Force, and in the interests of discipline that Ministers of the day should have unfettered control of the Force.'[108] Dunstall adds, however, that:

> In New Zealand, between 1898 and the First World War, there began an erratic shift from direct ministerial supervision and control towards the 'modern fiction'[109] that the police were the servants of the law rather than of the state. New Zealand Commissioners of Police, from Tunbrige onwards,[110] had a hand in establishing the concept of their 'independence' from ministerial direction. In doing so they drew upon the degree of managerial autonomy apparently achieved by the early Commissioners of the London Metropolitan Police and the doctrine of police independence of the executive espoused later by the courts.[111]

Just how 'erratic' this shift was over the ensuing seventy years or so is well illustrated by the accounts that follow this statement in the next six pages of Dunstall's book.[112]

Within four years of the *Blackburn* decision in England, Lord Denning's statement of the doctrine of police independence was being cited by a New Zealand judge,[113] and there is no doubt at all, as will be evident from what follows, that it has had a significant influence in shaping views about the police-government relationship in New Zealand ever since. As in Australia, court decisions in which the doctrine of police independence has been considered have been rare. During the last thirty years, however, there have been numerous occasions on which police ministers have indicated in parliamentary debates that it is not appropriate for them to intervene in 'operational matters.' The following remarks of the minister of police in 1981 are typical of such assertions: 'I know the police entered the factory following a complaint from the owners. The purpose was to inform the occupants that they had no legal right to remain there and that if they continued to do so they would be liable for trespassing. The issue for police is an operational one in which it would be improper for me to intervene.'[114] Similar sentiments were expressed in Parliament by the current minister of police twenty years later: 'I consider it my duty as Minister to be well briefed on current issues in order that I can make informed decisions on matters of policy, resources and administration. However, in matters concerning investigative practice, law enforcement decisions, or any of the responsibilities, authorities, or powers within the office of constable, I have no direct involvement in operational policing matters. Those are quite rightly the domain of the Commissioner.'[115]

A critical event that ignited public discussion of the police in New Zealand was the tour of the South African Springbok rugby team in 1981. The tour sparked enormous controversy in New Zealand, occurring in the context of the continuing regime of apartheid in South Africa, to which most New Zealanders were strongly opposed. Their opposition to that regime, however, sat uncomfortably with their historic passion for the game of rugby as a focus of national identity, so the proposed visit of the Springboks caused deep and damaging divisions within New Zealand society. The National government of Prime Minister Muldoon (or at least the prime minister himself) was determined that the Springbok tour should be allowed to go ahead. This insistence, however, was in the face of massive public protests throughout the country. The police, inevitably, were caught in the middle. Despite the best efforts of the police to prevent them, violent confrontations between the police and the protesters, and between the protesters and rugby fans who supported the decision to allow the tour to go ahead, not surprisingly ensued. Because the protesters included New Zealanders from every walk of life and every class, the public outrage voiced against the force that was inflicted on demonstrators by the police was almost certainly greater than it would have been if the police could have characterized the protesters as an unrepresentative 'radical' fringe. In the recriminations and public debates that ensued, questions inevitably arose as to whether, and if so to what extent, the police had been directed or influenced by the government in their policing of the demonstrations.

No definitive (or even tentatively certain) answers to such questions were ever to be forthcoming, as no subsequent official inquiry with a mandate to pose the questions was ever established.[116] What is clear from subsequent interviews with the former commissioner involved, however, is that he met with the Prime Minister and other ministers more than once to discuss the arrangements for the policing of the tour,[117] and this was not only not considered exceptional or unacceptable, but at that time was clearly expected under such circumstances. While what we know about the policing of the Springbok tour provides scant information about the realities of police independence in New Zealand in the early 1980s, therefore, I mention it here because it marks the beginning of a period in which questions about the relations between the police and the government took on particular salience in the public mind.

More recently the issue of police-government relations has been closely examined in three contexts: a governmental review of the administration and management of the New Zealand Police, controversy over the policing of a state visit by a foreign head of state, and the introduction of a bill to amend the existing *Police Act*. I consider each of these in turn below.

The Review of Police Administration and Management Structure
During the last two decades New Zealand has been at the forefront of what has been described as a 'revolution in public management,'[118] in which almost every aspect and institution of government has been the object of scrutiny and reform. Despite its long-standing claim to an arm's-length relationship to government (including the rest of the public service), the police service has not escaped attention in this process.[119] In April 1998, the minister of police announced a review of the

administrative and management structures of the New Zealand Police, the key objectives of which were to:

optimise the New Zealand Police's contribution to the Government's public safety objectives by ensuring that the most cost effective administrative and management levels and structures are in place; and ensure the most cost effective administrative and management structures for the New Zealand Police in achieving the Government's public safety objectives (including statutory obligations), without compromising front line capability.

Interestingly, the review was undertaken by a four-person private-sector team consisting of a management consultant, a constitutional lawyer and former police minister and prime minister, a company director, and a property consultant. The constitutional lawyer prepared a paper for the review on Constitutional Issues Involving the Police in which it was argued that:

There are some decisions made by the Police that have to be exercised on an independent basis free from Ministerial direction. There are other matters where the Police must follow Government policy. The distinction often comes down to the difference between policy and operations.

While the boundary may be difficult to draw in practice, it is clear that the Minister of Police cannot direct the Commissioner of Police in respect of the Commissioner's duty to enforce the criminal law either in particular cases or classes of cases. The Minister can however impose binding requirements in respect of matters of administration and the level of resources.'[120]

Sir Geoffrey Palmer argued that the current provisions in the *Police Act* and the *Police Regulations* inadequately delineate the desired relationship between the commissioner and the minister, and recommended 'that the line between policy and operations not be [statutorily] defined,[121] but its workings made transparent by amending the Police Act along the lines carried out in Queensland,[122] with appropriate adjustments for New Zealand circumstances.' He noted that 'such a change would allow the Minister of Police to give written directions to the Commissioner and these would be tabled in the House of Representatives.'[123]

In its report, the review noted that 'policing is a core function of the State, and as such the New Zealand Police, as an organisation closely resembles a Public Service department,' and that 'a number of the practices and processes adopted in the State sector for assigning accountabilities also apply to the New Zealand Police.'[124] The report went on to note that notwithstanding this, 'the New Zealand Police is distinguishable from a Public Service department in a number of respects.' Specifically, it reiterated verbatim Palmer's account of the constitutional constraints on the power of the minister to direct the commissioner, and commented that 'the difficulty in precisely defining the boundary between Government policy and Police operations has the effect of diluting the accountability of the Commissioner and the New Zealand Police, and has meant that the responsibilities of the Commissioner and the New Zealand Police have been defined in the broadest terms only.'[125] It noted too that 'whilst some parts of the State Sector Act[126] regime apply to the New Zealand Police, others do not, most notably, the appointment processes for Chief Executives, and the procedures for reviewing the performance of Chief Executives.'[127]

The report noted as well that the police 'manage assets of very substantial value, including a significant property portfolio' and mentioned the 'risk' that this entails.[128] It adopted Palmer's view that the 'central issue' with respect to governance arrangements for the police is 'how to strengthen the accountability of the Commissioner of Police consistent with their constitutional independence on law enforcement.'[129] Its recommendations in this respect bear quotation in full:

> The existing accountability arrangements could be strengthened and extended in a variety of ways:
>
> i) whilst it is not possible to clearly define the line between Government policy and New Zealand Police operations, it is possible to make its workings more transparent. This could be achieved by way of an amendment to the Police Act to prescribe a process for dealing with an impasse between the Minister and the Commissioner. Specifically where the Minister and the Commissioner are unable to agree on whether an issue falls within a Minister's role for decision-making, or the Commissioner's independent role, and where the Minister feels strongly enough to direct the Commissioner, then the Minister would be required to give that direction in writing and table it in the House of representatives.
>
> ii) the Police Act should be amended to clearly set out its purpose, to define the role of the Police, and to more clearly specify the responsibilities of the Commissioner;

iii) the Police Act could be brought more into line with those provisions in the State Sector Act which would enhance accountability including:

- clarification of the appointment process for the Commissioner and Deputy Commissioners including issues of tenure and removal;
- empowering the State Services Commissioner[130] to review and report on the performance of the Commissioner of Police;
- requiring the Commissioner of Police to report each year to the Minister on the financial performance of the Police;
- requiring the Commissioner to furnish a report on the operational components of New Zealand Police activities, and on issues which are subject to Ministerial direction; and
- the Commissioner's rights and responsibilities in dealing with issues of staff performance and discipline should also be lined up with the State Sector Act as appropriate.'[131]

Finally, the report recommended that, 'given the magnitude of the Crown's ownership interest in the New Zealand Police' and the risk associated with this, it would be advisable for the minister of police to appoint a 'Management Advisory Board, comprising persons with business skills and experience, to advise the Minister on the New Zealand Police's corporate intentions, including capital investments and divestments. This advice could also extend to assessing the adequacy of the business practices adopted by the New Zealand Police in managing its resources, and which in turn could feed into the State Service Commissioner's review of the Police Commissioner's performance.'[132]

Just over a month after the Review submitted its report, other events transpired which were to significantly influence debate over the police-government relationship in New Zealand.

The President of China's State Visit to New Zealand, September 1999
The President of China's visit to New Zealand in September 1999 was marked by public protests over China's alleged human rights abuses in Tibet. Under the pretext of ensuring that the president did not come to any harm from the protests, the police attempted, under threat of arrest, to disperse protesters and move them far away from sites that the president was visiting, including a hotel in Christchurch at which the Prime Minister of New Zealand was hosting a state banquet in his honour. It had been reported that the president had indicated that he would not attend the banquet while protests continued. Having moved

the protesters back away from the hotel, the police parked two buses in front of them in such a way that their protest banners could not be seen from the entrance of the hotel, and when the president eventually arrived, police sirens effectively drowned out the shouts of protesters. Several protesters were arrested and detained, but charges against them were eventually dropped. The police were accused of using excessive force and unlawfully interfering with the protesters' rights of peaceful assembly and free speech.

Some contemporary eyewitness accounts suggested that shortly before the police were deployed against the protesters at the hotel, the prime minister was in conversation both with the Chinese military official in charge of presidential security and with an assistant commissioner of the New Zealand Police, in the hotel lobby, and that the prime minister's chief of staff had 'remonstrated' with the assistant commissioner outside the hotel immediately prior to the police action to remove the protesters.[133]

These allegations were the subject of an inquiry by a parliamentary committee which submitted its report in December 2000.[134] The committee concluded that some of the police's actions (particularly the use of the buses and sirens) were 'unjustified' and constituted a prima facie violation of the protesters' rights under the *New Zealand Bill of Rights, 1990*. It found, however, that the allegations of improper interference in police operations by the prime minister and government officials were not supported by the evidence it had heard:

> We consider there is no evidence of members of the Government or their officials making either express or implied threats to the Police on this matter ... Nor is there any evidence that the Police felt their authority was being overridden. It is clear that the Police always knew that all decisions relating to the protesters were theirs to make, although they were made very conscious of the importance the Government placed on the dinner proceeding.
>
> As concerns the question of whether the then Prime Minister conducted herself appropriately, we consider that there is no evidence that Mrs Shipley attempted to direct the Police in the performance of their duties. Mrs Shipley was anxious about the attendance of the President and about the comfort of her large number of guests. A degree of liaison between Government officials and the Police is both important and inevitable in such circumstances.'

Having thus absolved the prime minister and government officials of any wrongdoing in this incident, the committee's report went on to emphasize the importance of appearances and perceptions in such instances:

> We wish to emphasise to all politicians and Government officials that care must be taken when interacting with the Police in a situation such as that which occurred in Christchurch. It is vital to have regard to the appearance to the public of any interaction between Government and the Police and to be alert to the inferences that may be drawn by the Police from any communication with politicians and Government officials. Care must be taken that boundaries are not blurred and that pressure is not unintentionally brought to bear on the Police. It is important that the boundaries between the political arm and the operational arm of the State are observed and maintained.

The committee felt that the evidence it had heard about the events at the hotel 'points to the need for clear guidelines, which will allow both the Government and the Police to have certainty about the boundaries of each party's respective authority. Such guidelines would assist the Police to resist anything that may be deemed to be inappropriate pressure. We acknowledge that guidelines can never provide absolute clarity of boundaries. However, we consider that the existence of guidelines would have assisted events on the evening of 14 September 1999.'

Noting that 'the powers of government relating to the maintenance of public order must be seen in the context of the relationship between the Government and the Police,' the committee went on to consider the legislative framework governing this relationship, and in particular 'the constitutional status of the police and the implications of the legislative framework for the operational independence of the Police.' The committee noted that 'the legislative framework needs to provide for clear legal boundaries between the Police and the Government.' As a result of its analysis of these issues, the committee recommended that:

> 1. Consideration should be given to clarifying the constitutional status of the police, as it is set out in New Zealand law. In particular, consideration should be given to examining the current legislative framework governing the Police, namely the Police Act 1958 and the Police Regulations 1992, to establish whether greater clarity[135] could be achieved in defining

the constitutional boundaries between the Police and the Government.

2. Consideration should also be given to enacting regulation 3 of the Police Regulations 1992 in primary legislation, and removing it from secondary legislation. This would be in accordance with the fundamental constitutional principle that regulations should be confined to dealing with matters of implementation and detail, whereas matters of policy and principle are dealt with in primary legislation.

Two aspects of the committee's arguments and conclusions deserve brief comment before moving on to consider the legislative aftermath of its report. In the first place, the committee's argument appears to expand the scope of the doctrine of police independence, so that it covers *all* police operations and not just those that may be considered to involve 'law enforcement' (however that may be defined). While some may argue that all police operations *do* potentially involve law enforcement, the committee's formulation of the doctrine certainly goes beyond the 'quasi-judicial' functions (of arrest, charging, and prosecution) that some earlier formulations of the doctrine envisaged.

Second, the committee's acceptance that 'a degree of liaison between Government officials and the Police is both important and inevitable' in situations such as that which arose during the Chinese president's visit, and its implicit acceptance that some direct 'interaction between Government and the Police' may be justified on such occasions, provided it is undertaken with 'care' and with due regard for appearances and possible police perceptions of government 'pressure,' is worthy of note. It does, however, raise the delicate issue of when the expression, in such circumstances, of 'legitimate' concerns or desires on the part of government officials may cross the line and reasonably be interpreted as inappropriate pressure or influence on the police in the performance of their duties.

The Police Amendment Bill (No. 2)

By the beginning of 2001 the New Zealand government had two reports in hand that recommended some legislative clarification of the appropriate relationship between the government and the police, each report having arisen out of quite different circumstances. Its response, in August 2001, was to introduce the *Police Amendment Bill (No. 2)* into Parliament.

The bill deals with a range of issues,[136] most of which have arisen out of the 1998 report of the Review of Police Administration and Management Structure, and many of which have proven quite controversial.[137] On the issue of the relationship between the police and government, the bill proposes a number of significant amendments to the *Police Act* along the lines of those recommended by the review report and the report of the Justice and Electoral Committee. The first group of these provides that the State Services commissioner shall have a leading role in managing the appointment process for a commissioner of police,[138] and in reviewing the commissioner's performance while in office.[139] The second group addresses specifically the respective roles of the commissioner and the minister, and the rights of the minister to give directions to the commissioner. Because of their importance in this respect, they deserve to be quoted verbatim here:

4 Responsibility and independence of Commissioner
   (1) The Commissioner is responsible to the Minister for –
      (a) the carrying out of the functions, duties, and powers of the police; and
      (b) tendering advice to the Minister and other Ministers of the Crown; and
      (c) the general conduct of the police; and
      (d) the efficient, effective and economical management of the police; and
      (e) giving effect to any directions of the Minister on matters of Government policy.
   (2) The Commissioner is not responsible to the Minister, but must act independently, in relation to the following –
      (a) enforcement of the criminal law in particular cases and classes of case;
      (b) matters that relate to an individual or group of individuals;
      (c) decisions on individual members of the police.

5 Minister's power to give directions
   (1)   The Minister may give the Commissioner directions on matters of Government policy that relate to –
      (a) the prevention of crime; and
      (b) the maintenance of public safety and public order; and
      (c) the delivery of police services; and
      (d) general areas of law enforcement.

(2) No direction from the Minister to the Commissioner may have the effect of requiring the non-enforcement of a particular area of the law.

(3) The Minister must not give directions to the Commissioner in relation to the following;

    (a) enforcement of the criminal law in particular cases and particular classes of case;

    (b) matters that relate to an individual or group of individuals;

    (c) decisions on individual members of the police.

(4) If there is a dispute between the Minister and the Commissioner in relation to any direction under this section, the Minister must, as soon as practicable after the dispute arises, –

    (a) provide that direction to the Commissioner in writing; and

    (b) publish a copy in the *Gazette*; and

    (c) present a copy to the House of Representatives.

A number of features of these provisions are worthy of note. In the first place, this is undoubtedly the most detailed attempt in any jurisdiction so far to legislatively specify the parameters of the relationship between a minister of police and a police commissioner.

Second, it will be noted that the matters with respect to which the commissioner is required to act independently (and with respect to which the minister is prohibited from giving directions to the commissioner) clearly extend beyond the realm of 'law enforcement' to any 'matters that relate to an individual or group of individuals'; any attempt to direct the police with respect to the handling of a particular public order situation such as that which transpired during the Chinese president's visit in 1999 would clearly be prohibited by this provision. A direction that related to the handling of such incidents generally, however (such as a direction that certain kinds of equipment or weaponry not be used in such situations), would presumably be permissible as a direction on a matter of government policy relating to the maintenance of public safety and public order. Given the breadth of the terminology prescribing the areas of the commissioner's independence, however, it is less easy to imagine what might be a permissible ministerial direction on a matter of government policy relating to 'general areas of law enforcement.' Clearly, there is room for interpretation of some of these provisions (and potential disagreement as to their application).

Third, while the provisions are specific with respect to ministerial 'directions,' their implications for less directive communications from the minister to a commissioner are not very clear. How forcefully would a minister be able to express the government's (or his or her own) 'views' or 'suggestions' about a situation before such expression (which might have considerable influence over a commissioner whose appointment is 'at pleasure') could be interpreted as an attempt at 'direction'?

Fourth, it will be noted that while directions by the minister of police are covered by these provisions, directions or communications by other ministers (including the prime minister) or government officials are not. Perhaps, however, the fact that the commissioner 'must act independently' in relation to those matters with respect to which ministerial directions are prohibited can be interpreted to imply that directions from any source on those matters would be equally unlawful.

Fifth, it is noteworthy that ministerial directions are only required to be reduced to writing if there is some dispute about them between the minister and the commissioner. This means that there need be no record of (and hence little or no accountability for) how frequently (or with respect to what matters) ministerial directions to the commissioner are given.

Finally, although the provisions are not explicit on this point, it may be implied from them that any ministerial direction in contravention of sections 5(2) or (3) would be unlawful, and that a commissioner would have a *duty* not to allow him- or herself to be influenced by such a direction (since it would concern a matter with respect to which the commissioner 'must act independently'). Would acquiescing in such a direction (assuming that this could be verified) amount to misconduct on the part of a commissioner? What recourse could there be against an overly submissive or compliant commissioner?[140]

Introducing the bill on Second Reading in Parliament, the acting minister of police was at pains to emphasize that it was not an attempt to achieve inappropriate government control over the police:

This bill acknowledges the need for the police to work in a non-partisan way, free from suggestions of political control and interference in operational matters. The bill enhances the constitutional separation between the police and politicians, putting the independence of the Commissioner on a statutory basis for the first time. In the future, the independence of the head of our police service will not simply rely on custom, convention, or case law; it will be spelt out in the Police Act. This bill puts the independence of the police on a clearer footing.

... The bill does not affect the role of the Commissioner of Police as this country's most senior law enforcer. It is absolutely essential that the police retain their operational independence. Nothing in the bill erodes that independence. Future commissioners will continue to have a strong operational policing background, and to be drawn from a pool of competent officers with New Zealand policing experience. The Government is committed to seeing that the police continue to be led by a credible and experienced Commissioner of Police.

The Opposition parties, and several of those who testified at committee hearings on the bill (including two former commissioners), however, were not convinced, one of the Opposition spokesmen referring to the bill as 'a constitutional outrage, in the truest sense of the words.' After receiving forty-two submissions, holding hearings that lasted just over three hours, and deliberating for a further six hours, the Law and Order Committee reported that it had been 'unable to reach a recommendation as to whether the bill should be passed.'[141] Since then, the bill has remained on Parliament's agenda but gone nowhere.[142]

Summary: New Zealand

As in Australia, the idea of police independence has had currency in New Zealand for quite a while, and it has been discussed primarily in the context of inquiries and legislative and broader government reform initiatives rather than in judicial decisions, as in England. The English *Blackburn* decision, however, has definitely had an important influence on recent thinking about police independence in New Zealand. Unlike in Australia, however, allegations of corruption have not provided an important context for discussions about police independence. Indeed, the main 'driver' for recent consideration of the issue in New Zealand has been the implementation, governmentwide, of major public service reform (the 'new public management').

Like Australia, and unlike England, New Zealand is currently exploring possibilities for legislative clarification of the relationship between the commissioner and the minister of police (and hence the scope of police independence). If enacted, the current proposals in this respect in the *Police Amendment (No. 2) Bill* will be the most detailed and specific anywhere.

Governments in New Zealand do not seem to have been as reluctant as some governments in Australia to recognize, in theory at least, a wide range of decision making with respect to which the police ought to be free from political direction. As in Britain and Australia, however, the autonomy of the commissioner is probably significantly limited in practice by the expectations of the new public management initiatives.

There is a recognition in New Zealand that widely defined independence must be accompanied by equally wide accountability requirements; in this respect, the very broad formulation of police independence in the *Blackburn* statement is not accepted.

The discussion around police independence in New Zealand, unlike in Australia, has generally focused on the relationship between the commissioner and the minister, rather than between the commissioner and the Prime Minister or other government ministers. Although there have certainly been many instances of significant government intervention in operational policing matters in the past, there now seems to be a broad acceptance by all political parties in New Zealand of a presumption against such intervention. There is not yet all-party agreement, however, that the proposed new legislative provisions in this respect provide the right delineation of the acceptable parameters of the commissioner–minister relationship.

Conclusion

This review of the development of the idea of police independence in the United Kingdom, Australia, and New Zealand demonstrates very clearly how much variation there is in these jurisdictions with respect to the content, scope, application, acceptability, and presumed implications of the idea. Noteworthy from the point of view of the concerns of the Ipperwash Inquiry is the fact that consultation between police commissioners and government ministers, including state premiers and prime ministers, prior to and during the course of public order policing operations does not seem to be regarded as untoward or unacceptable in either Australia or New Zealand, and in fact seems to be positively expected in some of these jurisdictions.

Despite the variation I have described, a common trend is discernible in all these jurisdictions, in which considerations and implications of more general public service reform are probably now having a much greater impact on the practical realities of the police-government relationship than purely legal doctrinal arguments. This trend, of course, is not unique to the police, but can be discerned in almost all areas of government.

There is also a clear trend, at least in Australia and New Zealand, towards a preference for legislative rather than judicial enunciation of the acceptable parameters of this relationship. It is too soon, however, to be able to determine what the implications of this trend may turn out to be for the degree of consensus about, and adherence in practice to, those parameters in those jurisdictions. But an important element of the trend is the insistence that whatever the scope and limits of ministerial direction and control settled upon, there must be more transparency (public accountability) – through the requirement that directives be in writing and published etc. – to the relationship between the police and the government. In any case, the experiences of the idea of police independence in the three countries examined provide a rich choice of ways to think about, define, and implement the concept.

NOTES

1 An idea that received judicial support from Lawton LJ in *R. v. Chief Constable of Devon and Cornwall, ex parte Central Electricity Generating Board*, [1982] Q.B. 458 at 474, and more recently by Lord Steyn in *O'Hara v. Chief Constable of the Royal Ulster Constabulary*, [1997] 1 All E.R. 129 (H.L.). This notion was implicitly rejected, however, in the New Zealand case of *Police v. Newnham*, [1978] 1 N.Z.L.R. 844. See also R. Hogg and Hawker, 'The Politics of Political Independence' (1983) 8(4) Legal Services Bulletin 160 and note 69 below.

2 J. Goldring and R. Wettenhall, 'Three Perspectives on the Responsibility of Statutory Authorities,' in *Responsible Government in Australia*, ed. P. Weller and D. Jaensch (Richmond, VA: Drummond, 1980), 136.

3 In a 1978 article, Geoffrey Marshall usefully distinguished between two possible 'modes' of accountability: what he called the 'subordinate and obedient' mode (in which accountability is directly linked to direction and control), and what he called the 'explanatory and co-operative mode' (in which it is not). Marshall argued that the 'explanatory and co-operative' mode (quadrant 4 in figure 4.1) is more appropriate for police, at least with respect to their law enforcement functions. In particular, he wrote that: 'If ... in the field of law enforcement we have to give a calculated and unprejudiced answer in 1977 to the question whether civil liberties and impartial justice are more to be expected from chief constables than from elected politicians (whether on police committees or in the House of Commons or in ministerial departments) many liberal democrats would feel justified in placing more trust in the former than in the latter.' Geoffrey Marshall, 'Police Accountability Revisited,' in *Policy and Politics, Essays in Honour of Norman Chester*, ed. D. Butler and A.H. Halsey (London: Macmillan, 1978), 61–3.

4 Interestingly, in a recent article about chief constables in Scotland, the idea
   of police independence is mentioned only in passing, and only English
   references to it (notably the report of the 1962 Royal Commission on the
   Police, discussed below) are cited: K. Scott and R. Wilkie, 'Chief Constables: A Current "Crisis" in Scottish Policing?' (2001) 35 Scottish Affairs
   54. For a much earlier discussion of the constitutional position of the police
   in Scotland, see J. Mitchell, 'The Constitutional Position of the Police in
   Scotland' (1962) 7 Juridical Review 1.

5 For a full discussion, in English, of the arrangements for police governance in the Netherlands, see T. Jones, Policing and Democracy in The
   Netherlands (London: Policy Institute, 1995): ch. 3 and 7, from which this
   brief account is derived.

6 For useful discussions of these two models, see H. King, 'Some Aspects
   of Police Administration in New South Wales, 1825–1851' (1956) 42(5)
   Journal and Proceedings of the Royal Australian Historical Society 205 and
   P. Stenning, Police Governance in First Nations in Ontario (Toronto: Centre of
   Criminology, University of Toronto, 1996), ch. 2.

7 The concern here was that although locally employed, such police were
   subject to law enforcement duties that were determined by state or national laws. It was felt to be inappropriate for local authorities to be held
   civilly liable for the performance of such duties by the police.

8 The main cases are: Enever v. The King, [1906] 3 C.L.R. 969; Fisher v. Oldham
   Corporation, [1930] 2 K.B. 364; and Attorney General for New South Wales v.
   Perpetual Trustee Company, [1955] A.C. 477. Relevant North American cases
   are reviewed in P. Stenning, Legal Status of the Police (Ottawa: Minister of
   Supply and Services Canada, 1982), ch. 4. See also (re Australia) Chapman
   v. Commissioner of the Australian Federal Police (1983), 76 FLR 428, and R. v.
   Commissioner of Police, ex parte Ross, [1992] 1 Qd. R. 289. The idea that a
   police officer is not a 'servant' of the Crown for the purposes of vicarious
   liability was rejected in the South African case of Sibiya v. Swart, (1950)
   S.A.L.R. 515.

9 One of the Australian judges (Dixon J) in the Perpetual Trustee case indicated that he felt constrained to follow and apply the court's earlier decision in Commonwealth v. Quince (1944), 68 CLR 227 (which involved a
   member of the armed forces, rather than a police officer), but that were the
   matter to be decided afresh, he would hold that the relationship between
   the Crown and a sworn staff member was an employment one: (1952),
   85 CLR 237 at 244. Similar sentiments were expressed by Marshall J in
   the later Australian case of Konrad v. Victoria Police (1998), 152 CLR 132
   at 143–4.

10 Most particularly, the following dicta of Griffith CJ in the Australian case of *Enever v. The King*, [1906] 3 C.L.R. 969: 'the powers of a constable, *qua* police officer, whether conferred by common law or statute law, are exercised by him by virtue of his office, and cannot be exercised on the responsibility of any person but himself ... A constable, therefore, when acting as a peace officer, is not exercising a delegated authority, but an original authority ...'

11 United Kingdom, Royal Commission on the Police, *Final Report* (London: HMSO, 1962), 74. Subsequent page references for quotations from this document are found in the main text.

12 There was no independent public prosecution service in England and Wales at the time (and indeed until the establishment of the Crown Prosecution Service there in 1985). Prosecutorial decisions were largely the responsibility of the police.

13 The commission noted that even with respect to these kinds of decisions chief constables were statutorily subject to the powers and authority of the director of public prosecutions in the case of 'certain grave offences.'

14 The commission noted that in Scotland 'a decision to prosecute, and the prosecution itself, are the concern of a judicial officer, the public prosecutor; and chief constables are required by s. 4(3) of the Police (Scotland) Act, 1956, to comply with such lawful instructions as they may receive from a public prosecutor in relation to the investigation of offences.'

15 Note that here once again the commission confounds issues of control and accountability.

16 It is not clear from the report whether this language was intended to refer only to what the commission had referred to as the 'quasi-judicial' law enforcement decisions respecting investigation, arrest, and prosecution in 'the enforcement of the law in particular cases,' or to a broader subset of 'activities concerned with law enforcement.'

17 Geoffrey Marshall, *Police and Government: The Status and Accountability of the English Constable* (London: Methuen, 1965), 120. See also Roach pages 22–4 and 56–7 of this volume for further discussion on Geoffrey Marshall's position.

18 Ibid., 119–20.

19 However, as indicated in note 3, above, his views on this later changed.

20 *R. v. Metropolitan Police Commissioner, ex parte Blackburn*, [1968] 1 All E.R. 763 at 769, per Lord Denning MR.

21 E.g., Marshall, 'Police Accountability Revisited; Stenning, *Legal Status of the Police*; G. Orr, 'Police Accountability to the Executive and Parliament,' in *Policing at the Crossroads*, ed. C. Cameron and W. Young (Wellington:

Allen & Unwin/Port Nicholson Press, 1986). Lord Denning's view was described as 'an extreme view, not consistently accepted by the bench nor by subsequent judicial inquiries' in Centre for Comparative Constitutional Studies (1997), 5. Paper commissioned by the Police Board of Victoria. Quotation in main text from L. Lustgarten, *The Governance of Police* (London: Sweet & Maxwell, 1986), 64.

22 One English chief constable, who had earlier been invited to conduct a review of the administration of the Victoria, Australia, Police Force (E. St Johnston, *A Report on the Victoria Police Force Following an Inspection* (Melbourne: Government Printer, 1971)), wrote that 'in operational matters a Chief Constable is answerable to God, his Queen, his conscience, and to no one else.' E. St Johnston, *One Policeman's Story* (Chichester: Berry Rose, 1978), 153.

23 [1981] 3 All E.R. 826 at 833.

24 [1988] 1 All E.R. 556 at 566.

25 [1999] 1 All E.R. 129.

26 Lord Scarman, *The Scarman Report: The Brixton Disorders* (London: HMSO, 1981). In his report, Lord Scarman commented: 'Community involvement in the policy and operations of policing is perfectly feasible without undermining the independence of the police or destroying the secrecy of those operations against crime which have to be kept secret.' He added, however, that 'there will, of course, be some operational aspects of policing – such as criminal investigations and security matters – which it would be wrong to make the subject of consultation and discussion with representatives of the community' (para. 5.56).

27 J. Alderson, *Policing Freedom* (Plymouth: MacDonald & Evans Ltd, 1979).

28 J. Anderton, 'Accountable to whom?' *Police* (10 February 1981) 6 at 10.

29 It is important to note that in the United Kingdom 50 per cent of funding for local police services is provided out of the national Treasury, but is dependent on satisfactory performance reports by inspectors employed by Her Majesty's Inspector of Constabulary (HMIC), who reports to the home secretary. This, of course, gives the central government considerable leverage over local policing policies and priorities.

30 S. 7 of the act required police authorities to set objectives, and s. 38 authorized the home secretary to require them to set performance targets.

31 It should be noted that, technically speaking, Lord Denning's statement in Blackburn was itself *obiter*.

32 United Kingdom, Independent Commission on Policing for Northern Ireland, *A New Beginning: Policing in Northern Ireland* (London: HMSO, 1999).

33 Ibid., 32–3. S. 33 of the *Police (Northern Ireland) Act, 2000*, however, defines the 'functions of the Chief Constable' of the PSNI in more or less identical terms to those used in s. 10 of the English *Police Act, 1996*, quoted above.

34 United Kingdom, Home Office, Communication Directorate, *Policing: Building Safer Communities Together* (London: Home Office Communication Directorate, 2003), i.

35 Ibid., 16.

36 S. 41A of the 1996 *Police Act*, as inserted by s. 5 of the 2000 *Police Reform Act*. Interestingly, in the original 2000 Police Reform Bill, this section authorized the home secretary to give directions to chief constables rather than to police authorities. This provision sparked an outcry, with claims that it was an attack on police independence, as result of which the provision was changed by the government: see G. Jones, 'Tories fight threat to police independence,' *Daily Telegraph*, 28 February 2002, and O. Letwin, 'Blunkett is laying the ground to make Britain a police state,' *Daily Telegraph*, 24 May 2002.

37 See http://uk.sitestat.com/homeoffice/homeoffice/s?docs2 .useoffirearms&ns_type=pdf.

38 The Bichard Inquiry Report: see http://www.bichardinquiry.org.uk/ 10663/report.pdf.

39 *The Queen on the application of the Secretary of State for the Home Department v. Humberside Police Authority and Westwood*, [2004] EWHC 1642 (Q.B.) at para. 12 of the judgment.

40 Ibid., at para. 11.

41 The issue in *Blackburn* was not whether politicians can or should give directions to the police, but whether the court could and should issue mandamus to compel the police commissioner to enforce a particular law.

42 Hogg and Hawker, 'The Politics of Political Independence,' 163.

43 *Enever v. The King* (1906), 3 C.L.R. 969 (Austr. H.C.) and *Attorney General for New South Wales v. Perpetual Trustee Co.*, [1955] A.C. 457 (J.C.P.C.).

44 For a more detailed analysis of these two cases and their relevance for the doctrine of police independence, see Marshall, *Police and Government*, 42–5.

45 Interestingly, the case that was relied upon in both of the Australian cases to support the conclusion that a police officer is not the 'servant' of those who employ him or her was an English case, *Stanbury v. Exeter Corporation*, [1905] 2 K.B. 838, in which the court had to consider whether an inspector appointed under the *Diseases of Animals Act, 1894* was to be considered a 'servant' of the local authority that appointed him. In that case, the court commented that the position of the inspector was analogous to that of a police officer in that his authority was not delegated to him by the local authority but conferred on him directly by the statute, and that his duties

thus transcended his local appointment. While this may arguably have been true of a locally appointed inspector (or even a constable) it is difficult to see how it could be true of a police officer appointed by the very state that enacts the legislation conferring authority on him, as was the situation in both of the Australian cases. For although there were once local municipal police forces in Australia, they had been replaced by state police forces, modelled on the Royal Ulster Constabulary, by the time these two Australian cases were decided.

46 *King-Brooks v. Roberts* (1991) 5 W.A.R. 500 (W.A.S.C.) and *R. v. Commissioner of Police, ex p. North Broken Hill Ltd.* (1992), 1 Tas.R. 99 (Tas. S.C.). In the former case, Lord Denning's *Blackburn* statement was directly cited with approval (at 517); in the latter case, Wright J only alluded to the fact that the police 'are not subject to the direction or control of any outside organization' (at 111).

47 In 1970, s. 6 the Queensland *Police Act* provided that the commissioner 'shall, subject to the direction of the Minister, be charged with the Superintendence of the Police Force of Queensland.' S. 9 of the Western Australian *Police Act* provided that the commissioner 'may make regulations, with the approval of the Minister for general management and discipline of the police force.' S. 8 of the Tasmanian *Police Regulation Act* provided that the commissioner 'shall, under the direction of the Minister, and subject to the provisions of this Act, have the control and superintendence of the police force.' S. 5 of the Victorian *Police Regulation Act* provided that the commissioner 'shall have, subject to the direction of the Governor in Council, the superintendence and control of the Force.' And S. 4 of the New South Wales *Police Regulation Act* provided that the commissioner 'shall, subject to the direction of the Minister, be charged with the superintendence of the police force.' S. 5AAA of the *Police Ordinance* of the Australian Capital Territory provided that the commissioner 'shall, under the direction of the Minister, be charged with the general control and management of the Police Force.' S. 8 of the *Police and Police Offences Ordinance* of the Northern Territory provided that the commissioner 'shall be charged and vested with the general control and management of the Police Force of the Territory and ... shall exercise and perform all powers and functions ... in accordance with such instructions as are given ... by the administrator.'

48 The premier was listed as a member of the General Committee of the Campaign for Peace in Vietnam which had supported the demonstration. South Australia, Royal Commission on the September Moratorium Demonstration, *Report* (Adelaide: Government Printer, 1971), 58. Page references for quotations from this report appear in parentheses in the main text.

49 South Australia, Royal Commission, *Report on the Dismissal of Harold Hubert Salisbury* (Adelaide: Government Printer, 1978), 50.

50 For a contemporary journalist's account of this case see S. Cockburn, *The Salisbury Affair* (Melbourne: Sun Books, 1979). For more academic accounts and analyses, see R. Plehwe and R. Wettenhall, 'Reflections on the Salisbury Affair: Police-Government Relations in Australia' (1979) 51(1) Australian Quarterly 75, and L. Waller, 'The Police, the Premier and Parliament: Governmental Control of the Police' (1980) Monash University L.R. 249.

51 South Australia, Royal Commission, *Report on the Dismissal of Hubert Salisbury*, 36.

52 Ibid.

53 She did not, however, choose to do so.

54 South Australia, Royal Commission, *Report on the Dismissal of Hubert Salisbury*, 20.

55 Again, beyond what follows, Mitchell J gave no specific examples.

56 The Australian Security Intelligence Organisation, a Commonwealth agency.

57 Hope J had chaired a royal commission into the Australian security services.

58 South Australia, *Report on the Dismissal of Hubert Salisbury*, 20.

59 Ibid. In support of this conclusion, Mitchell J quoted the comment in the final report of the English Royal Commission on the Police in 1962 that: 'The Commissioner of Police acts under the general authority of the Home Secretary, and he is accountable to the Home Secretary for the way in which he uses his Force.' United Kingdom, Royal Commission on the Police, *Final Report*, 1962: para. 91, p. 31.

60 T. Lawson, 'Report to Heads of Agencies Committee on Establishment of a Police Board in South Australia,' unpublished report, Southern Australia Attorney-General's Department, 1992. The committee comprised the commissioner of police (who had expressed opposition to the establishment of such a board in the state), the commissioner for public employment, and the chief executive officer in the Attorney-General's Department. For a critical reaction to this paper, see C. Stevens, 'A Report on the Concept of a Police Board in South Australia,' Current Issues paper #4, Police Association of South Australia: http://www.para.asn.au/paper04.htm (1995).

61 P. Stenning, *Legal Status of the Police* (Ottawa: Law Reform Commission, 1981) and R. Hann et al., 'Municipal Police Governance and Accountability in Canada: An Empirical Study' (1985) 9(1) Canadian Police College Journal 1.

62 The idea of establishing a police board, similar to those established in New South Wales and Victoria (discussed below), was apparently considered in South Australia in the early 1990s, but not adopted: see Lawson, Report, and Stevens, 'Report.'

63 No. 55 of 1998.

64 Queensland, Commission of Inquiry into Possible Illegal Activities and Associated Police Misconduct, Report (Brisbane: Government Printer, 1989), 35.

65 See his Barry Memorial Lecture on this topic, delivered in 1975. R. Whitrod, 'The Accountability of Police Forces – Who Polices the Police?' (1976) 9 Australian and New Zealand Journal of Criminology 7.

66 Quoted in Hogg and Hawker, 'The Politics of Political Independence,' 164.

67 Queensland, Commission of Inquiry, Report, 46.

68 The preceding account is based on the account of these events in the inquiry report at 35–46. Accounts by Whitrod and the police minister at the time, Allen Hodges, are reproduced in G. Pitman, 'Police Minister and Commissioner Relationships' (PhD dissertation, Faculty of Commerce and Administration, Griffith University, 1998), ch. 8.

69 The commission also recommended that the exercise of such powers by individual police officers should be subject to review by senior officers (ibid., 279–80).

70 Ibid., 278–9.

71 The secretary was the departmental head of the Police Department.

72 This provision has since been amended, broadening the power of ministerial direction to include written directions '(either specific or general) ... in relation to the use of common services': see now s. 37 of the act. For examples of recent directions issued by the minister under s. 37, see http://www.afp.gov.au/page.asp?ref=/AboutAFP/Legislation/ministerial.xml and http://www.afp.gov.au/page.asp?ref=/AboutAFP/Legislation/supplementary.xml

73 New South Wales, Commission to Inquire into New South Wales Police Administration, Report (Sydney: Government Printer, 1981).

74 Lusher J identified the main functions of the proposed board as: '1. The implementation of such of the recommendations of this report as are accepted by the Government. 2. The planning for and provision of a comprehensive planned police service in the State. 3. The oversighting of the resources employed in the provision of this service.' He then listed thirteen more specific functions. Ibid., 791–3.

75 Ibid., 789.

76 Act No. 135, 1983.

77 *Independent Commission Against Corruption Act,* 1988.

78 *Police Legislation Further Amendment Act, 1996,* No. 108, s. 34.

79 It is told well, and in great detail, in S. Williams, *Peter Ryan: The Inside Story* (Sydney: Viking/Penguin Books, Australia Ltd., 2002).

80 New South Wales, Royal Commission into the New South Wales Police Service, *Final Report* (Sydney: Government Printer, 1997), 244–5.

81 S. 8 currently provides: '(1) The Commissioner is, subject to the direction of the Minister, responsible for the management and control of NSW Police. (2) The Responsibility of the Commissioner includes the effective, efficient and economical management of the functions and activities of NSW Police.'

82 For an account of Ryan's final days as commissioner, see Williams, *Peter Ryan,* 305–24. Ryan's own list of 'operational' matters that the police minister had taken decisions on is reproduced at 318–19.

83 K. Milte and T. Weber, *Police in Australia* (Sydney: Butterworths, 1997), however, cited some examples of ministers invoking the doctrine of police independence (and its corollary of ministerial non-intervention in operational matters) in Commonwealth and Victorian Parliamentary debates during the 1970s (at 212–19). Other examples of conflicts between police commissioners and their police ministers in Australia are referred to in M. Finnane, *Police and Government: Histories of Policing in Australia* (Melbourne: Oxford University Press, 1954), 43–4.

84 Western Australia is currently the only Australian jurisdiction where the legislation does not explicitly specify that the police commissioner's exercise of his functions is subject to some executive direction. In 2003, this state established a Corruption and Crime Commission, headed by a corruption and crime commissioner who now shares with the police commissioner responsibility for the investigation or corruption and organized crime in the state: *Corruption and Crime Commission Act, 2003.*

85 The current chief commissioner of the Victoria Police Force, however, who previously served in the New South Wales Police during the Wood Royal Commission in the late 1990s, has recently argued strongly against the need or desirability of a royal commission to investigate current allegations of corruption within the Victoria Police Force: C. Nixon, 'Why Victoria Does Not Need a Royal Commission into Police Corruption,' http://www.police.vic.gov.au/showcontentpage.cfm (2004). She has been supported in this argument by the current minister of police: see M. Bachelard, 'Minister Changes Tune on Police Inquiries, *Australian,* 29 March 2004, 5.

86 See Victoria, *Board of Inquiry into Allegations against Members of the Victoria*

Police Force (Melbourne: Government Printer, 1976); and Western Australia, Royal Commission into whether there has been Corrupt or Criminal Conduct by any Western Australian Police Officer, *Final Report* (Perth: Government Printer, 2004).

87 St Johnston, *Report on the Victoria Police Force.*

88 Victoria, Committee of Enquiry, Victoria Police Force, *Report* (Melbourne: Government Printer, 1985).

89 Ibid., 12–13.

90 Ibid., 14. The provision inserted in the *Police Regulation Act* in 1873 provided that 'the Chief Commissioner shall have, subject to the directions of the Governor in Council, the superintendence and control of the Force.' S. 5 of the act is in identical terms today.

91 Victoria, Committee of Inquiry, *Report*, 19.

92 Ss. 4A–4G of the *Police Regulation Act*, inserted by the *Police Regulation (Amendment) Act, 1992*, No. 72 of 1992.

93 A more detailed description of the board and its functions can be found at http://www.uplink.com.au/lawlibrary/Documents/Docs/Doc56.html.

94 Police Regulation (Amendment) Act, 1999, No. 61 of 1999. See now s. 88 of the *Police Regulation Act* for the functions of the Police Appeals Board.

95 See J. Kennett, 1999.

96 Quoted in Victoria, Ministerial Administrative Review into Victoria Police Resourcing, Operational Independence, Human Resource Planning and Associated Issues, *Report* (Melbourne: Department of Justice, 2001), 36.

97 Ibid., 30.

98 In its report, the review commented: 'The Queensland provision would need some qualification in a Victorian context in order to safeguard the operational independence and accountability of the Chief Commissioner. For example, a restatement of Queensland paragraph (c) to refer to "the broad deployment of police numbers in accordance with policy objectives" would be consistent with the Review's [later] recommendations in Chapter 3' of its report (concerning human resource planning). Ibid., 55.

99 Ibid., 56. Interestingly, the Force Command, in its initial submission to the review, opposed giving such directive power to the minister, rather than to the governor in council, as the current Victorian legislation provides, on the ground that: 'if resort is had to the direction power, "the relationship between the Minister and the Chief Commissioner has probably become unworkable." In addition, as the current arrangements necessitate the Minister making a recommendation on the direction to the Governor in Council, they create an intrinsic safeguard, which accommodates "Ministers' historical caution about taking action that could be interpreted as

'political interference' in the administration of justice.'" Ibid., 52.

100 As noted above, however, serious allegations of corruption within the Victoria Police have recently surfaced, so it may well be that the state government is waiting until these are adequately addressed before proceeding with any overhaul of the state's police legislation.

101 See J. Chan, 'Governing Police Practice: Limits of the New Accountability' (1999) 50(2) British Journal of Sociology 251. The Labour government in Victoria, however, has committed to ending contracts and performance bonuses for senior police officers in the Victoria Police: Victoria, Ministerial Administrative Review, *Report*, 30.

102 See in particular M. Bersten, 'Police and Politics in Australia: The Separation of Powers and the Case for Statutory Codification' (1990) 14 Criminal L.J. 302.

103 S. 3 of the *Police Act*, 1958 provides that: 'The Governor General may from time to time appoint a fit and proper person to be the Commissioner of Police, who shall have the general control of the Police.'

104 P. Joseph, 'The Illusion of Civil Rights' (2000) (May) New Zealand L.J. 151 at 153.

105 This argument was subsequently supported by a parliamentary committee in its report on an incident that was alleged to have involved improper interference in police operations by the Prime Minister and a government official. The committee commented in its report that 'regulation 3 appears to confuse the constitutional status of the Police' (see New Zealand, House of Representatives, Justice and Electoral Committee, *Inquiry into Matters Relating to the Visit of the President of China to New Zealand in 1999: Report of the Justice and Electoral Committee*, http://www.gp.co.nz/wooc/i=papers/i7Aa-china.html.

106 H. Cull, 'The Enigma of a Police Constable's Status' (1976) 8 Victoria University of Wellington L.R. 148; B. Barton, 'Control of the New Zealand Police,' LLB thesis, Faculty of Law, Auckland University, 1978; G. Orr, 'Police Accountability' and T. Arnold, 'Legal Accountability and the Police: The Role of the Courts,' in *Policing, at the Crossroads* ed. C. Cameron and W. Young (Wellington: Allen & Unwin/Port Nicholson Press, 1986); G.A. Dunstall, *Policeman's Paradise? Policing a Stable Society, 1918–1945* (Wellington: Dunmore Press, 1999).

107 Dunstall, *Policeman's Paradise?*

108 Ibid., 12.

109 Cull, 'Enigma, 154.

110 Tunbridge served as commissioner from 1898 to 1903.

111 Dunstall, *Policeman's Paradise?* 13.

112 Ibid., 14–20. See also Orr, 'Police Accountability.'

113 *Osgood v. Attorney General* (1972), 13 M.C.D. 400; *Cullen v. Attorney-General and Commissioner of Police*, [1972] N.Z.L.R. 824; *Auckland Medical Aid Trust v. Commissioner of Police and Another*, [1976] 1 N.Z.L.R. 485. All of these cases involved the issue of vicarious liability for police wrongdoing. In the third the court held, distinguishing *Blackburn* and the earlier decisions cited therein, that for the purposes of the infringement of copyright action involved, the police officers in this case could be considered 'servants' of the Crown.

114 441 *New Zealand Parliamentary Debates*: 3433 (1981).

115 596 *New Zealand Parliamentary Debates*: 13080–81 (14 November 2001).

116 In chapter 8 of her fifth volume of the history of the New Zealand Police, entitled *More Than Law and Order: The New Zealand Police 1945–1992*, however, Susan Butterworth reports that in subsequent interviews, 'Retired Commissioner Walton remembers little communication with the government over the tour, and insists that he was never given any specific direction by either his own minister or the prime minister.' (In a more recent interview with former Commissioner Walton, he reiterated this insistence to me.) Chapter 8 of Butterworth's book (Oxford University Press) provides a full account of the policing of the Springbok tour.

117 See Orr, 'Police Accountability,' 57–8.

118 J. Boston, J. Martin, J. Pallot, and P. Walsh, *Public Management: The New Zealand Model* (Auckland: Oxford University Press, 1996).

119 Concerns over the governance and accountability of the police in New Zealand were also fuelled by a major scandal during the 1990s over huge cost overruns incurred in the course of an unsuccessful project to introduce a new information system for the police. For an account of this scandal, see T. Dale and S. Goldfinch, 'Pessimism as an Information Management Tool in the Public Sector.' http://www.cosc.canterburyiac.nz/tony.dale/papers/tr0202.pdf.

120 Chen and Palmer, *Constitutional Issues Involving the Police* (Wellington: 1988), 4. This section refers to 'Palmer' because it is generally understood that he, as the former Prime Minister of New Zealand, wrote the document.

121 Although Palmer did not explicitly say why he thought this should not be attempted, his reason may perhaps be surmised from his conclusion that an approach that sought to identify the 'components' of police independence 'still does not provide finite guidance as to the whereabouts of the split between those policy matters which might be considered to be matters for Ministerial direction and operational matters for which the Commissioner is solely responsible.' Ibid., 35.

122 S. 4.6(2) of the Queensland *Police Service Administration Act, 1990* provided that: 'The Minister, having regard to advice of the commissioner
first obtained, may give, in writing, directions to the commissioner
concerning – (a) the overall administration, management, and superintendence of, or in the Police Service; and (b) policy and priorities* to be
pursued in performing the functions of the Police Service; and (c) the
number and deployment** of officers and staff members and the number
and location of police establishments and police stations.' S. 4.6(3)
provided that: 'The commissioner is to comply with all directions duly
given under subsection (2).' (*Somewhat paradoxically, however, para.
4.8(2)(a) of the act provides that the commissioner's responsibilities
include responsibility for 'determination of priorities.' **It will be noted
that in Lord Denning's formulation of the doctrine of police independence (quoted above), deployment of officers is considered to be a matter
exclusively for the commissioner, with respect to which political direction
is not permitted.)

123 In connection with this recommendation, Palmer also referred to the
report of Wood Royal Commission on the Police in New South Wales, in
which the royal commissioner stated that 'it is desirable in principle that
the Police Service not be subject to undue political direction, and that the
ministerial role be confined to one of policy' (New South Wales, Royal
Commission *Final Report*, para. 3.28). The report also cited the provisions
of subsections (1), (2), and (4) of the *Australian Federal Police Act, 1979*,
which provided that: '(1) Subject to this Act, the Commissioner has the
general administration of, and the control of the operations of, the Australian Federal Police. (2) The Minister may, after obtaining and considering the advice of the Commissioner and of the Secretary, give written
directions to the Commissioner with respect to the general policy to be
pursued in relation to the performance of the functions of the Australian
Federal Police ... (4) The Commissioner shall comply with all directions
given under this section.'

124 The report mentioned particularly that '(i) the contribution of the New
Zealand police to the Government's Strategic Result Areas is specified,
and given operational effect through the six Key Result Areas,' and that
'(ii) leading from (i), the Commissioner of Police and the Minister negotiate an annual Purchase Agreement specifying the amount and quality of
the outputs to be delivered by the New Zealand Police. The Purchase
Agreement is reasonably specific, and does create the potential for the
Minister to alter law enforcement priorities consistent with the limits on
Ministerial direction incorporated in the Memorandum of Understand-

ing between the Minister and the Commissioner; and (iii) the financial
accountabilities and associated reporting requirements specified in the
Public Finance Act apply to the New Zealand Police.' New Zealand,
Review of Police Administration & Management Structure, *Report of
Independent Reviewer* (Wellington: New Zealand Police, 1998), para. 90.

125 Ibid., para. 91.

126 The *State Sector Act, 1988* is the principal legislation governing the public
service in New Zealand.

127 New Zealand, Review, *Report*, para. 91.

128 Cf. note 3, above.

129 New Zealand, Review, *Report*, para. 93.

130 This official is the head of the Public Service in New Zealand.

131 Ibid., para. 95.

132 Ibid., para. 96.

133 P. Joseph, 'Illusion of Civil Rights,' 152.

134 New Zealand, House of Representatives, Justice and Electoral Committee, *Report*.

135 Earlier in its report, the committee wrote that the constitutional boundaries between the Police and the government 'should be transparent and
unambiguous in the legislation. It is not adequate to say that legal boundaries are observed in practice.'

136 The bill formed the first part of a proposed two-stage reform process
dealing with the police's legislative framework. The second stage which
has now been officially announced is supposed to involve a 'first principles' rewrite of the *Police Act*.

137 The most controversial being a provision that would require a compulsory arbitration to take into account the commissioner's 'ability to fund
any resulting police expenditure' when making an award. This provision
has come to be referred to in some quarters as the 'Sweet F.A.' clause,
since it would insert a new paragraph (fa) into clause 24 of the Schedule
to the *Police Act*.

138 The commissioner will continue to be appointed by the governor general
'at pleasure.' The bill provides that the conditions of employment of the
commissioner are to be determined by agreement between the state services commissioner and the appointee, but only after the agreement of
the Prime Minister and the minister of state services has been obtained.

139 Such review, however, must be limited to those matters on which the
minister may direct the commissioner under the terms of the Bill (see
below).

140 Could it, for instance, be a defence to a criminal charge (e.g., of obstruct-

ing or assaulting police) or, in the case of a police officer, to a disciplinary charge of disobeying the order of a superior, that the police had been acting pursuant to an unlawful government direction?

141 New Zealand, House of Representatives, Law and Order Committee, 'Report on the Police Amendment Bill (No. 2),' No. 145–1. The Opposition parties released a separate report opposing passage of the bill ('Police Amendment Bill (No. 2),' n.d., 6 pp.)

142 In early 2004 some allegations of very serious historical and contemporary police misconduct resurfaced, in response to which a Commission of Inquiry into Police Conduct has now been established, which is not expected to report until later this year or early 2005. Under these circumstances, it seems unlikely that the *Police Amendment (No.2) Bill* will be proceeded with, if at all, before the commission's report is forthcoming. A spokesman for the minister of police was recently quoted in the press as saying that the bill was 'still good to go, but had been eclipsed by other, more urgent legislation' ('Code of Conduct Still in Draft Form,' *Dominion Post*, 25 May 2004, A2).

5 Accountability Mechanisms: Legal Sites of Executive-Police Relations – Core Principles in a Canadian Context

DIANNE MARTIN

Abstract

This chapter provides an overview, with examples and solutions drawn from policy documents, public inquiries, legislation, and case law, of the multiple sites where the governance of police in a democratic society is negotiated. Multiple factors, including political, institutional, and legal influences determine the ways that this intricately structured legal relationship functions in day-to-day situations. Bearing in mind the political and institutional contexts, this chapter examines the legal instruments and institutions that structure the relationship and help resolve the inevitable tension that arises. The central argument is that the relationship has evolved in various ways into a partnership, negotiated daily at various sites within the legal and constitutional systems.

Many of the negotiations take place informally and out of public view, while others are managed by the courts. Issues emerge only occasionally as a matter of public concern and are usually perceived as an aberration or crisis. The crises can be identified in particular contexts, for example, in Charter motions in criminal cases, in civil law suits against the police, or in institutional settings where the crisis has often been precipitated by media controversy. A minority of the issues generate sufficient challenge to legitimacy that special responses evolve or are called upon. These might include legislative change, new modes of civilian review, or public inquiries, which are often driven by community and media pressures. It is argued that in all cases better outcomes would be achieved if both police actors and judicial and political decision makers were better informed about the history of the relationship and the reasons for prevailing doctrines.

The arguments are supported with examples from many Canadian police

*services, including the RCMP, and with a case study of the governance of the
Toronto Police Service. The examples illustrate how police are actually regu-
lated and demonstrate how the theory of accountability to the rule of law
operates at different sites. The chapter concludes with a commentary by
Susan Eng, a former chair of the Toronto Police Services Board.*

Introduction

Few dispute the proposition that in a democratic society police must be
bound by the rule of law, accountable to civilian authority and the 'tool'
of no political master.[1] That is so regardless of whether the principle is
interpreted to argue for close civilian supervision, leaving only a narrow sphere of independence for police action, or for leaving residual
discretion in the hands of the police, thus supporting their independence and circumscribing the scope of civilian supervision and review.[2]
The choice is influenced by a number of factors, including political
ideology, and is examined here in light of a number of controversies
concerning the effectiveness of police management in Ontario in the
early years of the twenty-first century.

It is also widely acknowledged that law enforcement activities are
governed, or at least influenced, by an intricate web of rules and relationships operating at multiple sites[3] including the legal, constitutional,
political, social, and international. Multiple factors bear on the ways
that these intricately structured relationships are worked out in day-to-
day situations. These relationships between police officers and their
superiors, police officers and Crown attorneys, police managers and
civil authorities, and the police (both individually and collectively) and
the courts have evolved in various ways into mutually reinforcing if not
always amicable partnerships negotiated daily at various sites within
the legal and constitutional systems. Many of these negotiations take
place informally and out of public view and only occasionally break
down and emerge as matters of public interest or concern. When they
do, the crisis is usually presented and managed as an aberration in an
effort to preserve public confidence in the status quo.

Not surprisingly, that when an issue arises in a legal context it is
framed as an individual aberration. Most legal disputes are highly
individual; they occur, for example, between an individual and the
state, as in a criminal prosecution, or between an individual and someone else, as in a civil law suit. In the context of policing, a crisis in

governance only becomes a matter of public concern when a ruling or a judgment has considerable media interest, such as a ruling on a controversial subject.[4] A minority of these cases generate sufficient challenge to legitimacy that special responses evolve or are called upon, such as public inquiries, legislative changes, or reforms to modes of civilian review, often driven by community and media pressures.

While keeping in mind the broader context, this chapter will consider the legal strand in this complex web: the role of law in the regulation of police conduct and practice. It will provide an overview of the multiple sites where the legal governance of police in a democratic society is negotiated, and discuss examples drawn from the recent history of police governance in Ontario where the pendulum has swung from reforms introduced in the late 1980s and early 1990s to increase the scope and effectiveness of civilian oversight to reforms that reversed that approach in the mid-1990s. The dramatic changes enacted in 1996 are analysed together with the legislation and case law the legislation generated, with a view to assessing how effective the approach has been. A case study of the response to the 1989 misconduct of two officers of the Toronto Police Service illustrates the operation and effectiveness of the system the reforms replaced.

Despite recognition that there are valid concerns about overly complex mechanisms, the chapter concludes that locating responsibility for police governance in multiple sites ensures that issues ignored or dismissed at one site will be raised in another. This dynamic preserves a healthy transparency that serves to protect police freedom from inappropriate political interference.

A final introductory caution is in order. Discussion of the role of the law in police governance tends to focus on the ways that the law serves, or fails to serve, as a *limit* on police practice and a *curb* to police misconduct. This is because the law produces an accessible record of its role in governance in the form of decided cases, legislation and regulations, and legally constituted commissions of inquiry. It is important to remember, however, that there are limits to an analysis of legal rules and interventions. Two are particularly important. First, for the police the law is not a barrier or a threat, it is their 'tool' and they have considerable expertise in wielding it in their own interest.[5] Second, in most cases, the extent to which police control the 'facts' of an incident and the way the 'facts' are interpreted goes unchallenged and often determines both the outcome and the public perception of what happened and why. In this sense the 'facts' matter more than the rules, and processes that determine how evidence is gathered and shaped, and how it is analysed, are every bit if not more important in achieving accountability and transparency than the most elaborate set of substantive rules.[6]

Multiple Sites of Regulation: Complex or Comprehensive?

Police officers believe they are an over-regulated occupation relative to others and thus, by inference, are justified in resisting efforts to strengthen or improve regulation and governance. There is no doubt that police encounter a host of legal rules and expectations in all aspects of their occupational lives, and that many of those encounters have consequences for them both personally and professionally. The system of regulation and discipline faced by members of the Toronto Police Service has been described as 'unnecessarily complicated' and 'frequently reactive, slow, not fully transparent and unnecessarily bureaucratic.'[7] Police representative bodies such as the Toronto Police Association or the Canadian Association of Chiefs of Police have been highly effective in promoting this view,[8] which clearly influenced the reforms of the mid-1990s.[9]

From another point of view, criminologist John Braithewaite points out that 'a police service that is enmeshed in many webs of dependency will be vulnerable to the many when it corruptly does the bidding of one.'[10] Cases that excite public interest and raise concerns about accountability of the police tend to emerge because there are multiple sites where scrutiny of police conduct takes place. For example, in a recent case involving a Toronto Police plainclothes unit many strands combined to produce a crisis. An RCMP wiretap apparently recorded a Toronto police constable in incriminating circumstances; then a related corruption probe increased sensitivity to complaints from restaurant and bar owners about extortion of bribes so that they were taken seriously. Ultimately, a number of officers, including the sons of a former chief, were charged both criminally and under the *Police Services Act*.[11] As the scandal grew, so did demands for more effective accountability.[12]

Tension between these two views and debate on which is the best approach, or where the truth lies, has marked policing history for the past thirty years at least.[13] There is no easy answer, and many of the solutions proposed are usually found in personal perspectives on the issue. For individuals or communities harmed by police error or misconduct and not satisfied with the remedies on offer, it is clear that more effective discipline and accountability measures are required. It may be equally clear to a police manager finding it difficult to discipline or otherwise deal with a problem officer that faster, easier disciplinary measures and management tools are required. And for an individual officer faced with multiple levels of scrutiny, any one of which has the potential to end a career, increased measures for monitoring and sanctioning his or her decisions and conduct are regarded as oppressive. Other viewpoints may also be relevant.

In any event, some complexity is inevitable given the broad approach to governance prevailing in Canada. There has been an attempt to draw a bright line between policy and day-to-day operations, which is an extraordinarily difficult distinction to make. The basic rationale for the distinction is that policing policy is the province of elected and appointed civilian governors, while operations and the carrying out of policy are the province of the chief of police, who serves as a sort of chief executive officer employed by the civilian authority. All employees and officers report directly or indirectly to a chief of police and all discipline is administered in his or her name. The development, implementation, and supervision of policy is aimed both at the police service as a whole and at police officers as individual employees. At the level of a police service, the chief reports on the degree of operational success to a governing body, and receives policy direction from it.[14] At the officer level, the conduct or misconduct of individuals is managed through a hierarchical, highly structured, legalistic mechanism that sets standards and determines how allegations of misconduct will be investigated and determined. Conflicts about what is a policy and what is an operation are unavoidable and difficult to resolve. That the distinction might also lead to an overly bureaucratic and opaque management structure is also a clear risk. The following brief description of the structures in place will serve to illustrate the degree of complexity.

The Legislative Structure in Ontario

Despite their common law roots,[15] police services are creatures of statute and both their scope of practice and the modes of accountability are located in the legislation that creates them. In Ontario, authority for police to act flows from the *Police Services Act*[16] and from the minister of community safety and correctional services, who is charged with the monitoring of all police services and police services boards, and the issuing of policy directives.[17] The authority of the minister to govern is delegated to local police services boards,[18] and to the Ontario Civilian Commission on Police Services (OCCOPS), the members of which are appointed by the lieutenant-governor of the province. As amended in 1997, the act stipulates that every municipality maintaining a police service must have a police services board composed of three, five, or seven members, depending upon the size of the municipality to manage the police service. A board is composed of the head of the municipal council (or their designated representative), members of council, a civilian, and members appointed by the lieutenant-governor.[19]

Police services boards continue to be charged with the provision of police services in a municipality and are empowered to appoint the members of the service as well as the chief, determine police objectives and priorities, direct and monitor the performance of the chief, and establish guidelines for dealing with complaints. A board also has the jurisdiction to enact by-laws for the effective management of the police service.[20] The distinction between policy and operations is expressly entrenched in the act, which states that a board may not give orders to any member of a police force except to the chief.[21] The duties of police officers as well as the duties and powers of a chief of police, who reports directly to a police services board, are statutorily defined.[22] The act is supported by fifteen active regulations which contain among other things, a Code of Conduct for police officers setting out a range of prohibited activities from corrupt practice to restriction on police political activity.

The jurisdiction of OCCOPS was expanded in the 1997 restructuring to replace the public complaints review system. It was granted a new range of powers beyond its previous jurisdiction over local police services boards and as a forum for police officers' appeals from findings of misconduct. For example, OCCOPS is now empowered to conduct investigations and inquiries into complaints about the policies implemented or services provided by a police force, or the conduct of officers.[23] Also, OCCOPS may conduct inquiries on its own motion or upon the direction of the minister of community security and correctional services, a police services board, a chief of police, a municipal council, or a member of the public. An OCCOPS investigation or inquiry has all the powers of a commission under Part II of the *Public Inquiries Act*. It may impose wideranging sanctions, including the suspension or removal of a chief, members of a police services board, or an entire board;

disband a municipal police service; and appoint a replacement chief. Appeals from OCCOPS decisions are to the Divisional Court and must be made within thirty days of receiving notice of the commission's decision.[24]

Mechanisms that address allegations of misconduct against individual police officers are found in Part V of the act, which gives the chief of a police service broad discretion over all aspects of discipline, whether arising from a public complaint or from internally generated allegations of misconduct or employment infractions. Misconduct is a broad term that includes everything from quasi-criminal abuse of authority, withholding of services, or the inducement to misconduct of another officer in breach of the code of conduct of a municipal police service, to more strictly job-related behaviour concerning dress and appearance, firearms, personal property or money, punctuality, and the like. A chief may order an internal investigation into allegations of misconduct or may request that a member of an outside force, a judge, or a former judge, conduct an investigation.[25]

There are additional provisions concerning complaints about officers from members of the public, but essentially the chief is given broad discretion over all aspects of the public complaints process. An investigation is in the control of the police, including the decision *not* to investigate those complaints that a chief deems to have been made by a party not directly affected by the policy, service, or conduct, or to be 'frivolous, vexatious or made in bad faith.'[26] A chief may also decline to address a complaint made more than six months after the facts on which it is based occurred.[27] Otherwise, a chief must review or investigate all complaints, notifying the complainant and the implicated officer of the receipt of the complaint and of the decision whether or not to further investigate. A decision of a chief not to investigate a complaint may be appealed to OCCOPS. Any complaints regarding the conduct of a chief or a deputy chief are referred directly to the relevant police services board.[28]

Complaints by a member of the public, a board or a chief may be resolved informally or by way of a hearing. The powers of both a chief and a board are expansive and discretionary, and include dismissal, suspension, demotion, forfeiture of pay, and reprimand.[29] An appeal to OCCOPS within thirty days of a decision may be brought by a police officer, a complainant, or a police services board. A hearing conducted by the commission is an appeal, but new evidence into allegations of misconduct may be heard. Appeals from the decisions of OCCOPS are made to the Ontario Divisional Court, and may not be on a question of fact alone.[30]

While most matters of misconduct are investigated internally, whether brought by a police chief or superior officer or initiated by a complaint from a member of the public, cases of death or serious bodily harm that may have resulted from criminal offences committed by police officers are investigated by an independent agency. The Special Investigations Unit (SIU) was formed via a 1999 amendment to the *Police Services Act* as an independent agency. Investigations are conducted at the initiative of the director, who is not to be a police officer or former police officer, or at the request of the minister of community security and correctional services or attorney general. In a further attempt to maintain independence from the officers under investigation, the legislation also stipulates that an SIU investigator cannot work on an investigation that relates to members of a police force of which he or she was a member. The director can initiate criminal proceedings against an officer by laying an information and reporting the results of investigations to the attorney general for prosecution.[31] The act attempts to ensure compliance and states that 'members of police forces shall co-operate fully' with the SIU in the conduct of investigations.[32]

Under the 1999 Regulation 673/98, a chief of police is charged with the responsibility for securing the scene of an investigation until the SIU arrives, and with segregating the officers involved. Officers involved in the incident are prohibited from speaking to each other, but each is entitled to legal or union representation. The regulations also require each involved officer to appear for an interview with the SIU and to surrender their notes regarding the incident under investigation.[33] A distinction is drawn between 'subject officers' or those who caused the death or bodily harm, and 'witness officers,' a categorization the SIU is now required to make before speaking to the officers involved in the incident.[34] The regulations also stipulate that while a chief must also institute an internal investigation, it will be confined to the policies and procedures of the force and will be 'subject to the SIU's lead role in investigating the incident.'[35]

Accountability by Other Means

Legal measures that attempt to ensure accountability are not limited to the discipline, misconduct, investigation, and review mechanisms contained in the *Police Services Act*. Deaths at the hands of police are scrutinized not only by the SIU and by police supervisors, but also through the mechanism of a coroner's inquest. In addition, the actions and decisions of individual officers are scrutinized daily in the justice system, starting with the review of charges performed by a Crown attorney.[36] Courts, both civil and criminal, participate in assessing the propriety of that investigation. In all cases police officers, police services, and possibly even police services boards[37] may be subject to a civil law suit. All of these sites of legal decision making have the potential for generating public attention and may have significant consequences for the individuals and police services involved.

Criminal *or* Charter *Cases*

The criminal law impacts police practice through rulings, particularly *Charter* rulings that limit the admissibility of evidence or otherwise constrain police investigative practices.[38] Although police tend to protest *Charter* decisions, arguing that they frustrate the ability to maintain law and order, *Charter* values have undoubtedly altered the way in which policing in Canada is now conducted.[39] The courts also direct police practice through the interpretation of *Criminal Code* provisions such as the provisions which authorize arrest and detention[40] and the use of force. Section 25(4) justifies the use of force by a peace officer that is 'intended or likely to cause death or grievous bodily harm' when it is reasonably required to effect a lawful arrest (with or without a warrant), is reasonably necessary to prevent harm to the peace officer or to others, or to prevent a suspect's flight if not preventable by other means.[41] This provision often exonerates officers who are charged with use of force offences. Holding individual police officers accountable through direct criminal charges, especially around the use of force, has proved largely unsuccessful,[42] and even rare convictions or guilty pleas may not carry the severity of punishment that is usually regarded as serving a deterrent function, although the impact of merely being charged criminally should not be underestimated.[43]

Recent changes in police regulation designed to promote accountability have not been interpreted in a manner that facilitates criminal charges against officers. For example, the use-of-force reports made mandatory by the Ontario government under Premier Bob Rae have been ruled inadmissible as evidence in the criminal prosecution of police officers.[44] Also, the courts have generally protected the privacy of police officers in the context of attempts by defence counsel to compel disclosure of an arresting or investigating officer's disciplinary record. Pursuant to *R. v. Stinchcombe*,[45] the Crown must disclose to the defence all relevant material under its control; however, pursuant to *R. v. O'Connor*[46] and the related *Criminal Code* scheme, material in the hands of a third-party witness will be ordered to be produced only if a stringent test of relevance versus prejudice is passed. The issue then is the nature of the police disciplinary records and the role of the police in the prosecution process. In *R. v. Paryniuk*, in the Ontario Superior Court of Justice, an accused charged with narcotics offences sought to introduce evidence pertaining to an ongoing internal affairs investigation into potential misconduct involving members of the Toronto Drug Squad who arrested him. The Crown successfully argued that internal affairs' documents were third-party records and should be governed by the *O'Connor* principle, as well as by investigative, informant, and public interest privilege. The accused was not entitled to compel the production of the internal affairs investigative findings.[47] In *R. v. Altunamaz*,[48] the accused sought to compel production of the arresting officers' prior disciplinary or complaints records. The accused, charged with narcotics offences, brought an application for an order forcing disclosure of records of investigation by the Public Complaints Investigation Bureau, the Police Complaints Commission, and OCCOPS. The accused also sought disclosure of records of the internal affairs unit and the chief of police into past allegations of misconduct and disciplinary proceedings. The Ontario Superior Court held that the records held by the Police Complaints Commission and OCCOPS were third-party records.[49] However, in *R. v. Scaduto*, the court held that the accused was entitled to disclosure of records pertaining to past *Police Act* charges brought against several of the officers involved in his case. The court ruled that because the records in question had come into possession or control of the Crown, third-party status could not persist.[50] On a related matter involving the public complaints process, the Ontario Court of Appeal has ruled that an officer's section 7 *Charter* right against self-incrimination does not extend to an officer's notebooks, and that the police complaints commissioner was not prevented from relying on extracts from an officer's notebooks during a disciplinary hearing.[51]

Civil Cases
Civil actions against the police may also serve an accountability and supervisory function. For example, the *Jane Doe* case, which concerned

the investigation of a serial rapist, was a clear judicial sanctioning of police policy and operations.[52] The same individuals who may lay formal complaints regarding use of force or unjustified arrest or search may also launch civil suits against the police. These suits tend to involve allegations of malicious prosecution after charges are dropped, battery, or unlawful arrest or search.[53] The American experience with government 'pattern and practice' suits against systematically unruly police forces is another example of the way in which civil law can be used effectively to promote changes in police practice, although it should be noted that the process proceeds through settlement agreements, rather than trials.[54]

Coroners' Inquests

In Ontario, the coroner has a duty to investigate and hold an inquest into all deaths that occur while a person is 'detained by or in the actual custody of a peace officer.'[55] A defining feature of the modern Ontario coroner's system is its departure from its criminal law roots. The legislation itself clearly stipulates that an inquest proceeding is not to be construed as creating a criminal court of record, and prohibits any finding of legal responsibility.[56] However, inquests into police-related deaths in Ontario have developed into significant opportunities for public scrutiny. Despite or because of lengthy and often contentious proceedings involving complex legal wrangling, media coverage has been extensive and the issue of deaths at the hands of police are matters of considerable public concern.[57]

The Donaldson inquest in particular involved two of the key legal debates surrounding the modern police-related coroner's inquest; namely, the issues of standing for non-parties[58] and the matter of legal representation of institutional parties such as the police.[59] Both issues were crucial to obtaining a complete narrative of how the death occurred. Under the act, the test for standing is whether an applicant is 'substantially and directly interested in the inquest.'[60] There remains debate regarding the possibility of levels of standing at a coroner's inquest, given that section 41(2) grants a party with standing only the right to examine witnesses on matters 'relevant to the interests of the person with standing.' Traditionally, the police have sought to narrowly circumscribe the scope of coroner's inquests, resisting efforts to introduce evidence surrounding issues such as systemic biases, racial profiling, and the like.

Legal Activity versus Transparency and Accountability

The Rise and Fall and Rise Again of Civilian Oversight

The legal structure outlined above took effect in Ontario on 1 January 1998, replacing an equally sweeping reform introduced in 1990. The 1990 reforms favoured civilian oversight; the 1998 regime restricts both public access to the process and civilian oversight. Both approaches have received considerable criticism. In 2004, the third reform initiative in 20 years was set in motion and is widely expected to restore an increased measure of civilian oversight. On 19 April 2006 the Independent Police Review Act (Bill 103) was introduced for first reading that would create an independent civilian body within an independent review mechanism.[61]

Part of the history is attributable to the differing approaches to police governance of the political parties who were in office when these changes were made. The Liberals held office in 1990; they were followed by Progressive Conservatives in 1997, and came to office again in 2004. A large part of the development, however, is structural. The police enjoy a high degree of community support despite periodic concerns raised by high-profile scandals, and they are successful in resisting changes in governance and regulation from any source. Most citizen complaint and review schemes have been largely unsuccessful at reducing police misconduct or at increasing public accountability. In the introduction to his 1991 collection of articles detailing police accountability systems in England, Australia, Canada, and in American cities such as Chicago, Pittsburgh, Philadelphia, and San Francisco, Andrew Goldsmith identifies failures to reduce misconduct or to increase community confidence in police accountability in all of the jurisdictions. He notes that 'the widely attributed failure of internal complaints mechanisms reflects a loss of public confidence in the way in which the police have responded previously (or more to the point, have not responded) to expressions of citizen dissatisfaction and to evidence of misconduct more generally within their own ranks.'[62]

When change does occur, particularly change that increases oversight, it does so in the aftermath of a significant crisis in public trust. For example, public concerns during the 1970s about police misconduct and existing police-controlled complaint mechanisms led to the establishment in 1984 of a unique civilian review agency to deal with complaints concerning misconduct by Toronto police.[63] The Office of the Police Complaints Commissioner (PCC) was mandated to provide independent review and resolution of citizen complaints in Toronto, including the authority to sanction officers found guilty of misconduct, while leaving most initial investigations of complaints in police hands. The system was widely praised and offered as a model for other jurisdictions and was extended to cover all police services in the province in 1991.[64]

Successful[65] or not,[66] it did not last long. Following considerable police lobbying and a change in government, governance of police services in Ontario was once again studied, and revamped in 1997. As stated above, the changes came into effect on 1 January 1998. In a fairly brief report to the new government, Roderick McLeod, QC, successfully argued for the need to simplify and narrow the legislative foundation for governance of the police. Significant changes to the structure of civilian oversight followed the McLeod report and, while the new act did not make all the changes proposed in the report, it did include the abolition of the position of public complaints commissioner and the 'narrow legislative framework' McLeod had called for, and left the details of the conduct of investigations into complaints to the discretion of individual forces.[67] The Ontario experiment in civilian oversight seemed to be over. However, another cycle of scandal soon fuelled public dissatisfaction.[68] The failure of accountability mechanisms once more produced calls for reform[69] and, with another change in government in Ontario, civilian oversight is again being studied. In 2005, former Chief Justice Patrick LeSage completed a report dealing with complaints concerning police in Ontario.[70] The eventual passing of the Independent Police Review Act may be the result.

Police Discipline

The apparent failure of public complaint and internal discipline regimes to change police behaviour illustrates the inadequacy of reform strategies that concentrate on legalistic solutions. The police are used to viewing the criminal law as their tool. That perception sustains them in their work and in efforts to deflect public criticism and demands for public accountability. It encourages the belief that as members of the police force they are immune from criminal liability, and it dominates the structure and procedures around the disposition of citizen complaints.

Criminalizing the Discipline Process
Although the police are frequently bitter about the "inappropriate" benefits granted to accused persons by the criminal law, this view of the criminal law may, ironically, manifest itself in an almost evangelical

belief in the criminal trial process when it frees a police officer who has been accused of criminal conduct arising out of violence that the police perceive to be necessary.[71] An examination of Toronto Police Service attitudes towards internal employment discipline illustrates the phenomenon. Despite clear rulings from the courts that disciplinary proceedings against officers under the *Police Act* are *not* penal or quasi-criminal, but administrative and disciplinary in nature, [72] the proceedings remain shrouded in quasi-criminal trappings, primarily at the insistence of rank-and-file officers in attempting to bring some fairness to proceedings they view as inherently unfair. The procedures set out in the *Police Services Act* are interpreted to create a forum analogous to a criminal court for the disposition of serious misconduct allegations against officers, whether brought as citizen complaints or not. Experienced criminal defence lawyers represent the accused officer, rather than labour or administrative lawyers. Formal 'briefs,' identical to those used in criminal prosecutions, are prepared. The practices and procedures followed, from providing 'particulars' and 'disclosure' to 'setting dates' and imposing 'sentences,' reflect this perception and reinforce the adversarial and punitive aura of the proceedings. Yet no one is satisfied. Members of the public participating as victim witnesses are isolated from the process and are rarely satisfied by the outcomes of the hearings,[73] while individual officers feel that they have been selected as scapegoats by police management.[74]

A vivid illustration of strategic use of the special relationship that exists between police officers and the criminal law is found in the case of Toronto Police Constable Terence Weller, a case decided by the original Public Complaints Commission. Weller was ordered to resign when a public complaints tribunal found him responsible for a serious assault that ruptured a suspect's testicles and dislocated his knee. The Toronto Police Association, which had earlier 'declared war' on the public complaints tribunal, [75] was outraged that the officer had been denied the opportunity to 'clear' himself of the charges in a *criminal* trial. In order to give the officer that opportunity, a member of a neighbouring Police Association laid an information alleging that Weller had committed assault causing bodily harm. However, the attorney general stayed the proceedings on the ground that it was an abuse of the criminal process to lay a charge with no honest belief, based on reasonable and probable grounds, that an offence had occurred. This decision foiled the officer's bid to clear himself in what he and his colleagues perceived to be a forum more sympathetic to them than the one operating under the

Police Complaint Commissioner.[76] The police have employed other novel legal methods to counter disciplinary action. For example, there have been attempts to argue that both disciplinary and criminal proceedings violate an officer's section 11(d) *Charter* right against multiple convictions. However, in *R. v. Wigglesworth*, the Supreme Court of Canada held that disciplinary offences (in this case under the *RCMP Act*) are separate and distinct from criminal charges.[77]

Civil Challenges to Discipline
Police officers have also challenged disciplinary action by launching malicious prosecution suits against police services boards and disciplinary bodies. In *Bainard v. Toronto Police Services Board*, the officers had been charged with both disciplinary and criminal offences after allegedly assaulting a homeless man. After all proceedings were stayed, owing to delay and witness credibility issues, the officers brought an action for damages in relation to the disciplinary proceedings. The Ontario Superior Court dismissed the action, acknowledging that while the officers were victims of a 'very sloppy investigation,' there was no evidence of malice in relation to the investigation or the laying of the disciplinary charges.[78] In the 2004 case *Heasman v. Durham Regional Police Services Board*, Durham Region police officers sued the police services board for breach of fiduciary duty, negligent investigation, and abuse of public office for an investigation resulting in charges of neglect of duty and discreditable conduct that were later stayed. The court dismissed the claim, holding that the board had no fiduciary obligation to act solely in the interests of the plaintiff officers. Other lawsuits are pending.[79]

Judicial Review
Both the streamlined process introduced in the 1997 reforms and the predecessor provisions have been frequently challenged as police officers seek judicial review of disciplinary decisions and penalties.[80] *Browne v. OCCOPS*, one of two joined appeals, is the current leading case on the powers of OCCOPS under the new regime. Officers were initially successful before their chief and again at divisional court in securing a review of a successful appeal by the complainants, until the case eventually reached the Ontario Court of Appeal. The procedural arguments raised by the officers were dismissed. The court held that OCCOPS should not be held to a strict standard in reporting their decisions to the parties as long as the subject officers knew the case they had to meet.[81]

The predecessor legislation generated a considerable body of case law. Illustrating the role played by section 25 of the *Criminal Code* in disciplinary proceedings, *Duriancik v. Ontario (Attorney General)* considered the relationship between the board of inquiry hearings and the *Criminal Code* protection afforded to peace officers regarding the use of force. The Ontario Divisional Court held that the board erred in failing to consider section 25 of the *Criminal Code*, and that without considering section 25, the board could not have legally concluded that the officer had used unnecessary violence.[82] In *Tomie-Gallant v. Ontario (Board of Inquiry)*, the issue of the burden of proof in a board of inquiry hearing was addressed. The officer sought judicial review of a finding of guilt on charges of making an unlawful arrest under the *Police Act* regulations. The Ontario Divisional Court held that the board of inquiry had wrongfully reversed the burden of proof by requiring the officer to convince the board of more than the fact that she had reasonable and probable grounds for making the arrest.[83] In *Dulmage v. Ontario Police Complaints Commissioner*, the Ontario Divisional Court dealt with an officer's claim of reasonable apprehension of bias on the part of the board of inquiry. The case involved a complaint by a black woman regarding a strip search. The Congress of Black Women of Canada had made public statements condemning the officer's conduct. A member of the panel was also a member of the congress. The court held that the board, as then constituted, was prohibited from continuing the proceedings, finding that the test for reasonable apprehension of bias had been met.[84]

Complainants may also seek judicial review. The *Corp. of the Canadian Civil Liberties Assn. v. Ontario Civilian Commission on Police Services* is an example of complainant-driven judicial review. The chief of police had dismissed as unsubstantiated complaints respecting a decision to transfer young female protesters to a facility where police knew they would be strip searched. The decision was affirmed by OCCOPS and the complainants applied successfully for judicial review pursuant to section 72(5) of the *Police Services Act*. The court held that the standard of review is whether the decision of the commission was patently unreasonable. In reviewing the decision of the chief, the commission should have determined whether the alleged facts constituted a reasonable basis for the complaint. The court found that both the commission and chief applied the wrong evidentiary standard in determining whether a hearing should be held. Only evidence which 'may' constitute misconduct or unsatisfactory work performance is required; not 'clear and convincing' evidence, and the failure of the commission to apply the

Legal Sites of Executive-Police Relations 273

correct standard under act rendered its decision patently unreasonable. The complainants were held to be entitled to a hearing to be conducted by a different police force.[85]

Political and Civil Accountability

The Relationship between a Police Services Board and a Chief of Police
Given the nature of the relationship created by the *Police Services Act* between a chief of a police service and a police services board employing her or him, conflicts between them inevitably arise, particularly over the underdeveloped notion of the distinction between policy and operations. A police chief may feel that a board has overstepped its bounds by interfering in actual operations, while a board may clash with a chief over what it views as policy issues and a chief's failure to implement policy directions. That has certainly been the case in Toronto, where employment contract negotiations have also been highly contentious.[86] Tensions between the Toronto Police Services Board chair and the Toronto chief of police have on occasion been publicly acrimonious.[87] While the legislation appears to confer tremendous power on the boards, the ability to exercise this power has been limited by the actions or inaction of chiefs, and by a political reluctance to openly question the authority of the chief on what may appear to be operational issues, or to appear to be 'soft on crime' or 'anti-cop.'[88]

The search for an appropriate response to the problems of racism and racial profiling within the police service represents an example of a particularly difficult issue that has generated considerable tension between the board and various chiefs over the years. The interests of the chief and those of the board have been recognized as divergent on the matter of pursuing the racial dimensions of police violence, a conflict made public at publicized coroner's inquests – those of Raymond Lawrence and Lester Donaldson in particular – dealing with police shootings of young black males.[89] Although the courts have identified the phenomenon of racial profiling and the findings of the various commissions of inquiry have unequivocally noted the presence of racial bias in policing,[90] it has been difficult for Toronto police chiefs to acknowledge that racism may be systemic and unconscious as well as deliberate or malicious. Under its jurisdiction to set policy, the Toronto Police Services Board has sought to make the issue a priority, but these efforts have been met with extreme resistance and even denial by the union and by successive chiefs.[91]

The Relationship between Police Management and the Police Association

The relationship between police management and the police association has also become more confrontational and adversarial in recent years.[92] Perhaps the most hotly contested issue, however, has been the issue of political activities and endorsements by police associations, in particular the Toronto Police Association. The *Police Services Act* specifically limits the political activities of individual officers. Regulation 554/91 prevents the endorsement of political candidates or parties and permits an officer to voice political opinions on behalf of the force only when authorized to do so by the board or the chief.[93] The Toronto Police Association claimed that the regulation did not apply to the association and that it was the constitutional right of the Association to lobby, to express a political position, and to endorse candidates and political parties. The issue erupted in a controversy surrounding a fundraising campaign called 'True Blue.' The Toronto Police Association utilized telemarketers to solicit financial contributions from the public. In return for a contribution of a certain amount, donors would receive a Toronto Police Association colour-coded decal to denote the level of the contribution, which they could display, for example, in the windshield of their cars.[94] The association abandoned the campaign in the face of nearly unanimous public and political concern, but the general issue continues to arise.[95]

Other issues, such as the powers of the Special Investigations Unit (SIU) and antipathy towards civilian oversight in general have proven to be almost as contentious. As police chiefs attempt to deal sternly with misconduct, from officer use of excessive force to corruption, police unions respond with tactics such as holding unofficial 'votes of confidence' in their chief's performance. It was in this manner that the Toronto Police Association expressed its displeasure with Chief Julian Fantino;[96] however, the phenomenon has not been isolated to Toronto.[97]

Ironically, the Toronto Police Association itself has been rocked by a corruption scandal involving prominent members, including the association president.[98] The scandal, which resulted in criminal charges including breach of trust, fraud, influence peddling, obstruction of justice, and weapons-related charges, caused tension between the union and both the chief and the Police Services Board.[99] Because two of the accused were union officials at the time, the charges led to a re-emergence of the issue of whether union officials are technically police officers or whether they have immunity from Police Services Act provisions.[100] At the same time, the shocking charges have bolstered political support for proposed changes to civilian oversight structures in the province.[101]

A Case Study: The Junger and Whitehead Inquiry

Many of the issues discussed above were examined by the Ontario Civilian Commission on Police between October 1990 and May 1992. The commission was brought in to investigate the policies, practices, and procedures for internal investigations of the then Metropolitan Toronto Police Force. The issues were investigated in the context of the manner in which the misconduct and discipline of former Constable Gordon Junger and former Sergeant Brian Whitehead were handled. The context was explosive because the matter involved police corruption and police involvement in prostitution, and there was considerable public concern. In August 1992, the commission issued a comprehensive report that was equally critical of Toronto police officers, the chief, and the Police Services Board. The report made twenty-four wide-sweeping recommendations designed to improve the accountability and public trust they concluded had been lost.[102]

The Case of Gordon Junger

In the fall of 1989, Toronto Police Constable Gordon Junger and his girlfriend, Franklina (Roma) Langford, operated an escort service in Toronto called the 'Pleasure Can Be Yours Escort Service.' After Ms Langford complained to Toronto Police Internal Affairs about Junger's role in the escort service and a number of other matters of discreditable conduct, including possession of narcotics, Junger was arrested on 5 December 1989 in a hotel room where he was acting as an escort for a female client. The client was, in fact, a policewoman and the entire exchange with her was videotaped. Although charged with living on the avails of prostitution and possession of cannabis, Junger was never prosecuted.

In lieu of prosecution, Junger's lawyer negotiated a written agreement with the Internal Affairs Unit that would result in Junger resigning from the force as of 1 February 1990. In exchange, a charge of possession of narcotics would be withdrawn, no criminal or *Police Act* charges arising from or with respect to his personal and business relationship with Franklina Langford would be laid against him, all physical evidence relating to the investigation would be destroyed, and

Junger would not receive a negative employment reference. To all intents the agreement was fulfilled before any details of the agreement became public. Junger resigned, the charge was withdrawn, and the Metropolitan Toronto Police Services Board were simply advised, in brief report from the chief made in closed session, that an officer about whom there were allegations of drug use and prostitution-related activities had left the force. Apparently even the chief did not know all of the details in February when the deal was executed, but when he learned of the specific terms of the agreement in March he still did not advise the board about the deal. Instead, he asked the legal adviser for the Toronto police to develop guidelines for any future agreements of that sort.

The Case of Brian Whitehead

On 7 November 1989, a woman working as a prostitute was picked up by an off-duty police officer, former Sergeant Brian Whitehead, who threatened to arrest her if she did not comply with what he asked her to do. She complied but, after Whitehead told her he would continue his sexual abuse, she sought legal advice about what he had done to her and how to make him stop. The Toronto Police Internal Affairs Unit was advised, agreed to preserve the woman's confidentiality and, after a three-week investigation, arrested Whitehead on 22 November 1989 for sexual assault and extortion. Although arrested and detained briefly, Whitehead was not processed on those charges. Instead, on 11 March 1990, he was charged with corrupt practice under the *Police Services Act*. Pursuant to a plea agreement reached without any notice to the victim, 'Jane Doe,' Whitehead pleaded guilty to the charge of corrupt practice. Although a joint submission had been made for a penalty of 'days off,' he was instead demoted to constable on 11 May 1990. The criminal charges against him were withdrawn by the Crown. The promise of confidentiality was not kept and, in March 1991, Chief McCormack threatened to release the victim's identity. He was prevented from doing so on 19 March 1991, after Jane Doe was compelled to obtain an injunction.

The Media: 1990

The story of Jane Doe and former Sergeant Brian Whitehead did not appear in the press until March 1991, but considerable media attention was paid to the escapades of Gordon Junger and his controversial deal with Toronto police. A review of the print media produces a valuable record of what was said and what was not said, and by whom, before evidence at the inquiry clarified the facts.

In the first article on the Junger affair, written by *Toronto Star* reporter Alan Story,[103] Chief William McCormack claimed that no 'special deal' had been reached with Junger and that a thorough and impartial investigation had been conducted into possible criminal offences that he might have faced. The chief's explanation for the withdrawal of the possession of cannabis charges is that the evidence of a key witness (presumably Roma Langford) had changed. On the issue of a deal to drop charges against Junger, he is quoted as saying that the allegation by Junger that a deal had been struck 'does not dignify a reply.' In the days following, Chief McCormack insisted that he did inform the Police Services Board concerning the deal and the resignation. Some board members have no memory of being advised about such a remarkable case.[104]

Evidence called at the inquiry ultimately established that Roma Langford adamantly denied ever saying that she would recant her evidence concerning the drug charge against Junger. The inquiry believed her testimony. She had also told Internal Affairs about two officers on the force who had performed sex acts for money. With respect to Ms Langford's position, former Chief McCormack is quoted as saying; 'Who do you believe: the word of the police chief or that of a prostitute?' With respect to the matter of other officers (one of whom it is now known was his son Bill), McCormack is reported to have said that no evidence had been found to substantiate the claim, but that the continued publicity concerning the matter was hurting morale. The newspaper story recounting the exchange notes that Ms Langford provided police with a number of audiotapes of telephone conversations concerning the escort service as well as call sheets containing the officers' names.[105] This story is followed with the first of many strong editorials on the allegations and former Chief McCormack's responses:

> Metro Police Chief William McCormack has reacted angrily to allegations that the force suppressed a sex-for-money scandal involving force members. He insists the Metro force conducted a 'thorough' inquiry. Yet contradictory statements by a key player in the scandal have raised more questions. For example;
> • Was a thorough investigation conducted into all possible charges against the key officer about his running of the escort service before he left the force, without being prosecuted?

- Second, did the police force's internal affairs bureau conduct an exhaustive investigation before concluding that there was no evidence linking two other officers to the escort service? The woman involved in the service now says she has evidence showing their participation.
- Third, why were no drug charges laid against the key officer or his then companion when hash oil was found in their townhouse?

To his credit, McCormack has now invited the Ontario Police Commission – a body with investigative powers – to go through files on the case and put the doubts to rest. However, even without seeing the files, commission Chairman Douglas Drinkwalter yesterday called it 'a tempest in a teapot,' saying 'we don't have any big, grave concerns.'[106]

Media coverage of the evidence heard by the commission was extensive and continued to build up to the long-awaited report.

The Report: August 1992

In the introduction to their report, the commissioners set out four central criticisms. They concluded that 'there has been a tendency by the force to treat cases involving errant officers as an in-house problem, rather than a matter of public concern. In an effort to rid the force of an officer who was considered unsuitable, expediency has taken precedence over principle. Accountability for police discipline and civilian review has been compromised. Inadequate consideration has been given to victims of police wrongdoing.'[107] They identified as a key problem a culture of denial and insularity. That culture was demonstrated in the evidence of police witnesses who consistently minimized their errors and blamed anyone but themselves. They noted with concern:

The Metropolitan Toronto Police Force has maintained throughout this Inquiry that nothing seriously went wrong – nothing that a few procedural changes could not fix. The Chief of Police William McCormack told the Inquiry that the force has not been 'procedurally perfect,' but his officers have acted in good faith. It is significant that, as far as this Inquiry has been informed, not a single member of the force has been reprimanded in connection with these matters.

Internal Affairs, which conducted the investigations into Junger and Whitehead, has gone on record in its final submission (p. 2) as assessing its performance as flawless – 'totally proper, totally correct and totally legal' and in the best interests of the force and the community.[108]

Attitudinal and structural failures within the Metropolitan Toronto Police Forces were directly cited in the report as the origin of the crisis of public confidence in governance. The commissioners concluded their introductory remarks as follows:

> If the Metropolitan Toronto Police Services Board had reacted differently in April, 1990 when circumstances of the resignation of Gordon Junger first came to light in the media, this Inquiry need never have taken place. If the Board had used its own authority to uncover the facts of the Junger case and respond appropriately, the Ontario Civilian Commission on Police Services would not have felt obliged to intervene.
>
> If the Chief of Police for Metropolitan Toronto had responded vigorously and openly when he discovered the full details of the Junger resignation agreement, instead of keeping them confidential, the reaction to this whole matter would have been different.
>
> Had the force been less defensive and the Board less complacent at the outset, the public would have been assured that the issues were being addressed. This report would not have been necessary.[109]

They rejected entirely the former chief's rationalizations of the agreement reached with the former Constable Junger (the 'deal' the chief denied had taken place). Instead, they characterized it as an attempt to make the ends justify the means:

> The Inquiry heard a range of justifications from the force for the agreement, such as: it was worth it to get rid of a bad officer; there was no intention of complying with the terms anyway; the criminal case against Junger had fallen apart because the witness had changed her story; there was no hope of any other successful prosecutions; once he resigned, disciplinary charges were irrelevant; and it would have taken a long time to go through the disciplinary hearing process and would have cost the taxpayers a lot more to continue to pay Junger's salary on suspension until the case was resolved.
>
> All of these excuses amount to the end justifying the means. They are totally unacceptable.
>
> It is disturbing that the response of the Internal Affairs unit, which signed the agreement on behalf of the Chief, has been to continue to deny any error. The final written submission from Internal Affairs concluded that 'the conduct of Internal Affairs was appropriate, just and fair.' (p. 3) The motive expressed by Internal Affairs witnesses – their desire to secure

the resignation of an officer they believed should be off the force – may have been understandable, but their actions were wrong.

The commissioners are clear in placing some of the responsibility for the cavalier attitude of Internal Affairs on the chief and the Police Services Board. They said: 'The smugness of Internal Affairs in finding itself to be totally without fault is likely in part the result of the fact that no one has been censured for conduct in connection with any aspect of the Junger matter. According to testimony, the closest the force came to admitting a problem was to indicate that the agreement should have been shown to a lawyer before it was signed. This sounds like a procedural error only. It ought to have been recognized that in substantive terms, there were serious problems with the agreement.'[110] They were equally critical concerning their finding that Chief McCormack failed adequately to inform the Police Services Board or to act on what he learned:

Chief William McCormack testified that he was not fully aware of the details of the resignation agreement when he gave consent to it. The information he received about the agreement appears to have been second or third-hand. When he did see it, he was still not overly concerned because he believed that prosecution of the officer either in criminal court or a disciplinary hearing was not a viable option. He insisted that the agreement was not a 'deal' because neither party got anything out of it.

But he was sufficiently worried about public criticism when he saw the agreement that he thought it best to keep the agreement confidential.

The Chief of Police should have been fully informed – and should have ensured that he was fully informed – of the details of the agreement before his signature was attached to it. Once the Chief became aware of the agreement, he should have repudiated it and taken it to the Police Services Board. Keeping the agreement confidential, especially from his own Board, was an inappropriate reaction.[111]

Their conclusion that the response of the Police Services Board was 'wholly inadequate' included the board's failure to require answers from the chief. In other words, it is not adequate supervision simply to accept whatever information the chief chooses to provide.

Part 9 of the Report was devoted to the treatment of the victims of police misconduct; in this case, both Roma Langford and Jane Doe. In almost all cases the commissioners chose to accept the 'word of prostitutes' over that of police officers or the police chief. They also rejected the rationalizations for failing to proceed with criminal charges, which Jane Doe had advised them she was anxious to proceed with, and were critical of the way in which she was treated with respect to the *Police Act* charges. They said:

> Disciplinary hearings are not in-house matters to be dealt with in private by the force. Jane Doe should have been informed and involved. Furthermore, it is presumptuous and patronizing to make decisions on behalf of an adult who is capable of deciding on her own what is best for her. Police officers must take into account the greater good of the community in their decisions, but they should not presume to know what is best for an individual victim without consulting the person.
>
> The sad thing is that the response of the force to Jane Doe only got worse. She was not notified, as the key witness, of the disciplinary proceeding. Neither was her lawyer. Her statement was changed at the hearing by the prosecutor, at the insistence of Whitehead's lawyer, without her knowledge or concurrence. The prosecutor and defence agreed on a penalty of days' off (which was rejected by the hearing officer). During the hearing, in her absence, the promise to Jane Doe to protect her identity was ignored, and her name was entered into the transcript.
>
> The subsequent treatment of Jane Doe by senior management of the force seemed to emanate from a quite remarkable fog of ignorance. It is almost unbelievable that – having failed to notify Jane Doe of the disciplinary hearing, having reneged on a commitment to keep her name confidential, and having made unauthorized changes to her statement at the hearing - the force would call a news conference in which the Chief blamed Jane Doe for not showing up at the hearing and protecting her own interests. To add insult to injury, Jane Doe was also forced to go to court for an injunction to prevent her name being disclosed through public release of the transcript by the force.
>
> The force was simply too eager to deflect any public criticism from itself. It reacted defensively and in the process disregarded the interests of an individual who was twice victimized – by the original offence and by the police disciplinary system.[112]

The submissions on behalf of Jane Doe identified systemic gender bias as part of the explanation for the way that the complaints of Jane Doe and Roma Langford were handled. The commissioners accepted the need to investigate further the issue of gender bias:

Counsel for Jane Doe has suggested that a study be conducted into the treatment of women complainants and offences against women. We agree that more must be done to grapple with this issue. There is something seriously wrong when sexual assaults are going unprosecuted in cases where the accused is identified, and the allegations are substantiated by police investigators.

Police forces should be interested in ways of ensuring that more cases go to court. It is frustrating for police to substantiate that an offence has been committed and not be able to proceed because of the reluctance of the victim. For the victim, the longer-term consequences of avoiding facing the accused can be devastating.

We recommend that a task force be established by the Attorney General to develop practical means of supporting victims so as to encourage their cooperation in testifying against perpetrators of sexual crimes. The findings of the task force should help police forces to prosecute more sexual assaults successfully. The task force should not be limited to cases where the accused is a member of a police force, but it should give special consideration to that aspect of the issue.

Based on the practical measures developed by the work of the task force, all Police Services Boards should develop strategies to support victims of sexual assault and encourage their cooperation in prosecutions. Special consideration should be given to cases where the accused is a police officer.[113]

Lessons Learned, 1992–2004

The Chief of Police, 1992–1999
After the report was issued, former Chief McCormack continued to insist that he and his officers had done nothing wrong;[114] however, his most vigorous arguments in this regard were not made until after he retired and published a memoir, *Without Fear or Favour: The Life and Politics of an Urban Cop.*[115] He entitles the chapter concerning the Junger affair 'An Officer and a Gigolo,' and repeats the position rejected by the OCCOPS report that Ms Langford changed her evidence and thus the police had no option but to accept Junger's resignation. He then proceeds to blame the controversy concerning police handling of the case on the newly elected New Democratic government and on the inquiry panel itself.[116] In a position suggestive of more recent attacks on members of police services boards, he ends the chapter with an attempt to link Laura Rowe, a new Toronto Police Services Board member, with

Roma Langford, the woman who reported Gordon Junger to Internal Affairs. In McCormack's account, a traffic officer claims to have recognized Ms Rowe as a passenger in a car being driven by Roma Langford, who he charged with impaired driving. The officer selects Ms Rowe's photo from 'numerous others shown him by senior officers,' and is said to have 'also attended her swearing-in ceremony at headquarters the next day'; where, 'in front of television news cameras and everyone else in the room, [he] identified Laura Rowe as the passenger in Roma Langford's car.' Retired Chief McCormack gives no credence to Ms Rowe's statement that she was not there and did not know Ms Langford, nor to the statement from Lara Hoshowsky that it was she who was with Ms Langford. Instead, he offers the following questions as if they had not already been answered: 'What would Bob Rae's choice as the new member of the Police Board have been doing in a car with a drunken prostitute, on the eve of her swearing-in ceremony? Neither Rae nor Rowe, a lesbian activist, would say, which I thought very curious in light of the premier's oft-repeated declaration that an NDP government would be an open government. Nor did the province's top law official, Solicitor General Allan Pilkey, care to comment.'[117]

The political criticism continues in chapter 21 of McCormack's book, 'Bob Rae's Kind of People,' with a wideranging set of complaints about Susan Eng, who replaced June Rowlands as chair of the Police Services Board. His unhappiness with Ms Eng appears rooted in her insistence on full reporting to the board and on enforcing board policy.

The inability so clearly demonstrated in McCormack's memoir to accept or honour the approach that OCCOPS took to his and his senior officers' decisions in the Junger and Whitehead cases may be relevant to understanding the difficulties the board had in implementing the recommendations. If the chief of police is unable to accept criticism or direction from his or her employer, and resists acting on clear policy directives, the distinction between policy and operations will never serve the goal of accountability and transparency in executive-police relations.

The Toronto Police Services Board, 1992–1999

The Toronto Police Services Board under Susan Eng made consistent efforts to accept the twenty-four recommendations and to develop an accountability culture, but their efforts did not survive the term of the board members. The board's initial responses were encouraging. Within a month of the issuance of the report, they acknowledged the criticism and the need both to accept responsibility for the errors and to change the practices and the culture that had permitted the failures in governance.[118] In February 1993, they provided OCCOPS with the draft of what would become known as the '1992 Directive' and a 'firm commitment' to implement all of the Junger-Whitehead recommendations. However, by 1999, during the terms of a new chair (Norm Gardner) and a new chief (Julian Fantino), and with new legislation, OCCOPS said, 'Unfortunately, it is our conclusion that this commitment has yet to be fully met.'[119] It is not clear what role the changes in personnel and political culture may have played in this failure.

The first indication that all was not well came from a report on discipline in the Toronto force prepared in November 1996. The executive summary concluded that 'the discipline process currently in place at the Metropolitan Toronto Police Service is unpredictable and inefficient. The existing discipline process does not consistently inspire confidence and often the participants in the process are dissatisfied.'[120] The difficulties were not resolved. The 1999 report of OCCOPS highlighted the continuing difficulties the Toronto Police Services Board faces in governing the largest municipal police service in the country. In the first recommendation of the 1999 report, OCCOPS underscored the lack of any effective mechanisms to monitor the degree of implementation of the policy directives of the Police Services Board: 'The Metropolitan Toronto Police Services Board should develop mechanisms to improve its effectiveness in overseeing implementation of its policies by the force. The Board should have the capacity to monitor compliance with its policies on an ongoing basis and to investigate specific matters where necessary as they arise. The Board shall report to the Ontario Civilian Commission on Police Services within six months on the decisions it has made to respond to this recommendation.'[121]

The OCCOPS supported its concern and recommendation in some detail. First they identified the problem of 'fragmented information,' which is manifested in the filing and compiling rules and disciplinary information in a range of locations. The result of this fragmentation is that a 'multi-layered complex of policies, orders, directives and procedures that govern behaviour of civilians and police officers' are not made available to members in any way that ensures that the information is received, read and understood, and followed.[122] The same criticism could be applied to board directives. The question was what had happened in the few years since the Junger and Whitehead scandals.

The Police Services Board of 1992 committed itself to establish 'standards of conduct' and to put in place 'policies and procedures to ensure appropriate standards of conduct are complied with in the future.' It was determined to 'set in place mechanisms to ensure that the Chief, Internal Affairs, and the entire discipline system of the Force is monitored by the Board in order to ensure that appropriate standards of conduct are maintained.' Former Chief David Boothby advised the board of that time in February 1993 that these directions had been followed; however, something happened in the subsequent years and with the board that followed. In 1999, OCCOPS concluded that 'unfortunately, the Board did not follow through in auditing the Chief's implementation mechanism ... until recently the Board had no formal mechanism for monitoring compliance with Board policies. Consequently, reports are requested, but there is a tendency for them to "fall off the scope" over time, if no response is provided by the police service.'

To deal with this obvious problem, OCCOPS recommended a system of effective auditing implementation of board policy by the Police Service. The OCCOPS report also noted that the failure of the then chief to keep the Police Services Board apprised of allegations of serious misconduct, one of the key problems identified by the Junger and Whitehead Inquiry, was once more a concern.[123] Accordingly, the commissioners said in Recommendation 2: 'The Metropolitan Toronto Police Services Board should adopt a policy   stating clearly and unequivocally the obligation of the Chief to report fully on cases involving alleged wrongdoing by members of the force if the integrity of the force or the public interest is affected. The policy should state the obligation of the Board to be so informed. In addition, the Board should require regular status reports on serious disciplinary matters.'

Although it would clearly be unworkable for a chief to report every misdeed by a member of the service, the 1992 directive placed the balancing point in favour of reporting. This was no longer occurring. By May of 1998, then Chief David Boothby advised the board that he did not report all allegations. For example, he did not report allegations arising from complaints lodged through the Public Complaints Investigation Bureau; allegations made to unit commanders and investigated through the normal disciplinary process; allegations about the conduct of members of other police services; allegations about board members; and those which would endanger an individual or obstruct an investigation. In fact, reports were only generated when Internal Affairs opened

a criminal investigation file, which was reminiscent of a problem un-
covered by the Junger and Whitehead Inquiry. Not even cases involving
misconduct by senior management were being routinely reported to the
board. This was the case with Deputy Chief Reesor and the unautho-
rized handling of a revolver.'[124] Improvements in reporting were made,
and 'effective January 1999 the Board began receiving updates on public complaints of a 'serious' nature and relevant information regarding
issues involving officers of senior rank.'[125]

Not all of the Junger and Whitehead recommendations were seen as
requiring follow-up, however. For example, Recommendations 17 and
18 concerning gender bias and the treatment of victims were noted as
having been fulfilled.[126] In assessing what 'fulfilled' actually means, it
is helpful to keep in mind the experience and advice of Jane Doe on the
'successful' implementation of recommendations such as the appropriate investigation of sexual assault. The OCCOPS asked for a detailed
report from the board by 31 December 1999 on its progress in implementation of the Junger and Whitehead recommendations and its own
subsequent recommendations.[127] No report was received until 1 May
2000.[128] There was a change in chief during the time that OCCOPS
sought the report, so the delay was not unreasonable given an outgoing
chief's wish not to bind his successor. However, in the May 2000 response, the board claims to have substantially complied with all or
most of the recommendations of OCCOPS. The devil, as always, is in
the details of that implementation.

The Police Services Board, 1999–Present

The 'Final Response to Ontario Civilian Commission on Police Services
(OCCOPS) Regarding their Fact Finding Report' from the Toronto Police Services Board is found in an Extract from the Minutes of the
Meeting of the Toronto Police Services Board held on 1 May 2000
identified as number 156. It is a twenty-five-page document, with
twenty-eight recommendations. In response to the recommendation of
OCCOPS that the board must fulfil its governance role and assert
control over the systems and policies for which it is accountable by
periodically requiring audits of the service's implementation of its lawful directions and policies, little new is actually proposed. The response
acknowledges that the background to the OCCOPS recommendations
is the 1992 Junger-Whitehead directive, which was not properly implemented until 1997. On the issue of the need for periodic audits, the
response simply asserts that 'the issue of auditing is not new to the

Board,' lists a number of audits conducted from April 1991 to 2000, and notes that in February 2000 the board required the chief, in consultation with the city auditor, to develop an audit work plan. The board's response to Recommendation 16 is to require the chief to provide an annual report tracking the implementation of internal and external audit recommendations.[129]

Recommendation 11 of OCCOPS concerns the need for a review of the discipline process to improve efficiency and accountability and reduce delays in processing discipline charges. The response to that recommendation indicates that a complete review is dependent on improvements to information technology, improvements that are in the process of being implemented. Other measures include better caseload management across units, and the implementation of a team approach to the investigation of public complaints so that regardless of leaves or other occurrences one member of the team is 'continually addressing' each complaint. Finally, the board is advised that Chief Fantino, as part of the ninety-day review of operations he undertook upon becoming chief, 'is personally examining integrity issues.'

These are typical assessments and typical responses. They are difficult to analyse in the absence of concrete details and facts, and one is left to measure them against events, which may not be the most helpful approach. The most obvious events for that purpose are the corruption scandals that have erupted since the May 2000 response.

In January 2004, after a two-and-a-half-year investigation, criminal charges including fraud, theft, extortion, and perjury were laid against six former drug squad officers. The allegations stemmed from the officers' alleged treatment of suspects and accused persons in drug investigations, which included theft of money, assault, and perjury.[130] There is no doubt that the accused officers defended themselves vigorously against the allegations in the course of the investigation, and rumours surfaced about efforts to stonewall the RCMP probe, but Chief Fantino, who to his credit brought in a senior RCMP investigator, Chief Superintendent John Neilly, to lead the probe, resists any claim that there are widespread or systemic problems associated with the drug squad scandal.[131]

In answer to concerns initially raised by defence counsel with Chief Boothby, Chief Fantino not only brought in Chief Superintendent Neilly, he commissioned the services of retired justice George Ferguson, QC, on 29 November 2001 to prepare a report with recommendations for addressing the issues of corruption. Part I of the 'Review and Recommendations Concerning Various Aspects of Police Misconduct' addresses disclosure of police misconduct.[132] Part II addresses systemic issues, including recruitment, training and promotion, internal affairs, and officer abuse of alcohol and drugs. The report to the chief is dated January 2003. Chief Fantino did not provide the report to the Police Services Board until 26 February 2004.[133] No explanation has been provided for either the decision to retain Mr Ferguson without obtaining direction or advice from the Police Services Board, nor for the delay in providing the report to the board, although both have been criticized.[134] In any event, the drug squad scandal is not the only one facing the Toronto Police Service. In mid-April 2004 the news broke that more corruption charges were expected. First, the plainclothes unit at the downtown 52 Division was disbanded in response to a major investigation into an alleged shakedown of area bars.[135] Then the scandal spread as former chief Bill McCormack's eldest son was identified with it and linked to the Junger scandal of the 1990s.[136] Rick McIntosh, the head of the Toronto Police Association, stepped down because he too was linked to the scandal.[137] A third set of serious misconduct allegations involving officers involved with a drug addict included another of former chief McCormack's children and more charges.[138] Not surprisingly there have been calls for an independent inquiry[139] but Chief Fantino was left in charge of the issue, with the assistance of Mr Ferguson.[140]

Conclusion and Recommendations

Criminologist John Braithwaite argues that 'legal checks on abuse of power [are] difficult at best, counter-productive at worst,' and suggests instead two key 'counter-intuitive' strategies. He advocates replacing narrow, formal, and strongly punitive sanctions with broad, informal, and weak sanctions and separating enforcement targeting from the identification of the actor who benefits from the abuse of power – or removing investigation of the police from police hands. Specifically addressing the conflict between public concern over police misconduct and corruption and the police outcry over compromised independence, Braithwaite suggests that in order for the police to be resilient in resisting domination by any one structure or group (whether state, business, or professions like the law), the police must actually be dependent on all of them. That is, to promote both accountability *and* independence from political interference, the police structure must be receptive to checks on power from diverse sources, including oversight bodies, civil society, loosely organized community groups, a free press, the judiciary and, at the highest level, the executive branch of the state structure.[141]

Concern over the multiple sites of regulation dominated law enforcement concerns in the 1990s and continues to resonate in many circles, but an interest in returning to a broader range of oversight mechanisms appears to be somewhat on the rebound in light of recent events. One hopes so, as it is an important feature of both the accountability and responsibility aspects of police executive relations. When the executive is attentive to the complexities of the relationships and viewpoints, it is less likely that one perspective will prevail. A review of the recent history of the Toronto Police Service demonstrates how important it is that police governors, in this case the Toronto Police Services Board, be aware of the history and complexity of the institution they are responsible for. Perhaps the single most important reform one could recommend in this regard is the guarantee of some continuity of membership on police services boards so that essential history and appreciation of the multiple factors engaged when any change is attempted is preserved.

While complexity provides strength, it must not be a complexity of rules. Rather, the complexity should comprise multiple sites of observation and accountability and include many that are quite free from legal rules and doctrine. For example, the involvement of a community legal clinic in assisting Jane Doe in her struggle to hold former Sergeant Whitehead to account was instrumental in elevating the Junger Inquiry into a wideranging and significant tool of police governance.[142] Similarly, the catalyst for the Toronto Drug Squad investigation was the effort of a defence lawyer who had reason to trust the Professional Standards Branch of the Toronto Police and brought his concerns and evidence of corruption to Chief Boothby and then to Chief Fantino. In other words, there were resources in the wider community that acted as agents for investigation and accountability. Other examples abound and should be respected and supported rather than denigrated or merely tolerated. A similar catholicism of approach is required to ensure that the tension between policy and operations remains nuanced and evolving. The investigations of sexual assaults and sexual offences, for example, are a matter of operations, but these investigations generate significant policy issues that cannot be considered in a vacuum.[143] Once again, multiple sources of information and opinion should be encouraged.

Finally, without and perhaps even with a fundamental re-examination of the enterprise of policing and law enforcement in a postmodern world, one has to expect continued conflict and crises as we swing between independence and accountability, oversight and autonomy. The challenge is to appreciate that a pendulum always swings back and forth, and that the key is to strive for an appropriate balance regardless of ideological preference.

COMMENTARY BY SUSAN ENG

The great paradox in police accountability is the inadequacy of the law in holding those responsible for enforcing it to account for breaching it. The entire web of legislative instruments catalogued in Dianne Martin's paper relies on its multiplicity rather than the individual effectiveness of its constituent parts. Certainly, there are advances but the consensus among police watchers is that our accountability mechanisms have yet to fulfil their promise. And yet, one of the cornerstones of a liberal democracy is that all are treated equally under and before the law.

There is no shortage of erudite analysis of why this should be the case. From careful examination of the legal infrastructure to musings about a police subculture; from decrying lack of political will to criticizing the inattention of civilian overseers, it has all been done. So why does experience continue to trump expectations?

Perhaps it is the small-minded, not the high-minded, decisions that drive our reality. Here is one example. The disappearance of the Ontario Police Complaints Commissioner in 1997 could be said to be a hallmark of the political climate of this past decade. First established in 1981, the public complaints system had become accepted as part of the policing landscape in Toronto. But when the system was introduced provincewide, the loudest objections came not from the police lobby, as might be expected, but from the smaller municipalities who could not bear the cost of the hearings to decide on the complaints.

Costs skyrocketed when officers hired top-notch lawyers to represent them. If they were cleared, the municipality paid the legal expenses. From 1992 to 1996, Toronto paid out about $5.2 million in legal expenses for disciplinary matters, including public complaints. A proportionate sum would wipe out the entire budget of a smaller municipality. Perhaps that is why the provincially funded Special Investigations Unit was kept while the relatively less reviled Police Complaints Commission was disbanded. Thus, one very important vehicle for police accountability was sacrificed at the altar of municipal parsimony. The initial monetary savings are illusory because civil lawsuits have started to take the commission's place and the costs to defend them and payouts on successful claims may well exceed the cost of the public complaints system.

Those who are questioning why the Ontario government is reviewing the options for reintroducing a public complaints system rather than just dusting off previous legislation might do well to suggest to them that they simply set aside some funds to finance the hearings.

Or perhaps the reason why our reality does not match our expectations is that we have not demanded integrity, competence, and accountability from one of our most vital public services. Professor Martin points out in her paper that the 1992 Junger-Whitehead Directive was found not to have been in use by 1999, despite a wrenching public inquiry and stinging report. The only qualification I would make to those assertions, as one of the authors of the directive, is that it was fully implemented while the Police Services Board consistently demanded it. The directive was subsequently ignored without consequence until the review in 1999. That the executives of a professional organization would promptly disregard one of its own directives once the pressure was off should not be acceptable but it continues to happen in the policing realm.

Even when the judicial system finds its voice against overwhelming odds to point out misconduct, the organizational response is negligible. Listen to what Mr Justice Fraser said in rejecting Sergeant Kenneth Deane's testimony that he saw Dudley George holding a rifle and that he saw a muzzle flash. To explain why no rifle was found anywhere near the body, he testified that he saw Dudley throw the rifle away. To accept the defence argument, Judge Fraser said, the Court would have to believe that Dudley George, having just been shot in the chest, which fractured his clavicle, punctured his left lung, fractured his ribs and tore open a number of blood vessels, after all this, he decides to get rid of his rifle and manages to fling it across a road into a ditch!

Blatant cases of unbelievable testimony cannot help but to erode public confidence and tarnish the image of all police officers. And yet, no internal disciplinary action was taken on this aspect of the case. Would such a lack of institutional integrity and competence be acceptable in any other profession?

I suppose the question is 'acceptable to whom?' The common denominator in this examination is public opinion. Despite the public outcry when scandal hits, despite the soul searching of inquiries and symposiums, and despite the threat by the police union that they plan to target their critics, police chiefs bask in the reflected glory of nearly 100 per cent public approval ratings.

We are fond of explaining the police subculture in terms of 'us and them.' This does not tell the whole story. Rather, police buy into the social hierarchies the rest of us try to deny exist. The police subculture makes a distinction between people they will do things for, and people they "do things to."

Among the people the police do things for are their political masters, particularly if they inhabit the same quadrant of the political spectrum. Police service boards were conceived as a buffer between the political powers and the day-to-day workings of a police force. They were meant to guarantee the freedom from political interference that Kent Roach has addressed. And importantly, they are obliged to translate the needs and expectations of the public at large into policies that govern standards of behaviour in the police service.

There is a long history in Toronto surrounding the policing of public protests. The public interest in freedom of speech collides with the public interest in preserving public order. Traditionally, police interpret their greater mandate to preserve public order. They have a Public Order Unit in the police force; there is no Freedom of Speech Unit.

The public outcry over the alleged excessive use of force at the Economic Summit and subsequent public protests eventually, but not immediately, brought about the adoption of policies to require the Public Order Unit to engage with protest organizers to prevent unnecessary use of force. Up to that point, however, it can be argued that the protesters would be regarded by police as those outside the mainstream, not at all the people they did things for but people they did things to. What brought the change in policy was a police services board prepared to accord higher value to the freedom of speech. Indeed, in those heady days, it was possible to hope that not only civil disobedience, but even as Alan Borovoy[144] would argue, uncivil obedience, was protected.

Normative behaviour in the Toronto Public Order Unit had sufficiently changed by the time of the Queen's Park protests that the Toronto police were commended for their restraint while the OPP continued with a course of action that would land them in a public inquiry.

The point here is simply that a police services board acting as a buffer between what might be a majoritarian view and minority rights serves to uphold what society professes to value, in this case, the freedom to protest. And to apply one of the models of political intervention in the deployment of police resources referenced in Professor Roach's chapter of this book, such intervention was debated publicly and adopted only after full representation from the police service.

What if there is no buffer between that majoritarian view and minority rights? I would like to argue that only a police services board can provide that buffer – but I won't, since the make-up of those boards change. But in the case of the OPP and RCMP, there is no civilian governance body between the police service and the politicians, who we are calling here the executive branch.

What happens when the highest ranking of the people the police do things for conveys the majoritarian view, that the social disorder presented by the protestors is a graver issue than their civil right to protest? What happens to an operational directive that is based on the protection of civil rights and contemplates only the necessary level of restraint? One could argue that the protestors would then become the people that police do things to.

If this seems too harsh on indictment of police culture, we need only gauge our own reactions to the conviction of people not considered to be part of the 'criminal classes.' Did not the headlines scream with horror that Alan Eagleson, the lawyer and financial manager for many famous hockey players, who was convicted of fraud, might be required to wear an orange jumpsuit and pick up leaves around Queen's Park? The police are simply reflecting back to us the essential double standard of our society. While we universally profess to value equality before the law, we actually accept that some are more equal than others. The police are asked to choose for us and if they choose wrongly, or make the right choice at the wrong time, they are castigated.

The reality is that a significant enough proportion of the public do not see themselves as former Police Board chair Norm Gardner's 'scumbags,' but rather as upstanding citizens who need the protection of the police from such people. For that service, a windshield decal is cheap at twice the price. And just like a CAA sticker, it entitles you to service you might not otherwise get. That is why the Toronto Police Association launched its 'True Blue' campaign and expected the dollars to roll in.

But the 'True Blue' campaign was a watershed in another way. Although we might characterize the telemarketing scheme as a shake down or protection racket, there was little to distinguish that effort from the fear mongering that takes place every year at budget time. The only difference is that our politicians take the hit publicly for us when they question police spending, whereas these phone calls were coming into our homes. That was when the general public began to realize that they were being called on their double standards. Until the silent majority engages in the debate with the vocal minority about the proper role of the police in a liberal democracy, and together face the mixed messages that we send to our police agencies, the dissonance between what we hope for and what really happens will continue.

NOTES

Particular thanks to law student Katie Rowen for exceptional research assistance.

1 Jerome H. Skolnick, *Justice without Trial*, 2nd ed. (New York: Macmillan, 1975). But note that the extension of the doctrine of constabulary independence, which places the police 'above' politics, is much less·well supported.
2 See the chapters by Roach, Sossin, and Stenning for typologies of the dichotomy between civilian oversight and police independence.
3 'Sites' in this chapter refers to the points in the legal, policing, and other systems of civil society, where interactions between elements of the various systems takes place. Thus the points at which the activities and interests of a police chief intersect with the activities and interests of a police services board can be said to be a 'site.'
4 For example, the decision of Justice Anne Molloy of the Ontario Superior Court of Justice on 16 September 2004, in *R. v. Kevin Khan*, received considerable attention. Justice Molloy dismissed drug charges against Mr Khan on the basis that the Toronto police used racial profiling when they stopped him in his expensive car, and fabricated evidence to justify their stop and to link him to cocaine hidden in the car. Peter Small, 'Judge raps police in profiling case,' *Toronto Star*, 17 September 2004, A1. A subsequent story reveals that one of the officers involved was cited by a judge in 1993 for similar conduct. Jim Rankin and Betsy Powell, 'Officer Had 1993 Profiling Ruling,' *Toronto Star*, 18 September 2004.
5 Richard Ericson notes that the criminal law is a police officer's tool in reproducing order; it is a resource, not a restraint. This function of law as it relates to lawyers has been analyzed frequently by students of both law and sociology, 'Police Use of Criminal Rules,' in *Organizational Police*

Deviance: Its Structure and Control, ed. Clifford D. Shearing (Toronto: Butterworths, 1981), at 101. At the same time, the rule of law is taken for granted as the formal standard against which deviance should be measured and judged.

6 Few modern institutions are as successful as the police in shaping the discourse concerning them. From the initial shaping of the facts of an incident or arrest to conform to policing goals and legal or psychiatric discourse, through the presentation of the same facts in court, to portrayal of the case or of police work generally in the media police control of information is extraordinary. Richard V. Ericson, Patricia Baranek, and Janet B.L. Chan, *Representing Order: Crime, Law, and Justice in the News Media* (Toronto: University of Toronto Press, 1991).

7 Ontario Civilian Commission on Police Services, *Report on a Fact-Finding into Various Matters with Respect to the Disciplinary Practices of the Toronto Police Service*, July 1999, 3. This report dealt with a complaint from the Toronto Police Association that discipline was unfairly administered in the Toronto Police Service in that it was inappropriately lenient with regard to the misconduct of senior officers in comparison with the ways that 'rank and file' officers were treated. Although that complaint was not upheld, OCCOPS found a number of matters requiring improvement.

8 Linda Diebel, 'Mistrust of "suits" fills void behind badge,' *Toronto Star*, 2 May 2004, A1; David Hilderley, 'OPP adds support to Metro Police protest,' *Globe and Mail*, 26 October 1992, A19 (protest regarding use-of-force amendments to the *Police Act*); Philip Mascoll, 'Striking Metro police lock station doors,' *Toronto Star*, 27 January 1995, A1, A6 (labour action in response to charges laid against officer regarding the high-risk takedown of TV personality Dwight Drummond); Paul Walter, 'Investigative overkill poisons civilian review of police conduct,' *Toronto Star*, 10 February 1995, A19 (president of the Toronto Police Association argues the police force is subject to 'excessive' oversight); John Duncanson, 'Police chiefs getting ready to take on SIU,' *Toronto Star*, 13 March 2000, A4; John Duncanson, 'Fantino tries to change rules on SIU probes,' *Toronto Star*, 7 November 2000, A1, A26.

9 See Roderick McLeod, QC, *A Report and Recommendations on Amendments to the Police Services Act Respecting Civilian Oversight of the Police*, commissioned by the Ministry of the Attorney General and the Ministry of the Solicitor General (November 1996).

10 John Braithwaite, 'On Speaking Softly and Carrying Big Sticks: Neglected Dimensions of a Republication Separation of Powers' (Summer 1997) 47 Univ. of Toronto L.J. 305.

11 Cal Millar, John Duncanson, and Nicholaas Van Rijn, 'Police unit faces internal probe,' *Toronto Star*, 17 April 2004, A4; Christie Blatchford, 'Police probe corruption as union boss steps down,' *Globe and Mail*, 19 April 2004, A1, A9; John Duncanson, 'Betting scandal rocks police force,' *Toronto Star*, 20 April 2004, A1; Nick Pron and John Duncanson, '6 may face betting probe charges,' *Toronto Star*, 21 April 2004, A1, A16; John Duncanson and Tracey Huffman, 'Source: Police shielded drug dens,' *Toronto Star*, 24 April 2004, A1, A23; Nick Pron, 'Former chief's son facing charges,' *Toronto Star*, 26 April 2004, A1, A12; Christie Blatchford, 'Chief details charges against officers,' *Globe and Mail*, 27 April 2004, A10; Linda Diebel and Cal Millar, 'RCMP probing Toronto Police,' *Toronto Star*, 30 April 2004, A1.

12 John Barber, 'Enough with the few "bad apples,"' *Globe and Mail*, 24 April 2004, M1; Linda Diebel and Cal Millar, 'Police reform: "I want action,"' *Toronto Star*, 28 April 2004, A1, A19; 'Police require outside probe,' Editorial, *Toronto Star*, 28 April 2004, A22; Royson James, 'An independent inquiry is the only way to solve police mess,' *Toronto Star*, 28 April 2004, B3; Royson James, 'Fantino's message is loud, but is it clear?' *Toronto Star*, 29 April 2004, B1, B5, A4. Recent scandals in Ontario, coupled with the change in provincial governments, has led to a review of the civilian complaints process: Richard Brennan, 'LeSage to review police watchdog system,' *Toronto Star*, 10 June 2004, A1; Richard Brennan, 'Police complaints role "a challenge," former judge says,' *Toronto Star*, 11 June 2004, A20; 'Police complaints reform overdue,' Editorial, *Toronto Star*, 11 June 2004, A26.

13 See the chapters by Roach, Stenning, and Sossin in this volume.

14 When the relationship breaks down and this apparently simple chain of command is found wanting, or an event occurs that triggers outside intervention, further measures of accountability are engaged, which may have implications for the police service as a whole and for any individual officers who may be involved.

15 See the chapter by Roach in this volume.

16 *Police Services Act*, R.S.O. 1990, c. P.15. This is the model, broadly speaking, in place in all the provinces and territories and has similarities with the RCMP Act. In Ontario, the essential structure was not changed in the 1997 restructuring that eliminated the Office of the Public Complaints Commissioner.

17 *Police Services Act*, s. 3(2).

18 *Police Services Act*, ss. 27–40.

19 *Police Services Act*, ss. 21–7.

20 *Police Services Act*, s. 31.

21 *Police Services Act*, s. 31(3).

22 *Police Services Act*, ss. 41 and 42.

23 *Police Services Act*, s. 22(1)(a)(ii)(e).

24 *Police Services Act*, ss. 22, 23, 25.

25 *Police Services Act*, ss. 74–6. This occurred in Toronto in the case of allegations of drug squad corruption. Gay Abbate and Joe Friesen, 'Probe results
   in 22 charges filed against six officers,' *Globe and Mail*, 8 January 2004, A14;
   David Tanovich, 'Don't let cops investigate cops,' *Globe and Mail*, 31 August 2001, A13; Kirk Makin, 'Police chief denies "blue wall of silence" in
   corruption probe,' *Globe and Mail*, 21 January 2004, A6.

26 *Police Services Act*, s. 59.

27 *Police Services Act*, s. 59(4).

28 *Police Services Act*, s. 60(5).

29 *Police Services Act*, s. 68.

30 *Police Services Act*, ss. 70–1.

31 *Police Services Act*, s. 113 creates a complete code of powers for the SIU.

32 *Police Services Act*, s. 113(9). The SIU was and continues to be a lightening
   rod for police dissatisfaction with civilian oversight. Despite a legislative
   requirement to do so, police officers refused to cooperate with investigations, citing the Charter. In 1998 retired Justice George Adams, QC, was
   retained to devise ways to improve the relationship between police officers and the SIU. He suggested a distinction between subject officers who
   had the right to remain silent, and witness officers who were required to
   provide statements to investigators. 'Consultation Report of the Honourable George W. Adams, Q.C. to the Attorney General and Solicitor General
   Concerning Police Cooperation with the Special Investigations Unit,'
   14 May 1998. Many of his recommendations, including the creation of the
   two categories of officer, were implemented in January 1999 in Ontario
   regulation 673/98.

33 O. Reg. 673/98, ss. 3, 6, 8, 9, 11.

34 O. Reg. 673/98, s. 10.

35 O. Reg. 673/98, s. 11(1) and s. 5. These reforms may not be entirely successful. In 2003 the Supreme Court of Canada recognized the tort of
   misfeasance in public office in a case involving Toronto Hold up Squad
   witness officers who obstructed and thus failed to cooperate with an SIU
   investigation into a fatal police shooting. *Odhavji Estate v. Woodhouse*,
   [2003] S.C.C. 69.

36 The division of responsibility that leaves investigations and the decision
   to charge in the hands of police and the decision of how and whether to
   prosecute in the hands of the Crown is said to preserve police indepen-

dence and freedom from political interference. For example, the then
Attorney General of Ontario Roy McMurtry said in 1978: 'No one can tell
an officer to take an oath which violates his conscience and no one can tell
an officer to refrain from taking an oath which he is satisfied reflects a true
state of facts.' The Hon. R. Roy McMurtry, 'Police Discretionary Powers in
a Democratically Responsive Society' (1978) 41 RCMP Gazette no. 12 at
5–6; see also *R. v. Appleby Belisle, and Small* (1990), 78 C.R. (3d) 282 (Ont.
Prov. Ct). Charges of theft brought against a reporter and those who
leaked a copy of the upcoming federal budget (retrieved from a copy
room) were stayed on the basis that the officer who laid them had no real
subjective 'belief' that a crime had occurred, but laid them from 'excessive
zeal.' They were stayed despite the fact that no case was made for either
the reality or reasonable grounds for perception of political interference in
use of the criminal process, because no evidence was led that the source of
the officer's 'zeal' was political. The principle was recognized recently by
the Supreme Court of Canada in the context of the RCMP: *R. v. Shirose*,
[1999] 1 S.C.R. 565 at 591.

37 Although the claim was also allowed to proceed against the police chief
for not ensuring compliance with the SIU investigation, the Police Services
Board and the province were found in *Odhavji* not to owe similar private
law obligations. *Odhavji Estate v. Woodhouse*.

38 For example, *R. v. Golden* (2001), 159 C.C.C. (4th) 449 (S.C.C.) recognized
the intrusive and demeaning dimensions of personal searches and held
that strip searches as routine policy to obtain concealed evidence or check
for weapons cannot be justified under s. 8 of the *Charter*, and will always
be unreasonable if carried out abusively. *R. v. Brown* (2003), 173 C.C.C. (3d)
23 (Ont. C.A.) acknowledged the possibility of racial profiling in police
stops.

39 Reginald A. Devonshire, 'The Effects of Supreme Court Charter-Based
Decisions on Policing: More Beneficial than Detrimental?' 31 C.R. (4th) 82
recalls that the Canadian Association of Chiefs of Police (CACP) was
strongly opposed to the Charter. Between 1982 and 1993, 53 of 260 Charter
challenges involved allegations of violations by police officers, many of
which mandated a reform of police practices. The author conducted
interviews with officers of the Metropolitan Toronto Police, and evaluated
training material to assess the impact of Charter rulings, arguing that
police have generally been able to adapt to the most 'adverse' decisions
by altering investigative methods and procedures, and even abandoning
improper practices. The article lists some eighteen police practices sanctioned by the Supreme Court of Canada, and outlines the Toronto police

response to each ruling. In addition, the article sets out the rulings that have conditionally approved or wholly approved of particular police actions and practices. Devonshire concludes that there has been little attempt on the part of police to circumvent the Charter, with the Toronto police experts and manuals demonstrating 'a good knowledge of, and positive attitude towards the Charter.' The statistics indicate only nineteen cases where the Supreme Court found serious *Charter* violations and resolved the case in favour of the accused. During interviews with senior members of the Toronto police, the primary frustrations with the *Charter* appear to be that it has made investigations more difficult, labour-intensive and expensive, doubling paperwork and increasing trial times. Devonshire concludes that the CACP's concerns regarding the 'Americanization' of our justice system have not been borne out in the post-*Charter* period, in large part because the exclusionary rule in the *Charter* is not automatic, and because the police have been able to integrate *Charter* standards into their policies and practices.

40 *Priestman v. Colangelo*, [1959] S.C.R. 615. See Grant Smythe Garneau, 'Roberge: Judicial Extension of Police Powers' 33 C.R. (3d) 309. Garneau argues that the expansion of 'apparently committing' to reasonable and probable grounds for arrest is incorrect, and that the Court defeated the intentions of Parliament in regards to s. 25(4). *R. v. Roberge* (1980), 31 N.B.R. (2d) 668. See also Tracey Tyler, 'Conviction of officer a rare win by Crown,' *Toronto Star*, 11 January 1994, A1, A4.

41 Note also that s. 25 is frequently cited in the context of civil suits against officers arising out of the use of force; see, e.g., *Chartier v. Greaves*, [2001] O.J. No. 634; *Sherman v. Renwick* (2001), 2001 Carswell Ont 595.

42 Criminal convictions against police officers for actions occurring in the course of duty are notoriously difficult to obtain. See, most recently, the Otto Vass manslaughter case; Nick Pron and Betsey Powell 'Officers cleared in Vass case,' *Toronto Star*, 6 November 2003, A1. Traditionally, the Toronto Police Association has brought a great deal of public pressure to bear in regards to criminal prosecution of officers: Rosie DiManno, 'Police union follows its thin blue whine,' *Toronto Star*, 1 October 2003, A2 (discusses union response to Vass charges and the very public manslaughter trial of Constable David Deviney in the Lester Donaldson shooting). See also *R. v. Wighton* (2003), 176 C.C.C. (3d) 550; *R. v. Smith* (1998), 163 Nfld. & P.E.I.R. 179. For interpretation of s. 25 see *Bottrell v. R.* (1981), 22 C.R. (3d) 371.

43 *R. v. Cronmiller* (2004), 2004 B.C.P.C. 1. Six Vancouver police officers each plead guilty to three counts of assault in the beating of three men in

Stanley Park. The three men were arrested in the middle of the night at a downtown mall, and then driven by officers to a secluded area of the park, where the assaults occurred. Weitzel J held that while some leniency may be granted to officers who commit assault during a struggle while attempting to make arrest, the Stanley Park assaults, which he characterized as 'mob mentality' on the part of the police, were not such an occasion. He did, however, not incarcerate any of them.

44 *R. v. Wighton* (2003), 176 C.C.C. (3d) 550. The Ontario Court of Justice held that the admission into evidence of the report, made under compulsion of Reg. 926 under the *Police Services Act*, would violate the accused officer's right against self-incrimination, and that the admission of use of force reports in criminal proceedings generally would impair the effectiveness of the statutory reporting regime.

45 [1991] 3 S.C.R. 326. The right to disclosure was framed as a constitutional right in *R. v. Carosella*, [1997] 1 S.C.R. 80.

46 *R. v. O'Connor*, [1995] 4 S.C.R. 411.

47 *R. v. Paryniuk* (2002), 97 C.R.R. (2d) 151.

48 *R. v. Altunamaz*, [1999], O.J. No. 2262.

49 Ibid. (the judgement contains a summary of the different oversight bodies/complaints mechanisms in Ontario and their relationship to the Ministry of the Attorney General).

50 *R. v. Scaduto* (1999), 63 C.R.R. (2d) 155.

51 *Ontario (Police Complaints Commissioner) v. Kerr* (1997), 96 O.A.C. 284 (appeal by the commissioner of a Board of Inquiry finding that the notebook extracts were not admissible, resulting in the dismissal of the complaint).

52 *Jane Doe v. Metropolitan Toronto (Municipality) Commissioners of Police* (1990), 50 C.P.C. (2d) 92 (Ont. Div. Court); *Jane Doe v. Metropolitan Toronto (Municipality) Commissioners of Police* (1991), 1 O.R. (3d) 416 (C.A.).

53 *McLean v. Siesel* (2004), O.A.C. 122, 2004 Carswell Ont 200 (unreasonable force); *Hudson v. Brantford Police Services Board* (2001), 204 D.L.R. (4th) 645 (unlawful arrest and entry); *P.(P.) v. Pecorella* (1998), 1998 Carswell Ont 1887 (unlawful assault, false arrest and imprisonment); *Stevens v. Toronto Police Services Board* (2003), 2003 Carswell Ont 4612 (malicious prosecution, false arrest and imprisonment); *Lloyd v. Toronto Police Services Board (2003)*, 2003 Carswell Ont 58 (malicious prosecution, false imprisonment); *Bainard v. Toronto Police Services Board* (2002), 2002 Carswell Ont 2366 (malicious prosecution, false imprisonment); *Wason v. Gillis* (1996), 1996 Carswell Ont 1816 (wrongful arrest and battery); *Frazier v. Purdy* (1991), 6 O.R. (3d) 429 (malicious prosecution); see also *Odhavji*.

54 The 1994 *Violent Crime Control and Law Enforcement Act* gave the U.S.
    federal government the power to investigate and bring suit against any
    city whose police were routinely abusing their authority. Pittsburgh was
    the first large city where such a 'pattern and practice' suit has been settled
    through a consent decree (1997) following allegations of excessive force,
    false arrests, and improper searches by police. Vera reports that five years
    later, Pittsburgh has exhibited excellent compliance with the changes to
    police practices mandated by the consent decree, which listed seventy-
    four 'tasks' that the force had to perform to resolve the suit. 'Pittsburgh's
    Experience with Police Monitoring' (18 June 2003), online: *Vera Institute of
    Justice* http://www.vera.org/project project1_1.asp?section_id=2&project_
    id+13&sub_section_id=1&archive=.
56 *Coroner's Act*, R.S.O. 1990, c. C. 37, s. 10(4).
57 *Coroner's Act*, s. 2(2). See the discussion in Julian N. Falconer and Peter J.
    Pliszka, eds., *Annotated Coroner's Act 2001/2002* (Markham, ON:
    Butterworths Canada, 2001), 4.
57 Two of the most widely publicized inquests in recent years were held into
    the shooting deaths of Lester Donaldson and Raymond Lawrence, both
    killed by members of the Metropolitan Toronto Police Service. Jack Lakey,
    'Police acted as they should have, Donaldson probe told,' *Toronto Star*,
    18 March 1994, A9; Gail Swainson, 'Officer's testimony questioned by ex-
    pert,' *Toronto Star*, 24 March 1994, A6; Gail Swainson, 'Report contradicts
    officers, inquest told,' *Toronto Star*, 15 February 1994, A6; Gay Abbate,
    'Inquest wrangles over race,' *Globe and Mail*, 26 May 1993; Tony Wong,
    'Group wants race made an issue at inquest,' *Toronto Star*, 23 March 1993,
    A7; Gay Abbate, 'Lawrence used cocaine, toxicologist tells inquest,' *Globe
    and Mail*, 27 May 1993.
58 Both the Black Action Defence Committee and the Urban Alliance on Race
    Relations sought standing to pursue the racial dimensions of the case, the
    coroner denied both groups' applications, and judicial review was sought:
    Black Action Defence Committee v. Huxter, Coroner (1992), 11 O.R. (3d) 641
    (Div. Ct.), leave to appeal to Ont. C.A. dismissed. Ultimately the Urban
    Alliance on Race Relations alone was granted standing to pursue issues
    limited to cross-cultural sensitivity and the mentally ill. All other claims
    were denied. John Deverell, 'Racial issue ruled out for inquest,' *Toronto
    Star*, 23 February 1993, A7; Bob Brent, 'Black group tries new tack to get
    role at inquest,' *Toronto Star*, 4 September 1992, A9.
59 A conflict of interest issue arose over the question of whether one lawyer
    was entitled to jointly represent the officers implicated in the shooting, the
    Police Services Board, and the chief, at the inquest. The conflict of interest

inherent in such representation (given the diverse and potentially conflicting interests of these parites) was held to be sufficient to disqualify him.
Booth v. Huxter (1994), 16 O.R. (3d) 528 (Div. Ct). 'Court backs coroner over
conflict ruling,' *Toronto Star*, 15 January 1994, A13; Gail Swinton, 'No proof
of conflict, Donaldson inquest told,' *Toronto Star*, 27 October 1993, A12.

60 *Coroner's Act*, s. 41(1).

61 The immediate response from the Opposition Conservatives was to declare that they were approaching the proposed change 'with a degree of
trepidation' and claimed the previous system was working well and that
police morale would suffer. Legislative Assembly of Ontario, legislation
introduced by Hon. Bryant and opposed by Mr Runciman, 19 April 2006.

62 Andrew Goldsmith, 'External review and Regulation,' in *Complaints
Against the Police: The Trend to External Review*, ed. Andrew J. Goldsmith
(Oxford: Clarendon Press, 1991), 15–61, 19, 73–83, 227–63. See also Dawn
Currie, Walter DeKeseredy, and Brian Maclean, 'Reconstituting Social
Order and Social Control: Police Accountability in Canada' (1990) 2(1)
Journal of Human Justice 29 at 33–7. They identify both the failure of the
police to respond internally to misconduct and a failure of scholars and
others to address police intransigence on the issue.

63 Clare E. Lewis, who headed the expanded complaint commission that
followed this experiment, details the history of the system as a response
to growing public concern in 'Police Complaints in Metropolitan Toronto:
Perspectives of the Public Complaints Commissioner,' in *Complaints
against the Police*.

64 The *Police Services Act* was amended to add part VI (since repealed) to
deal with the complaints system. Part VI created a complete disciplinary
regime, including a civilian oversight component. Citizen complaints were
investigated at first instance by police officers assigned to the 'Police
Complaint Bureau.' Details of complaints and progress of the investigation
were reported monthly to the office of the Public Complaint Commissioner (PCC), which could intervene at any time. The results of the police
investigation of the complaint were then provided to the chief or his
designate for a determination. The chief had the authority to mediate a
resolution between the citizen and the subject officer, order a disciplinary
trial (as above), or take no further action. If the citizen was dissatisfied
with the result (90 per cent of complaints result in no further action) she or
he could appeal the result to the PCC. The PCC was required to review the
police investigation and authorized to reinvestigate the complaint in the
event of an appeal or dissatisfaction with the investigation, and could
order a trial before a 'Public Complaint Tribunal,' a three-person tribunal

chaired by one of a panel of lawyers appointed by the attorney general along with one member each from panels composed of appointees of the local Police Association (police union) and the attorney general. The tribunal had full disciplinary powers up to and including dismissal. See, for example, Werner E. Petterson, 'Police Accountability and Civilian Oversight of Policing: An American Perspective,' in *Complaints against the Police* at 280–3.

65 Susan Watt, 'The Future of Civilian Oversight of Policing' (2001) 33 Canadian Journal of Criminology 347. Watt describes the Ontario PCC as the first successful Canadian effort at the civilianization of police complaints procedures. She suggests that the Ontario system will ultimately be accepted by police and lead to the creation of similar systems in other Canadian jurisdictions.

66 In discussing the repeal of the PCC, criminologist Tammy Landau identifies some of the many criticisms that were made of the PCC. For example, the fact that the commission had very limited powers to investigate or initiate a complaint and that adjudicated decisions with respect to the outcome of complaints continued to rest with the chief. As part of the reason for its repeal, she points out that the rank and file never accepted the legitimacy of a civilian authority. Tammy Landau, 'Back to the Future: The Death of Civilian Review of Public Complaints Against the Police in Ontario, Canada,' in *Civilian Oversight of Policing: Governance, Democracy, and Human Rights*, ed. Andrew Goldsmith and Colleen Lewis (Oxford: Hart Publishing, 2000), 66–7.

67 Roderick McLeod, QC, *A Report and Recommendations On Amendments to the Police Services Act Respecting Civilian Oversight of the Police*, commissioned by the Ministry of the Attorney General and the Ministry of the Solicitor General (November 1996).

68 Far-reaching corruption scandals have plagued the Toronto Police Service in recent months: Nick Pron and John Duncanson, 'Officers face charges of fraud, theft and assault,' *Toronto Star*, 7 January 2004, A15; Christie Blatchford, 'Six officers to be charged in corruption investigation,' *Globe and Mail*, 7 January 2004, A9; Gay Abbate and Joe Friesen, 'Probe results in 22 charges filed against six officers,' *Globe and Mail*, 8 January 2004, A14; Kirk Makin, 'Police blocked corruption probe,' *Globe and Mail*, 20 January 2004, A1, A12; Kirk Makin, 'Police chief denies "blue wall of silence" in corruption probe,' *Globe and Mail*, 21 January 2004, A6; Christie Blatchford, '"Conscience is clean" Fantino says,' *Globe and Mail*, 21 January 2004, A6; Betsy Powell and Nick Pron, 'Weeding out corruption,' *Globe and Mail*, 22 January 2004, B1, B6; Cal Millar, John Duncanson, and Nicholaas Van

Rijn, 'Police unit faces internal probe,' *Toronto Star*, 17 April 2004, A4;
Christie Blatchford, 'Police probe corruption as union boss steps down,'
Globe and Mail, 19 April 2004, A1, A9; John Duncanson 'Betting scandal
rocks police force,' *Toronto Star*, 20 April 2004, A1; Nick Pron and John
Duncanson, '6 may face betting probe charges,' *Toronto Star*, 21 April 2004,
A1, A16; Katherine Harding, 'Mayor let down by chief's reply to corrup-
tion recommendations,' *Globe and Mail*, 23 April 2004, A12; John Barber,
'Enough with the few "bad apples,"' *Globe and Mail*, 24 April 2004, M1;
John Duncanson and Tracey Huffman, 'Source: Police shielded drug dens,'
Toronto Star, 24 April 2004, A1, A23; Christie Blatchford, 'Chief details
charges against officers,' *Globe and Mail*, 27 April 2004, A10.

69 The recent scandals have prompted calls for reform: Linda Diebel and Cal
Millar, 'Police reform: "I want action,"' *Toronto Star*, 28 April 2004, A1, A19;
Christie Blatchford, 'Judgment day for Toronto Police Service,' *Globe and
Mail*, 28 April 2004, A12; 'Police require outside probe,' Editorial, *Toronto
Star*, 28 April 2004, A22; Royson James, 'An independent inquiry is the
only way to solve police mess,' *Toronto Star*, 28 April 2004, B3.

70 The provincial government has responded by appointing retired Superior
Court Chief Justice Patrick LeSage to conduct a comprehensive review of
the civilian complaints process and issue recommendations for its overhaul: Richard Brennan, 'LeSage to review police watchdog system,' *Toronto
Star*, 10 June 2004, A1; Richard Brennan, 'Police complaints role "a challenge," former judge says,' *Toronto Star*, 11 June 2004, A20; 'Police complaints reform overdue,' Editorial, *Toronto Star*, 11 June 2004, A26. There is
some evidence that the Toronto Police Service has recognized the need to
be seen to be responding to the corruption crisis: Betsey Powell, 'Tipster
line for bad cops,' *Toronto Star*, 7 June 2004, E1 (force announces anonymous tip line, as per the recommendation of George Ferguson). The
report titled *Police Complaints System in Ontario* was completed 22 April
2005.

71 For example, the police distrust of courts and disdain for criminals who
'demand all the safeguards of due process' 'assumes thereby that they [the
safeguards] exist.' Doreen McBarnet, 'Arrest: The Legal Context of Policing,' *The British Police*, ed. Simon Holdaway (London: Arnold, 1979), at 25,
27.

72 *Re Trumblay et al.* (1986), 55 O.R (2d) 570 and cases cited therein at 590 and ff.

73 Goldsmith, ed., *Complaints against the Police*, at 15–61.

74 Richard Ericson identifies the use of internal discipline rules and procedures in order to maintain the belief that misconduct is isolated to 'bad
apples,' both within the police culture itself and in the community at large.
'Police Use of Disciplinary Rules,' in *Organizational Police Deviance*: *Its*

Structure and Control, ed. Clifford D. Shearing (Toronto: Butterworths, 1981), 97–101. See also 'Submissions on Behalf of Jane Doe: Ontario Civilian Commission of Police Services Inquiry (Junger Inquiry), Parkdale Community Legal Services, 1991.

75 Pat McNenly, 'Police Union vows fight to abolish complaints board,' *Toronto Star*, 20 December 1985.

76 The agent of the attorney general, in placing his reasons for the stay on the record, noted that Weller's 'conviction' by the Police Complaint Tribunal had been upheld on appeal to the Divisional Court. There was no doubt that the charge had been laid as a device, demonstrating a troubling belief in the tendency of criminal courts to acquit police officers who harm citizens while in the execution of their duty. *R. v. Terence Weller*, Ontario Court (Provincial Division) 21 April 1988, Kerr J., Scarborough (unreported).

77 *R. v. Wigglesworth*, [1987] 2 S.C.R. 541. See also *Armstrong v. Peel Regional Police Services Board* (2003), 2003 Carswell Ont 3331 (distinction between criminal and disciplinary proceedings); *Burnham v. Metropolitan Toronto Chief of Police*, [1987] 2 S.C.R. 572; *Trimm v. Durham Regional Police Force*, [1987] 2 S.C.R. 582; *Trumbley v. Metropolitan Toronto Police*, [1987] 2 S.C.R. 577 trilogy on s. 11(d) *Charter* compliance of disciplinary proceedings.

78 *Bainard v. Toronto Police Services Board* [2002], O.T.C. 504. See also (2004), 2004 W.L. 858890 (Ont. S.C.J.), 2004 Carswell Ont 1675 (officers suing board for breach of fiduciary duty, negligent investigation, and abuse of public office for investigation resulting in charges of neglect of duty and discreditable conduct, which were later stayed. The Court dismissed the claim, holding that the provisions of the *Police Services Act* and the *Public Service Act* create a complete code of discipline for the Ontario Provincial Police, leaving no gap in jurisdiction to hear the matter as a civil cause of action, and that the board had no fiduciary obligation to act only in the interests of the plaintiff officers).

79 *Heasman v. Durham Regional Police Services Board* (2004), 2004 W.L. 858890 (Ont. S.C.J.).

80 Although there have been successes, both by officers and complainants, the courts have generally been deferential to OCCOPS decisions. See *Townley v. Ontario (Police Complaints Commissioner)* (2000), 2000 Carswell Ont 343; *Ontario (Police Complaints Commissioner) v. Hannah* (1997), 145 D.L.R. (4th) 443; 105 *Thomas v. Ontario (Police Complaints Commissioner)* (1994), 1994 Carswell Ont 3222.

81 *Browne v. OCCOPS* (2001), 207 D.L.R. (4th) 415, reversing (1999), 127 O.A.C. 182 (Ont. Div. Ct.); and reversing (2000), 4 C.C.E.L. (3d) 153 (Ont. Div. Ct.).

82 *Duriancik v. Ontario (Attorney General)* (1994), 114 D.L.R. (4th) 504.

83 *Tomie-Gallant v. Ontario (Board of Inquiry)* (1995), 33 Admin. L.R. (2d) 34.

84 *Dulmage v. Ontario (Police Complaints Commissioner)* (1994), 30 Admin. L.R. (2d) 203.

85 See *Corp. of the Canadian Civil Liberties Assn. v. Ontario Civilian Commission on Police Services* (2002), 165 O.A.C. 79 (Ont. C.A.). for further confirmation that the standard of the review for a PCC Board of Inquiry decision is that of unreasonableness, as well as the deference generally afforded the Board of Inquiry by the courts.

86 Two former Toronto chiefs, Chief William McCormack and Chief Julian Fantino, have both been involved in public and sometimes hostile contract negotiations with the Toronto Police Services Board. Linda Diebel, 'No Fast Renewal of Chief's Contract: Miller,' *Toronto Star*, 22 January 2004, A1, A14. The Toronto Board decided well in advance of the expiry of Chief Fantino's contract not to offer him a second term and the search for the next chief commenced in the fall of 2004. Even so, power struggles over the issue were relentless. Linda Diebel, 'Battle still rages over Chief's future,' *Toronto Star*, 19 September 2004, A1.

87 See particularly the tensions surrounding the replacement of Chief Boothby and the conflict between Board Chair Susan Eng and Chief McCormack. John Duncanson, 'Boothby doomed as chief: sources,' *Toronto Star*, 8 May 1999, A4; Jack Lakey, 'Eng queries secret study on blacks,' *Toronto Star*, 12 February 1994, A8.

88 This may be seen as directly related to the proportion of the board composed of elected city councillors concerned about their prospects for re-election.

89 See, in particular, the discussion above of the Donaldson Inquest and the conflict of interest involving police lawyer Todd Archibald.

90 See, for example, *R. v. Golden*, [2001] 159 C.C.C. (4th) 449 (S.C.C.); *R. v. Griffiths*, (2003) 11 C.R. (6th) 136; *R. v. Brown* (2003), 173 C.C.C. (3d) 23. (Ont. C.A.). The accused, a black Toronto Raptor's basketball player, was stopped for speeding and required to give a breath sample. See also Kirk Makin, 'Police engage in profiling, chief counsel tells court,' *Globe and Mail*, 18 January 2004, A1, A26.

91 Jim Coyle criticizes Bromell's 'knee-jerk and petulant ... defiant and threatening' rejection of the judicial notice taken of the existence of police racial profiling in the Dee Brown case, and calls for a change in police union leadership. 'Bromell huffs and puffs and blows his credibility,' *Toronto Star*, 19 April 2003, A25. The Canadian Race Relations Federation

and others criticize the Toronto Police Service for not acting more quickly to respond to the Crown's admission of racial profiling and the recommendations of a recent summit on racial profiling in the justice system. Toronto police union president Craig Bromell and Chief Fantino continue to deny the existence of racial profiling. Catherine Porter, 'Action urged on race profiling,' *Toronto Star*, 19 January 2004, A11.

92 The aggressively activist union stance in Toronto stems from the 1995 widespread protests and job action against provincial use-of-force requirements that a report be filed every time an officer draws his or her weapon. The union undertook an illegal work-to-rule campaign that Chief McCormack was seemingly powerless to prevent. Jack Lakey, 'Police ignoring job action: Chief,' *Toronto Star*, 15 May 2003, B2; Philip Mascoll, 'Striking Metro police lock station doors,' *Toronto Star*, 27 January 1995, A1, A6. In his memoirs, the former chief presented the issue as a highly political, almost 'plot' against police by the government of the day. Bill McCormack, *Without Fear or Favour: The Life and Politics of an Urban Cop* (Toronto: Stoddart, 1999), ch. 21, 'Bob Rae's Kind of People.'

93 *Police Services Act*, amended to O. Reg. 89/98, s. 3.

94 Timothy Appleby, 'Toronto police union turns to telemarketing,' *Globe and Mail*, 22 January 2000, A23; John Duncanson, 'Drive not linked to force, chief says,' *Toronto Star*, 23 January 2000, A4; Virginia Galt and John Saunders, 'True Blue controversy shakes solidarity in the ranks of police, board says,' *Globe and Mail*, 31 January 2000, A16; Colin Freeze, 'Toronto police, board agree on fundraising issue,' *Globe and Mail*, 2 May 2000; John Duncanson, 'Chief brokers deal with board, union,' *Toronto Star*, 2 May 2000, B1, B4; Bagesheree Paradkar, 'True Blue gets mixed reviews from officers,' *Toronto Star*, 28 January 2000, A19; John Duncanson and Jennifer Quinn, 'Showdown! Police chief threatens union boss over True Blue fundraising scheme,' *Toronto Star*, 27 January 2000, A1, A24; Gay Abbate, 'Politicians launch crackdown on police union,' *Globe and Mail*, 28 January 2000, A1, A17; Paul Maloney and Bruce DeMara, 'New bylaw bans True Blue,' *Toronto Star*, 29 January 2000, A1, A21; Gay Abbate, 'Police union defies orders, leaders face sanctions,' *Globe and Mail*, 29 January 2000, A1, A27.

95 Linda Diebel, 'Police union resists board,' *Toronto Star*, 23 January 2004, F1 (complaints and court ruling sought on the issue of police union political endorsements); Rosemary Speirs, 'OPP union sends out a Long letter,' *Toronto Star*, 14 June 2000, A6; Paul Maloney, 'Police union endorsements split council,' *Toronto Star*, 26 August 2000, B1, B3; John Duncanson, 'Police union puts heat on candidates,' *Toronto Star*, 19 October 2000, D1, D4; Colin Freeze, 'Police union and politics and volatile mix,' *Globe and Mail*,

6 November 2000, A21; Royson James, 'City councillors are too fearful to bell Bromell,' *Toronto Star*, 20 November 2000, B1; Gay Abbate, 'Bully tag worked, union leader says,' *Globe and Mail*, 2 October 2003, A17; Gay Abbate, 'Police union accused of intimidation,' *Globe and Mail*, 27 January 2000, A1, A21.

96 Gay Abbate, 'Union puts Fantino's leadership to a vote,' *Globe and Mail*, 15 November 2001, A24; John Duncanson and Jennifer Quinn, 'Doubts raised over chief's leadership in police vote,' *Toronto Star*, 19 January 2002, A27; Jennifer Quinn and John Duncanson, 'Police chiefs feel heat of unions,' *Toronto Star*, 14 January 2000, A1, A18. See also Vanessa Lu, '8 officers sue police chief over fink fund case,' *Toronto Star*, 21 January 2003, A16; Colin Freeze, 'Drug squad officers blast police brass in civil suit,' *Globe and Mail*, 22 January 2003, A20; Gay Abbate, 'Pall cast over bargaining with police,' *Globe and Mail*, 22 November 2001, A30; Jim Rankin, 'Police union sues Fantino,' *Toronto Star*, 25 November 2001, A10; Jim Rankin and John Duncanson, 'Bromell blasts chief over charges,' *Toronto Star*, 20 September 2001, B1, B5.

97 Graeme Smith, 'Saskatoon police chief faces revolt in the ranks,' *Globe and Mail*, 2 July 2003, A5; Rod Mickelburgh, 'Rumours swirl around Vancouver chief,' *Globe and Mail*, 8 May 1999, A12.

98 Nick Pron and John Duncanson, '4 officers facing criminal charges,' *Toronto Star*, 4 May 2004, A1, A13; Jonathan Fowlie, 'Officers charged in "shakedown" case,' *Globe and Mail*, 4 May 2004, A1, A14; Jonathan Fowlie, 'McCormack defends his wife,' *Globe and Mail*, 7 May 2004, A13.

99 Jason Tchir, 'Hammer drops on four cops,' *Toronto Sun*, 4 May 2004, 1, 5; Jonathan Fowlie and Katherine Harding, 'McIntosh submits formal resignation,' *Toronto Star*, 21 May 2004, A11 (union boss resigns almost three weeks after being charged with four criminal offences in relation to the corruption scandal). The scandal has also caused division within the Toronto Police Association itself: Jonathan Kingstone, 'Union boss: I am the victim of smear,' *Toronto Sun*, 4 May 2004, 5; Nick Pron, 'Union trying to oust charged Officers,' *Toronto Star*, 5 May 2004, A1, A21; Jeff Gray and Jonathan Fowlie, 'Police union moves to oust its president,' *Globe and Mail*, 5 May 2004, A8; Robert Cribb and Nick Pron, 'Police union meets to oust pair,' *Toronto Star*, 6 May 2004, A16; Jonathan Fowlie and Jeff Gray, 'Police group won't discuss officers,' *Toronto Star*, 6 May 2004, A15.

100 John Barber, 'You go, Mike. We're counting on you,' *Globe and Mail*, 8 May 2004, M2. Barber cites the need for a definitive judicial finding on the subject of the jurisdiction of the *Police Services Act* over union officials.

101 Jennifer Lewington, 'Police oversight issue unifies city hall,' *Toronto Star*, 6 May 2004, A15.

102 The Ontario Civilian Commission on Police Services, *Report of an Inquiry into administration of Internal Investigations by the Metropolitan Toronto Police Force*, August 1992.

103 Alan Story, 'Morality officer ran sex-for-pay service,' *Toronto Star*, 7 April 1990, A1.

104 Tracy Tyler, 'Police board's memories vary on escort case,' *Toronto Star*, 11 April 1990, A7; Andrew Duffy, 'Chief promised no charges if officer quit,' *Toronto Star*, 12 April 1990, A8.

105 Cal Miller and Lisa Priest, 'Chief irate over publicity in escort case,' *Toronto Star*, 18 April 1990, A1. The matter of the other officers allegedly involved in the escort service surfaced again almost fifteen years later. Reports concerned the investigation into 52 Division shakedown scandal, disbandment of the 52 Division plainclothes unit, and allegations from eight transvestite prostitutes that they provided free sex to a police officer. Jonathan Kingstone and Rob Lamberti, 'T.O. cop extorted payoffs at clubs?' *Toronto Sun*, 18 April 2004. The story became more specific and linked allegations of the prostitution scandal to Bill McCormack Jr, son of former Chief Bill McCormack. McCormack Jr was Gordon Junger's partner at the time and implicated in the 52 Division shakedown scandal. The article links the prostitution allegations to the Junger scandal. Jonathan Kingstone and Rob Lamberti, 'Hooking police rumour,' *Toronto Sun*, 19 April 2004. Finally, it is confirmed that Bill McCormack Jr was suspended pending investigation (he was subsequently charged with a number of Criminal Code offences). Rumour links him to the Junger scandal, but he denies all wrongdoing. Mark Bonokoski, 'Rumour wed to lies,' *Toronto Sun*, 20 April 2004.

106 Editorial, 'The escort affair,' *Toronto Star*, 19 April 1990.

107 Ontario Civilian Commission on Police Services, *Report*, Part 2, 'Introduction,' 3–4.

108 Ibid.

109 Ibid.

110 Ontario Civilian Commission on Police Services, *Report*, Part 6, 'The Junger Agreement,' 1–2.

111 Ibid. 4–5.

112 Ontario Civilian Commission on Police Services, *Report*, Part 9, 'Treatment of Victims,' 2–4.

113 Ibid. 6–10, recommendations 17–20.

114 Rosie DiManno, 'The chief still doesn't get it,' *Toronto Star*, 29 August 1992, A4; Christie Blatchford, 'Shameless! Cops don't flinch at Junger report,' *Toronto Sun*, 29 August 1992, 5.

115 (Toronto: Stoddart, 1999).

116 Ibid. chap. 19.
117 Ibid.
118 Extract of the Minutes of the 10 September 1992 board meeting, Ontario Civilian Commission on Police Services, *Report on a Fact-Finding into Various Matters with Respect to the Disciplinary Practices of the Toronto Police Service*, July 1999, 33. This fact finding and report was made in response to a complaint from the Toronto Police Association that there was a double standard for discipline: senior officers were being treated more leniently than frontline officers. That allegation was not made out, but in the process of investigating it OCCOPS took the opportunity to revisit the implementation of the recommendations made following the *Junger/ Whitehead Inquiry*.
119 Ibid.
120 Report prepared by Thomas Lederer of the law firm Genest Murray Debrisay Lamek in response to the request by the Metropolitan Toronto Police Services Board to Conduct a Review in Accordance with the Resolution of the Board dated 14 November 1996, ii.
121 Ontario Civilian Commission on Police Services, *Report on a Fact-Finding into Various Matters with Respect to the Disciplinary Practices of the Toronto Police Service*, July 1999, 34–5.
122 Ibid.
123 Ibid., 36–7.
124 Deputy Reesor was 'counselled' by Chief Boothby for transporting a revolver he (legally) owned to sell (legally) to another police officer without obtaining a transfer permit (police officers do not require these permits for transferring their service revolvers). Police association head Craig Bromell used the distinction between this counselling and the dismissal of two civilian employees of the firearms unit when goods were found missing from the firearms unit. 'Police union boss plays politics,' *Now Magazine*, 7–13 May 1998.
125 Ontario Civilian Commission on Police Services, *Report on a Fact-Finding into Various Matters with Respect to the Disciplinary Practices of the Toronto Police Service*, July 1999, 39–40.
126 Ibid. 48–9.
127 Ontario Civilian Commission on Police Services, *Report on a Fact-Finding into Various Matters with Respect to the Disciplinary Practices of the Toronto Police Service*, July 1999, 4.
128 Extract from the Minutes of the Meeting of the Toronto Police Services Board held on 1 May 2000. Item #156/00, 'Final Response to the Ontario Civilian Commission in Police Services (OCCPS) Regarding the Fact-Finding Report.'

129 Ibid. 21–2.
130 Nick Pron and John Duncanson, 'Officers face charges of fraud, theft and assault,' *Toronto Star*, 7 January 2004, A15; Christie Blatchford, 'Six officers to be charged in corruption investigation,' *Globe and Mail*, 7 January 2004, A9; Gay Abbate and Joe Friesen, 'Probe results in 22 charges filed against six officers,' *Globe and Mail*, 8 January 2004, A14.
131 Kirk Makin, 'Police blocked corruption probe' *Globe and Mail*, 20 January 2004, A1, A12; Kirk Makin, 'Police chief denies "blue wall of silence" in corruption probe,' *Globe and Mail*, 21 January 2004, A6; Christie Blatchford, '"Conscience is clean" Fantino says,' *Globe and Mail*, 21 January 2004, A6; Betsy Powell and Nick Pron, 'Weeding out corruption,' *Globe and Mail*, 22 January 2004, B1, B6.
131 The issue of disclosing to the defence in a criminal trial the disciplinary records of investigating officers has been contentious in Ontario for a number of years. It was exacerbated by the decision to stay numerous drug charges investigated by the discredited officers. See generally *R. v. Paryniuk* (2002), 97 C.R.R. (2d) 151; *R. v. Altunamaz*, [1999] O.J. No. 2262; *R. v. Scaduto* (1999), 63 C.R.R. (2d) 155.
132 The report is significantly more narrow in scope than the terms of reference, which included an examination of organizational structure, the culture of policing, and fairly wide scope of integrity testing and background checks. Mr Ferguson chose (without providing a rationale for the choices except to say that these are areas where change is required) to report only on recruitment, training and promotion, the structure and function of internal affairs, and the use of alcohol and drugs.
133 In his 26 March 2004 letter to the Police Services Board, 'Response to recommendations of the Honourable Justice George Ferguson,' Chief Fantino said that Ferguson's report was received in March 2003.
134 Katherine Harding, 'Mayor let down by chief's reply to corruption recommendations,' *Globe and Mail*, 23 April 2004, A12.
135 Cal Miller, John Duncanson, and Nicholaas Van Rijn, 'Police unit faces internal probe,' *Toronto Star*, 17 April 2004, A4; Jonathan Kingstone and Rob Lamberti, 'T.O. cop extorted payoffs at clubs?' *Toronto Sun*, 18 April 2004.
136 Jonathan Kingstone and Rob Lamberti, 'Hooking police rumour,' *Toronto Sun*, 19 April 2004.
137 Christie Blatchford, 'Police probe corruption as union boss steps down,' *Globe and Mail*, 19 April 2004, A1, A9.
138 Christie Blatchford, 'Numbered firm received cheques,' *Globe and Mail*, 21 April 2004, A15; Jonathan Fowlie, 'A venerable police dynasty in turmoil,' *Globe and Mail*, 24 April 2004, A16; John Duncanson and Tracey

Huffman, 'Source: Police shielded drug dens,' *Toronto Star*, 24 April 2004, A1, A23; Shannon Kari, 'Addict-thief helped by officer in police probe,' *Globe and Mail*, 26 April 2004, A10; Nick Pron, 'Former chief's son facing charges,' *Toronto Star*, 26 April 2004, A1, A12.

139 John Barber, 'Enough with the few "bad apples,"' *Globe and Mail*, 24 April 2004, M1; Royson James, 'An independent inquiry is the only way to solve police mess,' *Toronto Star*, 28 April 2004, B3; Royson James, 'Fantino's message is loud, but is it clear?' *Toronto Star*, 29 April 2004, B1, B5; 'Police require outside probe,' Editorial, *Toronto Star*, 28 April 2004, A22.

140 Katherine Harding, 'Board backs Fantino's handling of probe,' *Globe and Mail*, 27 April 2004, A10; Linda Diebel and Cal Millar, 'Police reform: "I want action,"' *Toronto Star*, 28 April 2004, A1, A19.

141 Braithewaite, 'On Speaking Softly and Carrying Big Sticks.'

142 Discussed in Dianne L. Martin and Ray Kuszelewski, 'The Perils of Poverty: Prostitutes Rights, Police Misconduct and Poverty Law' (1997) 35 Osgoode Hall L.J., 835.

143 For example, the 'Jane Doe' case: *Doe v. Metropolitan Toronto (Municipality) Commissioners of Police* (1998), 39 O.R. (3d) 487; Melanie Randall, 'Sex Discrimination, Accountability of Public Authorities and the Public/ Private Divide in Tort Law: An Analysis of Doe v. Metropolitan Toronto (municipality) Commissioners of Police' (2001) 26 Queen's L.J. 451. See also *Odhavji*.

144 Executive director of the Canadian Civil Liberties Association and author of *Uncivil Obedience* (Toronto: Lester Publishing, 1991).

6 Steeped in Politics: The Ongoing History of Politics in Policing

MARGARET E. BEARE

Abstract

Much current controversy surrounding policing centres on two issues: the relationship between the police and politics, and the question of accountability. Dianne Martin's paper addressed the issue of accountability, and while the two issues overlap, I shall be looking specifically at the question of the links, formal and informal, between the police and politics. This chapter examines the operational realities of the police and executive linkages – beyond the official dictates of the law and the desired position expressed in ideological discourses on police independence. The chapter draws primarily on a content analysis of media coverage, historical and criminological literature and research, personal interviews, and public inquiries.

The central argument of this chapter is that, while there may be a somewhat clear-cut division between the 'policy' and the 'operational' control of the police by the state in law and in rhetoric, the reality is quite different. The relationship between the state and the police is a dynamic relationship that changes to reflect a number of factors, including the nature of the policing that is being carried out, the political interests of the party in power, and to some extent the personalities of the key players in both the police services and politics at a specific period in time.

This research indicates that looking for the 'smoking gun' – that is, the memo or document that in writing acknowledges a directive from the executive to the police – sidesteps the reality of the ongoing partnerships between politics and policing.

The chapter ends with a commentary by Tonita Murray, former director general of the Canadian Police College.

Introduction

This chapter draws from the historical record, recent trends, criminological theory, and interviews to examine the operational links (formal and informal) between policing and politics. The objective is thus to illustrate the complexity of the relationship between policing and politics and in the process to suggest how the truth of the relationship might be built into the formal policy, legislative, and accountability mechanisms.

An understanding of the organizational workings of the police is essential to any attempt to reconcile the tensions between the dictates of police autonomy and the restraints imposed on the police. In addition to examining cases involving state/political intervention in police operations, I shall be identifying the conditions that are vulnerable to this control over the police. I shall also be emphasizing that this control only becomes visible under certain conditions. The absence of an inquiry or protest does not necessarily speak to the absence of political influence in policing decisions. Political influence or dictates may be much more the 'norm' than the 'exception.'

Because the police and other agencies are created to carry out government intentions regarding law enforcement and security, and are dependent on government for their existence, authority, and resources, they are said to be part of the executive arm of government. Yet traditionally we maintain a belief in, repeat the rhetoric of, and in some cases protect the practice of, the independence of policing. We may be making false assumptions about the 'naturalness' of this independence.

In Canada we tend to trace our policing models back to England, and until fairly recently many of our police officers came from England. In countries that share this policing tradition, the ambivalent relationship between freedom to act unhindered by party interests while being held to account within the democratic process has been a concern from the days of the 'new' London police in 1829 through to the present. Jean-Paul Brodeur, however, reminds us that there was a different model in France in 1667 under Louis XIV, one which advocated rather than warned against the blatant use of police powers to advance state interests.[1] Similarly Louise Shelley, in her analysis of Soviet policing, describes the police involvement in the intimidation of political opponents for the benefit of political bosses as being an explicitly stated function of the police: 'the Communist Party sanctioned the elimination of class enemies, and political opponents by the police apparatus ...'[2]

Gerry Woods, in his research on the Los Angeles Police Department (LAPD) concluded that few gains were achieved from the movement away from the 'political machine' era, which characterized the highly politically controlled period of policing in the United States, towards the supposed professional and independent era. Woods's research illustrates that the police shifted from being controlled by politics to becoming 'political' in their own right through lobbying, intimidation of candidates, and an increasingly powerful and demanding union. Measurements of police effectiveness or efficiency also did not show a marked improvement.[3]

After the collapse of the Communist regimes in Eastern Europe, several countries are now faced with the task of re-examining the desired relationship between the 'new' governments and the (sometimes) 'new' police. Countries such as Hungary, Germany, Poland, the Czech Republic, and Slovakia are responding in different ways to this challenge. Shelley's analysis confirms that there has been no uniform movement towards what we might see as the 'appropriate' independence of the police from the state, but rather a move towards formalizing a 'high policing' model, with the police continuing to be assigned tasks aligned with the needs of those in political power.[4] These international examples reveal that there is little consensus around the potential for, or perhaps even the desirability of, our taken-for-granted 'ideal' independent model, and an examination of our own system may reveal political links that we typically wish to deny.

Obviously, we are concerned with those situations in which a political body or individual would 'instruct' the police as to whom to bring charges against, or not, whom not to investigate. At the beginning of this research, I considered these 'extreme' cases to be in some ways the least significant examples of police-political interference, because they are so obviously in violation of the accepted limits of political control over the police. However, as one identifies specific examples, distinguishing between 'policy' versus the 'operational' activities of the police blurs even in these cases. For example, it becomes evident that 'policy development' (deemed an area acceptable for government intervention) is problematic in that some policies determine the operational response of the police and are therefore not distinct from operational decisions.

While this chapter acknowledges some of those extreme cases, the intent is rather to show the ongoing 'normalized' degree of control by the state, or by government officials in positions of authority, over the operational activities of a police force – when it chooses to exert an influence. The difficulty arises that this control is most often accomplished with the willing complicity of the police service. This chapter argues that such complicity provides the curtain behind which the varying agendas of police and state can be advanced. An examination of police work reveals a mutual exploitation of the ambiguity that exists between the police and politics. The political direction into police operational decisions may only be seen when something goes wrong. As Robert Reiner says: 'Like riding a bike, policing is the sort of activity that is thought about mainly when the wheel comes off. When things are running smoothly it tends to be a socially invisible, undiscussed routine.'5 Perhaps more poetically, as Leonard Cohen might say, the various crises provide 'the crack' – 'That's how the light gets in'6 – and reveal that which usually remains hidden or unnoticed.

The task of this chapter is not to debunk the notion of independence – that would be too easy and too misleading. The evidence suggests a two-way relationship, with the political masters having direct involvement in police operational matters and the police becoming 'political' in their direct involvement into law making, decreeing policies, and selecting desirable political candidates. As Otwin Marenin and Gerry Woods separately describe, it was ironic that while arguing that their 'professionalism' entitled them to autonomy, the police turned increasingly towards the political arena in order to make their demands heard.7 Through a dramaturgical look at police work, we can see with some clarity the police as political actors, actively attempting to shape, mediate, and exploit their political environment. We can also see evidence of the politicians identifying the police as a valuable ally through which to gain desired political outcomes.

This chapter also acknowledges that all crime is in a sense political – but more so at various times in our history. What remains fairly constant is the attraction to crime rhetoric by the politicians. As Stuart Scheingold observed: 'Politicians in search of an issue have good reason to believe that campaigning on crime is good politics – at least if one takes a get-tough stand. Law enforcement officials are also well served by the fear of crime, since the result is frequently that more resources are directed to the agencies of criminal justice.'8

Bill Chambliss provides an analysis of the political dictate from New York. Rudolph Giuliani directed his police commissioner to establish a way of informing precinct commanders precisely where crime was occurring and to hold the precinct commander accountable for reducing the crime in his/her precinct. As Chambliss says: 'In what can only be considered a miracle, crime rates began to decline ... By the late 1990's the rates were heralded as demonstrating the success of get-tough laws.'[9] Following this success in New York, police chiefs in other big cities across the United States were pressured into replicating the New York strategies. This politically driven campaign was politically useful and useful to the police in terms of gaining large increases in resources. From 1991 to 2000 the size of the New York Police Department increased from 26,856 to 39,779 – an increase of over 12,000 officers.[10] The 'euphoria' was dampened only after the fact by evidence of police manipulation of crime data to produce these lower crime rates and the realization that other factors, such as demographics, a changing drug-use culture, and the huge increase in police resource played a significant role.

The 'mix' of a tight political agenda that coincides too closely with a policing agenda typically does not bode well for effective enforcement. In identifying the need to 'dampen' political rhetoric, Ted Gest concludes that the 'orgy of emotional but largely hollow and oversimplified talk' must be turned into rational decision making.'[11] 'Get tough' police crackdowns may assist both police and political agendas, but we see, in Canada and internationally, that some segments of our communities are more expendable and more easily exploited in the pursuit of organizational gains.

Adherence to a rhetoric of police independence rests on a belief in a number of contradictory notions. As Al Reiss points out,[12] the police must maintain the status quo (whatever it may be) until it is changed by legitimate political authorities. The police will therefore enforce the political stand at any given moment but must change with each change in political view while remaining politically neutral. Few criminologists have argued more strongly for a serious look at the police-and-politics relationships than Robert Reiner: 'Most police officers stoutly maintain that policing and politics don't mix ... it was an important part of the legitimating of the British police in the face of initial opposition that they were non-partisan. This notion of the political neutrality or independence of the police cannot withstand serious consideration. It rests on an untenably narrow conception of "the political." Restricting it to partisan conflict. In a broader sense, all relationships, which have a power dimension, are political. Policing is inherently and inescapably political in that sense.'[13]

Part of the justification for police independence is seen to rest on the ideological notion of community accountability – the idea of the police officer being a citizen-in-uniform. Rowan and Mayne, the first commissioners of the 'new' police force in London, were determined that the new force ' would be, in fact, but be believed to be, impartial in action' and that the best way to gain this impartiality was via the creation of 'political neutral, well-trained and disciplined professionals.'[14] In challenging the reader to look critically at the independence of the police Michael Brogden states: 'The ideological picture of accountability to the law is bound-up with an apparent duty on police officers to remove all vestiges of political direction and control, which they interpreted as control by constitutionally elected authorities ... an ideological view of policing that ignores the material practices of police work in British society, and represents a partisan conception of police-class relations (masked under the social construct of the community).'

Police and Politics Literature

Within an extensive literature pertaining to the relationship between police and politics, the following names stand out: David Bayley, Jean-Paul Brodeur, Michael Brogden, Richard Ericson, Alan Grant, Otwin Marenin, Wilbur Miller, Robert Reiner, C.D. Robinson, and J.Q. Wilson. The most useful criminological theorists reject extremes, or 'pure types,' including literature that presents the 'automaton' view that the police are a mere arm of the state, carrying out orders from some elite group or groups, or, conversely, that advances the view that the police are totally independent and that policy and operational issues seldom mix.

In between there is an alternative position. A most compelling description sees the 'independence' of the police serving as a mask that can be slipped on and off as needed. C.D. Robinson uses this description when discussing the bonds between the mayor and the police and argues that this was the actual political role of the police: 'to accept the punishment that might otherwise be received by others ... police serve as the convenient scapegoat for a variety of error, ineptitude, malfeasance, misfeasance, non-feasance, committed or permitted.'[15] The police can on occasion serve as the pawns of the state (as scapegoats, or lightning rods) who must take the blame for political decisions and for larger societal conditions that are in fact determined at the political level. Richard Rianoshek described, for example, the riots in the United States in the 1960s and 1970s. In these cases, the activities of the police were basically dictated by circumstances that had been determined by government decisions, followed by citizen responses to those decisions that left no alternative policing options. He stated: 'In this situation the police served as a social scapegoat, because their highly visible "brutality" directed attention from the real source of the protest movement and the riot growing out of it.'[16]

Mann and Lee quote Henry II's response to the problem posed by Thomas Becket: 'Will no one rid me of this troublesome priest?' In this form, a mere statement without a specific written order provides perfect deniability of responsibility if the query is taken up by some underling – especially if it results in controversy and blame.[17] The various alleged dictates of former Ontario premier Mike Harris to solve the Ipperwash Park situation may have echoed Henry's lament.

Very real ties connect the police to the governing body, and claims to the contrary – and claims of an independence outside of these ties – may result in a situation in which no one takes responsibility and no one can be held accountable. J.P. Brodeur[18] sites the example from the McDonald Commission where, after receiving explicit leads regarding RCMP crimes, the government appeared to prefer to insulate themselves with ignorance of the details of this lawlessness in order to justify their inaction. Likewise, RCMP commissioners can make a similar 'need not to know' defence.[19] In a related exchange concerning the then commissioner R.H. Simmonds regarding possible evidence that the government had been aware of and had sanctioned the RCMP 'dirty tricks' during the 1970s, Simmonds explained that he had not read the Nowlan Report (the RCMP internal investigation into their Security Service's 'dirty tricks') in order 'to prevent myself from becoming enmeshed in actions' that occurred before he had become commissioner.[20]

All of these views acknowledge, as stated by James Q. Wilson, that policing takes place 'under the influence of a political culture, although not necessarily under day to day political direction.'[21] In reality, most policing issues – either the target of the policing action or the nature of the incidents – are of no particular interest to the state. Within these 'zones of indifference'[22] the ideology of an autonomous police service can be true in fact as well as in belief. The situation changes when the state 'has a view.' Again, as discussed by J.Q. Wilson, these 'zones of indifference' may quickly become areas of great political concern given increased political significance of the particular issue. If politics can dictate this balance, the zone of indifference cannot be equated with real independence. Not to paint a picture of police subservience, the reverse may also be true. The police will protect their own interests, and while they may be willing to be seen as merely taking instruction on some occasions, they may make decisions based on their own perceptions of organizational or individual advantage.[23]

A thorough analysis of the ideology of political neutrality of the police has been undertaken by Manfred Brusten, who systematically examined each of the foundations upon which people claim the police to be politically neutral. He concluded that not only is each claim false, but that there is a danger in failing to determine the political views of the line officers since their political alignment may determine how they react in particular situations. In his research Brusten asserts the following:

- *Historically*, the police came into existence because of a given political situation and that their 'function' has always been to maintain the existing political power structure;
- *Structurally*, the argument that the police neutrally enforce 'law and order' ignores the fact that the status quo is nothing more than a certain state of the power structure. Manifestations of dissatisfaction within society will likely be perceived as being counter to law and order and will be suppressed, or at least 'controlled';
- *Politically*, the view that the police are neutral instruments in a democratic government, who may be used politically from time to time but do not make their own politics, ignores the role of political figures in appointing members of the policing regulatory boards, the role of politics in the police union, and the existence of secret security units as an integrated part of regular police work. He concludes with the warning that behind this political involvement by the police lurks political beliefs held by the police officers themselves, which are as yet untapped by empirical research.[24]

Resource dependency, renewal of police chiefs' contracts, fear of adverse publicity, socialization into a status quo supportive culture – all of these factors mean that the police organization will see itself as a partner of their political masters. The higher up the chain, the closer to the master. As Peter Manning states: 'In practise ... the police organizations function in a political context; they operate in a public political arena and their mandate is defined politically ... Patterns of police and politics within the community are tightly interlocked. The sensitivity of the police to their political audiences, their operation within the political system of criminal justice, and their own personal political attitudes undermine their efforts to fulfil their contradictory mandate to appear politically neutral.'[25]

Jean-Paul Brodeur's 'High Policing–Low Policing' Model

Jean-Paul Brodeur's thesis in *High Policing–Low Policing*[26] has made a significant contribution to the widely accepted concepts with which to differentiate 'political policing' from the rest (what he describes as the 'policing of conspicuous signs of disorder including criminal policing'). Brodeur argues that the political component is a core ingredient of what he terms 'high policing' – not a deviant aberration that numerous inquiries, courts, and other disciplinary mechanisms must eliminate and/or punish. As he states: 'High policing is actually the paradigm for political policing: it reaches out for potential threats in a systematic attempt to preserve the distribution of power in a given society.'[27]

According to Brodeur the police in North America are increasingly operating according to this 'high policing' paradigm, 'the long arm of the law being, so to speak, curtailed in favour of the wide eyes of the police.'[28] High policing is further described by Brodeur as having four key characteristics:

- 'Control' is accomplished in part by the storing of intelligence that encompasses any source of intelligence that might further state policies.
- Powers extend beyond those decreed by bifurcated systems that separate the powers associated with legislation from enforcement and the sanctioning of offenders.
- Protection of the community may be secondary to the use of enforcement to generate more information and hence more intelligence. 'Crime is thus conceived as something which lends itself to manifold exploitation.'
- Extensive use is made of undercover agents and paid informers and there is a willingness to 'advertise' this strategy – with part of the motivation being the amplification of fear among the populous.

As described by Brodeur, the 'high policing' model typically employs a certain set of strategies, and is typically 'political' in the sense that the issues are seen to be relevant to governments and this relevance legitimates the intrusiveness of the strategies that are employed. The use of such strategies and the rhetoric that accompanies them brings a much wider population of offences and offenders to the interest of the political masters. With the high policing model comes political interest and involvement.

Therefore, it isn't just the *cold* distinction between high and low policing but also how the state interprets the conduct as a 'threat' versus ordinary criminal activity. The political interpretation can shift quickly for reasons that have little to do with the actual activity and/or may be a political response to 'something going wrong.' A two-directional model might represent the categories of criminal activity and the likelihood that they will generate political involvement and/or interference (see fig. 6.1).

Three separate factors appear to feed into the increasing amount of 'high policing' if one utilizes Brodeur's model. First, 'low policing' is gradually taking on the rhetoric and strategies more traditionally attributed to 'high policing' in the sense that a wide array of 'normal' criminal conduct becomes discussed in 'threat rhetoric': Organized crime, drugs, and illegal migration all become 'threats' to either national security or the security of a section of an urban city. I shall demonstrate that within a large Canadian city, this racheting up of the potential impact from social problems and/or criminal incidents occurs because of the complex but increasing politicization of the police – and not vice versa.

Figure 6.1 Two-directional model: Type of criminal activity being policed and likelihood of political involvement

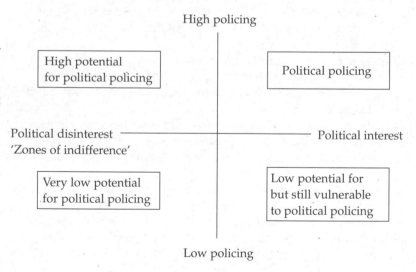

In this category of cases, politicization does not occur in order to combat the threat but rather because of the potential political advantage in defining the behaviour as a threat. In so doing, greater links to political interests are deemed to be justified.

The difficulty comes from the concept of 'political policing,' which at times appears to cover very diverse activities – that is, as Brodeur acknowledges, from policing the conduct of politicians to national security policing. A further issue is the fact that the concepts that represent the crimes or threats being policed, such as 'national security,' are to a large extent left to the police and politicians to define in an arena of secrecy. Brodeur acknowledges that the exploitation of crime for political advantage has a long history in police enforcement, and he mentions specifically morality offences such as prostitution, gambling, and drug and alcohol use. As Peter Manning argues: 'The matter of "political exigency," is of course highly flexible and is associated with the "high politics" of policing (Brodeur) ... the current situation suggests that a quasi-war can be declared by political fiat and congressional support for funding.[29] An active, democratic drama of policing, it seems, requires both opposition, i.e. forces that obstruct and oppose its strengths, as well as negation, i.e. those forces representing the evil and the marginal. These latter, the forces against which the "good" battles, in turn, have great flexibility, malleability and utility and can range from the reputatedly dangerous "squeegee men" of New York City under Mr. Bratton to terrorist threats to national security.'[30]

Second, the increasing use of surveillance and data collection and storage and the analysis of this information into intelligence may itself, according to Brodeur, transform low policing, as these 'policing strategies' come to resemble the political methods employed in high policing. As he states, brothels have long been a source of police intelligence gathering and extortion. Likewise, police discussions in Canada around issues such as the decriminalization of marijuana and the handing over of traffic patrolling to private police are debated in part in terms of the loss of intelligence gained from the policing of these 'offences.' The ability to stop and search is currently seen to provide information that in many cases has nothing to do with the traffic or drug possession violations. Ironically, given this obsession with collecting information, and despite decades of emphasizing the importance of information sharing and the need to make a commitment to analysis work in order to produce truly valuable strategic intelligence, sharing remains erratic and strategic intelligence remains vulnerable to an enthusiastic police manager. The police vow repeatedly to work better together and share together. This is substantiated by Manning, who states:

> While networked information systems are growing and linked databases more likely to emerge as a result of the 9.11 disaster, my observations suggest that the complexity of information technology in policing has not been met by an increased capacity of the police and other agencies to use such devices to their own benefit ... Furthermore, the web of control across policing organizations is technically flawed on the ground because the data bases are not wedded or linked; the software is incompatible; the management information system is a hodge-podge of ad hoc arrangements assembled over the last thirty years, and the introduction of new technologies, geo-coded data, enhanced 911, 311 non emergency call systems, has created new complexity and incomplete linkages.'[31]

A third explanation for an increase in high policing may relate more specifically to globalization (for want of a better word), which has propelled many aspects of law making and law enforcement into an international arena driven by agreements and conventions signed by governments – with hence a strong political link.

The final picture may be of a dialectic involving a policing organization, with requirements and interests of its own, policing a society made up of varying classes with varying degrees of political, social, and economic power, involved in matters ranging from critical concerns, to 'zones of indifference.' The result is a careful, but not always skilfully negotiated, order based on trade-offs, compromises, and the occasional episode during which the public becomes aware of discretionary policing based on corruption, and pay-offs, discrimination and bias, or political pressure, rather than objectivity, expertise, and efficiency.

Law Enforcement in Politically Charged Contexts in Canada

Lessons from History

The historical record demonstrates the enduring and mutually advantageous nature of the links between the police and their political masters, from nation building and the suppression of dissent, to policy advancement more generally, to the current 'security' policing environment. The public becomes alerted to political interests and involvement in operational policing decisions only in high-profile and media-worthy cases. This exposure is not restricted to any one type of incident – that is, the incidents in question are not necessarily international in scope or national security related – rather, almost any incident may become high profile when 'something has gone wrong.' When things go 'right,' it is business as usual – and 'usual' often involves a large amount of unofficial, unacknowledged, 'invisible' politization of police work.

Different forms of political influence and direction occur at the three different levels of government. This chapter begins at the federal level and works its way down through provincial arrangements to the local municipal level. All three levels are instructive in illustrating the ongoing and deep linkages between the police and political masters and the political process. The Royal Canadian Mounted Police (RCMP) are the Canadian federal police force; they also provide policing 'on contract' in a municipal and provincial capacity in various jurisdictions. Their influence in terms of policy compliance and policy making is significant. At the municipal level, this chapter focuses in some detail on the Metropolitan Toronto police force, which is the largest Canadian urban municipal force – our 'biggest' city police force.

Federal

The intent in this chapter is not to provide a thorough analysis of the politicized role of the RCMP but rather to indicate that its beginnings were, and current status is, rife with political direction. In a detailed study of the relationship between the police and politics in Great Britain, France, Germany, and Italy David Bayley argued that the role behaviour of the police in each country is a reflection of the 'purpose for which the force was created and the political culture of the country, especially the way in which authority is manifested by government officials.'[32] He saw the police role being more clearly involved in state politics where there were particular difficulties in 'state-building' – the process of penetration of a territory by a coherent set of institutions. He argues that violence and resistance must be seen to be 'political' before the police role will be expanded. Bayley's focus upon violence might not be particularly relevant in the traditional sense of the word, but the Canadian state faced violence from geographical conditions. As June Callwood has commented, the country is illogical: it runs east and west whereas the rivers, mountains, commerce, and people flow north and south.[33] Large-scale state intervention was thought to be necessary to protect the resources and territory as well as to develop and maintain the infrastructure to transport and develop raw materials.[34] There is general agreement that the Canadian state-builders perceived an immediate need to spread state control firmly and strategically across Canada.

Because of the interconnectedness of police and government, the evolution of the former has generally paralleled that of the latter. As government became stronger, more coherent, centralized, and interventionist (particularly in the twentieth century), so did the institution of the police. In many ways too, as government grew, it assumed greater control over the police. The evolution of government has also been a history of the evolution of policy making. In gradually bringing the police under control, the government has been able to enlist them in accomplishing its policy objectives.[35]

There are very few detailed Canadian case studies of the introduction of the 'new' police in Canada. However, two academic studies[36] on the North West Mounted Police (NWMP) trace their arrival in the Yukon and the transformation of law enforcement that occurred between the years 1885 and 1899, supplementing the literary accounts often written by the police or government officials. Both W.R. Morrison and Thomas Stone argue that the prime reason for the arrival of the 'Mounties' in mining communities during the late 1880s had little to do with improving the administration of justice. The Miners meetings were deemed to be quite successful at establishing and maintaining order in these communities. Rather than merely to serve the residents, the arrival of the police was intended to protect the territory, in particular from a takeover by the United States. According to Morrison: 'This system [Miners meetings] was bound to come into conflict with that of the Canadian Government which saw its distant possessions not as crucibles of self-government but as communities to be put under the benevolent but complete control of the central government.'[37]

Once the NWMP entered the north, representing the central government, the old Miners meeting system was doomed. The arguments made by Allan Silver, Wilbur Miller, and Eric Monkkonen[38] regarding experiences elsewhere also hold true in Canada: legal agencies such as the police perform a symbolic function as well as an instrumental function. The history of the NWMP is in many ways an account of how it made effective use of both functions to further the sovereignty aims of the Canadian government. The legitimacy of the Mounties reached 'beyond the creeks,' back to wherever the miners and adventurers might choose to settle, and served as an extension of the central government.

The NWMP stepped in to reconfirm, via law enforcement, not local community values but the control of the central government over the territory. It follows that when the first Inspector, Charles Constantine, went into the Yukon region, he was instructed to go not as a police officer but as an 'Agent of the Dominion Government.'[39] During the post-Confederation period, it was the desire for territorial expansion on the part of the Canadian government which led to the formation of the NWMP. Ostensibly instituted to settle conflicts in the west, they were just as purposefully, if more discreetly, to prepare the way for settlement and deter American plans for expansion. In contrast with the western United States, the Canadian prairies were governed and policed before they were occupied by settlers on any large scale. The police led the way for the introduction of an array of other government officials and agents.

In the 1940s, the voyages of the RCMP ship *St Roch* through the Northwest Passage served to show the Canadian flag. Again, for a short period in the 1980s, the Canadian government was again concerned with the protection of her sovereign territory, following the passage of American oil tankers and Russian submarines through the passage. As one gesture of sovereignty among others, the solicitor general of the day, accompanied by the commissioner of the RCMP, flew to the remote RCMP detachment of Resolute Bay, close to the Northwest Passage, to present a plaque commemorating, in French, English, and Inutituk, the voyages of the *St Roch*.[40] Even today, as the sole permanent representative of the Canadian government in many remote areas of the Canadian north, the RCMP continues to fulfil a sovereignty role that extends beyond 'policing.'

It was of course not only the European settlers over whom the early Canadian police ruled. The First Nations and Inuit in Canada's northern areas were brought under the sovereignty of the state. In addition to the more traditional 'policing' duties such as maintaining order, national security, and 'controlling' crime, the Mounties assumed responsibilities as diverse as:[41]

- running the penitentiary for prisoners and lunatics,
- managing the post office,
- accompanying the tax collector,
- enforcing customs and gold-smuggling laws,

- administration and regulation of government business and statutes, and
- furthering government policies on the imposition of temperance and prohibition; the assertion of sovereignty; and federal 'health and welfare' policies pertaining to the aboriginal populations.

A similar pattern occurred elsewhere in Canada. On the northwest frontier the RCMP fought prairie fires; arbitrated disputes between settlers and Native people; delivered mail; provided information, supplies, and veterinary services; identified and controlled epidemic diseases; helped new settlers adjust to pioneer life; and distributed food and clothing to Native people during times of hardship. In northern Ontario, the provincial police responded when disaster occurred. They were mobilized by the government, for example, when, between 1911 and 1922, a number of devastating forest fires destroyed millions of acres of forest, consumed whole towns, killed over 250 people, and left thousands of families homeless.

The order-maintenance problems outside of the municipalities grew as Canada began to expand economically. Large populations of single men who laboured building canals and railways, or were attracted to the gold rushes in northern Ontario, British Columbia, and the Yukon Territory, were seen to be a destabilizing force and frequently an actual threat to order. Governments created or enlarged existing policing mechanisms to control such populations.

Poor working conditions led to the formation of unions, organized strikes, and demonstrations. Among the most notable of these was the Winnipeg General Strike of 1919. While the policy of the leadership was non-violent, the strike was portrayed across the country as a Bolshevik uprising. After six weeks of strike action, the federal government ordered in the militia and the Royal North West Mounted Police (RNWMP). They broke up what began as a peaceful march and, in the confusion that followed, one spectator was killed and thirty wounded. Seven leaders of the strike were convicted by the courts of trying to 'overthrow' the state (rather than participating in a labour dispute). These convictions were based in large part on 'intelligence' that was at odds with the information being supplied by the RNWMP.[42] Another major incident was the On-to-Ottawa Trek in 1935, in which 1,300 unemployed men left Vancouver for Ottawa to protest on the grounds of Parliament. They were stopped at Regina by the RCMP, on orders of the prime minister. Riots ensued, which resulted in many injuries and the death of a member of the RCMP.[43]

During the 1920s and 1930s, the Communist 'threat' was seen to be entwined with the labour movement in Canada. Labour unrest took place against a backdrop of rising government fear of the radical socialism that had appeared in Europe. Many of the activists were immigrants; thus, immigrants, organized labour, radicalism, and subversion became linked in the popular mind. With government policy firmly against agitation, the police broke up strikes and arrested the leaders. They earned, as a consequence, the enmity of organized labour, who saw the police as strikebreakers, xenophobes, and capitalist hirelings. For their part, the police were following the policy of governments who regarded labour unrest as a movement to subvert Canada. Police showed little opposition to unionism itself,[44] and personal accounts of police of the period indicate some sympathy for the unemployed.[45] Both governments and police, however, demonstrated an inability to distinguish between dissent and subversion,[46] and so they tended to perceive the threat as greater than it was. The RCMP continued to be responsible for national security matters until 1984. Their role changed again post-9/11, when new Canadian anti-terrorism legislation brought the RCMP back into 'security' policing. It may change again post-Arar and the 2006 publication of the highly critical *Commission of Inquiry Report*.

Jumping from the earlier history to the recent, there has been a continuing blurring of federal policing and politics.[47] Some people argue that a fundamental change took place within the RCMP following the term of Commissioner Simmonds and his replacement by Norm Inkster. What caused the changes that coincided with Inkster's term as commissioner, we may never know. But in examining the politicization of police work, the personality and aspirations of the key players must not be ignored. This is perhaps most evident at the municipal level, where during various periods the police chief and the politicians can be seen 'duking it out' on the front pages of the local papers, but in a less visible manner the same is true for the RCMP, and perhaps with greater consequences for the wider administration of justice.

Paul Palango[48] makes the argument that the RCMP, particularly following the McDonald Commission in 1981,[49] was increasingly seen as problematic by the federal government and therefore as an institution that required political control: 'While Ottawa says it has simply been trying to be fiscally responsible, almost every move it makes seems intended to destabilize and demoralize the proud and loyal members of the RCMP. They know that, to be effective law enforcement officers, they must be independent of government, but almost to a man or woman these days, Mounties feel they have become subject to political control. The rule of law has been subverted by the rule of politics.'[50] Palango works his way through the various political scandals and the RCMP handling of them or failure to do so.

Palango's interpretation has its critics. A different interpretation of events might be that during the late 1980s and early 1990s the RCMP was being treated in a manner similar to all other federal government departments – that is, stripped of personnel and budget and asked to do not 'more with less,' but rather 'less with less.' Across government, departments were forced to undergo an intense exercise in identifying 'core' responsibilities and making decisions as to what could be/ should be contracted out or dropped entirely. It could be argued that during this period, working under these circumstances meant that the initiatives of all departments were being determined by central government to a greater extent than at previous times. Whatever the explanation, the period was rife with politically related incidents, while the merits of – or even the reality of – the shift towards a close political influence may remain debated.

The highest profile cases involving accusation of political interference involved Senator Michel Cogger and Doug Small. Cogger accused the RCMP of bias in their investigation of his activities, which included allegations of fraud, payments for lobbying, and money laundering. Commissioner Inkster set up a one-man board of inquiry under René Marin to investigate Cogger's claims. Inkster's critics argued that it was unheard of to hold an inquiry while a police investigation was ongoing and that doing so jeopardized the police investigation – and in their opinion, perhaps deliberately. This Tory senator was eventually convicted of accepting more than $200,000 from an entrepreneur who wanted government contracts; he remained in the Senate collecting his salary. In a second incident Doug Small, from Global Television, obtained a copy of the federal budget that was to be released the following day and held it up on the dinner-hour newscast on 26 April 1989. Charges of possession of stolen goods were laid against the journalist, even though, according to a complaint brought against the commissioner and the deputy commissioner, 'the RCMP knew or ought to have known that no crime had been committed.'[51] Prime Minister Mulroney was calling it a 'criminal act,' and the media immediately claimed that the charges were politically motivated.

One of the early findings from testimony given at the Ipperwash Inquiry[52] was the different 'independence versus accountability' structural reporting chain between the RCMP and the Ontario Provincial Police (OPP). Where the RCMP commissioner position is a 'deputy minister' level position with accountability to the minister and the government, the OPP commissioner is an assistant deputy minister who reports to a deputy minister. The RCMP argues that their system is necessary for accountability purposes; the OPP claim that their system is required for the sake of police independence from political influence. Some critics believed that during his time as commissioner (1987–94) Inkster came to see himself as an *actual* deputy minister, rather than holding deputy minister rank.

As commissioner, Inkster was politically sophisticated and moved easily among people who populated the upper echelons of the political and international social classes, rather than among police officers – even senior police officers. Palango quotes Inkster's response to accusations that the RCMP was becoming too political and too open to political interference: 'Any interpretation of this changed relationship which infers that the force can be used as a vehicle for political partisan purposes is sadly inaccurate and one I find totally unacceptable. Since 1985 the force has investigated over 30 cases involving persons appointed or elected to parliament ... Most of these investigations have been carried out amidst great public debate. Yet in each case I can find no evidence that members of the force did other than their duty without fear, favour or affection of or towards any person ...'[53] In follow-up questions Inkster revealed that there were fifteen ongoing investigations. In what might be seen as a 'damned if you do and damned if you don't' scenario, the immediate result of this disclosure was further accusations that this statement had 'warned' those fifteen political suspects to get home and destroy evidence.

Deputy Commissioner Jensen and Assistant Commissioner Stamler are quoted as having had concerns that the federal police had become co-opted by the political process specifically during the Mulroney era. Weekly meetings with the solicitor general of the day meant that critical information about ongoing investigations was being shared with their political masters. After Solicitor General Kelleher recommended Norm Inkster to replace Commissioner Simmonds upon his retirement, Kelleher made his own assistant deputy minister, Michael Shoemaker[54] – a civilian bureaucrat – deputy commissioner of the RCMP. The then deputy commissioner, Hank Jensen, maintains that Kelleher's original intention had been to make Shoemaker the commissioner, but that Simmonds and Prime Minister Mulroney had stopped it. As Jensen stated: 'As the force became more and more bureaucratic in its approach, the government was able to exercise more and more control over the operations of the RCMP ... My quarrel with Inkster and Shoe-maker is not that they made the force more business-like, but they made the RCMP an agency of government. They politicised it.'[55]

The expressed intent of the introduction of people like Michael Shoe-maker was to form a bridge between the RCMP and the Treasury Board, Privy Council, and Machinery of Government people. While the merits or motivations of appointing anyone to the deputy commissioner posi-tion from outside can be debated, Shoemaker was an intelligent man who had held senior positions in the ministry that dealt with policing. However, by the time Kim Campbell was Prime Minister, in a fevered bid to remain in power, the role of government departments across Ottawa – including the RCMP – appeared to be to get their ministers re-elected rather than serve the people of Canada.[56]

The interactions during the 2004 'sponsorship scandal' illustrate sev-eral aspects of this 'closeness' to politics. The first is funding. According to the auditor general's report, the RCMP basically 'laundered' $1,704,000 through the sponsorship program in order to buy horses and trailers and to increase their operating budget to compensate for the additional expenses incurred during their 125th anniversary celebrations.[57] This money travelled from the Communications Co-ordination Services Branch (CCSB) to three 'Liberal-friendly' Montreal ad agencies, who charged $1,326,290 for passing it on to the RCMP. The RCMP then opened a separate non-government bank account to house this money. This act, plus the fact that the funds were not transferred directly to the RCMP, supports the contention that the police were willing partners in a wider exploitation of government funds allotted for political reasons to Quebec and seemingly also to the RCMP. Ironically, of course, it is the RCMP who are responsible for criminally investigating the alleged sponsorship abuses. Lawrence Martin asks: 'Once implicated in the Adscam Scandal, were the Mounties then intent on covering it up? Back when the abuse of sponsorship monies first came to light in March 2002, the Alliance Party, through Rahim Jaffer, wrote to the RCMP requesting that it investigate the serious allegations. No action was taken. A couple of months later, Greg Weston of the *Ottawa Sun* con-tacted force headquarters to ask why not. The RCMP told him it was because they hadn't received a complaint. Given the Jaffer referral, Mr. Weston thought this was a rather perplexing response.'[58]

After the situation blew up with sustained media coverage, the RCMP claimed that their investigative efforts were being threatened by the insistence of the parliamentary inquiry in ordering the appearance of specific officials and the calling of witnesses. They claimed, perhaps correctly, that this inquiry process, in advance of the development of the police case, could affect the police investigation.[59]

Obviously, each of the separate political parties will have its own interpretation of the political ties of the federal police, and it is not my task to determine a definitive answer. However, there appears to be some objective evidence of linkages. The Quebec Superior Court ruling in the François Beaudoin case referred to the 'unspeakable injustice' of the RCMP raid on Mr Beaudoin's home, golf course, and cottage. Beaudoin – the bank executive who hesitated to grant a loan to a friend of Chrétien – won his wrongful dismissal suit and his annual pension and severance package were to be reinstated.[60] The Beaudoin case revealed that the Mounties had worked with Michel Vennat (a friend of Jean Chrétien) to destroy the former head of the Business Development Bank, who had challenged the prime minister in what became known as the 'Shawinigate File.'[61] This case involved allegations of political influence in the requesting and obtaining of government loans to expand the Auberge Grand-Mère and golf course, which had previously been owned by four friends, including the prime minister prior to being elected. The controversy rested on when he sold his shares and what influence and interests he maintained in the business venture.[62] Comparisons were made between the RCMP's 'diligence' in pursuing the former prime minister Brian Mulroney in the 'Airbus' controversy versus their reluctance to persevere in the Shawinigate Affair.

The 1997 APEC case provides an example of an incident where accusations of political influence resulted in a thoroughly investigated inquiry. As Lawrence Martin states: 'The force's independence from the political arm was seriously called into question ... After investigating the controversy over freedom-of-speech abuses at the summit in Vancouver in 1997, a commission of inquiry concluded that the RCMP buckled to political pressure from the PMO when it manhandled protesters. Specifically the report targeted Chrétien heavyweight Jean Carle who was fingered in the Beaudoin case.'[63]

In 2001, Commissioner Zaccardelli dispelled all concern regarding political influence in the RCMP! When asked by Randy White, the Alliance House leader, whether or not he was 'involved with the Liberals,' the commissioner stated: 'I have absolute and total independence and that independence has never been challenged or questioned.'[64]

Police Independence: Provincial versus Municipal Oversight

Within Ontario, debate over the independence of the police followed high-profile government corruption cases overlaid with organized crime 'threats' and the creation of the Ontario Police Commission in the early 1960s. Often when we see examples of state involvement in police operations there is a prevalent 'threat rhetoric' – the corrosion of society, organized crime, crime waves of one sort or another, political corruption, and/or highly visible public disorder.

It was assumed that if police matters were insulated from direct interference by municipal officials, then the result would be the avoidance of a conflict of interest and would ensure an independent police service. As Allan McDougall stated: 'The existence of a Minister to protect the police interest is necessary for police insulation to continue and remain. The importance to the populace of an impartial police service subject only to the law and the courts for its law enforcement activity, provides the rationalization for the maintenance of that status. Threats such as the corrosion of society by organized crime, crime waves, political corruption, and the increased visibility of public disorder reinforce this need, and reaffirm the policeman's belief in his mission.'[65]

According to his argument, the pressure for independence by the police and the perceived 'threats' from organized crime and corruption were seen to justify – or were *used* to justify – the extension of provincial policy. Of course, there is some irony in the manipulation of the organized crime threat as an argument for the need for police independence via a move away from municipal politics towards the provinces, since it was the corruption of an OPP officer (receiving bribes from gamblers in southwestern Ontario) that drove much of the hype and furore regarding the penetration of organized crime into Canada.[66]

Organized crime has always held a certain currency that elevates any discussion, especially when it directly links to political embarrassment or advantage. In the early 1960s, scandals involving organized crime and government corruption resulted in the attorney general establishing an administrative agency to fight these 'threats' and increase the efficiency of the police service in Ontario. The Ontario Police Commission was formed to assume responsibility for police policy.[67]

The establishment of a governing board was intended to ensure that the province would be reluctant to interfere with the operation of the police. The assumption was that the existence of this board 'provided some assurance that local politicians would not attempt to use their police department to their political advantage.'[68]

By the late 1960s the minutes from the Police Association of Ontario Annual General Meeting recorded the beginnings of a rhetoric that acknowledges that, while the police role was defined by the law, and their power determined by it, their role of preserving the peace and protecting the life and property of the citizenry went beyond law enforcement to include discretion based on: *commonly held social values and expectations ...*'[69] The Police Association recognized that encouraging citizen participation and emphasizing local autonomy would work to reduce any movement towards the legal restriction of the discretionary aspect of the police role. As commonplace as our current awareness of police descretion is, prior to the late 1960s it was seldom acknowledged. The identification of wide discretion of the police provides us with our link into municipal politics and municipal policing.

Local Politics/Municipal Policing

The RCMP are not only responsible for federal policing but are of course the provincial police in all but two provinces (Quebec and Ontario with shared responsibilities in Newfoundland and Labrador), Yukon and Northwest Territories, and serve on contract as the municipal police in 199 jurisdictions.[70] Different links to politics apply in each of these different situations. Chris Murphy argues that one of the reasons that some jurisdictions preferred to hire the RCMP on contract to do the local municipal level policing was because it was hoped that these contracts removed the police from local politics.[71] Murphy quotes one police committee member as saying: 'Oh, it was just impossible with the old police. You'd always be getting calls from people saying why did the police chief drive so and so home and why you arrest my son ... But with the RCMP you don't get that kind of thing ...'[72]

In addition to these sorts of complaints, there were also the 'cozy or corrupt' relationships between the police and the public where charges would be dropped and judges dismissed cases for friends. Some communities quite sincerely saw the policing of their communities very much as a 'community service' and therefore a service where local political interests were seen as a legitimate priority for the police. Political links in all of these forms were deemed to be closer between politicians and local independent police as compared to the RCMP. Being somewhat insulated from local politics did not, however, mean that the contracted RCMP were not susceptible to wider political pressures from Ottawa.

In this section I shall be looking at policing in Metropolitan Toronto. This study is by Canadian standards a study of 'big city' policing. The history of the force/service reveals a complex network of interdependent relationships between the police and politics – a varying but continual pattern of mutual exploitation between political and policing organizations. The data for this section was obtained from a qualitative and quantitative 'mapping' of the relationships pertaining to the police.[73] The intention is to trace and reveal the context within which the police interact with politics rather than to simply pinpoint incidents.

The issue of the relationship between the police and politics has been debated in Toronto from the amalgamation of the thirteen separate municipal forces into one force in 1957, to the present. A number of concerns that were first raised in 1957 later developed into larger political issues about the relationship between the chief of police and the chairman of the Board of Commissioners of Police, and in some cases the chairman of Metro Council and the mayor. The policing establishment survived and grew, along with the political careers of newsworthy political figures, via the execution of various 'clean-ups' and 'crack-downs.' These operations ranged in size and intensity from minor pet peeves of those citizens with influence to massive campaigns.

Metropolitan Toronto follows the Canadian model of having a non-partisan local government. Political parties are not supposed to have an active role in running the councils and they do not compete as parties for local council seats. Having said that, the first chairman of the Metropolitan Toronto Council was Frederick Gardiner. 'Big Daddy' Gardiner had been a corporate lawyer, a former reeve of Forest Hill, and the former vice-president of the Ontario Conservative Association.[74] In addition to membership on the executive committee, Gardiner attended sessions of the four standing committees, served on seventeen of the eighteen special council committees, and insisted on being appointed to the first board of police commissioners. As Colton describes him: 'Part tyrant, part showman, and part Philistine, Gardiner was the biggest story in town. His control over the metro agenda, his sense of theatre and timing, and his capacity for distilling a controversy into a pungent phrase (hysterical historical societies, the symphony played on a cash register, shovelling fog with a pitchfork ...) made for eye-grabbing copy and by-lines.'[75]

Gardiner's political ties serve as a good example of the early and continual presence of informal political pressures in the operation of the local governments – and specifically in the operation of the local police. In some ways, the political ties of someone like Gardiner were at least apparent and predictable. What we see when we analyse the operation of the Toronto police over a fifty-year period is a sometimes more subtle – but continual – pattern of political influence.

The first police chief of an amalgamated Toronto Police Force, John Chisholm, repeatedly asked his colleagues and trusted friends what Charles (Bob) Bick's real role was as chairman of the Police Commission. His view was that with Bick as both chairman of the police commissioners and Gardiner's right-hand man, and with Gardiner closely tied to the Tory party, surely they were planning a take-over of the police.[76] In the temporary police headquarters at King and Church Streets Bick's office was directly above the chief's, and Bick frequently buzzed chiefs Chisholm, Mackey, and Adamson in turn for consultation.[77] Bick held 10:30 a.m. daily conferences with the chiefs to ensure that the commission policies were being carried out – appropriately.

An editorial discussed the issue of who should be 'boss': the chief of police or the chairman of the Police Commission. The conclusion, of course, was that Bick should be boss. However, even this role was compromised. Bick had served with Gardiner on the original Metro Executive Committee. When Bick became chairman of the Police Commission, Gardiner as chairman of Metro Council had a seat on the commission. Even though Gardiner is quoted as having said, 'You run the police and I'll run the Metropolitan Council,' by 1958 he was publicly demanding that the Toronto police 'stop using powder-puff tactics with criminals and be prepared to shoot fleeing bank robbers, to kill.'[78]

While few chiefs are actually driven to despair by the fact of the role of the chairman of the Police Commission – with the possible exception of Chief McCormack under Susan Eng in the 1990s – Chief Chisholm was deeply distressed. After haunting Bick at his cottage and acting wildly out of character, Chisholm phoned Jocko Thomas on the morning of 4 July 1958 to say 'Chief speaking Jocko, special meeting of the Board at 12 noon – keep in touch' and went to High Park, where he committed suicide by shooting himself.[79]

Whatever the appropriate balance between the chief and the chairman, the chairman's position is clearly a powerful one, and when the holder of that position has political ties, political influences reach deep into policing. Bick remained chairman until 1977. The *Toronto Star* carried an article which suggested that three candidates were considered as his replacement. In all three cases, political motivations were identified as the reason for their candidacy. A reporter, Michael Best stated: 'The Police Commission deserves better than to serve as a bone-yard for tired provincial politicians or a convenient pasture for foes to be got out of the way.'[80] The process by which Bick was replaced by Phil Givens stank of political manoeuvring. Even before the position had been officially given to Givens, the impending appointment was not well-received by the police. As Jocko Thomas reported: 'nothing appears to have shaken the force in its 20 years as much as the threat that the job of head of the police commission is to be handled as a "political plus."'[81]

The accusation was that a deal had been made – and a peculiar deal it was. Givens was a Liberal rather than a Conservative – therefore why would he be given this position as a political reward from Premier Davis? The answer seemed to be that the seat he had successfully held – even against Mel Lastman – in North York was desired by the Conservative party. An appointment to the Police Commission offered to Phil Givens would move him out of his riding, which a Conservative candidate might then have a chance of winning. In fact, they were successful. Tory candidate Bruce McCaffrey won the riding Givens had given up. Givens was officially appointed chairman of the Police Commission and simultaneously made a judge, since one of the three provincial appointments to the board had to be a provincial judge. Bick had responded with the seemingly ultimate criticism – that political appointments to the Police Commission were an 'Americanization' of the Metro Force. It was how very blatant the Tory 'deal' was that troubled some critics: 'It would appear you get rewarded for what you don't do as well as for what you do, do.'[82]

Every period in the history of the metropolitan Toronto police reveals a similar pattern of political deals that impacted the police – in most cases, with at least senior police agreement and often with the support of the force as a whole. Three examples follow that reveal slightly different ways in which the police become 'directed' to carry out their police work in certain prescribed ways by their political masters.

The 'Hippie Threat'

'These youngsters go out and they take these rides ... [*trips, whispered Margaret Campbell*] ... take these trips – that's right – and they contribute nothing to society ... My opinion is that they are all a bunch of bums – there's no doubt about that opinion.'

Controller Allan Lamport[83]

In the 1960s we watched the police go from disregarding Yorkville as a location requiring targeting to implementing harassing move-along-tactics, saturating the area with undercover police, and assisting in directing fire trucks down the pedestrian-filled streets – all as Controller Allan Lamport criticized the police, the courts, and the legislators for being slow to react to his calls for action. The police were initially quite vocal in maintaining that Yorkville was not a significant policing problem area. This changed as the presence of the Yorkville hippies was raised by political voices to the level of a moral panic. The driving force was not the police, but rather the politicians.

This era in Toronto, like several others, revealed that defining 'dangerousness' is not the simple prerogative of the police but rather can involve all segments of the society that have the power to make their views known. While the police voice was non-existent at the beginning of the crusade against the hippies, the politicians (except for people like Donald MacDonald from the New Democratic Party) were developing a picture of an enticing, evil location that drew innocents to it. By June a *Toronto Star* editorial was critical of what was openly referred to as the political harassment of Yorkville by City Hall. Mention was made that Toronto developers were interested in putting high-rise building where the small coffee shops were located and the development would be impossible unless the city was able to expropriate large sections of Yorkville. Money, politics, and the police make for a powerful combination.

Urged by Controller Lamport, the Toronto Board of Control decided to send extra policemen into Yorkville to check on 'overcrowded living quarters.' The *Toronto Star* questioned why the city government did not care more about the involuntary over-crowding in slum areas rather than the voluntary overcrowding in Yorkville. Lamport's response was that Yorkville was a 'blot on the City' and he accused the magistrates of 'mollycoddling' these youth. The interference of the Board of Control into matters of law enforcement was hereby supplemented by their interference into judicial decision making. It was not until July of that year that the RCMP and the Toronto Police actively responded to Yorkville.

Nineteen-sixty-seven was the year of the President's Crime Commission in the United States, and the rhetoric over the border was increasingly of drugs and organized crime. Driven in part by the visits to Toronto of the U.S. organized crime 'experts,' the police began to link drug and 'mob' rhetoric with the Yorkville hippies. The next stage involved a partnership between the police and politicians in encouraging the use of old legislation such as the vagrancy laws to pile up long lists of charges. In addition, they created new licensing regulations that meant that any coffee house that charged admission had to be licensed as a public hall – and as a public hall had to close at 1:00 a.m. This of course resulted in an impossible dilemma for the coffee shops that needed the entrance fees to pay the musicians but also had to stay open beyond 1 a.m. in order to attract a sufficient crowd.

Eventually the police took a stand and resisted at least some of the pressures from the politicians. In mid-summer Lamport argued that there ought to be an 8 p.m. curfew in Yorkville and that youth should have to carry curfew cards. The Police Commission rejected these ideas as well as his plan to create a special police outpost in the 'hippie' area.[84] The editorial the following day stated: 'He wants to turn Toronto into a miniature police state to get a few "pot" and "acid" heads ... not even the police share his alarm.'[85] Initially urged on by the politicians to treat Yorkville as a 'threat,' by August the police were being accused of brutality in their interactions with the Yorkville youth. By November, with winter coming, the hippie 'problem' faded.

Law enforcement issues had never been so political as they were in the sixties: civil disobedience, marijuana, the sexual revolution, Vietnam. Law enforcement was itself an explosive political issue during these years.[86] The broader political nature of the Yorkville activities escaped Chief Mackey, who linked the disorder to 'world-wide moral breakdown.' According to Chief Mackey the social problems could be fixed by making Sunday school compulsory.

The 'Yonge Street Cleanup'

It was in terms of the 'doctrine of clear and present danger' that the control agents operated and it was the logic of their own definition of the situation which forced them to escalate the measures they took and proposed to take to deal with the problem.'

Stanley Cohen[87]

By the late 1970s the politicians had a different policing cause to push. The history of the Yonge Street Cleanup represents a complex story of manipulation for political mileage, rather than a response to community deterioration. The main 'crusaders' were the city politicians, in particular Mayor David Crombie. Paul Rock outlines the characteristics of a successful moral entrepreneur for government policy change. The picture is one of steadfast focus upon a single issue, endless speeches, writing, and commitment to one concern[88] – and David Crombie qualifies as a moral entrepreneur in Rock's sense. Yvonne Chi-Ying Ng traces some of the political manoeuvring around the Yonge Street 'crisis' and quotes an adviser to Crombie as declaring that following the death of the twelve-year-old shoe-shine boy, Emanuel Jaques, they no longer had to search for an incident to lend support to their clean-up campaign: 'Ironically, we didn't have to develop one. The murder accomplished that. Three weeks ago Crombie was a fascist for trying to clean up the street; now he's ineffectual for not doing it sooner.'[89]

Not unlike the Yorkville clean-up/clean-out political activity, lurking behind the Yonge Street crusade were political ambitions in partnership with economic interests that felt themselves better served by the replacement of the sex shops with 'legitimate' businesses. In 1977, the large Eaton's Centre complex opened in the middle of the controversial strip. Eliminating the existing residents and clients was the larger aim; rhetoric of crime, danger, and dirtiness was the means.

The politicians' objectives were advanced by the next phase, which involved evoking the dangers of organized crime. A committee of three aldermen was formed to study the situation, and they concluded the area was 'a dying business area dominated by organized crime.'[90] A former Ontario attorney general, Allan Laurence, found that pornography in a bookstore was distributed by two major organized crime families in New Jersey and Louisiana.[91] The timing was perfect. Two days later, CBC's *Connections* program on organized crime was released, and the circle was complete. As Hall and others said, 'Now the demons proliferate.'[92]

By the end of July 1977 City Council and the mayor were launching a 'major campaign' on the downtown sex industry. The politicians used in part the justification that they had received over four hundred letters from the public concerning the area, ignoring the years of attempting to convince the public as to those dangers via the media. This time we have the politicians saying: 'The community has indicated forcefully it's time to do something about Yonge Street and we as the City must act.'[93]

Private meetings were held between Mayor Crombie, Attorney General Roy McMurtry, and Deputy Chief Jack Ackroyd plus other city officials, the business community, and the church. A 'new plan' was devised and they used the term 'council of war' to describe their plans. Meanwhile, the media was extremely critical of the draconic approach being developed. An editorial argued, 'we are a society of laws, not a community where even well intentioned leaders can exercise arbitrary powers.'

In a dramatic fashion, Mayor Crombie sent a letter by car to Premier William Davis demanding 'immediate action.' The premier responded that he had 'immediately' sent the letter forward to the attorney general's office to be dealt with in the usual manner. Crombie responds: 'In other words, Mr. Premier, our concerns about cleaning up the yawning cess-pool on Yonge Street are lumped together in an administrative review of municipal authority to license chestnut vendors.'[94]

Describing the aldermen at a special meeting of city officials David Lewis Stein, reporter for the *Toronto Star* stated: 'of course they all protested they didn't want to go back to the bad old "blue-stocking days." But the more they protested, the more they sounded like as committee of zealots looking for a witch to burn.'[95]

By 5 August 1977, politicians were holding secret meetings and were reported to be plotting what they termed a 'secret war' on the sex shops. Metro Chairman Godfrey referred to plans to use imaginatively some new and some not so new laws. Calls for the return of the death penalty and demands that Ottawa bring back the vagrancy laws were part of this crackdown.

Metro hired a special lawyer (Morris Manning) to prosecute sex-shop operators and owners. Special court time and special judges were set aside to cooperate with the provincial government. Manning was encouraging a seldom-invoked 'disorderly houses act' which allows a county judge to close a premise if anyone there had been charged within the last three months of being a keeper or inmate of a common bawdy house. This statute had not been used since 1945. He referred to the measure as being one of a number of 'tactics' he was considering. An assistant Crown attorney was assigned the task of handling morals charges that were to be laid by a special Metro police task force.

Operating within this new structure, Metro police set up a special task force that would target the sex shops. A daily accounting of the number of arrests and charges were offered to their political masters and to the reading public. By-law officers travelled with the police and acted as customers to prove prostitution. Chief Adamson had forbade his officers to undress during these undercover operations; licensing inspectors were used instead because they had no such restrictions on their behaviour.[96]

One gets the picture of a street thronged with strolling aldermen, undercover 'everybody,' back-room special lawyers, prosecutors, and judges prepared to pounce on all potential suspects, while pondering new laws and new uses for old legislation. It was the era of Anita Bryant and the religious rights opposition to homosexuality. This hostility was shared by key columnists in the papers, as evidenced by the opinion piece by *Star* reporter Robert Nielson, who resented the involvement of homosexuals in the recent election and expressed his obvious inability to separate homosexuality from paedophilia: 'Some male homosexuals would dearly love to have a legal carte blanche to seduce young boys ... it would be dubious law that would compel a landlord, hotel keeper or salon keeper to let his place become a hang-out for homosexuals.'[97]

There were exceptions to the government's campaign to clean up the sexual conduct of the citizenry. Efforts in Ottawa and Toronto to reduce prostitution began to include the charging of male clients of female prostitutes. Almost immediately allegations of a cover-up arose during an investigation of organized prostitution in Ottawa. The names of four officers listed in a prostitute's 'trick book' were not processed because they were deemed not to be actual clients of the woman. While there could conceivably be a work-related reason why the names might be there, this did not appear to be the case. Editorials of the day emphasized the importance of fair and equal treatment of both client (the 'John') and prostitute. This prompted a 'review committee' to be formed by Attorney General Roy McMurtry and in December 1977 he concluded: 'The police have a duty to protect the politicians, members of the press and prominent businessmen who are listed in the "trick books" ...'[98]

Directed by politicians, the police had many 'duties' during these years – to follow and carry out the directions of their political masters in their enthusiasm to 'clean up' any sexual conduct defined as unacceptable while, in the process, protecting the reputations of any police, politicians, and prominent businessmen who might stray! Beginning in the early 1970s what Gerry Woods said was true in the United States was also true in Canada. A new kind of politicization of the police became apparent: 'Professional policemen now organize for overt, aggressive political action, supporting or opposing candidates and lobbying at all levels of government.'[99]

'Policing' the Gay Community

> As part of a celebrity profile on Chief Ackroyd, in response to the question: 'Behind my back my friends say ...?' Ackroyd, responded, 'My position has become too political.'
>
> *Toronto Star*[100]

The interweaving of political demands with law enforcement interests was never more apparent than during the 1980s. I shall analyse in some detail what became known as the 'bathhouse raids.' On 2 February 1981 the following quotation from Chief Jack Ackroyd appeared in the *Toronto Star*: 'We can't force people to give up their prejudices or their biases, not even policemen. But a cop has to be prepared to be professional ... I might have some personal prejudices about the lifestyle choice of homosexuals, but that cannot enter into my work. Legally and morally, they are entitled to the protection of the police department.'[101] Three days later, approximately three hundred police officers raided four steambaths. These simultaneous night-time raids with tools for breaking down walls were unique in terms of their size and aggression. Verbal insults and publicity via press photos added to the 'punishment' administered that night. In total, 289 men were charged as found-ins, twenty with being 'keepers,' one with assault, and a few other with minor charges. The following day three thousand people marched in protest at the scale and form of the police action against the gay community. The police were accused of engaging in selective policing and systematic harassment of this one specific community; the police intelligence bureau responsible for coordinating the raids was called an 'army of goons.' There were allegations of verbal abuse and unnecessary violence by the police. The chairman of the Police Commission at that time was Godfrey. He supported the police action and Mayor Flynn said it looked 'like a good bust.' When questioned as to the need for such a violent enforcement operation, the chief claimed that police investigations had indicated criminal code violations, and that charges could be laid therefore: 'I, as Chief, have no other course of action but to *go along with the direction of the Crown Attorney*'[102] [emphasis added].

The notion of the Crown attorney dictating the raid to Police Chief Ackroyd is an interesting transfer of responsibility. However, in May, Attorney General McMurtry denied all allegations that the size, timing, and nature of the raids had been discussed in his office. McMurtry did confirm that a York assistant Crown attorney 'was consulted in respect to some aspects of the raid.'[103] As Alan Borovoy stated: 'Nowhere in his letter does he [Ackroyd] answer why it was necessary to mount such an enormous operation for people who are nothing more than found-ins ... an incident like this, coming in a sequence of events, where police officers were openly involved in election campaigning against gay rights activities, is bound to generate considerable disquiet in the gay community.'[104]

Controversy that might have waned sparked again in March when a photograph of a protest rally revealed that the four 'protestors' at the head of the march carrying a large banner that read, 'Enough is Enough. Stop Police Violence,' were in fact undercover policemen who were later photographed making an arrest.[105] Police were accused of being *agents provocateurs*. Ackroyd's response was that 'anyone who doesn't understand the police blending into the crowd to keep the peace, doesn't understand police work.'[106] The chief appeared not to understand the difference between 'blending' and 'leading'!

How does this example relate specifically to politicization of the police? Like many of the police activities that appear to have been affected or determined by politics, the evidence remains inconclusive because the form that the political 'direction' takes is not usually a verbal command. Rather, it requires an analysis and understanding of the 'collegial' partnerships that may form between political officials and the police.

Questions were asked as to why a relatively new but very astute chief would willingly inflict upon himself the uproar and outrage he had to know would follow the raids. An analysis of the bathhouse raids, however, points to police motivations linked to election politics rather than to order, protection, or justice.

It is important to place the decisions regarding the timing and nature of the raids in the context of the prevailing political circumstances. Both the investigation by the intelligence squad and the raids were located between two elections. The six months of lead-up investigations into the bathhouses would have placed the initial concern by the police during the depths of the campaigning for the municipal elections that took place in November 1980; the actual raids took place on the first day of the forty-four-day election period leading up to the mid-March 1981 provincial elections.

The significance of the municipal elections rests with the police reaction to and intense lobbying against John Sewell, the incumbent candidate for mayor. Sewell was a vocal critic of police treatment of minorities – most specifically of blacks and gays. In addition, Sewell aligned himself with George Hislop, who ran for council on a platform that included protection of gay rights. The police union had actively campaigned against Sewell and Hislop, and anti-gay pamphlets were openly displayed in one police division.[107] In February 1980, the president of the Police Association announced in *News and Views* (the police magazine) that in all likelihood the association would endorse pro-police candidates in the November municipal election. Both Sewell and Hislop lost the election. The Police Association, big business, and the developers were fully behind Art Eggleton, who won. This result seemed to indicate that the gay community, when given an opportunity to vote for two candidates who supported their demands for equality, had failed, as a community, to come out in support.

With the municipal election over with, in 1981, candidates prepared themselves for the provincial elections. Certain factors are key to our appreciating the context. The Conservatives had been in office in Ontario continually since 17 August 1943. They had not, however, had a majority government since 1975, and a majority was very much what they wanted now. Premier Davis desired to take an active role in the big national issues relating to energy and the constitutional debate. The Conservatives needed to be able to take seats away from the New Democratic Party and the Liberals, and the previous election had indicated that the Conservatives had little to gain and much to lose if they supported the gay community. The thinking was that an attack on that community, however, might win them some Liberal votes and a few non-gay NDP votes. In addition, another 'voice' that was being heard was the 'Christian Right,' which had expressed concern about Premier Davis's government. Advertisements began to appear in newspapers across the country and their view was very clear: 'Having homosexuals in the school is the same as having a drunk drive the school bus.'[108]

In Ontario a coalition called the Pro-Family Political Action Committee was formed to make 'morality' a deciding factor in who should govern the province. Campaign Life, Family and Freedom, Renaissance International, and Positive Parents combined to form this lobby. They were powerful and were seen to be powerful. The director for the Progressive Conservative Party in Metro Toronto advised the federal Conservatives that they 'would profit by turning to the right.'[109] During 1981, the vice-president of the Progressive Conservatives in Metro was a staunch supporter of Campaign Life. A Metro Tory official had to resign when it became known that he had helped found the right-wing Edmund Burke Society and had publicly advocated the supremacy of specific races. In this environment, alienating gay activists would not cost the Conservative Party a block of votes or significant campaign funds but would serve to 'locate' it on one of the few issues where it was safe to be distinct from the other two parties: homosexual rights. The gamble was correct. The voters gave the Tories their majority.

This strategy might explain why the political party was pleased about the raids and their ability to 'stand behind' the judgment of the police chief. However, why would the police participate in it? Here is where simplistic answers do not work. The police were not likely 'told' to do the raids and to do them in a manner that was sure to provoke controversy. But in place of a clear directive we have a network of factors.

First, politics and the Metro Police were related in part because of the players involved. Every Tuesday morning Chief Ackroyd, Solicitor General/Attorney General Roy McMurtry, and the head of the Police Commission met for breakfast at the Park Plaza hotel. Chief Ackroyd could be seen as a 'colleague' of the Tory political core concerned with issues of state rather than as a fellow police officer managing his officers. One cannot assume that Chief Ackroyd – or any specific chief – would carry out the role according to 'traditional' methods; that is, Ackroyd was not the same type of chief as Adamson, Mackey, or Chisholm before him. As J.Q. Wilson states, "the most important way in which the political culture affects police behaviour is through the choice of police administrator and the moulding of the expectations that govern his role.'[110]

Aligning oneself socially, politically, and economically with the political elite can only serve to bring the interests of one's own group into line with the interests of the other, whether appropriately or not. The political issues 'become' policing issues. The priorities of the political masters were shared by Chief Ackroyd; in return, Chief Ackroyd's interests were advanced through their close working relationship. Ackroyd was chairman of the Canadian Association of Chiefs of Police during these years. The documents submitted by Ackroyd often indicated the support of McMurtry on issues related to legislative lobbying, policies, and practices of the police.

Second, many of the police – and Chief Ackroyd as well by his own admission – held a view as to the expendability of the bathhouse segment of the gay community. Police officers in the 1980s, and likely today as well, tend to be conservative in belief and in their voting behaviour. Police 'culture' is conservative and under a Conservative government is rewarded for being so. Twenty years later, in 2002, during another Conservative political era, the Toronto police raided a lesbian bathhouse. In this incident five male police officers confronted several hundred half-naked women. The Ontario Human Rights Commission concluded in a 'case analysis report' that these women were the targets of discrimination on the basis of their gender and sexual orientation. A public inquiry has since been called.[111] The point is made by Peter Manning and others that actors in any organization create and recreate their social worlds, defining the threats to which they will respond and those that they will and can ignore.[112]

The needs of any organization, according to Isaac Balbus, include the accomplishment of a task, legitimation within the system, and the growth and the maintenance of the organization itself.[113] Given the conservatism of the culture, the desire to fight boredom, the requirements of the organization itself – which include resources – politically targeted 'threats' that can be readily 'handled' by the police are seen (and welcomed) as actual enforcement problems. In some cases in Toronto's policing history, offences were seen to be committed even if the law had to be redefined, new laws created, or old laws resurrected to make it so! Hence, Ackroyd's claim that 'the law was violated. I had no choice' makes a headline but has no substance.

Third, Roy McMurtry was for five years (1978–82) wearing two hats – hats that many people viewed as being in conflict. As solicitor general of Ontario the provincial and municipal police forces are responsible to him. As attorney general, he is responsible for the administration of justice – including decisions such as charging police officers and determining the legality of specific police techniques. As one editorial stated (with reference to a RCMP matter): 'Policemen are supposed to obey the law and if they don't private citizens may lay criminal charges against them ... But, Solicitor General Roy McMurtry has been using his power as Attorney General of Ontario to disrupt this process.'[114]

Fourth, the chairman of the Board of Commissioners of Police, during these years, as we acknowledged, received his position as a result of a political deal. While this position is supposed to isolate the chief from the elected officials, in this case, and several notable periods since that time, it has actually served to unite the chief with the political masters. Rather than any notion of 'balance,' the media accounts during this period of the raids in Toronto reveal a three-member triumvirate composed of the chief of police, the chairman of the Police Commission, and the attorney general/solicitor general.

Unravelling why the police would 'go along' with the advancement of political careers involves many tangled strings. In some cases the advancement of police careers was at stake. At other times the same ideological positions as to the moral worth of alternative lifestyles were shared between the police and the city officials. The most obvious explanation is that the political demands usually meant increased police resources and profile. These resources allowed the police forces to grow in manpower, technological advancement, and legislatively granted police powers. A related reason reflects the dependence of the police on the goodwill of politically influential members of the society. 'Proof' of the need for more resources is less likely to secure those resources than are close friendly ties to the politicians who control the budgets.

What I have been attempting to illustrate with this example and the preceeding ones is the contradiction of the police wanting political independence and then actively seeking political roles and/or identifying their interest with the interests of the political masters. Likewise, the politicians appreciate the influence and strength that the police can offer to their issues. In combination, the notion of 'independence' is pretty shallow. Toronto is not unique, and the decades we were looking at are not unique. Gerald Woods makes the following point pertaining to his analysis of the 'professionalization' of the U.S. LAPD and their victory in becoming 'independent from politics': 'the department is apparently unsatisfied merely to be placed outside the legal control of elected politicians. It now takes an overt, aggressive role in city and country elections ... Formal and informal police organizations campaign for conservative office seekers. Threats have been issued that the election of certain candidates will result in mass resignations from the police force ... the powerful police lobby exerts considerable influence over municipal, county and state politicians. Thus the police hinder and occasionally obstruct the democratic process.'[115]

Michael Brogden speaks of the political interventions by the police in the United Kingdom being 'commonly dressed in the allegorical language of moral concerns.'[116] Further, according to T. Bowden: 'When the police become active as politico-moral censors, their political penetration of society is enhanced. By disguising political statements as views on social morality ... they enlist the moral support of the population ...'[117]

Michel Foucault argued that the sovereign state behind conventional power and control had dispersed into an infinite network of sites and processes of discipline and control. As he states, power becomes exercised not ' by right but by technique, not be law but by normalization, and not by punishment but by control.'[118] Police accountability is always contentious, and it is made more so by an alliance between the police and those officeholders who are meant to be concerned about accountability.

This history takes us back to Dianne Martin's accountability focus and brings us to what 1981 Police Commissioner Phil Givens referred to as 'Vigilante activists who could hold their meetings in a telephone booth' – that is, the Citizens Independent Review of Police Activities (CIRPA).[119] The appearance of CIRPA drew attacks from all of the groups that were supposed to have been interested in police accountability. McMurtry appointed Sid Linden to head a new commission to hear citizen complaints.[120] As Dianne Martin said: 'Godfrey's tactics [to malign CIRPA] are terribly reminiscent of those employed by Phil Givens, head of the police commission, and Solicitor General/Attorney General Roy McMurtry, and indeed reflect a larger problem with the people who direct the police.'[121]

Chief McCormack and Susan Eng: A New Era?

'I attributed some of the stress to the emerging profile of the Police Commission – later the Police Service Board ... not that I in any way objected to the notion that the police ought to be accountable to the public they serve. But I was becoming increasingly concerned by the presence on the Commission of certain members who appeared determined to bring the force to heel ... One of the people I was particularly concerned about was Susan Eng.'

Chief McCormack[122]

If policing were truly 'independent,' one might not expect to find a difference in the relationship between the police and their accountability masters depending on which political party was in power. However, what had to have felt like friendly, accommodating oversight ended with the election of the NDP in Ontario September 1990. A chapter in Chief McCormack's book called 'Bob Rae's Kind of People' sums up his lack of appreciation for the 'new people' with whom he had to interact. Susan Eng received the brunt of his various self-serving attacks. Unlike her predecessor, June Rowland, Eng had been tasked with a strong provincial mandate to bring about fundamental changes and no longer to serve as a rubber stamp for the chief.

At the 1992 annual Ontario Police Association meeting held in Ottawa, 21,000 police officers passed a non-confidence motion against the NDP, now in power in Ontario. Their 'Resolution,' dated 11 August 1992 states: 'Whereas the Premier, on behalf of his Government, has indulged in malicious statements implying that police in the province are racists and want to shoot people – instead of being supportive of law and order and racial harmony ... the delegates representing 21,000 member of the police service in Ontario ...unanimously declare a lack of confidence in Mr. Bob Rae and his government ...'[123]

This declaration was prompted by the release of the Provincial Task Force on Race Relations and Policing by Clare Lewis, which recommended among other things that the government should tighten up conditions in which a police officer could use deadly force (the fleeing felon controversy), and that the police should file a report when they draw or discharge their firearms. The 'Resolution' was reproduced as an open letter in the Ottawa newspapers. Rae countered by accusing the police of 'playing politics' in order to resist any of the police reforms that the government was advocating.[124] The outcome was a case of the 'duelling Lewis's.' Given the degree of angst apparently felt by the police at Clare Lewis's recommendations pertaining to greater accountability of police discretionary powers, Doug Lewis, solicitor general of Canada, seeing perhaps a valuable constituency, chose to confuse the situation further with a politically advantageous statement of his own, saying that his government should oppose anything 'which would cause police officers to become apprehensive and compromise the safety of themselves or the public.'[125]

The OPP also saw the benefit of taking their opposition to the public and playing politics with their demands. In 1992 the Ontario Provincial Police Association held a series of simultaneous news conferences and produced a fifteen-minute video detailing their anger with government cutbacks. The following year the Montreal Urban Community Police brotherhood staged a 'slow-down' in order to take their demand to the public. As Montreal Chief St Germain stated: 'From 12:30 or 1 pm I realized very clearly that as Chief of police I no longer had any control of public security on the territory of the MUC. All the responsibility, all the work of public security had been taken away from me and was now in the hands of the president of the brotherhood.'[126]

This degree of political involvement by the police was perhaps, as Susan Eng claimed, the result of the new freedoms the police had gained in Ontario in 1991 to engage in political activities, that is, to campaign for politicians during off-hours and to run for political office during leaves of absence.[127] The friction between Eng and McCormack never let up and ended only with the chief's retirement in 1995 and Eng's departure from the board. In the chief's 'long-goodbye' speech, given in October 1994, announcing his retirement in June 1995, he stated: 'I find it incomprehensible that a Chief of Police should be compelled to discharge his or her duties in an environment which is characterized by impertinence, disrespect, ignorance and capitulation by political appointees to the transitory whims of special interests ... I am concerned that continued political pressures being brought to bear by the individual vested interests of Board members through the media are resulting in very serious concerns for confidentiality and good working conditions between the Board and Command officers.'[128]

In an open letter to Chief McCormack, Alan Borovoy characterized this speech as 'heaping public scorn on your civilian masters' and as proof that the chief had failed to grasp the simple fact that he was accountable to his board.[129] The tension continued as the Police Association gained strength during the period that David Boothby served as chief. While there was less overt friction with the board, the police force, which had learned bullying and intimidation tactics from the 'top,' was increasingly out of control. The 2004 corruption inquiries, charges, and convictions may prove to be partially the consequence of the McCormack era.

All political attempts to hold the police to account appeared to vanish with the 1995 election, when Mike Harris's right-wing Progressive Conservatives defeated the left-wing New Democrats. The Harris government implemented a neo-liberal program of cuts to social spending and taxes (the 'Common Sense Revolution'), but with a strong 'law and order' policing agenda. The political position of the police changed dramatically with the victory of the Harris government, the election of Mel Lastman as mayor, and the appointment of Norm Gardner as head of the Police Services Board, with Craig Bromell as head of the Police Association. The result was a system of oversight that has been correctly described as 'outrageously tilted towards the cops.'[130]

In the Ontario general election of 2003, the Progressive Conservatives were defeated and Dalton McGuinty's Liberals won a majority government. With McGuinty as the new premier, David Miller as the new mayor, Alan Heisey appointed to and then resigning from the position of chair of the Police Services Board, and the Police Association (Union) in ruin from corruption allegations, the game is less certain. So 'uncertain,' in fact, that it appears that the police have taken matters into their own hands and leaked memos to the press in the attempt to undermine Heisey's authority. Although he claimed personal and professional reasons, in reality a split in the Police Board and the unprofessional conduct of two members who left a meeting rather than participate in a vote that might have seen an external investigation into the Metropolitan Police force caused Heisey to step down, leaving a gaping hole in an obviously important position.[131] As John Barber, a reporter for the *Globe and Mail*, said, 'the Toronto police board stumbles from scandal to scandal, its credibility sustaining ever-greater damage as more traps and tricks waylay both reformers and old guard alike.'[132] If the police were truly autonomous and 'independent' changes in governments would reflect minor changes in policies, rather than the angst or empowerment that each change brings.

Degrees of Vulnerability to Political Involvement: Vulnerable Offences and Vulnerable People

After reviewing the evidence presented throughout Toronto's history, it becomes obvious that the so-called consensual or victimless crimes are the more easily manipulated by politicians, supported and assisted by a horde of moral entrepreneurs. Drugs, vagrancy, prostitution, gay baths, and pornography – all held centre-stage for the antics of moral outrage and political manoeuvring. These are the offences that demand or at least allow for the widest discretionary policing. Due to the nature of these offences, all occurrences cannot be reacted to by the formal criminal process, and decisions regarding when to react, and with what force, and against who, become dependent on extralegal factors. Here is where politics plays its most prominent role.

While Alan Grant has observed that among the 'regular' policing activities, politics may dictate a focus on predatory rather than white-collar fraud or corruption (at least prior to the Enron-type massive crimes), we find in Toronto that political decisions reached through a broader range of major police initiatives. As the research shows, it was the 'newsworthy' political personalities who dictated much of the large-scale policing actions. It must be acknowledged that this political influence extended well beyond policy discussions deep into the operational aspect of policing.

Much of the political policing I have been discussing placed more emphasis on the 'doing' than on the 'results'; that is, what is 'political' is often being seen to be engaging in the enforcement activities that accompanied the political platforming. The results were of less importance. For example, Yorkville would necessarily calm down with the coming of winter, and the clean-up of Yonge Street allowed for development that would likely have followed the same course without the political and policing 'war.' The longer-term outcome of the bathhouse raids was greater friction between the police and not only the homosexual community but also a wider array of 'marginalized' groups, including race and ethnic communities.

Crime control strategies and political interventions cannot be applied indiscriminately against the entire population due both to the need to maintain broad public support and limited resources. The criminological cal research of people such as Clifford Shearing, Richard Ericson, John van Maanen, Wilbur Miller, Allan Silver, and the Commission on Systemic Racism in the Ontario Criminal Justice System[133] suggest the importance of an outsider or 'non-respectable' segment of the population that can serve as the focus of crime-control strategies without threatening the acceptance of the police by the 'significant' members of the society.

In the various research studies the police even have names for these 'non-worthy' members of the public. Shearing notes that the police differentiated between the 'scum' and the 'public'; Ericson speaks of the police designation of a 'puker' class; Van Maanen's research on the police refers to the 'asshole' group; and Silver's research specifies policing of the 'dangerous classes.' The Commission on Systemic Racism in the Ontario Criminal Justice System conducted a study in which a majority of black, Chinese, and white Toronto residents did not believe that the police treated everyone equally.[134] This study also revealed a belief in a hierarchy of negative treatment, in which blacks received the worst treatment, followed by Chinese, and then whites. The overall impression of unequal treatment revealed in the commission's findings confirmed earlier studies, such as the Clare Lewis Task Force on Race Relations and Policing from 1989. These attitudes remained largely unchanged at the time of a 1998 survey by Paul Grayson at the Institute for Social Research, which revealed that 38 per cent of respondents in Toronto believed that the 'police did not treat all racial and economic groups fairly.'[135] In 2003, we saw an identical pattern in the Ontario Human Rights Commission report, *Paying the Price: The Human Cost of Racial Profiling*.[136]

As argued by Harry Glasbeek, the criminal justice system perpetuates existing inequalities and power imbalances because of its inherent interest in protecting the status quo.[137] As their most visible agent, the police are empowered to enforce the moral, political, economic, and social consensus determined by the legislative and criminal justice systems. Charged with a mission of imposing order on chaos, and mythologizing themselves as the 'thin blue line' protecting the democratic consensus of acceptable behaviour from those who would seek to challenge it, it is unsurprising that police behaviour appears discriminatory to those who remain outside of the status quo, and equally unsurprising that they align themselves with their political masters.[138]

In addition to racial, ethnic, or sexual 'threats,' the 'dangerous classes' may also be largely invisible, such as organized criminals, drug dealers, or political activists. The early history of the RCMP saw 'foreigners,' radical labour unions, Bolshevists, and eventually students as the dangerous groups. Over the next 125 years different groups – but usually always some identified group – were singled out as a dangerous, often alien, threat. Together, these are the groups that the police and politicians can do things *to* rather than *for.*

Different periods during the history of the Metropolitan Toronto Police Service reveal different degrees of blatant discrimination. My task here is not to reproduce all of the literature on racism and the Canadian police, but merely to reflect on some of the key 'moments.' For example, in 1979 the Police Association's official internal publication included articles attacking gays as well as articles against Catholics, blacks, Pakistanis, and Jews.[139] With a circulation to over six thousand police officers, this 'minority' obviously felt confident that it had the support, or at least the tolerance, of the majority. Gays, blacks, and hippies might all be seen as 'expendable' during the periods in which they were the focus of so much policing activity.

James Q.W. Wilson discusses some of the dynamics of policing and governing heterogeneous communities where one group of voices can gain precedence over all others.[140] The police may feel themselves to be under intense political pressure to solve, or at least settle, competing demands from usually 'unequal' segments of society. As the police begin to work 'deeper' inside the community via a community-policing model, they and their political masters may hear most often and most stridently the voices of the most powerful or the most politically astute.

A number of studies of community policing point to the difficulty inherent in the fact that there is seldom one community, but rather several – of unequal power. In his study of Bill C-49, pertaining to the development and implementation in 1985 of changes to Canada's Criminal Code dealing with prostitution, Nick Larsen states: 'The controversy and conflict regarding street prostitution intensified in 1987 despite much more aggressive enforcement of Bill C-49. The Toronto police formed the Police-Community Prostitution Liaison Committee to facilitate cooperation and information sharing with residents, business owners, the Crown Attorney's office and local politicians. The one group which was not included was the prostitutes themselves ...'[141] He concludes that several different factors determined the 'control' of prostitution, including public pressure, corporate and redevelopment interests, and the 'political' activity of the Toronto Police. The most vocal groups were listened to while simultaneously an attempt was made to subvert local political activity to serve the interests of the police – most specifically, in order to lobby for increased police staffing, which, in some cases, was not used in prostitution enforcement. As Benedikt Fischer found in his study on community policing, this form of policing became an exercise in which community spokespersons together with the police, with the support of the politicians, determined which undesirables should be eliminated from the 'community.' The task became 'social ordering' along the lines of good/bad/ crime/safety/ community/ outsider, etc.[142] While recognizing that all crime has a political aspect to it, in some cases the reach is beyond crime to 'undesirability.' To some scholars, the *Safe Streets Act* and its targeting of 'squeegee kids' is the best (or worst) example of this partnership for orderliness.[143]

Although the perspective from the 'two sides' might be different, community policing impacts not only the citizens being policed but the police themselves, and perhaps in particular the chiefs of police engaged in this style of police work. A U.S. study of 115 chiefs of small town police agencies indicated that 44 per cent of their predecessors had left their positions due to political pressure.[144] While direct political involvement in policing may typically be more evident in the United States than in Canada, Canadian police executives across the country acknowledge that they operate in a small 'p' political atmosphere. They claim further that the movement towards community policing has increased the politicization of their work:

'To manage community policing effectively, police executives must build alliances with the community and win support for police strategies. Working like this is a delicate balancing act between competing demands. Police leaders must avoid offending some constituents while satisfying the demands of others. They must also apply the different policies of three levels of government, comply with the direction of a local civilian governing authority, and submit to one or more police oversight body ... maintain good relations with police unions, senior managers and operational officers ... take heed of the courts, understand the criticism of academics, implement the management policies of finance departments, resolve the conflicting demands of different interest groups, advocate the rights of minority groups, and be ready to speak when the media requires it.[145]

Community policing, however it is being put into operation, involves a different relationship with the public and a different relationship between the police and their politicians. In response to a hostile question in the House of Parliament, asking the then solicitor general of Ontario why he did not get rid of Susan Eng in order to stop the friction between the Police Commission and Police Chief McCormack, the Hon. Mr Christopherson stated: 'These are extremely difficult times. We are very much moving to community-based policing, a relatively new philosophy that requires a new dynamic between police and police services. The Metro leadership, given the circumstances that are in front of them and the difficulties they have faced, are doing as good a job as one can expect. In many ways, the work they are doing on a day-to-day basis is pioneering the new kind of community-based policing that is supported all across North America.'[146]

Current and Future Pressures and Influence from the Executive

Resource Dependency and Political Influence

Among all of the other factors, resource dependency is a crucial factor over police practices. As the Police Futures Group argue: 'through the power of the purse, governments have gained a much firmer control over policing and are more effective than formerly in holding police executives accountable.'[147] Related to this is the impact that this government influence has on dynamics within the police service. The new roles and responsibilities of police executives are not necessarily understood by the rank and file within police organizations: 'The executive may be perceived as "selling out," or being "weak," "political" or even "corrupt" by those police officers who do not understand the relationship of police to government.'

We must acknowledge the increasing role of the Treasury Board in determining police operational practices, and in more general terms, research emphasizes the critical role that the 'control' over the financial resources plays in police operations. As government funding of the police tightens and becomes more ear-marked for specific policing activities, the distinction between direction and interference blurs or vanishes. As Michael Brogden states: 'When resources are tightly defined and monitored centrally – where for example a fixed formula governs resource provision – the police institution is in a directly dependent relationship. Where, however, the factors determining resource provision are vague, and subject to modification by the police institution itself, a more independent relation can be said to exist.'[148]

Alan Grant has argued that much of what is seen to be 'police discretion' is in fact 'political discretion.'[149] Through resource allocations, political decisions and preferences can directly or indirectly encourage the police to focus on particular types of 'threats' and away from other offences. It is not so much a matter of the police deciding to enforce or not to enforce certain laws, but rather that they have the capability – granted through resources including facilitating legislation – to target a segment of all offenders. Because academics and the media concentrate on how police carry out their functions rather than why they are doing what they do, the link to political direction too often remains hidden.

The blanket term 'policy' direction is also insufficiently studied, especially since the distinction between 'policy direction' and 'operational decisions' rests at the core of our discussion. As the police themselves acknowledge, there are many layers of policy: 'There is framework policy, which is often expressed in legislation, by-laws, regulations and so on of governing bodies. These may be social, legal, economic, financial or administrative and generally they are understood as providing direction for actions. Then there are more specific policies on how certain things will be done. Both governing bodies and police agencies make policies at this level. For example, governments have issued quality standards for police operations, while police services have made policies on community policing. Where one starts and the other ends is often not easy to determine.'[150]

The transitory membership on some of the Police Boards, the replacement of senior police officers, and the 'rotation' of federal solicitors general (now called ministers of public safety and emergency preparedness) means that there is not always 'corporate' knowledge (and often limited substantive knowledge) within government or the various police departments to be adequately attuned to the division between appropriate and inappropriate government involvement.

During the 1980s, there were approximately six solicitors general of Canada, followed by another nine by 2006.[151] Frequent turnover in this portfolio is not uncommon and certain periods have been particularly unstable. As elections change, so do the ministers – and sometimes they change in between elections. Each minister tended to have his or her own set of priorities. One concentrated on police conduct and powers in the wake of the McDonald Commission of Inquiry[152] and the creation of the Canadian Security Intelligence Service, another on missing children, yet another on the suppression of the illicit drug trade, and another on international terrorism. A close examination of the numerous policies developed during this period would reveal that some had very little impact on the police or on society as a whole, while others directly impacted the police practices.[153] For example, major government policing-related initiatives funded during the 1990s included, among many others: the Child Sexual Abuse Initiative, Missing Children, the Family Violence Initiative, Canada's Drug Strategy, Brighter Futures, and the Aboriginal Justice Initiative. In each case there were direct implications for police operations as well as policy – that is, if the police wanted to benefit from the additional resources! Consider the operational changes 'thrust' upon the police following the approval of Canada's Drug Strategy. While the police – in this case the RCMP – have input, Treasury Board approval will only be granted for politically significant initiatives. The promise of funds is overwhelmingly attractive and serves to sway the preferences of the department who must vie for resources.

Canada's original National Drug Strategy in 1987 included fifty-one separate initiatives providing resources for specific enforcement activities, prevention activities, and international activities. A specific focus on this strategy, pertaining to policing, was the government's objective of being seen to create a 'made in Canada' approach to the control of drugs. The rhetoric spoke of an essential balance between demand reduction and supply reduction. As a consequence, the RCMP assumed a much larger, and better funded, 'prevention' role, with obvious direct operational implications. Funding was provided for drug prevention training programs, the development of lesson plans for use in schools, the development of a specific program called PACE (Police Assisting Community Education), and specific funding for police work with youth 'at risk.'

As part of this strategy, on the 'supply reduction' side Bill C-61, the *Proceeds of Crime Act*, was passed, making money laundering a criminal offence and giving the Crown powers to seize and forfeit the proceeds from designated drug offences and from approximately twenty-four additional 'enterprise crimes.' The addition of the enterprise crimes within Canada's National Drug Strategy was another 'political' aspect of the legislation. The provinces might never have agreed to the *Proceeds of Crime Act* if, as a result, only the federal government (via the prosecution of drug offences) would profit from the seizures of the illicit proceeds. But since the provinces would be involved in the prosecution of enterprise crimes, they too would profit and hence would see the merit in passing this significant piece of legislation. Police at all levels were thus 'brought' or 'bought' into the 'illicit proceeds' investigation approach to law enforcement.

The National Drug Strategy became 'Canada's Drug Strategy' when it was renewed in 1992. This strategy has been renewed approximately every five years up to the present. In 1992, the renewal included $33 million for the creation of three Integrated Anti-Drug Profiteering Pilot Units, located in Toronto, Montreal, and Vancouver. In a further renewal, these three sites were expanded to thirteen. Money laundering investigations have become a main policing strategy against organized crime and one could argue that this operational commitment was driven by Treasury Board and ministerial direction through the approval of the Memorandum to Cabinet submissions, in some cases with considerable pressure or influence from the international community.

Police-Operational Direction from International 'Political' Masters

In stark contrast to the account given by McDougall of the local constabulary who was largely limited to enforcing the law on his neighbour, when required by social outcry,[154] police officers today must 'march' to the tune of many international masters. Within a framework of globalization, we recognize the need for a degree of uniformity in law enforcement across jurisdictions in order to target transnational criminals. Pressures are put on countries to meet new international standards and to put into force legislation that is compatible with the laws and procedures in place in other jurisdictions.

Joint force operations within Canada are supplemented by operations between Canadian police and foreign police agencies. Several of the biggest organized crime cases that Canada has successfully completed have involved Canadian and U.S. policing agencies working collaboratively – often with policing officials from several other jurisdictions involved. Summer 1998 cases such as the arrest of the Sicilian Cuntrera-Caruana family members[155] and historic cases such as 'Operation Green Ice'[156] involved close and long-term partnerships between the RCMP and U.S. agencies including the FBI, DEA, and U.S. Customs, as well as police forces around the world.[157] These joint operations have had a profound effect on policing policies and practices.

It is important to recognize that policy and practice are intimately related to the cultural norms and mores of a society. Canada and the United States have distinct historical roots and different experiences of state-formation and statehood, and enjoy vastly different positions within the international arena. Simply put, the law, its enforcement as well as how it is interpreted, relates to historic traditions and notions of what is deemed an acceptable intrusion in the lives of the people by the state.

What happens to these cultural differences under political pressures to 'harmonize'?

In several notable cases, the lead (formally or informally) on international enforcement-oriented committees or in the various policing operations is taken by the United States. Ethan Nadelmann[158] describes the global U.S. police presence that includes a vast array of law enforcement representatives in foreign countries; a multitude of separate law enforcement agencies, each with their own reasons for operating abroad; and the U.S. linking of their 'war on drugs' with 'national security' which served to 'export' criminal investigatory techniques. The influence of the United States upon Canada is not always passively received or resisted; it is also often actively sought by Canadian law enforcement. Canadian police officers attend training courses in the United States, belong to associations such as the International Association of Chiefs of Police, and attend conferences such as the International Asian Organized Crime Conference, which alternates between Canada and the United States for their annual meetings. Policing weaponry is advertised in Canadian police magazines and displayed at policing conferences within Canada, and serves as the basis for some of the arguments made by the police for enhanced fire power, wider diversity of weapons and, in some cases, even the appearance of the uniforms.[159]

To return to Brodeur's characteristics of high versus low policing, the American-model of police work emphasizes high policing strategies: the storing of intelligence within a massive financial intelligence system (FinCEN); a blurring of the enforcement and the sanctioning of suspects via a focus on both civil and criminal forfeiture; and an extensive use of undercover stings and reverse sting strategies. As these policing strategies spread internationally, and most definitely across the U.S./Canadian border, 'normal' policing strategies will emulate high policing techniques that bring domestic policing closer into the political arena.

Not only are there international joint force operations, there are also internationally agreed-to conventions, protocols, and treaties, in addition to a maze of bilateral and multilateral agreements. Most of these have direct implications for the police, and many are signed by unelected officials on behalf of governments (or not), or are the product of equally unelected bodies set up to address specific 'global problems' – as defined by themselves. To question the relationship between 'police' and 'politics' thus becomes a much wider question – politics from where? Nondemocratically created agencies now affect 'policing' both within and among nation states.

The police may on occasion participate in these processes, but not always and they are not usually the driving force behind the operational consequences to be delivered via the scripted enforcement efforts. A body such as the Financial Action Task Force (FATF) would be but one example, but an example that has had significant impact in dictating specific legislation and police powers and policing strategies and targets. In the 'battle' against money laundering, for example, in addition to the FATF, there is the United Nations (including UNICRI, UN ODCCP and the Security Council), the IMF, the World Bank, the Egmont Group, the OECD, the Council of Europe, the European parliament, the World Customs Organization, and the Basle Committee. In 2006 Canada became head of the FATF for the year. Further it was announced that Toronto would become the first permanent home for the Egmont Group, which serves as the umbrella secretariat for all the internatinal financial intelligence units. These responsibilities place Canada in the centre of the international 'war' against money launderers.[160] All of these bodies have taken a position on how to control money laundering. Each group or organization has either drafted its own recommendations or concurred with the recommendations of others as to the harmonization of laws, policies, and, most germane to our discussion, police practices. While some of these international groups operate by way of persuasion (mutual evaluation by all partner states), others employ a more aggressive 'black-listing' approach. The result becomes accusations across borders as to who is or is not meeting their responsibilities in adequately responding to transnational criminal activities.

Nationally and internationally the 'policing' arena is filled with government officials, non-government officials, private contracted 'policing' persons, and joint-force operations involving multi-jurisdictions, plus the 'new' entities such as Europol along with Interpol. Untangling the political 'directives' now involves many different sources of political influence, from the local to the national and into the realm of the international political players.

Role of the Increasing 'Securitization' of Policing after 9/11

Since September 11, 'security' has become the objective with additional funds pumped in to alleviate some of the drought law enforcement had been experiencing. This is the category of police work that most naturally adheres to Brodeur's high policing model with direct political policing implications. Somewhat peculiarly, the police in Canada, rather than CSIS, benefited the most from the additional resources. Immediately following September 11, the RCMP received $59 million 'in support of its fight against terrorism.' In December 2001 the Canadian federal budget supplemented this amount to a total of $576 million to fund seventeen 'initiatives dedicated to national security efforts.'[161] As Errol Mendes states: 'In this new battlefield between crime and war, the governments and citizens of the leading democratic societies in the world raced to enact new legislation or strengthen existing legislation that aimed at providing enhanced security to its citizens.'[162]

There has been both a blurred conceptualization among organized crime, terrorism, and 'ordinary' criminal code violations and a blurring of the control agencies that address these separate forms of criminality. While everyone might agree that duplication of effort is wasteful and perhaps even counterproductive, some of the newer partnership arrangements and shifting mandates have been implemented without a policy debate or decision, with low visibility, and too often with low accountability. Traditional public policing is becoming increasingly intermingled with private security policing, with national security CSIS activities, and with military security activities.

National security offences were traditionally seen to be distinct from criminal code offences such as organized crime or drug enforcement, and at least in Canada were assigned to a separate body – specifically because of some of the problems that can arise when citizens are subject to surveillance by an agency that shares the mandate for both policing and national security. Some examples of blurring across mandates in Canada include the following three shifts, each of which brings the domestic police closer to the political machinery.[163]

First, our public police – particularly the RCMP – have adopted national security as a priority for the coming years. This of course is predictable. As we saw with the other Treasury Board–driven policing initiatives, the potential for additional resources brings additional police 'commitment' to those activities. However, questions are being asked whether the RCMP are in fact the best agency to develop the specialized political knowledge and language skills to deal with sophisticated international terrorists.[164] They do not have a good record of being able to distinguish dissent from terrorism. Whether CSIS has a better record is perhaps also questionable. The enhanced post–September 11 enforcement funding contributed to the creation of the Integrated National Security Enforcement Teams (INSETs); the Integrated Border Enforcement teams (IBETs); technological enhancements; Chemical Biological Radiological Nuclear Response teams (CBRN); and a Financial Intelligence Branch to target terrorist funding. Most of these teams and initiatives involve collaboration across control agencies, including CSIS, the DND, and occasionally with U.S. agencies including the Department of National Defence, the CIA, DEA, and FBI.

Second, our national intelligence agency (CSIS) has declared organized crime to be a national security threat, and thus organized crime and drugs have become a topic of increasing CSIS concern and involvement. Domestic intelligence gathering is by law restricted to very specific national security–related activities. What then happens when drugs and organized crimes are declared to be national security threats? All serious crimes are redefined as appropriate fodder for our intelligence agency. The relationships between the RCMP and CSIS converge over these offences.

Third, the military in Canada are increasingly being brought in to at least 'stand-by' in what is traditionally the policing of domestic unrest situations, such as the Oka stand-off (an Aboriginal community protest in Quebec) and the anti-globalization demonstrations (APEC in British Columbia, the Quebec City trade meeting). Mandates between military and domestic policing are very different and purposely so. The military also has a different relationship with the political masters. If you look at a Seattle or Quebec protest you see military strategies and responses that impact directly on the responses of the police – the consequence being a tendency to forget the democratic right to protest.[165] The increasing appearance of 'swat-wear' and intimidating technology and 'control' equipment used by the police in protest situations may be an indication of this militarization of the police.

Conclusion

The relationships between the police and politics are deep, varied, and sporadic. Political enforcement campaigns are very useful to politicians, and likewise political involvement in policing issues often means more resources and greater profile for the police. Acknowledging these links is critical to any approach that aims to bring predictability and accountability, let alone independence, to this ongoing interchange.

The search and possibly the discovery of evidence of the police being directed by politicians to take or not take a particular policing operational action ignores the context within which policing decisions are made, and likewise ignores the limited alternative tools at the disposal of politicians to deliver on the various promises that they have made. The police are very useful to politicians and will remain so. The police and politicians, along with the media, are locked into a mutually exploitable relationship. Is it possible to limit this relationship and in that way enhance the independence of the police? More visibility and more accepted procedures may assist, such as: First, all guidelines, policies, or legislation must acknowledge (rather than continue the pattern of denying) the factors that bind the police to politics. Second, political patronage must play no role in the assigning of police-related 'plums' (although no one near Toronto now considers any position on the Police Board as a 'plum'!). Third, the media could play a role in assisting the public to be wary of the 'war' rhetoric around crime. Once a community or a jurisdiction commits itself to the 'war on prostitution,' the 'war on drugs,' or any other clean-up/clear out 'war' campaign, the police will be marching side by side with politicians. Law enforcement in the sense of community safety will be secondary. Fourth, numerous royal commissions and task force reports have documented the racial discrimination and class bias within Canadian society. Neither police nor politicians are exempt from providing their quotient of discriminatory individuals. Decisions that effect the policing of citizens must acknowledge this potential bias, and in cases of violation those responsible must be held to account. This becomes one of the important reasons for curbing political interference into police work. When faulty decisions are made, it will be easier to locate their source in the absence of political hype and media hysteria. Fifth, increasingly, operational policing decisions are being made outside of Canada, with seemingly little Canadian policy or operational debate concerning these changes. This speaks to the need for wider and different accountability mechanisms regarding the pressures for specific police operational responses that come from international agencies and organizations to which Canadian political masters may at some different level be aligned. Canadian officials join or sign international initiatives for a host of different purposes. The fallout may include less-than-carefully considered policing directives. Sixth, the post-9/11 security roles being assumed by the RCMP will follow Brodeur's high policing model. Here the links with politics will be particularly close and less easily detached.[166] Visibility and greater accountability – and possibly a rethink as to the appropriate RCMP versus CSIS roles – may be in order.

COMMENTARY BY TONITA MURRAY

Politics in Policing

One of the difficulties in examining the question of politics in policing, as Dr Beare has done, is to define what we mean by 'politics.' Some of the chapters in this book have done a good job of carefully defining 'independence,' 'accountability,' and 'governance,' but 'politics' is used in relation to all of these terms as if it had a fixed definition. It is one of those words that we use a lot in very imprecise ways. Even the *Oxford English Dictionary* has nearly three pages devoted to nuanced definitions of the root word 'politic,' so perhaps we can be forgiven for not using the term very precisely. For example, we use 'political direction' in one sense to mean 'direction by a duly elected government,' but also in the sense of 'directed by partisan political interests.'

Margaret Beare has presented some vivid accounts of the second definition of the term. She has shown how the police were part of a number of political storms during the last fifty years or more; what is not always clear is whether they were integral or merely incidental players in the larger political drama. There may be alternative interpretations of the role of the police and the politicians in the events Dr Beare describes.

A case in point is the linking of the former commissioner of the RCMP, Norman Inkster, with political interests. I was working at the corporate level of the RCMP when Norman Inkster was commissioner and saw first-hand some of the *causes célèbres* of the day that Dr Beare and other contributors to this book have described. I know that he operated on a belief that the police had a social duty to serve all Canadians, including Aboriginal people, women, visible minorities, and gays and lesbians. He introduced community policing into the RCMP, and he instituted the internal Cogger Inquiry because he was concerned that due process and the rule of law had been breached in an RCMP investigation. He believed strongly in accountability to the community and to Parliament, both through the minister responsible for policing and through the parliamentary committee for justice and legal affairs, which comprises representatives of all political parties. His term in office could be characterized as enlightened and progressive. That a Conservative government was in office for most of his tenure was coincidental and not necessarily reason to suggest that in taking its legitimate policy direction he was unduly influenced by party politics.

Police View of Politics

What Dr Beare has demonstrated in her paper is how easy it is for the police to be drawn into a political maelstrom. The possibility of political influence over doctors, teachers, lawyers, correctional staff, or other agents who have control over our minds or bodies does not have the same ability to raise the social temperature. Nor do we spend so much time agonizing about the governance, independence or accountability of other branches of the executive arm of government. Generally, once we have set up the legal and accountability mechanisms, we leave other public sector institutions to function without a great deal of external oversight. This is sometimes puzzling, particularly in the case of regulatory agencies at either the federal or provincial levels, since their employees often possess some of the same powers as police officers.

Generally, the police are well aware of their vulnerability to being drawn into political controversy, but they are not always able to do anything about it. For example, when governing bodies make faulty policing decisions the police often have to suffer in silence because, as agents of the executive arm of government, they cannot criticize their masters publicly. As a consequence of such circumstances, police officers are often wary of legitimate political direction. Particularly at the municipal level and within police unions, the degree of suspicion of politics can extend even to describing their own chiefs as 'political' when they see them implementing government policies, balancing interests, priorizing resources, or making objective decisions that do not necessarily support the views of their employees. This has led to something of a gulf between police chief executives and rank-and-file police.

An excessive suspicion of politics may be partly driven by fear of being unduly influenced, but it may also reflect lack of knowledge of how government works and the place of the police in government. Usually recruit training does not provide the degree of knowledge and understanding necessary for police officers to gain a clear appreciation of their relationship to government; only those relatively few officers who reach the higher ranks learn much about the constitutional relationship between the executive arm of government and the police. Many police officers see themselves as solely accountable to the law and more independent from government than they really are. Consequently, the tendency is to view any policy direction as political interference. The danger is that they can become cynical about the motives of government and reluctant to implement legitimate government policies.

Governance

Of course, police suspicion of governance is not always misplaced, as Dr Beare and others have discussed in their contributions to this volume. We have a very patchy system of police governance. Ministers may be good governors or not, but if their appointed staff lack experience or do not understand the nature of the role and responsibilities of police, the direction from the executive of government will be largely ineffective. They will be unable to translate policy into police action.

The quality and effectiveness of municipal police services boards, which are the buffer between the police and elected officials, are particularly variable. While there are some knowledgeable and highly effective police board members, many newly appointed members frequently have little knowledge of police roles and responsibilities, and by the time they acquire sufficient knowledge to be wise governors their time is up and they are replaced by other new, inexperienced members.

Reasons for becoming members of police boards are also sometimes at odds with good policing. I have observed a significant number of members, such as small business owners, who are intent on holding down the cost of policing and thus municipal taxes rather than promoting good policing. Others come with other agendas for changing the police. Their intentions may range from the idealistic to the grinding of personal axes. In recent years there have been some good police services boards that have searched for and identified good chiefs to appoint. But in an appreciable number of cases, when progressive chiefs have run into trouble in implementing reform, the boards have capitulated to the critics and withdrawn their support from the chief.[167]

In the last decade, police governing bodies have shifted their focus from police conduct to police performance. This has been a result of the new public administration where fiscal has tended to dominate social policy, and where accountability has been required for the results rather than the means. Oversight of police conduct has largely been left to *Charter* interpretation by the courts, and to the external oversight bodies, while governments have tended to concentrate more on cost effectiveness, organizational streamlining, efficiency, and budget cutting than on overseeing policing according to democratic principles. The trend is evident in the notes to the papers reproduced in this volume. Many of the citations for the seminal studies on police accountability and conduct date from the 1970s and 1980s.

Margaret Beare's view that the tenure of Norman Inkster as RCMP commissioner during the late 1980s and early 1990s marked the beginning of closer ties to government may well be true, and the same observation might be made of other Canadian police services. This was a period when Canadian governments became preoccupied with budget control, value for money, performance, and achievement of results. On those occasions when extra resources were made available for policing, they were often earmarked for the support of particular government policy objectives. Through the power of the purse, governments were able to gain more policy direction of the police and to bring them more closely in line with other government departments. In Manitoba, this extended even to municipal police chiefs reporting to a city manager rather than a board or council. While this trend in public administration was seen by many observers as an expression of neo-liberal ideology, it still represented legitimate government direction and was practised by governments of many different political stripes.

There are then many inconsistencies and problems with police governance. In general, it can be said to be ineffective, sometimes misdirected, and often so weak as to be almost no governance at all. It is thus hardly surprising that events such as Ipperwash or APEC were thought by many to have been mishandled by the government. Nor is it any wonder that police, who are suspicious of politics, tend not to make a distinction between politics and legitimate direction by a governing body.

Conclusion

The problem simply put is that police tend to be unduly suspicious of even legitimate political direction while governing bodies are inherently weak in providing good direction. Police governance may well be in a crisis of failure. That accountable policing has not broken down completely can be credited to the courts, and to police leaders who have come through the 1980s and know that public confidence depends on police observing human rights and not abusing their powers. Nevertheless, everyone present at the symposium in which this paper originated could list a number of breaches of this record. Disinterested and competent political direction, coupled with attention to the means as well as the ends of policing, could create the mutual trust now lacking and result in better policing.

NOTES

1 Jean-Paul Brodeur, 'High Policing and Low Policing: Remarks About the Policing of Political Activities' (1983) 30(5) Social Problems 507. Repr. in

Understanding Policing, ed. K. McCormick and L. Visano (Toronto: Canadian Scholars' Press, 1992), 285.

2 Louise Shelley, *Policing Soviet Society: The Evolution of State Control* (New York: Routledge, 1996), 27.

3 J. Gerry Woods, 'The Progressives and the Police: Urban Reform and the Professionalization of the Los Angeles Police' (PhD dissertation, University of California, 1973).

4 Shelley, *Policing Soviet Society*, 196–7.

5 R. Reiner, *The Politics of the Police* (Oxford: Oxford University Press, 2000), 9.

6 Leonard Cohen, 1992. 'Anthem,' on *The Future* CD, Columbia, 1992.

7 Otwin Marenin, 6 'Parking Tickets and Class Repression: The Concept of Policing in Critical Theories of Criminal Justice' (1982) 6 *Contemporary Crises* 241; Woods, 'The Progressives and the Police.'

8 Stuart A. Scheingold, *The Politics of Law and Order: Street Crime and Public Policy* (New York: Longman, 1984), xii.

9 William Chambliss, *Power, Politics and Crime* (Boulder, CO: Westview Press, 2001), 41.

10 Two thousand were added under the Safe Streets, Safe City initiative in 1992; four thousand were added by Giuliani; and six thousand were transferred from Transit and Housing to the NYPD. See Bernard E. Harcourt, 'Policing Disorder: Can We Reduce Serious Crime by Punishing Petty Offenses,' Boston *Review*, 2000. Figures were taken by Harcourt from the U.S. Dept. of Justice FBI Crime Reports 1991 and 2000, Washington, 2001.

11 Ted Gest, *Crime and Politics: Big Government's Erratic Campaign for Law and Order* (Oxford: Oxford University Press, 2001), 270.

12 Al Reiss, 'Forecasting the Role of the Police and the Role of the Police in Social Forecasting,' in *The Maintenance of Order in Society*, ed. Rita Donelan (Ottawa: Ministry of Supply and Services, 1982), 132–50.

13 Reiner, *The Politics of the Police*, 8–9.

14 Commissioners Rowan and Mayne to J. Scanlon, 2 March 1842, mepol 1/41, letter 88301. Quoted and discussed in Wilbur Miller, 'The Legitimation of the London and New York City Police, 1830–1870' (PhD dissertation, Columbia University, 1973).

15 C.D. Robinson, 'The Mayor and the Police: The Political Role of the Police in Society,' in *Police Forces in History*, ed. G.L. Mosse (London: Sage, 1975), 278.

16 Richard Rianoshek, 'History, Ideology, and the Practice of Policing,' paper presented at the American Society of Criminology meetings, Denver, Colorado, 10 November 1983, 7.

17 Edward Mann and John Alan Lee, *RCMP: The RCMP vs. The People* (Don Mills, ON: General Publishing Co., 1979), 101.
18 McDonald Commission Report. Brodeur, 'High Policing and Low Policing,' 282.
19 Mann and Lee, *RCMP*, 99.
20 *Globe and Mail*, 10 January 1978, quoted in ibid.
21 J.Q. Wilson, 'Politics and the Police,' in *The Police Community: Dimensions of an Occupational Subculture*, ed. Jack Goldsmith and Sharon Goldsmith (Palisades, CA: Palisades Publ., 1974).
22 J.Q. Wilson, *Varieties of Police Behavior* (Cambridge: Harvard University Press, 1976), 233.
23 Marenin, 'Parking Tickets and Class Repression,' 257.
24 Manfred Brusten, 'Securing the State: Politics and Internal Security in Europe,' *Working Papers in European Criminology, No. 3, European Group for the Study of Deviance and Social Control* (1982), 53–76.
25 Peter Manning, 'Police: Mandate, Strategies and Appearances,' in *Criminal Justice in America*, ed. R. Quinney (Boston: Little, Brown and Co., 1974), 181–3.
26 Brodeur, 'High Policing and Low Policing.'
27 Ibid. 285.
28 Ibid. 287.
29 The present Bush administration has arrogated the ground of debate by calling the present state (28 January 2003) one of war, but it has not been declared. Whether this is a crisis in national security is presently being limply debated in the United States congress but not in the media.
30 'Three Modes of Security.' Draft paper prepared for the 'In Search of Security' conference sponsored by National Institute of Justice and the Law Reform Commission of Canada, Montreal, 19-23 February, 2003.
31 Ibid., 11.
32 David Bayley, 'The Police and Political Development in Europe,' in *The Formation of National States in Western Europe*, ed. Charles Tilly (Princeton, NJ: Princeton University Press, 1975), 375.
33 June Callwood, 'What Canadians care about,' *Toronto Star*, 20 April 1981, A12.
34 See S.D. Clark, *The Developing Canadian Community* (Toronto: University of Toronto Press, 1962).
35 From personal conversations with Tonita Murray.
36 Thomas Stone, 'The Mounties as Vigilanties: Perceptions of Community and the Transformation of Law in the Yukon 1885–1897' (1979) 14(1) Law and Society Review; W.R. Morrison, 'The Northwest Mounted Police and the Klondike Gold Rush,' in *Police Forces in History*, ed. Mosse.

37 Morrison, 'The Northwest Mounted Police,' 264.
38 See A. Silver, 'A Demand for Order in Civil Society: A Review of Some Themes in the History of Urban Crime, Police and Riot,' in *The Police: Six Sociological Essays*, ed. D.J. Bordua (New York: John Wiley and Sons, 1967); Miller, 'The Legitimation of the London and the New York City Police; Eric Monkkonen, *Police in Urban America, 1860–1920* (Cambridge: Cambridge University Press, 1981).
39 Stone, 'The Mounties as Vigilantes.'
40 Tonita Murray, correspondence.
41 William and Nora Kelly, *Policing in Canada* (Toronto: MacMillan of Canada, Maclean-Hunder Press, 1976), 21.
42 See S.W. Horrall, 'The Royal North-West Mounted Police and Labour Unrest in Western Canada, 1919' (1980) 61(2) Canadian Historical Review 169.
43 Correspondence with Tonita Murray.
44 Greg Marquis, *Policing Canada's Century: A History of the Canadian Association of Chiefs of Police* (Toronto: University of Toronto Press, 1993), 112–15.
45 Lynne Stonier-Newman, *Policing a Pioneer Province: The BC Provincial Police, 1858–1950* (Madeira Park, BC: Harbour Publishing, 1991), 192–8.
46 Keith Walden, *Visions of Order: The Canadian Mounties in Symbol and Myth* (Toronto: Butterworths, 1982).
47 There are two ways of analysing these linkages: tracing the changes that have occurred structurally and in terms of management within the RCMP, or, on a case-by-case basis, capturing the 'moments' when political interference has been more clearly illustrated. Unfortunately, there is neither time nor space to thoroughly catalogue the political aspects to the federal police following either of these methods. Some controversial decisions will be acknowledged.
48 Paul Palango, *Above the Law* (Toronto: McClelland and Stewart, 1994); *The Last Guardians: The Crisis in the RCMP ... and in Canada* (Toronto: McClelland and Stewart, 1998).
49 Canada, Commission of Inquiry Concerning Certain Activities of the Royal Canadian Mounted Police, *Certain R.C.M.P. Activities and the Question of Governmental Knowledge* (Ottawa: Ministry of Supply and Services, 1981).
50 Palango, *The Last Guardians*, 291.
51 Office of the Commissioner for Federal Judicial Affairs, [1994] 2 F.C. 562. *In the Matter of Parts V1 and Vii of the RCMP Act, R.S.C. 1985, c. R10, as amended by S.C. 1986, c.11.*
52 Ipperwash Inquiry, The Honourable Sidney Linden, Commissioner, ongoing at the time of writing (2005).

53 Norm Inkster, before the Standing Committee on Justice and the Solicitor General, 12 December 1989. Taken from Palango, *Above the Law*, 289.

54 Michael Shoemaker served under Commissioner Norm Inkster.

55 Hank (Henry) Jensen, quoted in Palango, *The Last Guardians*, 135.

56 Our role below the level of the deputy minister *previously* had been 'protected' from politics. We were to serve our particular stakeholders *and in so doing* the minister would be served. During those years in the early 1990s serving the political party rather than the public appeared to be the priority.

57 Canada, Auditor General, 'Government-Wide Audit of Sponsorship, Advertising, and Public Opinion Research,' *Report of the Auditor General*, 19–20.

58 Lawrence Martin, 'Police Force or political force? *Globe and Mail*, 18 March, 2004, A19.

59 Daniel Leblanc, 'Mounties tell MPs to slow up ad probe,' *Globe and Mail*, 21 April 2004, A1. The resulting Gomery Report has been seen to be partly responsible for the Liberal election defeat in 2006.

60 CBC News Online, 'Shawinigate bank exec wins dismissal suit,' 3 March 2004, http://www.cbc.ca/canada/story/2004/02/06/beaudoin040205.html (retrieved 8 January 2007).

61 Martin, 'Police Force or political force?'

62 CBC News Online, 'L'Affair Grand-Mere,' 6 February 2004, http://www.cbc.ca/news/background/chrétien/shawinigan.html (retrieved 8 January 2007).

63 Martin, 'Police Force or political force?'

64 Ibid.

65 Allan Kerr McDougall, 'Policing in Ontario: The Occupational Dimensions to Provincial–Municipal Relations' (PhD dissertation, University of Toronto, 1971), 414.

66 Ibid. 442.

67 It was also during this period that the Canadian Police Information Centre (CPIC), the Canadian Police College (CPC) in Ottawa, the Criminal Intelligence Service Canada (CISC), Forensic Laboratory Services, and the Identification Services were established.

68 Ibid. 422.

69 Ibid. 441.

70 *Organization of the RCMP*: http://www.rcmp-grc.gc.ca/html/organi_e.htm (accessed 9 August 2004).

71 This reason may have been in addition to the fact that until recently the federal government subsidized these contract arrangements. At one time the federal government assumed 60 per cent of the costs, then reduced

their contribution to 30/70. They now have a near-cost recovery rate: in 2005, municipalities with populations of 15,000 and over were billed 90 per cent of total costs.

72 Christopher J. Murphy, 'The Social and Formal Organization of Small Town Policing: A Comparative Analysis of RCMP and Municipal Policing' (PhD dissertation, Centre of Criminology, University of Toronto, 1986).

73 See Beare, 'Selling Policing in Metropolitan Toronto' A Sociological Analysis of Police Rhetoric 1957–1984 (PhD dissertation, Columbia University, 1987).

74 Timothy J. Colton, *Big Daddy: Frederick G. Gardiner and the Building of Metropolitan Toronto* (Toronto: University of Toronto Press, 1980), see particularly 77–89.

75 Ibid., 149.

76 Interview with Jocko Thomas, Courts Bureau Reporter for the *Toronto Star* and CFRB, 4 July 1983.

77 Jocko Thomas, 'Do police need a full-time commission chairman'? *Toronto Star*, 27 August 1977, A-6.

78 Colton, *Big Daddy*, 88.

79 Interview with Jocko Thomas, 4 July 1983. See also Jocko Thomas, *From Police Headquarters: True Tales from the Big City Crime Beat* (Toronto: Stoddart Press, 1990), 164–73.

80 *Toronto Star*, 25 April 1977, C-6.

81 *Toronto Star*, 19 May 1977, 1.

82 'Politicians divided on Givens police job,' *Toronto Star*, 25 August 1977, B-1.

83 Controller Allan Lamport. Recorded at a Board of Control meeting and reported in the *Toronto Star*, 21 September 1967, 41.

84 'Lampy fails to get Yorkville curfew,' *Toronto Star*, 4 August 1967, 23.

85 'Yorkville isn't Stalin's Moscow,' *Toronto Star*, 5 August 1967, 6.

86 'Law beyond the law,' *Globe and Mail*, 31 January 1969.

87 Stanley Cohen, *Folk Devils and Moral Panics: The Creation of the Mods and Rockers* (Oxford: Martin Robertson, 1980), 87.

88 Paul Rock, *A View from the Shadows: The Ministry of the Solicitor General of Canada and the Making of the Justice for Victims of Crime Initiative* (Oxford: Clarendon Press, 1986).

89 Yvonne Chi-Ying Ng, 'Ideology, Media and Moral Panics: An Analysis of the Jaques Murder' (MA thesis, University of Toronto, 1981).

90 'Toronto's tenderloin and organized crime,' *Toronto Star*, 13 June 1977, C-3.

91 Ibid.

92 S. Hall, C. Critcher, T. Jefferson, J. Clarke, and B. Roberts, *Policing the Crises: Mugging, the State and Law and Order* (London: Macmillan Press, 1979).

93 'Crombie's answer to city's sex shops: lock 'em up,' *Toronto Star*, 22 July 1977, 1.

94 Davis dallying on sex clean-up: city,' *Toronto Star*, 26 July 1977, B-1.

95 'City authorities are getting serious about Yonge Street – for better or worse,' *Toronto Star*, 28 July 1977.

96 'Paul Godfrey had ordered the licensing inspectors who posed as clients not to talk to the press,' *Toronto Star*, 13 August 1977, A-6.

97 'Opinion,' *Toronto Star*, 15 June 1977, B-4. Critical responses followed, such as 'No stopping homosexuals from winning rights. He says,' 21 June 1977, Letters to Robert Nielsen.

98 *Toronto Star*, 24 December 1977, A-3.

99 Woods, 'The Progressives and the Police,' 14.

100 'Close-Up' a celebrity profile. *Toronto Star*, 20 March 1983.

101 'Ackroyd still wants to be: a "better" cop,' *Toronto Star*, 2 February 1981, A-9.

102 'Protests mount over police raids on homosexuals,' *Toronto Star*, 10 February 1981, A-13.

103 'Didn't Plan Police Raid: McMurtry,' *Toronto Star*, 15 May 1981, A-11.

104 'Civil rights body wants raid probe,' *Toronto Star*, 25 February 1981, A-5.

105 'Police led homosexual march: star Photos Show,' *Toronto Star*, March 1981. The protest took place Friday, February 20 with over 4,000 people marching from Queen's Park to 52 Police Division.

106 'Police won't charge "embarrassed" marchers,' *Toronto Star*, 18 March 1981, A-3.

107 'Not after Sewell or Hislop police union boss insists,' *Toronto Star*, 21 October 1980, A-3 and 'Police display anti-homosexual leaflets,' 24 October 1980, A-16.

108 'Moral majority hit America (and the Ontario elector as well),' *Toronto Star*, 1 March 1981, B5.

109 'Tories in Metro lurch to the right,' *Toronto Star*, 19 June 1981, A-10.

110 James Q. Wilson, 'Varieties of Police Behavior: the Management of Law and Order in Eight Communities' (New York: Atheneum, 1976), 233.

111 17 June 2002, *Toronto Star*, 'Inquiry ordered in bathhouse raid,' A1 and A-23.

112 Peter Manning, *The Narcs' Game* (Boston: MIT Press, 1980), 19.

113 Isaac Balbus, *The Dialectics of Legal Repression* (New Brunswick, NJ: Transaction Books, 1982).

114 'McMurtry errs on RCMP suit,' Editorial, *Toronto Star*, 11 July 1981, B-2.

115 Woods, 'The Progressives and the Police,' 6.

116 M. Brogden, *The Police Autonomy and Consent* (New York: Academic Press, 1982), 153.

117 T. Bowden, *Beyond the Limits of the Law* (Harmondsworth: Penguin, 1978),
     81, quoted in *Police Autonomy*, quoted in Brogden, 153.
118 M. Foucault, *Discipline and Punish: The Birth of the Prison* (New York:
     Pantheon, 1977).
119 'Citizens Independent Review of Police Activities' – Dianne Martin was
     one of the founding members of this oversight committee.
120 'Sid the "softy" is talking tough,' *Toronto Star*, 21 July 1981, A-1.
121 'Citizens' group being maligned,' letter by Dianne Martin, *Toronto Star*,
     17 October 1981, B-3. Godfrey was chairman of the Municipality of
     Metropolitan Toronto.
122 William McCormack and Bob Cooper, *Without Fear or Favour* (Toronto:
     Stoddart, 1999), 219. D. Martin's chapter discusses further McCormack's
     views.
123 Police Association of Ontario, *Resolution*, 11 August 1992.
124 'Police ads on reforms out of line Rae warns,' *Toronto Star*, 14 August
     1992, A-5.
125 'Hostility hampers dialogue,' *Ottawa Citizen*, 12 August 1992, A10.
126 'Police slowdown leaves Montreal chief powerless,' Friday *Ottawa Citi-
     zen*, 9 July 1993, A-5.
127 *News Release*, 'Solicitor General Announces Discussion Paper on Political
     Activity Rights for Police Officers,' 24 June 1991. See also 'Police–NDP
     tensions keep escalating,' *Toronto Star*, 15 August 1992, D5.
128 'My Concern is ... a spirit of mistrust,' *Toronto Star*, 13 October 1994, A13-25.
129 'Talking Point: Hanging on just corrodes a worthy career,' *Toronto Star*,
     2 November 1994, A21.
130 Rosie DiManno, 'Police Board needs new direction, and some luck,'
     Toronto Star, 16 June 2004, A2.
131 John Barber, 'Decency destroyed at the Toronto Police Board,' *Globe and
     Mail*, 12 June 2004, M2.
132 Ibid.
133 See C. Shearing, 'Subterranean Processes in the Maintenance of Power:
     An Examination of the Mechanisms Co-ordinating Police Actions' (1980)
     18(3) Canadian Review of Sociology and Anthropology, taken from
     Understanding Policing, ed. K. McCormick and Livy Visano (Toronto:
     Canadian Scholars' Press, 1992), 349–65; R. Ericson, *Making Crime: A
     Study of Detective Work* (Toronto: Butterworths, 1981); J. Van Maaned, 'The
     Asshole,' in *Policing: A View from the Streets*, ed. P. Manning and J. Van
     Maanen (Santa Monica, CA: Goodyear Publ., 1978); W. Miller, *Cops and
     Bobbies: Police Authority in New York and London 1830–1870* (Chicago:
     University of Chicago Press, 1977); A. Silver, 'The Demand for Order in
     Civil Society: A Review of Some Themes in the History of Urban Crime,

Police and Riot,' quoted in Bordua, *The Police; Report of the Commission on Systemic Racism in the Ontario Criminal Justice System* (Toronto: Queen's Printer for Ontario, 1995).

134 Ibid., 341.

135 Frances Henry, Carol Tator, Winston Mattis, and Tim Rees, *The Colour of Democracy: Racism in Canadian Society* (Toronto: Harcourt Brace & Company, 2000), 173.

136 Ontario Human Rights Commission (December 2003). *Paying the Price: The Human Cost of Racial Profiling.* www.ohrc.on.ca

137 Harry Glasbeek, *Police Shootings of Black People in Ontario* (Toronto: Queen's Printer for Ontario, 1993), 27–31. (Taken from a draft report prepared by Catherine Tuey.)

138 Ibid.

139 'The Homosexual Fad' by Tom Moclair, S/Sgt. 14th Division, Police Association, *News and Views*, March 1979.

140 J.Q. Wilson, *Varieties of Police Behavior* (New York: Atheneum Press, 1976).

141 E. Nick Larsen, 'Urban Politics and Prostitution Control: A Qualitative Analysis of a Controversial Urban Problem' (June 1999) 8(1) Canadian Journal of Urban Research 28.

142 Benedikt Fischer, 'Community Policing: A study of Local Policing, Order and Control' (PhD dissertation, University of Toronto, 1998).

143 See, for example, Patrick Parnaby, 'Disaster through Dirty Windshields: Law Order and Toronto's Squeegee Kids' (2003) 28(3) Canadian Journal of Sociology 281.

144 Kenneth Tunnell and Larry Gaines 1992. 'Political Pressures and Influences on Police Executives: A Descriptive Analysis' (1992) *American Journal of Police* 11(1), 1–16 (quotes from Police Futures Group Study Series No. 3. p. 11).

145 Frederick Biro, Peter Campbell, Paul McKenna and Tonita Murray, *Police Executives under Pressure: A Study and Discussion of the Issues*, Police Futures Group Study Series #3 (Ottawa: CACP, 2000). 11.

146 http://www.ontla.on.ca/hansard/house_debates/35_parl/session3/l110.htm#P148_44603, 1994.

147 Biro et al., *Police Executives under Pressure*, 12.

148 Michael Brogden, *The Police: Autonomy and Consent* (London: Academic Press, 1982), 98.

149 Alan Grant, 'The Police – A Policy Paper,' Paper prepared for the Law Reform Commission of Canada (Ottawa: Minister of Supply and Services, 1980). This argument is discussed in our Introduction.

150 Police Futures Group, *Police Executives under Pressure*, 55.

151 Warren Allmand, Robert Kaplan, Elmer McKay, Perron Beatty, Pierre

Blais, Pierre Cadieux, and James Kelleher, followed by Doug Lewis,
Andy Scott, Herb Gray, Lawrence MacAulay, Wayne Easter, Anne
McLellan as minister of public safety and emergency planning Canada,
and Stockwell Day.

152 Government of Canada, Commission of Inquiry Concerning Certain
Activities of the Royal Canadian Mounted Police, *Report* (Ottawa:
Queen's Printer, 1981) (known as the McDonald Commission).

153 Sometimes governments decide on a policy ostensibly for one purpose
but in reality to achieve a quite different objective. As we have seen, a
Toronto Mayor seeking re-election may choose to launch a campaign to
clean up a sleazy part of Yonge Street and direct the police to concentrate
their attentions on the area. The question remains whether this is a
legitimate policy direction to solve a social problem or political interference with the police to gain personal advantage. Likewise, a decision to
build a prison or an RCMP detachment in a certain location may have
more to do with boosting the local economy, or ensuring the return of a
local member to Parliament by providing a constituency with a political
favour, than achieving operational aims. However, if there is a failure to
achieve the stated policy, the correctional or police officials are the most
likely to be criticized, not the policy decision makers.

154 Allan McDougall 'Policing in Ontario: The Occupational Dimensions to
Provincial-Municipal Relations' (PhD dissertation, University of Toronto,
1971), 418.

155 The Canadian RCMP, together with the Montreal Urban Community
Police and the Sureté de Quebec, worked for over two years with the U.S.
FBI, DEA, Customs, and Texas DPS as well as the Italian Raggrupamento
Operativo Speciale-Carabinieri and the Servizio Centrale Operative of the
State Police and Mexico's Procuraduria General de la Republica and
Federal Anti Drug Task Force on 'Project Omerta.' On 15 July 1998 key
members of the Cuntrera-Caruana Sicilian organized crime family were
arrested. At least fourteen arrests took place in North America, including
that of Alfonso Caruana, the alleged mob king-pin.

156 'Operation Green Ice' was headed by the DEA and involved collaborative
police work from Canada, Italy, Spain, Costa Rica, Colombia, the United
Kingdom and the Cayman Islands. The objective of this case was to
infiltrate money-laundering enterprises of targeted organized crime
operations headed by the major Colombian cocaine cartels. One phase of
this investigation culminated in a $1,075,000 seizure by the RCMP on
24 September 1992. This case was deemed important since it was one of
the first to establish the links between Colombian cocaine cartels and the
Mafia operating out of Italy. See Beare, *Criminal Conspiracies*, 131.

157 These cases are distinct from cases such as 'Operation Casablanca,' which was characterized by distrust between the U.S. and Mexican government and Mexican law enforcement. 'In this case, the Mexican officials were not informed about the U.S. investigation for fear of 'compromising the operation and placing the lives of US agents in danger.'

158 Ethan Nadelmann, *Cops across Borders: The Internationalization of US criminal Law Enforcement* (University Park: Penn State University Press, 1993).

159 The Ontario Provincial Police have adopted a new uniform and hat that resembles a U.S. trooper uniform. The Summer 1998 *Canadian Police Chief Magazine* tells the Canadian police that 'the look of authority Starts at the Top' – an advertisement for Stratton Hats from Illinois. The same magazine includes an advertisement for a firm out of California that will provide the written tests to enhance the capability of the police to hire appropriately. A number of the advertisements present 'tactical and survival' gear, body armour wear and video-based training courses.

160 Steven Chase, 'Top sleuths to set up home base in toronto,' *Globe and Mail*, 8 July 2006, A1–A4. The individual financial intelligence agencies include FINTRAC in Canada, FinCEN inU.S. and AUSTRAC in Australia. Egmont claims to co-ordinate the 'battle against money laundering in 101 countries.

161 RCMP site *Post-Sept 11th – The Fight Against Terrorism* http:// canadaonline.about.com/gi/dynamic/offsite.htm?site= http%3A%2 F%2Fwww.rcmp-grc.gc.ca%2Fnews%2F2002%2Fnr-02–18.htm (accessed 2 September 2003).

162 Editor-in-Chief's Introduction, 'Between Crime and War: Terrorism, Democracy and the Constitution,' Special Issue, National Journal of Constitutional Law 14(1) (2002).

163 Taken from Beare, *Policing with a National Security Agenda*.

164 Kent Roach, *September 11: Consequences for Canada* (Montreal: McGill-Queen's University Press, 2003), 194. The release of the 'Arar Commission Report' served to confirm many of these concerns. See *Report of the Events Relating to Maher Arar* (Ottawa: Public Works & Government Services Canada, 2006).

165 See, for example, Peter B. Kraska, ed., *Militarizing the American Criminal Justice System* (Boston: Northeastern University Press, 2001).

166 'I'm shocked – shocked.' In the days following the release of the Arar Commission report, a sequence of ministers publicly declared their surprise and ignorance of the RCMP mistakes. Who knew what, when, will remain open to debate.

167 Biro et al., *Police Executives under Pressure*.

Epilogue

Transcripts from the public hearings of the Ipperwash Inquiry help to put police governance theories into perspective and suggest that a sociological rather than a legal filtre might be more helpful in finding resolution. All the witnesses questioned on their understanding of the separate roles of government and police had no difficulty in assigning policy responsibility to government and operational responsibility to police, suggesting that this is the prevailing doctrine in practice. But police governance problems occur when there is no common understanding of what 'policy' and 'operations' consist. The concepts are slippery and mean different things in different situations.[1] The problem is compounded when people and institutions unconsciously slip from one role into the other.

The following edited extracts from the Ipperwash transcripts reveal the beliefs about police governance on which people acted in real-life situations. In practice, politicians, public servants, and even police sometimes had difficulty making a distinction between policy direction and operational independence. The extracts suggest that relatively short tenures in office, the need to manage crises, and lack of familiarity with the realities of policing on the ground sometimes lead politicians, political advisers, and generalist public servants to act as if they have more directive authority than it is practical for them to possess. Conversely, innocent questions or remarks can be construed as political interference, and fear of inadvertently straying into operational direction can prevent politicians and public servants from asking necessary questions of the police.

For their part, police can also cross the boundary between policy and operations when ostensibly providing operational advice. Indeed, because of their expertise, police often straddle the line. A police policy formulated without police advice has the potential to be unworkable. In practice, therefore, police may have more influence in the governance partnership than politicians, since politicians may have to rely heavily on the police for their ability to govern effectively. This may be an important reason why working and social relationships evolve between police and politicians. What legal theory cannot contemplate, pragmatism embraces.

The transcripts also suggest that police governance in practice is even more fraught with difficulties at the local level. The governance relationship and the role of local police governing bodies can become blurred by social and other community relationships between local politicians and the police. In such situations, politicians can act as if local relationships or the particular wishes of some constituents override the norms of police governance.

Ultimately, an important reason why ambiguity in police governance exists is because there has been little attempt to translate theories of police governance into working policies and procedures. Legislation has been eschewed for fear of introducing rigidity, which could become an obstacle in managing a crisis or a new situation. Yet the disinterest of judges or the discretionary powers of the police have not been seriously hampered by the existing rules that supposedly guide their decision making. Similarly, the utility of such ministerial guides as the *Discussion Paper* prepared in 1991 by Anne McChesney,[2] which was examined in the Ipperwash Inquiry, can be realized only if the principles they contain are rendered into operating policies and procedures for shaping the relations of ministers, their deputies, local governing bodies, and the police.

What follows is only a sample of the 'stated' understandings of some of the key witnesses at the Ipperwash Inquiry. Following these transcripts, *A Discussion Paper on Police Government Relations* and a series of questions that were used in the Ipperwash Inquiry process are reproduced in an appendix.

Larry Taman, Former Deputy Attorney General of Ontario and Deputy Minister of Native Affairs

Q: What in 1995 was your understanding about the relationship between the solicitor general and the police and, in particular, the Ontario Provincial Police?

A: My understanding was that the relationship was fundamentally similar to other ministries, including the Ministry of the Attorney Gen-

eral; that the minister is responsible for policy for all parts of the
ministry, including the Ontario Provincial Police. The Ontario Provincial Police, by law at that time, were plainly subject to ministerial
authority. The convention had developed that the minister did not
interfere with the work of the police in prosecutorial matters. And
secondly that, in operational matters, the minister did not give operational direction. The first of these, I think, was a legal restriction that is
quite strongly established in the law. The second, I think, is really more
a matter of practical judgment. If there's a police operation going on,
you can only have so many people in charge of it and the practical rule
that was followed, always, to the best of my knowledge, was that a
police operation on the ground was run by police officers on the ground
and the minister didn't interfere.

Q: With respect to policy and operations, how would you define the line
between policy and operations?

A: Policy has to do with rules that are of general application. The
government makes policy and says that, as a general matter, we will
strictly enforce speed limits in Ontario. And I think that's a matter of
policy and I think it's perfectly appropriate for the government to say
that there's zero tolerance of speeding in Ontario. In my view, that's a
government policy decision not a policing decision. I think that if there
then is an issue of how a given car chases a speeder down the road, I
think that's a policing matter. And I think everyone would think that a
solicitor general had lost her mind if she took to monitoring the police
bands and telling chase cars to go faster or go slower. So I think generally, it's the distinction between a rule and the application of a rule. The
rule is policy, the application of the rule is operations. But there's no
bright line between those two. I think there are many instances where
it's not perfectly clear whether some particular action falls on the policy
side or the operational side of the rule. And I think in those situations
there has to be cooperation between the policy people and the operational people.

**Charles Harnick, Former Attorney General of Ontario
and Minister of Native Affairs**

Q: In 1995, what was your understanding about the relationship
between the solicitor general's office and the police, the OPP in particular?

A: The rule in the Ministry of the Attorney General was that police officers lay charges and the Ministry of the Attorney General is responsible for prosecution. And there was a very definite line between those two functions. I did have a role to play in terms of police oversight. The police forces would be under the purview of the solicitor general. And it would be an obvious conflict if they were a stakeholder of the Ministry of the solicitor general and at the same time the solicitor general would be responsible for their oversight. I mean for instance the SIU [Special Investigations Unit] was a responsibility of the attorney general, the board of inquiry was a responsibility of the attorney general, but other than that there was not any role in terms of the attorney general being involved in policing.

Michael Harris, Former Premier of Ontario

Q: When you became premier in June of 1995, what was your understanding of the relationship between the government and the Ontario Provincial Police?

A: Well, we provided their budget through the Ministry of Solicitor General. We were well aware that there was a separation between the political arm of government and the police.

Q: When you say, 'We were well aware there was a separation between the political arm of government and the police,' what do you mean by that?

A: That policy, setting of laws, the regulatory process, those policy decisions were the purview of the politicians; that the police would have their own authority and as to how they would uphold those laws and how they would deal with it and that there was a separation there. And we were certainly well aware, I think, that was one of the fundamental tenets of democracy.

Q: What was your understanding as to the separation between the politicians and Ontario Provincial Police with respect to operational matters?

A: That politicians, including the solicitor general, would have no involvement in any operational decisions.

Q: And where did you gain that understanding, sir?

A: Well, I think I knew that growing up. I think I knew that from school. I think I knew that as a teacher. I think I knew that certainly as an MPP from 1981 on and certainly reinforced, I would suggest as minister of natural resources in 1985.

Q: And how would you define an operational matter back in 1995?

A: I'm not sure that I recall sitting down defining it.

Q: Today, what's your understanding of what's operational as opposed to policy?

A: Any situation that required intervention by the Ontario Provincial Police. I think it would apply to all police: municipality to police force and certainly federal government to RCMP. There would be no involvement in any operational matters – how the OPP conducted their affairs or investigations.

Debra Hutton, Executive Assistant on Issues Management to Premier Michael Harris

Q: Were you part of any briefings which focused on explaining the relationship or interrelationship between the government and the OPP in the early months of the government?

A: I don't recall specifically. It's not to say I wasn't. I had as I've indicated been in Opposition for seven years and I believe I had a – very clear – as I would argue the premier certainly seemed to have a very clear understanding of the distinction between what the OPP was responsible for and what the government was responsible for.

Q: What was your early understanding of that?

A: The only role that the Ontario government or that elected officials could play in government as it related to the OPP was one of a broad policy nature. So for example we certainly set policy as to number of OPP that the government would fund for example, those sort of broad types of policy areas and that's as far as it went.

Robert Runciman, Solicitor General and Minister of Correctional Services, 1995–1999, and Minister of Public Safety and Security, 2002–2003

Q: What was your understanding of the role of the solicitor general?

A: Essentially, oversight with respect to policing in terms of policy development, responsibility for the *Police Act* and ensuring it was adhered to, appointment of members to police services boards, policy development, of course, in terms of things like chase protocols, those kinds of issues that would come before a minister.

Q: And when you became the solicitor general what was your understanding of the relationship between you as the minister and the Ontario Provincial Police?

A: I think it was a pretty clear understanding that you didn't, in any way, shape or form, interfere with operational decision making on the part of the OPP or any police service for that matter. You established policy in consultation with police and a variety of stakeholders who would have an interest in policing in the province, and ensure that those policies were adhered to. And again, developing initiatives. I mentioned the police chase protocol as an example. Dealing with issues like allowing police services to use taser guns; pepper spray, when that came into use in Ontario, those kinds of initiatives, you would deal with as a minister.

Q: And what was the basis of your understanding in particular with respect to the role of the solicitor general and with respect to the OPP in operational matters?

A: Well, certainly not to provide any advice with respect to operational matters. I don't recall ever being apprised, in a detailed way, of operations of the police. There were occasions when I might be given a heads-up where there was a significant police effort with respect to drugs or something of that nature. Usually, I would be given notice that it was going to occur within an hour or something like that, so that at least I wouldn't be caught off guard by the media or by others. In terms of being given advance notice and being given the details of investigations or operational matters, that was not something that I asked for or expected to be informed of.

Q: And how would you define the difference between a policy matter and an operational issue?

A: I always primarily look at the legislation and the regulations and the policy directives that flow out of that and the protocols that were established over the years. So for the most part I would look at policy as being something in writing, something that people could refer to and could hopefully understand and agree upon. In terms of the operational decisions I would think in terms of the numbers of personnel for example that would be assigned to a given matter; the investigative techniques, the approaches made by the police in terms of their independence with respect to making decisions related to their responsibilities; those kinds of issues you would keep your nose out of. I certainly made every effort to keep my nose out of them. I think there were some areas that [were] a bit blurred where I might express an observation or a view which sometimes might have an effect or might not. One of the things that I continued to press over my years as solicitor general was that police officers were spending too much time in their cars. I'm not sure that it had much impact though.

Q: Can you give us some other examples?

A: We ultimately developed minimum standards for policing which were implemented across the province. We certainly wouldn't do this in isolation. It would have been done through extensive consultation with various stakeholders.

Dr Elaine Tondres, Deputy Solicitor General, 1995–1997

Q: With respect to your office, might you have received information of potential conflicts that you might encounter?

A: I called the then-director of Legal Services to my office and indicated to her that before the end of the day, I wanted a briefing from her on anything I needed to do to avoid conflicts of interest. I wanted, in detail, the separation of policy from operations and police. She gave me a very detailed briefing. And what I recall is something like the top ten (10) things to avoid doing. You don't call in the middle of a police investigation; whenever matters are before the courts, the minister is silent. Our briefing notes, she indicated to me, would often be disappointing in the sense that you would say we are familiar with the issue, no comment;

it's before the courts it's at the coroner's office, we can't speak to those matters; that sort of thing.

The commissioner reported directly through me to the minister, so we saw each other on a fairly frequent basis. He was not only the member of the senior management team, [h]e became the chair of my policy committee.

The kinds of conversations that he and I would have had would have been around things like: if we have a 40 per cent cut, where do you see your cuts? We spent a lot of time talking about technology. He was involved, and I led, a number of very important technology projects that had to do with radios and satellites and that sort of thing. We never discussed operations and it was very clear where the line was drawn.

Commissioner Thomas O'Grady (Rtd.), Ontario Provincial Police

Q: With respect to your role as commissioner of the Ontario Provincial Police and the solicitor general, what was your understanding when you became commissioner as to the distinction between your role and that of the solicitor general?

A: The *Police Act* of the day, on the face of it, said that I had the control and management of the Ontario Provincial Police, subject to the direction of the solicitor general. In practice, there was a deputy minister responsible under the solicitor general for operating as a buffer between the commissioner and the solicitor general. Although that did not preclude me from speaking directly to the solicitor general, most of my interaction was with the deputy minister of the day.

The solicitor general could impose general administrative and general policy that would affect the operation of the force and the solicitor general, I felt, was entitled to know in broad terms, the operations of the Ontario Provincial Police, but was not entitled to give any direction whatsoever in the day-to-day operational activities, nor to give any direction as to carrying out of operations. If there were things that were contentious, would gain wide media attention, [or] be a subject of discussion in the legislature, then he had to be informed of what the general action of the OPP was, but not the details of the matter.

Q: Can you give us some examples of policy?

A: Well I suppose the one that sticks in my mind was policy and legislation to allow the use of photo radar. That had been brought in by the previous government. After the arrival of the Conservative government who had campaigned on the issue, that regulation and legislation was changed, and so we no longer could use that technology.

Inspector Ron Fox (now Superintendent), Ontario Provincial Police, Seconded to the Solicitor General of Ontario to Advise on Aboriginal matters

We have included three separate sections from the Ipperwash transcripts related to this seconded police officer: the opening testimony of Inspector Fox; a section of the transcript that includes a recorded conversation between Inspector Fox and Inspector Carson and the cross-examination on that conversation; and, finally, the closing portion of the telephone conversation where Chief Superintendent Coles comes on the phone to warn Fox to be careful of both the amount and timing regarding the passing on of police information to 'them,' meaning government officials.

I was on loan to the ministry. My involvement with the Ontario Provincial Police while I was a special adviser was limited to more administrative matters than operational.

Q: Did you have any active policing responsibilities while you were the special adviser?

A: No, I did not.

Q: Did you continue to be subject to the *Police Services Act* of this province?

A: Yes, I did.

Q: Did you continue to have the duties of a police officer as specified by section 42 of that Act?

A: Yes, I did.

Q: Did the fact that you were working for the solicitor general, but still had duties as a police officer, cause you to be concerned that you could be put in a situation in which your responsibilities to the deputy solicitor general could conflict with your duties as a police officer under the *Police Services Act*?

A: There was a concern, yes.

Q: Were you, in your opinion, ever placed in such a conflict of interest position?

A: No.

Q: What steps did you take to avoid that?

A: I limited my information or information that was made available to me to only that which I might require to function in that position. I stayed away from very direct operational information and I offered no opinions with respect to operational information, how it may be or should be acted on, to those who were in an operational role within the Ontario Provincial Police.

Ron Fox to Inspector Carson

This testimony of Inspector Fox includes part of an edited transcript of a telephone conversation between Inspector Fox and Inspector John Carson, the incident commander for the Ipperwash Park incident. The tape illustrates the close interaction between the police and the political players that was facilitated by his seconded position.

Q: Superintendent Fox, I am going to play for you the recording of this telephone call, which is Exhibit P-428.

RF: Ron Fox.
JC: Hi Ronald, John here.
RF: I just want to let you know what went on at this Inter-ministerial Committee on Aboriginal Issues this morning.
JC: Okay. First of all the Premier's Office had representation there in the form of one Debra Hutton.
RF: Very much [em]powered. Basically the premier has made it clear to

her his position is there'll be no different treatment of people in this situation. In other words, native as opposed to non-native. And the bottom line is, wants them out and you know, was asking well what would the police do in a situation where there wasn't natives. I said well, I mean, you can't compare apples and oranges. I said, you know I come to your house and I plunk myself down and you ask me to leave and I don't. And you call for police intervention. Chances are I don't have Colour of Right for being there. Whether it's actual or perceived. And I said it's a little bit different here. We're talking about land claims and treaties. Well no! So I mean it's our property. And I said yes. By virtue of letters patent that were produced in 1929. But I said I mean these people refer to treaties that go back to pre-Confederation days. So I said, you know I'm not suggesting a course of non-action, but I said my theory has always been make hay slowly. And I said, what has to be done – I mean there's a whole whack of real steps that are in place now and I know are being done.

MNR [Ministry of Natural Resources] by the way, kind of were against getting an enjoining order. Preferring basically to pass it over and say well, you know I mean there's criminal code offences of mischief you know if you're lawful enjoinder, or use of property, trespass. So I very carefully explained to them that you know, under the trespass to property an officer could go serve process, escort somebody to the gate, and then they come back in. And we'll go on forever this way. And I explained the same with the criminal code and the provisions of the *Bail Reform Act* and how release procedures work. And I said quite clearly this is a civil dispute and it has to be adjudicated in a court of law, and the police given sufficient authority to act. So they finally agreed, the consensus is they'll get an enjoining order. And the MNR will provide a large part of the affidavit. But they wondered who they might speak to if they needed some perspective from the police. And I suggested yourself. So, in a nutshell what came up was about the service of this notice last night.

And these people, you know I mean they just get right in the minutiae. I'll tell ya, this whole fuckin' group is on some sort of testosterone high. Then I finally had to get right out and say look. I mean here's the strategy those folk will employ. The women and children will be at the forefront. And I said you got to understand that the provincial police will never shirk their responsibility. But read – their hands will get dirty

– read – so will the government's. And as long as we're prepared for that.

JC: That's right. But I doubt if they are.

RF: Mmmhmm. And let's not lose sight of the fact that this is a civil matter!

JC: That's right. That's right!

Q: Did you form any understanding based on this meeting as to why the premier's office was represented at it?

A: Other than the fact that it's within the Charter of the Interministerial Committee to have representation, no I did not.

Q: All right. So, they certainly had entitlement to be there, the premier's office? Now, based on your attendance, did you form any impression of Ms Hutton in her role as the premier's representative at this meeting?

A: She spoke as if she were the voice of the premier. I believe that's what I would have used in my conversation with John Carson, the word is 'empowered.'

Q: Now, carrying on with the transcripts, the next response is on page 1: 'And the bottom line is, wants them out, and you know, was asking, well, what would the police do in a situation where there wasn't natives. I said, well, I mean, you can't compare apples and oranges.'

Now, what did you intend to convey through this exchange with Ms Hutton?

A: What my intention was, was to bring to the matter at hand what I believed was the necessary complexity, as opposed to the simplicity. And I likened what would be a simple trespass, and I exampled myself going to her home, and being an unwanted guest, being asked to leave, not leaving, and the police had intervention. It would be entirely different if I were to go to someone's home, but I felt that there was a right and entitlement for me to be there. Again, that's something that any police officer would have a very difficult time trying to adjudicate.

Q: All right. Now, did Ms Hutton advise that she had personally spoken with Premier Harris in advance of this meeting; that he had communicated to her what his position was in the handling of the Park occupation?

A: The way she spoke, I can only assume that she had communication with the premier because she was speaking in his voice, if you will.

Q: All right, but did she actually – said she had been briefed or did you infer it?

A: No, she did not use those words that I recall, but she used the phrase: he wants this.

Q: Certainly she gave you the impression that she was speaking on behalf of the premier at this meeting?

A: That was my impression, yes.

Q: All right. And based on this exchange that we have just reviewed did you form any views as to what the premier's position regarding aboriginal land and treaty rights amounted to, in relation to the occupation at Ipperwash Provincial Park?

A: Once again, I don't see that the issue of aboriginal or treaty rights was taken into consideration. It was a dispute over property without the benefit of having any understanding, or at least acknowledging that there may be those with other interests in it. There was no response from Ms Hutton with respect to whether she understood or accepted.

Q: Now, can you tell me then what it was you were reacting to when you chose to characterize a group within the IMC [Interministerial Committee] as being on some sort of testosterone high?

A: My characterization there was that it would move forward and it was speaking to force. The force, generally, and I suppose, more pronounced in the male of the species and hence my comment. It was that there was no consideration for other ancillary thoughts, that one must move ahead solely on the fact that the property is owned and the document well titled and there was no other consideration to be had. And it was quite forcefully, I would suggest, put within that meeting.

Q: And you indicated that you said that, you know: 'Their hands will get dirty – read – so will the Government's.' What did you mean when you said that: 'Their hands will get dirty – read – so will the Government's.'

A: Well, again, it's rhetorical comment on my part and I think it was received in like and kind by Inspector Carson. The reality of it is going back to what I said. I said the strategy these folk will employ, the women and children will be in the forefront, and that comes from my personal experience. And I'm not suggesting it's right or wrong, I'm suggesting that's what occurs. For a simple trespass, if people are very strong in their conviction to be in a particular place, we will have to go in, if that was the decision of the police, and use force. In doing so, there is a good chance that someone will be injured. If the police do that we, in particular the Ontario Provincial Police, are a part of the government of Ontario. So by virtue of the activities that the police may undertake, the government, too, would be seen in that same light.

Q: And so, were you concerned that there would be a public perception that the actions of the OPP would be seen to be the actions of the government?

A: I think the perception comes from only this reality, that the OPP is a part of the Government of Ontario.

Q: But was this a public perception you were concerned about?

A: Well, perhaps it's a public perception and yes, that's always of concern, I think, to any practising police officer. More to the point, my concern was one for the safety of certainly the people who were in the park and I know that my concern would also be for the members of the Ontario Provincial Police that were responding.

Chief Superintendent Chris Coles (Rtd.), Ontario Provincial Police, Commander of Western Region, 1992–1996

Following the conversation between Fox and Carson, Chief Superintendent Coles came on the phone.

Chief: Hi, Ron.

Fox: Hi, Chief.

Chief: I've got a concern that we want to be careful what we're doing, that we don't give them, the people you're talking to, that we don't give them the information too fast. The problem with that, Ron, is that if you're not careful, you're going to run the issue there, as opposed to myself and the commissioner running it here. And so we better be careful. You're going to be the fastest source of information they've got, and now then we're going to end up in it – we're going to end up running it politically, and I don't want that. It's dangerous, if you think about it.

Gwen Boniface, Commissioner, Ontario Provincial Police, 1998–2006

Q: Now, one of the things that we've heard some evidence about was with respect to the command post and local politicians, provincial politicians being in the command post. What, if anything, has the OPP done with respect to that issue?

A: Well, we've had lots of discussion on it, and we will be preparing a policy that speaks to discouraging politicians in the command post. I think that there's always information that is valuable. I think the difficulty is it's best that it not be discussed or received in the Command Post itself. The training, as such, is to try to restrict it to police officers only, for two reasons. One is to keep the information in the proper containment, but secondly to alleviate confusion as people come and go. So it is quite clear that if you have people who need to speak to the incident commander or someone within the command post, then they should leave to be able to do that and do that off site.

Q: And the policy with respect to politicians in the command post that's being considered, are parameters being considered as to when that would be permitted or when it would not be permitted?

A: Our general principle will be it would not be permitted. But I think as you work, particularly in our rural communities, there's an ongoing relationship that exists by virtue of the type of communities we police. So our position would be that we would not have politicians in the command post, but obviously you would have to ensure that was communicated clearly so you don't get someone knocking on the door. You make your arrangements to meet off site.

Q: And I take it that, like all rules, there have to be exceptions, and presumably your policy will deal with that?

A: Yes. The incident commander would be required to explain why he or she would choose otherwise. I think that it is a matter of communicating clearly to the person who's requesting the meeting and to work from there.

Q: Municipally a chief of police will report to a police services board, right?

A: That's correct. The OPP after 1998 is required to have police service boards.

Q: And they're required to submit to their oversight in a manner of speaking.

A: The detachment commander would report to the police service board.

Q: Are [local] police services boards entitled to give orders, policy or otherwise, to detachment commanders?

A: There is local policy that can be established in terms of priorities for the community and such like.

Q: In circumstances where the commissioner makes an order to a detachment commander, that order would override any direction a police services board gave that detachment commander; is that not true?

A: They have a limit in terms of the oversight.

Q: I only ask you that because I want to be clear that while you have to work with police services boards and you're mandated to legislatively work with them, the truth is, they don't represent a civilian oversight body over the OPP, for example, the way police services boards do over municipal police services.

Marcel Beaubien, MPP for Lambton-Kent-Middlesex, 1995–2003

Q: Describe your relationship with the local OPP in 1995?

A: Well, at that particular point in time, I knew probably 90 per cent maybe 100 per cent of the officers in the detachment because we played ball together, we played hockey together. Some of them were clients. Some were personal friends and we ran into each other pretty well on a daily basis. Petrolia is not a very large town so if you stop at a coffee shop, chances are you might see somebody you know.

Q: Did you have any occasion to raise local constituency concerns with Staff Sergeant Lacroix, prior to September of '95?

A: Well, yes, there was the West Ipperwash issue which had been an ongoing situation for probably a couple of years by the time we were elected. There were reports from some of my constituents that they were being harassed, threatened. Some of them were complaining that the level of policing provided by the OPP was not adequate. So, I certainly made contact with Staff Sergeant Lacroix to get his side of the story whether the proper policing was in place.

Q: Upon becoming an MPP, did you participate in any orientation program at Queen's Park?

A: Yeah. There was a brief. I think it was a couple of hours one afternoon but it certainly was not an extensive briefing. We probably received written material but, you know I can't recall.

Q: Do you have any recollection of being specifically briefed on the concept of the division between police and government?

A: No.

Q: Did you have any understanding of that concept when you became MPP in June of 1995?

A: I think I had a fairly good concept of what the role of politician in relationship to a police officer or police department. I sat on a police commission for nine years, I attended meetings, I attended different conventions whereby the role was the topic. My view of it was quite clear that, as a politician, you look after the policy; when it comes to policing matters, you leave it to the police to do it.

Q: Just so that we understand what you mean by that concept, what do you mean by policing matters, non-interference with policing matters?

A: Well, for instance, if you have a policy [which sets] the speeding limit [at] a hundred kilometres, and if I'm doing a hundred and twenty I'm breaking the law. It's up to the officer to decide, you know, whether he's or she's going to give me a ticket, a warning, or what. It's not up to me to say I don't deserve a ticket or not. If I broke the law, it's up to the officer to decide what he or she is going to do. Very simplistic, but I think that's as simple as I can put it.

Q: And to your knowledge, were there any formal protocols or rules in place which set out, if you will, the do's and don't's of police-MPP contact?

A: Not that I'm aware of.

Q: Okay. Were you aware of any written rules which prevented any and all communications between MPPs and local police with respect to ongoing policing operations?

A: Not that I'm aware of.

Q: Do you have any understanding of any limits or restrictions, if any, on the content of communications which an MPP could have with police?

A: Not that I'm aware of.

NOTES

1 We see a similar issue arise in the *Analysis and Recommendations Relating to the Maher Arar Inquiry*. Ministerial directives were deemed to be essential but there was disagreement as to when the directives referred to 'policy guidance' versus more day-to-day enforcement decisions. See pages 322

and 330 of the *Report of the Events Relating to Maher Arar: Analysis and Recommendations, 2006.*
2 Anne McChesney, *Ministerial Control and the Ontario Provincial Police: A Discussion Paper* (Toronto: Legal Services Branch, Ministry of the Solicitor General, 1991).

Appendix

IPPERWASH DISCUSSION PAPER
GOVERNMENT/POLICE RELATIONS

IPPERWASH INQUIRY

Ontario

COMMISSION D'ENQUÊTE SUR IPPERWASH

250 Yonge Street, Suite 2910, P.O. Box 30
Toronto ON M5B 2L7

Tel: 416 314-9200

Fax: 416 314-9393

Web: www.ipperwashinquiry.ca

Bureau 2910, 250, rue Yonge, C.P. 30
Toronto ON M5B 2L7

Tél. :   416 314-9200

Téléc. :   416 314-9393

Internet : www.ipperwashinquiry.ca

MEMORANDUM

TO: Ipperwash Inquiry
            Parties with Part Two Standing
FROM: Nye Thomas
            Director, Policy and Research
            Ipperwash Inquiry
DATE: June 2006
RE: Discussion Paper on Police/Government Relations

1. INTRODUCTION

This is the first of three short discussion papers on major policy areas being considered in Part Two of the Ipperwash Inquiry. This paper considers the relationship between police and government and the scope of police independence from improper governmental influence. The Inquiry is also preparing discussion papers on policing and

Aboriginal peoples (including policing occupations) and Treaty and Aboriginal rights.

The purpose of this paper is to provide parties with notice of the issues that Part Two is considering on this subject. The paper also sets out a series of questions that are likely to arise in our deliberations. **Parties are encouraged to consider some or all of these questions and the issues raised in the discussion papers in their written and oral submissions.**

Neither the Commissioner, commission staff, nor the Inquiry's Research Advisory Committee have reached any conclusions on these issues. The Inquiry's policy staff and Research Advisory Committee have, however, provisionally identified a series of issues and questions that are likely to inform our analysis. The Commissioner will not be considering final recommendations on this or any other Part Two topic until the evidence is completed and all submissions have been received.

This discussion paper does not include references to the factual evidence or testimony heard at the Part One hearings. This paper will, however, discuss several policy topics or issues that have been discussed at the hearings. This is because many of the legal, policy and practical issues discussed at the hearings have been discussed in previous Inquiries, reports, and articles on this subject.

This discussion paper does not purport to address every relevant issue on this subject. Moreover, the issues and questions discussed here are neither exhaustive nor fixed. They are, rather a summary of major issues and questions that we have identified so far. We encourage parties to discuss or recommend other issues or questions we have not identified.

The focus of this paper is on provincial policy and processes.

2. THE IMPORTANCE OF POLICE/GOVERNMENT RELATIONS

The Ipperwash Inquiry is the fifth major Canadian public inquiry in the last 25 years to consider police/government relations.[1] The issue

---

1 In addition to the Ipperwash Inquiry, this issue was discussed at the APEC Inquiry, the Donald Marshall Inquiry, and the McDonald Commission. The issue is likely to be discussed at the Arar Inquiry as well.

has also been discussed at length in the United Kingdom, New Zealand, and Australia.[2]

The police/government relationship establishes the parameters and expectations of government involvement in policing policy and operations. The relationship is important because fundamental democratic principles and values are at stake. Police and policing are amongst the most basic functions of any state. Canadian democracy depends upon the police to fulfill their responsibilities equally, fairly, professionally, and without partisan or inappropriate political influence.

Yet the police/government debate is not simply about preventing police from becoming 'a law unto themselves' or inappropriate government influence. It is also about accountability and transparency for police and government decision-making.

Given this background, the Ipperwash Inquiry should attempt to develop recommendations that address both police and politicians/governments. The Inquiry may also attempt to provide guidelines for procedures to govern police-governmental relations generally and with respect to policing of Aboriginal protests and other public order events and crises. Finally, the Inquiry's should also presumably attempt to transcend individual governments, ministers, civil servants and police officials in order to accommodate a variety of different situations, political philosophies, and personal styles.

3. INDEPENDENCE, ACCOUNTABILITY AND TRANSPARENCY

The Report of the Independent Commission on Policing On Northern Ireland (the 'Patten Report') discussed the relationship between police independence, accountability and transparency at length.[3]

The Patten Report emphasized that while police should sometimes make decisions free from external direction 'no public official,

---

2 See Prof. Stenning's background paper for the Inquiry, *The Idea of the Political 'Independence' of the Police: International Interpretations and Experiences*, posted at www.ipperwashinquiry.ca/policy_part/relations/crp.html.

3 United Kingdom, Independent Commission on Policing for Northern Ireland (Rt. Hon. C. Patten, Chair), *A New Beginning: Policing in Northern Ireland* (London: 1999).

including a chief of police, can be said to be "independent"' at least in the sense of being 'exempted from inquiry or review after the event by anyone.'[4] The Patten Report also discussed the importance of police accountability and the types of police accountability:

> In a democracy, policing, in order to be effective, must be based on consent across the community. The community recognizes the legitimacy of the policing task, confers authority on police personnel in carrying out their role in policing and actively supports them. Consent is not unconditional, but depends on proper accountability, and the police should be accountable in two senses – the 'subordinate or obedient' sense and the 'explanatory and cooperative' sense.

> In the subordinate sense, police are employed by the community to provide a service and the community should have the means to ensure that it gets the service it needs and that its money is spent wisely. Police are also subordinate to the law, just as other citizens are subordinate to the law, and there should be robust arrangements to ensure that this is so, and seen to be so. In the explanatory and cooperate sense, public and police must communicate with each other and work in partnerships, both maintain trust between them and to ensure effective policing, because policing is not a task of the police alone.

> It follows there are many aspects to accountability. There is democratic accountability, by which the elected representatives of the community tell the police what sort of service they want from the police, and hold the police accountability for delivering it. There is transparency, by which the community is kept informed, and can ask questions, about what the police are doing and why. There is legal accountability, by which the police are held to account if they misuse their powers. There is financial accountability, by which the police service is ... held to account for its deliver of value for public money. And there is internal accountability, by which officers are accountable within a police organization. All of these aspects must be addressed if full accountability is to be achieved, and if policing is to be effective, efficient, fair and impartial.[5]

---

4 *Ibid* at 33.
5 *Ibid* at 22.

The Patten Report also noted the important relationship between transparency and accountability:

> People need to know and understand what their police are doing and why. This is important if the police are to command public confidence and active cooperation. Secretive policing arrangements run counter not only to the principles of a democratic society but also to the achievement of fully effective policing.[6]

4. WHAT ARE WE CONCERNED ABOUT?

The Inquiry's policy staff and Research Advisory Committee have provisionally identified several issues or questions in this area. Simply put, these are the policy problems we have been grappling with.

To start, we are obviously concerned with ensuring the professionalism of policing and preventing partisan policing or inappropriate government influence. We are also obviously concerned about police becoming 'a law unto themselves,' free from democratic input or control on appropriate issues.

We are further concerned about the accountability of both police and government decision-making. It appears that neither the statutory, constitutional, common law, nor policy rules in Ontario today clearly or adequately define the roles and responsibilities of the police and government respecting government intervention in, or influence over, certain kinds of police decision-making. Key concepts – including 'police independence,' 'policy' and 'operations' – are not defined in any statute, regulation or formal policy that we are aware of.

It also appears that the transparency of decision-making could be improved. Indeed, the importance of transparency cannot be underestimated. Transparency is necessary to hold decision-makers accountable.

Moreover, it appears that there is little agreement about which police activities fall within the ambit of police independence. Professor Stenning has written that there is 'very little clarity or consensus among politicians, senior RCMP officers, jurists ... commissions of inquiry, academics, or other commentators either about exactly what

---

6 *Ibid* at 25.

'police independence' comprises or about its practical implications ...'[7] As a result, the relationship can be confused or misunderstood, particularly during a crisis.

Nor is it clear *who* has the right to intervene in police activities. Both the *RCMP Act* and the Ontario *Police Services Act* give their respective Solicitor Generals the authority to direct the RCMP and OPP. Nonetheless, it appears that Ministers and officials other than the Solicitor General sometimes give police direction or guidance during specific incidents. This situation may challenge both the statutory provisions and ministerial accountability.

Finally, it appears that little comparatively little analysis has been given to police/government relations in the context of either public order policing or policing Aboriginal peoples. It may be that new or different rules are required in these situations.

To be fair, it is unlikely that everyone agrees that structural or systemic reforms are necessary. Many people likely believe that the most important safeguard in the police/government relationship is the personal integrity and professionalism of the individuals involved. They may also be skeptical of complex or costly institutional reforms that purport to clarify the real world of police/government relations. Or they may simply believe that practical experience has demonstrated that the existing system works well. These are important objections, particularly when voiced by observers with years of practical experience.

5. CURRENT LAW AND THEORY ON POLICE INDEPENDENCE

'Police independence' has a long and unsettled legal and theoretical history that we will not repeat here.[8] What follows below is a brief summary of the major legal and policy reference points in this debate.

a. The Ontario *Police Services Act*

The current statutory framework governing police/government relations in Ontario and the ambit of political independence is the *Police Services Act*.

---

7 Stenning at 5.
8 *Ibid* at 4–10.

Section 17(2) of the *Act* states: 'Subject to the Solicitor General's direction, the Commissioner has the general control and administration of the Ontario Provincial Police and the employees connected with it.' Section 3(2)(j) of the *Act* also gives the Solicitor General the authority to '[I] ssue directives and guidelines respecting policy matters.' These sections are similar to provisions in the *RCMP Act*.[9]

Moreover, neither the Act nor its regulations define 'police independence,' 'operational decisions,' or the scope of 'directives and guidelines.' Professor Roach concludes '[o]ne of the reasons for controversy and confusion about police independence in Canada is the general absence of clear statutory definitions of the concept.'[10]

The *Act* appears to create different standards for police independence as between the OPP and municipal police in Ontario. Section 31(4) of the *Act* says that local police boards will not direct the Chief of Police 'with respect to specific operational decisions or with respect to the day to day operations of the police'. There is no equivalent limitation on the provincial Solicitor General with respect to the OPP. As a result, the *Act* may give the provincial Solicitor General broad powers to intervene in OPP policy *and* operations.

b. *Campbell and Shirose (1999)*[11]

R. v. Campbell and Shirose is the Supreme Court of Canada's most extensive discussion of police independence. The case concerned whether the RCMP was covered by Crown public interest immunity when they conducted a reverse sting in a drug operation. Binnie J. rejected the claim of Crown immunity stating for the unanimous Court that:

A police officer investigating a crime is not acting as a government functionary or as an agent of anybody. He or she occupies a public

---

9 *Royal Canadian Mounted Police Act* R.S.C. 1985 c.R-10. Section 5 of the *Act* reads: '5. (1) The Governor in Council may appoint an officer, to be known as the Commissioner of the Royal Canadian Mounted Police, who, under the direction of the Minister, has the control and management of the Force and all matters connected therewith.'

10 See Professor Kent Roach's background paper for the Inquiry, *Four Models of Police-Government Relationships*, at pg. 8. This paper is posted at www.ipperwashinquiry.ca/policy_part/relations/crp.html.

11 *R. v. Campbell* [1999] 1 S.C.R. 565.

office initially defined by the common law and subsequently set out in various statutes.[12]

Binnie J. noted that the police 'perform a myriad of functions apart from the investigation of crimes' and that

[S]ome of these functions bring the RCMP into a closer relationship to the Crown than others ... [I]n this appeal, however, we are concerned only with the status of an RCMP officer in the course of a criminal investigation, and in that regard the police are independent of the control of the executive government.'[13]

The Court declared that the principle of police independence from the Crown in the exercise of its law enforcement functions 'underpins the rule of law' which 'is one of the "fundamental and organizing principles of the Constitution".'[14] Binnie J. further explained that:

While for certain purposes the Commissioner of the RCMP reports to the Solicitor General, the Commissioner is not to be considered a servant or agent of the government while engaged in a criminal investigation. The Commissioner is not subject to political direction. Like every other police officer similarly engaged, he is answerable to the law and, no doubt, to his conscience.[15]

---

12 *Ibid* at paragraph 27.
13 *Ibid* at paragraph 29.
14 *Ibid* at paragraph 18.
15 *Ibid* at para 33. Justice Binnie then cited Lord Denning's famous comments in *R. v. Metropolitan Police ex parte Blackburn* [1968] Q.B. 116 at 135–136 to the effect that: 'I have no hesitation in holding that, like every constable in the land, [the Commissioner of the London Police] should be, and is, independent of the executive. He is not subject to the orders of the Secretary of State, save that under the Police Act, 1964, the Secretary of State can call upon him to give a report, or to retire in the interests of efficiency. I hold it to be the duty of the Commissioner of Police of the Metropolis, as it is of every chief constable, to enforce the law of the land. He must take steps so to post his men that crimes may be detected; and that honest citizens may go about their affairs in peace. He must decide whether or no suspected persons are to be prosecuted; and, if need be, bring the prosecution or see that it is brought. But in all these things he is not the servant of anyone, save of the law itself. No Minister of the Crown can tell him that he must, or must not, keep observation on this place or that; or that he must, or must not, prosecute this man or that one. Nor can any police authority tell him so. The responsibility for law enforcement lies on him. He is answerable to the law and to the law alone.' *Blackburn* effectively establishes one end of the spectrum in the debate on police independence.

Campbell and Shirose suggests that the core of police independence is the exercise of law enforcement discretion and the conduct of criminal investigations in individual cases. The case does not, however, consider the outer limits of police independence from government. Nor does it address public order policing.

c. Other Reports and Developments

i. The McDonald Commission (1981)[16]

The McDonald Commission concluded that responsible Ministers should have extensive authority to direct, comment upon, or be advised of a wide range of police activities, including areas traditionally considered police 'operations.' The Commission defended Ministerial involvement on the basis of democratic principles:

> We take it to be axiomatic that in a democratic state the police must never be allowed to become a law unto themselves. Just as our form of Constitution dictates that the armed forces must be subject to civilian control, so too must police forces operate in obedience to governments responsible to legislative bodies composed of elected representatives.[17]

The Commission rejected any distinction between 'policy' and 'operations' that would insulate 'the day to day operations of the Security Service' from Ministerial review and comment. To do so would result 'in whole areas of ministerial responsibility being neglected under the misapprehension that they fall into the category of "operations" and are thus outside the Minister's purview.'[18] As a result, the Commission argued that democratic accountability required that the responsible Minister should have a right to be:

> ... informed of any operational matter, even one involving an individual case, if it raises an important question of public policy. In such cases, [the Minister] may give guidance to the [RCMP]

---

16 *Commission of Inquiry Concerning Certain Activities of the RCMP Freedom and Security under the Law* (Ottawa: Supply and Services, 1981).
17 *Ibid* at 1005–1006.
18 *Ibid* at 868.

Commissioner and express to the Commissioner the government's
view of the matter, but he should have no power to give *direction* to
the Commissioner.[19]

The Commission did not reject police independence entirely. It
concluded that police should be independent from government only
in the field of criminal process.

ii. The APEC Inquiry (1999)[20]

The APEC Inquiry considered allegations that the Prime Minister's
Office interfered with RCMP security operations. After considering the
issue at length, Mr. Justice Hughes recommended that:

• When the RCMP is performing law enforcement functions (investigation, arrest and prosecution) they are entirely independent of the
  federal government and answerable only to the law.

• When the RCMP are performing their other functions, they are not
  entirely independent but are accountable to the federal government
  through the Solicitor General of Canada or such other branch of
  government as Parliament may authorize.

• In all situations, the RCMP is accountable to the law and the courts.
  Even when performing functions that are subject to government
  direction, officers are required by the *RCMP Act* to respect and
  uphold the law at all times.

• The RCMP is solely responsible for weighing security requirements
  against the Charter rights of citizens. Their conduct will violate the
  Charter if they give inadequate weight to Charter rights. The fact
  that they may have been following the directions of political masters

---

19 *Ibid* at 1013 (emphasis in original).
20 Commission Interim Report Following a Public Inquiry into Complaints that took
    place in connection with the demonstrations during the Asia Pacific Economic
    Cooperation Conference in Vancouver (Ottawa: Commission of Public Complaints,
    RCMP, 23 July 2001). The APEC Inquiry was established under the public
    complaints provisions of the *RCMP Act* to consider the treatment of protestors
    during an international summit held at the University of British Columbia in 1997.

will be no defense if they fail to do that.

- An RCMP member acts inappropriately if he or she submits to government direction that is contrary to law. Not even the Solicitor General may direct the RCMP to unjustifiably infringe Charter rights, as such directions would be unlawful.[21]

Justice Hughes restricted police independence to the core functions of criminal investigations. He also recommended that the RCMP 'request statutory codification of the nature and extent of police independence from government' with respect not only to 'existing common law principles regarding law enforcement' but also 'the provision of and responsibility for delivery of security services at public order events.'[22] He did not explain whether public order policing was within the zone of police independence.

The APEC Report appears to suggest that the Charter may expand the ambit of police independence. Justice Hughes stated that 'weighing security requirements against the Charter rights of citizens' is exclusively a matter for the police and that they should refuse to follow 'the directions of political masters' if the result is to violate the Charter.

iii. The Patten Inquiry (1999)

As noted earlier, the Patten Report concluded that 'no public official, including a chief of police, can be said to be "independent" at least in the sense of being 'exempted from inquiry or review after the event by anyone.'[23]

Patten recommended replacing the phrases 'police independence' and 'operational independence' with 'police operational responsibility.' He argued that 'police operational responsibility' was clearer and more consistent with police accountability.[24]

---

21 *Ibid* at 10.4.
22 *Ibid* at 31.3.1.
23 See footnote 4.
24 *Patten* at 32.

Patten also recommended that the policing board should be able to require the Chief Constable to report on any operational matter and to ask the police complaints body also to investigate, including public order events. Its report also stressed that both the policing board and the police should be as transparent as possible.

iv. The Donald Marshall Commission (1989)[25]

The Commission into Donald Marshall's Wrongful Conviction also examined two cases where Nova Scotia cabinet members had been the subject of RCMP criminal investigations, but were not criminally charged.

The Marshall Commission, like the McDonald Commission before it, limited police independence to the process of criminal investigation. The Marshall Commission addressed the balance between account-ability and independence by recommending the creation of a Director of Public Prosecutions who would ordinarily be independent from the Attorney General but could be subject to written directives that would be published in the Gazette. This model was subsequently adopted in Nova Scotia.[26]

Professor Roach discusses the Nova Scotia model in his Inquiry background paper. He identified it a basis for a democratic model of police government relations because it respects the core of police independence while allowing the responsible Minister to intervene in policing matters in a transparent and accountable manner.[27]

v. Ministerial Directives

A number of governments have issued detailed ministerial directives governing how police and other enforcement agencies perform their work. They include directives that establish rules for activities arguably within the core zone of police independence – criminal

---

25 *Royal Commission on the Donald Marshall Jr. Prosecution* (Halifax: Queens Printer, 1989).
26 *Public Prosecutions Act* S.N.S. 1990 c.s21 as amended by S.N.S. 1999 c.16.
27 Roach at 43–44.

investigations. Directives of this sort are the 'policies of operations' described years earlier by the McDonald Commission.

The federal Solicitor General has issued directives to the RCMP. These directives address the following topics: information sharing agreements between the RCMP and other agencies; RCMP investigations into sensitive sectors such as unions and academia including policy guidance that the RCMP not interfere with the 'free flow and exchange of ideas normally associated with the academic milieu'; and requiring the RCMP to inform the Minister of investigations that are likely to give rise to controversy.[28]

The RCMP has publicly acknowledged that these directives establish a policy framework for areas of RCMP activities requiring clarification by the political executive; provide the RCMP with standards in selected areas of policing activity for achieving a balance between individual rights and effective policing practice; and inform the public about the character of supervision provided by the political executive to the RCMP.[29]

Ontario's Interim Enforcement Policy can also be seen as a form of Ministerial Directive. Subject to some enumerated exceptions, it requires approval of an MNR Assistant Deputy Minister before planned enforcement procedures including search warrants are undertaken with respect to the exercise of Aboriginal harvesting rights. It also provides for consultation with Aboriginal Chiefs before decisions are made to proceed with charges.[30] This directive provides policy guidance and procedures to govern the exercise of law enforcement discretion.

vi. Other International Developments

Professor Philip Stenning's background paper for the Inquiry discusses legislation and policy reform proposals in the United Kingdom, Australia, and New Zealand. Professor Stenning demonstrates that

---

28 Arar Commission *The RCMP and National* Security, December 2004 at 41–43.
29 RCMP submissions to the Arar Commission February 2005 at 27.
30 Interim Enforcement Policy amended October, 2005.

these questions are being asked in other jurisdictions as well. For example, legislation in some Australian states also contemplates Ministerial directives to the police. The legislative proposals introduced in New Zealand in 2001 represent the current outer limit of legal and policy reform in this area.[31] It is important to note, however, that the New Zealand proposal was recently withdrawn.

QUESTIONS FOR DISCUSSION

6. GUIDING PRINCIPLES

The Inquiry will likely begin by identifying several core principles to use as reference points for its analysis and potential recommendations in this area. The principles we have provisionally identified include:

- Ensuring the professionalism of police operations and non-partisan policing;
- Promoting accountable and transparent police decision-making;
- Promoting accountable and transparent government decision-making;
- Ensuring consistency with Canadian political traditions of Parliamentary democracy;
- Promoting clear and understandable lines of authority;
- Respecting the practical demands and operations of police and government, particularly in relation to the policing of protests.
- Respecting treaty and Aboriginal rights and the rule of law;

This is a long list. That said, the most difficult question for the Inquiry is likely to be how to balance competing principles, not simply to identify them. For example, it is sometimes argued that non-partisan policing requires 'buffers' to ensure a structural separation of politicians and police. This is part of the rationale for police service boards. The principle of non-partisan policing may also explain certain reporting or administrative relationships within government ministries. On the other hand, some people likely believe that 'buffers'

---

31 Prof. Stenning's paper includes a detailed analysis of developments in all three jurisdictions.

are unsound because they hamper Ministerial accountability and/or democratic input into police activities.

> *Question 1: Are these principles appropriate to guide the Inquiry's analysis and recommendations on police/government relations? Or, should there be others and what should they be?*

7. SCOPE OF POLICE DECISION-MAKING

a. Policy And Operations

What is appropriate scope of police decision-making? When does the government have the right to become involved?

The *municipal* provisions of the Ontario *Police Services Act* statute reflect the conventional theory of police/government relations in which police have independent authority for 'operations' and governments have authority to direct 'policy.' This theory is based, no doubt, upon fairly straightforward ideas about the appropriate balance between police professionalism/expertise for operations versus the need for democratic input and control of public policy.

As noted earlier, the *Act* does not explicitly prohibit the provincial Solicitor General from intervening in OPP operations. Nevertheless, it is likely that most provincial policy makers believe the policy/operations distinction applies to the OPP as well.

Patten, of course, believed that the phrases 'police independence' and 'operational independence' were themselves misleading. He preferred the phrase 'police operational responsibility.'

One important benefit of the policy/operations distinction is that it provides decision-makers with an apparent bright line demarking where police independence ends and permissible government intervention begins. The analytical problem is that 'policy' issues are not always clear and that policy issues can arise for the first time in the context of an ongoing operation. Moreover, a definitive definition of 'policy' and 'operations' may be both unwise and/or impossible. The Patten Report concluded that:

One of the most difficult issues we have considered is the question of 'operational independence.' Some respondents urged us to define operational independence, or at least to define the powers and responsibilities of the police ... We have consulted extensively in several countries, talking to both police and to those who are responsible for holding them accountable. The overwhelming advice is that it is important to allow a chief constable sufficient flexibility to perform his or her functions and exercise his or her responsibilities, but difficult if not impossible to define the full scope of a police officer's duties.[32]

It is difficult to use simple distinctions to guide decision-making in absence of understanding what values, interests or objectives the words 'policy' and 'operations' are intended to represent. As a result, the Inquiry may want to identify criteria that assist police and policy-makers to distinguish policy and operational issues. For example, an 'operational' issue could become a 'policy' issue when it affects constitutional rights, affects third parties or issues not directly in-volved in the situation/issue, raises interjurisdictional issues, sets a precedent for similar operations in the future, or where operational decision-makers do not have existing policies or protocols to guide them.

An alternative, but complementary, approach would be to encourage governments to issue transparent 'policies of operations' or to give the Minister or the police the option of requiring that any policy direction be written down so as to enhance transparency and accountability.

The Inquiry may want to identify a potential range of police activities in which governments should have the authority to become involved. Given our mandate, however, our analysis should perhaps focus on public order policing and whether or not this activity is within the zone of police independence. It may of course be true that some, but not all, public order policing is within that zone. Some public order events may raise important public policy questions because of their cost, effect on intergovernmental relations, effect on communities or third parties, or their effect as long-term precedents.

---

32 *Patten* at 32.

Aboriginal protests, occupations, and blockades are, of course, a crucial category of public order events that may inevitably raise public policy questions, particularly where a colour of right, treaty right, or other Aboriginal right is alleged.

It may be that 'policy' and 'operations' will always be fluid concepts, incapable of precise definition. If so, transparency and accountability for decision-making would appear to be crucial, no matter what definitions are used.

Question 2: Is it advisable to define police 'independence' definitively?

Question 3: In which areas should police have 'independent' decision-making authority? What criteria may assist decision-makers determine if an issue is 'policy' or 'operational?'

Question 4: Do Aboriginal and/or other public order events raise 'policy' issues in which governments can and should intervene?

Question 5: Should governments have the right to issue directions in 'policy' areas outside the core area of police activities in criminal investigations?

Question 6: Should governments have the right to intervene in the 'policies of operations?'

Question 7: Is the phrase 'police operational responsibility' preferable to 'police independence' and 'operational independence?'

b. Direction and Guidance

The McDonald Commission recommended that in some circumstances it was appropriate for government to provide the police with *guidance*, but not *directions* on policy and/or operational matters. This might occur when a government official says that he or she wants something to happen, but that they are not directing the police to do it. Some have criticized this distinction as untenable or impractical in the 'real' world, especially in the absence of a consensus about police independence. It is also not clear how governments can be made accountable for 'guidance' they may give to the police.

> Question 8:   Should governments have the right to give non-binding advice to police on operational matters? If so, how can this 'guidance' be made transparent or governments made accountable?

c. Accountability for Police Operations

The McDonald Commission concluded that the responsible Minister should always have a right to be informed of any operational matter, even one involving an individual case, if it raises an important question of public policy. The Patten Report similarly recommended in almost every case the policing board should be able to require a report from the Chief Constable even with respect to operational matters.

> Question 9:   Should governments have the right to be informed 'of any operational matter, even one involving an individual case, if it raises an important question of public policy?'

8. INSTITUTIONAL STRUCTURES AND PROCESSES

Most writers and reports on police independence doubt the ability of existing institutions to ensure accountability and transparency for either police or government decisions especially in crisis situations. That said, the Inquiry must be mindful of the practical realities of modern public administration. We presumably will have to be convinced that any new structure or process meets both our substantive recommendations and is workable and practical. What follows below is a high-level summary and analysis of some of the key questions that the Inquiry may address.

a. Current Accountability Mechanisms

The police are subject to disciplinary and civil actions and criminal prosecutions for their actions while responsible Ministers are subject to questioning in the legislature and the media and civil law suits, access to information requests and complaints to the Ombudsman or the human rights commission. The province has also just introduced new police complaints legislation. A fundamental question will be to decide if these mechanisms are sufficient to meet our substantive policy recommendations.

> *Question 10: Do current structures or processes ensure accountable and transparent decision-making by the police and government on police/government relations?*

b. Codifying Police Independence

The Inquiry will have to consider if and where its substantive recommendations should be codified. If so, where? The *Police Services Act*, regulations, ministry policies?

> *Question 11: Should police independence be codified? If so, where?*

c. Ministerial Accountability and *Police Services Act*

The plain language of the current *Police Services Act* in Ontario gives the provincial Solicitor General the authority to represent the government to the police. The Act also makes the Solicitor General accountable for the actions of the police to the public and legislature. This structure is consistent with the principle of ministerial accountability.

Does this structure reflect the realities of modern government? Professors Roach and Sossin in their papers for the inquiry have both pointed the need to consider the growing importance of central institutions in government and the challenges they present to traditional understandings of Ministerial responsibility. It could be argued that in its emphasis on Ministerial responsibility, the Ontario *Police Services Act* does not accord with the realities of modern Canadian governments.

The issue arises because ministers or officials *other* than the Solicitor General appear to be often involved in policing policy or directions, particularly during a crisis or operation. Does this challenge the legitimacy of the existing statutory arrangements and the principle of Ministerial accountability? At a minimum, it is clear that these officials should be bound by the same limits on government intervention as the Solicitor General.

Interministerial committees are an obvious and practical tool for managing issues or crises that involve more than one government ministry or agencies. What is the relationship between an inter-ministerial committee and the role and authority given to the Solicitor General by the *Police Services Act*? The composition of an inter-ministerial committee is an important issue. A committee of Deputy Ministers is clearly different than a committee of more junior government officials. A committee that combines political staff and civil servants is different again.

To what extent do policing issues involving Aboriginal people justify a different approach to the way that the government interacts with the police? Professor Gordon Christie discuses some of these issues in his background paper for the Inquiry. In particular, he discusses the role of central institutions with respect to Aboriginal affairs, the role of Ministry of Natural Resources officials who have some police powers and issues of Aboriginal and treaty rights.[33]

Question 12:   *Assuming the principle of ministerial accountability remains sound, are the existing provisions of the Police Services Act sufficient to protect and promote Ministerial accountability?*

Question 13:   *Should there be special rules governing non-Solicitor-General officials?*

Question 14:   *Do policing issues involving Aboriginal peoples justify unique police/government rules? If so, what are they?*

The Solicitor General and the Attorney General may have independent constitutional obligations. This may mean that in appropriate circumstances these ministers have some kind of duty to disregard the advice or direction of his or her Cabinet colleagues on policing policy issues or operations.

Question 15:   *Does the Solicitor General and/or Attorney General have the authority to disregard the advice or direction of his or her Cabinet colleagues on policing policy issues or operations?*

---

33 See Prof. Christie's background paper for the Inquiry, *Police-Government Relations In the Context of State-Aboriginal Relations*, posted at www.ipperwashinquiry.ca/ policy_part/relations/crp.html.

d. The Ontario Provincial Police

Most of questions so far have concerned legislative or organizational arrangements within the provincial government. The Inquiry may also want to consider institutional arrangements within the OPP.

> *Question 16: Should advice or directions from the government be directed to the Commissioner or through the Commissioner's office? How can operational decision-makers, incident commanders, and front-line officers within the OPP be insulated from inappropriate government directions or advice?*

e. Police Services Boards

The Inquiry may consider whether to recommend some kind of police service board for the OPP. Professor Roach notes that the OPP is 'somewhat anomalous' in not having a police board. He argues that

> ... a properly staffed police board might be able to spend much more time on policing than a Minister with multiple responsibilities in an expanding security portfolio. Such a board might also be more inclined to develop protocols and guidelines to deal in advance with issues such as the policing of protests. Police boards could also facilitate the inclusion of Aboriginal people and other vulnerable groups in the democratic model of policing. At the same time, it could be argued that adding another body ... might only cause confusion and diffuse accountability.[34]

A related issue concerns *public* participation in policing issues. The police/government literature typically discusses the relationship between the executive and the police. The issue of public participation in the government/police relationship is largely missing. This is unfortunate as it is widely understood that modern public institutions depend on pubic participation to function most effectively. As a result, the Inquiry may consider institutional structures that promote public participation on policing issues.

Some of the arrangements we may consider – police service boards, for example – have attendant public processes or reporting

---

34 Roach at 38–39.

arrangements that could promote participation, accountability and transparency. The Inquiry must ask, however, whether a police service board model of public participation can be effectively reproduced at a provincial level or is otherwise advisable.

> Question 17: Should there be a Police Service Board for the OPP? Are there other ways of facilitating greater public participation in formulating and discussing the policies that govern the OPP?

f. Transparency and Directives

How can policy directions be more transparent? This is an important issue irrespective of whether the direction comes from government, a Minister or a police board. As discussed above, one model to increase transparency is the use of Ministerial directives.

> Question 18: Should there be greater use of Ministerial Directives to the OPP? Should all governmental directions be reduced to writing and made public? Should the Commissioner have the option of asking that governmental direction be reduced to writing in the form of a Ministerial directive?

g. Government Intervention during a Crisis

When can governments intervene? The RCMP Ministerial Directives are detached from particular events or investigations. Conversely, the Nova Scotia Director of Public Prosecutions model contemplates 'real time' policy direction with respect to an ongoing prosecution or event. Professor Stenning notes that consultation between police commissioners and government ministers, including state premiers and prime ministers, prior to and during the public order operations is not considered inappropriate in either Australia or New Zealand and may, in fact, be seen positively. Government intervention may be more complicated during a crisis because it may be difficult to record government directives, advice, etc. in a constantly changing and face-paced environment.

The APEC report concluded that accountability for government interventions during an event was best achieved through appropriate record keeping and effective case management. In this way, government directives or interventions would be recorded for posterity and subsequent review.

> Question 19: How should governmental directions to the police be recorded during a crisis? If government issues directions during a crisis, how should they be transmitted and recorded?

9. THE MINISTRY OF NATURAL RESOURCES

Policing, especially with respect to Aboriginal people, is not only carried out by the OPP and municipal police forces, but also by MNR officials. The *Fish and Wildlife Conservation Act* gives conservation officers limited powers to arrest and issue warrants. These powers raise questions about police independence and conservation officers and the appropriate balance between accountability and independence for MNR enforcement activities. They also raise questions about government and Ministerial accountability. As noted earlier, the Ministry's Interim Enforcement Policy is an interesting example of a transparent 'policy of operations.'

> Question 20: Does the principle of police independence apply to the law enforcement actions of conservation officers? How should the government and the responsible Minister be held accountable for direction given to conservation officials?

10. CONCLUSION

As noted above, the purpose of this paper is to provide parties with notice of the issues that Part Two is considering. Parties are encouraged to consider some or all of these questions and the issues raised in the discussion papers in their written and oral submissions.

Please contact me with any questions or comments.

QUESTIONS ON GOVERNMENT/POLICE RELATIONS

> Question 1: Are these principles appropriate to guide the Inquiry's analysis and recommendations on police/government relations? Or, should there be others and what should they be?

Question 2: Is it advisable to define police 'independence' definitively?

Question 3: In which areas should police have 'independent' decision-making authority? What criteria may assist decision-makers determine if an issue is 'policy' or 'operational?'

Question 4: Do Aboriginal and/or other public order events raise 'policy' issues in which governments can and should intervene?

Question 5: Should governments have the right to issue directions in 'policy' areas outside the core area of police activities in criminal investigations?

Question 6: Should governments have the right to intervene in the 'policies of operations?'

Question 7: Is the phrase 'police operational responsibility' preferable to 'police independence' and 'operational independence?'

Question 8: Should governments have the right to give non-binding advice to police on operational matters? If so, how can this 'guidance' be made transparent or governments made accountable?

Question 9: Should governments have the right to be informed 'of any operational matter, even one involving an individual case, if it raises an important question of public policy?'

Question 10: Do current structures or processes ensure accountable and transparent decision-making by the police and government on police/government relations?

Question 11: Should police independence be codified? If so, where?

Question 12: Assuming the principle of ministerial accountability remains sound, are the existing provisions of the Police Services Act sufficient to protect and promote Ministerial accountability?

Question 13: Should there be special rules governing non-Solicitor-General officials?

Question 14: Do policing issues involving Aboriginal peoples justify unique police/government rules? If so, what are they?

Question 15: Does the Solicitor General and/or Attorney General have the authority to disregard the advice or direction of his or her Cabinet colleagues on policing policy issues or operations?

Question 16: Should advice or directions from the government be directed to the Commissioner or through the Commissioner's office? How can operational decision-makers, incident commanders, and front-line officers within the OPP be insulated from inappropriate government directions or advice?

Question 17: Should there be a Police Service Board for the OPP? Are there other ways of facilitating greater public participation in formulating and discussing the policies that govern the OPP?

Question 18: Should there be greater use of Ministerial Directives to the OPP? Should all governmental directions be reduced to writing and made public? Should the Commissioner have the option of asking that governmental direction be reduced to writing in the form of a Ministerial directive?

Question 19: How should governmental directions to the police be recorded during a crisis? If government issues directions during a crisis, how should they be transmitted and recorded?

Question 20: Does the principle of police independence apply to the law enforcement actions of conservation officers? How should the government and the responsible Minister be held accountable for direction given to conservation officials?

Bibliography

Abbate, Gay. 'Bully tag worked, union leader says.' *Globe and Mail*, 2 October 2003, A17.

– 'Inquest wrangles over race.' *Globe and Mail*, 26 May 1993.

– 'Lawrence used cocaine, toxicologist tells inquest.' *Globe and Mail*, 27 May 1993.

– 'Pall cast over bargaining with police.' *Globe and Mail*, 22 November 2001, A30.

– 'Police union accused of intimidation.' *Globe and Mail*, 27 January 2000, A1, A21.

– 'Police union defies orders, leaders face sanctions.' *Globe and Mail*, 29 January 2000, A1, A27.

– 'Politicians launch crackdown on police union.' *Globe and Mail*, 28 January 2000, A1, A17.

– 'Union puts Fantino's leadership to a vote.' *Globe and Mail*, 15 November 2001, A24.

Abbate, Gay, and Joe Friesen. 'Probe results in 22 charges filed against six officers.' *Globe and Mail*, 8 January 2004, A14.

Adams, the Honourable George W., QC. 'Consultation Report' to the Attorney General and Solicitor General Concerning Police Cooperation with the Special Investigations Unit.' 14 May 1998.

Addario, Frank, and Marcus Pratt. '*R. v. Ghorvei*: The Ontario Court of Appeal Polishes Up Some Bad Apples.' (2000) 29 C.R. (5th) 111.

Alderson, J. *Policing Freedom*. Plymouth: MacDonald & Evans Ltd, 1979.

Allen, T.R.S. 'The Rule of Law as the Rule of Reason: Consent and Constitutionalism.' (1999) 115 L.Q. Rev. 221.

Anderton, J. 'Accountable to whom?' *Police* 13 (10 February 1981): 6.

Appleby, Timothy. 'Toronto police union turns to telemarketing.' *Globe and Mail*, 22 January 2000, A23.

Archibald, B. 'Coordinating Canada's Restorative and Inclusionary Models of
    Criminal Justice: The Legal Profession and the Exercise of Discretion under
    a Reflexive Rule of Law.' Presentation to the Canadian Association of Law
    Teachers, 1 June 2004.
Armstrong, Jane. (2004) 'B.C.'s Campbell left reeling from liberal dose of
    sleaze.' *Globe and Mail*, 1 January 2004, A1.
Arnold, T. 'Legal Accountability and the Police: The Role of the Courts.' In
    Policing at the Crossroads, edited by C. Cameron and W. Young. Wellington:
    Allen & Unwin/Port Nicholson Press, 1986.
Asia Pacific Economic Cooperation Conference in Vancouver (Ottawa: Com-
    mission of Public Complaints, RCMP, 23 July 2001): http://www.cpc-
    cpp.gc.ca/defaultsite/ at 30.4.
Bachelard, M. 'Minister changes tune on police inquiries.' *Australian*,
    29 March 2004, 5.
Balbus, Issac. *The Dialectics of Legal Repression: Black Rebels before the American
    Courts*. New York: Russell Sage Foundation, 1973.
– *The Dialectics of Legal Repression*. New Brunswick, NJ: Transaction Books,
    1982.
Barber, John. 'Alan Heisey? It's just plain scary.' *Globe and Mail*, 17 January
    2004, M1.
– 'Decency Destroyed at the Toronto Police Board.' *Globe and Mail*, 12 June
    2004, M2.
– 'Enough with the few "bad apples."' *Globe and Mail*, 24 April 2004, M1.
– 'You go, Mike. We're counting on you.' *Globe and Mail*, 8 May 2004, M2.
Barton, B. 'Control of the New Zealand Police.' LLB thesis, Faculty of Law,
    Auckland University, 1978.
Bayley, David H. *Democratizing the Police Abroad: What to Do and How to Do It*.
    Washington, DC: U.S. Department of Justice, 2001.
– 'The Police and Political Development in Europe.' In *The Formation of
    National States in Western Europe*, edited by Charles Tilly. Princeton, NJ:
    Princeton University Press, 1975.
Bayley, David H., and Clifford D. Shearing. *The New Structure of Policing:
    Description, Conceptualization, and Research Agenda*. Washington, DC: Na-
    tional Institute of Justice, U.S. Department of Justice (July, NCJ 187083),
    2001.
Beare, M.E. *Criminal Conspiracies: Organized Crime in Canada*. Toronto: Nelson
    Canada, 1996.
– *Policing with a National Security Agenda*. Prepared for Heritage Canada.
    www.canadianheritage.gc.ca/progs/multi/pubs/police/security_e.cfm
    (accessed 8 July 2006).

- 'Selling Policing in Metropolitan Toronto: A Sociological Analysis of Police Rhetoric 1957–1984.' PhD dissertation, Columbia University, 1987.
Benzie, Robert. 'John Tory vows boost for cities.' *Toronto Star*, 7 May, 2004.
- 'Police role in politics examined; Union has backed candidates Province seeks legal opinion.' *Toronto Star*, 5 February 2004, A4.
Bersten, M. 'Police and Politics in Australia: The Separation of Powers and the Case for Statutory Codification.' Criminal L.J. (1990) 14, 302.
Bich, Marie-France. 'Organisation des forces de police au Canada.' (1989) 23 R.J.T. 279.
Biro, Fred, Peter Campbell, Paul MacKenna, and Tonita Murray. *Police Executives under Pressure: A Study and Discussion of the Issues*. Ottawa: Canadian Association of Police Chiefs, 2000.
Blatchford, Christie. 'Chief details charges against officers.' *Globe and Mail*, 27 April 2004, A10.
- '"Conscience is clean" Fantino says.' *Globe and Mail*, 21 January 2004, A6.
- 'Judgment day for Toronto Police Service.' *Globe and Mail*, 28 April 2004, A12.
- 'Numbered firm received cheques.' *Globe and Mail*, 21 April 2004, A15.
- 'Police probe corruption as union boss steps down.' *Globe and Mail*, 19 April 2004, A1, A9.
- 'Shameless! Cops don't flinch at Junger report.' *Toronto Sun*, 29 August 1992, 5.
- 'Six officers to be charged in corruption investigation.' *Globe and Mail*, 7 January 2004, A9.
Bonokoski, Mark. 'Rumour wed to lies.' *Toronto Sun*, 20 April 2004.
Boritch, Helen, and John Hagan. 'Crime and the Changing Forms of Class Control: Policing Public Order in 'Toronto the Good,' 1859–1955' (1987) 66(2) Social Forces 307.
Boston, J., J. Martin, J. Pallot, and P. Walsh. *Public Management: The New Zealand Model*. Auckland: Oxford University Press, 1996.
Bothwell, Robert, Ian Drummond, and John English. *Canada since 1945: Power, Politics and Provincialism*. Toronto: University of Toronto Press, 1981.
Bowden, Tom. *Beyond the Limits of the Law: A Comparative Study of the Police in Crisis Politics*. New York: Penguin, 1978.
Braithwaite, John. 'Accountability and Governance under the New Regulatory State.' (1999) 58 Australian Journal of Public Administration 90.
- 'On Speaking Softly and Carrying Big Sticks: Neglected Dimensions of a Republication Separation of Powers.' (1997) 47 Univ. of Toronto L.J. 305.
Brennan, Richard. 'LeSage to review police watchdog system.' *Toronto Star*, 10 June 2004, A1.

– 'Police complaints role "a challenge," former judge says.' *Toronto Star*, 11 June 2004, A20.

Brent, Bob. 'Black group tries new tack to get role at inquest.' *Toronto Star*, 4 September 1992, A9.

Bright, Mr Justice (Commissioner). South Australia Royal Commission on the September Moratorium Demonstration. *Report*. Adelaide: Government Printer, 1971.

Britton, N. 'Civilian Oversight of Police.' (2000) 40(4) British Journal of Criminology 639.

Brodeur, J.P. 'High Policing and Low Policing: Remarks about the Policing of Political Activities.' (1983) 30(5) Social Problems: 507. Repr. in *Understanding Policing*, edited by Kevin McCormick and Livy Visano. Toronto: Canadian Scholars' Press, 1992.

Broeker, G. *Rural Disorder and Police Reform in Ireland, 1812–36*. London: Routledge & Kegan Paul, 1970.

Brogden, M. *The Police: Autonomy and Consent*. New York: Academic Press, 1982.

Brogden, Mike, Tony Jefferson, and Sandra Walklate. *Introducing Police Work*. London: Unwin Hyman Ltd, 1998.

Brusten, Manfried. 'Securing the State: Politics and Internal Security in Europe.' *Working Papers in European Criminology* (No. 3, European Group for the Study of Deviance and Social Control, 1982), 53–76.

Buerger, M.E. 'Supervisory Challenges Arising from Racial Profiling.' (2002) 5(3) Police Quarterly 380.

Butler, D., and A.H. Halsey. *Policy and Politics Essays in Honour of Norman Chester*. London: Macmillan, 1978.

Butterworth, Susan. *More Than Law and Order: Policing a Changing Society, 1945–1992*. Dunedin, New Zealand: Otago University Press, 2005.

Callwood, J. 'What Canadians care about.' *Toronto Star*, 20 April 1981, A12.

Canada. Commission of Inquiry Concerning Certain Activities of the RCMP. *Freedom and Security under the Law*. Ottawa: Supply and Services, 1981.

Canada. 'Deputy Prime Minister Tables Consultation Paper on National Security Committee for Parliamentarians.' Ottawa: Public Safety and Emergency Preparedness Canada, 2004.

Canada. Auditor General. *Report of the Auditor General*. 'Government-Wide Audit of Sponsorship, Advertising, and Public Opinion Research.' Ottawa: Office of the Auditor General of Canada, www.oaq-boq.qc.ca/domino/reports.nsf/html/03menu_e.html (accessed 8 July). 2004. November 2003.

Canada. Commission of Inquiry into the Actions of Canadian Officials and Relation to Maher Arar: *Report of the Events Relating to Maher Arar*. Ottawa: Public Works and Government Services, 2006.

Canada. *Report of the Royal Commission on Aboriginal Peoples*. Ottawa: Indian

and Northern Affairs, 1996. www.ainc.qc.ca/ch/rcap/sq/59/_e.html#0
(accessed 8 July 2006).

Canadian Association of Chiefs of Police. 'A Brief Concerning the Proposed
Resolution Respecting the Constitution of Canada.' Presented by the Law
Amendments Committee of the Senate/House of Commons Special Joint
Committee on the Constitution of Canada, Ottawa, 27 November 1980.

Carter, Mark. 'Current Tensions in the Federation: Provincial Prosecution
Policy.' Presentation to the Canadian Association of Law Teachers, 31 May
2004.

CCLA. 'Proposed Amendments to the Police Civil Complaint System.' Brief
prepared for the Attorney General for Ontario (January 2004).

Centa, R., and P. Macklem. 'Securing Accountability Through Commissions of
Inquiry: A Role for the Law Commission of Canada.' (2001) 39 Osgoode
Hall L.J. 117.

Centre for Comparative Constitutional Studies, University of Melbourne.
*Governance and Victoria Police: Discussion of Issues Concerning the Constitution
of Victoria Police and its Relationships with the System of Government.*
Melbourne: Centre for Comparative Constitutional Studies, Faculty of Law,
University of Melbourne, 1997.

Chambliss, William. *Power, Politics and Crime.* Boulder, CO: Westview, 2001.

Chan, J. 'Governing Police Practice: Limits of the New Accountability.' (1999)
50(2) British Journal of Sociology 251.

Chan, Janet B.L. *Changing Police Culture: Policing in a Multicultural Society.*
Cambridge: Cambridge University Press, 1997.

Chase, Steven. 'Top Sleuths to set up home in Toronto.' *Globe and Mail*, 8 July,
A1 and A4.

Chen, Mai, and Sir Geoffrey Palmer. *Constitutional Issues Involving the Police:
An Analysis for the Independent External Review of the Police Administrative and
Management Levels and Structures.* Wellington: Chen & Palmer, 1988.

Chi-Ying Ng, Yvonne. 'Ideology, Media and Moral Panics: An Analysis of the
Jaques Murder.' MA thesis, University of Toronto, 1981.

Chong, Gordon. 'Who controls police?' *Toronto Star*, 6 May 2004.

Choudhry, Suijit, and Kent Roach. 'Racial and Ethnic Profiling: Statutory
Discretion, Democratic Accountability and Constitutional Remedies.' (2002)
40 Osgoode Hall L.J. 1.

Clark, S.D. *The Developing Canadian Community.* Toronto: University of Toronto
Press, 1962.

Cockburn, S. *The Salisbury Affair.* Melbourne: Sun Books Pty. Ltd., 1979.

Cohen, Leonard. '*Anthem.*' On *The Future* CD, Columbia, 1992.

Cohen, Stanley. *Folk Devils and Moral Panics: The Creation of the Mods and
Rockers.* Oxford: M. Robertson, 1980.

Cole, Daniel H. 'An Unqualified Human Good: E.P Thomson and The Rule of Law.' (2001) 28(2) Journal of Law and Society 177.

Colton, Timothy J. *Big Daddy: Frederick G. Gardiner and the Building of Metropolitan Toronto*. Toronto: University of Toronto Press, 1980.

Cotterell, Roger. 'Professional Guardianship of Law.' In *The Sociology of Law: An Introduction*. London: Butterworths, 1984.

Cowell, D., T. Jones, and J. Young, eds. *Policing the Riots*. London: Junction Books, 1982.

Coyle, Jim. 'Bromell huffs and puffs and blows his credibility.' *Toronto Star*, 19 April 2003, A25.

Cribb, Robert, and Nick Pron. 'Police union meets to oust pair.' *Toronto Star*, 6 May 2004, A16.

Cull, H. 'The Enigma of a Police Constable's Status.' (1976) 8 Victoria University of Wellington L.R. 148.

Cummins, Bryan David. *Aboriginal Policing: A Canadian Perspective*. Scarborough: Prentice Hall, 2003.

Currie, Dawn, Walter DeKeseredy, and Brian Maclean. 'Reconstituting Social Order and Social Control: Police Accountability in Canada.' (1990) 2(1) Journal of Human Justice 29.

Dale, T., and S. Goldfinch. Pessimism as an Information System Management Tool in the Public Sector: Lessons from the INCIS Fiasco in the New Zealand Police Force. http://www.cosc.canterbury.ac.nz/tony.dale/papers/tr0202.pdf.

Delacourt, Susan. 'Flurry of civil suits expected within days.' *Toronto Star*, 11 May 2004, A6.

– 'To serve and protect its political bosses.' *Toronto Star*, 17 April 2004, F03.

DeMara, Bruce. 'Officers Defend Endorsements.' *Toronto Star*, 30 April 2004.

Desbarats, P. *Somalia Cover-Up: A Commissioner's Journal*. Toronto: McClelland & Stewart, 1997.

Deverell, John. 'Racial issue ruled out for inquest.' *Toronto Star*, 23 February 1993: A7.

Devonshire, Reginald A. 'The Effects of Supreme Court Charter-Based Decisions on Policing: More Beneficial than Detrimental?' (1994) 31 C.R. (4th) 82.

Dicey, Albert Venn. *Introduction to the Study of the Law of the Constitution*, 8th ed. Holmes Beach, FL: Gaunt, 1996.

Diebel, Linda. 'Battle still rages over chief's future. *Sunday Star*, 19 September 2004, A1.

– 'Mistrust of "suits" fills void behind badge.' *Toronto Star*, 2 May 2004, A1.

– 'No fast renewal of chief's contract: Miller.' *Toronto Star*, 22 January 2004, A1, A14

– 'Police union resists board.' *Toronto Star*, 23 January 2004, F1.

Diebel, Linda, and Cal Millar. 'Police reform: "I want action."' *Toronto Star*, 28 April 2004, A1, A19.
– 'RCMP probing Toronto Police.' *Toronto Star*, 30 April 2004, A1.
Diefenbaker, John. *One Canada: The Years of Achievement, 1957 to 1962*. Toronto: Macmillan, 1976.
DiManno, Rosie. 'The chief still doesn't get it.' *Toronto Star*, 29 August 1992, A4.
– 'Heisey should step aside.' *Toronto Star*, 17 January 2004, E1.
– 'Police Board needs new direction, and some luck.' *Toronto Star*, Wednesday 16 June 2004, A2.
– 'Police union follows its thin blue whine.' *Toronto Star*, 1 October 2003, A2.
Docking, M. *Public Perceptions of Police Accountability and Decision-Making*. 2003. Home Office Online Report. http://www.homeoffice.gov.uk/rds/pdfs2/rdsolr3803.pdf (accessed 28 May 2004)
Dominion Post. 'Code of conduct still in draft form.' 25 May 2004, A2.
Downes, D., and T. Ward. *Democratic Policing: Towards a Labour Party Policy on Police Accountability*. London: Labour Campaign for Criminal Justice, 1986.
Duffy, Andrew. 'Chief promised no charges if officer quit.' *Toronto Star*, 12 April 1990, A8.
Duncanson, John. 'Betting scandal rocks police force.' *Toronto Star*, 20 April 2004, A1.
– 'Boothby doomed as chief: sources.' *Toronto Star*, 8 May 1999, A4.
– 'Chief brokers deal with board, union.' *Toronto Star*, 2 May 2000, B1, B4.
– 'Drive not linked to force, chief says.' *Toronto Star*, 23 January 2000, A4.
– 'Fantino tries to change rules on SIU probes.' *Toronto Star*, 7 November 2000, A1, A26.
– 'Police chiefs getting ready to take on SIU.' *Toronto Star*, 13 March 2000, A4.
– 'Police union puts heat on candidates.' *Toronto Star*, 19 October 2000, D1, D4.
Duncanson, John, and Tracey Huffman. 'Source 2004, Police shielded drug dens.' *Toronto Star*, 24 April 2004, A1, A23.
Duncanson, John, and Jennifer Quinn. 'Doubts raised over chief's leadership in police vote.' *Toronto Star*, 19 January 2002, A27.
– 'Showdown! Police chief threatens union boss over True Blue fundraising scheme.' *Toronto Star*, 27 January 2000, A1, A24.
Dunstall, G.A. *Policeman's Paradise? Policing a Stable Society, 1918–1945*. Vol. 4 of *The History of Policing in New Zealand*. Wellington: Dunmore Press, 1999.
Dyzenhaus, D., and M. Moran, eds. *Calling Power to Account*. Toronto: University of Toronto Press, 2004.
Editor-in-Chief's Introduction. 'Between Crime and War: Terrorism, Democracy and the Constitution.' (2002) 14 National Journal of Constitutional Law 1.
Editorial. 'The escort affair.' *Toronto Star*, 19 April 1990.

Editorial. 'Police complaints reform overdue.' *Toronto Star*, 11 June 2004, A26.

Editorial. 'Police require outside probe.' *Toronto Star*, 28 April 2004, A22.

Edwards, John. 'The Attorney General and the *Charter* of Rights.' In *Charter Litigation*, edited by Robert Sharpe. Toronto: Butterworths, 1987.

– *Ministerial Responsibility for National Security*. Ottawa: Supply and Services, 1980.

– 'The Office of the Attorney General – New Levels of Public Expectations and Accountability.' In *Accountability for Criminal Justice*, edited by P. Stenning. Toronto: University of Toronto Press, 1995.

– *Walking the Tightrope of Justice*. Halifax: Queen's Printer, 1989.

Eliot, Robin. 'References, Structural Argumentation and the Origin of Principles of the Constitution.' (2001) 80 Can. Bar Rev. 67.

Ericson, Richard. *Making Crime: A Study of Detective Work*. Toronto: Butterworths, 1981.

– 'Police Use of Criminal Rules.' In *Organizational Police Deviance: Its Structure and Control*, edited by Clifford D. Shearing. Toronto: Butterworths, 1981.

– 'Police Use of Disciplinary Rules.' In *Organizational Police Deviance: 'Its Structure and Control*, edited by Clifford D. Shearing. Toronto: Butterworths, 1981.

Ericson, Richard V., Patricia Baranek, and Janet B.L. Chan. *Representing Order: Crime, Law, and Justice in the News Media*. Toronto: University of Toronto Press, 1991.

Etter, B., and M. Palmer, eds. *Police Leadership in Australasia*. Sydney: Federation Press, 1995.

Etzioni-Halevy, Eva. *Bureaucracy and Democracy: A Political Dilemma*. London: Routledge, 1985.

Falconer, Julian N., and Peter J. Pliszka, eds. *Annotated Coroner's Act 2001/2002*. Markham, ON: Butterworths Canada, 2001.

Finkelman, Paul. 'The Second Casualty of War: Civil Liberties and the War on Drugs.' [1993] S. Cal. L. Rev. 1389.

Finnane, M. 'Police and Politics in Australia: The Case for Historical Revision.' (1990) 23 Australian and New Zealand Journal of Criminology 218.

Finnane, M. *Police and Government: Histories of Policing in Australia*. Melbourne: Oxford University Press, 1994.

Fischer, Benedikt. 'Community Policing: A Study of Local Policing, Order and Control.' PhD dissertation, University of Toronto, 1998.

Foucault, M. *Discipline and Punish: The Birth of the Prison*. New York: Pantheon, 1977.

Fowlie, Jonathan. 'Fantino lashes out as Liberals cancel helicopter funds.' *Globe and Mail*, 6 November 2003.

– 'McCormack defends his wife.' *Globe and Mail*, 7 May 2004, A13.
– 'Officers charged in "shakedown" case.' *Globe and Mail*, 4 May 2004, A1, A14.
– 'A venerable police dynasty in turmoil.' *Globe and Mail*, 24 April 2004, A16.
Fowlie, Jonathan, and Jeff Gray. 'Police group won't discuss officers.' *Toronto Star*, 6 May 2004, A15.
Fowlie, Jonathan, and Katherine Harding: 'McIntosh submits formal resignation.' *Toronto Star*, 21 May 2004, A11.
Freeze, Colin. 'Drug squad officers blast police brass in civil suit.' *Globe and Mail*, 22 Jan-uary 2003, A20.
– 'Police union and politics and volatile mix.' *Globe and Mail*, 6 November 2000, A21.
– 'Toronto police, board agree on fundraising issue.' *Globe and Mail*, 2 May, 2000.
Freiman, Mark. 'Convergence of Law and Policy and the Role of the Attorney General.' (2002) 16(2) S.C.L.R. 335.
Friedland, Martin. 'Controlling the Administrators of Criminal Justice.' (1988–9) 31 Crim. L.Q. 280.
– *Controlling Misconduct in the Military: A Study Prepared for the Commission of Enquiry into the Deployment of Canadian Forces to Somalia*. Ottawa: Ministry of Public Works and Government Services Canada, 1997.
– 'Military Justice and the Somalia Affair.' (1992) 40 Crim. L.Q. 360.
– 'Reforming Police Powers: Who's in Charge?' In *Police Powers in Canada*: *The Evolution and Practice of Authority*, edited by R.C. Macleod and David Schneiderman. Toronto: University of Toronto Press, 1994.
Galt, Virginia, and John Saunders. 'True Blue controversy shakes solidarity in the ranks of police, board says.' *Globe and Mail*, 31 January 2004, A16.
Garneau, Grant Smythe. '*Roberge*: Judicial Extension of Police Powers.' (1983) 33 C.R. (3d) 309.
Gest, Ted. *Crime and Politics: Big Government's Erratic Campaign for Law and Order*. Oxford: Oxford University Press, 2001.
Glasbeek, Harry. *Police Shootings of Black People in Ontario*. Toronto: Queen's Printer for Ontario, 1993.
Globe and Mail. 'Charge of reporter may signal tougher stand on secrets.' 1 June 1989.
Globe and Mail. 'Decency destroyed at the Toronto Police Board.' 12 June 2004, M2.
Globe and Mail. 'Law beyond the law.' 31 January 1969.
Globe and Mail. 'Leak charges not political, Tories say.' 31 May, 1989.
Goldring, J., and P. Blazey. 'Constitutional and Legal Mechanisms of Police

Accountability in Australia.' In *Keeping the Peace: Police Accountability and Oversight*, edited by David Moore and Roger Wetttenhall. Sydney: Royal Institute of Public Administration Australia/NSW Office of the Ombudsman, 1993.

Goldring, J., and R. Wettenhall. 'Three Perspectives on the Responsibility of Statutory Authorities.' In *Responsible Government in Australia*, edited by P. Weller and D. Jaensch. Richmond, Vic.: Drummond, 1980.

Goldsmith, Andrew J., ed. *Complaints against the Police: The Trend to External Review.* Oxford: Clarendon Press, 1991.

– 'External review and Regulation.' In *Complaints against the Police: The Trend to External Review*, edited by Andrew J. Goldsmith. Oxford: Clarendon Press, 1991.

Goldsmith, Andrew, and Colleen Lewis, eds. *Civilian Oversight of Policing: Governance, Democracy, and Human Rights.* Oxford: Hart Publishing, 2000.

Grant, Alan. 'The Control of Police Behaviour.' In *Some Civil Liberties Issues in the Seventies*, edited by Walter Tarnopolsky. Toronto: Osgoode Hall Law School, 1975.

– *The Police: A Policy Paper*. Prepared for the Law Reform Commission of Canada. Ottawa: Minister of Supply and Services, 1980.

Gray, Jeff, and Jonathan Fowlie. 'Police union moves to oust its president.' *Globe and Mail*, 5 May 2004, A8.

Griffith, John. 'Ideology in Criminal Procedure or a Third Model of the Criminal Process.' (1970) 79 Yale L.J. 359.

Haag, P. 'Constitutional Status of the Police: Complaints and Their Investigation.' (1980) 13 Australian and New Zealand Journal of Criminology 163.

Hall, S., et al. *Policing the Crises: Mugging, the State and Law and Order*. London: Macmillan Press, 1979.

Hann, R., J. McGinnis, P. Stenning, and S. Farson. 'Municipal Police Governance and Accountability in Canada: An Empirical Study.' (1985) 9(1) Canadian Police College Journal 1.

Harding, Katherine. 'Board backs Fantino's handling of probe.' *Globe and Mail*, 27 April 2004, A10.

– 'Child-porn controversy hits police board.' *Globe and Mail*, 15 January 2004.

– 'City Police Board in Disarray.' *Globe and Mail*, 28 May 2004.

– 'Heisey cleared of breaching rules.' *Globe and Mail*, 26 March 2004, A13.

– 'Mayor gets Fantino's apology.' *Globe and Mail*, 21 February 2004.

– 'Mayor let down by chief's reply to corruption recommendations.' *Globe and Mail*, 23 April 2004, A12.

– 'Panel on youth crime praised.' *Globe and Mail*, 20 February 2004.

Harrison, John. 'Faith in the Sunshine State: Joh Bjelke-Petersen and the

Religious Culture of Queensland.' PhD dissertation, University of Queensland, 1991.

Henry, Frances, et al. *The Colour of Democracy: Racism in Canadian Society*. Toronto: Harcourt Brace & Company, 2000.

Hilderley, David. 'OPP adds support to Metro Police protest.' *Globe and Mail*, 26 October 1992, A19.

Hogg, Peter. *Constitutional Law of Canada*. 3rd ed. Toronto: Carswell, 1992.

Hogg, Peter W., and Allison A. Thornton. 'Reply to "Six Degrees of Dialogue."' (1999) 37 Osgoode Hall L.J. 529.

Holland, K. 'The Political and Public Accountability of the Police.' (1983) 8(5) Legal Services Bulletin 221.

Hogg, R., and Hawker, B. 'The Politics of Police Independence.' *Legal Services Bulletin* 8(4): 160–5 and 8(5): 221–224.

Hume, Mark. 'Bribery suspicions prompted B.C. raid.' *Globe and Mail*, 3 March 2004, A5.

– 'Judge gives first insight into BC police raid.' *Globe and Mail*, 2 April 2004, A9.

Hutchinson, A. 'The Rule of Law Revisited: Democracy and Courts.' In *Recrafting the Rule of Law: The Limits of Legal Order*, edited by D. Dyzenhaus. Oxford: Hart Publishing, 1999.

James, Royson. 'City councillors are too fearful to bell Bromell.' *Toronto Star*, 20 November 2000, B1.

– 'Fantino's message is loud, but is it clear?' *Toronto Star*, 29 April 2004, B1, B5, A4.

– 'An independent inquiry is the only way to solve police mess.' *Toronto Star*, 28 April 2004, B3.

– 'Police Board paralyzed again.' *Toronto Star*, 31 July 2004.

Jang, Brent. 'Police probe won't disrupt B.C. budget, minister says.' *Globe and Mail*, 1 January 2004, A4.

Jefferson, T., and R. Grimshaw. *Controlling the Constable: Police Accountability in England and Wales*. London: Frederick Muller Ltd./ Cobden Trust, 1984.

Johnson, John. Ministerial Administrative Review into Victoria Police: Resourcing, Operational Independence, Human Resource Planning and Associated Issues. *Report*. Melbourne: Department of Justice, 2001.

Jones, G. 'Tories fight threat to police independence.' *Daily Telegraph*, 28 February 2002.

– 'Tories fight threat to police independence. '*Daily Telegraph*, 24 May 2004.

Jones, T. 'The Governance and Accountability of Policing.' In *Handbook of Policing*, edited by T. Newburn. Cullompton, UK: Willan Publishing, 2003.

– *Policing and Democracy in the Netherlands*. London: Policy Studies Institute, 1995.

Joseph, P. 'The Illusion of Civil Rights.' (2000) (May) New Zealand L.J. 151.

Jowell, J., QC. 'Beyond the Rule of Law: Towards Constitutional Judicial Review.' (2000) Pub. L. 671.

Kaplan, Robert P. 'Who Watches the Watchdogs? The Clark Affair Underlines the Vital Importance of R.C.M.P. accountability.' (22 March 1999) 153(11) *Time International* 19.

Kaplan, William. *Presumed Guilty: Brian Mulroney, the Airbus Affair and the Government of Canada.* Toronto: McClelland and Stewart, 1998.

Kari, Shannon. 'Addict-thief helped by officer in police probe.' *Globe and Mail*, 26 April 2004, A10.

Kelly, William and Nora Kelly. *Policing in Canada.* Toronto: Macmillan Canada, Maclean-Hunter Press, 1976.

Kennett, J. 'Labor Launches Assault against Police Independence.' http://www.dpc.vic.gov.au/domino/web_notes/pressrel.nsf/ 4a2562ce0017cf654a2562 ... (accessed September 1999).

Kerr McDougall, Allan. 'Policing in Ontario: The Occupational Dimensions to Provincial-Municipal Relations.' PhD dissertation, University of Toronto, 1971.

King, H. 'Some Aspects of Police Administration in New South Wales, 1825–1851.' (1956) 42(5) Journal and Proceedings of the Royal Australian Historical Society 205.

Kingstone, Jonathan. 'Union boss: I am the victim of smear.' *Toronto Sun*, 4 May 2004, 5.

Kingstone, Jonathan, and Rob Lamberti. 'Hooking police rumour.' *Toronto Sun*, 19 April 2004.

– 'T.O. cop extorted payoffs at clubs?' *Toronto Sun*, 18 April 2004.

Kraska, Peter B., ed. *Militarizing the American Criminal Justice System.* Boston: Northeastern University Press, 2001.

Kymlicka, Will, ed. *Citizenship in Diverse Societies: Theory and Practice.* New York: Oxford University Press, 2000.

Lakey, Jack. 'Eng queries secret study on blacks.' *Toronto Star*, 12 February 1994, A8.

– 'Police acted as they should have, Donaldson probe told.' *Toronto Star*, 18 March 1994, A9.

– 'Police ignoring job action: Chief.' *Toronto Star*,15 May 2003, B2.

– 'Probe requested of chief's words.' *Toronto Star*, 12 December 2003.

Lambert, J. *Police Powers and Accountability.* London: Croom Helm, 1986.

Landau, Tammy. 'Back to the Future: The Death of Civilian Review of Public Complaints Against the Police in Ontario, Canada.' In *Civilian Oversight of Policing: Governance, Democracy, and Human Rights*, edited by Andrew Goldsmith and Colleen Lewis. Oxford: Hart Publishing, 2000.

Larsen, E. Nick. 'Urban Politics and Prostitution Control: A Qualitative Analysis of a Controversial Urban Problem.' (1999) 8(1) Canadian Journal of Urban Research 28.

Law Enforcement and Criminal Liability White Paper. Ottawa: Department of Justice, Criminal Law Policy Section, 2000.

Lawson, T. 'Report to Heads of Agencies Committee on Establishment of a Police Board in South Australia.' Unpublished South Australian Attorney-General's Department, 1992.

Leblanc, Daniel. 'More charges likely to be laid in ad sponsorship scandal.' *Globe and Mail*, 10 March 2004, A4.

– 'Mounties tell MPs to slow up ad probe.' *Globe and Mail*, 21 April 2004, A1.

Letwin, O. 'Blunkett is laying the ground to make Britain a police state.' *Daily Telegraph*, 24 May 2002.

Lewington, Jennifer. 'Police oversight issue unifies city hall.' *Toronto Star*, 6 May 2004, A15.

Lewis, Clare E. 'Police Complaints in Metropolitan Toronto: Perspectives of the Public Complaints Commissioner.' In *Complaints against the Police: The Trend to External Review*, edited by Andrew J. Goldsmith. Oxford: Clarendon Press, 1991.

Lewis, Claire E., Sidney B. Linden, Q.C., and Judith Keene. 'Public Complaints against Police in Metropolitan Toronto: The History and Operation of the Office of the Public Complaints Commissioner.' (1986) 29 Crim. L.Q. 115.

Livingston, Debra Ann. 'Brutality in Blue: Community, Authority, and the Elusive Promise of Police Reform.' (1994) 92 Mich. L. Rev. 1556.

Loader, I. 'Democracy, Justice and the Limits of Policing: Rethinking Police Accountability.' (1994) 3 Social & Legal Studies 521.

Loader, Ian, and Aogan Mulcahy. *Policing and the Condition of England: Memory, Politics and Culture*. Oxford: Oxford University Press, 2003.

Loveday, B. 'Waving not Drowning: Chief Constables and the New Configuration of Accountability in the Provinces.' http://www.psa.ac.uk/cps/1998%5Cloveday.pdf

Lovett, Frank. 'A Positivist Account of the Rule of Law.' (2002) 27 Law & Soc. Inquiry 41.

Lu, Vanessa. '8 officers sue police chief over fink fund case.' *Toronto Star*, 21 January 2003, A16.

Lunn, Hugh. *Joh: The life and political adventures of Johannes Bjelke-Petersen*. St Lucia: University of Queensland Press, 1979.

– *Johannes Bjelke-Petersen: A Political Biography*. 2nd ed. St Lucia: University of Queensland Press, 1984.

Lusher, Mr Justice E. (Commissioner). *Commission to Inquire into New South Wales Police Administration Report*. Sydney: Government Printer, 1981.

Lustgarten, L. *The Governance of Police*. London: Sweet & Maxwell, 1986.

Maloney, Paul. 'Police union endorsements split council.' *Toronto Star*, 26 August 2000, B1, B3.

Maloney, Paul, and Bruce DeMara. 'New bylaw bans True Blue.' *Toronto Star*, 29 January 2000, A1, A21.

Makin, Kirk. 'Plan would require disclosure of past misconduct to civilians.' *Globe and Mail*, 27 February 2004, A11.

– 'Police blocked corruption probe.' *Globe and Mail*, 20 January 2004, A1, A12.

– 'Police chief denies "blue wall of silence" in corruption probe.' *Globe and Mail*, 21 January 2004, A6.

– 'Police engage in profiling, chief counsel tells court.' *Globe and Mail*, 18 January 2004, A1, A26.

Manitoba. *News Release*. 'Manitoba Refuses to Prosecute Firearms Registration Offences.' 2003. http://www.gov.mb.ca/chc/press/top/2003/04/2003-04-15-02.html

Mann, Edward, and John Alan Lee. *RCMP: The RCMP vs. The People*. Don Mills, ON: General Publishing Co, 1979.

Manning, Peter. *The Narcs' Game: Organizational and Informational Limits on Drug Law Enforcement*. Cambridge, MA: MIT Press, 1980.

– 'Police: Mandate, Strategies and Appearances.' In *Criminal Justice in America: A Critical Understanding*, edited by R. Quinney. Boston: Little, Brown and Co., 1974.

– *Police Work: The Social Organization of Policing*. Prospect Heights, IL: Waveland Press, 1997.

– 'Three Modes of Security.' Draft paper prepared for the *In Search of Security* conference, sponsored by the National Institute of Justice and the Law Reform Commission of Canada, 19–23 February 2003.

Manson, Allan, and David Mullan, eds. *Commissions of Inquiry: Praise or Reappraise?* Toronto: Irwin Law, 2003.

Marenin, Otwin. 'Parking Tickets and Class Repression: The Concept of Policing in Critical Theories of Criminal Justice.' (1982) Contemporary Crises 241.

Marin, René. *Policing in Canada*. Aurora, ON: Canada Law Book, 1997.

Mark, Sir Robert. *In the Office of the Constable*. London: Collins, 1978.

Marquis, Greg. *Policing Canada's Century: A History of the Canadian Association of Chiefs of Police*. Toronto: University of Toronto Press, 1993.

Marshall, Geoffrey. *Constitutional Conventions*. Oxford: Oxford University Press, 1984.

– 'Police Accountability Revisited.' In *Policy and Politics: Essays in Honour of*

Norman Chester, edited by D. Butler and A.H. Halsey. London: Macmillan, 1978.

– *Police and Government: The Status and Accountability of the English Constable.* London: Methuen, 1965.

Marshall, G., and B. Loveday. 'The Police: Independence and Accountability.' In *The Changing Constitution*, edited by J. Jowell and D. Oliver. Oxford: Clarendon Press, 1994.

Martin, Dianne L., and Ray Kuszelewski. 'The Perils of Poverty: Prostitutes' Rights, Police Misconduct and Poverty Law.' (1997) 35 Osgoode Hall L.J. 835.

Martin, L. 'Police Force or political force? *Globe and Mail*, 18 March 2004, A19.

Martin, Maurice. *Urban Policing in Canada: Anatomy of an Aging Craft.* Toronto: University of Toronto Press, 1995.

Mascoll, Philip. 'Striking Metro police lock station doors.' *Toronto Star*, 27 January 1995, A1, A6.

Matas, Robert. 'Mounties target B.C. ministers' staffers.' *Globe and Mail*, 29 December 2003, A1.

Miller, Mayor David. 2004. Address to North York, Etobicoke, and Scarborough Chambers of Commerce (March 9). http://www.city.toronto.on.ca/mayor_miller/speeches/c_of_c_030904.htm See also http://www.toronto.ca/legdocs/2004/agendas/committees/pof/pof040224/it023a.pdf

McBarnet, Doreen. 'Arrest: The Legal Context of Policing.' In *The British Police*, edited by Simon Holdaway. London: Arnold, 1979.

– *Conviction: Law, the State and the Construction of Justice.* London: Macmillan, 1981.

McChesney, Anne. *Ministerial Control and the Ontario Provincial Police: A Discussion Paper.* Toronto: Legal Services Branch, Ministry of the Solicitor General, 1991.

McCormack, Bill, and B. Cooper. *Without Fear or Favour: The Life and Politics of an Urban Cop.* Toronto: Stoddart, 1999.

McCormick, K., and Livy Visano, eds. *Understanding Policing.* Toronto: Canadian Scholars' Press, 1992.

McDougall, Allan. 'Policing in Ontario: The Occupational Dimensions to Provincial-Municipal Relations.' PhD dissertation, University of Toronto, 1971.

McIntosh, Andrew. 'Mounties conducted secret probe of spending.' *National Post*, 13 February 2004.

– 'Senior Mountie queried sponsorship funds in '98: *National Post*, 2 June 2004.

McLeod, Roderick, QC. *A Report and Recommendations On Amendments to the Police Services Act Respecting Civilian Oversight of the Police*, commissioned by the Ministry of the Attorney General and the Ministry of the Solicitor General (November). Toronto: Government of Ontario, 1996.

McMurtry, The Hon. R. Roy. (1978) 'Police Discretionary Powers in a Democratically Responsive Society.' (1978) 41 *RCMP Gazette* 125.

McNenly, Pat. 'Police union vows fight to abolish complaints board.' *Toronto Star*, 20 December 1985.

Mickelburgh, Rod. 'Rumours swirl around Vancouver chief.' *Globe and Mail*, 8 May 1999, A12.

Miller, Cal, John Duncanson, and Nicholaas Van Rijn. 'Police unit faces internal probe.' *Toronto Star*, 17 April 2004, A4.

Miller, Wilbur. 'The Legitimation of the London and New York City Police, 1830–1870.' PhD dissertation, Columbia University, 1973.

Miller, W. *Cops and Bobbies: Police Authority in New York and London, 1830–1870.* Chicago: University of Chicago Press, 1977.

Miller, Cal, and Lisa Priest. 'Chief irate over publicity in escort case.' *Toronto Star*, 18 April 1990, A1.

Milte, K., and T. Weber. *Police in Australia*. Sydney: Butterworths, 1997.

Mitchell, J. 'The Constitutional Position of the Police in Scotland.' (1962) 7 Juridical Review 1.

Mitchell, Madam Justice R. (Commissioner). South Australia Royal Commission. *Report on the Dismissal of Harold Hubert Salisbury.* Adelaide: Government Printer, 1978.

Monahan, Patrick. *Constitutional Law.* 2nd ed. Toronto: Irwin Law, 2002.

Monkkonen, Eric. *Police in Urban America, 1860–1920.* Cambridge: Cambridge University Press, 1981.

Moore, Kathryn. 'Police Implementation of Supreme Court Charter Decisions: An Empirical Study.' (1992) 30 Osgoode Hall L.J. 547.

Moran, Mayo. 'Case Comment on *Jane Doe.*' (1993) 6 CJWL 491.

Morgan, J. *Conflict and Order: The Police and Labour Disputes in England and Wales 1900–1939.* Oxford: Clarendon Press, 1987.

Morris, Ramona. *Ontario Police College Recruit Profile, September 1998–September 2003.* Toronto: Queen's Printer for Ontario, 2004.

Morrison, W.R. 'The Northwest Mounted Police and the Klondike Gold Rush.' In *Police Forces in History*, edited by G.L. Mosse. Beverley Hills, CA: Sage, 1975.

Murdoch, Caroline, and Brockman, Joan. 'Who's on First? Disciplinary Proceedings by Self-Regulating Professions and Other Agencies for 'Criminal' Behaviour.' (2001) 64 Saskatchewan Law Review 29.

Murphy, Christopher J. 'The Social and Formal Organization of Small Town Policing: A Comparative Analysis of RCMP and Municipal Policing.' PhD dissertation, University of Toronto, 1986.

- 'Policing Postmodern Canada.' (1998) 13 Can. J.L. & Soc. 1.

Nadelmann, E. *Cops Across Borders: The Internationalization of U.S. Criminal Law Enforcement*. University Park: Pennsylvania State University Press, 1993.

Neesham, T., QC, Chair. Committee of Inquiry, Victoria Police Force. *Report*. Melbourne: Government Printer, 1985.

New South Wales. Commission to Inquire into New South Wales Police Administration. *Report*. Sydney: Government Printer, 1981.

New South Wales. Royal Commission into the New South Wales Police Service *Final Report*. 3 vols. Sydney: Government Printer, 1997.

New Zealand. Commissioner of Police. *Final Report on the Review of Police Administration and Management Structures*. Wellington: New Zealand Police, 1998.

New Zealand. House of Representatives, Justice and Electoral Committee. *Inquiry into Matters Relating to the Visit of the President of China to New Zealand in 1999: Report of the Justice and Electoral Committee*. http://www.gp.co.nz/wooc/i-papers/i7Aa-china.html.

New Zealand. House of Representatives, Law and Order Committee. 'Report on the Police Amendment Bill (No. 2),' No. 145-1. The Opposition parties released a separate report opposing passage of the Bill ('Police Amendment Bill (No.2),' n.d., 6 pp.).

New Zealand. Review of Police Administration & Management Structure. *Report of Independent Reviewer*. Wellington: New Zealand Police, 1998.

Nixon, C. 'Why Victoria does not need a Royal Commission into police corruption.' 2004. http://www.police.vic.gov.au/showContentPage.cfm

Oliver, I. *Police, Government and Accountability*. London: Macmillan Press Ltd., 1987.

O'Neil, Peter, Jim Beatty, and Lori Culbert. 'B.C. legislature raid involved possible fraud, source says.' *National Post*, 14 January 2004, A7.

Ontario Civilian Commission on Police Services. *Report on a Fact-Finding into Various Matters with respect to the Disciplinary Practices of the Toronto Police Service*. Toronto: Queen's Printer of Ontario, July 1999.

- *Report of an Inquiry into Administration of Internal Investigations by the Metropolitan Toronto Police Force*. Toronto: Queen's Printer of Ontario, 1992.

Ontario. Commission on Systemic Racism in the Ontario Criminal Justice System. *Report of the Commission on Systemic Racism in the Ontario Criminal Justice System*. Toronto: Queen's Printer for Ontario, 1995.

Ontario Human Rights Commission. *Paying the Price: The Human Cost of Racial Profiling*. 2003. www.ohrc.on.ca.

O'Rawe, Mary. 'Transitional Policing Arrangements in Northern Ireland: The Can't and the Won't of the Change Dialectic.' (2003) 26 Fordham Int'l L.J. 1015.

Orkin, Andrew J. 'When the Law Breaks Down: Aboriginal Peoples in Canada and Governmental Defiance of the Rule of Law.' (2003) 41 Osgoode Hall L.J. 445.

Orr, G. 'Police Accountability to the Executive and Parliament.' In *Policing at the Crossroads*, edited by C. Cameron and W. Young. Wellington: Allen & Unwin/Port Nicholson Press, 1986.

Ottawa Citizen. 'Hostility Hampers Dialogue.' 12 August 1992, A10.

Ottawa Citizen. 'Police slowdown leaves Montreal chief powerless.' 9 July 1993, A5.

Packer, Herbert. 'Two Models of the Criminal Process.' (1964) 113 U. Penn. L.Rev. 1.

Palango, Paul. *Above the Law*. Toronto: McClelland and Stewart, 1994.

– *The Last Guardians: The Crisis in the RCMP ... and in Canada*. Toronto: McClelland and Stewart, 1998.

Paradkar, Bagesheree. 'True Blue gets mixed reviews from officers.' *Toronto Star*, 28 January 2000, A19.

Parnaby, Patrick. 'Disaster through Dirty Windshields: Law, Order and Toronto's Squeegee Kids.' (2003) 23(3) Canadian Journal of Sociology 281.

Patten, Rt. Hon. C., Chair. United Kingdom Independent Commission on Policing for Northern Ireland Report. *A New Beginning: Policing in Northern Ireland*. London: Crown copyright, 1999.

Petterson, Werner E. 'Police Accountability and Civilian Oversight of Policing: An American Perspective.' In *Complaints against the Police: The Trend to External Review*, edited by Andrew J. Goldsmith. Oxford: Clarendon Press, 1991.

Pincione, Guido. 'Market Rights and the Rule of Law: A Case for Procedural Constitutionalism.' (2003) 26 Harv. J.L. & Pub. Pol'y 397.

Pitman, G. 'Police Minister and Commissioner Relationships.' PhD dissertation, Griffith University, Queensland, Australia, 1998.

Plehwe, R. 'Some Aspects of the Constitutional Status of Australian Police Forces.' (1973) 32 Public Administration (N.S.W). 268.

Plehwe, R., and R. Wettenhall. 'Reflections on the Salisbury Affair: Police-Government Relations in Australia.' (1979) Australian Quarterly 75.

'Police union boss plays politics.' *Now Magazine*, 7–13 May 1998.

Porter, Catherine. 'Action urged on race profiling.' *Toronto Star*, 19 January 2004, A11.

– 'Lawyer to probe Heisey's comments.' *Toronto Star*, 16 January 2004.

– 'Police probe fails to find who leaked Heisey memo.' *Toronto Star*, 15 May 2004.

– 'Union stays out of federal race.' *Toronto Star*, 3 June 2004, B3.

Powell, Betsey. 'Tipster line for bad cops.' *Toronto Star*, 7 June 2004, E1.

Powell, Betsy, and Catherine Porter. 'Police board gets action plan.' *Toronto Star*, 26 February 2004, B2.

Powell, Betsy, and Nick Pron. 'Weeding out corruption.' *Globe and Mail*, 22 January 2004, B1, B6.

Pron, Nick. 'Former chief's son facing charges.' *Toronto Star*, 26 April 2004, A1, A12.

– 'Union trying to oust charged officers.' *Toronto Star*, 5 May 2004, A1, A21.

Pron, Nick, and John Duncanson. 'Officers face charges of fraud, theft and assault.' *Toronto Star*, 7 January 2004, A15.

– '4 officers facing criminal charges.' *Toronto Star*, 4 May 2004, A1, A13.

– '6 may face betting probe charges.' *Toronto Star*, 21 April 2004, A1, A16.

Pron, Nick, John Duncanson, and Kerry Gillespie. 'Tory gets police union's support.' *Toronto Star*, 29 October, 2003.

Pron, Nick, and Betsey Powell. 'Officers cleared in Vass case.' *Toronto Star*, 6 November 2003, A1.

Pue, Wesley W. 'Executive Accountability and the APEC Inquiry: Comment on *Ruling on Applications to Call Additional Governmental Witnesses*.' (2000) 34 U.B.C. Law. Rev. 335.

– *Pepper in Our Eyes: The APEC Affair*. Vancouver: UBC Press, 2000.

– 'Policing, the Rule of Law and Accountability in Canada: Lessons from the APEC Summit.' In Pue, ed, *Pepper in Our Eyes*.

– 'The Prime Minister's Police? Commissioner Hughes' APEC Report.' (2001) 39 Osgoode Hall L.J. 165.

– 'Why the APEC allegations are so serious.' *Globe and Mail*, 5 October 1998.

Queensland Commission of Inquiry into Possible Illegal Activities and Associated Police Misconduct (Fitzgerald Inquiry). *Report*. Brisbane: Government Printer, 1989.

Queensland Public Service Management Commission. *Review of the Queensland Police Service*. Brisbane: Queensland Public Service Management Commission, 1993.

Quinn, Jennifer, and John Duncanson. 'Police chiefs feel heat of unions.' *Toronto Star*, 14 January 2000, A1, A18.

Randall, Melanie. (2001) 'A Sex Discrimination, Accountability of Public Authorities and the Public/Private Divide in Tort Law: an Analysis of Doe V. Metropolitan Toronto (municipality) Commissioners of Police.' (2001) 26 Queen's L.J. 451.

Rankin, Jim. 'Police union sues Fantino.' *Toronto Star*, 25 November 2001, A10.

Rankin, Jim, and John Duncanson. 'Bromell blasts chief over charges.' *Toronto Star*, 20 September 2001, B1, B5.

Rankin, Jim, and Betsy Powell. 'Officer had 1993 profiling ruling.' *Toronto Star*, 18 September 2004.

Rawlings, P. *Policing: A Short History*. Cullompton, UK: Willan Publishing, 2002.

RCMP. News Release dated 29 December 2003. 'Search Warrants Executed on BC Legislature: News Release.' http://www.rcmp-bcmedia.ca/printablepressrelease.jsp?vRelease=4218 (RCMP Media Relations website).

RCMP. *Post-Sept 11th – The Fight against Terrorism*. http://canadaonline .about.com/gi/dynamic/offsite.htm?site=http%3A%2F%2Fwww.rcmp-grc.gc.ca%2Fnews%2F2002%2Fnr-02-18.htm (accessed 2 September 2003).

RCMP. http://www.rcmp-grc.gc.ca/html/organi_e.htm (accessed 9 August 2004).

Réaume, Denise. 'The Constitutional Protection of Language: Security versus Survival.' In *Language and the State: The Law and Politics of Identity*, edited by David Schneiderman. Montreal: Yvon Blais. 1991.

– 'The Demise of the Political Compromise Doctrine: Have Official Language Use Rights Been Revived?' (2002) 47 McGill L.J. 593.

Reiner, R. *Chief Constables: Bobbies, Bosses, or Bureaucrats*. Oxford: Oxford University Press, 1991.

– 'Police Accountability: Principles, Patterns and Practices.' In *Accountable Policing: Effectiveness, Empowerment, Equity*, edited by R. Reiner and Sarah Spencer. London: Institute for Public Policy Research, 1997.

– *The Politics of the Police*. 3rd ed. Oxford: Oxford University Press, 2000.

Reiner, R., and Sarah Spencer, eds. *Accountable Policing: Effectiveness, Empowerment, Equity*. London: Institute for Public Policy Research, 1997.

Reiss, Al. 'Forecasting the Role of the Police and the Role of the Police in Social Forecasting.' In *The Maintenance of Order in Society*, edited by Rita Donelan. Ottawa: Ministry of Supply and Services, 1982.

Rianoshek, Richard. 'History, Ideology, and the Practice of Policing.' Paper presented at the American Society of Criminology meetings, 10 November 1983, Denver, CO.

Roach, Kent. 'The Criminal Process.' In *The Oxford Handbook of Legal Studies*, edited by P. Cane and M. Tushnet. Oxford: Oxford University Press, 2003.

– 'Did September 11 Change Everything? Struggling to Preserve Canadian Values in the Face of Terrorism.' (2000) 47 McGill L.J. 893.

– *Due Process and Victims' Rights: The New Law and Politics of Criminal Justice*. Toronto: University of Toronto Press, 1999.

– 'The Evolving Test for Stays of Proceedings.' (1998) 40 Crim. L.Q. 400.

– 'Four Models of the Criminal Process.' (1999) 89 J. Crim. L and Criminology 691.

– 'The Role of the Attorney General in Charter Dialogues Between Courts and Legislatures.' Paper prepared for conference in honour of Ian Scott, Queen's University, Fall 2003.

– *September 11: Consequences for Canada*. Montreal: McGill-Queen's University Press, 2003.

Robb, J. 'The Police and Politics: The Politics of Independence.' In *Police Powers in Canada: The Evolution and Practice of Authority*, edited by R.C. Macleod and David Schneiderman. Toronto: University of Toronto Press, 1994.

Robinson, Cyril D. 'The Mayor and the Police: The Political Role of the Police in Society.' In *Police Forces in History*, edited by G.L. Mosse. London: Sage, 1975.

– 'Police and Prosecutor Practices and Attitudes Relating to Interrogation as Revealed by Pre- and Post-Miranda Questionnaires: A Con-struct of Police Capacity to Comply.' (1968) 3 Duke L.J. 425.

Rock, Paul. *A View from the Shadows: The Ministry of the Solicitor General of Canada and the Making of the Justice for Victims of Crime Initiative*. Oxford: Clarendon Press, 1986.

Royal Commission into the New South Wales Police Service. *Final Report*. 3 vols. Sydney: Government Printer, 1997.

Russell, Peter. *Freedom and Security: An Analysis of the Police Issues before the Commission of Inquiry*. Ottawa: Commission of Inquiry Concerning Certain Activities of the Royal Canadian Mounted Policy, 1978.

Sammonds, N. 'The Slow March Towards Democratic, Civilian Oversight of Security Forces.' (2001) 359(1) The Round Table 213.

Savoie, Donald. *Breaking the Bargain: Public Servants, Ministers and Parliament*. Toronto: University of Toronto Press, 2003.

– *Governing from the Centre: The Concentration of Power in Canadian Politics*. Toronto: University of Toronto Press, 1999.

Scarman, Lord. *The Scarman Report: The Brixton Disorders*. London: HMSO, 1981.

Scheingold, Stuart A. *The Politics of Law and Order: Street Crime and Public Policy*. New York: Longman, 1984.

Schneiderman, David, ed. *Language and the State: The Law and Politics of Identity*. Montreal: Yvon Blais Ltéé, 1991.

Scott, Colin. 'Accountability in the Regulatory State.' (2000) 27 Journal of Law and Society 38.

Scott, Ian. 'Law, Policy and the Role of the Attorney General: Constancy and Change in the 1980s.' (1989) 39 U.T.L.J. 109.

Scott, K., and R. Wilkie. 'Chief Constables: A Current "Crisis" in Scottish Policing?' (2001) 35 Scottish Affairs 54.

Shearing, Clifford. 'Subterranean Processes in the Maintenance of Power: An Examination of the Mechanisms Co-ordinating Police Actions.' (1980) 18(3) Canadian Review of Sociology and Anthropology 283.

Shelley, Louise. *Policing Soviet Society: The Evolution of State Control*. New York: Routledge, 1996.

Silver, A. 'A Demand for Order in Civil Society: A Review of Some Themes in the History of Urban Crime, Police and Riot.' In *The Police: Six Sociological Essays*, edited by D.J. Bordua. New York: John Wiley and Sons, 1967.

Simon, J. 'Governing through Crime.' In *The Crime Conundrum: Essays on Criminal Justice*, edited by G. Fisher and L.M. Friedman. New York: Westview Press, 1997.

Simon, Jonathan. 'Speaking Truth and Power, Presidential address and commentaries.' (2002) 36 Law and Society Review 37.

Skolnick, Jerome H. *Justice without Trial*. New York: Macmillan, 1975.

Small, P. 'Judge raps police in profiling case.' *Toronto Star*, 17 September 2004, A1.

– 'Police union sues Star over race-crime series.' *Toronto Star*, 18 January 2003, A6.

Smith, D. 'The Police and Political Science in Canada.' In *Police Powers in Canada: The Evolution and Practice of Authority*, edited by R.C. McLeod and D. Schneiderman. Toronto: University of Toronto Press, 1994.

Smith, Graeme. 'Saskatoon police chief faces revolt in the ranks.' *Globe and Mail*, 2 July 2003, A5.

Smith, G. 'Saskatchewan police probe finds anti-Native prejudice.' *Globe and Mail*, 22 June 2004, A1.

Sossin, Lorne. 'Discretion Unbound: Reconciling Soft Law and the *Charter*.' (2002) 45 Canadian Public Administration 465.

– 'The Politics of Discretion: Towards a Critical Theory of Public Administration.' (1993) 36 Canadian Public Administration 364.

– 'Speaking Truth to Power? The Search for Bureaucratic Independence.' (2000) 55(1) University of Toronto L.J. 1.

South Australia. Royal Commission on the September Moratorium Demonstration. *Report*. Adelaide: Government Printer, 1971.

South Australia. Royal Commission. *Report on the Dismissal of Harold Hubert Salisbury*. Adelaide: Government Printer, 1978.

Speirs, Rosemary. 'OPP union sends out a Long letter.' *Toronto Star*, 14 June 2000, A6.

Spencer, S. *Called to Account: The Case for Police Accountability in England and Wales*. London: National Council for Civil Liberties, 1985.

St Johnston, E. *A Report on the Victoria Police Force Following an Inspection.* Melbourne: Government Printer, 1971.

– *One Policeman's Story.* Chichester: Barry Rose, 1979.

Stein, Janice Gross. *The Cult of Efficiency.* Toronto: House of Anansi/Canadian Broadcasting Corporation, 2001.

Stenning, Philip C. 'Accountability in the Ministry of the Solicitor General of Canada.' In *Accountability for Criminal Justice: Selected Essays*, edited by Philip C. Stenning. Toronto: University of Toronto Press, 1995.

– 'Independence and the Director of Public Prosecutions: The Marshall Inquiry and Beyond.' (2000) 23 Dal. LJ. 385.

– *Legal Status of the Police.* Ottawa: Law Reform Commission of Canada, 1981.

– *Legal Status of the Police.* Ottawa: Minister of Supply and Services, 1982.

– *Police Commissions and Boards in Canada.* Toronto: University of Toronto Press, 1981.

– *Police Governance in First Nations in Ontario.* Toronto: Centre of Criminology, University of Toronto, 1996.

– 'Someone to Watch over Me: Government Supervision of the RCMP.' In *Pepper in Our Eyes: The APEC Affair*, edited by Wesley W. Pue. Vancouver: UBC Press, 2000.

– 'Trusting the Chief: Legal Aspects of the Status and Political Accountability of the Police in Canada.' PhD dissertation, University of Toronto, 1983.

Stevens, C. 'A Report on the Concept of a Police Board in South Australia.' Current issues paper #4, Police Association of South Australia. 1995. http://www.pasa.asn.au/paper04.htm.

Stone, Thomas. 'The Mounties as Vigilanties: Perceptions of Community and the Transformation of Law in the Yukon 1885–1897.' (1979) 14(1) Law and Society Review 81.

Stonier-Newman, Lynne. *Policing a Pioneer Province: The BC Provincial Police, 1858–1950.* Madeira Park, BC: Harbour Publishing, 1991.

Story, Alan. 'Morality officer ran sex-for-pay service.' *Toronto Star,* 7 April 1990, A1.

Stuart, D. 'Policing under the *Charter.*' In *Police Powers in Canada: The Evolution and Practice of Authority*, edited by R.C. Macleod and David Schneiderman. Toronto: University of Toronto Press, 1994.

Stuart, Don. '*Burlingham and Silveira*: New Charter Standards to Control Police Manipulation and Exclusion of Evidence.' (1995) 38(4) C.R. 386.

Sutherland, S. 'Responsible Government and Ministerial Responsibility: Every Reform Is Its Own Problem.' (1991) 24 Canadian Journal of Political Science 91.

Swinton, Gail. 'No proof of conflict, Donaldson inquest told.' *Toronto Star*, 27 October 1993, A12.
– 'Officer's testimony questioned by expert.' *Toronto Star*, 24 March 1994, A6.
– 'Report contradicts officers, inquest told.' *Toronto Star*, 15 February 1994, A6.
Tanovich, David. 'Don't let cops investigate cops.' *Globe and Mail*, 31 August 2001, A13.
Tchir, Jason. 'Hammer drops on four cops.' *Toronto Sun*, 4 May 2004, 1, 5.
Teubner, G. *Law as an Autopoietic System*. London: Blackwell, 1993.
Thomas, J. Courts Bureau Reporter, Interview for *Toronto Star* and CFRB, 4 July 1983.
Thomas, J. 'Do Police Need a Full-Time Commission Chairman?' *Toronto Star*, 27 August 1977, A-6.
Thomas, Jocko. *From Police Headquarters: True Tales from the Big City Crime Beat*. Toronto: Stoddart Press, 1990.
Toronto Police Service. *Ferguson Report*. 2004: http://www.torontopolice .on.ca/modules.php?op=modload&name=News&file=article&sid=916.
Toronto Police Services Board. Extract From the Minutes of the Meeting of the Held on 1 May 2000 Item #156/00 'Final Response to the Ontario Civilian Commission in Police Services (OCCPS) Regarding the Fact-Finding Report.'
Toronto Star. 'Ackroyd still wants to be a "better" cop.' 2 February 1981, A-9.
Toronto Star. 'Citizens' Group being maligned.' 17 October 1981, B-3.
Toronto Star. 'City authorities are getting Serious About Yonge Street – For better or Worse.' 28 July 1977.
Toronto Star. 'Civil rights body wants raid probe.' 25 February 1981, A-5.
Toronto Star. 'Close-Up,' a celebrity profile.' 20 March 1983.
Toronto Star. 'Court backs coroner over conflict ruling.' 15 January 1994, A13.
Toronto Star. 'Crombie's Answer to City's Sex Shops: Lock 'Em Up.' 22 July1977, 1.
Toronto Star. 'Davis Dallying on Sex Clean-up: City.' 26 July 1977, B-1.
Toronto Star. 'Didn't plan police raid: McMurtry.' 15 May 1981, A-11.
Toronto Star. 'Inquiry ordered in bathhouse raid.' 17 June 2002, A1 and A23.
Toronto Star. 'Lampy fails to get Yorkville curfew.' 4 August 1967, 23.
Toronto Star. 'McMurtry errs on RCMP suit.' 11 July 1981, B-2.
Toronto Star. 'Moral majority hit America (and the Ontario elector as well).' 1 March 1981, B5.
Toronto Star. 'My Concern is ... a spirit of mistrust.' 13 October 1994, A25.
Toronto Star. 'Not after Sewell or Hislop Police Union boss insists.' 21 October 21: A-3.
Toronto Star. 'Ottawa admits it intervened before budget charges laid.' 1 June 1989.

Toronto Star. 'Paul Godfrey had ordered the licensing inspectors who posed as clients not to talk to the press.' 13 August 1977, A-6.

Toronto Star. 'Police ads on reforms out of line Rae warns.' 14 August 1992, A5.

Toronto Star. 'Police display anti-homosexual leaflets.' 24 October 1980 A-16.

Toronto Star. 'Police led homosexual march: Star photos show.' March, 1981.

Toronto Star. 'Police-NDP tensions keep escalating.' 15 August 1992, D5.

Toronto Star. 'Police won't charge "embarrassed" marchers.' 18 March 1981, A-3.

Toronto Star. 'Politicians divided on Givens police job.' 25 August 1977, B-1.

Toronto Star. 'Protests mount over police raids on homosexuals.' 10 February, 1981, A-13.

Toronto Star. 'Sid the "softy" is talking tough.' 21 July 1981, A-1.

Toronto Star. 'Talking point: Hanging on just corrodes a worthy career.' 2 Nov-ember 1994, A21.

Toronto Star. 'Tories in Metro lurch to the right.' 19 June 1981, A-10.

Toronto Star. 'Toronto's tenderloin and organized crime.' 13 June 1977, C-3.

Toronto Star. 'Yorkville isn't Stalin's Moscow.' 5 August 1967, 6.

Townsend, Derek. *Jigsaw: The Biography of Johannes Bjelke-Petersen: Statesman – Not Politician*. Brisbane: Sneyd & Morley, 1983.

– *Don't you worry about that! The Joh Bjelke-Peterson memoirs*. North Ryde, NSW: Collins/Angus & Robertson, 1990.

Tunnell, Kenneth, and Larry Gaines. 'Political Pressures and Influences on Police Executives: A Descriptive Analysis.' (1992) 10(1) American Journal of Police 1.

Tyler, Tracey. 'Conviction of officer a rare win by crown.' *Toronto Star*, 11 January 1994, A1, A4.

– 'Police board's memories vary on escort case.' *Toronto Star*, 11 April 1990, A7.

United Kingdom. Home Office, Communication Directorate. *Policing: Building Safer Communities Together*. London: Home Office Communication Directorate, 2003.

United Kingdom. Independent Commission on Policing for Northern Ireland. Report. *A New Beginning: Policing in Northern Ireland*. London: Crown copyright, 1999. http://www.pixunlimited.co.uk/pdf/news/Northern_Ireland/fullreport.pdf

United Kingdom. Royal Commission on the Police. *Final Report*. Cmnd. 1728. London: H.M.S.O., 1962.

Van Maaned, J. 'The Asshole.' In *Policing: A View from the Streets*, edited by P. Manning and J. Van Maanen. Santa Monica, CA: Goodyear Publishing, 1978.

Vera Institute of Justice. 'Pittsburgh's Experience with Police Monitoring.'
    18 June 2003. http://www.vera.org/project project1_1.asp?section_id=
    2&project_id+13&sub_section_id=1&archive=.
Victoria. Board of Inquiry into Allegations against Members of the Victoria
    Police Force. *Report*. Melbourne: Government Printer 1976.
Victoria. Committee of Inquiry, Victoria Police Force. *Report*. Melbourne:
    Government Printer, 1985.
Victoria. Ministerial Administrative Review into Victoria Police Resourcing,
    Operational Independence, Human Resource Planning and Associated
    Issues. *Report*. Melbourne: Department of Justice, 2001.
Wade, William, and Christopher Forsyth. *Administrative Law*. 8th ed. Oxford:
    Oxford University Press, 2000.
Wald, Michael et al. 'Interrogation in New Haven: The Impact of *Miranda*.'
    (1967) 76 Yale L.J. 1518.
Walden, Keith. *Visions of Order: The Canadian Mounties in Symbol and Myth*.
    Toronto: Butterworths, 1982.
Wall, D. *The Chief Constables of England and Wales: The Socio-Legal History of
    a Criminal Justice Elite*. Aldershot: Ashgate/Dartmouth Publishing Co.,
    1998.
Waller, L. 'The Police, the Premier and Parliament: Governmental Control of
    the Police.' (1980) 6 Monash University L.R. 249.
Walter, Paul. 'Investigative overkill poisons civilian review of police conduct.'
    Toronto Star, 10 February 1995, A19.
Waters, D.W.M. *The Law of Trusts in Canada*. 2nd ed. Toronto: Carswell, 1984.
Watt, Susan. 'The Future of Civilian Oversight of Policing.' (2001) 33 Canadian
    Journal of Criminology 347.
Wear, Rae. 'Johannes Bjelke-Peterson: The Lord's Premier (UQP).' In *The
    Bjelke-Petersen Premiership 1968–1983: Issues in Public Policy*, edited by Allan
    Patience. Melbourne: Longman Cheshire, 1985.
– *Johannes Bjelke-Petersen: The Lord's Premier*. St Lucia: University of Queens-
    land Press, 2002.
– *Johannes Bjelke-Petersen: A Study in Populist Leadership*. St Lucia: University of
    Queensland Press, 1998.
Weber, Max. *The Theory of Social and Economic Organization*. Translated by
    A.M. Henderson. New York: Free Press, 1947.
Western Australia. Royal Commission into whether there has been Corrupt
    or Criminal Conduct by any Western Australian Police Officer. *Final Report*.
    2 vols. Perth: Government Printer, 2004. http://police.royalcommission
    .wa.gov.au/publications/publications.nsf/PoliceRC?openpage.
Wettenhall, R. 'Government and the Police.' (1977) 53 Current Affairs Bulletin
    12.

Whitaker, Reg. 'Designing a Balance between Freedom and Security.' In *Ideas in Actions: Essays on Politics and Law in Honour of Peter Russell*, edited by J. Fletcher. Toronto: University of Toronto Press, 1999.

Whittington, Les. 'Opposition questions timing.' *Toronto Star*, 11 May, 2004, A01.

Whittington, Les, and Miro Cernetig. 'Fraud charges rock Liberals.' *Toronto Star*, 11 May, 2004, A1, A7

Whitrod, R. 'The Accountability of Police Forces: Who Polices the Police?' (1976) 9 Australian and New Zealand Journal of Criminology 7.

Wilson, J.Q. 'Politics and the Police.' In *The Police Community: Dimensions of an Occupational Subculture*, edited by Jack Goldsmith and Sharon Goldsmith. Pacific Palisades, CA: Palisades Publishing, 1974.

– *Varieties of Police Behaviour: The Management of Law and Order in Eight Communities*. New York: Atheneum Press, 1976.

Williams, S. *Peter Ryan: The Inside Story*. Sydney: Viking/Penguin Books Australia Ltd., 2002.

Winter, Jane, and Natasha Parassram Concepcion. 'Current Human Rights Concerns Arising from the Conflict and Peace Process in Northern Ireland.' 9 NO. 2 Hum. Rts. Brief 6. 2002.

Wiseman, Nelson. 'Hand in Glove? Politicians, Policing and Canadian Political Culture.' In *Pepper in Our Eyes: The APEC Affair*, edited by Wesley W. Pue. Vancouver: UBC Press, 2000.

Wong, Tony. 'Group wants race made an issue at inquest.' *Toronto Star*, 23 March 1993, A7.

Woods, J. Gerry. 'The Progressives and the Police: Urban Reform and the Professionalization of the Los Angeles Police.' PhD dissertation, University of California, 1973.

Young, Margot E. '"Relax a Bit in the Nation": Constitutional Law 101 and the APEC Affair.' In *Pepper in Our Eyes: The APEC Affair*, edited by Wesley W. Pue. Vancouver: UBC Press, 2000.

Yourk, Darren. 'Lapierre politicizing RCMP and probe: Opposition.' *Globe and Mail*, 22 April 2004.

CASES CITED

Altunamaz, R. v., [1999] O.J. No. 2262.

Appleby, Belisle, and Small, R. v. (1990), 78 C.R. (3d) 282.

Armstrong v. Peel Regional Police Services Board (2003), 176 O.A.C. 358.

Arnault v. Prince Albert (City) Police Commissioners, [1996] 4 W.W.R. 38, 136 Sask. R. 49, 28 C.C.L.T. (2d) 15.

Attorney General for New South Wales v. Perpetual Trustee Company, [1955] A.C. 457.

Auckland Medical Aid Trust v. Commissioner of Police and Anotherr, [1976] 1 N.Z.L.R. 485.

Badger, R. v., [1996] 1 S.C.R. 771.

Baie d'Urfe c. Quebec, [2001] J.Q. no. 4821 (Que. C.A.).

Bainard v. Toronto Police Services Board, [2002] O.T.C. 504.

Bisaillon v. Keable and Attorney General of Quebec (1980), 17 C.R. (3d) 193, C.A. 316, 62 C.C.C. (2d) 340, 127 D.L.R. (3d) 368.

Bisaillon v. Keable and Attorney General of Quebec, [1983] 2 S.C.R. 60, 37 C.R. (3d) 289, 4 Admin. L.R. 205, 2 D.L.R. (4th) 193.

Black Action Defence Committee v. Huxter, Coroner (1992), 11 O.R. (3d) 641, 16 Admin. L.R. (2d) 88.

Booth v. Huxter (1994), 16 O.R. (3d) 528, 111 D.L.R. (4th) 111.

Bottrell, R. v. (1981), 22 C.R. (3d) 371, 60 C.C.C. (2d) 211.

Brown, R. v. (2003), 9 C.R. (6th) 240, 36 MV.R. (4th) 1, 170 O.A.C. 131, 64 O.R. (3d) 161, 173 C.C.C. (3d) 23.

Browne v. Ontario Civilian Commission on Police Services, [1999] CarswellOnt 3592, 127 O.A.C. 182.

Burnham v. Metropolitan Toronto Chief of Police, [1987] 2 S.C.R. 572, 32 C.R.R. 250.

Campbell v. Attorney General of Ontario (1987), 35 C.C.C. (3d) 480, 60 O.R. (2d) 617, 42 D.L.R. (4th) 383.

Campbell, R. v., [1999] 1 S.C.R. 565.

Carosella, R. v., [1997] 1 S.C.R. 80, 112 C.C.C. (3d) 289, 98 O.A.C. 81, 4 C.R. (5th) 139.

Chapman v. Commissioner of the Australian Federal Police (1983), 76 FLR 428.

Chartier v. Greaves, [2001] O.J. No. 634.

Chief Constable of Devon and Cornwall, ex parte Central Electricity Generating Board, R. v., [1982] Q.B. 458.

Commissioner of Police, ex p. North Broken Hill Ltd., R. v. (1992), 1 Tas.R. 99 (Tas. S.C.).

Commissioner of Police, ex parte Ross, R. v., [1992] 1 Qd. R. 289.

Committee for the Commonwealth of Canada v. Canada, [1990] 1 S.C.R. 139.

Commonwealth v. Quince (1944), 68 C.L.R. 227.

Corporation of the Canadian Civil Liberties Assn. v. Ontario Civilian Commission on Police Services (2002), 165 O.A.C. 79, 61 O.R. (3d) 649, 97 C.R.R. (2d) 271, 220 D.L.R. (4th) 86.

Cronmiller, R. v. (2003), 2004 B.C.P.C. 1.

Cullen v. Attorney-General and Commissioner of Police, [1972] N.Z.L.R. 824.

Darroch v. Metropolitan Toronto Police Services Board (1996), 20 O.T.C. 334.

Delgamuukw v. British Columbia, [1997] 3 S.C.R. 1010.

Dowson v. The Queen, [1983] S.C.R. 144, 35 C.R. (3d) 289, 7 C.C.C. (3d) 527.

Dulmage v. Ontario (Police Complaints Commissioner) (1994), 30 Admin. L.R. (2d) 203, 21 O.R. (3d) 356, 75 O.A.C. 305, 120 D.L.R. (4th) 590.

Duriancik v. Ontario (Attorney General) (1994), 114 D.L.R. (4th) 504, 75 O.A.C. 27.

Enever v. The King, [1906] 3 C.L.R. 969.

Felderhof, R. v., [2003] O.J. No. 4819 (C.A.).

Fisher v. Oldham Corporation, [1930] 2 K.B. 364.

Frame v. Smith, [1987] 2 S.C.R. 99.

Frazier v. Purdy (1991), 6 O.R. (3d) 429.

G. (P.) v. Ontario (Attorney General) (1996), (*sub nom. P.G. v. Police Complaints Commissioner*), 90 O.A.C. 103.

Gage v. Ontario (1992), 90 D.L.R. (4th) 537, 55 O.A.C. 47.

Gauthier v. Toronto Star Daily Newspapers Ltd., [2003] O.J. 2622 (Sup. Ct.), affirmed [2004] O.J. 2686 (C.A.).

Gladstone, R. v., [1996] 2 S.C.R. 723.

Golden, R. v., [2001] S.C.J. No. 81, 47 C.R. (5th) 1, 159 C.C.C. (4th) 449.

Griffiths, R. v., (2003), 11 C.R. (6th) 136, 106 C.R.R. (2d) 139.

Guerin, R. v., [1984] 2 S.C.R. 335.

Hadfield, R. v. (1985), 85 N.B.R. (2d) 208.

Haida Nation v. British Columbia (Minister of Forests), (2002) B.C.C.A. 462.

Hayes v. Ontario (Police Complaints Commissioner) (1995), 33 Admin. L.R. (2d) 34, 88 O.A.C. 96.

Heasman v. Durham Regional Police Services Board, [2004] WL 858890, 2004 Carswell Ont 1675.

Hodgkinson v. Simms et al., [1994] 3 S.C.R. 377.

Hudson v. Brantford Police Services Board (2001), 204 D.L.R. (4th) 645, 158 C.C.C. (3d) 390, 150 O.A.C. 87, 48 C.R. (5th) 69, [2001] O.J. No. 3779.

Jane Doe v. Metropolitan Toronto (Municipality) Commissioners of Police (1990), 50 C.P.C. (2d) 92, 40 O.A.C. 161, 74 O.R. (2d) 225, 72 D.L.R. (4th) 580, 5 C.C.L.T. (2d) 77 (*sub nom. Doe v. Metropolitan Toronto (Municipality) Commissioners of Police*) 1 C.R.R (2d) 211.

Jane Doe v. Metropolitan Toronto (Municipality) Commissioners of Police (1991), 1 O.R. (3d) 416.

Jane Doe v. Metropolitan Toronto (Municipality) Commissioners of Police (1998), 39 O.R. (3d) 487.

Johnson v. Halifax (Regional Municipality) Police Service, [2004] N.S.H.R.B.I.D. No. 4.

Judges Remuneration Reference, [1997] 3 S.C.R. 3.

Keegstra, R. v., [1990] 3 S.C.R. 697.

Khan, R. v., Ont. S.C.J., Malloy J, 16 September 2004, (unreported).

King-Brooks v. Roberts (1991), 5 W.A.R. 500 (W.A.S.C.).

Konrad v. Victoria Police (1998), 152 C.L.R. 132.

Krieger v. Law Society of Alberta, [2002] 3 S.C.R. 372.

Lac Minerals Ltd. v. International Corona Resources Ltd., [1989] 2 S.C.R. 574.

Ladore et al. v. Bennett al., [1939] 3 D.L.R. 1 (P.C.).

Lalonde v. Ontario (2001), 56 O.R. (3d) 505.

Law v. Canada (Minister of Employment and Immigration), [1999] 1 S.C.R. 497.

Lloyd v. Toronto Police Services Board, [2003] CarswellOnt 58.

Marshall, R. v., [1999] 3 S.C.R. 456.

McCann v. Ontario (Police Services Act Board of Inquiry) (1994), 69 O.A.C. 78.

McLean v. Siesel (2004), 182 O.A.C. 122.

McCleave v. City of Moncton (1902), 32 S.C.R 106.

Metropolitan Police ex parte Blackburn, R. v., [1968] Q.B. 116.

Metropolitan Police ex parte Blackburn, R. v., [1973]. Q.B. 241.

Nicholson, R. v., [1999] B.C.J. No. 330, [1999] CarswellBC 1287.

Noel (Committee of) v. RCMP, [1995] 9 B.C.L.R. (3d) 21, 12 M.V.R. (3d) 50, 7
     W.W.R. 479.

O'Connor, R. v., [1995] 4 S.C.R. 411.

Odhavji Estate v. Metropolitan Toronto Police (2001), 194 D.L.R. (4th) 577.

Odhavji Estate v. Metropolitan Toronto Police, [2003] 3 S.C.R. 263.

Odhavji Estate v. Woodhouse (2003), S.C.C. 69, 19 C.C.L.T. (3d) 163, 233 D.L.R.
     (4th) 193, 180 O.A.C. 201.

O'Hara v. Chief Constable of the Royal Ulster Constabulary, [1997] 1 All E.R.
     129.

Ontario (Police Complaints Commissioner) v. Will (1993), 67 O.A.C. 317, [1993]
     CarswellOnt 1158.

Ontario (Police Complaints Commissioner) v. Hannah (1997), 145 D.L.R. (4th) 443,
     1997 CarswellOnt 820.

Ontario (Police Complaints Commissioner) v. Kerr (1997), 96 O.A.C. 284, 143
     D.L.R. (4th) 471.

Ontario Provincial Police Commissioner v. Silverman (2000), 49 O.R. (3d) 272, 188
     D.L.R. (4th) 758, 135 O.A.C. 357.

Osgood v. Attorney General (1972), 13 M.C.D. 400.

Osoyoos Indian Band v. Oliver (Town), [2001] 3 S.C.R. 74.

P. (P.) v. Pecorella, [1998] CarswellOnt 1887.

Paryniuk, R. v., (2002), 97 C.R.R. (2d) 151.

Peart v. Peel Regional Police Services Board, [2003] CarswellOnt 2447.

Polewsky v. Home Hardware (2003), 66 O.R. (3d) 600 (Div. Ct.).

Police v. Newnham, [1978] 1 N.Z.L.R. 844.

Power, R. v., [1994] 1 S.C.R. 601.

Prescott (Town) v. Ontario (2003), 178 O.A.C. 192, 233 D.L.R. (4th) 93.

Priestman v. Colangelo, [1959] S.C.R. 615, 124 C.C.C. 1, 19 D.L.R. (2d) 1.

Prue, Re, [1984] A.J. No. 1006 (Q.B.)

The Queen on the application of the Secretary of State for the Home Department v. Humberside Police Authority and Westwood, [2004] E.W.H.C. 1642 (Q.B.).

Reference re Secession of Quebec, [1998] 2 S.C.R. 217.

Regan, R. v., [2002] 1 S.C.R. 297, 161 C.C.C. (3d) 97, 209 D.L.R. (4th) 41, 282 N.R. 1.

Roncarelli v. Duplessis, [1959] S.C.R. 121.

Roberge, R. v., (1980), 31 N.B.R. (2d) 668, 75 A.P.R. 668.

Scaduto, R. v., [1999] 63 C.R.R. (2d) 155, [1999] O.J. No. 1906, 97 O.T.C. 307.

Scott v. Ontario, [2002] CarswellOnt 3606.

Sherman v. Renwick, [2001] CarswellOnt 595.

Shirose, R. v. (1999), 237 N.R. 86, 133 C.C.C. (3d) 257, *(sub nom. R. v. Campbell)* [1999] 1 S.C.R. 565, 42 O.R. (3d) 800, 171 D.L.R. (4th) 193.

Sibiya v. Swart, [1950] S.A.L.R. 515.

Small, R. v. (1990), 78 C.R. (3d) 282.

Smith, R. v. (1998), 163 Nfld. & P.E.I.R. 179, 503 A.P.R. 179, 163 Nfld. & P.E.I.R. 179.

Somerset County Council, ex parte Fewings, R. v., [1995] 1 All E.R. 513 at 524.

Sparrow, R. v., [1990] 1 S.C.R. 1075.

Stanbury v. Exeter Corporation, [1905] 2 K.B. 838.

Stevens v. Toronto Police Services Board, [2003]) CarswellOnt 4612.

Stinchcombe, R. v., [1991] 3 S.C.R. 326, [1992] 1 W.W.R. 97, 68 C.C.C. (3d) 1, 130 N.R. 277.

T. Weller, The Queen v. Ontario Court (Provincial Division) 21 April 1988, Kerr J, Scarborough (unreported).

Taku River Tlingit First Nation v. Ringstad, [2002] BCCA 59.

Thomas v. Ontario (Police Complaints Commissioner), [1994] CarswellOnt 3222.

Tomie-Gallant v. Ontario (Board of Inquiry) (1995), 33 Admin. L.R. (2d) 34, 88 O.A.C. 96.

Townley v. Ontario (Police Complaints Commissioner), [2000] CarswellOnt 343.

Trimm v. Durham Regional Police Force, [1987] 2 S.C.R. 582, 37 C.C.C. (3d) 120, 24 O.A.C. 357, 45 D.L.R. (4th) 276, 32 C.R.R. 244.

Trumbley v. Flemming, [1987] 29 Admin. L.R. 100, 81 N.R. 212, 24 O.A.C. 372, *(sub nom. Trumbley v. Metropolitan Toronto Police)* [1987] 2 S.C.R. 577, 32 C.R.R. 254, 37 C.C.C.(3d) 118, 45 D.L.R. (4th) 318.

Van der Peet, R. v., [1996] 2 S.C.R. 507.

Wason v. Gillis (1996), 3 O.T.C. 307.

Wewaykum Indian Band v. Canada, [2002] 4 S.C.R. 245.

Wiche v. Ontario, R. v., [2003] CarswellOnt 291.

Wighton, R. v. (2003), 176 C.C.C. (3d) 550, 13 C.R. (6th) 266.

Wigglesworth, R. v., [1987] 2 S.C.R. 541, [1988] 1 W.W.R. 193, 61 Sask. R. 105, 60
    C.R. (3d)193, 24 O.A.C. 321, 45 D.L.R. (4th) 235.

Index

Aboriginal Justice Initiative, 359
Aboriginal peoples: assumption of
  Canadian sovereignty, 167–70;
  discretion in rule of law, 132–3;
  preservation of culture, 153–4;
  self-policing of, 12. *See also*
  Aboriginal peoples in police-
  government relationship
Aboriginal peoples in police-
  government relationship: activities to avoid in, 173–4; assumption of Canadian sovereignty,
  170–2; conflict of interest in
  fiduciary relationship, 179n22,
  180n35, 181n41; in fiduciary
  relationship, 11, 159–66, 180n33;
  history of, 65, 147, 155–8, 174–5,
  327–9; Ipperwash Inquiry, 83;
  legal and constitutional status,
  147, 152–4, 162–6, 178n9; on
  police boards, 69; policing of, 76,
  91n99, 129; project of reconciliation, 165–6; self-policing, 12;
  treated as 'minority populations,'
  147, 149–52; treaty rights, 9, 11,
  66, 154–8, 178–9nn11–23, 180n35
abuse of process application, 46

accountability mechanisms: absent
  from *Blackburn* decision, 199–200;
  in Australia, 212–14; balanced
  with police independence, 185,
  193, 221–2, 244n15; chain of command, 261, 263, 296n14; community, 318; coroners' inquests, 105,
  265, 267, 273, 301n58; differences
  between RCMP and OPP, 330–1;
  as distinct from oversight, 120;
  formal police-government relations, 73–5, 94n128, 288–90, 367;
  information or influence, 69–72,
  349–50; internal investigations,
  290–4; litigation, 56, 266–7; media as, 66–7, 117, 260–1, 296n12;
  ministerial, 21, 48, 51, 63, 88n53,
  88n56, 88n58, 92n113, 94n124;
  ministerial as lacking, 101–2, 118;
  ministerial in democratic policing,
  59–60; as multi-layered, 13–14,
  120–1; at national and provincial
  levels, 24; in New Zealand, 230–3,
  253n119, 254n124; for police discipline, 278–82; police independence and, 91n103, 184–5, 192,
  207, 274; and police mandate, 5;